The Other Grand Dukes

Sons and Grandsons of Russia's Grand Dukes

By

Janet Ashton
Arturo E. Beéche
Coryne Hall
Grant Hayter-Menzies
Greg King
John van der Kiste
Marlene Eilers-Koenig
Penny Wilson

Foreword By
H.R.H. Prince Michael of Kent

Introduction By
Charles B. Stewart III

EUROHISTORY.COM

ISBN 978-0-9854603-9-6
Copyright © 2012 Arturo E. Beéche
First Edition – December 2012

All rights reserved. No part of this book covered by the copyrights hereon may be reproduced or used in any form or by any means without prior consent of the publisher, except for brief passages covered by reviewers. Reproducing passages from this book by any means, including mimeographic, photocopying, scanning, recording, or by any information retrieval system is an infringement of copyright law.

Published by:

Eurohistory.com

6300 Kensington Avenue
East Richmond Heights, CA 94805 USA
Telephone: (510) 236-1730

Email: books@eurohistory.com
URL: http://www.eurohistory.com

Cover design by David W. Higdon
Editing by David W. Higdon & Katrina Warne
Layout by Eurohistory
Proudly printed and bound in the USA

Cover Photo – Eurohistory Royal Photographic Archive: Imperial Russia.
A Romanov Gathering: Seated from left: Grand Duchess Maria Pavlovna Sr., Empress Alexandra Feodorovna, Tsar Nicholas II, Grand Duchess Helen Vladimirovna, Grand Duke Boris Vladimirovich, Grand Duke Andrei Vladimirovich. Standing, same order: Grand Duchess Tatiana Nikolaevna, Duchess Antonia of Mecklenburg-Schwerin, Grand Duchess Victoria Feodorovna, Grand Duchess Olga Nikolaevna, Grand Duke Kirill Vladimirovich, Princess Elisabeth of Greece, Princess Olga of Greece, Grand Duchess Anastasia Nikolaevna, Princess Marina of Greece, Grand Duchess Maria Nikolaevna.

To Eurohistory's Readers...

You all make it possible.

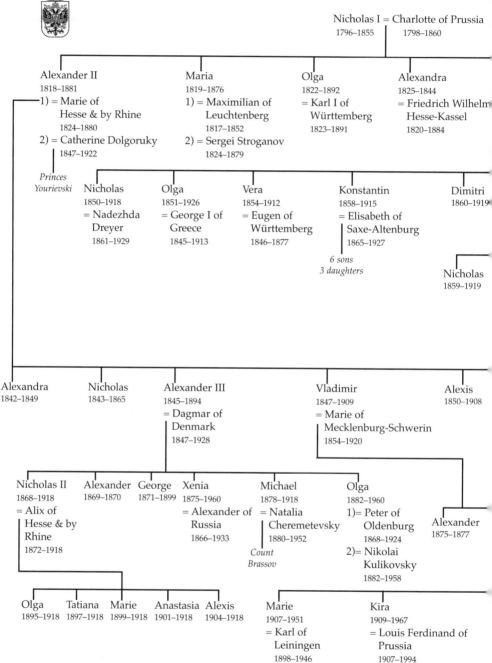

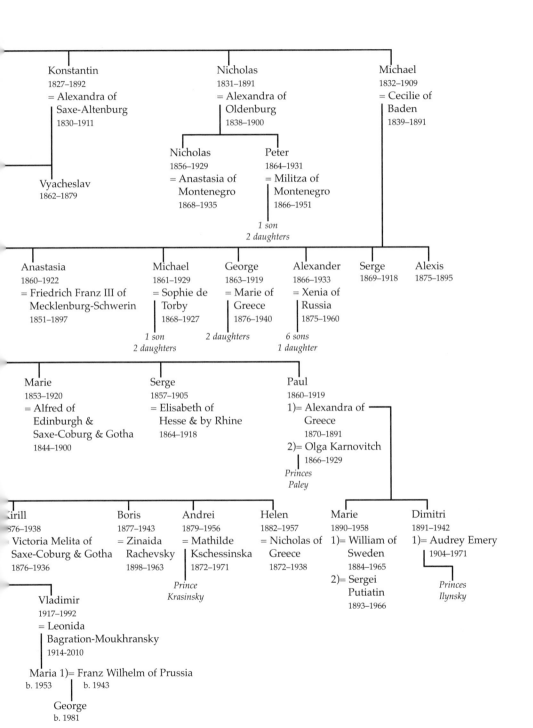

Table of Contents

Foreword   i

A Word from the Publisher   iii

Acknowledgments   v

Introduction   vii

Chapter I – The Sons of Grand Duke Vladimir Alexandrovich

Grand Duke Kirill Vladimirovich	1
Grand Duke Boris Vladimirovich	20
Grand Duke Andrei Vladimirovich	25

Chapter II – The Son of Grand Duke Kirill Vladimirovich

Grand Duke Vladimir Kirillovich	34

Chapter III – The Grandson of Grand Duke Vladimir Kirillovich

Grand Duke George Mikhailovich	44

Chapter IV – The Son of Grand Duke Paul Alexandrovich

Grand Duke Dimitri Pavlovich	47

Chapter V – The Sons of Grand Duke Konstantin Nikolaievich

Grand Duke Nicholas Konstantinovich	59
Grand Duke Konstantin Konstantinovich	80
Grand Duke Dimitri Konstantinovich	122
Grand Duke Vyacheslav Konstantinovich	133

Chapter VI – The Sons of Grand Duke Nicholas Nikolaievich

Grand Duke Nicholas Nikolaievich Junior	139
Grand Duke Peter Nikolaievich	156

Chapter VII – The Sons of Grand Duke Michael Nikolaievich

Grand Duke Nicholas Mikhailovich	169
Grand Duke Michael Mikhailovich	183
Grand Duke George Mikhailovich	195
Grand Duke Alexander Mikhailovich	203
Grand Duke Serge Mikhailovich	214
Grand Duke Alexis Mikhailovich	220

Endnotes Notes 223

Bibliography 237

Name Index 241

Photo Section 120-121

Family Trees

Table #1: The Russian Imperial Family	
Table #2: The Vladimirovichi and Pavlovich Lines	18
Table #3: The Konstantinovichi Line	138
Table #4: The Nikolaievichi Line	168
Table #5: The Mikhailovichi Line	212

FOREWORD

I am very flattered to have been asked to write this foreword. The biographical works of Arturo Beéche are well respected among my wider family and have come to be regarded as something of a gold standard.

The first Russian influence on me came through my grandmother Yelena Vladimirovna, who died in 1957. She was a formidable lady with whom I used to stay in the 1950s in her house in Athens, surrounded by cats. She remained staunchly in that city throughout the Second World War.

Her own mother,, Grand Duchess Vladimir, was indomitable. There is a story about her after 1918 when she was living in the country in the Caucasus. She and her lady-in-waiting, Turia Galitzine, had heard the ominous news that the Bolsheviks were surrounding the house. So she called Turia and said that if the worst came to the worst, and those people came into the house, the two ladies would sit on the sofa in the drawing-room, side by side, doing their crochet, looking down at their work and not raising their eyes, and talking always in English. Shortly afterwards they heard loud noises and took up their positions on the sofa. The drawing-room doors burst open, and there appeared a motley group of drunken, unshaven specimens of humanity, armed to the teeth with pistols of every kind. The ladies continued their conversation and ignored them. They could hear the trespassers debating amongst themselves in Russian who should pull the trigger first. "You do it!" they shouted to the leader. "No" he replied. "Our little Ivan should do it because we know he is the best shot" and so on. Eventually, after what must have seemed like hours, the ruffians shambled out of the house and never reappeared.

Everyone has their own idea of what makes them proud to be a Romanov descendant. This is mine.

H.R.H. Prince Michael of Kent
Kensington Palace, London
June 2012

The Other Grand Dukes

ACKNOWLEGEMENTS

The authors would like to extend their appreciation to everyone involved in the publication of this extensive two-volume book project. It is a truly unique work of royal biography in itself,. We hope that our work will become a book of choice when readers wish to learn about the Romanov Dynasty and Imperial Russia.

Janet Ashton would like to thank Katrina Warne, William Lee, and, as always, Greg King.

Coryne Hall would like to thank, "my husband Colin, for once again reading all my drafts and offering constructive criticism."

Grant Hayter-Menzies would like to express his appreciation to the following for their assistance and encouragement: Arturo Beéche, Xenia von Besack, Carl Reeves Close, Peter Kurth, Marion Mienert, Stephen O'Donnell, and Odette Terrel des Chenes.

John van der Kiste would like to "thank my wife Kim Van der Kiste who read through the drafts for me as ever."

Marlene Eilers Koenig wishes to thank, "My cats, Edison and Sienna Rose Koenig...and all those who read our books!"

Penny Wilson would like to express, "Special thanks to Anne Barrett and Helene Deramonde for their work on our behalf in the National Archives, Washington DC, and to Stephanie Hoover."

Last, but by no means least, Arturo Beéche would like to "thank David W. Higdon, my husband, for his unquestioned support in every single project I have designed at Eurohistory. My work would be impossible to complete without his encouragement, unequalled patience, frank suggestions, interminable willingness to be an asset, and loving companionship. I must thank our sons Zac and Nicholas Higdon Beéche for allowing their stay-at-home dad the time and space he needed to complete this book."

"I would also like to thank all of my collaborators, in particular Charles Stewart, Janet Ashton, Coryne Hall, Grant Hayter Menzies, Marlene Eilers Koenig, Penny Wilson, Greg King, Ilana Miller, Lisa Davidson William Lee, Zoia Belyakova and John van der Kiste. I would also like to express my deepest appreciation to all the contributors to this book for their diligence, enthusiasm and patience. Particular appreciation goes to Katrina Warne and Dr. Mary Houck for their continued efforts in making our projects a success. Many more are those who must be thanked. I apologize in advance if I forget to mention you, but we know your aid came out of love for history in general, the Romanovs in particular, and that you did not help us just to be thanked."

"I would like to thank HRH Prince Michael of Kent for writing the foreword to this volume. Also many thanks are due to Prince Alexander of Yugoslavia for loaning us his mother's diaries, to Princess Barbara of Yugoslavia and Archduchess Helen of Austria for their continued support on this and other projects, as well as to Prince Dimitri of Yugoslavia, Count Hans-Veit and Hereditary Count Ignaz zu Toerring-Jettenbach for their advice, encouragement, interest, accessibility and support."

"Many years my dear friend Jacques Ferrand suggested the publication of this two-volume work. He did so during one of our regular meetings in Paris. His encouragement greatly propelled the effort that now culminates with this book. Sadly, a tragic accident took Jacques from us just months before the publication of the first volume. I know he would have been pleased with both books and posthumously wish to thank him for inspiring me.

Lastly, I wish to express our sincerest appreciation to the staff of Thomson-Shore for their incredible support, guidance and attention to detail. They truly form an amazing team that has helped us print three books in one year...and we hope countless more in years to come!"

Finally, enjoy the reading...

A Word From the Publisher

During the Summer of 2004, I was busily preparing for two events: the publication of *The Grand Duchesses – Daughters and Granddaughters of Russia's Tsars*, and our wedding. Both took place the same week. It was a stressful yet exciting time, as the reader can imagine.

However, both events have brought me, as a publisher and a husband, endless joy. Soon after *The Grand Duchesses* began selling, I realized that we had to produce a companion book, which logically would be titled "The Grand Dukes – Sons and Grandsons of Russia's Tsars." My dear friend the late Jacques Ferrand suggested that I ought to do so as well. *"The Grand Duchesses is excellent...you should do one or two volumes about the Grand Dukes,"* Jacques said. Two years later I had finished choosing the authors, every single one of them an expert in their field, and work began in earnest. The end result amounted to nearly seven hundred pages of text, which just before going to print forced us to make the decision to publish the book as a two-volume set. This allowed for an easier book to handle, as well as giving us the chance to include more pictures than if we had retained the original idea of having the book be a single volume. This is the second volume in the series. The first volume, *The Grand Dukes*, was published in late 2010, sadly too late for Jacques to enjoy.

Publishing these books was not the easiest enterprise, I must admit. The contributors came from the USA, the United Kingdom, Canada and Russia. We had to have guidelines, spelling consistency, cohesiveness, agreeing on editing, formatting and content. At times it proved to be a challenge, but we overcame difference and now rejoice when seeing the fruits of our labor. We did it!

What readers now hold in their hands is the product of an amazingly talented group of today's leading royal biographers. Among us we have written more then 60 books, as well as hundreds of magazine and journal articles – something to be extremely proud of no doubt.

The Grand Dukes and *The Other Grand Dukes* came to life after a challenging Summer 2010 during which I battled a life-threatening illness and faced countless radiation sessions that lasted more than half a year. I felt debilitated and powerless; at times despondent. I was afraid that I would not be around to see our sons grow into productive members of society. I was petrified when thinkning of what Dave's life would be as a single parent. My well-being came first and for that to happen, it was necessary for all Eurohistory business and projects to stop. This decision infuriated some people, who lost little time in expressing their anger in most unfriendly ways. Yet, thinking about completing the book provided me with ample sources of inspiration and the will to overcome the challenges I faced. Once the illness's defeat allowed my return to the office at Eurohistory, I jumped in the fray and three weeks later the book's first volume went to print. Now, nearly two years after, the circle is completed.

I am inspired by the end result. *The Grand Dukes* and *The Other Grand Dukes* are sure to become among those "must-have" titles in our European royal history book collection. Hopefully, the reader will agree with our own perception of the words we authored in these two volumes.

Before letting the reader continue, one word of caution. Imperial Russia followed the Julian calendar, *"a reform of the Roman calendar, was introduced by Julius Caesar in 46 BC, and came into force in 45 BC. It was chosen after consultation with the astronomer Sosigenes of Alexandria and was probably designed to approximate the tropical year, known at least since Hipparchus. It has a regular year of 365 days divided into 12 months, and a leap day is added to February every four years. Hence the Julian year is on average 365.25 days long."*

The rest of the Western world followed the Gregorian calendar. *"The Gregorian calendar, also known as the Western calendar or the Christian calendar, is the internationally accepted civil calendar. It was introduced by Pope Gregory XIII, after whom the calendar was named, by a decree signed on 24 February 1582."* Furthermore, the motivation for the Gregorian reform was that the Julian calendar assumes that the time between vernal equinoxes is 365.25 days, when in fact it is about 11 minutes less. The accumulated error between these values was about 10 days when the reform was made, resulting in the equinox occurring on March 11 and moving steadily earlier in the calendar. Since the equinox was tied to the celebration of Easter, the Roman Catholic Church considered that this steady movement was undesirable.

Consequently, countries following the Julian calendar were behind a few days. Russia was one of them. In the XVIII century Russia was eleven days behind the Western world. In the XIX century the difference was 12 days, while in the 20th century that number rose by one to 13. Hence, when appropriate, authors have used Western dates, and if Julian calendar dates were used, we have added the "O.S." after the used date. O.S. stands for Old Style, meaning the Julian calendar. In some instances, authors have chosen to use both dates.

One last word. Of late some authors have taken to addressing members of the Imperial Family by the title of "Grand Prince" or "Grand Princess." Although this is a translation perhaps closer to the original Russian title, we feel it erroneous, and this is the reasoning why. The Imperial Court was quite clear about this matter. The manual published by it and handed to Western diplomats serving in Russia established that the title of members of the Imperial Family was "Grand Duke" and "Grand Duchess." For some modern authors to contradict the Imperial Court itself, I personally find erroneous and historically inaccurate.

Also, and for obvious reasons, we have not included in this volume those Russian Grand Dukes who died in infancy.

With that said, enjoy *The Other Grand Dukes* – we hope it brings alive a world long gone – a world devoured by the passions of brutal men and their inability to appreciate and respect history.

Arturo E. Beéche
East Richmond Heights, CA
June 2012

INTRODUCTION

There may never have been a time when "Grand duchy" didn't conjure a castle in Fairyland, nor when "Grand Duke" did not evoke a silver-haired aristocrat sporting a monocle whose chest was festooned with too many sashes and medals, and whose life was adorned with too many comforts and sycophants. Unlike kings, who come in a variety of images, ranging from paternally wise to battle horse-mounted to gold-greedy, grand dukes are quaint stereotypes, at best vague, at worst absurd. Even when the last living member of this species, the ruler of Luxembourg, is remembered, no substantially different figure comes to mind. Rather the reverse.

But once upon a time there were grand dukes of a different sort. Medieval grand dukes, bearded and wrapped in fur-lined capes wielded sword and icon against pagans on the steppes. Soldier grand dukes swarmed on the capital between wars filling theatre balconies with applause or waiting impatiently in closed carriages for a prima ballerina to make her last curtsey on stage. And émigré grand dukes sipping someone else's champagne in the lounge of a 20th century Parisian hotel they could no longer afford. Russia's dukes, throughout their history, were like Russia's literature; sweeping, mysterious, and tragic. In short, grand. These men grew Russia, and spent it, and their like is no more to be seen.

Grand Duke is the traditional English rendering of the Latin *magnus dux* and *magnus princips*. After the fall of the Byzantine Empire in 485 C.E., Europe's marauding tribes spread out and began to settle down and establish boundaries which they could defend against rivals. Skilled warriors made themselves chieftains and, if they could aggrandize the tribe's territory and pass leadership down among kinsmen, they emerged from the Dark Ages as dukes and princes, adopting those titles from the commanders of the old Roman Empire.

Among these, Gonçalo Mendes (fl. 950–997) in northwestern Iberia may have been the first to take a higher title, *magnus dux portucalensium* ("great duke of the Portuguese") in rebellion against his liege lords, the kings of León around 980 C.E. In 1435 Duke Philip *the Good* of Burgundy (1396–1467) declared himself "Grand Duke of the West," but neither he nor his son Charles the Bold (1433–77) achieved broad recognition of the title or succeeded in expanding their Flemish base into a revived kingdom of Arles. In 1569 the Medici family rendered permanent their domination of Florence when Pope Pius V conferred upon them the rule of the new Grand Duchy. In 1576 the Holy Roman Emperor dropped his protest against this elevation and confirmed the Grand Dukes of Tuscany as vassals within the Empire. Tuscany passed, upon extinction of the Medici, to the Habsburgs and remained Europe's best known independent grand duchy until absorbed into the kingdom of Italy in 1859.

In Eastern Europe, duchies and principalities evolved differently than in the West and South. Unlike "grand dukes" whose territories were of insufficient size and clout to obtain international recognition as kings, the typical grand prince in Eastern Europe was more likely to lead a loose confederation of tribes in war or migration. The princes over whom he exercised jurisdiction were likely to be kinsmen or allies, authority over sub-tribal groups being retained by each group's own leaders. The Grand Prince (Nagyfejedelem) of the Magyars emerges in the 9th century with a following of seven tribes. They merged with three Khabar tribes of Turkish origin by 881, spreading out over the Carpathian mountains. The grand princedom thrives until 1000 C.E., when St Stephen converts this Magyar/Turk amalgamation into the Christian kingdom of Hungary.

The "grand dukedoms" of Transylvania and Finland were largely titular, as no independent prince ever held them. The titles simply identified these territories as subject provinces of foreign monarchs. In 1765 Empress Maria Theresia upgraded her province, the Principality of Transylvania, into a grand princedom (Großfürstentum), but it continued to be administered by a Hungarian governor in her name. Pursuant to the Austro-Hungarian Compromise of 1867, Transylvania ceased to be administered separately within the Austro-Hungarian Empire, and was fully integrated as an additional province into the kingdom of Hungary, although the Habsburgs continued to include "Grand Prince of Transylvania" among their hereditary titles.

Under Sweden, Finland was also a sovereign grand princedom in name only from 1581 to 1809, sending representatives to Stockholm's Parliament and having no independent government. Following the defeat of Sweden in the Finnish War in 1809, the country switched allegiance from the King of Sweden to the Emperor of Russia who became the new grand duke. Although Russia remained an autocracy, during the war resistance to its conquest was sought by promising the Finns internal autonomy. Thus, Finland was governed separately, according to the laws and administrative system closer to that developed under its old suzerain, Sweden. Russia's tsar contented himself with appointment of a Finnish governor-general resident in Helsinki. However, from 1899 until the Russian Revolution, Finland's independence and progressive legislation was thwarted as the tsar's regime imposed "russification" in an effort to consolidate Russian rule and to thwart nationalist tendencies. With the abolition of the Russian monarchy in 1917, the Finnish grand princedom ceased to exist. The Finnish Diet looked briefly to the Duke of Urach (a morganaut of the German royal House of Württemberg, like the Duke of Teck) and a Prince of Hesse to establish an independent monarchy – this time as a kingdom. But revolutionary fervor for a republic prevailed and the Hessian's invitation to a royal coronation in Helsinki was rescinded on 14 December 1918.

Another medieval dynastic model of grand ducal status is illustrated by the Gedyminids in Lithuania. Grand Duke Mindaugas (c.1200-1263) arose in 1220 to form a Baltic state in Lithuania, becoming a Christian and allying with the Order of Livonian Knights. Although in the last decade of his reign he was crowned king, he is the first known Grand Duke of Lithuania, having been recognized in youth as inheriting senior rank among Lithuania's 16 native Balt princes and dukes. Considered a nation-builder despite constant struggles with Tatars and rebellious relatives who finally assassinated him, he remains a heroic grand ducal figure.

Gediminas (c.1275-1341) was a successor, though not a descendant, of

Mindaugas. He rejected Lithuania's Chrisian royal crown in favor of grand ducal status in 1316 and spent his reign fending off Christian encroachment in defense of the predominant pagan population. His numerous sons and daughters firmly entrenched his dynasty in Lithuania as the House of Jagiellon, where they reigned as grand dukes while ruling Poland as kings until 1572. Subsequent rulers of Poland retained rule of the grand duchy of Lithuania but it became one of many subordinate lands and titles held by these Polish kings. However, several prominent families of the nobility in Russia and Poland legitimately descend from Gediminas.

Contrary to popular opinion, at no time was there a "Grand duchy of Warsaw." Napoleon would reduce Poland to a mere duchy. Then after 1807 Poland was divided as the spoils of war, the emperors of Russia ruling as kings of "Congress Poland" and the kings of Prussia as "Grand Dukes of Posen."

Grand duchies came late to Germany arriving, in fact, only after the abolition of the Holy Roman Empire in 1804 and Napoleon's elevation of his brother-in-law Joachim Murat as Grand Duke of Berg. In the vacuum left by the Habsburgs, the landgraviate of Hesse-Darmstadt declared itself henceforth to be the Grand Duchy of Hesse and by Rhine and the margrave of Baden took the title of Grand Duke. They were soon followed by the now independent dukes of Saxe-Weimar, Mecklenburg-Schwerin, Mecklenburg-Strelitz and Oldenburg. Even the Congress of Vienna engaged in title inflation, carving out the grand duchy of Luxembourg for the Princes of Orange as newly-minted kings of the Netherlands in 1830.

Unlike some of the earlier, titular grand princedoms, these small 19th century realms were real and the internal authority of their grand dukes was undiminished, theoretically, by any overlord. But they were dwarfed by the imperial powers aggrandizing around them, forged by 19th century nationalism. The German grandduchies were obliged in 1815 to join the German Confederation and, in 1871 the German Empire established under Prussia's Hohenzollerns. Luxembourg joined too, despite its allegiance to the Dutch king and Tuscany's Habsburg grand duke was replaced by a 95% vote of his subjects to transfer their allegiance to the Savoyard king of Italy.

There remained one more grandduchy from the medieval era on the outskirts of Europe which, unlike those which became secondary statelets, evolved into the main realm of its dynasty and ultimately, into a European super-power. During the course of that evolution, the title of grand duke changed in usage and meaning in Russia, but survived there for as long as monarchy did.

Slavic lore once maintained (and now resists) the notion that Rurik (c.830–c.879) was a Viking prince who led a migration of Scandinavians (the Varangians) to Russia. He established his rule as a prince ("knyaz"), in Novgorod among a host of warring Slavic and Baltic petty rulers around 860 CE. His numerous descendants successfully expanded their authority in all directions over generations to follow. Primogeniture was unknown among them, so at every generation each Rurikid prince received a fraction of the patrimonial territory, liegemen and his kin's support to establish or conquer his own principality. Thus Kiev was taken by Rurikid Varangians in 882 and the grandduchy of Kieven Rus' was born, the political and cultural womb of modern Russia, the Ukraine and Belarus. Ruled by Rurik's descendants, Kiev became the first Russian grandduchy in 1015, until fratricidal conflict and invasion by the Mongols in 1237 brought about its collapse.

Scattered and reduced, Rurik's descendants nonetheless survived. A few climbed back up to grand ducal status, now under the dominion of the Golden Horde. It was at this point that a distinction arises among the Rurikids between those who held only princely rank and their theoretical suzerains, the grand dukes of Vladimir-Suzdal, Muscovy and Galicia–Volhynia. Previously, the distinction between the 'velikiy knyazi' (grand princes) and the 'udyelniye knyazi' (local princes) was largely a matter of prestige. The Mongols made it a matter of authority. In 1252 Sartak Khan made Prince Alexander Nevsky of Novgorod the new Grand Duke of Vladimir-Suzdal, then foremost of the Rurikid principalities. Muscovy transformed from principality to grand duchy in 1283. With the approval of the Mongol overlords, the grand dukes exercised authority over the other Rurikid princes, their policies reflecting awareness of the fact that rival Rurikids were eager to supplant them.

Once Peter, Metropolitan of All Rus, moved his seat from Vladimir to Moscow in 1325 it was clear that Muscovy had become the premier Rurikid power in the Rus. In 1328 Ivan I Kalita ("the Moneybag"), Prince of Moscow, obtained appointment from the Great Khan of the Golden Horde as Grand Duke of Vladimir, thereby becoming suzerain over the other Rurikid princes, in particular Ivan's rivals, the princes of Tver and Nizhny Novgorod. His descendant Ivan III the Great repelled the Golden Horde's exactions and tripled Muscovy's area in what is known as "the gathering of the Russian lands."

Ivan IV the Terrible took the decisive step, having become Grand Duke of Muscovy in 1533 (occasionally styling himself tsar as had some of his ancestors, notably Ivan III) of officially crowning himself Tsar and Autocrat of All Russia in 1547. Henceforth the sons and daughters of Russia's rulers added to their grand ducal title that of 'tsarevich' or 'tsarevna'.

'Tsar' was the Russian term for the ancient rulers of Byzantium and other monarchs of imperial stature, and the word is related to the Latin 'Caesar'. Nonetheless by the time of Peter the Great, the word was no longer synonymous with 'emperor'. The only European monarch of imperial rank was the Holy Roman Emperor, who had long been referred to in Russia as "kesar" rather than as tsar. However, the tsar was also Autocrat ("Samoder-ec"), a title which unequivocally implied the monarch's absolute authority over the Russian land and people.

Ivan the Terrible gave meaning to tsarist autocracy by introducing the Oprichnina ("separation") to Russia. A time of terror for prince and peasant alike, during this period of focus on the rights and lands of the Tsar, now become absolute, those of the nobility were deprecated. Ivan pursued a policy of isolating himself from and degrading the nobility, including his own kin who until recently had reigned over principalities inherited, like Ivan's tsardom, from their common ancestor Rurik the Varangian. Officially, all subjects of the realm were declared to be serfs of the Autocrat and, while retaining their personal estates, the rights of the many Rurikid families over their properties and peasants were curtailed, their princely privileges revoked and effaced. Princes and boyars, including those like the Gedyminians who descended from foreign sovereigns, while not stripped of their nobility relative to the rest of society, were declared to share neither status nor prerogatives with the Tsar. Thanks to Ivan's own familial brutality his line soon came to an end, and with him the rule of the Rurikids in Russia.

The first Romanov to become Tsar in Russia did so through an obscure connection in the female line to the last tsars of the House of Rurik. After an interregnum (the so-called "Time of Troubles") during which the country was occupied by Polish-Lithuanians, Russia's Zemsky Sobor (assembly of the land) bypassed the numerous squabbling Rurikid princely branches who had, anyway, lost any claim to dynastic status during the Oprichnina, to award the vacant throne to Michael Romanov in 1613. Descended from Muscovite boyars, his paternal grandfather's sister, Anastasia Romanova, had become the first consort of Ivan the Terrible in 1547. Officially, Michael was not elected tsar from among the Russian people at large, but was 'called' to the throne as one of the nearest collaterals of Tsar Theodore I. Every sector of Russian society was called upon to prevent recurrence of the Time of Troubles by publicly and unreservedly swearing allegiance to Michael and the heirs of his body as their new dynasty of sovereigns.

In 1721 Peter assumed a different title, one unknown in Russia save to those fluent in Latin: Imperator. The consort of the imperator was declared to be the 'Imperatritsa'. The titles for imperial children of 'tsarevich' and 'tsarevna' were abandoned in favor of similar but newly-coined terms; 'Caesarevich' ('Tsesarevich' in Russian) and 'Caesarevna' ('Tsesarevna') essentially blended together the Slavic and the Latin, East and West — just the image Peter intended to evoke. Grand Duke and Grand Duchess fell into desuetude, although they remained titles belonging to the older generation of Romanovs, Peter's siblings and nieces.

When the childless Caesarevna Elisabeth Petrovna Romanova became empress, she summoned from Germany her late sister Anna Petrovna's son, Duke Karl Peter of Holstein-Gottorp, to take up his place in Russia as her heir. After converting to Orthodoxy, he was proclaimed successor to the throne, granted the title of grand duke and the style of Imperial Highness. Use of the old titles for this new heir was apparently intended to re-assure Russians that a new, foreign dynast could be inserted into the line of succession to Russia's throne without alarm. After all, Karl Peter was a grandson of the revered Peter the Great, whose name he adopted. When the young Peter's own son Paul Petrovich (by Princess Catherine of Anhalt-Zerbst) was born he, too, was proclaimed a grand duke – although designation as the official heir to the throne was omitted. When Peter's wife seized the throne from him, beginning her reign as Catherine the Great, Paul Petrovich was, again, promptly recognized as 'Grand Duke', but not as heir, in keeping with the Emperor Peter's law which allowed the Autocrat to name his or her successor. For the next 40 years, Russia's heir presumptive was known to the public simply as the Grand Duke Paul Petrovich.

Traditionally the title velikiy knyaz had no specific rules of descent: it belonged to all dynasts, and additionally, dynasts were created by the act of granting the title to some other heirs. Until the 19th century, the Russian Imperial House was usually in a precarious situation, often having no more than a couple of living male dynasts, if even that many. Empress Elisabeth, after all male-line descent had been exhausted, made her sister's son, the future Peter III of Russia a dynast and a Grand Duke.

In 1797, Peter III and Catherine II's disaffected son, Emperor Paul, having languished during his mother's reign under fear of being disinherited by imperial fiat, decreed the Fundamental Laws of the Russian Empire, which fixed the rules of succession for the duration of the monarchy. It is widely believed that Catherine's mistreatment of Paul left him in such a state of misogynistic paranoia that as soon as he became tsar he banned women from the throne forever. The opposite is true: Not only did he affirm that Romanov descendants in female line could inherit the throne, but Paul stipulated that any female dynast was to reign in her own right if the succession fell to her, and could not be bypassed in favor of her male issue. He also stipulated in law that every male Romanov upon attaining adulthood, and each new monarch during coronation, had to swear to uphold the succession laws unaltered.

However, no woman could succeed to the throne of Russia so long as there remained any males in the dynasty. Despite the execution of several males of the Imperial family besides her father and brother, there were still many Romanov grand dukes and princes who escaped from the Russian Revolution, the last of whom died in exile only in 1992.

Russian monarchical law stated that once the last Romanov male died (who would also have been emperor/tsar, at least in theory), that male's nearest female relative, or her descendant, automatically inherited the throne. This is known in Europe as 'semi-Salic' succession because, unlike the Salic law of history, it did not ban female succession altogether. But it meant that instead of an emperor's daughter or sister succeeding to the crown, a distant male relative, perhaps of a junior branch of the family, might inherit. Moreover, if he died without male issue his own daughters and sisters would have a prior claim to the crown than those of the previous emperor.

Semi-Salic law only distinguishes between females based on nearness of kinship to the last emperor, not dynasty. Thus it gave no preference to Romanovs per se, and none to Russians over foreigners, or to the Orthodox over the non-Orthodox.

Another complexity is the application of requirements for 'equal' marriage to Russia's dynasts. In 1820, the Fundamental Laws were modified to require that spouses of Romanovs had to be born of a "royal or sovereign family" if the issue were to have rights of succession to the Russian throne. Although Alexander III tightened this law in 1886 by altogether forbidding unequal marriages, in 1911 Nicholas II eased the restriction by ukase, allowing princes and princess of the Blood Imperial – but not grand dukes or grand duchesses – to marry unequally under three conditions: 1. the marriage had to obtain the emperor de jure's prior consent; 2. the issue would have no succession rights or membership in the imperial house; and, 3. Imperial consent would only be granted if the prince or princess first renounced his/her own personal right of succession as well.

Although three Romanovs complied with this law when they married (Princess Tatiana Konstantinovna in 1911, Princess Irina Alexandrovna in 1914, and Princess Catherine Ioanovna in 1937), three Romanovs violated it: Grand Duke Michael Aleksandrovich in October 1912, Grand Duchess Olga Alexandrovna in November 1916, and Grand Duchess Maria Pavlovna Jr. in

September 1917 (in post-revolution Russia). Under monarchical law, these last three weddings were void, since a 1797 Fundamental Law declared that marriages of members of the imperial dynasty were only legal if contracted with the emperor's prior approval, and such approval could not legally be granted to dynasts of grand ducal rank.

Because the Fundamental Laws only applied to sons and daughters of the imperial dynasty in the male line, the marriages of female Romanovs (whether grand duchess or princess) were fully subject to restriction, while those of their offspring – even though possessing Russian succession rights if descended from an approved marriage – were not (the sole exception were the children of Nicholas II's sister, Xenia, who had married a Romanov cousin).

The emperor was traditional and legal head of the Orthodox Church in Russia and his consort was expected to be Orthodox as well. Included in Russia's Fundamental Laws were Articles 184 and 185. The two laws regulated, but distinguished between, the marriages of male dynasts who were distant enough in the line of succession that their wives were unlikely to become empress, and those who, by contrast, could be expected at the time of marriage to be called to wear Russia's crown.

Article 184 applied to the former group, allowing them to marry non-Orthodox princesses dynastically. Article 185 was unspecific, affording the sovereign discretion, but in practice it was applied to the emperor's heir-apparent or heir-presumptive and their near heirs, to require them to marry Orthodox brides. Who decided which dynasts could only marry within the church? The Emperor. Of course it was always possible that a distant cousin would unexpectedly succeed to the crown. But in that case his or her consort could, under law, convert.

This religious compromise reflected the fact that when the Fundamental Laws were adopted, Russia was the only Orthodox dynasty reigning in Europe. It would have limited the bridal selection pool too much if the Romanovs had been rigid about Orthodoxy. Contrary to a popular misconception, it made no legal difference in the Romanov dynasty whether the child of an equal and approved marriage was born to an Orthodox mother so long as the child adhered to Orthodoxy in the event of inheritance of the throne.

Strictly speaking, all of Peter III's male-line descendants and their wives were also "Duke/Duchess of Holstein-Gottorp, Count/Countess of Oldenburg." In practice, these titles were only added to the Emperor's long string of secondary titles. Russia exchanged its claim to Gottorp for Oldenburg in 1777, and then donated the latter to a German branch of Holstein cousins. But the ducal and county titles continued to descend according to the rules of the Holy Roman Empire and, later, those of the German Empire within which the territories lay.

In 1762 Catherine II's son Grand Duke Paul Petrovich was accorded the title 'Tsesarevich' as heir apparent (or more commonly spelled *Tsarevich*). Until then, there had been no special title for the emperor's or tsar's eldest son. Paul's eldest son, Alexander, was likewise tsesarevich from 1797, after Paul was crowned Emperor. Paul's children, mostly born while he was heir apparent, were grand dukes and grand duchesses, which became the customary style for the emperor's children and other male-line descendants.

When Catherine the Great introduced French as the court language at St Petersburg, 'grande duchesse' was already the customary translation in that language, as was 'grand duchess' in English. Some linguists and historians consider this usage a modern mistranslation. But Catherine, being fluent in German, Russian and French, was better situated than anyone to assess the relevant nuances and alternatives. Thus, whatever its provenance, 'grand duchess' reflects sovereign choice rather than ignorant error.

In 1886, Alexander III restricted the title of grand duke to children and male-line grandchildren of an emperor, along with the attribute of Imperial Highness. Great-grandchildren were princes of the Blood Imperial with the style of Highness. Each of these great-grandsons' heirs-male in perpetuity (and their consorts) was also entitled to be addressed as Highness, while the remainder of male-line descendants were princes and Serene Highnesses. This latter style being fairly common among Russia's many non-royal princely families, in 1911 a group of grand dukes petitioned the emperor to extend the grand ducal title to additional generations of Romanovs, and to allow princes to marry unequally while retaining their dynastic rights. Nicholas II formally rejected these requests as is documented in the Frederiks Memorandum.

What, then, of the claim to be a 'grand duke' made by Vladimir Kirillovich (1917-1992)? And of his even more ambitious claim to be the de jure Emperor, entitled to exercise the Imperial prerogative even in the long years of Romanov exile following the Russian Revolution? And finally, what of the claim that his daughter, Maria Vladimirovna (b.1953) inherited headship of the Imperial dynasty upon her father's death despite the fact that there are a dozen or more males alive who descend in the legitimate male line from one or another of Russia's emperors?

These questions are closely bound together and usually accompanied by many more questions and doubts as to the rightful claimant to the defunct throne of the Romanovs. But upon examination, they appear answerable by reference to a few facts, seldom acknowledged in this context.

The rules governing succession and titles are legally non-existent and unenforceable since the overthrow of Russia's monarchy in 1917. Most Romanov descendants have lived outside Russia for generations now and use either no title at all or one conveniently made up and recognized by others as a courtesy. On the other hand, any discussion of Romanov claims and titles, whether historical, genealogical, political or purely hypothetical is meaningless unless the rules that were in force when the monarchy existed structure the conversation. Yet the challenges to the dynastic claims of Kirill Vladimirovich, Vladimir Kirillovich, Maria Vladimirovna and/or George Mikhailovich invariably ignore – and demand that others ignore – the steps taken by them to comply with Russia's Fundamental Laws governing the succession at enormous personal sacrifice, while ignoring the contradictions or inadequacies of the objections raised to their claims. Sometimes it seems as if only the Vladimirovichi are held to a standard of legality or tradition in order to qualify as claimants to headship of the Romanov dynasty. Others who assert such leadership or repudiate claims, too often do so without addressing questions about their own standing, according to law or tradition, as Romanov dynasts, or about the reasoning they apply in determining the validity of others' claims to dynastic status: a chorus of "never mind!" is too often submitted as the only reply to any questioning of alternative rationales or assertions.

Never mind, for instance, that other dynasties have lost thrones, wealth, citizenship, and lives (Spain, Bulgaria) during revolution, but equal status (so-called *"ebenbürtig"*) marriage remained the norm in their dynasties (even during exile) until the heads of their dynasties changed the norms – and not before.

Never mind that post-Revolution the Vladimirovichi branch of the Romanovs managed to contract four marriages between 1925 and 1976 into families previously recognized as ebenbürtig, apparently not finding it impossible to comply with Russia's dynastic (Pauline) law on marriages in exile.

Never mind that twenty years after the 1917 revolution, three of the four surviving grand dukes and two adult Romanov princes not only recognized Vladimir as the rightful head of the dynasty according to Pauline law, but signed an affidavit affirming *"that the rights of each one of the Members of the Imperial House of Russia are precisely defined by the Fundamental State Laws of the Russian Empire and the Statute on the Imperial Family, and are well known to all of us and we have all committed ourselves by a special oath to observe them."*

Never mind that as soon after the revolution as 1924, Grand Duke Alexander Mikhailovich provided his signature and those of four of his adult sons on a similar pledge of allegiance to Grand Duke Kirill Vladimirovich, which stated, *"We submit ourselves to you and are ready to serve our beloved country as our fathers served it, and according to their principles."* Excluding the two of Alexander's sons who never signed (Dimitri and Vassili, both of whom pre-deceased Vladimir Kirillovich, leaving no sons), there were only two adult male Romanovs living who, by 1938, had not agreed in writing to continue to be bound by the Pauline succession laws: Prince George Konstantinovich, who died unmarried the next year, and Prince Roman Petrovich.

Never mind that Roman Petrovich's son, Nicholas Romanovich, as President of the Romanoff Family Association, stated in an official declaration published in *Point de Vue* on 12 May 1992, that *"Kirill's rights were incontestable,"* yet Kirill, as acknowledged head of the dynasty, never recognized the 1921 marriage of Roman's parents as dynastically valid. Never mind that of the four members of the Romanoff Family Association (alleged to be dynasts) who have rejected the dynasticity of Vladimir Kirillovich and/or his daughter Maria Vladimirovna, two are themselves children of marriages deemed morganatic by the man they or their fathers accepted in exile as rightful head of the Romanov dynasty. The other two are Dimitri Romanovich (b. 1926) and the late Princess Vera Konstantinovna (1906-2001), neither of whom produced dynastic offspring eligible to claim legal heirship to Nicholas II, Peter the Great or Michael Romanov.

For émigrés, monarchists, sticklers and dreamers, article 53 of the Fundamental Laws remained crucial long after the Romanovs were executed or exiled: *"On the demise of the Emperor, his heir accedes to the Throne by virtue of the law of succession itself, which confers this right upon him. The accession of an Emperor to the throne is counted from the day of the demise of his predecessor."*

Properly, this means that for those who reject the legality (if not the reality) of the Russian Revolution, there has been no interregnum since 1917. The laws that governed Romanov succession and titles under the monarchy are considered still valid, regardless of de facto obstacles to their enforcement. Therefore, if one applies the formula of the Fundamental Laws to the House of Romanov to determine who would today be Russia's monarch, that person's right to use of the titles and prerogatives of the Russian Emperor follows automatically, regardless of what discretion is deemed politic to employ in the real world.

There are, in other words, living grand dukes in today's world. We have but to acknowledge the tradition they incarnate to know them.

Charles B. Stewart
Los Angeles, CA
June 2012

1

The Sons of Grand Duke Vladimir Alexandrovich

Grand Duke Kirill Vladimirovich
(1876-1938)

By John van der Kiste & Arturo E. Beéche

Vladimir Alexandrovich and the former Duchess Marie of Mecklenburg-Schwerin married at St Petersburg on 12/24 August 1874. Upon entering the Russian Imperial Family, she adopted the Russian name Maria (Marie) Pavlovna, but was also referred to as the *"Grand Duchess Vladimir."* The second son of Grand Duke and Grand Duchess Vladimir, Grand Duke Kirill Vladimirovich was born at Tsarskoe Selo on 30 September/12 October 1876.[1] Their first son, Alexander, died in infancy six month's after Kirill's birth. Later there would be two more brothers, Boris and Andrei, and a sister, Helen.

From boyhood the sea fascinated Kirill. In his memoirs, he recalled, *"To master the elements, one thing was essential above all others, and that was sail, its management, and the ability to maneuver in all the possible and seemingly impossible situations with which the cunning and the vicious nature of the sea could confront one."*[2] He entered the Imperial Navy at the age of fourteen. Two years later Kirill began preparations and studies for the intermediate Naval College examination, which he undertook in 1895. In the meantime, he served on various ships and ironclads, while focusing on gaining further experience as a sailor.

As was the case with most Romanovs, Kirill was to become very fond of foreign travel. Vladimir Alexandrovich and Marie Pavlovna were inveterate, tireless travelers and every year saw them visiting relations and friends, as well as attending royal events, throughout Europe. When he was seventeen, Kirill accompanied his parents on a major tour of the Iberian Peninsula. Besides visiting schools, institutions and factories, the traveling Vladimirs also visited the Spanish royal family, *"Queen Christina of Spain...I remember her pretty gait and her elegant and truly queenly bearing. The King was a rather naughty little boy, always running away from his nurse,"* Kirill later recalled.[3]

Kirill enjoyed a happy childhood with his brothers and sister. All the Vladimirovichi children were to remain deeply attached, as well as fiercely loyal, to one another. Given what life had in store for them, this was one of the most precious gifts their parents could have passed on to the children. Kirill recalled that his early years were filled with dedicated English nannies that taught the Vladimirovichi children the English language before they even learned their native Russian. In fact, Kirill's English accent was to be much clearer, than that of his future wife Victoria Melita, who always spoke with a guttural accent reminiscent of her German ancestors and roots.

Grand Duke Vladimir and his wife were very attached to one another and in three and a half decades of marriage there was never a word of marital discord. They were also deeply fond of their children, for whom they would move heaven and earth in due time. Grand Duke Vladimir, who was said to have been jealous of his brother Alexander III, was particularly proud of his strong, virile sons. One can certainly imagine his satisfaction at producing such sturdy children in comparison to the weakling sons of Tsar Alexander III. Not that Grand Duke Vladimir's sons would turn out to be paragons of virtue, mind you. In the end the two youngest, in particular, Boris and Andrei, were to be quite a disappointment as they matured into selfish and spoiled men, simply too fond of an easy life of privilege and unwilling to sacrifice any of their whims to benefit of anyone but themselves. Their romantic entanglements, as we will see later, were to be the source of untold chagrin, particularly to their ambitious mother.

In spite of the differences between Tsar Alexander III and his brother Vladimir, Kirill was always deeply fond of his uncle. In the summer of 1894 Kirill was honored with an invitation from his bear-like Uncle Sasha. The young Grand Duke was serving on the *Vovin*, a fully rigged frigate that served as a training ship. While onboard, Kirill was summoned by the ship's captain, who told him, *"Your Imperial Highness is to report to His Majesty…There is a torpedo-boat alongside which will take you to the Imperial Yacht."*[4] Alexander III, who was convalescing, happened to be sailing on the *Tsarevna*. Knowing that Kirill was on a training ship nearby, the Tsar invited his nephew to spend some days in his company. Even in later years, Kirill remembered those days fondly, *"I spent two delightful days with them* [Alexander III and some of his family], *and had, to use the schoolboy expression, a real treat."*[5]

Along for the visit Kirill found Grand Duke Alexis Mikhailovich, who although a first cousin of Alexander III, was but a year older than Kirill. To keep the boys entertained during their stay, Alexander III challenged them to a race. Michael Alexandrovich, Alexis Mikhailovich and Kirill Vladimirovich were asked to row their own dinghy in a competition to test their seamanship and strength. Kirill easily beat his cousins and Alexander III rewarded him handsomely.[6] Sadly, it was to be the last memory Kirill would have of both his Uncle Sasha and cousin Alexis; the Tsar and the young Grand Duke would be dead within a year.

Although Kirill was not in Livadia to witness the death of Alexander III, he was present at his funeral. The Tsar's passing was a deathblow to the dynasty. Kirill recalled that, *"Never again was there to be that same of spirit of understanding among us, that easy fellowship and gay merriment. All that had come to a final conclusion. It was a harsh stroke to Aunt Minnie, whose personality had been ideal for the exalted position which she had so admirably occupied…a dismal tragedy for Russia, the full extent and real nature of which is clearer to me now more than ever before."*[7]

Tsar Nicholas II, thoroughly unprepared for the great task that his father's death placed on his young shoulders, was overwhelmed with sadness and foreboding. Not only had he lost a parent he loved deeply, but also he was tsar now. At a time when he should have been enjoying his recent engagement to Alix of Hesse and by Rhine, Nicholas II found himself unwillingly performing the perfunctory obligations of presiding over his father's funeral, as well as the inauguration of a new reign during troubling times for Russia. Due to the special circumstances caused by the Tsar's untimely death, Nicholas' marriage ceremony was quickly organized. To marry Nicholas II, Alix became an Orthodox and took the name Alexandra Feodorovna. Kirill, along with his brothers Boris and Andrei, and their cousin Michael Alexandrovich, served as best men at Nicholas' wedding, a show of family loyalty that would, in later years, disappear.

More than a year later, Kirill traveled to Moscow, a city that had caused a deep impression on him several years before. This opportunity had deeper meaning, for at hand was the coronation of Tsar Nicholas II. Kirill later remembered that, *"On the day of the Coronation we assembled outside Moscow at the Petrovsky Palace for our entry into the capital...I was riding a grey charger, a present to my father from the Emir of Buchara...The Emperor entered Moscow on a white charger, heading a brilliant cavalcade. He was followed by his uncles all in the different uniforms of their regiments, next came we and the Royal delegates from all the monarchies of Europe."*[8] Kirill was deeply impacted by the mysticism involved in the coronation ceremony and he would never forget his impressions of the exciting days spent in Moscow. However, and interestingly, he did not dwell much on the tragedy of Khodynka Field for which his Uncle Serge Alexandrovich was responsible. Perhaps in an effort to protect the memory of his assassinated uncle, Kirill's reference to the negligence exhibited on that tragic day was rather succinct, *"The organization* [of the coronation]*, barring one disastrous oversight, was quite impeachable."*[9] This oversight, better known as the Khodynka Field tragedy, not only caused the trampling to death of nearly 1400 people, but also the injury of more than a thousand others. It was to be remembered as an ominous beginning to what turned out to be a disastrous reign.

The coronation was not the only aspect of Kirill's trip to cause a deep impression within him. His heart, it seems, was also set aflutter by the presence of his first cousin Grand Duchess Victoria Melita of Hesse and by Rhine. She was there accompanying her husband the Grand Duke Ernst Ludwig, only surviving brother of Nicholas II's wife. Furthermore, Victoria Melita was no stranger to Russia for after all her mother was the indomitable Grand Duchess Marie Alexandrovna, who back in 1874 had married Prince Alfred, Duke of Edinburgh and later Saxe-Coburg & Gotha, Queen Victoria's second son. The coronation, no doubt was an unforgettable experience, but just as thrilling was the entanglement that would come out of it.

In 1897 Grand Duke Kirill joined the ship *Rossyra* on her maiden voyage to England. While there he participated in the naval review that formed part of Queen Victoria's Diamond Jubilee celebrations that summer. His English uncle, Alfred, who was an Admiral of the Fleet, presented Kirill to Queen Victoria during the Jubilee festivities. It was a thrilling experience for the impressionable youngster. Unlike his parents, who were believed to be Germanophiles, Kirill greatly admired the English. Of the old and imposing Queen and Empress he recalled, *"We lunched with Queen Victoria, whom we found very amiable. She made an very favourable impression upon me – there was something quite distinctive about her, which only a strong personality can convey on the first acquaintance."*[10]

At around this time, Kirill reconnected again with Victoria Melita. Of course their 'friendship' was very discrete since she was still married, albeit unhappily. Nonetheless, prudence was of the essence and neither party wanted their deep attraction to become *vox populi* among the vicious wagging tongues at various European courts. The fact that Kirill and Ducky were grandchildren of Tsar Alexander II helped provide cover for their close relationship. Kirill's father, Vladimir, was an older brother of the Duchess of Edinburgh and Saxe-Coburg and Gotha, Marie Alexandrovna. Kirill's mother and Duchess Marie also happened to be very close friends, not just sisters-in-law.

Victoria Melita of Edinburgh was born on the island of Malta in 1876.[11] At the age of eighteen she married her first cousin the Grand Duke Ernst Ludwig of Hesse and by Rhine. Their grandmother, Queen Victoria, encouraged the alliance as she felt the characters and personalities of groom and bride suited them. She, along with her grandchildren and their families, was to be deeply disappointed. Ernst Ludwig and Victoria Melita loved a good joke, while enjoying laughter and pranks. None of these endeavors made for a good, solid, lasting marriage. The first cracks in their relationship were apparent by the time a daughter was born in 1895. By then what kept Ernst Ludwig and Victoria Melita together was an endless row of parties and weekend guests. Kirill, as it turned out, was one of those invited to join in the fun.

Throughout his life, particularly after the Russian Revolution, Kirill was to be constantly accused of nefarious plots to do away with Tsar Nicholas II. As a ruler, Nicholas ineptly stumbled from one crisis to the next, while the country's future appeared increasingly uncertain. The fact that by the end of the century the Empress had only given birth to girls, only served to muddy the imperial rumor mill. If Nicholas produced no sons, then the succession would pass to his brothers. First in line was the deathly-ill Grand Duke George Alexandrovich; second in line was Grand Duke Michael Alexandrovich, of whom not much was expected or thought of by the Imperial Family at large. It was quite feasible that since Grand Duke Vladimir and his sons came after Michael, Kirill could inherit the Russian throne at some point. Given that relations between the Vladimirovichi and Nicholas II seemed to be tense, as the Tsar was much in awe of his uncle, rumors about plots to dispose of the ruler were ripe. Earlier in 1899 even *The New York Times* published a short article, rumor-based as it turned out, in which *"a plot against the Tsar…has been discovered, the object of the conspirators being to take advantage of the state of the Tsar's health to remove him from power."*[12] The scurrilous report mentioned that given George Alexandrovich's worrisome health (he would die later that year), the overthrow of Nicholas II was seen as a solution to restore strong-arm rule in Russia. Nothing came of the alleged plot, of course, but innuendo of this sort was to become part of the lore surrounding the Vladimirovichi in general, Kirill in particular.

In August 1899 Kirill was invited to Wolfsgarten, the country estate of Ernst Ludwig and Victoria Melita, whose turbulent married life was under increasing strain. His brother Boris had received a personal invitation from Ducky, as she knew it would be inadvisable to invite Kirill directly. Rumors of their liaison were already widely whispered about; no one was fooled, and hence discretion was tantamount. On his second visit a year later, they knew they were falling in love; *"the three weeks which I spent at Wolfsgarten in the autumn of 1900,"* he wrote later, *"were decisive for the whole of my life. Thereafter we were to meet as often as possible."*[13]

Queen Victoria had been greatly responsible for bringing the Grand Duke and Duchess of Hesse and by Rhine together, and while she was still alive they had tried to make their marriage work. However, once she was gone, Ernst Ludwig and his wife agreed to divorce, much to the consternation of their families. For a time, Ducky was treated as a virtual outcast by most of her relations. In 1903, the death from typhoid fever of their only child Elisabeth signaled a final break from the Darmstadt days. Victoria Melita placed her Hessian Order inside her daughter's coffin at the funeral. By doing so, she symbolized that a new beginning was at hand and a chapter had been closed.[14]

Once divorced from Ernst Ludwig, and while living under her mother's roof in Coburg and the Château Fabron near Nice, Victoria Melita continued receiving the visits of her beloved Kirill. Their courtship was an open secret. The longer they went without seeing each other, the more their love deepened. The 'secret' was already out and even Alexandra Feodorovna was well aware that Ducky and Kirill were more involved than they let on. She had always tried to counsel her own brother and his wife, hoping that by doing so she would help their floundering marriage. The Empress wished to protect her brother's reputation at all costs. For that she begged her sister-in-law's aid in asking that all people needed to know, was that the divorce came as a consequence of the couple finding it impossible to *"get on together."* In a letter to Grand Duchess Xenia Alexandrovna she asked for help in, *"curtailing any gossip you might hear, for the sake of the whole family."*[15]

Perturbed by the limbo in which Ducky's relationship with Kirill left the couple, Marie Alexandrovna decided to take matters into her own hands. She wrote a letter to Nicholas II's mother asking for her intervention with the Tsar. In it Marie asked the Dowager Empress' support to obtain Nicholas II's permission for Kirill and Victoria Melita to marry secretly. Nicholas II denied the request and sent Boris Vladimirovich to Coburg to inform Aunt Marie of his decision. Relations between the Dowager Duchess of Saxe-Coburg & Gotha and her imperial nephew suffered greatly because of this refusal, which all involved felt was more Alexandra Feodorovna's doing than her husband's.

Meanwhile, Kirill was about to be sent on naval service to the Far East. During a spell of leave before setting sail, he and Ducky had dinner one evening by themselves. It was a bittersweet occasion, for the object of his affections, he noted, was in exile and he was, *"going to the unknown, to the uncertainty of a blank future."*[16]

Several months later, after his ship *Peresviet* docked at Vladivostok, he received a telegram from Tsar Nicholas II, ordering him to stay in the Far East indefinitely. He knew pressure was being brought on him to keep Kirill and Ducky apart. It was followed by a dispatch from his father, to the effect that he should submit to the Tsar's will for his own good. Considering that Tsar Nicholas was most in awe of his Uncle Vladimir, this was an ominous sign. Kirill was being asked to subordinate his own personal hopes and wishes to the cause of family unity. Furious at the thought that plots were being hatched behind his back, he felt as if being condemned to unofficial exile. Tension rose.

By Christmas 1902 he was in Singapore, where he received a watch from Ducky as a present. Previously that summer, Kirill had been on an official visit to Japan with the expressed object of fostering better relations and increasing trade with that nation.[17] On his return voyage he spent three weeks in Singapore, and mingled freely with members of the British Pacific squadron in port. He made friends with a British sloop commander, who had served with the Grand Duchess' late father and knew the Edinburgh family well. Reminders of whom and what he had left behind haunted him daily.

Early in 1903 Kirill returned to the Mediterranean, and at Villefranche he learned that a steamer was to be put at his father's disposal. As he had expected, Grand Duke Vladimir came and tried half-heartedly to persuade Kirill to give up any hope of marrying the former Grand Duchess of Hesse and by Rhine. Kirill remained obdurate and his doting father gave in with good grace and without much resistance. The latter had nothing but sympathy and good wishes for his son, who was determined to marry his beloved in the face of such odds. He appeared basically supportive of the couple, no matter what the rest of the Imperial Family might think.

Later that year, during the summer, after returning to Russia on naval leave, he spent a few quiet weeks with his parents before going to Coburg, to visit with Ducky, her younger sister and their mother. He and Ducky did a good deal of motoring together, visiting several cities while also becoming acquainted with much of historic Germany. While visiting his parents at Tsarskoe Selo, he had an interview with the Tsar, who was his usual affable and sympathetic self but refused to give any indication as to the future prospects of a marriage with Victoria Melita, beyond a vague suggestion that, *"things would, possibly, straighten out."*[18] He allowed Kirill to visit Coburg, which was significant as in accordance with imperial law, no member of the Romanov Dynasty, unless on active service, could leave Russia without the sovereign's express permission.

Meanwhile, Victoria Melita's youngest sister, Beatrice, was in the midst of an entanglement of her own. Beatrice, known to the family as Bee or Baby Bee, had fallen madly in love with Grand Duke Michael Alexandrovich, Nicholas II's only surviving brother, and until the birth of Tsarevich Alexis Nikolaievich in 1904, his heir as well. The problem rested on the fact that the Russian Orthodox Church banned marriages between first cousins. As was the case with Kirill and Ducky, Baby Bee and Michael were also first cousins. Unlike the other lovebirds, Michael and Baby Bee did not have as many opportunities to see each other. In a letter Michael sent to her in Summer 1903, he expressed his utter jealousy about it, while also mentioning that Nicholas II is shy and feels overwhelmed by the excessively protective *"actions of the Vladimirs."*[19]

By then the tension raised at the Imperial court by Kirill's relationship with Ducky had reached a boiling point. In a letter to Bee Michael Alexandrovich wrote that, *"Mother says it is a grave mistake to allow Kirill and Ducky to see each other, as it only makes it worse. I understand why she tells me this, so I stop thinking that I may be allowed to see you. Can you understand how horrible this situation is?"*[20] Fearful of not being permitted to see Michael, Beatrice told her mother about the relationship the cousins shared. Marie of Coburg was a doctrinaire social martinet about many things. However, when it came to the love affairs of her children, she usually tried to help them survive these entanglements unscathed. No sooner than Baby Bee had made her mother privy to the secret, that Marie Alexandrovna took matters into her own hands. From Russia, Michael wrote to Bee saying that, *"For the first time I have spoken openly to your mother about our feelings and she was endearing. I cannot begin to tell you how happy I am about this."*[21] Nicholas II's reaction to Michael and Baby Bee's affair was just as unbending as that which he had demonstrated toward Kirill and Ducky. However, unlike Kirill, Michael Alexandrovich ended backing away from Baby Bee and eventually entered a morganatic marriage with a divorced commoner, much to the utter chagrin and devastation of his brother. One is thus left to wonder how differently history may have been had these relationships received the Tsar's approval, not his interference and derailing commands.

Not surprisingly, much animosity between the various Romanovs was caused by Nicholas II's position on these matrimonial matters. In a previously unknown letter sent by Michael Alexandrovich to Baby Bee, and which Ana de Sagrera first revealed in her dual biography of Beatrice and Queen Victoria Eugenia of Spain, he dared ask what were Bee's impressions of Alexandra Feodorovna. *"Alix has returned to Darmstadt after a four year absence, which makes her very happy. I have never asked you before if you like her or not. A stupid question perhaps. However, I would like to have an answer,"* the tsar's brother wrote.[22] There is no trace of Bee's answer. One can perhaps assume that it could have also revealed what both her mother and Ducky felt concerning Alix and her supposed role in Nicholas II's refusal to allow Kirill and Michael to continue with their respective relationships. However, as it now seems, the refusal of permission rested solely on Nicholas' shoulders.

The Tsar probably thought that this infatuation between his cousins would run its course. He had been as appalled and astonished as the rest of the family by Ducky's divorce, describing it in a letter to his mother as, *"a terrible and unexpectedly grave event,"* and adding that in such a case as this *"even the loss of a dear person is better than the general disgrace of a divorce."*[23] He thought Kirill would never dream of asking his permission to marry a divorced woman whose previous husband was still alive.

Two events in 1904 stiffened the resolve of Kirill and Ducky to become husband and wife. The first was his narrow escape from death in the Russo-Japanese war. Baby Bee, who had been traveling in Egypt in an effort to recover from the collapse of her affair with Michael Alexandrovich, heard of Kirill, along with his brother Boris, having joined the war effort. *"Very sad to know about this war, it is horrible to think of the pain it will bring. My two cousins, Kirill and Boris, are there as well. May God help in everything ending well."*[24]

Kirill and Boris volunteered for service in the rapidly developing conflict in the Far East. Nicholas II was very proud of his cousins' desire to serve in what was hoped would be a short, and of course victorious campaign. On 27 February, Kirill headed to war. Earlier that afternoon Kirill had visited Nicholas II to take leave of his cousin. Later that day at the train station in St Petersburg there was a touching scene as he bid farewell to his obviously emotional parents. Grand Duchess Vladimir *"broke down at the last moment and wept as she embraced her son* [Kirill],"[25] showing to all present that even an imperial mother feared for the safety of her soldier son. Boris and Andrei, there to lend moral support, held Kirill in a long brotherly embrace. Grand Duke Vladimir fared no better and shed countless tears as the train slowly rolled away from the station.

Indeed, off to war Kirill went. Just nearly six weeks after his emotional departure from St Petersburg, tragedy struck. He was First Officer on board the flagship *Petropavlovsk* as it entered Port Arthur on 13 April and was blown to smithereens by a Japanese mine. Of the 711 officers and men on board, only 80 were saved. Kirill was badly hurt: he suffered serious burns and his back muscles were strained. On top of that, he suffered from shell shock. The press reported Kirill's miraculous survival in glowing prose saying that he *"was blown some distance by the force of the explosion."* Furthermore, Kirill survived, *"owing to his skill as a swimmer…was able to remain a long time above water, refusing to be rescued till the weaker were saved."*[26]

Kirill's injuries were to be long lasting and would change his life forever. One newspaper article said that as a consequence of the explosion, he suffered, *"displacement of the heart, resulting from extreme weakness."*[27] In fact, as it turns out, the Grand Duke suffered from post-traumatic stress disorder brought about by shell shock. He developed a visceral fear of the ocean and felt, from then on, deeply challenged when performing his naval obligations. His recovery was painfully slow. Three weeks after the sinking, he was brought back to St Petersburg, where Kirill, arrived quietly, and only his family and a few friends were at the railroad station to greet him. As soon as he was fit enough to do so, he traveled to Coburg, where Ducky and her sister greeted him with much anticipation on what turned out to be an unforgettable reunion, at which he felt, *"like one who was returning from the land of the dead to new life."*[28]

The second important event that year was Kirill's position in the Russian line of succession. As long as the Empress continued giving birth to daughters, Kirill was seen as a likely successor to the Imperial throne. Not many in St Petersburg considered Michael Alexandrovich worthy of the position, plus his dalliances with unsuitable women only contributed to that misconceived perception. The succession had been at the heart of Vladimir Alexandrovich's half-hearted efforts to dissuade his son from marrying a first cousin, and a divorced woman. The birth of the Tsarevich Alexis on 30 July/12 August 1904 altered the situation and Kirill's chances of inheriting the throne now seemed remote. This made Kirill feel more at ease with his choice of bride and he believed that Nicholas II would thus have a lesser issue with allowing the marriage to proceed, particularly if presented with an accomplished fact.

As we mentioned before, once he was able to leave St Petersburg, Kirill obtained permission to convalesce in Europe. He had been suffering from post-traumatic stress disorder and believed that a stay with Ducky, in Germany and the South of France, would do wonders for his physical and mental sanity. Of course, he had other plans in mind as well. Kirill traveled to Coburg and later spent time with his Aunt Marie and Ducky at the Château Fabron. In the eyes of his cousins, Kirill had become a legendary figure, what with his surviving the tragedy in the Far East and his military exploits, he seemed turned into an irresistible figure. Bee loved to sit around and listen to Kirill's war stories, particularly those related to his surviving the sinking of the *Petropavlovsk*. "*What had saved me were my clothes,*" Kirill recalled.[29] Furthermore, he continued reminiscing, "*It was bitterly cold, and the water incidentally, was just a few degrees above zero. I was dressed in a padded coat, underneath which I had a fur-lined jacket and an English woolen sweater. This very likely gave me some buoyancy, otherwise I would have gone to join the rest of the six hundred and thirty-one* [men] *who perished.*"

Kirill also recalled that upon returning from the Far East, he was welcomed by his Uncle Serge Alexandrovich in Moscow. It was the last time Kirill saw him, as within a year Serge would be blown to pieces by a nihilist's bomb. Once in St Petersburg, Kirill had an audience with his cousin Tsar Nicholas II. He expected the Tsar to be interested in obtaining his impressions of the war and the conditions facing Russians in the Far East. However, Kirill was to be disappointed for during the audience, "*it struck me as odd that he did not ask me about the Petropavlovsk disaster...nor did he refer to the war or ask how it was progressing. The conversation was confined to an exchange of the usual politenesses which generally concern themselves with health and weather. He seemed tired and overwrought.*"[30]

Being under great strain and suffering from nightmares and stress, Kirill's stay in Europe was destined to bring him much calm and rest. Undoubtedly, having Ducky by his side, as well as living under the roof of his indulging Aunt Marie, greatly contributed to his mental and physical recovery. Meanwhile, efforts to obtain Nicholas II's approval for his marriage to Ducky were renewed. At one point the Tsar asked that Kirill wait and let time settle the matter. Kirill always believed that in saying so, Nicholas II had given him tacit approval for the wedding plans. As he would find out soon enough, Kirill was deeply mistaken.

In the Fall 1904 Kirill returned to Russia and received a staff position at the Admiralty. His work centered on advising on a new type of ship that the Russian fleet was looking into building. He described this work as, "*neither exacting nor interesting.*"[31] He did recall later that it was at that same time when the Admiralty approached the Russian emperor with the idea to send the Baltic Fleet to relieve the Russians under attack at Port Arthur. Nicholas II listened to the naval 'experts' and sided with them. It was not just an erroneous decision, but it would prove to be one of his reign's worst mistakes.

Kirill had always intended to rejoin the Russian Navy as soon as his health allowed, but in May 1905 the fleet was decisively defeated by Japan at Tsushima. Checkmate! Russia could not, any longer, pursue such a hopeless conflict. Peace was promptly signed in August. In the meantime, the financial and social strain caused by the war brought the country to a standstill. Riots were widespread, as were strikes. Violence became commonplace and the revolutionaries renewed their efforts to target the Romanovs. To his mother, Nicholas II wrote, "*It makes me sick to read the news! Nothing but strikes in schools and factories, murdered policemen, Cossacks and soldiers, riots, disorder, mutinies. But the ministers, instead of acting with quick decision, only assemble in council like a lot of frightened hens and cackle about providing united ministerial action... ominous quiet days began, quiet indeed because there was complete order in the streets, but at the same time everybody knew that something was going to happen – the troops were waiting for the signal, but the other side would not begin. One had the same feeling, as before a thunderstorm in summer! Everybody was on edge and extremely nervous and of course, that sort of strain could not go on for long.... We are in the midst of a revolution with an administrative apparatus entirely disorganized, and in this lies the main danger.*"[32]

Earlier that year, Grand Duke Serge's assassination sent a thunderbolt of shock through the Romanov Dynasty. The country teetered on the brink of disaster and violence spread like wildfire. Even the farthest confines of the empire were ablaze. Left without any other choice, Nicholas II was forced to submit to stark reality. On 5 August 1905, the Tsar issued a manifesto calling for the convocation of a popularly elected legislative body. The Duma had come into existence. It was the end of autocracy.

Kirill and Ducky spent the rest of that summer in Germany visiting Coburg and Munich, where he was a regular outpatient for treatment at a sanatorium. He also went to Langenburg, where he had *"a jolly visit"* with Ducky's sister Alexandra and her husband, the amiable Hereditary Prince Ernst of Hohenlohe-Langenburg.[33] Prior to his departure from St Petersburg, Kirill sought the advise of a prelate close to Empress Alexandra Feodorovna. He hoped that if the priest gave him clarity on the matter, this would make it easier for Nicholas II to finally grant permission for him to marry Ducky. Father Yanishev, confessor of the Imperial Family, assured him that from the point of view of canon law, there was no objection to him marrying his divorced cousin. Kirill felt encouraged by this and began preparing his wedding, which would take place after cessation of hostilities with Japan.

The preparation for his wedding presented Kirill with a few complications. Earlier that summer Nicholas II had again expressed his opposition to the marriage and cautioned Kirill against it.[34] No Russian priest would dare perform the wedding vows for fear of offending the Tsar and causing a swift reaction from the Holy Synod. Hence, his choice fell on Aunt Marie Alexandrovna's private confessor, Father Smirnoff, who officiated a small private ceremony at Tegernsee, near Munich, on 8 October 1905. No one from the groom's family was present. His ever-supportive Uncle Alexis Alexandrovich, who was in Munich at the time, was invited to Tegernsee, though without being told in advance of the reason why. He was delayed by the weather and arrived during the feast that followed the wedding ceremony. When told of what had happened, he was dumbfounded at first, but then warmly congratulated the couple. Yet, a new storm brewed and when news hit the Imperial court, the Tsar was livid.

After a few days' honeymoon, Kirill returned to St Petersburg with much trepidation. He went there to inform the rest of the family of what he had done. His worried parents were not surprised. He intended to tell the Tsar the next day, but was forestalled when on the evening of his arrival Count Vladimir Fredericks, the court minister, came to see the family after supper and while they were playing bridge. He brought an ultimatum from the Tsar announcing that Grand Duke Kirill Vladimirovich was to be deprived of his honors and income, struck off the Imperial Navy list, and had forty-eight hours to leave Russia. In none of their previous interviews had the mild-mannered sovereign given any hint of such severe penalties if his cousin disobeyed.[35] Kirill and his parents were in shock and they believed the Empress was behind it. Alexandra Feodorovna's critics blamed her for convincing Nicholas to severely punish Kirill and make an example of him. Alexandra's myrirad critics also said it was her latest attempt to seek revenge on Ducky for divorcing Ernst Ludwig. They were all mistaken, as it now seems.

Grand Duke and Grand Duchess Vladimir were enraged and horrified by the Tsar's decision. She poured out her fury in a long letter to her uncle, Prince Heinrich VII Reuß zu Köstritz, telling him that, *"the blind vindictiveness and rage of the young Empress has, for sheer malice, exceeded everything the wildest imagination could conceive."* The matter, she went on, had *"been dealt with as though some terrible crime had been committed and judgment has been passed in this sense."*[36] Marie, perhaps blinded by her maternal pain and fury, was most unfair to Alexandra Feodorovna. The Empress and Victoria Melita, contrary to popular belief, had always been fond of one another. As granddaughters of Queen Victoria, Alix of Hesse and Ducky of Edinburgh had spent part of their childhood under the aegis of their English grandmother, not just as visitors to Osborne House on the Isle of Wight, but also at Windsor, Balmoral and Buckingham Palace.

Several historians have gone as far as claiming that Alix felt displaced by Ducky after her English cousin married Ernst Ludwig. However, letters recently published point to the polar opposite. In these testaments to history, Alix is filled with concern for Ducky's well being, while she constantly inquires as to her emotional state and asks for Ernst Ludwig to have Ducky write to her more often. Every letter Alix received from Ducky was the cause of much joy. In 1898 Alexandra Feodorovna heard of Marie of Romania's unconventional behavior in Bucharest and pitied her. *"Poor little thing, I wish she had a more sensible and severe husband to prevent her foolishness. It comes all from her bringing up – always the beauty, the painter and told in her face,"* Alexandra wrote. In the Empress' opinion Ducky, who was *"a thousand times more handsome & clever & deep,"* was a far better character than her sister Marie. *"How can parents have favourites & when a girl is pretty & vain they ought not to tell it her,"* was Alexandra's final sentence.[37] These are hardly the words of a woman holding a visceral grudge against a cousin who 'displaced' her in Darmstadt.

It is very likely that Tsar Nicholas, surrounded on all sides by misbehaving Romanovs, among them his own siblings, sought to make an example of Kirill's predicament. Let us not forget that at the time, Nicholas II had already been dealing with various domestic scandals emanating from within the confines of the Imperial Family. Paul Alexandrovich, Michael Alexandrovich and Olga Alexandrovna, the Tsar's uncle, brother and sister, caused three of these scandals that threaten to taint the image of the dynasty. As if it was not enough that Nicholas II was busy dealing with a worsening political situation within Russia, now he had to contend with turmoil and disobedience within his own family. This would have never happened under Alexander III, many whispered. Enough was enough! Either Kirill would have to obey his imperial cousin or face serious consequences. Consequently, he was made an example. All other Romanovs were thus made aware that the Tsar had had enough of their shenanigans.

Turmoil within the Romanov Dynasty was always present, but up until then, it remained hidden from public view. That changed with Nicholas II's uncle. Grand Duke Paul Alexandrovich firstly married Princess Alexandra of Greece, who died in childbirth in 1891. Left a desolate widower with two children, Paul felt lonely and sought companionship elsewhere. A lady friend with whom he eventually settled into quiet domesticity provided this solace. In 1897 Paul and Olga von Pistolkhors (née Karnovitch), who was still married to her husband Eric, produced a son, Vladimir Pavlovich, who would later receive the title of Prince Paley and attain widespread recognition as an acclaimed poet. Paul asked Nicholas II for permission to marry Olga, but was denied it. Undeterred by his nephew's refusal, Paul left Russia and married his lady friend in 1902. Banned from entering the empire, the wayward Paul settled in Paris, where he had already transferred a large portion of his fortune in anticipation of the Tsar's reaction.

Further worry was caused by the shenanigans of Nicholas II's brother and sister, Michael and Olga. Michael Alexandrovich had carried on a dalliance with their cousin Bee of Edinburgh, even though he had been told in no uncertain terms that their marriage was not a possibility. Following this fiasco, Michael fell in love with Alexandra Kossikovskaya, a lady-in-waiting to his sister Olga Alexandrovna. When he asked Nicholas II for permission to marry her, the Tsar was appalled and furious. Michael was forced to give her up and sent away on an extended foreign tour in the company of his mother. As if that had not upset the family enough, Michael went one step further when he fell in love with Natalia Cheremetevsky whom he would ultimately marry.

Not to be outdone by both her uncle and brother, Grand Duchess Olga Alexandrovna, unhappily married to Duke Peter of Oldenburg, a known homosexual, began a liaison with a Blue Cuirassier Guards officer. Michael Alexandrovich, of all people, introduced them, and Olga and Nikolai Kulikovsky soon became romantically involved. Olga asked Peter for a divorce, but he refused the request. Instead, the pliable Oldenburg appointed Kulikovsky as an aide-de-camp and allowed him to live at the Oldenburg mansion in St Petersburg – a modern menage a trois!

Back to Kirill we must now return. His departure from Tsarskoe Selo took place after Grand Duke Vladimir's famed stormy meeting with Nicholas II. Kirill and Victoria Melita met in Berlin and continued to Coburg, where her mother provided them with a small town palace located behind the Edinburgh Palais, the vast home she had built decades before. Coburgers knew this smaller structure as the 'Kirill Palais'. They also traveled along with the Marie Alexandrovna as she visited her various residences away from Coburg. Château Fabron remained, one of their favorite destinations.

The years he was to live in exile, Kirill considered among the happiest in his life. Not much seemed to dampen his spirits for after all he was, *"in spite of the loss of my career, my position, and all the rest that the world can give,"* able to keep *"what was dearest"* to him.[38] They also traveled around Europe in his motorcar and visited friends and relations near and far. Besides spending time in Coburg and at Château Fabron, the newlyweds also became frequent visitors to Langenburg, Munich, Strasburg and Paris. Although Kirill's access to his private fortune was hindered by banishment from Russia, his income was helped by support from his parents and Ducky's mother. If anything, exile, which Nicholas II perhaps designed as punishment, meant a time Kirill was able to spend without much worry, or having to perform official and military obligations.

The couple's first child, Maria Kirillovna, was born at the Edinburgh Palais in February 1907. The previous month, Ducky was received into the Russian Orthodox Church. In a letter to her daughter Helen in Athens, Grand Duchess Maria Pavlovna shared Kirill's delight with his wife's decision, as *"it will only make matters simpler for all, particularly when done before the baby's birth."*[39] It turned out to be the beginning of the couple's long road toward rehabilitation and their eventual return to Russia.

One year later Grand Duke Alexis Alexandrovich died suddenly while in Paris, a playground for much of his debauchery. His remains were transported to St Petersburg, where a funeral was held at the SS Peter and Paul Fortress. Kirill having been terribly fond of his uncle, Grand Duke Boris asked Nicholas II for permission for his brother to be present. The Tsar granted the request and allowed Kirill to wear military uniform. Kirill was also able to spend a couple of days with his parents before returning to France, where Ducky and their daughter awaited. It was the last time he was to see his father alive. Grand Duke Vladimir, whose health was giving his wife much concern, took a turn for the worse and died in February 1909. Kirill attended the funeral. Vladimir's passing was a great personal loss to his eldest son, *"for during his life…he had not only been a loving father but also a kind friend and a source of strength in times of trouble and sorrow."*[40] It was the last step before Nicholas II backtracked and allowed Kirill's permanent return to Russia.

Already a year after the Grand Duke's marriage, the Tsar relented, and agreed to recognize the wedding. Just before Grand Duke Vladimir's death, Nicholas II made Ducky a Grand Duchess, Victoria Feodorovna. *"Ta femme est grande duchesse,"* Marie Pavlovna telegraphed her son.[41] A decisive factor, as it turns out, had been Grand Duke Vladimir's declining health. Sadly, as mentioned before, Vladimir did not live long enough to see his son fully rehabilitated.

As the reader may recall, Ducky already had one daughter Maria Kirillovna, born in 1907, and a second, Kira Kirillovna, was born in 26 April/9 May 1909. Later that May Kirill was appointed as second-in-command to the cruiser *Oleg*, and took part in fleet exercises in the Baltic and the Mediterranean. In April 1910 he was promoted to Captain, and in the following month Kirill and Victoria Melita, accompanied by her daughters, arrived on Russian soil, albeit separately. At last they could begin their married life at home in Russia, and settled at Kavalersky Dom, Tsarskoe Selo. For the next two years Krill served in the Naval Academy.

During the 1912 Summer Olympics, Kirill was in Stockholm as Russia's official representative. Nicholas II had asked his cousin to be head of the Russian Imperial delegation, a commission the Grand Duke accepted with much glee. Kirill sailed to Stockholm on board the *Oleg* and while there received a visit from King Gustaf V, who wore the uniform of a Russian Admiral. Kirill recalled that as captain of the *Oleg* he reported to the Swedish king in Russian. Gustaf, broad smile on his face said that the Grand Duke's words did, *"not convey anything to him, but he was sure that"* Kirill's report was correct.[42] Ducky was present as well, but she stayed on the Admiralty's yacht. While in Sweden, Kirill and Ducky also spent time with his cousin Marie, daughter of Paul Alexandrovich, and her husband Prince William of Sweden, Gustaf V's son.

In the Autumn 1912 Kirill was ordered with *Oleg* to the Mediterranean, but his nerves got the better of him, he had to leave the ship and return to Reval. On two subsequent occasions he tried to put to sea again, but 'holy terror' prevented him from doing so, and he had to consider his career in the navy at an end.

It is rather likely that Kirill was still suffering from post-traumatic stress disorder caused by his experiences in the Far East, as well as accentuated by the difficulties unleashed by his marriage. In a letter to her daughter Alexandra of Hohenlohe-Langenburg, Marie Alexandrovna provided a private insight into Kirill's predicament and trauma. *"Kirill looks well but au fond* [after all] *he is still in a deplorable condition as to nerves,"* she said. *"Imagine that the other day he was going off to Cronstadt to see his former ship and was looking forward to it. Ducky took him to the steamer on the Neva and he went on board, but the moment the ship was going to move, he suddenly was taken with a real frantic fright, and hobbled off on shore again before all the officers! It was a terrible scandale and he was in such despair, that he howled for hours after it! Only fancy not having the courage to face the water even on a river! Of course I did not talk to him about it, all seems too hopeless and he still clings to the naval service. The doctor here says it is all nerves and that he does not find his heart at all in a bad condition."*[43]

The Tercentenary of the Romanov Dynasty was celebrated in 1913. By then Kirill and his wife were fully incorporated into court life. The government sought to celebrate the election of the first Romanov to the Russian throne as a far-reaching event responsible for propelling the country into European prominence. Kirill supported the propaganda by stating that, *"Russia and they* [the Romanovs] *are inseparable. They are linked together in one destiny."*[44] Throughout Russia there were celebrations to honor the dynasty and its accomplishments. In several of the newsreels we can watch today, Kirill and Ducky are among the many Romanovs who attended countless official public gatherings. No one could imagine that within a year the Russian Empire would be at war.

As the summer of 1914 rolled in, Kirill rejoiced in the delivery of a brand new motor yacht he had commissioned in England and looked forward to a relaxing time spent sailing leisurely on along the Baltic coastline. With Ducky and their daughters by his side, the Grand Duke embarked on a cruise along the Gulf of Finland. One can but hope, for the sake of crew and passengers that his fear of the seas had subsided by then.

Once the cruise was finished, Kirill focused on his other hobby, motoring. Grand Duke Kirill was an enthusiastic motorist. Once the motorcar became the rage, Kirill lost little time adopting this new mode of transportation and investing in it as much time and money as he possibly could. While living in exile he had relished the opportunity to travel from Coburg to Nice by car. His many motoring excursions also took Kirill to other cities in France, Switzerland, Italy, Austria and Germany. One time he even motored from Russia to Coburg, Ducky by his side.

There is no doubt that Kirill embraced motoring with serious enthusiasm, and not just as a driver, but also as a supporter of further technological development. Kirill, for example, commissioned the building of a very modern contraption, a motorized sleigh. In December 1910 the said *"automobile sleigh,"* which was *"propelled by means of a turbine wheel, which acts in relation to the air as a steamship screw does in water,"* was presented during a ceremony on an island on the River Seine near Paris. The vehicle was designed with Russia's bitter winter in mind and it would *"travel across the snow-covered Russian steppes at the rate of sixty miles an hour."*[45] Clearly, as was the case with many of his family and friends, Kirill enjoyed the thrill of speed provided by motor travel. This however, got him in trouble on several occasions. One time he was speeding toward the German-Danish border, when he collided with a butcher cart. The authorities deemed that the high rate of speed at which the Grand Duke was driving was responsible for the ensuing collision. The butcher cart was overturned and its occupants called the police after the speeding caravan failed to stop. Along with Kirill, in three other automobiles, were not only his cousin Grand Duke Dimitri Pavlovich, but also a coterie of Russian and German aristocrats. Problems for the careless drivers caught up with them at the border, where the police detained them. Reprimanded for not stopping at the scene of the accident, Kirill and his racing companions were only let go, *"after depositing the money to pay for the damage."*[46]

As an enthusiastic motorist, he had participated in various rallies. One particular yearly trek took him driving along the Baltic provinces in the company of other aristocratic motorists. It was while on the last evening of the 1914 Baltic rally, that he was informed of Russia's state of war with Germany. He had planned to drive to Coburg next, where they would spend the rest of the summer in the company of Ducky's mother. That long drive, however, remained forever unaccomplished.

Not hesitating to fight for his country, Kirill returned to St Petersburg immediately and volunteered to join the war effort. In spite of his patriotism, the Grand Duke was painfully aware of how completely unprepared Russia was. *"Our army was still in the process of reorganization and by no means ready to engage Germany's military machine with much hope of success. We had just emerged from less than ten years before from the disastrous war with Japan and from a revolution which, though it shook the structure of the Empire badly, had not led to its collapse, but it gave some indication of the kind of thing that lay in store for us in case of another unsuccessful war,"* Kirill wrote many years later.[47]

Unable to serve in the Russian Navy, Kirill joined the General Staff, while Ducky became deeply involved with hospital work. She was indefatigable in her efforts to bring much-needed aid and care to thousands of wounded soldiers who came through her hospital trains. In a letter to her sister-in-law Helen, Ducky shared her impressions on the overwhelming task at hand, *"Our chief base has been Warsaw since the beginning and those German brutes are still attacking the environs, but our side thank God is doing well. The amount of wounded is stupendous and the work greater than any efforts can suffice to cope with. One week over 39,000 passed through Warsaw's hospitals and trains."*[48] Ducky also shared her frustration at being kept from continuing her work because her husband had come down with an unexpected illness. *"For two weeks I have been shut up in military confinement with Kirill who has mumps and who was ejected from the terrified staff within a few hours as if he had the pest. This quarantine has stopped all my work for a time,"* she revealed.[49]

She also did not mince words when criticizing her own mother-in-law, for she believed the Grand Duchess Vladimir, at times, hindered the hospitals by wanting all attention and praise focused on her own efforts, rather on the work at hand. *"I had a few little tiffs with her over work, the first I have ever had with her since I am in Russia,"* Ducky wrote. *"She accused me of jealousy and wanting the glory to myself while God knows I think it is the other way round. Half Russia as far as I can see sails its hospital flags under her name and I really only want the good to be got as much as humanly possible out of our organizations and work and after all I have worked and she orders, and the orders are futile I cannot help saying so and will continue to do so. She does everything en grand, I might rather say en enorme and in consequence we are always in many difficulties and she won't understand it."*[50] Surely Grand Duchess Vladimir, who had always assumed leadership of everything around her, was not about to let her daughter-in-law outshine her. In fact, as the war progressed and malaise within Russia deepened, relations between Maria Palvovna and Kirill and Ducky only became ever more strained.

By Summer 1915, hope for victory over Imperial Germany had began to dissipate. Kirill continued in his work at the front, but was visiting St Petersburg and Tsarskoe Selo more frequently as his responsibilities demanded his presence in the capital. As for the rest of the family, Ducky provided a glimpse in a letter written to her adored sister-in-law Helen Vladimirovna. In this short missive Ducky shared many of her worries and concerns about the Tsar and others within the family circle, saying that, *"What Nicky and Alix think one never knows as on the rare occasions one meets they never talk of anything at all except small details or episodes. Dimitri…looks atrociously ill. Olga and little Marie [Marie Pavlovna Jr.] continue their nursing work and do well. I believe, especially Olga has never been home once. Aunt Minny was ill and Ksenia [Xenia] too."*[51]

Meanwhile. Russia headed toward the abyss. As the Empress fell ever more under the influence of Rasputin and as government ministers became increasingly dependent on her approval to remain in office, Kirill's widowed mother Grand Duchess Vladimir became widely seen as the unofficial family spokesman for discontent with the Tsar and Alexandra Feodorovna. Grand Duchess Vladimir was already suspected of being overly ambitious for her sons. Critics said she was at the center of conspiracies. The Grand Duchess did not mince words either. She was accused of saying that the Empress must be 'removed' or 'annihilated' if the Russian empire was to avoid a fatal crash. As criticism increased and rose in virulent tones, relations between Alexandra Feodorovna and the Grand Duchess Vladimir worsened. Opponents of the Tsar's conduct of the war rallied around Grand Duchess Vladimir, whose continued vituperative language and poignant criticism became the talk of St Petersburg. Danger was in the air.

Even Kirill and Ducky were fearful of the sort of people the Grand Duchess Vladimir was surrounding herself with. Throughout the war, Ducky continued having run-ins with her mother-in-law, encounters that ended in *"these terrible scenes,"* responsible for causing her much pain. Ducky blamed Maria Pavlovna for much of her frustration with war work, writing to Helen Vladimirovna that, *"thanks to your Mama, my best work has been stopped."* Relations between Kirill and Ducky and his mother became a rollercoaster. *"Now she is outwardly decent again and we meet most rarely but she continues to surround herself with such awful people in all her organizations. Bugs are so plentiful that one does not know where to turn. Kirill fumes and is rude to them which does not add any comfort to the situation. It would not matter so much if public opinion did not so severely criticize her, but how on earth are we to make her understand it."*[52]

Furthermore, the greatest intriguer in the universe of the Grand Duchess Vladimir was none other than her youngest son Andrei, who *"encourages her and is her only confidant, but to me he pretends to be out of everything and gets up and leaves whenever I tell him anything. So it's all no use. One is bound hands and foot and must struggle on in silence and disgrace vis a vis of her."* Kirill, Ducky said, *"fumes and is rude to them which does not add any comfort to the situation. It would not matter so much if public opinion did not so severely criticize her, but how on earth are we to make her understand it."*[53] This does much to counter the historically accepted version of events that places the Vladimirovichi opposed in unison to Nicholas and Alexandra. In fact, union within the Imperial family had frayed and broken a long time ago, which only accelerated the bloody and violent reckoning the dynasty was about to suffer.

Kirill and Ducky, who were expecting another child, were in St Petersburg when revolution broke out in March 1917. They were particularly struck by the absence of leadership that filled the power vacuum that opponents of tsardom and revolutionaries were only too happy to fill. Eager to avoid a total collapse of law and order, Kirill offered his services to the provisional government. At the time it was not officially a revolutionary body, and to him it was the last *"certain thing among the wreckage."* Still commander of the naval guards, he had to make an instant decision as to whether to lead them to the Duma, which had issued an appeal to all troops and commanders to show their allegiance. The Duma asked for them to march to the building and show their loyalty. This was a last ditch effort to avoid complete chaos and mayhem, as well as the bloodbath that would ensue. Kirill believed there was no alternative but to lead his troops to the Duma. In years to come, he would pay dearly for this action as myriad critics would use it to accuse the Grand Duke of betraying Nicholas II, while seeming to exempt the weak, irrational and isolated Tsar of any blame for the empire's collapse. Did Nicholas II not violate his sacred oath to defend his inheritance for future generations by running the empire aground?

The move succeeded in reestablishing order, albeit briefly, but at great personal cost. The French Ambassador, Maurice Paléologue, noted disdainfully in his diary that Grand Duke Kirill had not merely, *"come out openly in favor of the revolution,"* but had apparently forgotten or dismissed the oath that bound him to his Emperor. Instead Paléologue rather theatrically accused Kirill of placing the services of his men *"at the disposal of the mob."*[54] Some members of the Imperial family regarded him as a turncoat, a coward even, and never forgave him. However, in the grand scope of events, Kirill's actions had little to do influencing the course of events that by then had gone out of the control of the Romanov Dynasty. Kirill's critics failed to realize that the one Romanov who ought to be blamed for the destruction of Imperial Russia was none other than Tsar Nicholas II, who when the empire needed a leader, was only too quick to continue hiding in the unreal world he and his wife created. Critics of Kirill may argue that he betrayed the Tsar, yet these same critics tend to extend Nicholas II an excuse, at every conceivable turn, for his own betrayal of the sacred oath he had sworn at his coronation. In the turmoil of the revolution, Nicholas II was the first to forget his responsibility not just to the realm and the throne, but also to the rest of the Imperial family. Faced with that ultimate betrayal, can one truly fault the other Romanovs for wanting to save themselves and families from the cataclysm swallowing Russia?

His actions during those terrible revolutionary days may have saved the lives of himself and his children, but it was too late to save the doomed Romanov dynasty. The Tsar abdicated in his own name and in that of his son and heir, his brother Michael refused to accept the crown, and the Russian empire was no more. Meanwhile, many within the family were scathing in their criticism of Kirill's behavior. There is no question, of course, that it was both a flawed move on his part, as well as one with deep political implications for his future role as future Tsar-in-exile.

Kirill, Ducky and their children were treated with great respect, but they realized that it would be expedient to leave Russia. They were invited to stay with friends in Borgo, Finland, and in June 1917 they left St Petersburg, the last time they ever set foot on Russian soil. Their palace was not ransacked by the mob, but they were forbidden to take anything of value with them, beyond such clothes as they could carry, and any jewelry they could conceal about themselves. Soon after their arrival at Borgo, Ducky gave birth to a son, whom they named Vladimir after his late grandfather.

They stayed there until the Autumn 1919, a year after the world had been shocked by the murder of the Tsar and his family. From Finland, they went briefly to Berlin, before continuing to meet the Dowager Duchess of Saxe-Coburg and Gotha in Munich, and then traveling together to Zurich. When meeting her mother, Ducky found nothing short of a ghost of the once mighty Marie Alexandrovna.

Kirill's own mother managed to flee Russia just in time and before falling in the hands of the advancing Bolshevik armies. Raggedy, exhausted, penniless, yet filled with her famous pride, Grand Duchess Vladimir made it to the Black Sea, where at Novorossisk her niece Olga Alexandrovna saw her. *"Disregarding peril and hardship, she stubbornly kept to all the trimmings of bygone splendour and glory. And somehow she carried it off... When even generals found themselves lucky to find a horse cart and an old nag to bring them to safety, Aunt Miechen made a long journey in her own train. It was battered all right – but it was hers. For the first time in my life I found it a pleasure to kiss her...,"* Olga recalled.[55] Maria Pavlovna made it out of Russia and the safety of her favorite spa, Contrexéville, in France, where she owned a villa. By then, however, her life had run its course. The Grand Duchess Vladimir died there on 6 September 1920. Although she was cash strapped, she did leave her children an amazing jewel collection that would come in handy in later years.

Seven weeks after the death of Kirill's mother, it was Ducky's turn to lose her own beloved mother. The Dowager Duchess of Saxe-Coburg & Gotha died in October 1920, leaving Ducky the Edinburgh Palais at Coburg, as well as a considerable part of her jewels. For the next few years, Kirill and Ducky divided their time between this home and their home at Nice, Château Fabron, which they also inherited from her mother. Both were increasingly despondent at the state of post-war Europe, particularly England's *"attempts at recognizing the Bolsheviks as a respectable and legitimate government,"* and the policy of her Prime Minister, Lloyd George, in inviting the Bolsheviks to the 1919 peace conference, an action *"considered by Russia a crime such as history has never known."*[56]

Around 1923, Kirill had a nervous breakdown, and for a while was unable to cross the street without holding his wife's hand, or sleep unless she sat up next to him. She pulled him through these difficult few months, and encouraged him in regaining his self-confidence, even to the extent of a grand if empty gesture the following year. In the summer of 1924 he proclaimed himself guardian of the imperial throne, following this action a few weeks later with a signed manifesto in which he assumed the title of Tsar. As it was beyond doubt that Nicholas II, his wife and their children and Grand Duke Michael, the next in succession, had been murdered, and as the Russian laws of succession did not permit the imperial throne to remain vacant, he was therefore laying claim to the title of Tsar of all the Russias. He also elevated his three children to grand ducal status. His critics argued that this was done in direct contravention of a Romanov family statute whereby only children and grandchildren of sovereigns in the male descent could bear this distinction. Yet, as Emperor-in-exile and *de jure* Head of House Russia, he could maintain that the statute originally drawn up by his grandfather was now null and void.

His actions were bitterly criticized by many aristocrats living in exile. They pointed out that his cousin Grand Duke Nicholas Nikolaievich, former Commander-in-Chief of the Russian army, had a better claim in view of his superior war record and seniority, even though genealogically Nicholas was further down the line of succession. It would have been absurd, not to mention in contradiction of the Fundamental Laws, to witness Nicholas Nikolaievich succeeding instead of his cousin Kirill, but the younger Romanov's critics cared not one iota about such legal matters. They also resented Kirill's actions during the revolution in 'yielding' to the provisional government and breaking his oath of loyalty. From her retreat at Hvidøre in Denmark, the Dowager Empress declared that there was no dynastic issue to consider as her son, along with his family, were still alive. Later that year she published a letter in the *New York Times*, admitting that it had been the will of God to call her beloved sons and grandson, but nevertheless she feared that Kirill's manifesto would, *"create a schism and in so doing will not improve but on the contrary will worsen the position in Russia which is already sufficiently tormented."*[57]

The legal mechanisms regarding the Imperial succession were rather different than those supported by both the Dowager Empress and Grand Duke Nicholas. Their positions relied more on emotion and popular standing, than on actual legalities. The Pauline Laws were very clear in establishing the line of succession. In 1917, after Tsar Nicholas II, Tsarevich Alexis and Grand Duke Michael Alexandrovich, next came Kirill, his dynastic descendants and his brothers and their own dynastic descendants, if any. After the Vladimirovichi line came the line of Grand Duke Dimitri Pavlovich, who was then followed by the dynastic male heirs of Grand Duke Konstantin Nikolaievich. Only after the Konstantinovichi could, therefore, Grand Duke Nicholas, his brother and nephew, exercise succession rights. The Russian Imperial succession was not an 'elected' office; it was clearly established and stipulated and ruled by its own set of laws. Grand Duke Nicholas may have been more popular than Kirill, but popularity was not a rocket up the line of succession. As for the approval of the Dowager Empress, although it may have carried moral weight, of course, it lacked any legal weight on succession matters.

Critics of Kirill's actions have argued that his marriage cancelled his succession rights. Not true. Whereas the Russian Orthodox Church did not kindly look upon first cousin marriages, these could be had with dispensation. Besides, if the Tsar recognized the marriage as equal (as Nicholas II did by including the birth of Kirill's daughters in the Imperial Family registry), as the ultimate authority within Russia, then the Church's position was pointless in these matters.

In late November 1925, Maria Kirillovna married Hereditary Prince Karl of Leiningen, a distant relation. The wedding ceremony took place in Coburg and was attended by a bevy of royal relations. Shortly afterwards, the Grand Duke and Duchess purchased the house that would become their permanent base in France, Ker Argonid, located near the fishing village St Briac-sur-Mer. In future years Kirill and Ducky would frequently travel from St Briac to Paris and Amorbach, home of Marie Kirillovna, who also gave her parents seven grandchildren, beginning with the birth of Prince Emich of Leiningen, born at Coburg, in 1926.[58]

Meanwhile, Kira Kirillovna was developing into a rather splendid beauty. By her twentieth birthday there were rumors that Kira was to be engaged to King Boris of Bulgaria.[59] However, nothing came of this. Later, and because of Kira's frequent visits to Romania, there were efforts to get her married to her first cousin Prince Nicholas.[60] Yet again, nothing came of this friendship. Surely, the cousins may have been fond of each other, but alas their feelings were of friendship and nothing else. Then late in 1937 the outside world was informed of a grand alliance between the Houses of Hohenzollern and Romanov. On 30 December at a family gathering in Potsdam, Grand Duchess Kira

The Vladimirovichi & Pavlovich Lines

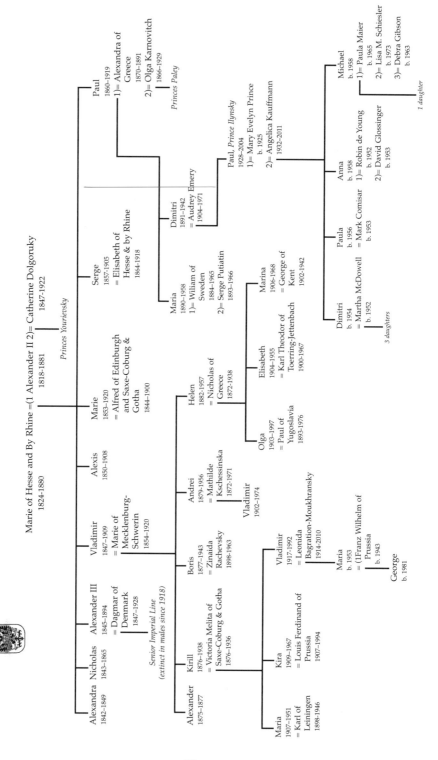

Kirillovna of Russia and Prince Louis Ferdinand of Prussia announced their engagement.[61] The civil ceremony and Orthodox wedding took place there on 2 May 1938. Two days later the couple wed again, this time in a Lutheran ceremony, at Haus Doorn, in the Netherlands, the home of Kaiser Wilhelm II, Louis Ferdinand's grandfather.[62] Through this marriage the blood of the Romanovs was united, once again, with that of the Hohenzollerns. Kira and Louis Ferdinand were a devoted couple.

In October 1928 the Dowager Empress died. Kirill attended the funeral at Roskilde Cathedral. The Danish press made much of *'Tsar Kirill, Keeper of the Throne'*, conspicuous as he left his seat in the cathedral to conduct members of Danish royalty to their seats. Olga Alexandrovna, the late Dowager Empress's youngest daughter, was angry that so many who had paid her mother scant attention when exiled, lost little time heading to Copenhagen to attend her funeral. Olga was especially bitter toward Kirill, *"who should have had the sense to stay away."*[63] That Kirill stayed at the Amalienborg Palace as a guest of the King of Denmark only irked his critics even further. Not that they cared much for the fact that the Danish monarch saw Kirill as the *'de-jure'* Head of House Russia, but Queen Alexandrine was a first cousin of Kirill's as well. By then, just about anything Kirill did or said, whether appropriate or not, mattered little to those who had resented him for so very long. In their eyes, Kirill would never be anything but a turncoat and usurper.

In January 1929 Grand Duke Nicholas died, and Kirill's position as *Tsar-in-exile*, for what it was worth, was unchallenged. The Grand Duchess supported her husband in his self-proclaimed leadership as he went through the perfunctory motions of such empty actions as receiving reports on the state of Russia every morning from his secretary-general, issuing imperial orders, offering thanks, and signing promotions from his study desk. Interestingly enough, both Kirill and Nicholas Nikolaievich led political movements in favor of a monarchical restoration in Russia, while also offering themselves as options against the Soviets. What Kirill and Nicholas only realized too late, was that Moscow-sponsored spies had infiltrated their political movements. These moles took advantage of the animosity between the grand dukes and spent considerable energy, as well as funds raised by Kirill and Nicholas, in causing bad relations between the contending Romanovs. Recapturing the Imperial throne became an elusive dream.

While much turmoil surrounded Kirill's political activities, his family life had remained an oasis of peace and comfort. Yet even that was to be spoiled by a misstep made by the Grand Duke. Marie, widowed Queen of Romania, was a regular guest of her sister and brother-in-law at St Briac. In the summer of 1933 she wrote to a friend that her sister had, *"had an overwhelming soulgrief which has shattered her conception of life and humanity."*[64] Kirill, it was assumed, had had an affair. Though Russian Grand Dukes had rarely been noted for their fidelity, she took it very badly, and she was never the same again. Her will to live was lost. She was seriously ill in the winter of 1935, had a stroke early in the New Year, and died on 2 March 1936.[65]

Ducky's death shattered Kirill, himself already seriously ill. For some years he had suffered from arteriosclerosis, a hardening of the arteries that caused increasing problems with his circulation and eyesight. In December 1934 Queen Marie of Romania had described him as a *"poor ruin,"*[66] and as a widower he soon fell into decline. He started dictating his memoirs, but never reached further than the family's departure from Russia after the revolution. His son Vladimir completed them. The book was published in 1939 as *My Life in Russia's Service*. He lived long enough to attend the wedding of his younger daughter Kira to Prince Louis Ferdinand of Prussia, but as he lingered on that summer at St Briac, his health was visibly failing. In September gangrene set in, and he was admitted to hospital in Paris, where he died in his sleep on 12 October 1938.[67]

Grand Duke Boris Vladimirovich
(1877-1943)

By Coryne Hall

Grand Duke Boris was born on 12/24 November 1877 in St Petersburg, the second surviving son of Grand Duke Vladimir and Grand Duchess Marie Pavlovna. (A son born in 1875, had died in March 1877). At the christening on 11/23 January 1878 in the Winter Palace church Boris's godparents were his grandfather Tsar Alexander II, German Emperor Wilhelm, Grand Duchess Alexandra Iosifovna and the Dowager Princess Caroline Reuß.

Boris was very close to his elder brother Kirill and younger siblings Andrei and Helen. They grew up between their country palace at Tsarskoe Selo and the Vladimir Palace in St Petersburg with its opulent staterooms, exotic Moorish boudoir, three libraries, winter garden, gothic dining-room, two large banqueting halls and interminable gas-lit passages. There were visits from Alexander II, who gave his grandsons small stuffed dolls dressed in the various Guards' uniforms and also a wooden slide that they loved to career down watched by their English nurse Millicent Crofts. Thanks to *Milly*, English became Boris' first language. She taught him nursery rhymes and read English books aloud, including *Barnaby Rudge* and *Oliver Twist*.

After the assassination of Alexander II in 1881, the children became especially close to the family of Alexander III, whose youngest son Michael was a year younger than Boris. He often invited his cousins to spend the weekend at Gatchina. In winter they skated, tobogganed and played snowballs, while in spring they rowed on the palace lake.

When they left the nursery behind, Mlle Delevskaya came every day to teach them Russian and General Alexander Daller was appointed the boys' governor. He chose their tutors and sent progress reports to the Grand Duke and Duchess when they were away. Father Alexander Diernoff gave Religious instruction, Vsevolod Chernavin taught Russian history, Vyacheslav Chernavin geography, and there were special tutors for English, French and German. They were mischievous boys, who one day hoisted Helen up a flagpole instead of the flag, although she was a willing participant. Boris entered the Nikolaevsky Cavalry School from which he graduated in 1896 and was gazetted a Cornet in the Life Guards Hussar Regiment.

At eighteen, Boris was a *"charming and attractive young man with a husky voice and a lisp."*[1] The sociable Boris liked nothing more than to drink and have fun. He found plenty of opportunity in the spring of 1896 at the coronation of his cousin Nicholas II. Royalty from all over the world had gathered in Moscow, among them Boris' cousins the elder daughters of Prince Alfred Duke of Edinburgh, Marie and Victoria Melita. Boris was immediately attracted to Marie, *Missy*. Twenty-year-old Missy was a great beauty – but she was also the wife of Crown Prince Ferdinand of Romania and the mother of two young children. During her three-week stay she did nothing to discourage Boris' attentions. That autumn Boris visited Romania. Missy found him an amusing companion, so much so that his *"lengthy stay and obvious adoration"* provoked criticism from her mother and from members of the Court.[2]

The romance continued on and off for several years. Although generally considered to be an Anglophobe, Boris built an English Cottage-style dacha at Tsarskoe Selo.

When Missy visited Russia she often bicycled over to see the progress of the building. By the autumn of 1899 she was pregnant. Refused permission to give birth in Coburg, she told King Carol flatly that, *"she wanted a divorce, and that the child she was carrying was Boris's."*[3] Whatever the truth, Crown Prince Ferdinand accepted the subsequent child as his own but Boris' gift of a Fabergé walkingstick handle remained one of Missy's favorite possessions. Boris declared himself her *"cavalier for life"* and thirty years later thanked her for having *"always remained a lovely dream."*[4]

Boris was now a confirmed boulevardier, primarily interested in his own pleasure and incapable of living within his considerable income. His doting mother often lent him money and the total debt reached half a million rubles. He has been described as *"Russia's favorite spender"* and his exploits frequently made the newspapers. On a whim he once took a bowl of goldfish from the house of a high-ranking old lady whom he had been visiting. When she complained to the Empress, Boris was forced to apologise.[5] He gambled in Cannes and Monte Carlo, played baccarat in Biarritz while the champagne flowed freely, and was a frequent visitor to Paris. His chief preoccupation was deciding where to lunch and dine. Dinner over, Boris frequently turned the restaurant into a parade ground, coercing guests into performing impromptu military manoeuvres.[6]

In 1902 Boris set off on a world tour, meeting Kirill in Port Said. They visited Thebes, Memphis, Luxor and the temples at Karnak, before being taken back to Cairo in the Khedive's private yacht. After travelling to Colombo on his brother's ship Boris watched a Ceylonese Temple dance. In America he drank champagne from the slipper of a chorus girl and tipped shop assistants with twenty-dollar bills. His wild and unpredictable behaviour became renowned but even for Boris the excess had begun to pall. He once remarked sadly that after a while, *"every woman is the same, nothing is new except the face."*[7]

In January 1904 the Russo-Japanese War broke out and on 26 February Boris departed for the front after a grand ceremony at the Nikolaevsky railway station. He was on the hill above Port Arthur when Kirill's ship exploded and sank. Only by chance was he not on board himself. The Serbian Prince whom Boris was accompanying had suggested they go on board *"as it was a golden opportunity to witness a fight at sea"* but Boris vetoed the idea.[8] Hurrying down to the harbour he had no real hope that Kirill was alive. Later he was told that Kirill had miraculously been rescued. Kirill was carried on board Boris' private train, where doctors attended him during the long journey home.

Maybe it was the sudden realisation that life could be quickly snatched away that prompted one of Boris' few serious attempts to settle down. In the Isle of Wight in around 1903 he met King Edward VII's niece Princess Victoria Eugenie of Battenberg, known to the family as 'Ena'. Boris was immediately smitten by Ena's cool blond beauty but she was only fifteen. In 1905 they met again in Nice. Ena was now seventeen and even more beautiful. He proposed and Ena hesitated. Boris agreed to say no more until she had come "out" into society later that year. Ena's season was such fun that she quickly forgot about the Russian Grand Duke and the following year married King Alfonso XIII of Spain.[9]

For Ena it was a lucky escape. Boris had a string of mistresses. A liaison with Jeanne Lacroix produced a son, Jean Boris Lacroix, born in Paris in 1905.[10] Boris was responsible for the engagement of Mlle Demidov, member of a very prominent society family, being broken off almost on the eve of her wedding. Another assignation involving a married lady came to the ears of the Chief of Police and was soon the talk of St Petersburg.[11]

Two severe blows hit Boris in these years. The first was the banishment of Kirill, for marrying Victoria Melita in defiance of the Tsar's ban. The second was the death of his father in 1909.

With parents as cultured as Grand Duke Vladimir and Grand Duchess Marie Pavlovna, Boris had ample opportunity to appreciate the finer things of life. He patronized the arts, was a client of Fabergé, a supporter of the impresario Serge Diaghilev and an admirer of the ballerina Anna Pavlova. He held wild parties at his dacha and attended the lavish parties of friends, particularly those of Mathilde Kschessinska where guests sat around her sunken bath drinking champagne. He liked to play cards but did not like to lose. Occasionally he was called upon to do something serious. In December 1911 he represented the Tsar at the coronation of King Vajiravudh of Thailand and in 1916 paid an official visit to Persia.

When war broke out in 1914 Boris was appointed Major General commanding the Ataman Cossacks of the Guard, although his duties were vague. He was allowed to travel more or less as he liked, even visiting the Crimea on one occasion. His frequent periods of leave were punctuated by visits to the theatre or parties at the house of Prince Serge Obolensky and other friends. In 1915 he spent over 25,000 rubles on meals, 16,000 rubles on servants, 8,000 on automobiles but gave only 46 rubles to the Church.[12] Later he was attached to military headquarters where the Tsar had taken command of the army, leaving the government in the hands of the Empress and Grigory Rasputin.

In February 1916 he requested the hand of Grand Duchess Olga Nikolaievna. The Empress was scandalised. *"The oftener I think about Boris, the more I realize what an awful set his wife would be dragged into,"* Alexandra wrote to Nicholas. *"....To give over a well used half worn out, blasé young man, to a pure, fresh girl 18 years his junior and to live in a house in which many a woman has "shared" his life. Only a "woman" who knows the world and can judge and choose with eyes open, ought to be his wife… But an inexperienced young girl would suffer terribly, to have her husband 4th, 5th hand or more…"*[13] The Tsar and Tsarina's refusal caused Boris to became ever more critical of Alexandra's disastrous government as the situation went from bad to worse.

In June 1916 Boris and some friends were having supper with a British officer, Major Thornhill. After a few drinks, Boris suddenly accused the British of sitting in their trenches while the French army was massacred at Verdun. *"You can be certain that the moment peace is signed with Germany we shall go to war with you,"* he added. The outburst was reported and Boris was reprimanded both by the Tsar and the commander of the British Mission, General Sir Alfred Knox. Although he apologised, the damage was done and the incident did no good to Boris' reputation.[14]

The murder of Rasputin did little to ease the internal situation. Boris was one of the Grand Dukes who signed a letter asking for clemency for Grand Duke Dimitri Pavlovich, exiled to Persia for his part in the plot. When the letter had no effect, Grand Duchess Vladimir dared not telephone Boris, *"fearing that in his anger he might do something rash."*[15]

All the Grand Dukes were now convinced that Nicholas must be replaced and Alexandra's influence neutralised. Meetings were held, plots were discussed but they could not agree on any one course of action. While the family hesitated the Tsar acted. On 8 January 1917 Nicholas told Grand Duchess Marie Pavlovna that she, Kirill and Andrei should leave the capital for a while. As the situation spiralled into revolution, Boris remained in the capital attending parties and going to the ballet. When supplies of bread ran out, demonstrators filled the streets. On 24 February he telegraphed his mother informing her of riots. By the end of February the situation was alarming and on 2 March Nicholas abdicated.

Boris was at Moghilev with Grand Duke Serge Mikhailovich when Nicholas returned to say goodbye to the army. He remained at Stavka until Nicholas left under arrest for Tsarskoe Selo.

On 15/28 March Boris was arrested at his dacha. An indiscreet letter from his mother, in which she stated that *"the only hope for Russia was in* [Grand Duke] *Nicolai Nicolaievich,"* had been intercepted and read by the Provisional Government.[16] A few days earlier some letters from Boris had been found in Mathilde Kschessinska's house. As she was accused of bribery and the sale of artillery contracts Boris' correspondence with her also placed him under suspicion. By July his arrest had been lifted and he had left the army. By late August, still at Tsarskoe Selo, he was reportedly depressed but had the foresight to obtain permission to travel.

The Honourable 'Bertie' Stopford, who worked for the British Embassy (and also probably the Secret Intelligence Service) dined with Boris two or three times a week and they hatched a plan to save Grand Duchess Vladimir's jewels. Disguised as workmen, with the aid of a loyal caretaker they gained access to the Grand Duchess' safe in the Vladimir Palace. Stopford put the jewels into two old Gladstone bags and carried them back to London, where he placed them in a safe deposit box. He took the cash to Kislovodsk, concealed in his boots.

In September Boris joined his mother and Andrei in the Caucasus. With him went his mistress Zinaide and her French friend Marie. Zina, described as fair in colouring and *"like a piece of delicate Dresden china,"*[17] was the daughter of General Serge Rashchevsky and some twenty years Boris' junior. Born on 3/15 November 1898, she had married Nicholas Elissiev in 1913 and divorced him the following year. She had lately often acted as Boris' hostess at his parties at the Tsarskoe Selo dacha, where her slim figure was a stark contrast to the plump Boris. In Kislovodsk Grand Duchess Marie Pavlovna refused to let Zina share her villa. She had to rent a separate house, as did Andrei's mistress Mathilde Kschessinska.

In October came news of the Bolshevik revolution. Banks were nationalised, accounts frozen and private property was confiscated. Soon the Bolsheviks made their presence felt in Kislovodsk and by January 1918 house searches and confiscations were a frequent occurrence. Everyone lived in fear. Boris was arrested in June but released after four hours. The following month rumours spread that the Tsar had been shot at Ekaterinburg.

During the night of 7/20 August soldiers carried out a search of Marie Pavlovna's villa and arrested the two Grand Dukes. Boris and Andrei were taken to the State Hotel in nearby Piatigorsk, where the local Soviet pressed for their execution. Their freedom was secured by a lucky chance. In Paris several years earlier Boris had bought some paintings from a struggling artist. This artist was now the Bolshevik Commander.

The Commissar advised them to flee into the mountains. Armed with false papers stating they were on a mission for the Soviet, Boris and Andrei wandered through the Kabarda until they found a safe place to settle. Only after five weeks did they feel it safe to return to Kislovodsk. The following morning everybody had to flee from the Bolsheviks.

Protected by loyal Cossacks they headed for Tambiev. By day they travelled in wagons and by night slept where and how they could. It was a difficult and dangerous journey. After several days the Grand Ducal party reached Baltapachinska, where they remained for few days, before moving on to the coastal town of Anapa where they arrived in late October. A retired General loaned his house to the Grand Duchess and her sons. Zina and Mathilde stayed at the town's only hotel.

November 1918 brought the end of the war and, later, the arrival of allied ships. The Grand Duchess refused to leave Russia but, to her great distress, Boris decided to go to Europe.

In January 1919 the British Representative in Constantinople contacted the Foreign Office in London on behalf of Grand Duchess Vladimir, who asked permission for Boris to come to England. Unfortunately for Boris, neither King George V nor the government wanted the Romanovs. *"We know H.M.'s wishes on the subject,"* an official wrote in the margin of the document. *"Reply that it is regretted that permission cannot be granted at the present moment." "I agree. He is no good,"* commented someone else, probably recalling Boris' anti-British outburst in 1916.[18] The official refusal was phrased more politely. Denied a visa for England, in March 1919 Boris and Zina left Russia via Constantinople. On 12 July they were married in Genoa and settled provisionally in Nice.

Marie Pavlovna and Andrei left Russia in 1920. When the Grand Duchess died in September of that year in Contrexéville, Boris, his mother's favorite child, inherited her fabulous emeralds.

In 1922 Boris and Zina moved to a large residence called 'Sans Souci' on the route des Gardes at Meudon, near Paris. The Grand Duke, as much of a reprobate as ever despite his marriage, was happy in the atmosphere of a city he knew well. The Romanov family and the Russian émigrés, however, had little to do with Zina and few could find a good word to say about her. They considered her, *"disreputable, vulgar and low born."* The cosmopolitan nouveaux riches flocked to Zina's salon, excited by proximity to a *"real Grand Duke."* Presumably Boris had sold his mother's emeralds for he was financially secure. Queen Marie of Romania was also generous in helping her less fortunate relatives. Boris indulged his wife's every whim, *"and perhaps also made some profit from the acquaintance of unscrupulous industrialists and bankers of obscure origin."* Many people believed that Boris' money came from Zina.[19]

In the winter of 1925 they sailed to New York, checking in at the Ritz Carlton with Boris' 22 trunks of luggage and Zina's 300 dresses. Although his visit was purportedly to *"see friends and enjoy life,"* a prominent New York Congressman accused Boris of *"travelling with tickets given to him by rich Americans"* who were clamouring to curtsey to these unemployed scions of royalty.[20]

Boris supported Kirill's claim to be 'Tsar' in exile, even though Kirill declared his brother's marriage to Zina was *"illegal and void."*[21] In October 1938 Boris and Andrei were summoned to St Briac, where Kirill was gravely ill. They moved him to the American Hospital in Paris but despite the doctors' best efforts he died on 12 October.

The following year the Second World War broke out. Boris and Zina were at their Biarritz villa when the Germans reached Paris in June 1940. Refugees began pouring in, including Andrei and Mathilde who had fled from Paris. On 26 June the Germans reached Biarritz. After three months Andrei and Mathilde returned home, Boris and Zina followed.

At the end of 1942 Boris and Zina moved to the rue de la Faisanderie in Paris. It was here that in 1943 Boris became critically ill. Alerted by telephone on 9 November, Andrei hurried over but was too late. Boris, the *"one more likely to be shot by a husband than an assassin,"* had died quietly in his bed.[22] After the funeral in the Russian Church three days later, his body was placed in the crypt. Later, it was transferred to the Orthodox chapel in Contrexéville, southern France, where Boris was laid to rest with his doting mother.

Zina lived on in Paris without much contact with her Romanov relations. She died there on 30 January 1963.

Grand Duke Andrei Vladimirovich (1879-1956)

By Coryne Hall

The youngest of Vladimir and Marie Pavlovna's sons was Grand Duke Andrei Vladimirovich. He was born at their country palace at Tsarskoe Selo at 3:00 am on 24 May 1879 and christened at 10:30 am on 12 June by Their Majesties' Confessor in the church of the Catherine Palace at Tsarskoe Selo. The godparents were his grandfather Tsar Alexander II; Grand Duchess Alexandra Petrovna (great-aunt); the Prussian Crown Prince Friedrich Wilhelm (later, briefly, Kaiser Friedrich III); and his maternal great-grandmother the Dowager Grand Duchess Alexandrine of Mecklenburg-Schwerin.

Andrei grew up in the magnificent Vladimir Palace on the Dvortsovaya Embankment, just along the River Neva from the Winter Palace. There was an opulent suite of staterooms, an exotic Moorish boudoir, three libraries, a winter garden, a gothic dining room and two large banqueting halls. The palace's magnificent wine cellars were extensive and the palace even had it own Russian banya (sauna). In summer there were visits to Tsarskoe Selo, where Andrei and his siblings Kirill, Boris and Helen could row on the lake or ride in the park. Thanks to their English nurse Milly Crofts they all had a good command of the English language. As Grand Duke Vladimir was President of the Russian Academy of Arts from 1876, the children had Leon Bakst as a drawing master.

Andrei grew up to be *"tall, handsome,...fun-loving,"*[1] and entered the Mikhailovksy Artillery School with a view to following the traditional military career expected of a Russian Grand Duke. His mother's hopes that he would make a suitable marriage, however, were doomed to failure on the night in early 1900 when Andrei met the prima ballerina Mathilde Kschessinska and fell under her spell.

Grand Duke Andrei was twenty to Mathilde's twenty-seven. She had been Nicholas II's mistress before his marriage and was currently under the 'protection' of Grand Duke Serge Mikhailovich. Nevertheless, Andrei soon found himself smitten and by the summer of 1900 the pair had became lovers. Because of the difference in their ages, not to mention Mathilde's reputation, there was some hostility within Andrei's family. The main focus of this opposition was his mother. Grand Duchess Marie Pavlovna was determined that her three sons would make good, suitable marriages. These plans certainly did not include her youngest son forming a liaison with the now notorious Mathilde Kschessinska.

Nevertheless, the affair continued, even though Mathilde was living with Serge. In the autumn of 1901 Andrei and Mathilde met in Venice, moving on to Padua, Rome, Assisi, Perugia, Florence, Pisa and Genoa. Shortly afterwards Mathilde discovered she was pregnant. When her son Vladimir ('Vova') was born at Strelna on 18 June 1902 no one knew which of her two Grand Ducal lovers was the father. Mathilde, writing her memoirs during Andrei's lifetime, later maintained it was Andrei but there is no proof either way. Vova was given the patronymic 'Sergeievich', indicating that, officially at least, he was regarded as Serge's son.

That autumn Andrei entered the Military Law Academy in St Petersburg and the following year he acquired his own home, the former von Dervis mansion in St Petersburg. The opulence of the Florentine-style rooms did not encourage Andrei to set up home. He and Mathilde were able to meet there, away from Serge's gaze, but Andrei never replaced the von Dervis coats-of-arms with his own. He gave many parties, inviting members of the Imperial family as well as artists from the Imperial theatres.

Occasionally he was entrusted with a diplomatic assignment. In 1907 the Tsar sent Andrei and his father on an official mission to Bulgaria. Andrei's sense of humour came to the fore and he promptly appeared before the ruling prince, Ferdinand of Saxe-Coburg (a Turkish vassal) wearing a Turkish decoration on his breast. On a second visit to Sofia four years later he teased Ferdinand again, recording the incidents gleefully in his diary.[2]

In 1908 he accompanied Kschessinska to Paris, where she was appearing at the Opéra, although they did not stay at the same hotel. Andrei, who gave a dinner for the Opéra's director when he visited St Petersburg, had oiled the wheels for this 'invitation'.

Afterwards Andrei, Mathilde and six-year-old Vova had a holiday in Ostend, where they were photographed bathing in the sea. Andrei showed no signs of making a 'suitable' marriage and continued to shower Mathilde Kschessinska with jewels. Among them were a sapphire and diamond diadem, and two enormous cabochon sapphires once owned by Andrei's distant cousin Duchess Zinaida de Leuchtenberg.

In 1911 Andrei was in Kiev, attending the military manoeuvres. During his stay the Prime Minister Peter Stolypin was assassinated at a gala performance at the Kiev Opera House in the presence of the Tsar. A few weeks later Andrei faithfully followed Kschessinska to London, where she was appearing at Covent Garden. He threw several parties for the ballet company at the Savoy Hotel and organised a trip to see Windsor Castle. They spent the spring in Monte Carlo and Andrei found the climate there so agreeable that he decided to lease a villa for the following year.

In the autumn of 1912 the Grand Duke's health, never strong, began to give cause for concern. He suffered from acute bronchitis and was seriously ill in bed for the whole of August. The doctors, fearing tuberculosis, dispatched him to the Crimea. Grand Duke Nicholas Nikolaievich lent Andrei a house on his estate, Tchair, where he remained until November. From there he entered a sanatorium at Reichenhall, near Munich to take advantage of the mountain air. Unfortunately, this did not bring the expected improvement so at the insistence of Grand Duchess Marie Pavlovna, Andrei was moved to the Kulm Hotel in St Moritz where Mathilde joined him for a while. He missed the Romanov Tercentenary Celebrations earlier in the year but was able to take part in those held in Kostroma and in Moscow.

In 1913 Andrei bought Villa Alam, at Cap d'Ail in the South of France, where with Mathilde, he spent the following spring. He and Mathilde intended to spend every spring there but the outbreak of war ended their old life forever.

At the end of September 1914 Andrei left for the northwest front, where he was attached to General Ruzsky's staff. The following year, when his health had improved, he commanded the Horse Artillery Brigade of the Guard, although this was not a united command.[3] Soon afterwards the Tsar took over command of the Russian army, leaving the government in the hands of Empress Alexandra and Rasputin. The Empress soon complained that Andrei had been hanging around in the capital for two years – *"is there no nomination for him anywhere out at the war – active?"*[4] she wrote to the Tsar. In fact, since the summer of 1915 Andrei, Boris and Dimitri had been frequent guests for lunch at Grand Duke Michael Alexandrovich's home, where they were strongly critical of the Empress. Andrei was at the front by October, returning in mid-December.

By now all the Grand Dukes were of the opinion that the Empress' interference in government must be stopped. After the murder of Rasputin in December 1916, Andrei made it clear that he supported his cousin Grand Duke Dimitri Pavlovich, who was implicated in the plot. The Grand Dukes held various meetings, including at least one in Andrei's palace on 21 December, with a view to obtaining more lenient treatment for Dimitri, banished after his involvement in the murder. He was one of the signatories of the collective letter from the family asking the Tsar to rescind the order for Dimitri's banishment because of his poor health. Andrei, a well-educated man with a keen, enquiring mind, recorded his impressions of events in long diary entries. *"We are at war, the enemy is threatening, and we are busy arguing such incidental things,"* he wrote on 21 December. *"It is a shame to make so much noise over the murder of a dirty scoundrel. Shame on us all."*[5]

Dimitri's banishment was a terrible shock to Andrei – but more was to follow. On 1 January 1917 Grand Duke Nicholas Mikhailovich was exiled to Grushevka, his Ukrainian estate, for supporting Dimitri and speaking out against the Empress. Andrei recorded that this left the Imperial family stunned.

There were meetings, plots and counter-plots. Many of the Grand Dukes were now convinced that Nicholas must be dethroned and Alexandra's influence neutralised, but they could not decide on a course of action. Some wanted a regency for Tsarevich Alexis but they could not agree on who was to be regent.

While the family hesitated the Tsar, for once, acted. On 8 January Nicholas told Grand Duchess Marie Pavlovna that in their own interests she, Kirill and Andrei should leave the capital for a few weeks. The Grand Duchess left for Kislovodsk, a health spa in the Caucasus. Kirill went to Archangel on a tour of inspection. On 16 January Andrei went to the Alexander Palace for an audience with Nicholas. He was received courteously and the audience was normal, although Andrei later recorded that it lasted less than five minutes. Later that day he left to join his mother, officially to take the cure. Boris remained in the capital, since 1914 renamed Petrograd.

Andrei arrived at Kislovodsk on 21 January, happy to leave the chaos of Petrograd that was, quite literally, making him ill. In his diary he recorded the sheer relief of leaving the atmosphere of lies and deceit that permeated the capital.

Kislovodsk was the most fashionable spa resort of the Northern Caucasus, which lay in the south of Russia in the strip of land between the Black and the Caspian Seas. The region was peaceful and Grand Duchess Marie Pavlovna rented a villa. Then, on 24 February they received a telegram from Boris informing them of rioting in the capital. Soon afterwards more telegrams arrived and by 1 March it was obvious that the situation was serious. As rumours flew around Kislovodsk Andrei and his mother had no definite news about what was happening.

On 4 March came the news that Nicholas had abdicated for himself and the Tsarevich, and that Grand Duke Michael Alexandrovich, called to the throne so unexpectedly, had refused. The news hit Andrei *"like a thunderclap."* He found the effort of writing it all down more than he could manage. *"All the former grandeur of Imperial Russia has collapsed in a single day!"* he wrote incredulously. *"It has collapsed irreversibly! Where shall we all go now? Misha's appeal to have general elections now is the worse news of all! What can he be thinking at such a time?"*[6]

A few days later Andrei decided to go 300 miles south to Tiflis to meet Grand

Duke Nicholas Nikolaievich, 'Nikolasha' who, in one of his last acts, Nicholas II had re-appointed Commander-in-Chief of the Russian armies. Nikolasha ordered Andrei and his mother to remain in Kislovodsk until further notice. Andrei received a taste of what was to come when revolutionaries while returning to Kislovodsk stopped his train. On 13 March he swore allegiance to the Provisional Government.

Soon afterwards Grand Duchess Marie Pavlovna was placed under house arrest at the Semyonov Villa, where she had been living. Andrei appealed to the Minister of Justice, Alexander Kerensky, asking that either charges be brought against her immediately or that she be released. Her already failing health, he said, had been greatly affected and unfounded attacks on her good name had recently been appearing in the press. Not until June was the order for her house arrest lifted.

All court property, including the palaces and private estates, was transferred to the state at the beginning of April. The Minister of Agriculture commandeered Andrei's palace. All the Romanovs now ceased to receive their incomes from the Imperial Appanages, millions of acres of Crown Lands set aside by Catherine the Great to provide incomes for the Imperial family. Soon Andrei and his mother were relying on The Honourable 'Bertie' Stopford to bring messages from Boris in Petrograd as well as much-needed cash, which he smuggled in thousand rouble revolutionary notes hidden inside his boots.

In July Mathilde and Vova, who had lost almost everything when the ballerina had to flee her Petrograd mansion before it was looted by the mob, joined Andrei. At his mother's insistence Andrei rented a separate villa for them nearby. Soon afterwards Boris arrived with his mistress Zina Rashchevsky. She was also forced to live elsewhere.

At the end of October 1917 came news of the Bolshevik revolution and with it they lost all hope of ever returning to Petrograd. The banks were nationalized and private bank accounts frozen. Overnight, Andrei and his family had become penniless.

By January the Bolshevik presence was making itself felt in Kislovodsk, with house searches and confiscations a frequent occurrence. One evening, during a small dinner party at Mathilde's villa, a gang of Red soldiers burst in to see the bourgeoisie. Andrei was wearing a Cherkeska, the Cossacks' coat-like garment with a row of imitation cartridges along the breast, with a dagger. Hearing that the men were looking for weapons he quickly put the dagger in the hall. One of the soldiers noticed its absence and asked where it was, whereupon Mathilde told him, to avoid any problems. They even tried to confiscate Vova's small dagger but one of the servants protested that he was just a child. Later one of the men returned and warned them to put out all the lights and disperse, or they would all be in danger.

In June, as the grip tightened, Boris was arrested but luckily soon released. The following month rumours circulated that the Tsar and his family had been murdered at Ekaterinburg.

On 7 August 1918 soldiers entered the Grand Ducal villa, posting a guard around the building and sentries outside the bedrooms to stop the inhabitants communicating with one another. After a systematic search Andrei and Boris were arrested. They were taken to the State Hotel in nearby Piatigorsk for interrogation. Lydia Davydova, one of the most prominent members of Kislovodsk society, interceded with Commissar Lestchinsky to try and obtain their freedom. She was even able to visit the Grand Dukes at the hotel and assure them that everything possible was being done. Meanwhile, the local Soviet were pressing for their execution. Commissar Lestchinsky secured their freedom at almost the eleventh hour and returned them to Kislovodsk under escort. He strongly advised them both to flee into the mountains for their sake of their safety.

Commissar Lestchinsky gave them papers with false names, stating they were on a mission for the Soviet. Then, in a two-horse brake Boris and Andrei headed for the Kabarda where the chief Circassian tribe, the Kabards, lived on the north slope of the mountain. They wandered at first from village to village before finding a safe place to settle. It was almost five weeks before they were finally able to return to Kislovodsk. They were just in time. The following day everyone had to flee from the Bolsheviks.

Travelling on wagons, in difficult terrain and often under fire, the column of refugees headed first for Tambiev, escorted by a small group of Cossacks. At night the party slept how they could, huddled in blankets. All around them were Bolshevik forces, and when they heard singing in the night they did not know if it was from Reds or Whites. After a journey of several days they finally reached Baltapachinska, where it was possible to remain for a while and recover from their flight. Now they had to decide where to stay until the Southern Caucasus was quiet again. One of the generals advised the Grand Ducal party to go to the coastal town of Anapa where things were reasonably calm.

After a night crossing in an old trawler, they reached Anapa on 22 October 1918. A house loaned by a retired general was made available to the Grand Duchess and her sons. The others stayed at the town's only hotel.

With the end of the war in November 1918 General Poole arrived in Anapa to try and persuade the Grand Duchess to leave. She refused. Boris left Russia in March but Andrei remained with Mathilde and his mother. Later that month the cruiser *Montrose* arrived and Commander Goldschmidt conveyed to the Grand Duchess another offer to bring her and Andrei to Constantinople in case of danger. Again Marie Pavlovna refused. Shortly afterwards Andrei was invited to tea aboard the *Montrose*, where he and Commander Goldschmidt discussed the rumours circulating about the Tsar's murder. Andrei said that he had no news either way, but the Commander insisted on drinking the Tsar's health, leaving the Grand Duke with the impression that Goldschmidt was unable to tell him all that he knew on the subject.

In May 1919 they returned to Kislovodsk, where life had returned more or less to normal. The White Army were victorious and they expected soon to hear of the fall of Moscow. Then victory turned to defeat and by the end of the year the situation became critical. In December Andrei suffered a great loss when his ADC F. F. von Kube, who had served him for many years, died of typhus.

Soon afterwards they were forced to flee once more. Early in January 1920 they arrived in Novorossisk, where they spent six weeks in a railway carriage. By now even the Grand Duchess was convinced that the only course open to them was to leave Russia, and they were finally able to take passage on an Italian ship bound for Venice. After six days in Novorossisk harbour the ship sailed on 19 February. Andrei was the last Grand Duke to leave Russia.

In Constantinople everyone had to disembark for fumigation. Finally they reached Venice, where Andrei and Mathilde had supper at the restaurant where they had dined as young lovers nineteen years earlier. Now they were émigrés. Andrei boosted their confidence by placing his Fabergé cigarette case prominently on the restaurant table.

The following day they left by special train for the South of France. Andrei accompanied his mother to Cannes, before joining Mathilde and Vova at Villa Alam later. Because the villa was bought in Mathilde's name, and she was not a member of the Romanov family, it was not sold during the war when the Tsar ordered the family to repatriate their assets held abroad. Therefore, Andrei and Mathilde still had a home. The first thing they did was mortgage the villa to pay the staff and buy clothes, although Andrei was in the fortunate position of having left some luggage behind when they left the villa in 1914.

With the death of Grand Duchess Marie Pavlovna in September 1920 the only real obstacle to Mathilde and Andrei's marriage was removed. They married in Cannes on 30 January 1921 with the consent of Grand Duke Kirill, who Andrei now acknowledged as head of the Imperial Family. Andrei also adopted Vova, giving him official recognition as his own son. Kirill granted Mathilde the title of Princess Krasinsky, while Vova became Prince Krasinsky. In 1935 she became Her Serene Highness Princess Romanovsky-Krasinsky.

Despite their somewhat reduced circumstances Mathilde and Andrei maintained as much as possible the lifestyle of members of the Imperial family, living off the proceeds of the rubies inherited from Andrei's mother. At Villa Alam they had a cook, butler, gardener and a maid. They lunched at Claridges in Nice, danced at the Carlton in Monte Carlo, gambled at the Casino and made regular trips to Paris. Like other prominent émigrés Andrei was engaged in charity work. He was patron of the Alexandrino School in Nice, for which he collected funds and every year organised fund raising galas at the Hotel de Paris. At one of these galas King Gustaf V of Sweden won three first prizes, insisting on loading them into his car as presents for his granddaughters.

Other old friends and members of the family visited, although many others (including Kschessinska's former lover Grand Duke Serge Mikhailovich) had perished in the revolution. In 1920 Andrei met Nicolai Sokolov, the White investigator. Sokolov had compiled a dossier on the deaths of the Tsar and his family at Ekaterinburg and of Serge and other members of the family at Alapaievsk. He now had no doubt as to their ultimate fate and that all had perished. Andrei sat up all night copying by hand the most important documents.

In 1922, with the deaths of the Tsar, Tsarevich and Grand Duke Michael almost certain, Kirill proclaimed himself Guardian of the Throne. Two years later he proclaimed himself 'Emperor'. This action divided the Romanov family and Andrei was one of the few Grand Dukes who supported his brother's action.

Then in 1925 a rumour circulated through the Royal courts of Europe. A sick, unidentified young woman had been pulled from a Berlin canal five years earlier after attempting suicide. It was believed she was Russian but she refused to answer any questions. She was now believed by some people to be the Tsar's daughter Grand Duchess Anastasia and the only survivor of Ekaterinburg. Although many former courtiers tried to formally identify the young woman, they were unable to reconcile their memories of the plump, lively Grand Duchess with the tubercular girl in the Berlin hospital. Finally she was visited by Grand Duchess Olga Alexandrovna, who later issued a statement saying she was unable *"to find the slightest resemblance between Grand Duchess Anastasia"* and the unknown woman in Berlin,[7] now known as Frau Tchaikovsky.

Andrei, a graduate of the Military Law Academy of St Petersburg, had been one of the last members of the family to see Nicholas' daughters. He tried to interest other members of the family in the matter. With the Dowager Empress and her daughters maintaining a *"negative attitude,"* Andrei requested their permission to conduct his own investigation, *"in order to protect his family from further embarrassment."*[8]

The question of Frau Tchaikovsky's identity split the Romanov family. The Danish Minister in Berlin, under pressure from his government, now reluctantly informed Andrei that he would not be able to support her either morally or financially after 1 February 1927. He hoped Andrei, who was working with the family's permission, would take over. This situation left Andrei with a problem of considerable magnitude. His own efforts to raise money for 'Anastasia' amongst the émigrés had netted less than 500 Marks and he had no means of financing her mounting hospital bills himself. Nevertheless, he sent a small gift of money to indicate his goodwill. Luckily, George Romanovsky de Beauharnais, Duke of Leuchtenberg (a great-grandson of Tsar Nicholas I and therefore Andrei's distant cousin), offered her a home at his Bavarian Castle. There she remained for the next year as the investigation continued.

Andrei had decided that a more objective approach could be maintained if he refrained from meeting Frau Tchaikovsky. Not until 31 January 1928 did he finally meet the woman on whose behalf he had been battling. Andrei and Mathilde travelled to Paris, where it had been arranged that he would meet the Anastasia claimant before she left for America to stay with his cousin Princess Xenia, Mrs William B. Leeds. When the meeting took place it was, in Andrei's own words, an *"unshakable recognition."* He left the meeting in a state of shock. *"I have seen Nicky's daughter,"* he repeated over and over again saying that he was in no doubt that she was Anastasia. The resemblance was remarkable but Andrei expressed his surprise that she did not speak to him and merely sat sobbing. Andrei remained convinced that he had met the only survivor of Ekaterinburg. When this fact was made public, against his wishes, it provoked *"a real storm"* amongst his relatives.[9]

In the autumn of 1928 twelve members of the Romanov family issued a signed statement declaring 'Anastasia' an impostor. Andrei continued his investigation, defying Kirill's order to *"cease all activity in Anastasia's interest,"* but even he became disillusioned as the case began to turn into a hunt for the Tsar's fortune. This was something in which Andrei did not wish his name to become involved. Nevertheless, he remained the only Grand Duke to acknowledge "Anastasia."[10] Although it was reported in the press that Andrei was about to go to America to help establish the young woman's identity, nothing came of this proposed visit.

Andrei continued his investigation, stipulating that on his death the dossier be kept secret, *"until the public release of documents in the German general staff, documents the Kaiser had, and documents in the Kremlin."*[11] Although DNA tests have now proved that Anna Anderson (as Frau Tchaikovsky came to be known) was not Anastasia, the dossier has never been made public.

Meanwhile, by 1928 Andrei and Mathilde's own financial situation had become critical. The gaming tables of Monte Carlo had taken most of their money and, it was rumoured, Mathilde's fabulous jewels. A brief glimmer of hope came from Poland, where Andrei still owned some land, but in the redistribution of the frontiers the area was restored to the Soviet Union. Somehow they had to make some money.

Like all the Grand Dukes, Andrei was unfitted for life in the real world. Brought up in vast palaces, with a host of servants to satisfy every whim, they had no knowledge of the value of money, let alone how to earn it. Vova, spoilt from childhood, was little better. Mathilde, therefore, was the one being in the household with any financial sense.

Early in 1929 they moved to 10 Villa Molitor, in the 16th Arrondissement of Paris and Mathilde opened a ballet school in a nearby studio in order to support the whole family. At first Andrei kept the books and dealt with the financial side of the business. Then in late 1930 he was once again taken seriously ill, spending three months in hospital. It was Easter before he was permitted to return home and even then was confined to bed for some time. That summer they went to Evian to enable Andrei to recover his health.

The ballet school went from strength to strength during the 1930s but on a family level things were less rosy. The death of Kirill's wife Victoria Melita, and then that of Kirill himself upset Andrei. In 1934 his niece Princess Marina of Greece became a member of the British Royal family when she married Prince George, Duke of Kent, son of King George V. Neither Andrei nor Boris was present at the wedding and when Marina visited Paris and failed to call at Villa Molitor Andrei was deeply hurt.

The outbreak of war in 1939 brought new trials. People were advised to leave Paris, which was expected to be one of the first places to be bombed. Andrei, Mathilde and Vova therefore moved to a house in Le Vesinét, about eleven miles from the capital. Mathilde continued to commute into Paris every day to run her school. No bombs fell. This was the period of the 'phoney war' and after enduring four months of bitterly cold weather they decided to return to their house in Paris.

Then in 1940 the Germans invaded France. Andrei and his family boarded an overcrowded train and fled to Biarritz, where they stayed with Boris in his villa for three months. Soon it became apparent that the Germans would over-run France and they therefore returned to occupied Paris. Without the money earned from the ballet school they had no means to live.

The German invasion of Russia on 22 June 1941 brought new problems. Vova was arrested by the German police and held in an army camp at Compiègne. Despite Andrei's entreaties to prominent members of the émigré community to help obtain his freedom, they refused to assist because of Vova's previous involvement in a political movement. Meanwhile Andrei and Mathilde sent parcels to Vova and were occasionally able to visit, all the while living in constant fear of arrest themselves. After over four months in prison Vova was finally freed.

The years under German occupation were hard. A curfew was in force, the black market was flourishing and various commodities were completely unavailable. In 1943 Boris died suddenly, before Andrei could reach his bedside. Vova, who also suffered from indifferent health, entered a nursing home for a serious operation the following year. As the war dragged on life became more and more of a struggle.

In 1944 Paris was finally liberated. Welcome food parcels arrived from friends abroad and with the end of the war in 1945 life finally returned to normal.

In the post-war years Andrei was a familiar sight around Paris, shopping for food at the market. He still enjoyed playing bridge, but only for small stakes, and nearly every week there was a reception at Villa Molitor. He also enjoyed female company, not for romance, but to while away the hours when Mathilde was teaching at the studio.

In October 1956 Andrei suffered a bout of influenza, which left him weak. Nevertheless, his sudden death on 30 October at the age of 77 was a shock to everyone. He had broken by six months the longevity record set by Grand Duke Michael Nikolaievich in 1909. Andrei's body lay in state in the drawing room of Villa Molitor, now converted into a mortuary chapel, while hundreds of people attended the twice-daily services. The funeral service at the Russian Church in Paris on 3 November was conducted by Metropolitan Vladimir and witnessed a vast outpouring of Russian émigrés. The church was so crowded that people spilled out into the courtyard and even into the streets beyond. Among the mourners were Grand Duchess Marie Pavlovna the younger and Princess Irina Youssoupov. Afterwards his coffin was taken to the small chapel, and then two months later was moved to the crypt.

Alwaays living in strained financial circumstances, Mathilde survived until 1971. Her son Vova died three years later. They all now rest together in the Russian cemetery of St Geneviève des Bois outside Paris.

2 The Son of Grand Duke Kirill Vladimirovich

Grand Duke Vladimir Kirillovich (1917-1992)

By Arturo E. Beéche

*I*n late winter 1917, and as the Russian Empire crumbled, *"disorder in the rear of the front increased,"* Grand Duke Kirill Vladimirovich recalled, *"There was a noticeable shortage of food in the capital, especially of bread...Crime and violence increased daily and the police were frequently attacked by gangs of hooligans."*[1] Within weeks Tsar Nicholas II abdicated, governmental structures collapsed, Imperial Russia was no longer.

The chaos that ensued after the February Revolution would not only consume Russia as the world knew the colossus to be, but it would also obliterate the Romanov Dynasty. In the midst of overwhelming uncertainty, the Imperial family became targets for the ire of an increasingly embittered, ominous and bloodthirsty mob. Kirill Vladimirovich sought to evacuate his young family from Petrograd, while also securing that his pregnant wife would be able to give birth in the regular tranquility of an area where the revolutionaries could not get a hold of them. With this in mind, the Grand Duke obtained permission to leave St Petersburg, where *"an uncanny calm before the great storm"* had settled in.[2]

With permission from the government, Kirill arranged for his family to travel to Finland. In June 1917 he boarded a train, with his daughters Maria and Kira, and left the capital, never to set eyes on it again. Victoria Melita, almost seven months' pregnant with the couple's third child, traveled separately from her husband and daughters. In his memoirs, Kirill recollected his departure longingly, *"Before me lay the unknown, behind me the gathering shadows of the night."*[3]

Once in Finland, Kirill rented two houses in Borgo, near Haiko. Along with them came servants and nannies, equerries and a master of the household. The grand Duke had chosen this location because he had friends, the Etter family, who owned a large estate in the vicinity. It was while living at Borgo that Victoria Melita gave birth to her last child, the long-awaited heir to the Vladimirovich line, Vladimir Kirillovich. The birth took place on 17/30 August 1917.[4] The baby's christening took place some three weeks later, his godparents being Grand Duchess Maria Pavlovna (Sr) and Grand Duke Boris Vladimirovich. They were not present, for at the time they were still at Kislovodsk. The ceremony was conducted by Protopresbyter Alexander Dernoff, Head of the Court Clergy and Dean of the Cathedrals in the Winter Palace.

However, the security found at Borgo and Haiko, where Kirill moved his family after Vladimir's birth, was only a temporary respite from the gathering storm. The Grand Duke feared that as Russia rapidly fell into political disarray, even Finland was not far away enough from the maelstrom. This increasing sense of insecurity, vulnerability even, was confirmed one day when a group of sailors from the Baltic fleet, stationed at Helsingfors, showed up unexpectedly at the Grand Duke's home and produced a search warrant. By then the majority of the Romanovs were either in prison or under house arrest, and Kirill certainly did not want to suffer the same fate.

A year passed by. The situation within Finland deteriorated further and the former grand duchy found itself in the midst of a civil war between Reds and Whites. Killings of landed gentry became commonplace as the Communists tried, desperately and eventually unsuccessfully, to take over Finland. In the end, the Finnish Whites, under the command of General Mannerheim, were able to overcome the Reds and some sense of calm was restored.

After the end of the Great War, Kirill was confronted with an even more uncertain future. Remaining in Finland no longer seemed a viable option, particularly as their finances were in complete disarray and the country's weather was wreaking havoc among his staff. The Swedish monarch, Gustaf V, made approaches and offered his aid in helping the Russian exiles travel out of Finland and perhaps on to Germany. However, the situation there was no better as the defeated German Reich had crumbled and the Kaiser sent into exile. Victoria Melita's own mother, a Germanophile, was even encouraged to settle outside the country's borders, doing so in Switzerland. Still, Marie Alexandrovna owned considerable property on the French Riviera, Coburg and Bavaria, which would certainly provide the Kirills with a roof over their heads.

From Finland they traveled to Berlin, where Victoria Melita's sister, Fürstin Alexandra of Hohenlohe-Langenburg, met the rag-tag group of impoverished exiles. After two very emotional days, they continued to Munich, where Marie Alexandrovna awaited their arrival. From there the group continued to Switzerland, where the Dowager Duchess of Saxe-Coburg & Gotha had spent a considerable part of the First World War.

The safety provided by exile was fraught with ample uncertainty nonetheless. Chief among these new worries was the precarious state of health the family found both of Vladimir Kirillovich's grandmothers, Maria Alexandrovna and Maria Pavlovna (Sr.). These grand duchesses had been indomitable figures of Tsarist Russia, paragons of every aspect of the magnificence that surrounded the Imperial court. Now, what Kirill and Victoria Melita shockingly discovered, were two bent old ladies, ghosts of their former selves. Death did not wait long to make pay its unwanted visit. Grand Duchess Maria Pavlovna (Sr.) died at Contrexéville on 6 September 1920.[5] The Dowager Duchess of Saxe-Coburg & Gotha, last surviving child of Tsar Alexander II and Empress Maria Alexandrovna, died on 24 October.[6] Death took her while living in a Zürich hotel, a far cry from the splendor in which most of her life had played out.

These family deaths, as painful as they must have been, also brought a ray of sunshine to Vladimir Kirillovich's financially strapped parents. Maria Pavlovna and Maria Alexandrovna had been amazingly wealthy. Although cash-poor at the time of death, Vladimir's grandmothers left behind sizable fortunes in jewels, artwork and real estate. From his mother, Kirill received all her pearls, not a small portion of her large jewelry collection. The sale of some of these pieces guaranteed the Grand Duke a certain degree of solvency in years to come. From her mother Victoria Melita inherited, besides some of her magnificent jewelry, important real estate, the crowning piece of these holdings being Coburg's Edinburgh Palais, the home Maria Alexandrovna had built for herself across from the Ehrenburg, her husband's family seat. These two inheritances assured Vladimir's parents of a permanent roof over their heads, a relatively peaceful environment in which to raise their growing children, and a reduction of their financial travails. Coburg became a peaceful refuge away from the uncertainties they had lived through since the assassination of the Austrian heir, Archduke Franz Ferdinand, and his wife Sophie, ignited the powder keg responsible for obliterating the world of the Romanovs. Extended periods of time were spent in France as well, where Kirill and his wife always felt welcomed.

While living in Coburg, the Kirills of Russia were in excellent terms with Duke Carl Eduard of Saxe-Coburg & Gotha, the dual duchy's last ruler. Charlie, as the duke was called within the family circle, was also a first cousin of Victoria Melita's. Under a regency presided by Hereditary Prince Ernst of Hohenlohe-Langenburg, starting in 1900, Charlie succeeded Duke Alfred, Maria Alexandrovna's husband. Hence, while in Coburg both families maintained a close relationship, which extended to their children as well. After all, Vladimir Kirillovich was only a year younger than Friedrich Josias, Charlie Coburg's youngest son and eventual heir. Vladimir's sisters, Maria and Kira, were of the same age as Charlie's elder children, Johann Leopold, Sibylla and Hubertus. Many are the photos showing the children of these two families playing, riding and performing tableaux vivants.

However, when it came to finding husbands, Vladimir's sisters looked farther than their Coburg cousins. In 1925 Maria Kirillovna married a distant cousin, Hereditary Prince Karl of Leiningen (1898-1946). The wedding took place in Coburg and the couple settled at Amorbach, the groom's family seat. From then onward, this sleepy German town located in Germany's Odenwald was to have a close connection to Vladimir and his parents. In fact, it was while visiting Amorbach that Vladimir's mother died in 1936. It was there where Vladimir Kirillovich would spend part of the Second World War. Kira's marriage was spectacular, but more about that later.

In the mid-1920s Vladimir's parents relocated to France. Kirill's political activities did not sit well with the German government. France, instead, provided a far more tolerant climate from which to launch his imperial ambitions. With proceeds from the sale of the Coburg Palais, Kirill and Victoria Melita were to purchase a house in St Briac-sur-Mer, Brittany. Not only was the village close to the coast and English Channel, but it was also a four-hour train ride from Paris, where Vladimir's parents also obtained a pied-a-terre. Paris, with its large Russian exile community was a welcoming city to the Romanovs.

When it came time to focus on Vladimir's education, his attendance at a local school was out of the question. On one hand the parents did not believe that the future Head of the Imperial House of Russia should attend a local school with commoner boys, while on the other hand, Kirill and his wife were truly worried that their son's security would be compromised if attending such an establishment. Consequently, and without another options, they decided that the boy was to be instructed at home, just as previous generations of Romanovs had been. In the process, Vladimir became a polyglot and was fluent in five languages: Russian, English, French, German and later in Spanish. At one point he seemed to be headed to Winchester, a prestigious school in England, but his mother decided against it.[7] Neither of Vladimir's parents was too fond of Albion and in fact many suspected them of harboring anglophobic opinions, mainly due to what was seen as George V's abandoning of the Romanovs during the Russian revolution. This did not prevent Kirill and Victoria Melita, with Kira and Vladimir in tow, from having a rather jolly time in London while attending the wedding of Marina of Greece and the Duke of Kent.

During the mid-to-late 1930s Vladimir attended a Russian school in Paris, as well as King's College in London. Just before he entered this school, Vladimir, accompanied by Kirill and Kira, stayed at his Aunt Beatrice's home in Kew. During the stay in London, Kirill complained of *"not feeling well."*[7] He returned to France for the holidays, while Vladimir and Kira went to Cecilienhof, Potsdam, where on 23 December Kira became engaged to Prince Louis Ferdinand of Prussia. Their engagement was made public a week later. In the New Year Vladimir returned to London and continued his studies, but his education came to a quick end upon becoming an orphan in 1938.

Let us stop for a second and take a quick look at *"Aunt Beatrice."* Born Princess Beatrice of Edinburgh in 1884, she was the youngest of the five children of Prince Alfred and Grand Duchess Maria Alexandrovna. Like her eldest sister Marie, who became Queen Consort of Romania, Beatrice was blessed with extraordinary good looks, a gift that eluded her middle sisters Victoria Melita and, certainly, Alexandra. For several years Beatrice was involved in a liaison with Grand Duke Michael Alexandrovich, her own first cousin. In the end the dalliance came to naught and the young, broken-hearted Beatrice was left to find herself another suitor. That very lucky man was none other than the Infante don Alfonso of Spain (1886-1975), eldest son of the Infante don Antonio and his scandalous, yet endearingly royal, wife, Infanta doña Eulalia, an aunt of King Alfonso XIII. The Infante don Alfonso owned considerable properties in Sanlucar de Barrameda, and this region was later to play an important role in Vladimir Kirillovich's life. On her sister's deathbed, Beatrice promised Victoria Melita that she would always look after Vladimir. *"She knew we were there and on the first day she whispered thankfully to each one of us,"* the Infanta remembered. *"At the head of her bed, my sister asked that I look after and watch over Vladimir as if he were my own son. I promised her to do so."*[8]

Now let us fast forward a bit. As the reader may recall in a previous chapter, Victoria Melita died suddenly in early 1936 while visiting her daughter Maria at Amorbach. Kirill, a ghost of his former handsome self, survived his wife by two years, dying at Neuilly on 13 October 1938. *"On October 12 my sister and I, father's brothers, and sister, Princess Nicholas of Greece, were summoned to the hospital,"* Vladimir recalled. *"We all gathered at his bedside. There was still a lingering flame of life in him…he passed away in his sleep. The expression of his face was so calm that it seemed as though he realized that he had at last found peace and quiet after six months of uninterrupted suffering."*[9]

Soon after his father's death Vladimir, who had been elevated to the title of Grand Duke by his father, published manifesto. In this pronouncement the young Romanov not claimed headship of house, but also expressed his hope of one day serving All Russians. In the meantime, rumors in the press claimed that Vladimir was planning on having secret talks with Hitler concerning his future role in a non-Communist Russia. Vladimir lost little time in publicly contradicting these claims, saying that he *had* no intention of becoming a puppet emperor. *"I have never been approached nor would I ever lend my name to any act tending to dismember the Russian empire,"* said Vladimir to accusations that he was being sought as Hitler's puppet ruler for the Ukraine.[10] Furthermore, Vladimir said that his visit to Germany had no other purpose than spending the holidays at Amorbach, as a guest of his sister Maria Kirillovna.

In 1939 Vladimir returned to England and worked as an ordinary mechanic in an automobile plant. Vladimir's argument to explain such a puzzling choice was rather simple, *"he just wanted to what the life of a working man was like."*[11] One author suggested that it could have also been an English attempt to Anglicize a young man who was raised by Anglophobic parents. Whatever the true reasons behind Vladimir's proletarian experiment, it was to be short-lived. When summer arrived, Vladimir returned to France, where the start of war caught him. His time in the automobile plant was to be Vladimir's only real job, for the rest of his life he dedicated himself to the cause of monarchical restoration, while living off his investments.

Much ink has been spent on trying to portray the Grand Duke as a supporter of Germany during the conflict. Yes he was partly raised in Germany, a fact that is not a secret to anyone. He had ample Germanic bloodlines and his sisters were married to German princes. He felt very comfortable speaking the language and enjoyed paying visits to the country, where he always had many friends, besides countless relations. However, to use these well-known aspects of the Grand Duke's life as an excuse for calling him a supporter of National Socialism smacks this author as an allegation bordering on the scurrilous.

Vladimir remained ensconced in France during the German occupation. His travel choices were rather limited and crossing borders was no longer as easy as it had once been, particularly for European royalty. At one point, the German authorities, which had always kept him under surveillance, arrested Vladimir and transported him to Germany. Berlin had wanted him to publish a manifesto asking Russians to support Nazi Germany's invasion of the Soviet Union. Vladimir refused to do such a thing. Instead, accompanied by his closest collaborators, he was housed in a concentration camp at Compiègne. *"In 1944 the Germans forced me to pack up and leave St Briac, where I had been under surveillance,"* Vladimir once recalled.[12] He was taken to Amorbach, where he lived at his sister Maria's home.

In later years, the Grand Duke was falsely accused by his enemies of cavorting with the Nazis. He categorically denied the libelous insinuating. When denying the insidious rumor, he recalled that the Germans, *"had no particular reason to treat me as a prisoner and no particular reason to consider me an ally. They could not suspect me of approving of their policies in Russia...they wanted to make Russia a German province, and they knew that they could not obtain my support for such a scheme."*[13] Whereas Kirill and Victoria Melita may have been supporters of the German fascists because they convinced themselves, as did many of their cousins, that the movement's ultimately goal was restoration of the monarchy, there is no evidence that Vladimir shared his parents' position.

As the Third Reich began its slow death, Vladimir managed to get himself out of Germany via Austria and tried entering Switzerland. The Swiss would not have him and instead Vladimir had to stay in Feldkirch, Austria. Once the British occupation forces grated permission, Vladimir was allowed to fly to Spain, where he lived with his aunt Beatrice in Sanlucar de Barrameda, near Seville. It was there that he met the woman with whom he was destined to start a family.

Enter Princess Leonida Bagration-Moukhransky. Born in Tbilisi, Georgia, on 6 October 1914 (O.S.)[14], Leonida was the daughter of Prince George Bagration-Moukhransky and of his wife, the former Elena Zlotnicka. This made the baby a member of a family that had once ruled over Georgia. In fact, the Bagrations have always claimed to be among the oldest Christian ruling dynasties. In 1801, however, Tsar Paul had annexed Georgia into the Russian Empire, following which the Bagrations became a leading family of the Russian nobility, serving in the Tsar's army and at court in St Petersburg.

Leonida's family did not leave Russia until a few years after the revolution. By then her paternal grandfather was executed and the family lived in constant fear for their lives. Leonida's father removed his family from Georgia, only to return some time later. However, as Bolshevik rule became more oppressive, the Bagrations were forced to accept the inevitable and exile, therefore, was their only option.

Exile brought the Bagration family to France, where Leonida's grandmother and relations had already settled. Russian aristocrats in Paris were a dime a dozen and most lived in very strained circumstances. It was there that the young princess met and married a wealthy American, Sumner Moore Kirby. Their wedding took place in Nice in 1934, but ended in divorce three years later. One child was born from this union, Helen Kirby. In 1945 Leonida's ex-husband had a harrowing end in a concentration camp. Helen was one of the beneficiaries of his large estate.

As war intensified, Leonida and her daughter relocated to Spain. The country remained untouched by the conflict raging across Europe. Spain's dictator, General Franco, saw much political capital in not joining his former allies in Berlin. Anyhow, Leonida's decision to find refuge in wartime Spain was to prove fateful.

In 1946, while hosted by a prominent aristocratic Spanish family, Leonida made the acquaintance of a young man who would change her life. His name was Vladimir, his past was Russia, his future was uncertain. In her memoirs, which were authored in the late 1990s, Grand Duchess Leonida recalled how she met her husband, *"one night, the Grand Duke Vladimir came to dine with us. He was living at his aunt's, the Infanta Beatrice of Spain, who owned a property nearby. He was also very close to our hosts. It was during this gathering that I truly came to know Vladimir."*[15]

Soon after their acquaintance, Vladimir moved to Madrid, where he was offered employment. Money being tight, he received an allowance from his aunt Beatrice. Vladimir needed this job quickly. Leonida followed. Their liaison continued while both lived in the Spanish capital, even though Leonida recalls they were also seeing other people. It was all a love dance as Vladimir took his time making a decision. Finally, *"One night he excused himself from being able to accompany me to the cinema because he had an engagement with some Hungarians,"* Leonida recalled. *"I knew he also was seeing a German lady. 'That's fine', I said indifferently. I have plans to go out with a friend nonetheless."*[16] Apparently, consumed by jealousy, that night the Grand Duke never stopped calling Leonida's flat. His excuse being that he had left his glasses behind. Grand Duchess Leonida remembered that, *"Well, that was a problem…he did not wear any glasses!"*[17] One month later they became engaged.

Opposition within his close family circle rose almost immediately. From Paris, Princess Nicholas of Greece, Vladimir's paternal aunt, expressed her consternation at his choice of bride. She is said to have sent out a message to Orthodox priests across Europe demanding that none officiate the wedding ceremony. From Sanlucar, Aunt Beatrice was equally disconcerted. *"In spite of the many pleas from Infanta Beatrice, who did not like the Georgians, the Grand Duke was intent on marrying Leonida,"* a noted Spanish author tells us.[18] The wedding, a small Orthodox ceremony, took place in Lausanne on 12 August 1948. *"The Infanta cut off all contact with them and never spoke of her nephew because his wedding caused her such grief. Apparently some royal families also frowned upon Vladimir's choice, as can be seen in the correspondence of Queen Victoria Eugenia of Spain,"* the author noted.[19] After spending their honeymoon in Palma de Majorca, Vladimir and Leonida settled in Madrid. From there he continued his involvement with exiled Russian monarchist organizations, publishing edicts and manifestos on all matters Russian with some frequency. Visits to St Briac were renewed since Vladimir had inherited his parents' house. Leonida once said that her sisters-in-law were always welcoming and never raised any issues about her marrying Vladimir. Peculiarly enough, as mentioned before, both Maria and Kira were to die while guests of their brother's. Visiting Madrid in 1951, Maria Kirillovna, a war widow by then, suffered a fulminating heart attack. There was nothing that could be done to save her life. In 1967 while visiting the Vladimirs at St Briac, Kira Kirillovna suffered an embolism. She died a few hours later at a local hospital.[20]

Leonida gave birth to Vladimir's daughter in 1953. The baby was named Maria, in honor of her father's two grandmothers. It was a very difficult pregnancy and the mother once recalled that she had to, *"spend eight months in absolute rest in order to complete the very difficult pregnancy."*[21] This Leonida always remembered as the most difficult aspect of her last pregnancy since she considered herself, *"a woman with a very dynamic temperament."*[22] The happiness brought to Vladimir and Leonida by the arrival of their daughter Maria was soon to turn sour. Firstly, there were those who claimed that Leonida had never been pregnant and that her claim to have spent eight months in bed was nothing but an attempt to fake a birth. Outrageous. Secondly, there were those who continued raising opposition to Vladimir's spousal choice, falsely claiming that the Bagration bride was a morganatic spouse.

In fact, prior to his involvement with Leonida, the Spanish royal family asked Vladimir if Prince Irakly Bagration-Moukhransky, Leonida's brother, was of royal standing. Irakly was going to marry the Infanta María de las Mercedes, a niece of King Alfonso XIII. In his response to the inquiry Vladimir explained that the Bagrations were a dynasty that had once ruled over a kingdom that Russia conquered.[23] As part of the settlement the dynasty signed with Tsar Paul I, they retained many of their properties, but became members of the Russian aristocracy. So, were they royal, these Georgian princes? Indeed, just like the Orléans, and the Parmas and Two Sicilies were all cadet branches of the Bourbon dynasty. They belonged to a dynasty that had once being ruling and sovereign. Imagine how preposterous it would be to think that the descendants of the Duke d'Orléans, for example, were not of royal lineage!

Opponents of Vladimir's choice also raised myriad issues. Among these were: Vladimir was not a member of the Romanov dynasty due to his parents' *"irregular"* marriage; Kirill was not really the heir because the Dowager Empress opposed his 1924 manifesto; Leonida was a divorcée; she was a morganatic wife; Maria could not succeed because of her *"morganatic"* status; and finally, grasping a straws because she was a female. Infinite pages have been written to combat these allegations, perhaps too numerous for us to discuss in greater detail. I would urge the reader to visit the excellent websites maintained by François Velde (*http://www.heraldica.org/*) and Guy Stair Sainty (*http://www.chivalricorders.org*), two of the world's foremost authorities on dynastic matters. There one can read excellent explanations of the Grand Duke Vladimir's status not only as a Russian dynast, but also as Head of the Imperial Russian House.

In 1969 Vladimir, upon Maria reaching the age of sixteen, declared that she would become *"Curator of the Russian Throne,"* in case he died. By then all other Romanov males had married morganatically, thus preventing their offspring from being in the line of succession. Vladimir wanted to assure himself that his daughter, the child of an equal marriage, would thus be clearly perceived as the future head of House Russia. This act did not sit well with several of the morganauts and the level of their acrimonious banter bordered on vulgarity. Led by a son and grandson of Grand Duke Peter Nikolaievich, they formed a group called *"The Romanoff Family Association,"* and began a campaign to present themselves as a valid option for the Russian succession.

Grand Duke Vladimir enjoyed a financial situation that was much improved from that of his exiled parents. He had invested his money well and received the support of many loyalists from around the world. Added to that was Leonida's own finances, which included her settlement from the Kirby divorce, as well as control of the

Kirby inheritance of her daughter Helen. In Madrid the couple first inhabited a vast apartment in a prestigious address. Later on they purchased a villa in a very distinguished neighborhood where many other royals owned homes. While living in Spain, they maintained very close relations not only with the Spanish royal house, but also with many other exiled royals, among them those from Bulgaria and Albania. A royal historian who visited the Grand Duke in the 1970s described him thus, *"Lives the life of passionless ease, without the stresses and dangers earlier Romanoffs [sic] endured. Idleness does not seem to bother him; he is capable of spending hours in contemplation. For him the past is full of glory; the present is bland and insubstantial…a brooding prisoner of his ambitions and resentments. He has allowed himself only one great passion: contempt for his opponents."*[24]

Physically, Grand Duke Vladimir evoked views of his Romanov ancestors. One author described that the Grand Duke, *"dresses like a French businessman, talks like a British solicitor, and looks a bit like an American hero. He is handsome and strong: he has a certain look in the eyes that one might guess a Romanoff [Sic] could not avoid – a certain air of autocracy, a suggestion of fear, and a clarity of breeding. Vladimir, a great-grandson of Queen Victoria of England, is related to virtually all the royal dynasties of Europe. He gives the impression of being capable and energetic."*[25] The Grand Duchess Leonida, the same visitor, said, *"is an arresting beauty in the classical sense: a wonderful profile, thick dark hair, and a superb voice. She exudes an aura of peaceful but forceful authority."*[26]

The Vladimirs of Russia were doting and vigilant parents as Maria was their only child. Born at a time when her mother neared the age of forty, she was not expected to have siblings. Like her parents, Maria Vladimirovna is a polyglot and has a deep love of everything Russian. After attending schools in Madrid, she entered Oxford University. Vladimir and Leonida lived in England during the years that their daughter was enrolled at the prestigious university. Visits to Madrid and St Briac became part of their regular yearly trek, as were visits to various Russian émigré communities around the world.

Once Maria Vladimirovna concluded her stay at Oxford, the question of the succession, once again, became tantamount for the dynasty's future. Given the immense amount of criticism Vladimir was the object of concerning his choice of Leonida, it was imperative for Maria Vladimirovna to find a suitable husband. The solution to this quandary was provided at a soirée organized by Prince Louis Ferdinand of Prussia. Maria attended the elegant gathering and while there she met the man who would in time become her spouse. His name was Prince Franz Wilhelm of Prussia. He was the son of Prince Karl Franz Josef (1916-1975)[27] and of his wife, the former Princess Henriette of Schönaich-Carolath (1918-1972).[28] Franz Wilhelm's paternal grandfather was Prince Joachim of Prussia, Kaiser Wilhelm II's youngest son. Henriette's mother was the former Princess Hermine Reuß, who in 1922 became Wilhelm II's second wife, to the chagrin of many within his family. Franz Wilhelm was the eldest of twins, but his baby brother Franz Joseph died three months after their birth, which took place in 1943. Within two years the family fled their Eastern German lands and sought refuge in the western part of the country, witnessing how many of the ancestral lands of the Hohenzollerns were now under the control of the Soviet Union. After escaping capture by the communists, they lived in Switzerland and The Netherlands, before eventually settling in Hamburg.

Given all the tragedy and stress lived by Franz Wilhelm's parents, it was not a wonder that their marriage did not survive long. They were divorced in 1946, two years after the birth of a third child, Franz Friedrich. The dissolution of the marriage of Franz Wilhelm's parents meant that the children were passed along from one school to the next, from one relation to another. Henriette never remarried, while her husband migrated to South America and died in Chile in 1975.²⁹ Grand Duchess Leonida remained convinced that the unstable family life surrounding her future son-in-law was surely to become a major obstacle for the couple. In the end, she was to be correct about her fears.

In her memoirs, Grand Duchess Leonida expressed, in no uncertain terms, her apprehension regarding Franz Wilhelm. *"Franz Wilhelm was a boy already hardened by the trials that life had not spared him,"* she said.³⁰ Furthermore, she recalled that Prince Louis Ferdinand, who happened to be the prospective groom's godfather, also begged for Maria not to *"marry him."*³¹ It was all to no avail. Maria Vladimirovna was in love with the tall, blond and blue-eyed prince. Their engagement was announced in July 1976 and their religious wedding was celebrated two months later in Madrid.

Not long after the wedding ceremony, which was attended by a galaxy of royals, both ruling and exiled, problems arose. Leonida, obviously not a fan of her daughter's husband, as well as fearful for the future, had already demanded that the couple sign a pre-nuptial agreement. Franz Wilhelm had agreed at first, but then relented, only to change his mind once again. He converted to Orthodoxy, abandoned his birth name and became Grand Duke Michael Pavlovich. The situation must have been fraught with tension, it seems. In fact, in her memoirs Grand Duchess Leonida did not even bother mentioning the collapse of her daughter's marriage, a result she apparently expected from the beginning. As she once said, *"Preventing the marriage of Maria was impossible, the divorce not at all."*³²

On 13 March 1981, Maria Vladimirovna gave birth to a baby boy. The child was baptized with the name of George Mikhailovich and was a Russian Grand Duke from birth. Not surprisingly, he was to be his parents' only offspring. Within a few years Franz Wilhelm and Maria Vladimirovna parted ways rather acrimoniously. Ricardo Mateos, an expert on the familial relations of Queen Sofía of Spain, said that as Franz Wilhelm's marriage collapsed, *"he requested the aid of Queen Sofía who, in a show of affection and consideration, expressed to him her support and made it all easier for him in Spain. In fact, it was the Queen who even found him a lawyer in Madrid to help him through the divorce. Since then, his life has never been easy, even though he remained living and working in Madrid."*³³

Back in Madrid, the collapse of the Iron Curtain caught the Russian exiles by surprise. Vladimir had always hoped to live long enough to witness the fall of Communism. His wishes came true on 9 November 1989, as the Berlin Wall, that monstrous symbol of human lunacy cracked and crumbled. Revolution spread like wildfire across Eastern Europe and within months Poland, Eastern Germany, Czechoslovakia, Hungary, Bulgaria, Yugoslavia, and even Romania had done away with their pro-Soviet dictators.

Within the Soviet Union the situation also became untenable as Communism, after all, proved to be a broken, corrupt and unsustainable economic system. Mikhail Gorbachev's Perestroika had unleashed forces unforeseen and even his regime eventually ended in the dustbin of history. In the new Russia, led by Boris Yeltsin, there was certain degree of nostalgia, yearning even, for long-forgotten Imperial glory. The Romanovs suddenly became an important chapter of the nation's history, not one maligned in history books by Soviet dictators and apparatchiks.

Consequently, Grand Duke Vladimir visited St Petersburg in November 1991 when Anatoly Sobchak, Mayor of St Petersburg (also previously known as Petrograd and later Leningrad), extended an invitation. It was the Grand Duke's life-long dream. On the flight there, he told a journalist, that, *"As soon as I received the invitation to go back to Russia, I immediately accepted, but on one condition: that as Russians neither I nor my wife should need a visa to enter the country."*³⁴ While in St Petersburg, Vladimir was asked what his role would be in the new Russia, to which he replied, *"I hope that my presence as representative of the Romanov family may help to rekindle the religious and ethical values which have been oppressed for so many years, but which I believe are still alive in the hearts of the Russian people."* It was an emotion-filled sojourn and one that a deeply moved Grand Duke Vladimir relished greatly. The visit was to be one of his last joys.

In April 1992 Grand Duke Vladimir traveled to the United States. The voyage was designed as a goodwill visit to attract American investors to Russia. On 21 April, during a news conference in Miami, just prior to giving a speech to *"a forum of civic and business leaders,"* Grand Duke Vladimir Kirillovich collapsed and died. Grand Duchess Leonida remembered the tragic day when she became a widow, *"in the morning he awakened in great spirits…all night long he had held my hand…during a conference at a local bank, he took a coffee and rejoined a group of journalists. I was seated just a few meters away from him. Suddenly, he collapsed on a table while responding to a question. People rushed to him. As for me I sat nailed to my seat. My brain refused to consider the worst and had made me consider it was simple drowsiness. Everyone ran, terrified, and I did not move. A world collapsed!"*[35] An aneurism brought a sudden and painless end to a long, well-lived life. As his wife once said, *"he died as he lived, serving his country."*[36]

Upon receiving the awful news of her father's passing, Grand Duchess Maria Vladimirovna decided on a flight to Miami. Her mother dissuaded Maria from doing so and instead asked that she travel to Paris to meet her and Vladimir's remains. Meanwhile, negotiations began in earnest to bring the remains to St Petersburg for burial. Anatoly Sobchak, with the cooperation of President Boris Yeltsin, made it all happen. On 29 April Grand Duke Vladimir Kirillovich's funeral was celebrated at the imposing St Isaac's Cathedral. Afterward, he was housed inside the Romanov Crypt at the Peter and Paul Fortress. He was the first Romanov to be honored this way since the death of Grand Duke Konstantin Konstantinovich in 1915. Yet, not wanting to cause a stir among a jittery public still dealing with the turmoil engulfing their country, the press stated, *"the honorable funeral was regarded by civic and Russian authorities as an obligation to the Romanov family rather than a step toward restoration of the monarchy."*[37] *"His whole life outside, all his feelings and efforts, Grand Duke Vladimir Kirillovich dedicated to a country he considered his own,"* Patriarch Aleksy exclaimed in his eulogy. *"His faith and long patience were not in vain."* On the eve of his passage to the other world, he stepped on his native soil."*[38]

Just months before his death, Grand Duke Vladimir said, *"For me the throne is not as important as my desire to be of some use to my country."*[39] The Grand Duke born in exile had come full circle.

In an interview Vladimir granted in the late 1970s, he defined for posterity how he saw the future of Russia: *"everything depends on the circumstances of the change. Perhaps democracy would be a good idea, though not for the start. After a firm government, one would have to adopt another firm government, at least for the beginning, until new conditions emerge. A monarchy of the future would have to be different from what we had in 1905 or 1917. It's the principle that counts, not the form."*[40]

Grand Duchess Leonida survived her husband by eighteen years, dying in Madrid on 23 May 2010.[41] She rests with Vladimir Kirillovich inside the Grand Ducal Vault adjacent to the Cathedral of SS Peter and Paul in St Petersburg.

3

The Grandson of Grand Duke Vladimir Kirillovich

Grand Duke George Mikhailovich
(b. 1981)

By Arturo E. Beéche

The arrival of the long-await heir came on 13 March 1981, in Madrid, Spain. On that day, Grand Duchess Maria Vladimirovna was delivered of a healthy baby boy: George Mikhailovich. His birth, coincidentally, took place on the centennial anniversary of the assassination of Tsar Alexander II, the baby's great-great-great-grandfather. George's baptism took place in Madrid, *"in the presence of the miraculous icon of the Mother of God of Kursk."*[1] Among those in attendance were: King Juan Carlos I and Queen Sofía of Spain, King Simeon and Queen Margarita of Bulgaria, as well as King Constantine II of the Hellenes, the boy's godfather.[2]

The birth of George Mikhailovich caused considerable consternation among the morganatic Romanovs. *"The Romanov Family Association hereby declares that the joyful event in the Prussian Royal House does not concern the Romanov Family Association since the newborn prince is not a member of either the Russian Imperial House or of the Romanov family,"* a rather unkind press communiqué released by the non-dynastic Romanovs announced.[3] Acrimonious statements flew between the warring camps, but since all other Romanovs had married in contravention of the Fundamental Laws of the Imperial family, the opinions held by Vladimir's opponents had little dynastic value. However, foolish, and bitter, this reaction by the morganauts may have been, it did little to dampen the enthusiasm of the baby's parents and grandparents; what it achieve, was adding plenty of coal to the simmering fires between Grand Duke Vladimir and his extended morganatic Romanov cousins.

From the beginning, Grand Duchess Leonida argued, the family had concerns about Maria's choice of husband. In her memoirs, Leonida argued that her own brother-in-law, Prince Louis Ferdinand of Prussia, cautioned Vladimir against the marriage and begged for the parents to, *"not allow Maria to marry him."*[4] Leonida and her husband found it *"impossible to prevent"* their daughter to marry Franz Wilhelm.[5] However, and just in case, he agreed to sign an agreement for separation of property. Furthermore, the children had by the couple would bear the name Romanov and would be the recognized heirs to the imperial throne. Franz Wilhelm also accepted to convert to Orthodoxy and adopt a Russian name, which he did (Michael Pavlovich). Yet, nothing could prevent the expected outcome and five years after George's arrival, Maria and Michael

Pavlovich parted ways. Theirs was an acrimonious divorce, made more so by the countless accusations and press interviews granted by the spouses and their families. Grand Duchess Leonida's indomitable character had never warmed to her Prussian son-in-law and she was among his main critics. Her book of memoirs serves as living testament of her strong words on the matter.

Relations between Franz Wilhelm, who returned to his German name after his divorce, and Maria have always remained distant and tense, at best. He once declared to the press that his son was *"a Prussian prince,"*[6] a statement that only irritated his former in-laws even further. George has never been seen in public in the company of his father. In fact, in August 2011 while attending the Potsdam wedding of Prince Georg Friedrich of Prussia, Maria and George ran into Franz Wilhelm.[7] They entered the festivities separately and left the same way. Whether they spoke to each other, or took photos together remains a mystery.

George Mikhailovich had a rather international early life. Along with his mother and grandparents he lived between Madrid, Paris and St Briac-sur-Mer in Brittany. While in Madrid and Paris he attended prestigious schools and in 1999 graduated high school. George then continued his studies at Oxford University. As is the case with most members of his family, he is a polyglot. George is fluent in Spanish, French, English and Russian.

In her memoirs, Grand Duchess Leonida spoke fondly of the boy. *"He is nineteen now,"* she said.[8] *"How far away it is since he was a small boy whom I awaited outside the Stanislas College when we lived in Paris, and inhabited an apartment blocks away from the Palais Talleyrand, which had been the home of Tsar Alexander I!"*[9] She also mentioned that his upbringing, although focused on the legacy George is to inherit, also resembled that of a boy his age. Besides enjoying fencing, George Mikhailovich *"loves riding and videogames,"* his adoring grandmother wrote.

The young Grand Duke is also a convinced Russophile. At the age of ten his grandmother gave him a Cossack uniform, which the child enjoyed wearing very much. His religious instruction in the Russian Orthodox faith took place in Paris. He is said to be deeply interested both in history and his ancestors. Tsar Peter the Great seems to be George's favorite Romanov. He also has a deep passion for Russian literature, the works of Pushkin being his favorite.

The death of Grand Duke Vladimir was a great loss to his only grandchild. Grand Duchess Leonida remembered her grandson's reaction, *"It affected him deeply. It was as if he lost his own father since they were so close to one another. This loss, if anything, convinced him to focus on his education as future heir to the Russian throne."*[10] Furthermore, in 2000, Leonida described her grandson as *"living like most of the princes of his age…While also profoundly anchored in his times and completely prepared to play the role History and His people may confer on him at some point…When I see him, I pray and hope, I wish he accomplishes, as History wishes, the service to His people that his birthright destined him to."*[11]

George Mikhailovich first visited Russia, under rather painful circumstances, in 1992. The occasion was the burial of his beloved grandfather Grand Duke Vladimir. Since that sad date, George has visited his Motherland many times, *"always showing a lively interest in all aspects of the life of the people. Russia's ancient Orthodox churches, and what George considers their uniquely special prayerful atmosphere, have made an indelible impression."*[12]

This author happens to have met the young Grand Duke at the funeral of the Countess of Paris, celebrated at St Louis de Dreux on 5 July 2003.[13] George Mikhailovich was there representing the Russian Imperial family. He seemed to a bit shy and circumspect, although always displaying a welcoming look and a friendly disposition. That was seven years ago now, and since then much has happened in his short life.

Opponents of his mother, mainly those within the morganatic Romanov ranks, allege that since George is a "Hohenzollern" by birth, he cannot inherit the Russian Imperial claims. However, they forget that the last living Romanov was Tsarina Elisabeth, Peter the Great's daughter, who died in 1761. Her heir, Tsar Peter III, was a Holstein-Gottorp by birth. Married to a princess of Anhalt-Zerbst, the future Catherine the Great, Peter was most likely not the biological father of his only son, the future Tsar Paul I. However, since Peter III never denied the paternity of his son, history has assumed that Paul was his father's son. And that is just for starters. The Romanovs are not the only dynasty in which the succession will pass through the female line. Such cases abound in European royal history, and one need only think of the following examples: Denmark, where the Glücksburgs will be succeeded by a son of the Count de Monpezat but the dynasty will retain the same name; The Netherlands, where the last Orange-Nassau by birth was Queen Wilhelmina, the grandmother of the present queen, yet the dynasty has retained the ancient name; Romania, where King Michael's grandson, a commoner by birth, was elevated to the princely rank; Sweden, where the Bernadottes will eventually be succeeded by a child of a commoner father, also elevated to the princely rank; Great Britain, where the House of Windsor (actually Saxe-Coburg & Gotha) will be succeeded by the Mountbatten-Windsors (actually the Glücksburgs); and many other examples. Hence, to claim that because George Mikhailovich's father was a Prussian prince by birth the young man cannot succeed his mother, is not only erroneous, but also sexist and historically myopic.

To her critics, Maria Vladimirovna, Head of House Russia, has replied, *"Attempts to disparage my rights have originated with people who, firstly, do not belong to the Imperial Family, and, secondly, either do not themselves know the relevant laws or think that others do not know these laws. In either case, there is unscrupulousness at work. The only thing that causes me regret is that some of our relatives waste their time and energy on little intrigues instead of striving to be of some use to their country. I have never quarreled with anyone about these matters and I remain open to a discussion and cooperation with all, including, of course, my relatives. But there can be no foundation for cooperation without respect for our dynastic laws, fulfilling these laws, and following our family traditions."*[14]

After completing his studies, Grand Duke George worked at the European Parliament for a few years. Later he moved to Luxembourg where he was employed at the European Commission's Directorate-General for Atomic Energy and Security. On 12 December 2008, George Mikhailovich was appointed an aide to the Director General of MMC Norilsk Nickel, a major Russian nickel-mining company.[15] Whether he continues in this position or not, is something that this author does not know.

All along, he has become increasingly involved in his mother's role as the Head of the Romanov Dynasty. George and Maria are inseparable and devoted to one another. In the years since Leonida's passing, they are more regularly present at family and royal events around Europe, particularly in France and Germany. Among George Mikhailovich's closest friends is Baron Axel de Sambucy de Sorgue, the eldest son of Princess Chantal of France, herself the youngest child of the late Count and Countess of Paris.

Grand Duke George Mikhailovich, the hope of the Romanov Dynasty, is single, and whether he will be expected to marry a royal, or not, remains to be seen. He is the only, and hopefully not the last, Grand Duke of Russia.

The Son of Grand Duke Paul Alexandrovich

Grand Duke Dimitri Pavlovich
(1891-1942)

By Grant Hayter-Menzies

Compared to the vigorous, sparkling Grand Duchess Marie, her younger brother Grand Duke Dimitri Pavlovich seemed even in infancy to hold in his large dark eyes all the remote sadness of a life already spent in struggle – an expression which was never to alter – not from his cradle to the pictures taken before his death, at fifty-one, in a Swiss sanatorium.

The irony of Dimitri's young life is that long before he, like all his family, lost everything in the 1917 revolution, there was every reason for this grand duke of the house of Romanov to anticipate a glorious future. Favored in looks and character, as coolly elegant in his white and gold Chevalier Guards uniform as he was wearing a duster behind the wheel of one of his 100-horsepower automobiles, Dimitri was the toast of the empire during the tinseled period known as Russia's Silver Age. Yet despite these gifts, both the earned and inherited, Grand Duke Dimitri went from a solemn little boy to a solemn man, gazing out from a face that by turns was strikingly handsome and chillingly expressionless – blank as the façade of a palace emptied of all living occupants.

Again unlike Marie, whose fighter instinct took her out of Bolshevik Russia and on to a life filled with creative efforts to make her way in an alien world, Dimitri seemed not to have the will to do much more than turn his mournful gaze toward charismatic women often older than he – his sister Marie, Countess Brassova, couturière Coco Chanel, millionairess Audrey Emery – and bask in a glow he could not emanate on his own. The ennui that claimed so many among his generation of Romanovs might well have trapped him for certain death in the Russia of Lenin had not an amazingly foolhardy act propelled him out of the shadow of the Bolshevik scaffold and into the limelight normally reserved for national heroes – the half-botched murder of Grigory Rasputin on 17 December 1916.

It was characteristic of Dimitri to say as little about the events of that night in the Youssoupov Palace on the Moika Canal as if he had not even participated in them. Therein is reflected the pact made between the plotters to never speak of what happened at Prince Youssoupov's macabre tea party. But for the rest of his life, Dimitri also seemed to carry with him a palpable awareness of the mistake he had made in becoming involved in Rasputin's murder, along with a haunting sense that he had helped open the floodgates that swept away his world and everyone in it. Hence, that distracted expression which, years later and in a room full of smiling faces, riveted the eye with curiosity, sympathy, and pathos.

Though most babies are the cynosure of attention at their birth, the newly born Dimitri literally took a back seat to the drama surrounding the illness of his mother Alexandra Georgievna. In September 1891, the former Alexandra of Greece and her fond husband, Grand Duke Paul Alexandrovich, were visiting the latter's brother, Grand Duke Serge, at Illinskoe, his country estate outside Moscow. Why the Countess von Bothmer, in an 1899 monograph on Grand Duchess Paul's mother Queen Olga of Greece, would write that Paul's wife died from the effects of a 'carriage accident' must remain a mystery because the reality was far more tragic. During her visit, Grand Duchess Alexandra, who was seven months pregnant, fell whilst jumping into a boat. The next day she collapsed during a ball and went into labour. Every effort was made to save her and the child she was carrying, but it must have been clear to more than a few of those present that the Grand Duchess was already beyond reach of the period's crude medical assistance.

One may imagine the tensions pacing the creaking floors of the old dacha during the illness of Grand Duchess Alexandra Georgievna, and even more so the shadows that sank over the place when she grew worse and entered a coma. For six days, the twenty-one-year-old princess lay between life and death. On 18 September she gave birth to a son (whether induced or spontaneous is not known). Shortly thereafter, Alexandra was pronounced dead.

In the chaos of unavailing doctors, midwives, distraught husband, relatives, and servants in Illinskoe's small square rooms, the premature and weakly Dimitri was left on a chair wrapped in blankets, where he was found, so Grand Duchess Marie heard later, by his sister's sturdy English nurse, "Nannie" Fry. Only when the news of Grand Duchess Alexandra's demise had seeped into the collective Illinskyan brain was the newborn thought of and attention turned to responding to his care with the same assiduity. Fry's attentiveness was a presage of her future reign: she and her assistant, Lizzie Grove, were to prove such important influences in the childhood of both Marie and Dimitri that by 1897, their new governess, Yelena Djunkovskaya, was "horrified" to discover that neither child understood Russian and that, moreover, they spoke English with the "h" dropped, as their nurses did.[1]

The era of incubators and other medical equipment for the care of premature babies being decades away, the physicians at Illinskoe devised something very similar for the tiny boy by wrapping him in a cottony-wool bundle and placing him in a cradle lined with hot water bottles. Severe-featured Grand Duke Serge, without whose assent anything so much as breathed of its own accord at either Illinskoe or Moscow, tenderly gave the child the *"bouillon baths"* prescribed by the doctors to strengthen his constitution. Because or perhaps in spite of this post-natal care, the future founder of the Russian Olympics and equestrian par excellence survived these first crucial weeks of his life.

The Pavlovich children were left at Illinskoe for some months while their heartbroken father returned to St Petersburg to bury his young wife among the Romanov tombs in the Cathedral of SS Peter and Paul. A photograph from this Illinskoe period shows Marie and Dimitri seated outside in bentwood highchairs at a table all but covered by the implements of teatime. The bonneted heads of the two infants are turned toward the camera; and even at this tender age the aggressive expression of inquiry in Marie's face contrasts abruptly with the smooth pale stare of her younger brother. No one, least of all the children, could know that far from being a temporary dwelling place, Uncle Serge's Illinskoe was in due course to become one of Marie and Dimitri's childhood homes.

In St Petersburg, Marie and Dimitri lived with their father in his Italian Renaissance mansion on the English Embankment, from which one could see the River Neva fluttering with sails in summertime. In the nursery on the second floor, Nannie Fry and Lizzie Grove reigned over Marie and Dimitri in splendid isolation; even their father only came to see them–in the fashion honored by most parents at the time – in the morning and evening.

Grand Duke Paul seems to have been a curious mixture of iron discipline and overpowering affection – a milder version of his brother Serge. No one could approach him, wrote his daughter, without a sense of being inexorably drawn to him. Yet there was about this tall gentleman with the beautiful hands and receding hairline a delicate reticence not unlike that exhibited by his son in later years – Dimitri, in fact, resembled his father more than anyone else in the family, except that the cool architecture of Grand Duke Paul's features was warmed by lustrous blue eyes not untouched by a fugitive glint of *Schwärmerei* (enthusiasm). For though it appears Paul did love his children very much, he seems to have done so with a heart haunted by the death of their mother.

Therefore it was a surprise that the woman Paul did fall in love with was the young wife of an officer of the Chevalier Guard, who he had come to know as the regiment's commander.

That this first meeting in 1895 between the sad Grand Duke and the commoner with the ivory cameo face was to lead to no fleeting affair became clear when, two years later, Paul's lover, Olga Valerianovna von Pistolkors, bore him a son, Vladimir. Matters also became clear to Madame von Pistolkors' husband, Eric Augustinovich. It was then that he knew that a divorce was inevitable.

Thus the love of Paul's life was not only a commoner, but also now a divorced one. When he married Olga in a secret ceremony in Italy in 1902, he and his unsuitable new wife were exiled from Russia by a Tsar who was to watch Romanov-to-commoner marriages spring up like weeds in the imperial gardens: Nicholas' younger brother, Grand Duke Michael, would marry the twice-divorced daughter of a lawyer, while his sister, understandably unhappy with her joyless marriage to the homosexual Prince Peter of Oldenburg, divorced him and married her own commoner lover, Captain Nikolai Kulikovsky.

Under orders from Nicholas, the Pavlovich children were placed in the care of Grand Duke Serge and his wife, the Hessian Princess Elisabeth, known as "Ella." Not for a year would Marie or Dimitri be allowed to see their father and then only with their Uncle Serge present and the dangerous Mme von Pistolkors hidden safely away.

Life at idyllic Illinskoe was not easy for Paul's orphans. For one thing, the childless Ella was not thrilled to have two children on her hands and was not particularly hospitable.

Even more confusing than consistently chilly Aunt Ella, Uncle Serge could be a steely disciplinarian one moment and embracingly affectionate the next. Consuelo, Duchess of Marlborough met him around this time and thought him one of the handsomest men she had ever seen, with the qualification that he also would have made *"a magnificent Mephistopheles."* He exhaled an evil air, she thought.[2] Many agreed with her. Limited in his affections (Marie's words) he may well have been, but much of this

49

may have been due to the fact that certain of Serge's affections had to be strictly limited – and even then, Grand Duke Alexander Mikhailovich relates the mockeries of Serge that took place in officers' messes, showing the cat (Serge's homosexuality) was very much out of the bag. As painfully demonstrated by the furtive diary entries and anguished letters of such "closeted" homosexuals as Grand Duke Konstantin Konstantinovich and composer Peter Ilyich Tchaikovsky, it was not easy being gay either in the Russian Imperial Family or in Russian society itself. Therein may lie a good many of the emotional "limitations" for which Serge is so infamous.[3]

Luckily, Dimitri had a steadier male presence in his life in the form of fifty-year-old General Paul Alexandrovich Laiming, named the ten-year-old prince's governor in 1901. General Laiming and his wife gave both Dimitri and his sister a glimpse of what a serenely ordinary marriage and household could be like. At the Laimings' apartment in Uncle Serge's St Petersburg palace, Dimitri and his sister were never brushed off whenever they asked a question as they were by Ella and their assorted governesses and governors. They learned that married people could also be friends, something new to the charges of Serge and Ella. (The happy, gentle Laimings were to remain dependable up until the revolution in 1917: one of the old general's last acts of service for Dimitri was to arrange for the sale of the crimson-walled Beloselssky-Belozerzsky Palace on the Nevsky Prospekt which the Grand Duke had inherited years before from his uncle.)

But Dimitri's time as foster son was not to last for long. Russia and Japan went to war in February 1904, over, among other things, Port Arthur on Korea Bay. This war went from bad to worse as the Japanese turned out to be something more than the "yellow monkeys" Nicholas' advisors disparagingly thought them to be.

As the dominos of Russian military defeats toppled one against another, revolutionary pressures began to break lava-like through the heretofore placid crust of the empire, particularly escalating after the gunning down of a deputation of unarmed workers near the Winter Palace in St Petersburg in January 1905 – an event entered in the history books as "Bloody Sunday." A little over a month later, having just left the Kremlin's Nicholas Palace in Moscow, Grand Duke Serge paid the very heaviest of prices for parading his conservative old regime policies in the face of revolutionary reaction: a bomb, hurled into his coach, blew him literally to pieces. The reign of stiff, strange Serge Alexandrovich, as Governor General of Moscow and petty tyrant at home, was at an end.

Ella has made a macabre place for herself in historical memory by her spontaneous act of rushing out to the bloody snow of the square and gathering up her husband's body parts with her bare hands. But what is also remembered of the Grand Duchess is the great character change that overcame her in the wake of this horrifying shock. Released from Serge's over-lordship, she accepted another disciplinarian in the form of Jesus Christ, taking the veil and founding the Convent of SS Martha and Mary in Moscow. Though Ella ultimately became the clear-eyed, sensible woman who by her opposition to Rasputin fearlessly incurred the displeasure of her sister the Empress, at this time she was not the person to be in charge of anyone, let alone two teenagers. It was deemed a protective measure to send Marie and Dimitri north to stay with the Tsar and his family.

For Marie, this period in the bosom of Nicholas and Alexandra, surrounded by the quaint English cosy-corners and anti-macassared divans favored by the home-keeping Empress, was not of long duration. In 1907, Ella virtually affianced her niece to Prince William of Sweden without the girl's assent. Marie herself was actually resigned to the idea of being joined to the lanky, tight-lipped second son of King Gustaf although later, Ella expressed some doubt.

With his sister married off by the spring of 1908 and his father living in gilded exile in Paris, the sixteen- going on seventeen-year-old Dimitri could at this point in his life truly be said to be dependent on the kindness of strangers. It was as if fate was preparing him to be dependent, as he soon would have to be, on no one but himself.

Even before Grand Duke Serge's death, Dimitri's life was running in the channels smoothed before him by generations of Romanovs. In 1903 at the age of twelve, he was entered in the lists of the Chevalier Guard regiment and outfitted with a variety of uniforms (the so-called *petite tenue* was for everyday, while the *grande tenue*, in which the wearer was harnessed with enough military ornamentation to shame a Christmas tree, was for court wear). In the Cavalry Academy, Dimitri applied himself to his studies to a degree that compromised his ever-delicate health, but he emerged one of the finest horsemen of his time, ably competing (though taking no medal) in the 1912 Olympic Games in Stockholm, the only Romanov ever to do so. Perhaps because for once a trophy proved beyond his reach, Dimitri went one better and laid the groundwork for the first Russian Olympiad in 1913, which after the revolution would be appropriated by the Soviet government as its own.

Between visits to his increasingly unhappy sister in Sweden, Dimitri gave himself over to the army, taking part in the summer military maneuvers at Krasnoe Selo in winter, making St Petersburg and Moscow his playgrounds in the company of his boyhood friend, Prince Felix Youssoupov.

Dimitri also continued spending time with the Imperial Family – he was so close to them that a possible marriage was rumored between the young Grand Duke and the Tsar's eldest daughter, Grand Duchess Olga. It was obvious by then that the Tsarevich, whatever Rasputin's powers of persuasion, was not going to get better and probably would not live to full adulthood. Surrounded by one flourishing Romanov morganatic marriage after another, particularly that of his surviving brother Michael, in 1912, Nicholas II was starving for an heir. Though not next in line, Dimitri would have been just the thing; his birth near Moscow led the populace of that jealous town to claim him as *"our grand duke,"* and bookish Olga declared herself interested only in marrying *"a Russian"* – which national, if not ethnic, profile fit Dimitri about as well as any of the other Romanovs, including Olga herself.

But before too long Dimitri, called by the endearing name of *"Goula"* or "Little Dove" in the Imperial Family, was to show how much fathers live in sons by falling in love, to a degree almost devoid of judgment, with the pretty, witty morganatic wife of his cousin Grand Duke Michael – Natalia (Countess) Brassova, twice-divorced when Michael married her and already something of a Russian Wallis Simpson.

For most of the world, the year 1914 was to become not only a real dividing line between the old and new worlds but also between the world of the living and of the dead. In between was an oppressive no-man's-land of disaster looming in the distance. Grand Duchess Marie, newly divorced and returned to Russia, sensed the chill in the air. But at least the Pavlovichi were all together again: the Tsar had in 1912 given his Uncle Paul–along with his wife and their three children – permission to return to Russia, where the grateful couple built a French-designed, antique-filled villa in Tsarskoe Selo and were cordially received by the formerly tart-tongued empress.

When war broke out in August of that year, the whole family got involved – Dimitri as an officer, Marie as a nurse, and their father Paul as inspector general of the Chevalier Guards. Dimitri earned the coveted St George Cross in only the first few weeks of the war when he rescued a wounded corporal (and his horse) under heavy battery. Thus by December 1914, the gilt of his reputation was enjoying its highest lustre. Like his father and sister, he touched something in people of all classes that the reigning family never dreamed existed and he was liked all the more for joining this talent with good looks and a sprightly manner. Baron Carl von Wrangell-Rokassowsky remembered seeing Dimitri at the Hotel de Russie in Yalta, appareled in the elegant white uniform of the Chevalier Guard, surrounded by a crowd which he himself had to smilingly ask to give way. *"Loud hurrahs acclaimed the young prince,"* the baron recalled.[4]

With this halo about his head, Dimitri can perhaps be forgiven for seeing a world bathed in the same warm glow. But when he met his cousin Michael's wife – eleven years Dimitri's senior – at a train station that December, he threw not only reality but caution to the wind. A striking woman who turned heads everywhere, Natasha's coquettish reaction was somewhat ill-considered because she seems to have realized neither how hot were the passions of this young man toward her nor the burning jealousies of her battle-harassed husband at the front, to whom she veritably bragged in her letters about the latest exploits of the prince whom she charmingly called *"Mr. Lily-of-the-Valley."*[5]

Perhaps willfully oblivious to the fire with which he was playing, in January, Dimitri felt able to corner Natasha in her Moscow hotel room and declare his love for her outright. In her defense, at no time does Natasha seem to have felt much more for Dimitri than the same maternal concerns shown by the empress and his own sister. Alexandra's tended to emerge in little notes to her husband, *"Don't let him go to that lady so often"* and *"Such society is his ruin,"* while Natasha shared with Michael her more practical feelings. She worried that Dimitri would be given a Cossack squadron in the Caucasus despite suffering from tuberculosis so advanced he coughed up blood – red stains which, when Natasha pointed them out on his handkerchief, he laughed away. (Rasputin's blood on the covers of his car seats was to evoke a considerably more somber response from him in the very near future.)[6]

Whatever Natasha did to defuse the scene in her hotel room, it appears to have worked: if the Grand Duke continued to flutter around his cousin's wife like a moth to a flame, he did so from a safer distance. And for these two, bliss was simply not to be: even when they were to come together again years later in English exile, Michael's handsome ghost would stand between them as sturdily as had his handsome body when alive. Though Natasha was to be just one of the several strong women who supported Dimitri's passive personality, he does seem to have truly been in love with her. She was among the first people he wrote to when the revolution lifted the sanction on his communications to and from Russia. *"Be happy and do not forget me,"* he scribbled. Happy, Natasha was not destined to be, but forget him she never did.[7]

Comte Louis de Robien of the French embassy noted in his diary in April 1917 that Prince Felix Youssoupov had once claimed to have been cured of a *"liver complaint"* by none other than the man he was in the future to murder – Grigory Rasputin, that strange combination of faith healer and court jester so dear to Empress Alexandra's heart. That Felix was fascinated with the ugly, unkempt muzhik with the pulsating blue-gray eyes is obvious enough from his own accounts. That he went to visit Rasputin more than once prompted the glib fellows in the chancery to wonder, per the Comte de Robien, whether the fabled sexual athlete from Siberia was not actually treating Felix, *"a little lower down....."*, demonstrating just how seriously either was taken in official quarters.[8]

The truth of Felix' feelings toward and about Rasputin may never be known, but we do know this: that on the night of 16/17 December 1916, he lured Rasputin into a room in the basement of his palace on the Moika Canal – a room which had been got up decorated with all the bear-rugged and fringed frippery of a Belasco drawing-room drama – where he first tried poison in cakes and wine and then, when this had no effect, shot the *"staretz"* with a Browning pistol borrowed (he claimed) from Grand Duke Dimitri, waiting upstairs with the other accomplices. The prince, the Grand Duke, the Duma delegate, the Preobrajensky Guard officer, and the cyanide-bearing physician thought that by removing Rasputin from the scene of Russian power, they were automatically returning the empress to equilibrium and saving the Russian throne for the temporarily befuddled Nicholas.

But they were mistaken. Unfortunately, Rasputin was not even half the problem. Alexandra, driven nearly mad by the hemophilia she herself had bequeathed to her suffering son, and never less than mildly hostile toward anyone who did not selflessly see things her way, would have performed the job of regent in Nicholas' absence in just as unbalanced a fashion without Rasputin as with him. As for Nicholas, his weaknesses stemmed from having never been properly prepared for his job as Tsar and from a fatalism that came not from his Orthodox-convert wife but was as much a part of him as his sea-blue eyes and remote smile.

Dimitri spent time with the Tsar at his Moghilev headquarters after Nicholas had ill-advisedly taken command of the Russian army in 1915, and as he told his sister, each time he talked to Nicholas he became *"more and more persuaded of the hopelessness of the situation."* The Tsar, he told Marie, had no clue that a *"terrible abyss"* was yawning at his feet. Dimitri and many who thought like him felt themselves in the position of officers aboard a ship of state which, Titanic-like, was heading straight for an iceberg. But instead of removing the captain whose steering was amiss, they tossed overboard his drunkard valet, thinking this would make the difference. That they (and the Grand Dukes who later unsuccessfully planned to overthrow Nicholas and place the Empress safely in a convent) were willing to try anything to reverse the ship's direction is understandable given the fact that it was actually the directionless Alexandra attempting to navigate it.[9]

As noble as the assassins' motives may have been, that December night they committed cold-blooded murder. Dimitri was deeply enmeshed: there may be controversy over whether or not he actually lent his gun for the first bullet, but there is no question that he drove the bleeding body of Rasputin to the Petrovsky Bridge nor is there any doubt that he watched his compatriots topple it into the icy waters of the "Little Neva." Dimitri was also the first to have doubts that what had been accomplished was not merely badly, nastily done, but largely irrelevant to the real dangers hovering over imperial Russia. He told his sister how frightened he was by the *"gathering consequences"* of the murder, entirely opposite of what he had been expecting.[10] Grand Duke Alexander Mikhailovich was to put it more bluntly: *"Rasputin alive was just a man, known to everybody as a drunkard peasant reaching for money. Rasputin dead stood a chance of becoming a slaughtered prophet."*[11]

These consequences were in keeping with the irony-laden atmosphere of that last Christmas-tide of old St Petersburg. Any other such accomplice to the murder of a legally innocent man would have swung from a rope beside the one who pulled the trigger. Yet though Nicholas thought Dimitri *"a monster,"* he nonetheless handed down to him the one sentence that ultimately saved his life: he exiled him to the Persian front under command of General Baratoff of the Caucasian Army. When everyone from

Grand Duke Paul to other members of the Romanov family tried to persuade the Tsar to ease up on the punishment, they received a pedantic yet truthful reply: *"No one is permitted to commit murder."* This did not prevent people all over Russia from hurrying to their churches *"to light candles before the icons of Saint Dimitri,"* as French Ambassador Maurice Paléologue recalled.

The Rasputin affair cut across Grand Duke Paul's family with particular bloodiness because the elder sister of Princess Paley (as Olga Valerianovna had become), Lubov Golovina, was a partisan of Rasputin. The princess' eldest son by her first marriage to Eric von Pistolkors was brother-in-law to Anna Vyrubova, another of the Empress' court fools and a Rasputin zealot. And yet another of the princess' children, Countess Marianne Zarnekau, was quite the opposite and was happy to have Rasputin put out of the way. As Grand Duchess Marie was to write with supreme understatement, describing that Christmas spent in the company of lovers and haters of the horse-trader's son from Pokhrovskoie: *"The gathering was odd."*[12]

Marie saw her brother off at the station where the dry snow, still air, and half-lit buildings made an appropriately mournful setting for a leave-taking which, so far as anyone knew, might last for untold years. Far less oppressed by the turn of events, Prince Youssoupov, thrilled with his instant fame, suffered the comparatively lighter sentence of being banished to his estates in Kursk province. He, too, would survive the revolution, escaping Russia with a handful of his family's famous jewels and paintings and a popular reputation that earned him much more interest than all his valuables put together.

Within two months, the Tsar would abdicate the throne, for himself and his son. Nicholas' brother, Michael, was Tsar for twenty-four hours before he, too, abdicated. The revolution that freed Dimitri from the bonds of his exile also kept him from returning to his native land. He was never to see Russia again.

Dimitri spent a bit less than two years in Persia and far less than that in conditions of imperial exile. The Persian front actually seemed to suit him – he was welcomed by the officers there, his reputation for the Rasputin assassination having preceded him – and the arid climate could not have done harm to the tubercular condition noted by Countess Brassova. When the dynasty fell and the Provisional Government invited him to return to Russia a few months later, Dimitri declined returning. Instead, he quit the disintegrating army, and lacking both friends and money, he lived precariously on his own.

By spring 1917, Sir Charles Marling, head of the British legation in Tehran, who practically adopted the once-again abandoned Romanov grand duke, effected Dimitri's rescue from Persia. Sir Charles did his career no good by shielding Dimitri at a time when no Russian Grand Duke was even permitted to so much as set foot in England lest Russia's new masters have their noses put out of joint. But in true British fashion, Marling carried out his self-imposed job as protector with splendid and fearless ease, taking Dimitri with him when he and his family left Persia in 1918; his own wife nursed the Grand Duke when he fell ill with typhoid fever at Cairo.

Dimitri himself showed Anglo-Saxon fortitude by asking for a commission in the British army, which would make his abhorrent Romanov presence far more palatable to *"Cousin Georgie's"* ministers. He arrived in London with the Marlings in December 1918, roughly a month after his sister Marie and her second husband, Serge Putiatin, had escaped to the Romanian royal court, and a month or so before their father was shot in the neck at close range by Cheka guards at the Fortress of SS Peter and Paul, together with several other captive Romanovs. Eventually, Dimitri and

Marie were to become fully apprised of the holocaust that had included the Imperial Family, Aunt Ella, their half-brother Vladimir Paley, and other Imperial cousins unlucky to have been slow to quit the kingdom of Lenin.

For a year Dimitri shared a London house and his depreciated rubles with his sister and brother-in-law, trying to avoid the ever-sensational Felix Youssoupov. This proved difficult, as Felix both postured himself as the self-crowned savior of Imperial Russia and demonstrated real heroism by assisting destitute émigrés with his own funds; and in any case was always on the tip of the Russian colony's collective tongue. And not only theirs. The former Consuelo Vanderbilt seems to have been one of the few friends to whom Dimitri spoke of the events of 17 December 1916, though with no new confession, merely giving a vague outline of the by then well-known scenario. She was a witness, however, to Rasputin's continued haunting of his most reluctant hangman. On arriving for a luncheon at the house of "Emerald" Lady Cunard, Dimitri's daffy hostess announced him to her astonished guests as, *"The Grand Duke Dimitri, the murderer of Rasputin!"* Dimitri had come with the sympathetic Consuelo. Though Emerald Cunard's political luncheons usually comprised no more than ten persons, given this small and knowing audience, Dimitri decided it was in everyone's best interest to make a dignified but speedy exit.

In the course of this trying time spent among the British aristocracy, Dimitri was to give Consuelo a sampling of some pique not normally associated with his easygoing character. At a house party organized at her estate of Crowhurst, Consuelo's dinner table was set ringing by the anti-Kaiser arguments offered with stentorian zeal by former British Prime Minister Herbert Asquith: *"The Kaiser should be hanged!"* Afterward, Dimitri turned to Jacques Balsan, Consuelo's future husband, and said, *"De quel droit ces gens-là permettent-ils de nous critiquer?"* ("What right do such people have to criticize us?") It isn't known how firmly Dimitri's tongue was in his cheek when making this remark, but when Consuelo heard of it she was wryly reminded of something Lord Randolph Churchill once said on seeing a portrait of Louis XVI, grand and stupid in velvets and ermine: *"Now at last I understand the French Revolution!"*[13]

By 1920, Dimitri was back in Paris, on his own this time, not far from the Bois de Boulogne villa that had belonged to his father. He got a job serving on the board of a champagne firm – Grand Duke Alexander Mikhailovich was referring to Dimitri when he wrote in his memoirs of a young Grand Duke who decided he could make a living off his knowledge of his favorite beverage: *"The cursed stuff cost me so much money before, that surely it ought to support me now."*[14]

American journalist Frederick L. Collins had to chase Dimitri around the city for days, finally nabbing him in a Paris restaurant called The Acacias, where he noted all the features that women and men found so attractive: *"He is, in his slender, well groomed person, all that a grand duke should be – especially if you like your grand duke young, clean-shaven, and concave at the waist-line. He has a figure like Rudolph Valentino's and a head like Charles Dana Gibson's."* Amid the noise of their fellow diners, Dimitri opened up to Collins about his military service in Persia and his lack of clothes to stand up in on leaving there with the Marlings, but omitted to mention his part in the killing of Rasputin. As Collins pointed out later in his 1923 book, *This King Business*, Dimitri did not seem *"to realize that his own act, more than any other one thing, precipitated the revolution and the resulting chaos in which he now finds himself."*[15]

Collins later found out that Dimitri's "grand plan" to go into business was related to his sister Marie's embroidery atelier at 48, rue François Premier, which the intrepid American visited on invitation of Dimitri's brother-in-law, Serge Putiatin.

Collins was not impressed: *"I entered a dark, low passage with cement walls, such as we put in our cellars,"* he recalled, *"but with no such luxurious whitewashing as any good American house would give them. The pink bow and yellow curls of the janitor's scrubby child were the only touch of color between the narrow street door and the blind turn at the end of the passage."* There, in the cramped space where Marie, her elderly father- and mother-in-law Prince and Princess Putiatin, and her titled employees created lengths of shimmering Russian-inspired embroidery in bird-of-paradise colors, Collins had a moment of shame at his arrogant American opinions of fallen nobility. *"I saw* [in the young women working in the atelier] *the brains and courage of long generations of gentlewomen,"* he wrote, *"and I saw another thing, a strange thing, in such a place and on such a tired, pin-pricked hand. I saw, on the engagement finger of* [a young woman], *a marvelous cabochon sapphire – a sapphire deep and lustrous as her eyes."*

He further wrote:

"These Russians, for all their grimly silent courage, are human. Underneath the sophisticated manner of Dimitri, the busy brusqueness of the young Poutiatine [sic], *the cheerful industry of the old prince, and the insistent contentment of the old princess, there lies, so close to the surface that a jewel may scratch it, the tragedy of the human heart."*[16]

But Marie's atelier at 48, rue François Premier was not Dimitri's preferred hangout spot. He preferred to be where the action was, and before long he found himself a mistress in opera singer Marthe Davelli. In a curious double connection with his sister, who provided embroideries to France's premiere *couturière*, Gabrielle Chanel, Davelli emphasized her resemblance to Chanel by wearing nothing but "Coco's" fashions. And it was Davelli who is said to have introduced Dimitri to Coco at an all-night party braying with jazz and alcoholic gossip. *"You take him,"* the singer allegedly offered her old friend. *"He's too expensive for me."*

Always ready for a challenge – she bragged about how many millions she had squandered on men – Chanel took on the grandson of Tsar Alexander II, and by spring 1922 they were lovers. Chanel biographer Axel Madsen claims Dimitri gave Chanel *"Romanov pearls,"* which in their *echt* splendor served as prototypes for her instantly successful faux jewelry, charming the eye in its implausible opulence the way its genuine prototypes had once done. It's hard to say whether Dimitri was ever in a position to give a woman wealthier than he was jewels she could have bought for herself (and did – one of her favorite pearl necklaces was purchased from a former maid-of-honor to the dowager empress). Though Chanel was later to cast aspersions on *"those grand dukes,"* claiming there was nothing to them but *"vodka and the void,"* she confessed to being intoxicated by the Russians blown to Paris by the Bolshevik explosion. (What Consuelo Vanderbilt approvingly described as Dimitri's *"long blue eyes"* and his attractively stealthy, wolf-like walk had something to do with it, too.)

In 1922, Chanel was intoxicated enough to purchase a villa in order to be alone with her Imperial lover, whose presence in her life seems to have coincided with, rather than sparked, the Russian influence on her designs of the time. While it's clear Chanel never cared for Dimitri as much as he did her – his son Paul was to recall how, years after the affair had ended, it was his father who still thought of none but Coco – and though the relationship ended, at least officially, some time around 1923, Dimitri could not keep away from the alluring *modiste*. Some sources claim he was still escorting her about after his 1926 marriage with the American heiress Audrey Emery, a marriage for which Dimitri's sister, always looking out for her beloved brother, claims responsibility in her memoirs. Indeed, Dimitri must have brought some good luck to Chanel because he was with her the night she met the immensely wealthy

Duke of Westminster, whose lover she became from 1925 until his marriage to the daughter of Lord Ponsonby five years later.

Audrey Emery herself had a connection to the British peerage: her widowed and very rich mother had married into it. Audrey was quite rich in her own right – rich unto pre-Depression millions – and also entirely to her favor was the fact that Grand Duchess Marie was fond of her. The natives of Cleveland, Ohio and Illinskoe, Moscow Province, were joined together in Biarritz, scene of Dimitri's past Chanelian glories. A press blitz followed with photos of the smiling heiress and the somber Grand Duke interspersed with breathless accounts of the wedding expenses.

The marriage was not to last, but before it officially ended in 1937, Audrey procured from the self-proclaimed "Tsar," Grand Duke Kirill Vladimirovich, the title of "Princess Romanovsky-Ilyinsky," which title devolved on their son Paul. Freed from one prince, Audrey married another, also named Dimitri but of the Georgian Royal house, and settled with him on a horse farm in Virginia, USA. (She was rumored, after her next divorce, to be interested in marrying Prince Pierre of Monaco, father-in-law of another American girl, Grace Kelly. But Audrey declared her marrying days over and went to live in Palm Beach, Florida, of which city her son was to become mayor.) When Audrey and Paul left France at the outbreak of war in 1939, Dimitri gave his son a collection of lead soldiers and kissed him goodbye. That was the last Paul Romanovsky ever saw of his shadowy father.

Dimitri still had champagne – his job at the firm – and he still had Chanel, with whom he gadded about Paris. These, however, were pale distractions for a man dispossessed of his birthright, unlucky in love, and now physically ill. The bloody handkerchief noted by Countess Brassova so many years before, in that world now at the bottom of the sea, was just one indication of how weak was the flesh surrounding Dimitri's equally wavering will. Given to depression, Dimitri may well have sought escape in something stronger than champagne, which would not have improved his condition. For Rasputin rose up from the dead again and again when Felix published his controversial book, *Rasputin: His Malignant Influence and His Assassination* in 1927, and shortly after when Rasputin's daughter, Maria, brought suit for nearly a million dollars against Felix and Dimitri for having deprived her of her father's companionship by their premeditated murder of him in 1916. A French judge threw out the case (based on the killing having been a "political act" in long-defunct Imperial Russia), but Dimitri had never been proud of that bloody, snowy night on the Moika – the last thing he wanted was to be reminded of it in *aeternum*. According to Grand Duchess Marie, once Felix' book appeared, Dimitri never spoke to him again.

And so the years passed by. There is a picture, taken in 1938 at Doorn, Kaiser Wilhelm's home in The Netherlands, on the occasion of the marriage of his grandson Prince Louis Ferdinand of Prussia and his bride, Grand Duchess Kira Kirillovna, daughter of Grand Duke (and Tsar) Kirill. Represented on this celebratory day on the very edge of another world about to explode, were the royal families of Russia, The Netherlands, and Prussia, along with various other titled and elderly luminaries, roped in pearls and prinked with plumes. In this picture, besides the happy, handsome couple, one sees Crown Princess Cecilie of Prussia, who though middle-aged, still had the look of a girl about to burst out laughing; the benign Grand Duke Kirill, tilting a little in his chair; and the future Queen Juliana of The Netherlands, sitting on the floor with a regal grandeur absent in Kirill's sprawling, scowling son, Grand Duke Vladimir. Their smiles gleam pearly, as if time which stops for no one has for a while, and to their relief, stopped for them. Behind them, more than half in shadow, stands a thin-faced man whose high forehead catches the gleam from a window, whose tired eyes gaze off sadly to some bleak middle distance unknown to those around him. This man is Grand Duke Dimitri Pavlovich of Russia, favorite of the last Tsar of Russia, once the most spoiled, wealthy, and charming young royal bachelor old Europe was ever to know.

Perhaps in the middle of this joyous launching into life of a loving young couple, Dimitri was being more than just the proverbial melancholy Russian, musing amid gaiety upon his own mortality. He had been in and out of sanatoriums for several years, mostly due to his recurring tuberculosis. Between war and revolution, Dimitri had had many a narrow escape from death, but when death came for him for the last time, it found him among the alpine snows of Davos, Switzerland, three years into World War II on 4 March 1942. The official cause of death was attributed to complications from tuberculosis, but the espionage-thick atmosphere of wartime suggested it was something rather more doubtful, even sinister, than that.

The eminent *émigré* physician, Dr. Eugene de Savitsch (whose hyper-monarchist father, Constantin, had helped the former Imperial children's French tutor, Pierre Gilliard, write *La fausse Anastasie*), visited the Davos sanatorium after Dimitri's death and chatted about the case with the head surgeon. To his surprise, the x-rays indicated lesions old and long healed. According to the head surgeon, Dimitri had been in *"highest spirits"* the day he died, having been told that he was cured. These high spirits seem to have prompted him to loquacity, for he told the surgeon about German negotiators sent to talk to him about joining the German army and commanding a Russian contingent, all part of Hitler's effort to stamp out Joseph Stalin. Dimitri went on to say that he had refused because he was basically pro-English and was mortified by the thought of a Romanov being in the ranks of an army set on crushing Russia, even if Stalin was doing a good job of that himself.

Apparently still jubilant, Dimitri had organized a Russian fête that evening to which all hospital personnel were invited. Hence the head surgeon's surprise when he was urgently summoned to Dimitri's room later that night where he found his patient in the bathroom "blue-faced" and dead.

"Poisoning was a not unnatural deduction," wrote Dr. de Savitsch. But Jacques Ferrand, in his biographical study of Grand Duke Paul's family, indicates that Dimitri was carried off *"par une crise d'urémie"* – an attack of uremia. Though uremic poisoning can cause its sufferers to collapse into a coma and, if not treated immediately, to die, a more gradual degeneration of kidney function and overall health is usually indicated with this disease. With warning symptoms commonly including bleeding, weight loss, nausea, and pericarditis (to list the nicer ones), how chipper could Dimitri have felt the day he died? Or as may be the case, had he concealed the seriousness of his condition? Perhaps his early training, according to which a prince must always turn a smiling face to the world, proved the most enduring as well as the most tragic of Dimitri's many lost inheritances.[17]

After his long detour through Tehran, Biarritz, and Palm Beach, Dimitri would finally come home. When the Grand Duchess Marie was interred in 1958 in the chapel of Mainau, her son Count Lennart Bernadotte's island castle in Lake Constance, Dimitri's remains were exhumed, borne on a sleigh from his snowy alpine grave, and brought to rest beside the first woman who had mothered and loved the last grand duke of old Russia.

5 The Sons of Grand Duke Konstantin Nikolaievich

Grand Duke Nicholas Konstantinovich
(1850-1918)

By Penny Wilson

Nicholas, the eldest of the four Konstantinovich sons, was born on 2/14 February 1850 at the Marble Palace in St Petersburg. It was Valentine's Day; an ironic birthday for the man who would one day find himself at the center of one of the Romanov Dynasty's most sordid sexual scandals. The proud parents, Grand Duke Konstantin Nikolaievich and Alexandra Iosifovna, nicknamed the little Grand Duke "Nikola."

The infant Nicholas was intended for the Imperial Navy, where his father served – and initially, it seems that the boy had some significant interest in his future career at sea. In January 1857, Nicholas's uncle, the Emperor Alexander II presented his own young son, Grand Duke Alexis, with his first miniature naval dress uniform. The six-year-old Nicholas Konstantinovich proved to be intensely jealous. *"He takes comfort in the thought that soon he, also, might be so favored,"* Konstantin Nikolaievich wrote of his son to Alexander. *"It will be nice to see both of our little sailors in matching parade uniforms."*[1]

Outside of the apparent frivolity of this exchange over the children's naval uniform, Konstantin Nikolaievich and Alexandra Iosifovna emphasized a liberal education for their six children, and sought to expose them to the best in terms of political education and the humanities; they employed specialist tutors in history, the sciences, literature, civil law, religion, Russian, German, French and English. In addition to this breath-taking curriculum, there was a piano teacher who instructed the children twice weekly, and a dancing master that inculcated in the young Grand Duke the dances and behavior that were considered necessary social skills.[2]

Nicholas Konstantinovich proved to be an adept student: clever, skillful and quick-brained. But he was stubborn in his liberal Republican ideas – something that may well have pleased his notoriously liberal father – and this drove his masters to despair. Nicholas particularly enjoyed tormenting his French tutor, Monsieur Ricard. One day, Ricard assigned the young Grand Duke to write a verse in French. Nicholas's poem ended with the bold and insightful couplet: *"Et sous ce veston civil, Chacun me traitera de manant"* ("And under a civilized guise, Each one will treat me as a churl"). On reading this pointed barb from his charge, the angry tutor became so irate that he ended the lesson, left the schoolroom, and immediately extended his resignation to Konstantin Nikolaievich, who refused to accept it.[3] In the end, however, Ricard had no success with Nicholas, and was eventually dismissed from his post by Alexandra Iosifovna after Nicholas insulted some Imperial relatives by quoting some particularly vehement Republican passages from Victor Hugo in their presence.[4]

In 1860, at the age of ten, Nicholas Konstantinovich had his first dose of life at sea when he took up a post alongside his equally young cousin Alexis Alexandrovich aboard the frigate *Zabavu* as she cruised the Gulf of Finland.[5] Nicholas drilled with a naval quartermaster, and, while he generally enjoyed the time he spent with Alexis, with whom he was close, he found that a life at sea was not to his taste.[6] Although Konstantin Nikolaievich was disappointed, he came to realize that Nicholas would not be happy as a naval officer, so he released his son from this obligation; but as a Grand Duke, Nicholas had, perforce, to take up military duty in some capacity – and so he entered the Imperial Army.

By the time Nicholas reached his late teens, he had grown into a tall, slim young man, with a reputation for being kind and generous; he had, recalled Countess Marie Kleinmichel, *"fine manners."* He had also inherited his parents' musical abilities and, as Kleinmichel recalled, *"possessed a very fine voice."*[7] Yet he was also intensely stubborn and selfish. As a small child, Nicholas had been the favorite of both of his parents; because of the vicissitudes of Imperial life, he was sometimes ignored and overlooked – and then was spoiled and indulged in a way that almost certainly contributed to his increasingly wayward behavior. Konstantin Nikolaievich enjoyed spending time with his eldest son, playing games and sports with him, allowing him to accompany him on official duties and inspections, and he took a lively interest in Nicholas's school reports – but he had no patience or ability to deal with Nicholas's temper tantrums, emotional outbursts, and episodes of obstinacy. At such times, the father would merely instruct Nicholas's tutors to be severe and punishing with him – and whether this was the intention of such instruction, the tutors would sometimes resort to beating the young Grand Duke into some form of submission.[8]

Alexandra Iosifovna took little active interest in her son's development as he reached his teenaged years. Perhaps her lack of attention was a function of her disappointment in her husband and the ultimate failure of their marriage, but Nicholas himself would later complain that she was always a cold woman, consumed with hypochondria, and interested only in her spiritualists and in the ceremonial grandeur of her life as a Grand Duchess.[9]

With a disinterested mother, and a father heavily involved with his own duties and concerns – including a growing second family with the ballerina Kuznetsova – there was no-one to advise and counsel Nicholas following his entry into the Imperial Army, and he fell in with a thoroughly disreputable group of friends. Unsupervised, Nicholas gave free rein to his emotions, whims and desires, and he began to spin out of control. It was rumored in St Petersburg that he was caught up in a social group that encompassed not only the usual "fast" elements of social climbers, ballerinas and high-priced whores, but also several known revolutionaries, including Sophie Perovskaya, one of the future assassins of Alexander II.[10] Nicholas, truly his father's son, sincerely believed that widespread liberal reform was the best hope of the Romanov Empire. *"It was rumored among the intelligentsia,"* recalled Elisabeth Naryshkin-Kurakin, tongue firmly in cheek, *"that the Grand Duke was the only member of the Imperial Family who was earnestly engaged in social studies and research."*[11]

Very quickly, the young Grand Duke became utterly abandoned to the pursuit of pleasure, and his vices and dissolute habits showed in his person. One night, it is said, he had his adjutant, Captain Victor Vorpovsky, bring a number of cheap prostitutes into the Marble Palace, where he proceeded to preside over a drunken orgy. Soon after, a flagrant and carelessly conducted affair with one of his mother's Maids-of-Honor resulted in the young woman's banishment from Imperial service. Before too long, it was whispered in the capital that Nicholas Konstantinovich was suffering from the effects of syphilis.[12]

Harriet Blackford, Nicholas's passionate American mistress, painted a glowing description of the Grand Duke when she first met him: *"I will never forget his beauty…He was a young man, a little bit over six feet tall, magnificently built, with broad shoulders, and a waist both supple and elegant. His form suggested strength joined with grace."* His face, she noted, *"was a perfect oval, with pale skin and a broad forehead. His golden brown hair was fine and curled, though rumpled, for he habitually ran his fingers through it when he was nervous."* His light mustache, carefully trimmed and brushed, betrayed his youth. She watched his eyes – *"deeply set,"* and with *"a color that flickered like fire, illuminated with joy and passion, and glittering like emeralds. Sharp, spiritual in conversation or reasoning, sometimes hard, the Grand Duke penetrated with his scrutinizing gaze to the depth of your heart."* Although he appeared healthy, she noted that he was *"somewhat pale, for he was often indisposed."*[13]

Harriet first saw Nicholas in the last flush of his youth, when he still appeared as a fairytale Prince. Unfortunately, too much indulgence, too much drinking, too little sleep and too many women caught up with him, and his looks fled. Nicholas's eyes may indeed have *"flickered like fire,"* but his face had grown into an unpleasant copy of that of his father. His golden brown hair was receding rapidly, and his "supple and elegant" waist sported an unbecoming paunch, the result of too much rich food and too much of the "fast" life; by the age of twenty-two, the Grand Duke looked ten years older, his eyes circled with dark shadows and his face puffy.

When her eldest son's "fast" life and dissolute habits became evident to her, Grand Duchess Alexandra Iosifovna feared that Nicholas was on his way to following in his father's footsteps, and she attempted to curtail Nicholas's excesses. She pored over her Almanach de Gotha, searching for a suitable princess for her aimless son. She eventually settled on Princess Friederike of Hanover, her own niece and Nicholas's first cousin. The Russian Orthodox Church forbade such close unions, but exceptions had been made in the past, and it fell to the Emperor, as Supreme Guardian of the Russian Church, to grant this rare approval. Perhaps the Grand Duchess assumed that by presenting her son's increasingly alarming lifestyle to Alexander II, the Emperor would agree to this marriage as Nicholas's only hope for salvation from himself. In the end, however, no proposal was made, and Alexandra's sole attempt at finding Nicholas a suitable wife fell by the wayside when Friederike, deep in her own entangled romantic adventures, adamantly refused to consider any Russian alliance.[14]

Nicholas Konstantinovich, who had taken little interest in his mother's marital machinations, was not unduly disturbed by this development, and promptly returned to his disreputable life. Then – disastrously for all – in the autumn of 1873, he met Harriet Ely Blackford. The scandal ignited by their deeply passionate love affair stunned the Imperial Family and sparked a diplomatic incident that shook the Western world.

Golden blonde and beautiful, Harriet Blackford – almost three years Nicholas' senior – was born in March 1847, the youngest daughter of famed

Philadelphia cleric, the Reverend Dr. Ezra Stiles Ely.[15] By the time of Harriet's birth, her father, once a rising star of the Presbyterian Church and correspondent of Presidents Jefferson and Jackson, was over sixty-years-old, and had fallen on hard times. Bad investments had left the once wealthy Ely perpetually short of cash, and he is said to have been *"accused and tried for shady dealings,"* in which he swindled his own parishioners.[16]

In 1836, eleven years before Harriet's birth, Ely's first wife died.[17] Seven years later, Ezra Ely did the unthinkable, and married again; his new bride, Caroline Thompson Holmes was, at twenty-three, thirty-four-years younger than her husband. An unseemly May-December second marriage following so close on the heels of Ezra's financial failures scandalized prim Philadelphia society, and he was shortly replaced as pastor to the wealthy congregation at the city's Old Pine Street Church and sent to a far less prominent suburban parish.[18]

A stroke in 1851 deprived him of even this position, and his death in 1861 left his young wife Caroline to raise their two children, Harriet and her younger brother Zebulon, as best she could on a meager income.[19] Harriet could not ignore the contrast between the smart new dresses and shining black carriages of her school-friends and half-siblings, and her own world of genteel poverty. The lesson that money and power equaled social acceptance was not lost on the young girl, but it was not only luxury that was missing from her life. The lack of security that money brings was also desperately felt in the Ely household. Harriet yearned for the better lives of those around her, and she developed a deep-seated attraction to the very things most conspicuously missing from her life. *"That which shines,"* Harriet later recalled, *"always had the ability to captivate me."*[20]

Above all, she recalled, her *"girlish imagination"* was captivated by Imperial Russia, and the story of Peter the Great. *"I avidly read about Peter's romantic life as a carpenter; the ice palace constructed by Empress Anna; and of the wild splendors of the great and cruel Catherine. My imagination was vividly impressed by this land covered in snow, with frozen mighty rivers like the Neva, where one could cross the ice impetuously, in a horse-drawn sleigh, descending hills of ice at vertiginous speed, and especially by the promise of summer nights, where darkness does not happen."*[21]

Two weeks after her seventeenth birthday, Harriet eloped with a young man named Beale Steenbergen Blackford; they were married on 18 April 1864, in Oakland, Maryland.[22] In short order, she became pregnant, gave birth to a daughter, Caroline, and watched as her husband died of consumption.[23] Harriet had not long been a wife, and was determined not to drape herself in widow's weeds; her brief marriage to Beale had not brought her the security and freedom from care that she sought. Trusting her life and future to another had brought disappointment; now, her resolve was strengthened, and she would never again abdicate control of her own destinies to another. Rebelling ferociously against the hidebound Victorian morality that would have kept her impecunious and desperate, she proceeded to launch herself into a series of romantic liaisons that stunned the proper dowagers of Philadelphia society. It was the start of Harriet's adventures.

Harriet's first forays out into the social world of post-Civil War Philadelphia were measured steps, designed to test the waters, but the details of her initial entrée are murky. Perhaps taking pity on a young widow, her wealthy half-brothers and half-sisters launched her on society. In any event, she soon found that she was able to attract considerable attention. In a sea of dark-haired young women, Harriet's luxuriant blonde curls, cascading richly about her shoulders and framing her charming face, set her quite apart. There was a luminous quality about her, but it was more than that.

In convivial surroundings, especially when she found herself the center of attention, Harriet glowed. She quickly learned to flatter, not by speaking, but simply by focusing her attention on those around her. There was about her an unquestionable aura of self-promotion, though Harriet largely managed to conceal it behind a façade that was all wide-eyed innocence. If, in the end, she dared to strike out against convention, it was largely due to the fact that, beneath the demure, feminine exterior, beat the heart of a confirmed, if as yet unwitting, narcissist. Harriet was driven by a determination to be the center of attention and focus of interest wherever she went, which turned society's matrons against her.

The attentions of wealthy men soon followed and Harriet's situation improved through questionable liaison after questionable liaison. Leaving her young daughter to live with her mother and brother, she moved in to a mansion on Philadelphia's stylish Rittenhouse Square, which won for itself a reputation as a house of ill repute. Various men were seen coming and going at all hours of the day and night, and Philadelphia society openly scorned her. Filled with more confidence than common sense, Harriet followed the established social custom of the day, and duly left her calling card, now marked with the pompous nom de guerre of "Madame Henrietta Blackford," with the proper butlers who answered the doors of her neighbors' elegant houses, though no one dared return the courtesy. The new name, an attempt to both cultivate an air of sophistication and also to distance herself from her former life, fooled no one, but it fit the respectable, cultured image Harriet had embraced. Society dowagers cast disapproving looks at the mansion in the Square; hiding behind a veneer of social respectability, they eagerly listened to every new tale concerning Mrs. Blackford, and tongues clucked in an endless stream of gossip. Her days in Philadelphia ended when she became too hot for the city to hold. Caught extorting $50,000 from an *"indiscreet pillar of Philadelphia society,"* the new "Henrietta" followed the suggestion that she leave the city immediately.[24]

Before long, Harriet was in New York, but only to board an ocean liner heading for Europe; she was broadening her horizons. She spent time in Paris, London, and Vienna, embarked on what would prove her most difficult task: recreating herself as a European courtesan.[25] Philadelphia had snuggled comfortably in its own sense of superiority, but in Europe, Harriet encountered a world of extravagance, where the façade of social respectability never quite covered the moral excesses and sybaritic splendor of the continent's elite. One night, she took in a performance of the comedy Fanny Lear, the story of a sailor's daughter who – having received a large inheritance – moved to Paris to find a wealthy husband among the city's aristocracy. The story eerily echoed Harriet's own, and she quickly adopted the play's romantic illusion to forever separate her from her prosaic past; from now on, Harriet Ely of Philadelphia, sometimes known as Madame Henrietta Blackford would also be known as Fanny Lear.[26]

By November 1871, Harriet was ready to take on Russia, where, it was said, the richest men in the world lived.[27] She boarded a train in Paris, and set off for St Petersburg.[28] During the course of her border interrogation, however, she was detained because of her lack of a visa. She had the presence of mind to mention that the Director of the Imperial Theaters in St Petersburg was an acquaintance. Cables were hastily dispatched, and the next morning a reply came from General Trepov, Chief of the St Petersburg Police, allowing her entrance to Russia. *"Thus,"* Harriet wrote in her memoirs, *"I entered into Russia as I was to leave it, by General Trepov's special orders."*[29]

Arriving in the Imperial capital, Harriet eagerly set about conquering

St Petersburg. As a beautiful young American woman, she undoubtedly possessed a certain novelty; most American visitors to St Petersburg had been diplomats, businessmen, journalists, and occasional travelers, and although the city had seen its share of English, French, German, and other European courtesans, it had never welcomed an American in that role. Harriet impressed with her educated, refined manner; her demure demeanor; and her language skills, easily slipping from English to French, with a smattering of German and a growing knowledge of Russian. Soon, with her reputation secured, Harriet was being called *"the American Beauty,"* and *"La Belle Fanny"* by members of the city's aristocracy.[30]

Then, on the fateful evening of 15/27 December 1871, Harriet attended the masquerade ball at the Mariinsky Theater. When she arrived at the theater, she quickly found a group of young officers she knew from her numerous outings; *"many offered me their arms,"* she recalled, but Harriet declined, instead taking the arm of a tall young man whom she did not know.[31] *"He accepted me graciously,"* she recalled. *"Because of his great height, he bent closer to speak, and looked closely at me."*[32]

"I speak very little English," he said.

"That's alright," she said. *"I know French, and I will speak enough for both of us!"*[33]

This remark seemed to delight him, and he began to ply her with questions. Harriet had no idea that she had just met a Grand Duke, and she continued to banter with him, and tease him in her usual languid, apparently casual manner. In short order, she captivated him.

"Do you know who I am?" he suddenly asked.[34] He asked her if she would like to sit with him, and she agreed. He took her arm and led her across the dance floor, where a number of gilt chairs stood in rows between tall banks of orchids and roses; as they walked through the theatre, Harriet remembered, *"I noticed how quickly people got out of his way, and respectfully saluted."*[35] She had inkling now that he might be someone important. Instead of stopping at the chairs, he continued through a door, turned up a staircase carpeted in a gold-edged runner, and stopped at the first tier of the theater. Here, a footman in scarlet and gold livery embroidered with the Imperial double-headed eagle opened a door to a private box and bowed low as the couple passed. Harriet found herself in a box high above the dance floor, its elaborately carved and gilded archway hung in red velvet fringed with gold bullion, and its sofa and chairs upholstered in gold damask with more Imperial eagles.[36]

Once settled in the Imperial box, Harriet turned uncharacteristically shy, perhaps frightened by her obvious success, perhaps uncertain of how to proceed with a man from this lofty pinnacle of society. Nicholas teased her for a few moments before confessing his identity; he asked her to remove her mask so that he could judge her beauty for himself. Nervously, or perhaps coquettishly, Harriet turned away, and declined several times to remove her domino.[37] At last, she let it fall from her face, and raised her eyes to his, watching him look at her. *"I don't believe I could ever look enough at you,"* he told her with a sudden ferocity.[38] Harriet, accustomed to manipulating those around her, she now found herself in a curious, new position. *"I reddened with pleasure,"* she admitted frankly. Openly desired, not by some rich businessman or minor aristocrat, but by the Emperor's nephew, her imagination quickly wove the possibilities into an enchanted tapestry. *"I saw myself at that moment as Madame de Maintenon, or Madame de Pompadour,"* she confessed, mistresses who had enriched themselves and cemented their places in history through their royal liaisons. *"My imagination soared,"* she remembered. *"I suddenly felt my own strength, and this gave me confidence."*[39]

It was the Grand Duke who broke the spell, asking if he could join her for supper at her hotel. Harriet half-protested, saying that it was far too late to expect the hotel restaurant to be open, but adding cautiously that she would be happy to "entertain" him in her own rooms. *"How could I resist him?"* she later wrote, though she had no wish to do so.[40] Her measured protests, her coquettish flirtations, and her carefully contrived façade of innocence had all woven a spell on other men as she enticed them toward her bed, but none of it seemed necessary with this eager Grand Duke. She replied by rote, from habit, not inclination, yet she sensed something urgent in his request that she had no wish or ability to forestall.

It became clear to Harriet that Nicholas considered this something far more than an evening's divertissement, though she had no idea at that point of the passion that burned within him. Here, in her hotel suite, was a handsome, wealthy young Grand Duke, scion of perhaps the world's richest and most powerful ruling family, and a man ninth in line to the Throne of Imperial Russia. If he was playing a game, if she was to be used and then cast aside, the material rewards, at least, promised to be spectacular.

When morning came, Nicholas Konstantinovich went to her desk, sat, and wrote the following on a piece of her stationery: *"I swear by everything I hold sacred never to speak to anyone without my master's permission. I swear, as a well-born American, to faithfully maintain this oath, and declare myself, body and soul, the slave of Grand Duke Nicholas Konstantinovich of Russia."* Harriet was startled; she looked up at Nicholas, and he said, *"Sign it."* Perhaps she was as captivated and intrigued with him as he was with her, for Harriet duly signed the strange statement and, as Nicholas crept away at sunrise, he promised her that he would return to her that night.[41]

The passionate affair that began in Harriet's suite that snowy St Petersburg night quickly blossomed into an elaborate and dangerous dance enacted without discretion across the capital before the eyes of a startled aristocracy and scandalized Imperial Family. Together, they attended balls; drove in the Grand Duke's crested sleigh down the crowded Nevsky Prospekt; watched performances at the theater and opera; and dined in fashionable restaurants, their passions – for once – concealed behind the closed doors of wood-paneled private dining rooms.[42] With each outing the couple grew bolder. One night, Nicholas took Harriet to the Marble Palace, creeping in through a small side door that led through a warren of corridors to Nicholas's private apartments. Harriet later recalled the endless Persian carpets; the walls hung with stag's heads; the smell of the leather-bound books in his library; the crisp white linen that shrouded his table; and the heavily veined marble walls of his bathroom. He fed her, drank with her, and made love to her in his bed, bidding her to remain at his side all night.[43]

It is difficult to gauge the depth of real love between Nicholas and Harriet. Certainly, Nicholas lavished her with expensive gifts, *"out of proportion with those usually accorded a mistress,"* as Alexandre Tarsaidze wrote.[44] And while the Grand Duke was at Krasnoe Selo with his regiment, he arranged to have Harriet, disguised as an Adjutant, smuggled into the camp to cater to his amorous needs.[45] But despite their dependence on one another, in Nicholas's earliest letters to Harriet, there is evidence of the business arrangement that originally existed between them. A short message on his engraved notepaper reads: *"Here is the money, my dear, thank you for your duties to me. I will return today at 3."*[46]

Soon, the couple traveled to Europe together, ostensibly, as Nicholas explained, on the order of his doctor, to rest.[47] It became evident, however, that resting was not on Nicholas's agenda; the couple behaved as scandalously in Europe as they had in Russia; before too long, they were on the run from the agents of the Imperial Police, who had been detailed to follow the errant Grand Duke, and tracked the lovers from hotel to hotel.

Nicholas and Harriet's relationship became increasingly volatile as their hedonistic lifestyle spun out of control. Following one turbulent argument over a beautiful Hungarian woman to whom Harriet believed Nicholas had paid too much attention, Nicholas beat Harriet, threw her against a wall. The lovers parted for several days, and Harriet began to cast around her for a new protector.[48] Nicholas, however, discovered that Harriet was essential to his happiness, and he enticed her back with the highly unusual step of taking her on a trip to visit his sister, the Queen of the Hellenes, at the villa of Mon Repos in Corfu. Queen Olga greeted Harriet cordially, and made a gracious and friendly impression on the American, who found her *"very pure, very innocent, and the most sympathetic person you could find."* This visit gave Henrietta a surprising insight into Konstantinovichi family relationships; *"I was astonished,"* she wrote in her memoirs, *"that the Grand Duke had for his sister an affection that approached idolatry."*[49]

It appears from her memoirs that Henrietta took this introduction to Nicholas's sister as his family's tacit approval of their relationship – and, by extension, that of the Emperor. But she was, despite a talent for exquisite manipulation, still too naive to the ways of royalty to understand that the friendly smiles from the courtiers meant nothing; behind her back, news of her presence in Mon Repos had reached Nicholas's father, Grand Duke Konstantin Nikolaievich, who became enraged that Nicholas had so far forgotten himself as to introduce his mistress to his sister the Queen. Together with the secret police's information on the couple's scandalous European escapades, it was all too much for the Imperial Family to bear. Secret policemen were dispatched to America and to various places in Europe to compile a dossier on Henrietta's past at Alexander II's request; a dossier that – if it be filled with appropriate evidence – could one day be used to separate her from the Grand Duke.

Suddenly, Nicholas was recalled to Russia, with orders to continue on to Khiva in Central Asia with his regiment. Harriet went to Paris, and the Grand Duke reluctantly returned to St Petersburg; here, he found that the details of their trip had duly been reported, and at great length, to both Konstantin Nikolaievich and to Alexander II. Shortly before he was to leave for Khiva, Nicholas was summoned to his father's study, where Konstantin Nikolaievich soundly berated his son for his involvement with a woman he now deemed *"an adventuress."* During the interview, the Grand Duke was restrained, listening as his father reproached him, saying that – as Nicholas later confided to Harriet – *"I might need a mistress, but I shouldn't have displayed you all over Europe. He said it was immoral."* Nicholas calmly replied that he was not to blame. *"It's in my blood,"* he said to his father, and went on to cite the examples of Peter the Great, Anna, Elisabeth, Catherine, Paul, Nicholas I, his uncles, and, finally, his own father, who himself was famously involved with a mistress.[50]

In the end, Nicholas was sent away from the danger of his American *"adventuress"* to the danger of war. The Empire's soldiers were engaged in a protracted campaign against the Khan of Khiva, attempting to coerce him into acceptance of Russian supremacy throughout Central Asia. The Khan had resisted diplomatic overtures, and the situation erupted into a military conflict when his soldiers seized fifty Russians as prisoners, hoping to use them as bargaining chips in an effort to stave off Russian expansionism. Nicholas's letters to Harriet now included a chronicle of his progress, as he traveled from Orenburg by sleigh across some two hundred miles of snow, then up into the Urals, and finally to the arid desert of Central Asia. He became the first Romanov to set foot in these contentious lands, and he found that – at least before reaching Khiva – he was greeted as a hero by the various nomadic tribes at war with the Khan. When he arrived in any town, the Grand Duke was quickly surrounded by hundreds of curious, cheering spectators, who pushed and fought for a chance to touch his sleeve, his boots, and his horse. Nicholas, however, remained largely unmoved, consumed as he was with anguish over being separated from Harriet. He wrote to her: *"My dear little Grand Duchess of all the Russias!! I am entirely desolate; it is ten days since I received a letter from my dearest Fanny Lear; I am so thirsty in this terrible desert, to have no news of you. For an entire month now, I have seen nothing but sand dunes, yellow and red snakes, tortoises, and all kinds of insects, all more or less dangerous. The only thing that comforts me is the medallion that I wear around my neck that contains your hair."*[51]

The campaign was a harsh one, conducted in winter over snow and ice. By spring, when the Russians were near Khiva, Nicholas was given command of one of four advance battalions that was to storm the rebel city. Horses and sleighs were exchanged for camels as they reached the edge of the desert Steppe. The Russians were unprepared for the ravages of the terrain: men sank up to their knees in the swirling sands, and icy winds whipped the desert into a blinding, impassable fury. After struggling for several weeks, the advance battalions finally reached the boundary of Khiva and a hastily built fort. As the Russians advanced, the Grand Duke was entranced at the hostile surroundings. Water, he reported, was in short supply, yet if it could somehow be brought in and the land irrigated, it would become a tropical garden ringed by snow-capped mountains. He filled his letters with descriptions of the sun-dried mud streets and the little, curious houses he encountered; the thriving, colorful bazaars that, he said, smelled terribly, but that were packed with enticing goods that he duly purchased *"for our apartment,"* as he explained. Woven carpets, pottery, silver, and exotic silks were all carefully crated and sent back toward St Petersburg on camels.[52] It is clear from his letters that although Nicholas was at war in sometimes-perilous situations, his first thoughts were constantly with Harriet: *"Before I found you,"* he wrote, *"I had no family; the Marble Palace had become odious to me. This can be said of me: I was looking for another family. I met a princess, whom I wanted to marry; but this plan fell through. I continued to search among the ladies of St Petersburg...Finally, I met the pretty little blonde called Fanny Lear (but I don't like blondes!), spirituelle, and, which is more important, desirous of me. And it was done...my home was found."*[53]

In May 1873, the Russians slowly tightened the noose around Khiva. *"The enemy focused his might on us,"* Nicholas wrote. *"The bravest galloped within four paces of us, shooting as they circled. We shot back. I saw several fall dead or wounded, and horses dragging them away. I must give credit; they never leave their wounded behind, but ride up swiftly and lift them to their saddles under our fire. It was a noble sight."*[54] He pushed on; when he saw the enemy begin its retreat, *"I raised my saber, giving the signal, and then I noticed that the Cossacks were bowing and crossing themselves, and I understood that this was the most dangerous moment of my life."*[55] It was the climactic battle of the campaign, and the Russians emerged victorious. Now, it fell to Nicholas Konstantinovich, as the Emperor's most senior representative, to present the demands for surrender directly to the Khan.

Following his victory, Nicholas summoned Harriet from Paris to join him in Samara, where he had taken a house. He wrote to her passionately: *"I hold you in my arms, I pin you down with my legs, I kiss you everywhere, and I fall at your feet insane with* love and longing."⁵⁶ Henrietta traveled by train and river-steamer to get there, but once in Samara, the reunion was so passionate and heart-felt, that by the time the pair returned to St Petersburg, and to the comfort of the apartment the Grand Duke had purchased for Harriet on the fashionable Mikhailovskii Square, they had come to an agreement over their future together, and Nicholas was determined to act. Contrary to Konstantin Nikolaievich's order for discretion, however, the pair was soon spotted in public: attending balls, dining in restaurants, and driving through the city.

Soon the Imperial capital was alive with gossip over the scandalous and uncontrolled romance between the Grand Duke and the wild American woman. Nicholas threw all caution to the wind, and among other outrageous marks of favoritism toward his mistress, he obtained a pass for Harriet to attend the marriage of his cousin, Grand Duchess Marie Alexandrovna, to Prince Alfred, Duke of Edinburgh, on 11/26 January 1874; with other spectators, Harriet took her seat in the gallery overlooking the hall along which the Imperial Family would pass on their way to and from the Palace Cathedral.⁵⁷ The Grand Duke even provided Harriet with a special pass that enabled her to observe the wedding dinner and the grand ball that followed in the Nicholas Hall. She found a friendly servant, who brought ice cream, cake, oranges and sweets to her in her alcove.⁵⁸

Then, one night that winter of 1874, while his mother was at Pavlovsk, the Grand Duke collected Harriet and took her to the Marble Palace. A handsome young Cornet named Savin accompanied them, and they took a number of bottles of champagne from the Palace's wine cellars. Nicholas led the pair up a service stair to his mother's bedroom, where they spent several hours drinking. According to the most salacious version, he and his guests stripped and, together, made love on Alexandra Iosifovna's bed. At the end of the evening, apparently without Harriet's knowledge, Nicholas Konstantinovich broke off several of the large diamonds in a jeweled crown adorning an icon given to his mother by Emperor Nicholas I on the occasion of her marriage; the next day, the Grand Duke gave them to his Adjutant, Captain Vorpovsky, to pawn.⁵⁹ Unknown to them, Nicholas and Harriet had shared their final, devastating assignation.

Within hours of the delirious and dangerous romantic encounter between Nicholas Konstantinovich and Henrietta Blackford at the Marble Palace, the stones missing from Alexandra Iosifovna's wedding icon were noticed. Servants were summoned and questioned, all without result. Without considering the most likely explanation, and not thinking about the possible implications for his family, Konstantin Nikolaievich informed his brother the Emperor. In his turn, the Emperor ordered Count Peter Shuvalov, head of the infamous Third Section of His Majesty's Chancellery, the Okhrana, and General Feodor Trepov, Chief of the St Petersburg Police, to begin an investigation into the affair. Soon, Vorpovsky was arrested and interrogated; under torture, he admitted what had taken place. Savin, likewise, was arrested and, after confessing his role, was exiled to Siberia; he later managed to escape to America.⁶⁰

Alexander II kept news of the investigation from his brother. Konstantin Nikolaievich only learned of his son's involvement when, following his interrogation of Vorpovsky, Count Shuvalov called on him at the Marble Palace and informed him that Nicholas had stolen the jewels. Konstantin Nikolaievich recorded in his diary on 12/24 April 1874: *"Trepov reported that the diamonds from the icons were found in a pawn-shop!!!! And that they were pawned by my son's adjutant. The arrested adjutant testified that Nikola gave him the diamonds and Nikola ordered him to pawn them."*⁶¹

At first, Konstantin Nikolaievich refused to believe what he heard, laying the blame for the thefts squarely on Harriet. When Nicholas learned of this, he went straight to Harriet's apartment. When she opened the door, she saw that his clothes were disheveled, and his face ashen. He begged her to immediately take all of his letters, their private agreements, and her jewels to the American Legation and deposit them with the American Minister for safekeeping. Then he told her: *"Get together everything you can manage, and leave Russia, and do not return. I see now that I will never have any peace here. And if they decide to send you to Siberia, it will be accomplished, they would be persuaded."*[62]

Harriet asked why on earth she would be sent to Siberia – and Nicholas told her that he had kept in her apartments compromising papers, which would make one believe that he was part of a revolutionary conspiracy.[63] Nicholas was calm, but firm, and insisted that Harriet carry out his instructions. Harriet did as Nicholas requested, gathering her papers, including personal letters from Nicholas, and his pledges and financial arrangements with her concerning legacies and bequests he planned to make in her favor, and together with her jewelry, delivered them to the American Legation in St Petersburg. Marshall Jewell, the new American Minister to Russia, took them from her without question and placed them in his safe. Then she returned to her apartment and waited. Contrary to Nicholas's wishes, she did not hurry to leave Russia, or even to make herself more difficult to find.

On 15/27 April, Shuvalov was back at the Marble Palace, where he renewed his accusations. Many in the Imperial Family and in St Petersburg, firmly believed that Shuvalov was somehow behind the entire incident, attempting to use it to discredit Konstantin Nikolaievich, whose liberal policies he despised.[64] When the Count insisted, Konstantin Nikolaievich summoned his eldest son to the meeting, where Shuvalov confronted him with all of the evidence. Nicholas, however, denied everything; before he stormed out of the room, he demanded that Shuvalov be arrested for treason.[65] Konstantin Nikolaievich described it as a *"horrible scene,"* noting that his son showed *"no repentance,"* only *"obduracy, and not a single tear."*[66]

As soon as the interview ended, Nicholas went straight to Harriet's apartment. Harriet was still in the dark over Nicholas's trubles; she asked him repeatedly what they were. Finally, he told her that several jewels from the crown of an icon belonging to his mother were missing, and that Vorpovsky had been accused of the theft. *"In order to keep his innocence,"* he related, *"he was forced to say that I had stolen them. And I will be arrested, imprisoned, and declared insane. As for you, you will be interrogated, and searched, and then driven from Russia."*[67] Harriet was aghast, but assured Nicholas that she believed him, and loved him no matter what happened. He told her later that day that he had ordered a ring for her, engraved with his name and the date beginning their romance; but he was not going to be able to get it for her. Instead, he drew a ring from his left hand and placed it on her finger, telling her that he considered her his wife, and would love her forever.[68]

Nicholas left Harriet to go to the Marble Palace and dine with his father. Despite his promise, however, he did not return to his mistress. Hours later, a worried Harriet made her way to the Marble Palace, and entered through the porte cochere, finding herself in the familiar hallway outside Nicholas's apartments. His door stood closed, and there was a large key sticking out of the lock; turning the key with difficulty, Harriet opened the door and ventured to look inside. To her astonishment, Nicholas's rooms were empty. She hurried back the way she had come, intending to return quickly to her apartment; but as she left the Marble Palace, she remembered a friendly dvornik who had helped her on her first visit to the Palace. She thought she would try and find him; hopefully, he could tell her what was happening. Harriet hurried back to the entrance of the Palace, and, as she entered the service door, she was shocked to catch sight of Nicholas, held under guard by his father's officers and adjutants. Abandoning her mission, she left the Palace and went home.[69]

The next morning, 16/28 April, Harriet received a brief note from Nicholas, informing her that he had been arrested and was a prisoner in the Marble Palace. She spent the morning preparing for her own arrest; she put on a new dress and prepared her toilet as though being dressed by a couturier. And then she waited. By five in the afternoon, she was tired from her sleepless night, and nothing untoward had happened – so Harriet got ready for bed. As soon as she had donned her nightgown and undone her hair, there was pounding at her door and fifteen officers of Shuvalov's Third Section stormed into her apartment.[70] Drawers were opened, their contents strewn on the floor; books pulled off shelves, flung into the air to dislodge any hidden papers, and left to fall to the carpet with a thud; sheets were ripped from the beds and mattresses overturned; wardrobes were stripped of their contents, dresses carefully examined for any evidence. Harriet's jewelry was confiscated, along with 7,000 rubles that she kept in her desk.[71]

Harriet herself was placed under arrest and told she would have to accompany the men, not to the American Legation, nor to Police Headquarters, but rather to the ominously named House of Detention, where she was to be kept a prisoner. Here she spent an uncomfortable and uncertain night, in a tiny, cold cell guarded by a barred door. Over the course of the next several days, she locked horns with Count Shuvalov as he attempted to bully and coerce her out of the property given to her by Nicholas. It seems as though Shuvalov was looking for certain, very specific items, and that Harriet was not entirely aware of what he wanted. She was determined to give him nothing, and reminded him repeatedly that she was a foreign national, an American citizen, and as such, did not fall under his jurisdiction, especially given his refusal to allow her to contact the American Legation in St Petersburg.

Unbeknownst to Harriet, the American Legation had been desperate to assist her. At ten o'clock in the evening of April 16/28, one of Harriet's servants managed to slip away from the apartment on Mikhailovskii Square while it was being searched and ran to the American Legation, demanding to see the Minister or his Secretary. The Secretary, Eugene Schuyler, interviewed the maid almost immediately, and heard her appeal for protection for herself and for her mistress; Harriet, the maid said, had asked of the Russian police permission to contact the American Legation, and the presence of a Legation member for the duration of the search, but both requests were refused.[72]

On learning of Harriet's detention, Marshall Jewell, the American Minister in St Petersburg, quickly dispatched a note to General Trepov, the Prefect of the St Petersburg Police: *"The Minister Plenipotentiary of the United States has the honor to send his regards to His Excellency the Aide-de-Camp Trepov, and to say that the apartment of Madame Blackford, an American citizen, in the Gerbine House, Mikhailovskii Square, was entered this evening by the police. The apartment was searched and many objects removed. Mrs. Blackford was arrested. The Envoy hopes the General will inform him – tonight, if possible – as to why the police have arrested her, of what crime she is being accused, and where she is at present. The Envoy does not wish to hinder the administration of justice, but as he believes he knows already the cause of this affair, he wishes to assure himself that Madame Blackford will not be deprived of the protection of the law."*[73]

To this, Trepov frostily replied: *"I, Adjutant Trepov, send my utmost regards to His*

Excellency Marshall Jewell, Ambassador Plenipotentiary, and have the honor to inform him in response to his note of April 16/28 (No. 43) that it is under the orders and the depositions of Count Shuvalov that Madame Blackford was, with great regard and care, transferred to a place where she will lack no care and where she will be in good health and calm in spirit."[74]

Jewell was not satisfied. He directed another message be sent, not as an unofficial inquiry to the Police, and in Russian, but as a formal communication on behalf of the United States Government to the Russian Minister of Foreign Affairs, M. de Westmann. It asserted that Harriet was an American citizen being held without recourse to the American Legation. It repeated the questions asked in the previous, less formal note, and reminded de Westmann that the courtesy of a direct reply was required.[75]

De Westmann made it clear to Marshall Jewell that any matter that involved not only the Okhrana but also a member of the Imperial Family was beyond the jurisdiction of the Foreign Office; de Westmann hesitated even to mention the case to Count Shuvalov. De Westmann additionally advised Jewell to consider Harriet's infamous reputation, and cautioned him against pursuing the matter any further.[76]

Despite such warnings, Jewell resolved to act. He contacted the senior members of St Petersburg's Diplomatic Body, the Portuguese Minister the Viscount de Figanniere, and the British Ambassador, Lord Augustus Loftus, both of whom agreed on the seriousness of the case. They advised a continued and insistent personal approach to the Russians, coupled with an official approach to the Diplomatic Body, who would then act in concert with an application to the Emperor. But before any of this could happen, on 18/30 April, a messenger finally delivered a note from Harriet to the American Legation. In this note, Harriet asked that the American Minister release to Count Shuvalov all the items that she had deposited with him for safekeeping some three weeks before. Eugene Schuyler quickly found Jewell and advised him of the arrival of Harriet's urgent and unusual request. Neither man was entirely convinced that the letter had not been coerced, but Jewell asked Schuyler to go at once to the House of Detention and meet with Mrs. Blackford.

Schuyler found Harriet exhausted, but with her mind made up. She asked Schuyler to bring her boxes from the Legation to the House of Detention, so that she could go through them with General Trepov and Count Shuvalov. When the boxes arrived at the prison, there were three items of contention: A diamond parure; and two documents written by Grand Duke Nicholas Konstantinovich. One promised that a monthly allowance would be paid to Harriet for the rest of her life. The other had a more detailed arrangement in which Harriet, should she be parted forcibly from Nicholas, would be paid 5,000 rubles per month for life; in the event that Nicholas would predecease her, this arrangement would be terminated with a final payment from Nicholas's estate in the amount of 100,000 rubles.[77]

In the end, and after much wrangling, Harriet was able to retain the diamonds only after making a payment to Nicholas's father in the amount of 10,000 rubles. Harriet also accepted a flat sum of 50,000 rubles (approximately $500,000 in current figures) in lieu of Nicholas's written promises and bequests.[78] When these issues were settled, Schuyler was permitted to return the rest of Harriet's property to her – a collection of smaller jewels, and personal letters from the Grand Duke that she refused to part with, though she had to endure the humiliation of having to open every one and allow Shuvalov to read them.[79]

Harriet was shortly released from the House of Detention, but her jailer went with her to her apartment, where she remained under house arrest until an order arrived that she was to leave Russia within forty-eight hours. Before she left, however, she was summoned to an uncomfortable meeting with General Trepov. He told her that at first, he had had great hopes of being able to use her testimony on the Grand Duke's behalf in the matter of the theft, but there was no opportunity. The case had quickly fallen into Shuvalov's hands, and from there, the matter had become public knowledge; once the public knew that a member of the Imperial Family was a thief, there was no way to settle things quietly.[80]

Harriet told Trepov that Nicholas was a kleptomaniac, stealing small and inexpensive things but she added that he had never taken anything of great value. Trepov agreed, saying that items found in Nicholas's rooms at the Marble Palace supported her assertion: there were miniatures, paper-knives, bottles of scent, purses, cigarette cases, lace handkerchiefs, small table bells, and small objects made of porcelain, all of low value and all jumbled together in the greatest disorder.[81]

After this, a guard escorted her to a waiting train. Clutching a case containing her letters from the Grand Duke, she entered her compartment and held it tightly in her lap. From the windows of the carriage, she gazed out upon the broad Nevsky Prospekt, with its ornate palaces where she and Nicholas had danced and dined as society watched in disbelief. At noon on Sunday, 10 May 1874, the train steamed slowly out of St Petersburg, on its way to Paris. Harriet would never see Russia, or Nicholas Konstantinovich, again.

In the end, Harriet took her revenge against Alexander II, Konstantin Nikolaievich, Count Shuvalov – the whole Russian Government that had separated her from Nicholas – by writing a scandalous account of her adventures with the Grand Duke, entitled *Le Roman d'une Americaine en Russie*, that appeared the following year in Belgium and in Paris. Copies were quickly suppressed; the Belgian police, acting under intense pressure from the Russian Government, seized many of the volumes. Others that survived had some twenty pages excised from the bound text, comprising most of the personal letters that Nicholas Konstantinovich had written to her.[82]

Finding life without the Grand Duke intolerable in Europe, Henrietta briefly returned to Philadelphia, only to find the city even more openly hostile toward her than it had been before. In 1885, she returned to Europe, this time to Italy, where she lived quietly for a few months before falling ill; her doctor diagnosed consumption. In an effort to prolong her days, she went to the south of France, hoping that the warm climate and sea air would prove beneficial, but she only became worse. She died in Nice on 15 May 1886.[83]

Nicholas himself became a victim of the Imperial machine, *"sacrificed,"* as Eugene Schuyler wrote in a dispatch to Washington, in order to preserve the public face of the Romanov Dynasty.[84]

In the end, it is not possible to determine who believed that Nicholas was genuinely guilty of the theft of which he was accused, and who believed that this was merely a young man's sexual escapade gone terribly awry. And in the end, it did not matter if Nicholas was guilty or innocent; no Romanov Grand Duke could be allowed to be sentenced to prison for theft. It was far preferable that he somehow be removed from the Imperial stage. In order to accomplish this, Alexander II charged a commission to investigate the Grand Duke's sanity, an incredibly hypocritical action, given the Emperor's own romantic misalliance. Alexander may have felt this, however, for the entire episode, as he confessed to Princess Dolgorukaya, left him *"quite depressed."*[85]

Then, for a short time, it appeared as though an alternative solution had been found: Shuvalov produced a former convict who expressed himself willing to shoulder the blame for Nicholas for a consideration. Nicholas's own father, who was fearful that Shuvalov might one day use this information to blackmail Nicholas and the Imperial Family at large, rejected this idea.

"What to do with Nikola?" Wrote Konstantin Nikolaievich in his diary. The Imperial Family met in council to decide the fate of the wayward Grand Duke, and their final determination was that Nicholas should be declared insane and therefore not responsible for his criminal actions. *"After long vacillation, we decided to wait for the doctor's evaluation and no matter what it says, publicly declare him spiritually ill and lock him away. That will be enough for the public. But for Nikola, he will be locked away in strict solitary confinement with a punitive and correctional regime.... I told myself: "No matter how painful and hard, I can be the father of a sick and mad son, but being the father of a criminal, publicly stunned by the blow, would make my future impossible."*[86]

Cynically – and despite the final decision having already been made – the psychological examination of Nicholas proceeded. A team of physicians, led by a Doctor Balinsky, examined the Grand Duke; they were to report on their findings, but their results were already a foregone conclusion.[87]

In August of 1874, after almost four months of examination and observation, the doctors stated as a certainty that the Grand Duke was indeed suffering from mental instability. *"In mental facilities,"* their report concluded, *"the Grand Duke deviates from observed norms."*[88] With this official diagnosis, Nicholas Konstantinovich was formally declared to be insane, although the announcement convinced no one.[89] On Alexander II's instructions, on 12 September 1874, the Minister of the Imperial Court dispatched a secret memorandum to the Minister of Justice, in which the, *"incurable mental illness"* of the Grand Duke was announced; the memorandum also requested that legal proceedings begin to deprive Nicholas Konstantinovich of his freedom.[90] In the interim, Nicholas was placed under the control of two officials, both doctors: Nicholas Zdekauera and Professor Ivan Balinsky, who had headed the psychological investigation.[91]

In protest and seemingly entirely sane, Nicholas Konstantinovich wrote: *"Am I a madman or a criminal? If I am a criminal, try me and sentence me. If I am a madman, put me under treatment, but in any case give me some hope that I may one day come back to life and liberty. What you are doing is cruel and inhuman."*[92] But the Imperial Family was adamant – and it seems that their plan had advanced a step: To convince Nicholas himself that he was mentally ill and in need of treatment. Reporting again to Washington, Eugene Schuyler wrote that the Grand Duke was being held in confinement in an isolated house in the countryside outside of St Petersburg, and that *"he...has been allowed to see no one except his father and the aides-de-camp and physicians who had immediate charge of him. I have been told by one of these gentlemen that his physical health is perfect and that it would be very difficult for a casual observer to notice any signs of mental malady. It has been, however, if I am correctly informed, the aim of all the persons charged with his surveillance to impress upon him in every possible way that he is insane."*[93]

In the late summer of 1874, Nicholas' treatment began. He was forced to endure long, *"therapeutic"* baths of ice water; he was beaten and drugged into submission if he rebelled; if he refused to eat, he was fed by force. This regimen eased somewhat in the autumn, when the Grand Duke was sent to a remote farm near the village of Elizavetino, where he was forced to work as a laborer, cleaning manure from barns and mowing hay.[94] On 11 December 1874, Alexander II signed the official decree that Grand Duke Nicholas Konstantinovich was *"seriously unwell,"* and required *"special treatment under the constant care of specialists."*[95] By the summer of 1875, the decision had been taken to move Nicholas further away from St Petersburg, and he was sent to

Oreanda in the Crimea, where he was confined to his father's estate above the Black Sea.[96] Here, the harsh and cruel physical regime imposed on him at Elizavetino was relaxed, and the Grand Duke was allowed to take walks and engage in painting and musical pursuits.[97]

For most of a year, Nicholas Konstantinovich lived a quiet life – but he was still a young man, and was not ready to accept his lot and retire from society. When out walking one day in 1876, the Grand Duke met a woman: Twenty-one-year-old Alexandra Abaza Demidova, the estranged wife of Alexander Demidov, a minor Crimean official. Nicholas and Alexandra were captivated with each other, and soon fell in love. Despite constant surveillance, the resourceful Grand Duke managed to initiate and pursue an extended physical affair with Alexandra, who soon enough became pregnant with his child. A girl they named Olga was born in May 1877.[98] The situation could no longer be kept secret, and details of the romance and the failure of security surrounding Nicholas were reported to a furious Alexander II in St Petersburg.[99]

The Emperor lashed out immediately, and ordered the Grand Duke exiled to remote Uman, in the Cherkassk Province. A determined Demidova soon followed, bringing their daughter with her. When she sought entrance to the estate where the Grand Duke was being kept under strict and heavy guard, she was turned away on Imperial order. But a sympathetic guard eventually smuggled her in, and, a year later, she gave birth to the Grand Duke's son, Nicholas.[100]

The situation escalated. Alexander II, realizing that Nicholas was unlikely to voluntarily give up his new family, ordered that the Grand Duke be returned under the heaviest of guards to Oreanda. A second Imperial order was given: That Nicholas would never be allowed again to see Alexandra Demidova or his son and daughter.[101] Nicholas was enraged, and he declared to his household, *"I shall go amongst the people, wearing the Cross of St Andrei and they will rise to my defense."* This threat of rebellion was reported to the Emperor, who then ordered this decoration seized, and called down on his nephew a still harsher regime of imprisonment.[102]

By this time, Grand Duke Konstantin Nikolaievich had also taken up semi-permanent residence in the Crimea with his mistress and, appealing to his brother, he requested that his son be moved further away, this time to Orenburg in central Russia. This effectively removed Nicholas from the realm of Alexandra Demidova, who found it not so easy to follow the Grand Duke with two infants in tow – but it did not end Nicholas's romantic adventures.

In Orenburg, the Grand Duke met Nadezhda Dreyer and married her in February 1882, by which time Alexander II had been assassinated, and had been succeeded by Nicholas's cousin, Alexander III. The bride was the nineteen-year-old daughter of Orenburg's Chief of Police, the man charged with maintaining strict security around Nicholas's household. The union was morganatic, but although his family tried to force an annulment, the Grand Duke refused.[103] In so angering the new Emperor, Nicholas found himself exiled further to the east, to Tashkent in Central Asia, where he would spend the rest of his life.

Some years previously, the Grand Duke had encountered Central Asian territory during the military campaign in Khiva. His interest in the region now rekindled, Nicholas Konstantinovich set about a comprehensive program designed to transform the dusty desert into a lush, tropical garden. He used his annual Government stipend as Grand Duke to finance archaeological and scientific expeditions into the surrounding countryside, editing and writing several scholarly articles and journals on the subject that his family in St Petersburg attempted to suppress in an effort to ignore his continued existence. One of his longest articles concerned the history of Tashkent, which outlined the Grand Duke's plan to turn the arid desert town into an oasis. The article was smuggled abroad and published in an English magazine, but when sought, permission to publish inside Russia was firmly denied by Alexander III.[104] Nevertheless, under Nicholas's direction and financing, irrigation canals were dug and water brought to the surrounding countryside, allowing Tashkent for the first time to develop a serious agricultural industry. Nicholas planted trees along the city's dusty streets and laid out green gardens for the public; he also founded several workers' clubs, charitable institutions, and even provided Tashkent with its first cinema.[105]

The Grand Duke spent many of his days hunting. He kept a fine stable of horses, and would ride out into the surrounding mountains to shoot duck and pheasant, and stalk tigers, antelope, and bear.[106] These expeditions, led by nomadic local chiefs, were always an exercise in exotic precision. The Grand Duke, atop a black stallion, carried an ivory-handled dagger in one hand; the other, clutching hold of the reins, also held a long leash, on which a trained leopard trotted. The swirling pack of hounds would chase prey across rivers and up mountains; when cornered, Nicholas Konstantinovich would then release his pet leopard, which easily pinned down the animal, allowing the Grand Duke in for the kill.[107]

The Grand Duke built himself a small, elegant palace in the center of the city. Designed by Albert Benois and erected between 1889-90, it was a constructed atop a raised ground floor, its mellow, golden brown stone façade bristling with arches, carved architraves, decorative pilasters, and statuary beneath a steep, mansard roof. Within, a suite of rooms were adorned by local craftsmen in a mixture of Gothic, medieval, Middle Eastern and Oriental motifs, with stained glass windows, tall, multi-tiled porcelain stoves, and a handsome marble staircase with a thick red carpet. Here, the Grand Duke displayed his immense collection of art: paintings by German, French, and Italian masters hung alongside the works of Russian artists and between tapestries collected by Nicholas during his trips to Europe. In addition to the paintings and tapestries, he also possessed a unique collection of porcelain from Japan, China, and India. Its exotic garden, bordered by a thick grove of oaks, was filled with roses, Japanese dwarf trees, reflecting ponds, and graceful iron bridges beneath the shade of the tall palms. He also maintained a private zoo, with monkeys, pelicans, peacocks, flamingoes, his pet leopard, and other wildlife.[108]

In 1883, Nicholas Konstantinovich became a father once again, when Nadezhda gave birth to a son who was named Artemi. In the space on his birth certificate listing his father, the presiding official wrote *"Top Secret, by Decree of the Highest Authority."* It was a transparent attempt to maintain the secret, because his godparents were duly named as Grand Duke Konstantin Nikolaievich and Queen Olga of the Hellenes.[109] Although he refused to allow the Grand Duke to return to St Petersburg, Alexander III did relent and grant morganatic titles to his son, providing him with the title and style of His Highness Prince Iskander.[110] A second son, Prince Alexander, was born in November of 1889. Nicholas Konstantinovich was not yet forty-years-old, and for the first few years he proved himself a devoted father, doting on his two sons and settling into a life of comfortable, if imposed, exile. But, like his restless father, Nicholas was incapable of faithfulness to one woman.

Although he never divorced Nadezhda, in 1895 Nicholas bought a sixteen-year-old girl, Darya Chasovitinova, from a local Cossack chief, for a hundred rubles, and installed her in a small house near his own palace in Tashkent. In the three years that followed, Darya gave birth to three children, all of whom the Grand Duke acknowledged as his own: Darya, born in 1896; Sviatoslav, born in 1897; and Nicholas, born in 1898.[111] Five years later, he fell in love with a sixteen-year-old student named Valerie Hmelnitskuju during a tour of her school in Tashkent. He purchased a house for her and – secretly and bigamously – married her. When word of this union reached St Petersburg, the Emperor Nicholas II ordered the officiating priest stripped of his office, and banished Valerie from Tashkent.

Perhaps goaded into action by Nicholas's outrageous actions, other Konstantinovichi began to visit Nicholas in the place of his distant exile. In 1904, after traveling to Tashkent, Queen Olga of the Hellenes – who had taken introduction to Nicholas's mistress Harriet Blackford in her stride thirty years previously – concluded that by this time Nicholas had, *"completely lost all moral sense of what he can do, and what is demanded of him."*[112] Konstantin Konstantinovich also visited him in Tashkent in these same years. On the first evening of his stay, he later said, he found his brother *"quite normal."* After the following evening, he had changed his opinion, deeming Nicholas Konstantinovich *"rather strange."* By the third day, Konstantin Konstantinovich had decided that his brother was, *"not entirely sane."*[113]

Princess Anatole Bariatinsky, visiting Tashkent after the turn of the century, found the exiled Grand Duke, *"a man of great force of character, iron will, and indomitable energy,"* but noted that he was, *"subject to violent fits of rage, in which he lost all control over himself and became quite unaccountable for his actions. Once, when he was in one of these ebullitions of temper, he dug a hole and for no apparent reason buried his wife up to her waist in the sand."*[114]

Nicholas Konstantinovich, the Princess remembered, presented an eccentric appearance. *"His head and face were clean-shaven, and he wore an eyeglass. His costume consisted of a red shirt, something in the style of the peasants' garment, a black velvet suit, and, winter and summer alike, a sealskin cap. His favorite color was red, and this predominated everywhere in his surroundings. His house, carriages, the liveries of his servants, even to the harness of his horses – everything was of a bright red."* Despite these peculiarities of appearance, however, she found him, *"a good conversationalist and linguist, and highly cultivated in every respect; but he was an original in every sense of the word. The Governor-General often found him trying, as he was in the habit of going into the town incognito and mixing freely with all classes of people, which sometimes led to complications owing to his uncontrollable temper."*[115]

During her stay in Tashkent, Princess Bariatinsky received an invitation from the Grand Duke's wife Nadezhda to take tea. She found her, *"one of the most eccentric and peculiar women I have ever met. She wore the most extraordinary clothes, usually quite unsuited to the occasion; thus, for instance, she would appear in the afternoon in an evening dress trimmed with sequins, paillettes, a tiara on her head, a big diamond necklace sparkling down over her bosom, and generally ablaze with jewelry. Her clothes were always of the most showy colors."* On arriving at the Grand Duke's palace, Princess Bariatinsky was, *"…ushered into a semi-dark room in the Moorish style, where I felt by no means at ease. I was met by an enormous greyhound, barking vociferously, which always followed at [Nadezhda's] heels. This time she wore a remarkable tea gown with a long train. The whole room was covered with carpets into which the feet sank so that no sound could be heard but the rustling of her silk dress. She told the dog to lie down and showed him the whip. Then, turning to me, she said, 'Don't be alarmed Princess, the dog is quite tame. Would you not like to see my monkeys?' 'No, thank you', I exclaimed hastily, fearing that she might bring them in. My only wish* was to escape into God's air and light out of this menagerie. Suddenly, with muffled steps, a Sart appeared carrying a cup of chocolate, though the weather was boiling. This reception bordered on the grotesque, and she told me, by way of consolation, that a bear she had in her possession nearly devoured her a short while before, and she was obliged to give it to the Zoological gardens. I beat my retreat from this extraordinary house of pleasure."[116]

The final decade of the Grand Duke's life played out in the peculiar routine of his life in Tashkent; he worked tirelessly to improve the agricultural, financial and cultural circumstances of the city, and, a fond paterfamilias, he watched his five children grow up. At the time of the Revolution, Prince Alexander Iskander, Grand Duke Nicholas's second son with Nadezhda Dreyer, was living in St Petersburg with his first wife, Olga Iosifovna Rogovskaya. Alexander Nikolaievich had been allowed to join the Blue Cuirassiers Life Guards Regiment in St Petersburg, and, his paternity well-known, he moved freely through aristocratic circles.[117] Prince Alexander married Olga Iosifovna in Tashkent in May 1912, and two years later, Grand Duke Nicholas's first grandchild, Kirill, was born on 5 December 1914. The baby prince was named Prince Romanovsky-Iskander. On 21 January 1917, Kirill was joined in the Iskander nursery by his small sister Nathalia. Grand Duke Nicholas was delighted with this welcome news.

A scant six weeks later, Nicholas also welcomed news of the Revolution, and the collapse of the Romanov Dynasty. Certain that Russia's best days now lay ahead, the Grand Duke happily attended revolutionary meetings in Tashkent, suggesting reforms and offering financial assistance; he also sent a cable of congratulations to Alexander Kerensky on the latter's assumption of control of the Provisional Government.[118]

Having thrown in his lot with the Bolsheviks and publicly supported their regime, he was largely ignored in Tashkent, but he was not to enjoy the new regime for long. For many years, Nicholas was – if referred to at all – described as the first Romanov executed by the Bolsheviks.[119] The truth, however, was less dramatic. In the winter of 1918, Nicholas Konstantinovich fell ill with pneumonia; the illness progressed rapidly, and he died in his palace in Tashkent on 13/26 January 1918, in the arms of Darya, his illegitimate daughter by Chasovitinova.[120] He was sixty-eight. He had the singular distinction among the imperial family of being the only member of the former Dynasty to be given a full, state funeral by the Bolsheviks. On the day of the ceremony, thousands of people crowded the streets of Tashkent to pay their respects, and an escort of Bolshevik soldiers formed a guard-of-honor that surrounded his coffin as it lay in state in the Cathedral of the Transfiguration in the city. The most decorated and fierce revolutionaries were picked to lower his body into a special vault in the Cathedral at the end of the service.[121]

Nicholas Konstantinovich had been the most troublesome and singular member of his generation of Grand Dukes; a man tormented by his own brilliant and excitable mind; a forward thinking liberal in a conservative, reactionary dynasty. He was ultimately a victim of his time and his circumstances, neither of which allowed for the change he craved. When the Revolution brought about this change, it was fortunate that Nicholas did not live to see it, for it swept up his beloved family and destroyed them.

On the orders of Emperor Alexander III, Nicholas had not been permitted contact with his first and illegitimate family with Alexandra Abaza Demidova. Alexandra herself, having been forbidden to travel to the province where Nicholas was exiled, lived quietly in straitened circumstances in the Crimea, where she eventually met and married Count Paul Sumarokov-Elston, brother of Zenaida Youssoupov's husband, Felix. Count Paul generously agreed to raise Grand Duke Nicholas's children, Nicholas and Olga, as his own, and he proved himself to be a wonderful stepfather. Following Alexandra's death from tuberculosis at Koreiz in 1894, Count Paul applied to Alexander III for assistance with the children's nebulous social and legal status. The Emperor granted the children the name of Volinsky, changed their legal status, and allowed them to enter into the upper reaches of Russian society.[122]

Nicholas Volinsky attended several cadet academies in St Petersburg, after which he joined the Imperial Guard as a Sub-Lieutenant in the Emperor's Own Cuirassiers Regiment. During the Russo-Japanese War, he was promoted to Captain of the 2nd Regiment of the Nertchinsk Cossacks, serving in the Trans-Baikal Region along the Trans-Siberian Railway. Nicholas II granted Volinsky the rights of a hereditary noble within the Empire, further cementing his place in genteel society.[123] Nicholas Volinsky predeceased his father the Grand Duke, dying either in 1913 in Italy or in 1914 while fighting with his regiment in the First World War.[124]

Olga Volinsky also died young. In her youth, she began to exhibit signs of mental illness, and after the death of her mother her behavior grew more bizarre and unstable. Although Count Paul continued to look after her in the Crimea while pursuing every possible cure, eventually her insanity became obvious to everyone. Considered a danger to herself and to others, she was sent to Germany, where she was committed to asylum. Here, in 1910, she died, lost in a haze of madness.[125]

Darya Chasovitinova, the Grand Duke's Cossack paramour, apparently died in 1922 in Tashkent. Her three children with the Grand Duke suffered varied fates. Sviatoslav was executed at the age of eighteen by the Bolsheviks in the midst of the Civil War, while his brother Nicholas choked to death on fumes from a stove left burning in his mother's house one winter night in 1922. Their sister Darya, in whose arms Nicholas Konstantinovich had died, left Turkestan and settled in Moscow, where she died at the age of seventy in 1966.[126]

Nadezhda Dreyer survived her husband by a decade, years in which the goodwill of the Bolsheviks toward the Grand Duke dissipated as memories faded and the Civil War took hold. In 1919, Prince Artemi Iskander died while fighting with the White Army in the Civil War, and his involvement with the anti-Bolshevik forces was to have dire consequences for his mother. In early 1920 the Bolsheviks confiscated the Grand Duke's Palace, forcing Nadezhda to leave her home.[127] She died in 1929 from poverty and exposure.[128]

Prince Alexander Iskander was more fortunate than his siblings and half-siblings. At some point in these difficult years, he divorced his wife Olga and, leaving her and his two young children amidst the chaos of Soviet Russia, fled to Europe. Here, he married a second time, in Paris on 11 October 1930, to Nathalia Konstantinovna Khanykova, a thirty-seven-year-old émigré from St Petersburg. The couple had no children. He died in Grasse, France, on 26 January 1957 – ironically the thirty-ninth anniversary of his father's death in Tashkent.

Alexander's first wife, Olga, took her two children to Moscow where, in an effort to conceal their Romanov origins in the new Soviet Union, she remarried and changed their surname to that of her new husband, Androsov. A neighbor soon learned their true identity, however, and threatened to report them to the GPU; in terror, the family was forced to flee, hiding themselves in a shabby basement flat on Moscow's Arbat.[129] Olga was among the millions of nameless Russians who disappeared during Stalin's purges in the 1930s. Her son, Prince Kirill Romanovsky-Iskander, slipped quietly into obscurity before his death in Moscow in 1992. Her daughter, Princess Nathalia, spent much of her life hiding in plain sight while performing in a circus as a trick motorcyclist, and became famous for her fantastic stunts. During her career, she took many falls and endured many accidents, yet enjoyed great popularity, assisted by her great beauty and penchant for posing in studio publicity portraits dressed as a man.[130]

Given her fame, it is not surprising that the KGB approached her and asked her to work on their behalf; the Princess first refused, then – perhaps recognizing the tenuous nature of her position as a Romanov descendant in the Soviet Union and the threats that she would be shot if she did not cooperate – changed her mind.[131] In the 1990s, with the fall of the Soviet Union, Princess Nathalia again enjoyed a measure of celebrity, as curious journalists sought her out and told her remarkable story in newspapers, magazines, and in books. In 1998, she was one of the guests who attended the burial service in St Petersburg for the remains of Nicholas II and his family. Princess Nathalia had married Nicholas Dostal in the 1940s. On 24 July 1999, she died in Moscow, the last of Nicholas Konstantinovich's line.

Grand Duke Konstantin Konstantinovich (1858-1915)

By Greg King, Penny Wilson & Arturo E. Beéche

*I*n the midst of these upheavals, the life of one member of the Konstantinovichi family was – much to the satisfaction of Alexander III – settling in to expected routine. Of all the Romanov Grand Dukes, Konstantin Konstantinovich never gave cause for worry or speculation; never offered critics of the Dynasty any ammunition; never found himself at the center of unwelcome gossip; nor was he even, as with his somewhat staid brother Dimitri, the object of polite mockery. And yet, ironically, it is in the life of the irreproachable Konstantin Konstantinovich that one finds one of the most closely-held secrets of the Romanov Dynasty.

Grand Duke Konstantin Konstantinovich was perhaps the most capable and intelligent of all the Romanovs in the last generation to rule. He was born on Sunday, August 10/22, 1858, at five in the morning in the Palace at Strelna on the Gulf of Finland. Three days after his birth, his father wrote proudly to his brother Alexander II that, *"everything here is going well, thank God,"* and adding, *"my wife's milk has begun to appear now; her breasts are full, though swollen a good deal which makes her rather uncomfortable."* As for the baby, Konstantin Nikolaievich declared, *"Our little Kostia is doing well, and spends the days in bed with his mother."*[1] The baby's christening was delayed for nearly seven weeks, and only took place on Friday, 26 September/8 October 1858. His godparents included his uncle and aunt, Emperor Alexander II and Empress Marie Alexandrovna; at his christening ceremony, he was endowed with a number of Imperial orders, signifying what would become a life of service: the Order of St Andrei, the Order of St Alexander Nevsky, the Order of the White Eagle, and the Order of St Anna.[2]

According to the dictates of his father, Grand Duke Konstantin Nikolaievich, Konstantin – like all of his brothers and sisters – received a comprehensive, liberal education. His first nanny was an Englishwoman, following the trend of the day that embraced all things British. Assisting her was Varvara Mikhailov, the daughter of one of Grand Duke Konstantin Nikolaievich's servants, who assumed general charge of the children's early instruction when the English nanny left.[3] As a young boy, he was particularly close to his Mikhailovichi cousins, the Grand Dukes Nicholas, Michael, Alexander, and George, as well as Alexander II's youngest son Grand Duke Paul. Grand Duke Peter, youngest son of Grand Duke Nicholas Nikolaievich Sr., also became a close confidant; with his mother having abandoned St Petersburg for a convent in Kiev and his father completely absorbed in his affair with a ballerina, the young Peter often spent many months living with the Konstantin Family in the Marble Palace and at Pavlovsk. Of all of these cousins, however, Konstantin Konstantinovich was perhaps closest to Grand Duke Serge Alexandrovich; the two children often shared lessons, and were instructed together in the Orthodox Faith by Abbot Leonid of the Savvino-Storozhevsk Monastery.[4]

This instruction was to have a lasting effect on both boys, who grew up pious and embraced the role of religion in their daily lives. It is a curious aspect of their histories that both Grand Dukes shared so many commonalities, even as young men: they were artistic, well-read, and exceptionally taken with the practice of Orthodoxy. Later, both cousins would deal with their homosexuality in vastly different ways, but in a manner that left little doubt as to the pervasive influence of Abbot Leonid as they struggled to remain true to themselves and to their deeply held faith.

When he was seven, Konstantin Konstantinovich was given a male tutor, who was placed in general charge of his educational career, and who brought specialists in history, the sciences, literature, civil law, religion, and politics, to the palace to lecture his young charge. A host of tutors and teachers followed over the years: instructors in the Russian language, as well as tutors in German, French, and English; a piano teacher, who gave lessons twice weekly; and a master who drilled the young Grand Duke in the dances considered necessary social skills.

With Grand Duke Konstantin Nikolaievich's deep love of the sea, it was perhaps inevitable that he would enlist all of his sons in the Imperial Navy. The young Grand Duke Konstantin was duly entered as a cadet in the Imperial Naval Academy, but he generally received his lessons away from the other pupils at the hands of Lieutenant N. A. Zelenoy, who served as his father's Fligel-Adjutant. He was allowed to attend general lectures with the rest of the cadets only on special occasions. He duly went to sea when he was twelve, serving aboard several training ships and frigates. Lengthy reports on his progress arrived regularly at the Marble Palace: *"Following prayers at 9AM,"* reported Konstantin Konstantinovich's minder, *"I asked the Grand Duke to repeat what he had learnt before. He made several mistakes but on the whole it was quite decent. After lunch, from 2 to 4PM, the Grand Duke trained with the 2nd Cadet Team. The Grand Duke's health is always excellent. His face is brown up to his eyes and his cheeks are rosy."*[5]

In 1874, when he was sixteen, Konstantin Konstantinovich joined the crew of *HMS Reefer*.[6] A year later, he was appointed to the frigate *Svetlana*, commanded by his cousin Grand Duke Alexis Alexandrovich, for an extended voyage through Europe and the Mediterranean, during which he visited various ports in Denmark, England, Spain, Italy, and Greece. By 1876, on reaching his eighteenth birthday, Konstantin was promoted to Midshipman under the command of Rear Admiral Grigory Butakov, who assumed control of *Svetlana* in preparation of a possible war against the Ottoman Empire.[7]

These voyages, while interesting, did nothing to awaken in Konstantin Konstantinovich an appreciation for the sea, and although the young man endured the continued course of training for the sake of his father, he could muster no real passion for life at sea. Worse still, he often suffered from debilitating sea-sickness, a condition he never managed to overcome.[8] His experience in the Navy, however, had sharpened Konstantin Konstantinovich's social skills. Lady Augusta Stanley, visiting Russia in 1874, found herself seated next to him at a dinner. He was, she wrote, *"an enchanting companion;"* he was *"very good looking,"* she said, *"very clever, and quite un homme du monde."*[9]

The young Grand Duke struck all whom he encountered as a serious, dutiful young man. But his dedication was to the ideal of expected service, rather than to his father's personal dream that his sons follow in his love of the sea. It is ironic that of the three sons who lived to adulthood – Nicholas, Konstantin, and Dimitri – all three, even though enrolled at birth in the Imperial Navy, later chose to join the Imperial Army and thus ignore the wishes of their father. By the time he was twenty, Konstantin Konstantinovich had reached his decision and, pulling together his courage, he told his father of his wish, as his brother Nicholas had done before him, and his brother Dimitri was to do after him. In this move, all three sons were supported by their mother, who perhaps relished the opportunity to side against the husband who was, at the time, engaged in his very public humiliation of her with his affair with Kuznetsova.

Konstantin Konstantinovich duly won his battle with his strong-willed father, and joined the Imperial Army at the age of eighteen. He served first with the Izmailovsky

Life Guards Regiment; by the age of twenty, he had risen to the rank of Colonel-in-Chief of the 15th Tiflis Grenadiers Life Guards Regiment, with whom he saw action during the Russo-Turkish War of 1877-78.[10] During the campaign, his regiment was dispatched to the front in the Danube basin, and the Grand Duke came under enemy fire several times, *"responding with exceptional calm and bravery,"* as one military official reported. *"In his actions, His Imperial Highness served as an inspiration to his men, refusing to accept defeat."* On 3 October 1877, he participated in the successful bombardment of a Turkish steamer in the midst of a heavy round of hostile artillery fire. His quick thinking and action won him the praise of his superiors, and in recognition of his act, Alexander II awarded him the Cross of the Order of St George, 4th Class.[11] It was the young Grand Duke's first and only taste of military battle, and one that left him profoundly affected.

By his twentieth birthday in 1878, Konstantin was made an Adjutant-General to his uncle Alexander II and, on Sunday, 26 November/8 December 1878, the Grand Duke took his Oath of Allegiance to the Emperor in the Cathedral of the Winter Palace as his father and mother looked on. He also took an Oath of Allegiance to the Armed Forces.[12] Shortly after this, he joined the famed Preobrajensky Life Guards Regiment, with whom he would continue his military career and obligations until his death. But the Grand Duke was not merely content to lead the pleasant, often aimless and debauched life of a young aristocratic officer. During his tenure in the Izmailovsky Life Guards, he founded the Izmailovsky Dossugui, or Literary Society, through which he began to impose his own cultivated and artistic tastes. Given the motto, *"Valor, Purity, and Beauty,"* the Society was a distinctly non-military organization: its emblem, designed by Konstantin Konstantinovich himself, depicted an officers' saber piercing a lyre, the whole ringed with flowers.[13]

Whether in barracks in St Petersburg, or on maneuvers at the military camp of Krasnoe Selo just outside of the Imperial capital, the Society regularly met each week in sessions presided over by the Grand Duke, spending their time discussing Russian literature and poetry; it was on these evenings, surrounded by his most trusted and sympathetic comrades, that the Grand Duke first began to publicly offer up his own fledgling examples of poetry. The admiration and warm response they drew convinced him to seriously pursue his literary talents.[14]

The Society did not stop with Russian literature and poetry, however. Soon, the works of Russia's great playwrights were also commonly discussed, and eventually a small troupe of amateur actors, drawn from the Izmailovsky Regiment, began to act selected scenes from assorted comedies and dramas. When they had reached a satisfactory level of skill, these performances were extended to complete plays, enacted before audiences composed of their fellow soldiers. At first, men took all of the roles, often appearing in full costume as the women characters, but as their confidence grew, the Grand Duke invited actresses from the Imperial Dramatic Corps to join in their presentations. These activities left the young Grand Duke with two burgeoning talents: That of a poet, and that of a capable and gifted actor – qualities he would later put triumphant use. *"Everyone who was anybody,"* recalled a contemporary, *"felt eager to be present, and invitations were eagerly sought."*[15]

By 1884, Grand Duke Konstantin Konstantinovich was a tall young man, standing six-feet-four-inches, thin, with auburn hair, deep blue eyes, and a trim beard and mustache. *"In appearance,"* wrote one contemporary, *"he resembles his father, though he has a much finer and more delicate countenance."*[16] Baroness Sophie Buxhoeveden recalled him as *"very good looking, with his mother's regular features and the short fair beard of a Renaissance portrait. He was the member of the Imperial Family with the most all round culture and a patron* of all arts."[17] Another contemporary called him *"one of the simplest men, and although of imposing presence, was most unassuming in his manner. Always amiable, he had the gift of placing those he conversed with completely at their ease."*[18]

He had traveled widely, not only to Europe, but also to Greece, North Africa, and Palestine. But it was his time spent in Italy in 1882 that was to have the most profound effect on the young man. Visiting Rome, Venice, Florence, and Palermo, he absorbed the country's rich artistic heritage and beauty, capturing his impressions in a number of vivid poems. The Grand Duke was becoming a deeply artistic, cultivated man. He adored the famous *Wanderers* school of painters, and *Night on the Dneiper* by Arkhip Kuindzhi, which hung in his study, was his favorite.[19] Like his father, Konstantin was an adept musician, and especially enjoyed performing Chopin on the piano. But more often than not, he could be found sitting in his study, immersed in a book and surrounded by a swirl of smoke from his favorite cigars.[20]

That same year – 1882 – during a visit to his mother's native Saxe-Altenburg, Konstantin met Princess Elisabeth Auguste Marie Agnes, daughter of Prince Moritz of Saxe-Altenburg and his wife Auguste, formerly a Princess of Saxe-Meiningen. Born on Wednesday, 25 January 1865 in Meiningen, the seventeen-year-old Princess was a slim young woman with a long neck and narrow waist, and light brown hair coiled in a fringe atop her head. The Grand Duke's mother, Alexandra Iosifovna, pushed the pair toward marriage; Princess Elisabeth seemed amenable enough to the idea, but Konstantin Konstantinovich was less certain. It took nearly two years for the young Grand Duke to finally work up the courage to propose. He could have remained a bachelor, but family pressure on him was enormous; by this time, his brother Nicholas Konstantinovich had been living in disgrace in exile for ten years, and there was little doubt that his father's estates would devolve upon Konstantin – a fact that would necessitate heirs. Expectation may have pushed the Grand Duke toward a proposal. In the end, it is difficult to say what his true feelings about Elisabeth may have been.

In 1883, Grand Duke Konstantin Konstantinovich returned to Saxe-Altenburg. In the time that had passed, he had maintained a correspondence with Elisabeth, and had even written several poems about her as he tried to come to terms with the idea of marriage. When he finally worked up the courage to propose, Princess Elisabeth accepted. Six months later, she came to Russia for her wedding. Grand Duke Konstantin Konstantinovich, accompanied by his mother, went to the German border to collect her and bring her back to St Petersburg aboard a special train. *"Within just a few minutes,"* he wrote in his diary, *"Elisabeth was in Russia. She saw for the first time a Russian Church and was especially impressed with the simplicity of the people. I latched myself close to her side, and watched the Honor Guard with her and Mama. We wrote telegrams, ran quickly back and forth, had lunch at midday, and wrote more hurried telegrams."* His fiancée, Konstantin noted, *"was very tired, and slept closely against me with her head on my chest. In the last little bit of time, she must have much to handle."*[21]

Elisabeth refused to convert to Russian Orthodoxy. Although she wished to marry Konstantin, she apparently said she would abandon the marriage if conversion were forced upon her. *"She was very religious,"* her son Gabriel later wrote, *"and believed very sincerely in God. Her faith became one of the things that supported her through the years."*[22]

Alexander III did not require that Elisabeth renounce her faith, making clear that any children born of the union would nevertheless be considered members of the Imperial House and would retain full succession rights. She was granted the title of Grand Duchess Elisabeth Mavrikievna, with the style of Imperial Highness, but her title was not preceded with the customary appellation of Blagovernaya, or *"The Truly*

Believing," as a reminder that she had not converted. Her decision caused a great deal of consternation in the Imperial Family, and especially to her fiancé. On their journey back to St Petersburg, as he noted his diary, *"I argued with her, and she listened to my reasoning that one cannot fully serve a people without being at one with their customs. She said that God has not thus far moved her to convert, and so she won't. I wanted her to note that this makes me sad, so sad that I don't know what to do with all my grief, except to pray to God. Was there ever such a heavy blow? I am reminded that I promised myself earlier that I would not marry someone of another faith."*[23]

The Grand Duke, as he confessed to his diary, was terribly worried over how his sister, Queen Olga of the Hellenes, would take this news, and how she would treat Elisabeth. *"I am afraid,"* he wrote, *"that our Olya will not like her so much."* In Konstantin's eyes, Elisabeth compounded her error by admitting that, since their engagement, she had become very close to his aunt, Grand Duchess Vera, and that *"she likes very much Vera's German point of view. That was to me very disagreeable and unpleasant, although I must see that this is completely understandable, and that her honesty is praiseworthy."*[24]

The train bearing the Grand Duke and his fiancée arrived in St Petersburg on Tuesday, 10 April 1884. At Gatchina, they were met by Queen Olga and Dimitri Konstantinovich, who presented Elisabeth with a bouquet of flowers tied with a ribbon that bore the inscription: *"From Your Future Cousins."* As they neared the capital, Elisabeth changed into a white dress, *"in which,"* Konstantin noted, *"she looked fine."* A band played the German and Russian National Anthems as the train pulled into St Petersburg; along the platform stood a Guard-of-Honor of the Izmailovsky Life Guards Regiment, and Alexander III and all of the members of the Imperial Family. The Emperor greeted the Princess by kissing her hand, and saying, *"Permit me to wish you welcome. I am very glad to make your acquaintance,"* while Marie Feodorovna embraced and kissed her.[25]

The couple drove through the streets of St Petersburg to the Marble Palace, where Grand Duke Konstantin Nikolaievich waited to greet his future daughter-in-law; he was, wrote his son, *"sick and weak, with swollen cheeks."* Elisabeth, Konstantin noted, *"passed all these tests well by behaving simply, even the one with Olya [Olga], which I had been worried about, and which was very important to me."* The couple then went to the Palace Church, where Archimandrite Ioann waited with a Golden Cross to bless them. *"With pounding heart,"* Konstantin later wrote, *"I waited to see what would happen. After the Sovereign, the Empress, and all the senior members of the family, Mama and Papa paid their obeisance to the Cross. But Elisabeth did not. For me, this was bitter, hurtful and sickening. All saw, and recognized her refusal, and this gave the entire congregation pause for thought on this painful moment. The short service was soon ended, and we of the Orthodox Faith again kissed the Cross, including the Lutheran Marie Pavlovna [Grand Duchess Vladimir]. All alone, Elisabeth bowed her head, and kissed it not. Olya and I stood there shamefaced, and let our heads hang."*[26]

A reception followed in the Palace's Marble Hall, during which Alexander III and Marie Feodorovna presented Elisabeth with a magnificent diamond and sapphire necklace. But for Konstantin Konstantinovich, the day had been hopelessly spoiled by his fiancée's refusal to kiss the Cross. As soon as the members of the Imperial Family departed, he sent for a Lutheran Minister, Father Findeisen, *"in whom we placed our trust and hope."* His talk with the Princess, the Grand Duke wrote, *"Brought about a concession. He told her that she could kiss the Cross, and that this only meant that she was paying homage to the Country and customs of her people, and not that she embraced the Orthodox Religion. This eased our concerns somewhat."*[27]

Elisabeth tried to reassure her fiancé of her deep devotion. On the morning of their wedding, she dispatched a short letter to him, in which she told Konstantin that she had prayed for him the previous night, and asked that God would grant him understanding to respect her decision to remain a Lutheran. Her refusal to convert, she declared, had nothing to do with her love for him, which she said was far greater than she could ever convey in writing. *"I pledge to you that I will do nothing to hurt or anger you because of our different religions,"* she wrote, adding that she would try, for his sake, to understand the sacraments of his Church. She ended: *"Yours, today, and for the rest of my life."*[28]

The wedding took place on Sunday, 15/27 April 1884, in St Petersburg. The pair was united in two ceremonies. The Orthodox service, conducted by Father Ioann Yanishev, took place in the Cathedral of the Winter Palace, and was immediately followed by a Lutheran service in the Palace's Alexander Hall. Konstantin wore the Parade uniform of the Izmailovsky Life Guards Regiment, while Elisabeth, he noted, "was very beautiful, in diamonds under a small, diamond-covered crown." The Grand Duke wrote: *"After the words, 'Our Lord and God', before You and this entire company I marry this couple, 'I saw Elisabeth already as my wife, whom I should care for, love, and embrace for life. The moment the priest led us to the altar was particularly solemn for me. I felt light and free."* It was, he said, *"as if a stone has rolled from my heart."*[29]

For the first few years of their married life, the couple settled into a quiet routine. The new Grand Duchess was a beautiful, vibrant young woman. Called "Mavra" within the Imperial Family, and "Lilinka" by her husband, she was not particularly intelligent, but she was stubborn and willful, and in time, her refusal to change her religion led to much resentment within the Imperial Family as well as within the country at large.[30] She regularly attended her own services at the Lutheran Church in Tsarskoe Selo. Reportedly her refusal to convert to Orthodoxy angered other members of the Imperial Family, but Elisabeth resisted all the pressures on her, finding in her faith the strength and comfort necessary to face the uncertain years ahead.

The nine children of Konstantin Konstantinovich were raised in an atmosphere of liberal education and duty and respect for their position in life. Although they studied English, German, and French, the latter under Professor Bailly Comte of the University of St Petersburg, their father was careful to insist that only Russian should be spoken in the household, and that the nursery should be staffed by Russian women.[31]

The Konstantinovichi children were considered delicate in their childhood, and the elder sons, in particular, seem to have been rather sick when they were young. Even into their youths, Ioann and Gabriel suffered from various illnesses that often made them the object of jokes among members of the Imperial Family. Baroness Sophie Buxhoeveden, who often played with the Konstantinovichi children, later recalled: *"Alas, I knocked them down and maltreated them sadly, for they were puny, weedy little fellows, still treated as babies in the nursery, while I was a lusty damsel of nearly six, and tall and strong for my age."*[32] And Grand Duchess Marie Pavlovna, who – with her brother Dimitri Pavlovich – often visited Pavlovsk, recalled: *"We went sleigh riding with the boys, and as we were much more enterprising than our cousins, our animation added to the occasion."*[33]

Ioann and Gabriel Konstantinovich, in particular, were both often sick, and together spent more than a year of their childhood living at Oreanda in the Crimea with a doctor and several servants. Their health improved in the climate, and the boys enjoyed their time spent on the beaches and in short tours around the peninsula. The time spent with only each other for company forged a strong sibling relationship that was to last to the ends of their lives.[34]

Despite the drawback of their delicate health, but partly because they were being strictly brought up, the Konstantinovichi children were among the very few Romanovs whom Empress Alexandra Feodorovna accepted as playmates for her own children. The English periodical *The Tatler* noted in an issue early in 1906 that Grand Duke Konstantin Konstantinovich's children were the favorite cousins of the Emperor's children, and the ones most often to be found in their company.[35] On these visits to the Alexander Palace at Tsarskoe Selo, Gabriel Konstantinovich, at least, took in Empress Alexandra's redecorations with a critical eye. He noted that the wood paneling, art nouveau-style cozy corners, and multitude of chintz and patterned fabrics *"did not at all fit the style of the Alexander Palace, which had been uniformly built along classical, Empire-style lines."*[36]

In 1908, Grand Duke Konstantin Konstantinovich recorded in his diary: *"Our little ones were invited to tea with the Emperor's children. Igor went too. Little Anastasia was thrilled with him, kept calling him a nice little boy, and gave him flowers when they said good-bye."*[37]

Other family occasions, however, left a less pleasant impression. After his wife lunched with the Imperial Family, Grand Duke Konstantin Konstantinovich recorded Tsarevich Alexis's bad behavior in his diary: *"He wouldn't sit up, ate badly, licked his plate, and teased the others. The Emperor often turned away, perhaps to avoid having to say anything, while the Empress rebuked her elder daughter Olga, who sat next to her brother, for not restraining him. But Olga cannot deal with him."*[38]

Grand Duchess Elisabeth Mavrikievna was, recalled Serge Smirnov, *"a dedicated mother."*[39] To the nurseries at the Marble Palace and Pavlovsk she brought a sense of Teutonic efficiency, installing a German nanny, Angelika Klein, whom the children called *"Ika."*[40] One of the reasons that the censorious Empress Alexandra Feodorovna readily welcomed the Konstantinovichi children into her own home was that she and Elisabeth Mavrikievna shared similar attitudes and outlooks. Both doted on their children, and both attempted to transplant traditional, homey values from their native Germany into their Russian homes.

Konstantin was a loving but strict father and, as his son Gabriel recalled, all of his children were frightened of him, more as imposing, worshipful presence than as a stern man. He wanted his children to grow up independent, with spirit and responsibility. The children all regularly visited him in his study each day, a room that, remembered his son Gabriel, *"always smelled so nice from his lovely cigars."*[41] The Grand Duke was not a distant father: there were no bows or handshakes, but rather hugs, as he swept his children up in his arms or held their hands with his long, bejeweled fingers.[42] For his eldest son Ioann, these early visits proved to be something of an ordeal. The Grand Duke kept a large bearskin rug on the floor in front of his desk, and each time the young Prince saw it, he burst into screams and ran wildly from the room, incidents that his father mercilessly teased him over in his later life.[43]

Prince Ioann Konstantinovich was the eldest of Grand Duke Konstantin Konstantinovich and Grand Duchess Elisabeth Mavrikievna's children. He was born on the morning of Monday, 23 June/5 July 1886, at Pavlovsk. During the labor, the Grand Duke nervously smoked in his bathroom, and read *The Thoughts of Marcus Aurelius*. As he waited for news, he noticed that he had simply thrown on the white shirt he had worn the previous day; King Ludwig II of Bavaria had died mysteriously only ten days earlier, and the shirt bore a broad black mourning band around its left sleeve. Noticing this, Konstantin – as he later confided in his diary – wondered if he should have worn such an ill-omen on what was a happy personal occasion.[44] Nevertheless, the wearing of this mourning shirt became for the Grand Duke a peculiar ritual, and he put it on to sit through the births of all his children.⁴⁵

At Konstantin Nikolaievich's request, the new baby was given the Slavic name Ioann – the first time the name had been used in the Imperial Family for hundreds of years.⁴⁶ Konstantin Konstantinovich and Elisabeth Mavrikievna would follow this pattern with their other children. Called "Ioannchik" within the family, Ioann was the first child born into the Imperial Family after Alexander III's Ukase restricting the title of Grand Duke or Grand Duchess to the children and grandchildren of an Emperor; had he been born a year earlier, he would thus have been Grand Duke Ioann Konstantinovich. His mother – and indeed, all of the Konstantinovichi – was clearly irritated, believing that the Emperor's decision had come about owing to the proliferation of sons born to Grand Duke Michael Nikolaievich. In a letter to her father, Elisabeth Mavrikievna complained: *"Our first thought was also the marriage contract! It certainly is clear on the religion of the children, but has nothing about rank! The whole cousinship stands upon the oath of allegiance document, wherein the one who signs before, though of the same rank, takes precedence before the same Heir dies. There is a law from Emperor Paul concerning our grandsons. Alas! But it came out that the previous Emperor had already thought of it. It comes because of the many Mikhailovichi. Therefore, our children will not be Romanovs, but instead will be called Princes of Russia – Kniyaz Rossiya. That is still a consolation, otherwise it would have sounded too morganatic. Alexandra Iosifovna is entirely infuriated and wants to say to you that she no more burns for the Emperor as she once did. In the beginning, I was very indignant, but I say to myself now: Dear, ordinary, worthy Princes, and not worthless Grand Dukes. In public, people are highly dissatisfied with the Ukase. It is not only against the finances, but against the masses that we are losing prestige. The Emperor allowed Alexandra Iosifovna to send him a message through Minny, which she did, telling him that he was making strangers of us. And also, that despite whatever he says, we are still royalty!"*⁴⁷

In keeping with his ukase, Alexander III issued a manifesto on 3/15 July that proclaimed Ioann Konstantinovich to be a Prince of the Imperial Blood, with the style of His Highness.⁴⁸ A week later, on Friday, 11/23 July, the new Prince was christened in a ceremony conducted in the Church of Pavlovsk Palace. The ceremony began at half-past one in the afternoon, and was conducted by Father Ioann Yanishev, Personal Confessor to the Emperor and Empress. At his christening, the names of Ioann's illustrious string of godparents was read out, and included Alexander III; his great aunt Olga Nikolaievna, Queen of Württemberg; his grandfather, Grand Duke Konstantin Nikolaievich; his aunt Olga, Queen of the Hellenes; and from his mother's family the Duke of Saxe-Altenburg; the Dowager Duchess of Saxe-Meiningen; his grandfather Prince Moritz of Saxe-Altenburg; and his aunt the Hereditary Princess of Schaumburg-Lippe.⁴⁹

Ioann, recalled his brother Gabriel, was *"a nervous child,"* prone to fits of weeping and uncontrollable fear.⁵⁰ He eventually grew out of this and, in September 1900, at the age of fourteen, Ioann Konstantinovich was inducted into 1st Cadet Corps, under his father's supervision.⁵¹ On Sunday, 6/19 January 1908, Prince Ioann took his Oath of Allegiance to Nicholas II and the Imperial Army in the Church of the Catherine Palace at Tsarskoe Selo; this came when Ioann was twenty-two, a rather late age, for other members of the Imperial Family usually took their Majority Oaths when they turned twenty.⁵² He joined the Chevalier Life Guards Regiment, fulfilling the military duties expected of him, though the Prince's true passion lay elsewhere.⁵³

Ioann was a quiet, sensitive, unpretentious young man, given to solitude and reflection.⁵⁴ He was also deeply religious, often talked of renouncing his title and taking monastic vows and his brothers regularly teased him over his piety.⁵⁵ Such a vocation would probably have suited the rather ordinary-looking Prince, whose only notable physical feature was his extreme thinness coupled with his great height, which made him look rather like a column in one of his father's palaces.[56]

Three years later, much to the surprise of the Imperial Family, Ioann married. His bride was Princess Elena Petrovna, daughter of King Peter I of Serbia, of the Karageorgievich Dynasty; her mother, Zorka Lyubika, had formerly been a Princess of Montenegro. She was supposedly the same age as her future husband, officially having been born on 23 October 1886, at Rijeka, Serbia; there is, however, some dispute about this, and conflicting accounts also record her birth as having taken place on 4 November 1884, making her two years older than Ioann Konstantinovich. The Princess, niece to both Grand Duchess Militza and her sister Grand Duchess Anastasia, daughters of King Nicholas I of Montenegro, had been brought to Russia under their protection, to be educated, as they had been, at St Petersburg's Smolny Institute for Young Ladies of Noble Birth, after the premature death of her mother.

It was apparently another of the Montenegrin sisters, Elena, who became Queen of Italy, who arranged the initial meeting between her niece and Prince Ioann, inviting both to a carefully contrived party at which the pair was thrown together all evening. The Princess had a fine figure and features, though her head was rather large and sat somewhat uneasily above slender shoulders; in personality she tended to be headstrong and somewhat domineering. But Ioann was clearly taken with her, and much to the surprise of his family rather quickly proposed, an offer the ambitious young Elena accepted with equal alacrity. On learning of the news, Nicholas II wrote to his mother: *"How did you like Ioannchik's engagement to the daughter of the King of Serbia? It happened like a flash of lightning! I should think it must be a risky thing to marry Ioannchik, he ought to become a monk, which he himself talked of doing."*[57]

The marriage was celebrated on Sunday, 21 August/3 September 1911, in the Church of the Grand Palace at Peterhof in the presence of most of the Imperial Family. A reception and banquet followed, given by Dimitri Konstantinovich in the Marble Hall at Strelna just down the Gulf of Finland; the palace had not yet been electrified, so the guests dined in the light of a thousand candles shimmering in the ormolu chandeliers above. In the middle of the banquet, however, the candles – which had been put in too haphazardly and quickly – began first to drip and then fall onto the guests, a few at the beginning, and ending with a fiery torrent that eventually sent the guests fleeing the room.[58] After the marriage, the young couple moved into apartments in the Marble Palace. Ioann returned to his Horse Guards Regiment, while Elena, always independent, announced that she intended to study medicine at the University of St Petersburg in order to become a doctor.[59]

This ambition was cut short when the Princess became pregnant in the summer of 1913. On the evening of Tuesday, 7/20 January 1914, she gave birth to a son, Vsevelod Ioannovich, in the Marble Palace. In a manifesto issued on Wednesday, 8/21 January 1914, Nicholas II decreed Vsevelod to be a Highness and a Prince of the Imperial Blood; four days later, the Emperor, along with his wife Alexandra and his mother, Dowager Empress Marie Feodorovna, attended the Prince's christening, in a late afternoon service conducted in the Chapel of the Marble Palace by Father Kedrinsky, Personal Confessor the Imperial couple.[60] Along with the boy's grandmother Grand Duchess Elisabeth Mavrikievna, Nicholas II was appointed one of his godparents.[61]

The second of Grand Duke Konstantin Konstantinovich's children, Prince Gabriel, was born on the afternoon of Thursday, 2/14 July 1887, in the State Bedroom of Empress Marie Feodorovna, consort of Paul I, at Pavlovsk. Three days later, Alexander

III issued a manifesto announcing his title as a Prince of the Imperial Blood with the style of Highness.⁶² He was christened on the early afternoon of Monday, 29 July/9 August 1887, in the Palace Church at Pavlovsk by Father Ioann Yanishev. His godparents included Alexander III; King George of the Hellenes; his grandmother Grand Duchess Alexandra Iosifovna; his aunt Grand Duchess Vera Konstantinovna, Duchess of Württemberg; his uncle Grand Duke Dimitri Konstantinovich; the Duke of Saxe-Meiningen; the Duchess of Saxe-Altenburg; his maternal great-grandmother the Dowager Duchess of Saxe-Meiningen; and his maternal grandmother Princess Auguste of Saxe-Altenburg, Duchess of Saxony.⁶³

From a very early age, Gabriel was passionately devoted to his father and to all things military. In his memoirs, he recalled: *"Since the age of seven, I dreamed of entering the Nikolaievsky Cavalry School."*⁶⁴ In 1900, he was allowed to join the 1st Moscow Cadet Corps as preparatory training; in 1903, he finally received permission to join the Nikolaievsky School. *"Having worn a cadet's uniform for five years,"* he wrote, *"at last my dream came true, and I became a real military man."*⁶⁵ On Sunday, January 6/19, 1908, Gabriel Konstantinovich took the Oath of Allegiance to Nicholas II in a ceremony held in the Church of the Catherine Palace at Tsarskoe Selo.⁶⁶

Unlike his serious and reserved brothers, Gabriel was much more social, and, to his father's chagrin, he began to associate with an aristocratic crowd considered "fast" by the strict standards of the day. He was a regular visitor to the elegant, art nouveau-style mansion of the famous Mathilde Kschessinska, the former prima ballerina and mistress before his marriage to Nicholas II. The great ballerina's parties were legendary: *"We all sat there and smoked and talked,"* recalled her friend and fellow dancer Lydia Kyasht. *"She was a wonderful hostess, and her parties were very popular."*⁶⁷

At the time, Kschessinska was openly living with two Romanov Grand Dukes, Serge Mikhailovich and Andrei Vladimirovich. Serge Mikhailovich was so enamored with the scheming ballerina that he raised no objection, and soon all of St Petersburg knew of the unusual ménage à trois. Mathilde, in turn, openly boasted of her sexual game and amorous success in keeping both men at her side, sharing her house and her bed with two Romanovs. She relished the scandal and courted the publicity that came with the complicated liaisons, leading to barely-disguised accounts in the city's racier periodicals.⁶⁸ When Prince Konstantin Radziwill declared to her, *"You should be proud to have two Grand Dukes at your feet,"* she replied imperiously, *"What's surprising about that? I have two feet."*⁶⁹

Matters were further complicated when Mathilde became pregnant in the fall of 1901. When she gave birth to a son, Vladimir, the following summer, no one knew with any certainty if the father was Grand Duke Serge Mikhailovich or Andrei Vladimirovich. The latter recognized the boy as his own, though Vladimir himself openly expressed doubts.⁷⁰ Kschessinska relished the publicity, appearing in increasingly expensive jewels as gossips clicked their tongues in astonishment at the situation. Vladimir Teliakovsky, Director of the Imperial Theaters, became Kschessinska's most enthusiastic critic. He found her personal life offensive, her constant demands at the theater petty and vindictive, and her stage technique rapidly fading. He termed her *"morally impudent, cynical and brazen,"* a woman *"living simultaneously with two Grand Dukes, and not only not concealing the fact, but on the contrary, weaving this 'art' as well into her stinking, cynical wreath of human offal and vice."*⁷¹ All St Petersburg knew of Mathilde's affairs, and her bastard son of doubtful paternity, and her mansion soon became a center of scandal and intrigue, a place where aristocratic men could be guaranteed to meet attractive, eager young women set on attracting their attentions and taking them as lovers.

It was to this elegant mansion of ill repute that, in August 1911, Prince Gabriel Konstantinovich came to attend a small ball. Kschessinska had prepared carefully for the occasion, providing a suitable collection of eager young women waiting for the opportunity to attract a suitable lover. One of these was Antonina Rafailovna Nesterovskaya, a twenty-one-year-old dancer. Born in St Petersburg on 13 March 1890, she came from a family of impoverished nobility. Just before the turn of the century, she and her sister Lydia had been accepted as pupils at the famous Imperial Ballet School, where they first encountered Kschessinska, who was then nearing the end of her official career. In 1906, Antonina was accepted as a member of the prestigious Mariinsky Ballet Corps, and between 1908-11, she also appeared as a member of Serge Diaghilev's famous Ballet Russes during several European tours.[72]

Antonina, recalled Lydia Kyasht, *"was a great friend of mine. She was not at all beautiful, but was the wittiest and most amusing conversationalist I have ever met. She could describe persons and places so vividly that anyone listening to her felt they were actually meeting with them in the flesh. After listening for only a short period to her conversation, one forgot that she was stout and plain because her interesting personality absorbed one."*[73]

Kschessinska herself later proudly recalled that Antonina *"carefully noted my way of living and entertaining...and soon adapted herself to her new milieu."*[74] Called "Nina," the young dancer was, at five-feet-three-inches, nearly a foot shorter than Gabriel Konstantinovich. Vladimir Krymov, a chronicler of aristocratic St Petersburg, later modeled a character in his novel *For the Millions* on Antonina: *"Always dressed a bit pretentiously, always in Paris gowns, and only now during the war, a few things from Brissac. She won't wear anything else. She makes a pouty little face, minces and says all kinds of silly things, repeating the same thing several times if it sticks in her head for some reason."*[75]

For all her air of sophistication, however, Antonina was quite naive. She once joined Lydia Kyasht on a tour of southern Russia, appearing at a number of provincial theaters and staying in indifferent hotels. At Baku, Antonina checked them in to the distinctly uncomfortable Hotel l'Europe, whose lobby was crowded with shady characters and whose porters promptly stole their luggage. At night, the two dancers were startled by the constant screams and *"horrible shrieks"* coming from adjoining rooms in their hotel. After their performance, the dancers were presented to the Governor-General of Baku, who inquired about their stay. When they confided details of their lodgings, the official was horrified. *"Do you mean to say that you have been staying at the brothel?"* he asked incredulously. *"It is the hot bed for white slave traffic!"*[76]

Soon after the meeting at Kschessinska's mansion, Gabriel and Antonina became lovers. In 1912, they joined Kschessinska and Grand Duke Andrei Vladimirovich on a trip to the Riviera, staying in Cannes and Monte Carlo; to mark the trip, Gabriel presented Antonina with an English Bulldog puppy that she called Carlo. When Gabriel went to take him to have his tail cropped, as was customary, Antonina objected strenuously, afraid that it would hurt the dog. Thereafter, *"Carlusha,"* as the pair called the dog, rambled around her flat in St Petersburg, happy wagging his tail for his devoted mistress.[77]

"When I first heard about the romance between Nina and the Grand Duke Gabriel," recalled Kyasht, *"I thought in my own mind it must have been an attraction of opposites; for he was very thin whereas she, to put it politely, was very plump. He was devoted to her just the same, and installed her in a wonderful palace in St Petersburg. They were the most hospitable couple, and kept open house for their friends. Guests favored with an invitation to their parties could rest assured of getting the most delicious food and the rarest wine. We spent many delightful evenings there playing poker, which was one of our chief amusements in Russia. The Grand Duke proved a*

most generous lover, and indulged all Nina's whims. She appeared insatiable in her demands, especially when she found she had only to express a desire for anything to have her wish instantly gratified. I shall never forget one day when I went to their house and found Nina awaiting me in a state of great excitement. She refused to give me any explanation but insisted on my accompanying her upstairs. When we arrived there she flung open a door and ushered me into a new and most perfectly appointed nursery. What was my astonishment, on going toward the beribboned cot that filled the place of honor in the center of the floor to find it occupied by a hideous black and white bulldog instead of the infant I had half anticipated. This animal turned out to be Nina's latest acquisition and pet, and she explained to me that the nursery had been specially designed for its occupation. When I suggested a kennel would have been more suitable, she called me cruelhearted! The dog was really a most ferocious beast. It had an unpleasant habit of biting any guest to whom it took a dislike. But in spite of this, Nina persisted in regarding it with eyes blinded by love, and called it by the most ridiculous-sounding pet names."[78]

Gabriel pressured Antonina to quit the Ballet Corps; she agreed, and thereafter he was a regular visitor to the extravagant house he had purchased for her on Kamennostrovsky Prospekt in the capital.[79] Gabriel was devotedly in love, but there was little he could do about the situation. The Romanov Family Statutes, introduced by Emperor Paul I in 1797, along with the Fundamental Laws of the Russian Empire, expressly forbid any such morganatic union between a member of the Dynasty and one of unequal rank. He appealed to his aunt Olga, Queen of the Hellenes, to intercede on his behalf and, sympathetic, she duly went to see Nicholas II, requesting permission for her nephew to marry. The Emperor, however, flatly refused, saying that if he allowed Gabriel to contract a morganatic marriage, other members of the family would undoubtedly attempt to follow his example.[80] But Gabriel would not be denied, and the pair was secretly engaged shortly before the First World War.[81] Through the twists and turns of the many years that followed, he remained passionate in his devotion to the dancer, determined that one day he would overcome the obstacles and marry his mistress.

Princess Tatiana Konstantinovna, Konstantin and Elisabeth's first daughter, was born on 11/23 January 1890, in the Marble Palace in St Petersburg. The name Tatiana had not previously been used in the Imperial Family, and it seems to have been the choice of her grandfather, Grand Duke Konstantin Nikolaievich who, it is said, had scrawled the name in his shaky hand on learning of her birth.[82] Although later rumor would speculate that Konstantin Konstantinovich had selected the name from Alexander Pushkin's *Eugene Onegin*, there seems to be no evidence to support this.

Tatiana was a quiet girl, with a talent for the piano inherited from her father.[83] A fringe of luxuriant hair framed her blue eyes, and also served to conceal an ugly childhood scar. Her brother Gabriel had owned a large pink cockatoo that he attempted to teach to talk; tiring of his efforts, he gave the bird to his sister. Tatiana was playing with the pet outside of its cage one day when the bird suddenly turned on her and lashed out with its beak across her forehead; although the wound was superficial, the scar remained.[84]

She made her first official Court appearance on 11/24 August 1904, at the christening of the new Tsarevich Alexis Nikolaievich in the Church at the Palace of Peterhof. Early that morning, she had joined her family as they left the nearby Palace of Strelna in a string of carriages and made their way along the coast of the Gulf of Finland to the Emperor's estate. During the ceremony, Princess Tatiana appeared for the first time in Russian Court dress, her arms cloaked in long white gloves, a string of her mother's pearls around her neck, and a satin kokoshnik with a large bow atop her hair.

Two years later, Tatiana Konstantinovna celebrated her sixteenth birthday. To mark the occasion, her parents gave a magnificent ball for her at Pavlovsk Palace in February 1906; also sharing the night, as a kind gesture by Konstantin Konstantinovich and Elisabeth Mavrikievna, was Grand Duchess Marie Pavlovna, who had come from Moscow with her aunt, the recently widowed Grand Duchess Elisabeth Feodorovna. Nicholas and Alexandra also came from nearby Tsarskoe Selo. The ball began at six in the evening in the Palace's Italian Hall, with a cotillion followed by a midnight supper before the festivities ended. It was, recalled Grand Duchess Marie Pavlovna, *"a great event,"* and that night Pavlovsk sparkled with music and laughter.[85]

Grand Duke Konstantin Konstantinovich's thoughts soon began to turn to his eldest daughter's possible marriage. At one time, he considered the idea of suggesting a match with Nicholas II's brother Grand Duke Michael Alexandrovich, but apparently abandoned the idea when Tatiana showed absolutely no interest, and Michael became entangled with his future morganatic wife, Natalia Cheremetevsky.[86] In the spring of 1911, Tatiana Konstantinovna was staying with her family in their wooden dacha at Oreanda in the Crimea when, on 1 May, she became engaged to the dashing Prince Konstantin Alexandrovich Bagration-Moukhransky.[87] The pair had met the previous year in St Petersburg, though their romance was to take a curious course that involved important matters related to the Imperial succession that continue to loom large in the present day controversies over who today is the Head of the House of Romanov in exile and claimant to the former throne.

Born on 2/14 March 1889, in St Petersburg, Prince Konstantin Bagration-Moukhransky had been educated at the elite Corps des Pages in the capital; on leaving the institute in 1909, he was commissioned a 2nd Lieutenant in the Erivan Grenadier Life Guards Regiment. A tall, dashing young man with a short little mustache, he had a charming manner, and soon attracted the Princess's attention. One contemporary wrote that the Prince, *"was as handsome as a Greek God."*[88] His romance with Tatiana would lead Nicholas II to make his only formal amendment to the Fundamental Laws of the Russian Empire.

As a member of the Imperial House, and a dynast with succession rights to the Imperial Throne, Princess Tatiana was bound by a number of articles contained within the Fundamental Laws. According to Article 183, *"Permission of the Reigning Sovereign Emperor is required in the marriage of every member of the Imperial House."* Tatiana thus had to seek Nicholas II's permission to marry, and her choice presented a conundrum because Prince Konstantin, according to the standards of the Imperial Government, was not of equal rank to his bride. According to Article 36 of the Fundamental Laws, if a dynast married *"a person not of corresponding birth, not belonging to a Royal or Sovereign House,"* any children born of the union were to be deprived of any succession rights to the Imperial Throne.[89]

There is no indication that this was an issue for Princess Tatiana; there were so many eligible male dynasts alive in 1910 that her place in the Imperial succession was very low. But the question of Prince Konstantin's status nevertheless became a source of intense argument. When Tatiana first raised the possibility of an engagement with her father, he is said to have refused on the grounds that it would be a morganatic union.[90]

"Father and mother," Prince Gabriel Konstantinovich recalled, *"were positively opposed to the marriage. Papa requested that Bagration be sent from St Petersburg to Tiflis."* Tatiana, he noted, *"was so upset and sad that she fell into a deep depression and became ill. This, in turn, exacerbated an accident she had while tobogganing at Pavlovsk, a blow to her spine, and this forced her to rest in bed for a long time. All winter, she barely got up, and then only to lay on the balcony in the sunshine. Mother was worried over Tatiana, and did not know how to revive*

her spirits." Eventually, she dispatched one of her courtiers to purchase some books on Georgian history for her daughter, and Tatiana read them avidly. Among the most influential was a small book on St Tamara of Georgia; reading this tale, Gabriel remembered, seemed to give his sister strength. *"She was certain,"* he added, *"that if she prayed to Tamara, she would see her fiancé again."*[91]

The Prince was a member of the oldest ruling Christian dynasty in the world; the Bagrations had occupied the throne of Georgia for a thousand years as independent sovereigns, beginning their reign in 886. In 1783, Catherine the Great signed the Treaty of Georgievsk with King Irakly II of Georgia, in which she recognized the Kingdom's sovereign status and guaranteed that Russia would respect and "preserve forever" the independence of the Georgian Throne and honor the sovereignty of its Bagration Dynasty. She further stipulated that the treaty was to be binding on her own heirs and successors in recognizing the Bagrations as "Sovereign Kings and Princes" of Georgia. In 1798, Irakly's successor, King George XII – fearing Persian expansion – suggested that Georgia be incorporated into the Russian Empire, on the condition that the Bagrations remained sovereigns and retained all the rights and privileges of Catherine's treaty. Emperor Paul I, however, took advantage of the chaos and in 1800 simply seized the country in violation of the Treaty of Georgievsk, forcibly incorporating it and its rulers into the Empire.[92]

Although King George XII protested, there was little he could do; thereafter, the controlling powers in the Russian Empire simply ignored both the sovereign history of the Bagration Dynasty and Catherine II's treaty, officially listing members of the former Royal House of Georgia as *"titled nobles within the Russian Empire."*[93] The Bagrations, who had been forcibly deprived of their sovereign status, thereafter declined to be listed in the *Almanach de Gotha* as mere princes of the Russian Empire.[94] Technically, the Bagrations fell into the somewhat nebulous category of former ruling houses that no longer reigned but whose members were considered *Ebenburtigkeit*, or of equal status for the purposes of marriage. This list, at the time of Princess Tatiana Konstantinovna's romance, included the House of Bourbon in France; the Houses of Bourbon-Two Sicilies, Bourbon-Parma and Habsburgs of Tuscany in Italy; the Houses of Hanover, Nassau and Hesse-Kassel in Germany; and the Houses of Orléans and Napoléon in France.[95]

Many members of the Imperial Family believed that a marriage between Princess Tatiana and Prince Konstantin would be a morganatic one. Marie Alexandrovna, the Duchess of Edinburgh and Alexander II's only surviving daughter, wrote to her daughter Crown Princess Marie of Romania: *"Did you hear that Uncle Kostia's daughter Tatiana is engaged to a Caucasian* [sic] *Prince Bagration? The first morganatic female marriage in our family. She was simply dying and swindling away on account of this morganatic love and now it has been sanctioned. A dangerous beginning in our family and the opening of a new social era."*[96] Yet this is flatly contradicted in Grand Duke Konstantin Konstantinovich's diary, where he recounted a conversation he had had with Nicholas II on the issue before the pair was engaged. According to the Grand Duke, the Emperor declared that he, *"would never look upon her marriage to a Bagration as a morganatic one, because that House, like the House of Orleans, is descended from a once-ruling Dynasty."*[97] Whether such considerations had proved a hurdle in the negotiations is not known, but by the spring of 1911, Nicholas II gave permission for the Prince to ask for Tatiana's hand. On 1 May – ironically the day of St Tamara in the Orthodox Church – the couple was formally betrothed in the Church of the Intercession of the Virgin at the Imperial estate of Livadia.[98]

That summer, the looming marriage ceremony caused Nicholas II to initiate a round of formal enquiries concerning the issue. The Emperor convened a special meeting of various Grand Dukes to discuss the forthcoming marriage and the question of allowing possible unequal unions, as there was much talk within the Imperial Family that Princess Tatiana's marriage, if recognized, would set a precedent for morganatic marriages. In a letter written to the conclave by Count Vladimir Fredericks on the Emperor's behalf, the Minister of the Imperial Court declared Nicholas II's decision: Grand Dukes would not be allowed to contract morganatic marriages, but Princes and Princesses of the Imperial Blood, on receiving the Emperor's permission, would be allowed to do so. If they elected to enter into a morganatic union, the Emperor would grant new surnames and coats-of-arms to the spouses and to their descendants to signify the change in status. The Emperor further declared that henceforth there would be only two categories of marriages he allowed: those unions equal for the purposes of dynastic succession, and morganatic unions.[99]

This, in turn, led Nicholas II to amend the Fundamental Laws of the Russian Empire. Two weeks before Princess Tatiana married, he issued a decree that stated, as an addendum to Article 188, *"Henceforth no Grand Duke or Grand Duchess may contract a marriage with a person of unequal birth, not belonging to a Royal or Sovereign House."*[100] The change, initially brought about by questions over the proposed union of Princess Tatiana, was expressly conceived as a measure to prevent Nicholas II's brother Grand Duke Michael Alexandrovich from marrying his longtime mistress and mother of his bastard child.

The marriage between Princess Tatiana Konstantinovna and Prince Konstantin was celebrated in the Church of the Pavlovsk Palace on 21 August/2 September 1911. As Nicholas II, Empress Alexandra, and their four daughters looked on, the bridal couple appeared, followed by Tatiana's parents. The Princess wore a beautifully embroidered Russian Court dress of silver tissue, with a long veil held in place by a diamond kokoshnik in her hair.[101] The Princess formally renounced her rights of succession to the Imperial Throne in accordance with Article 37 of the Fundamental Laws of the Russian Empire; this renunciation has been taken as a sign that the marriage was unequal, but seems to have been done as was customary when a female dynast married a spouse considered to be a foreign prince. On 24 August 1911, Nicholas issued the following decree: *"Her Highness Princess Tatiana Konstantinovna has presented to Us, over her own signature, a renunciation of her of succession to the Imperial Throne of All the Russias, which belongs to her as a member of the Imperial House of Russia."*[102] There was no mention or provision made, however, for any children born of the union, who technically retained succession rights, although their mother did not. Again, the issue was a formality, to avoid the throne passing to foreign descendant. Additional weight to this argument is lent by the later comments of Tatiana's only son, Prince Teymuraz Bagration-Moukhransky, who apparently recounted how his mother had often told him that Nicholas II himself had instructed Prince Konstantin Bagration-Moukhransky to sign the marriage register as *"Prince of Georgia,"* an indication of his family's previous sovereign status and a clear signal that the marriage was not a morganatic one.[103]

Despite his assurances to Grand Duke Konstantin Konstantinovich on the issue, Nicholas II never formalized his opinion that the marriage between Princess Tatiana and Prince Konstantin was an equal one. His announcement of the marriage, in a formal ukase to the Imperial Senate, made no mention of the union as being morganatic, another sign that he regarded it as an equal union; unequal unions were always described as such in official documents. Nor, as the Emperor had earlier decreed, were the children born to the marriage granted new surnames and coats-of-arms, as he had specified in the case of morganatic descendants.[104] The couple had two children. The first, a son, was called Prince Teymuraz Konstantinovich. He was born at Pavlovsk on 21 August/2 September 1912, the first anniversary of his parents' marriage. A daughter, Princess Nathalia Konstantinovna, was born on 19 April/2 May 1914, at Oreanda in the Crimea.

Prince Konstantin Konstantinovich, the fourth child of Grand Duke Konstantin Konstantinovich, was born on the afternoon of Thursday, 20 December 1890/1 January 1891, in the Marble Palace in St Petersburg. He was christened on the afternoon of Sunday, 13/25 January 1891, in the Chapel of the Marble Palace, in a service conducted by Father Ioann Yanishev. His godparents included Alexander III; Queen Marie of Hanover; the Grand Duke of Saxe-Weimar-Eisenach; Grand Duchess Elisabeth of Oldenburg; his grandfather, Grand Duke Konstantin Nikolaievich; Grand Duchess Alexandra Petrovna; Grand Duke Alexis Alexandrovich; Grand Duchess Alexandra Georgievna; Grand Duke Peter Nikolaievich; Grand Duke Michael Nikolaievich; his maternal grandmother Princess Auguste of Saxe-Altenburg; and his aunt, Princess Louise of Saxe-Altenburg.[105]

Like his brothers, he entered the Imperial Cadet Corps, destined for a life in the military.[106] Called "Kostia" within the family, the Prince grew into a tall, *"charming young man,"* exceptionally thin, with an angled face, a small, trim mustache, and deep blue eyes.[107] He joined the Nizhegorodski Cadet Regiment and later, the Imperial Guards Regiments.[108] Quiet and reserved, he made a good impression on those whom he encountered. He showed little interest in pursuing any romantic alliance, and in the end, did so only at the instigation of others. In 1911, the Dowager Duchess of Saxe-Coburg thought that he would make a suitable husband for her granddaughter, Princess Elisabeth of Romania. Prince Konstantin Konstantinovich had to be prodded by his mother into expressing any interest. Whatever Elisabeth Mavrikievna told her son appears to have worked, for in a few months Marie Alexandrovna reported: *"The young Kostia is seized now with terror that she will be snatched away, as he says, before he has even made her acquaintance. The young man seems really quite nice, is much liked in his regiment and they have really been very well brought up. This one is full of life and they always have a pleasant existence at home, full of interests."* In the end, however, Elisabeth's mother Crown Princess Marie refused to consider the possible match, and Konstantin Konstantinovich never again expressed any interest in a possible alliance.[109] He remained unmarried, a well-mannered and pleasant young man, greatly liked by his relatives.

Prince Oleg Konstantinovich was born at two on the afternoon of Sunday, 15/27 November 1892, at the Marble Palace. *"While it was happening,"* recalled Prince Gabriel, *"my father, brother, and I were playing billiards. Then we were taken to my mother. I saw her lying on her bed, and Father Arseni, with Oleg in his arms, was reading prayers in front of the icons."*[110] He was christened at two on the afternoon of Thursday, January 3/15, 1893, in the Church in the Marble Palace by Father Ioann Yanishev. His godparents included Empress Marie Feodorovna; the future Nicholas II; his grandmother Grand Duchess Alexandra Iosifovna; Princess Marie of Prussia; Princess Marie of Greece; Prince Adolf of Schaumburg-Lippe; the Hereditary Princess of Schaumburg-Lippe; Duke Alexander Petrovich of Oldenburg; Prince Ernst of Saxe-Meiningen; and Prince Friedrich of Saxe-Meiningen.[111]

Oleg, more than any of the other Konstantinovichi offspring, was his father's son: handsome, quiet, introspective, and immensely talented. He showed an early gift for music, poetry and drawing, and a love for architecture; Grand Duke Konstantin Konstantinovich decided that, alone of his children, Oleg would be allowed to pursue a regular educational course rather than a military one.[112] He was enrolled as an external student at the Polotsk Military Academy, and attended classes in the university course at the Emperor Alexander Lyceum, where he did well, much to the consternation of several of his brothers, who recognized that he was their father's favorite and receiving special treatment. At the Lyceum, Oleg performed to a standard much higher than that set for the classes, so it was decided that he would do better in an independent study program, under the supervision of Major-General N. N. Ermolinsky. The result of his study of the humanities was a brilliant work on the judicial ideas of Feofan Prokopovich, for which the Prince was awarded the Pushkin Medal.[113]

Despite his dislike of the military, Oleg could not escape his obligations as a member of the Romanov Dynasty. He served as Cornet in His Majesty's Life Guards Hussar Regiment, cutting a dashing figure in his uniform. Just before the First World War, he became unofficially engaged to his sixteen-year-old second cousin Princess Nadezhda, daughter of Grand Duke Peter Nikolaievich and his wife Grand Duchess Militza. The fiery and proud Militza apparently put up something of a fuss over the romance, protesting that marrying into the Konstantinovichi family was beneath her daughter's dignity, but family objections fell in the face of the burgeoning romance. No announcement was made, however, and the engagement simply faded away with the beginning of the First World War.

Prince Igor Konstantinovich was born on Saturday, 29 May/10 June 1894, at Strelna. He was christened on Tuesday, June 21/July 3, 1894, at Strelna. His godparents included Alexander III; his grandmother Grand Duchess Alexandra Iosifovna; his uncle Grand Duke Dimitri Konstantinovich; Grand Duke Vladimir Alexandrovich; the Grand Duke of Mecklenburg-Schwerin; Princess Eugenia Maximilianovna of Leuchtenberg; Duchesses Elsa and Olga of Württemberg; Prince Peter Alexandrovich of Oldenburg; and his maternal grandmother Princess Auguste of Saxe-Altenburg.[114]

Igor grew up to be a pleasant, somewhat aimless young man, tall and broad-shouldered, with a chubby face and sparkling eyes. With his brother Konstantin he studied in the Cadet Corps, where he managed to slip through his studies rather than win any laurels.[115] Ballerina Lydia Kyasht later called him *"the most irresponsible man I have ever known."* Among his family and friends, he was called "Baby-Boy," a reflection of his marked immaturity and tendency to let his emotions dictate his behavior.[116] Wild pranks and loud shouts or guffaws were often followed by fits of temper or bursts of unexpected tears, leaving those around him always on guard against his inability to control his uncertain emotions. Igor was rather a challenge. His brother Gabriel later recalled that Igor *"always seemed to speak in shouts,"* and he had trouble keeping his feelings in check. Once, while dining with Nicholas II, Igor loudly interrupted the Emperor and launched into his own conversation. Nicholas, polite though he was, shouted across the table, *"I am talking!"* and fixed Igor with a stony look. But Igor was unable to stop himself; rather than cease speaking, he became even more excited, explaining in a loud voice that he had not been breathing when he was born, and had to be slapped, and that this accounted for his vocal level.[117]

He cared little about his military obligations and, like his uncle Grand Duke Dimitri Konstantinovich, seemed to be obsessed with horses. He took great pride in his stable, and it was said that when he appeared in the streets of the capital driving his brightly painted troika, strollers paused in admiration.[118] Despite his somewhat peculiar character, Igor was genuinely liked by his relatives, known to be kind-hearted and generous.[119] Ironically for a young man so known for his nearly constant shouting, as he reached maturity he began to suffer from problems with his lungs, and constant illnesses and colds led to pneumonia that eventually prevented regular military service.[120]

Prince George Konstantinovich was born on Wednesday, 23 April/6 May 1903, in the Marble Palace. He was christened on Thursday, 29 May/11 June 1903, in the Church of the Marble Palace. His godparents included Empress Alexandra Feodorovna; Grand Duchess Elisabeth Feodorovna; his grandmother Grand Duchess Alexandra Iosifovna; Grand Duke George Mikhailovich; his brother Prince Ioann, and his sister Princess Tatiana; Princess Victoria of Sweden; the Duke of Saxe-Meiningen; Prince Edward of Anhalt; and Prince Maurice of Schaumburg-Lippe.[121] At the age of ten, he was enrolled as a Cadet in the Orlovsky Cadet Corps.[122]

A genial, good-natured boy, he became one of the few friends allowed Tsarevich Alexis Nikolaievich, his junior by a year, and the pair frequently played together on visits to the Alexander Palace. Grand Duke Konstantin Konstantinovich later recalled how, on one occasion, Alexis *"hugged him and played happily with him on the slide, and on learning that Georgie wants to be a chauffeur when he grows up, offered his services as his assistant."*[123]

Princess Nathalia was born on 10/23 March 1905, at Pavlovsk. Christened exactly one month later, she was destined to live only two months. On 10/23 May 1905, she died in her mother's arms from peritonitis and inflammation of the brain. Her brother Prince Oleg Konstantinovich, then eleven-years-old, recorded her passing in his diary. He had been in the Crimea with his older brothers and sister, Tatiana, when she was born, and only returned to St Petersburg after her death. *"So we never saw Natushya at all,"* he noted sadly. He also noticed the curious coincidence of her birth, christening, and death, on, respectively, March 10, April 10, and May 10. *"Always the 10th,"* Oleg commented.[124]

Princess Vera Konstantinovna, the youngest and last of Grand Duke Konstantin Konstantinovich's children, was born in 1906 at Pavlovsk. On visits to the Alexander Palace, her proud father noted, Nicholas and Alexandra's daughters *"made a fuss"* over her, and *"carried her in their arms."*[125] Princess Vera Konstantinovna, in fact, later vividly remembered these frequent visits with her Imperial cousins and their parents. Nicholas II, she recalled, once came to tea at Pavlovsk with her parents while she was forced to endure a music lesson away from the grownups. Before she left, however, *"the Emperor turned to me, looked at me attentively, caressed me on my head, and said some kind words. He charmed me then."* There were also visits to the Alexander Palace at Tsarskoe Selo. Princess Vera remembered being served *"wonderful chocolate cream"* during one meal there with her brother Prince George. *"When we were offered an additional portion, I and my brother ate it. Then they offered some more again. We wanted it very much but we decided that it would be against the rules of etiquette, and grudgingly refused."* The four Grand Duchesses, she later said, *"were a little bit ashamed of their titles, and everybody at home called them simply by names. And in their everyday life they were very modest."*[126]

Tsarevich Alexis, who was two years older than Vera, did not often join in the children's games. Often, as Vera later recalled, this was a blessing, for he could be demanding and rude. Once, he interrupted a tea party given by his sisters for Vera, stealing the little pastries on their plates and wolfing them down, then wiping his dirty hands on their dresses. On another occasion, Vera arrived in the garden of the Alexander Palace in a new, white party dress with a blue sash; catching sight of her, Alexis pointed at a large mud puddle, saying, *"I order you to jump in there!"* Although she knew her dress would be ruined and that she would be punished, Vera meekly obeyed. Alexis, she once observed, had been a *"beautiful young child,"* but also *"a little tyrant."*[127]

On another occasion, Princess Vera recalled being entrusted to carry a message from her father to the Emperor. In the way of children, she created a drama around the short trip, involving being pursued by enemy soldiers intent on taking the message from her. She forced her small pony to greater and greater speeds, weaving in and out and around the trees and lakes in the park between Pavlovsk and the Alexander Palace. Arriving at the Alexander Palace, she pulled her pony up in a Wild-West stop, threw herself off his back, and raced up the steps into the entryway, to be greeted by the startled faces of several servants, who had come to see what the noise was all about.[128] Years later, after War and Revolution had stripped Vera of family, country, and possessions, these memories remained vivid, alive in a sparkle in her clear, blue eyes.

In the late summer of 1894, Alexander III participated in the usual Army maneuvers at Krasnoe Selo. It was to be the Emperor's last public appearance; a few weeks later, while hunting in Poland, he felt increasingly unwell, and doctors diagnosed a fatal case of nephritis. In an attempt to prolong his days, they advised Alexander III to travel to the warmer climate of the Crimea. Queen Olga of the Hellenes offered her villa of Mon Repos on Corfu, but by the time the Emperor reached Livadia he was too weak to continue his travels. Fearing the end, members of the Romanov Family and royal relatives from across Europe rushed to the Crimea, including Olga Konstantinovna. The widowed Grand Duchess Alexandra Iosifovna had also rushed to Livadia, bringing with her the renowned priest Father Ioann of Kronstadt, revered as one of the saintliest men in all Russia.[129] They – along with the rest of the family – watched helplessly as the Emperor rapidly faded, dying on the afternoon of 20 October 1894. Thirteen years of conservative, autocratic, and reactionary rule had come to an end, but hopes for reform were soon dashed under the new Emperor, Nicholas II.

Although Alexandra Iosifovna had retired from public appearances, for the wedding of Nicholas II and his bride Alexandra, as her son Konstantin Konstantinovich noted, she *"decided to take part in the Imperial procession, dressed in a Russian gown of silver brocade with pearls."*[130] Soon afterward, recalled Baroness Sophie Buxhoeveden, Empress Alexandra began to pay court to the elderly Grand Duchess, showering her with *"all the charming little attentions by which a bright young woman can cheer the old people."*[131]

The Grand Duchess was actually in a somewhat peculiar position. Although Alexander Mosolov, the Head of Nicholas II's Court Chancellery, described her as a formidable grande dame, who regarded St Petersburg as too modern and morally corrupt, there was another side of the elderly widow of which few knew.[132] A few years earlier, during an intimate family meeting with Alexander III, the subject of the future Nicholas II's private life had been raised. The Emperor, who hoped to mold his son into a model of masculinity, had proposed a liaison with some suitable mistress. It was the straight-laced Alexandra Iosifovna who apparently suggested an affair with Polish ballerina Mathilde Kschessinska, asserting that she combined *"beauty, elegance, passion, sentimental tenderness, and passionate melancholy."*[133] Although such machinations seem starkly at odds with Alexandra's reputation, soon enough Tsarevich Nicholas had taken Kschessinska as his mistress; in a bold and brazen – not to mention ironic – move, Kschessinska was soon installed in the house at No. 18 English Prospekt formerly occupied by Konstantin Nikolaievich's mistress Anna Kuznetsova, allowing Nicholas to literally follow in his great-uncle's footsteps.[134]

While Alexandra Iosifovna thus apparently had entangled herself in Nicholas II's personal life, her son Grand Duke Konstantin Konstantinovich had never cared for, or involved himself in the sphere where he might have provided equal influence, that of politics. As accomplished as he was, recalled Grand Duke Alexander Mikhailovich, Konstantin Konstantinovich *"hated politics and feared politicians. He wanted to be left alone with his books, his plays, his scientists, his soldiers, his cadets, and his own happy family."*[135] And

Princess Radziwill asserted: *"During his whole life he has carefully abstained from taking any part in, or even expressing an opinion on, politics or any subject concerning them."*[136]

Konstantin thought he knew the reason. In his diary he confided: *"In the highest circles, I am considered a liberal, a dreamer, a fantasist, and am presented as such to the Emperor. And he, I think, holds just about the same opinion of me. He does not see me in the light of public opinion, the opinion of the non-ruling classes; the Emperor, it seems to me, does not quite trust me."*[137]

He certainly refused to involve himself in the political struggles of the day, although increasingly he confided his feelings to his diary as Nicholas II's reign progressed, and he found himself drawn ever closer to the drama unfolding. A week after Nicholas inherited the Throne, Konstantin described a conversation he had with Grand Duke Nicholas Mikhailovich: *"I was most struck by what he said about Vladimir and Serge supposedly trying to influence the young Emperor and bend him to their will. Nicholas thinks that they might just achieve their aim. But I think that Nicholas could be wrong. While I hope that the young Emperor will not succumb to anyone's influence, I fear that my wish will not be realized. Nicholas has warned me that the Emperor will want to use me. Others are predicting a prominent post for me. I myself have a vague inner feeling. But I am also afraid; I am certainly not going to push myself forward."*[138]

This naive view, he found, was soon shattered. He at first found the new Emperor's obligations an annoying distraction: *"I miss very much the simple relations I previously enjoyed with Nicky. We used to see each other almost every day during the two years that he served with us. Now there can be nothing like that happy past. I would not call on him without an invitation, as this would be impolite and unseemly, while he has more than enough to do without me, but I am of course unhappy that I am not summoned."*[139]

Yet as a Romanov Grand Duke, he was propelled into the usual round of public ceremonies that, during Nicholas II's reign, often took on unfortunate political overtones. In May 1896 the Grand Duke – along with most of his family – journeyed to Moscow to celebrate Nicholas II's Coronation; even Grand Duchess Alexandra Iosifovna temporarily abandoned the seclusion of her widowhood to witness the spectacle. According to protocol, no fellow crowned and consecrated sovereign was allowed to participate in the ceremonies or witness the Coronation service itself; two exceptions, however, were made to this rule in 1896, one for Nicholas II's mother, Dowager Empress Marie Feodorovna, and the other for Queen Olga of the Hellenes, who arrived in Moscow with her sons George and Nicholas to attend the festivities. Her sister Vera Konstantinovna, Duchess of Württemberg, had also come, bringing her twin daughters, Princesses Elsa and Olga.

Konstantin Konstantinovich and his family were participants in nearly every major ceremony that took place over the next few weeks. He was enchanted by an evening concert, watched by the Imperial Family on the evening of 8 May from the balcony of the Petrovsky Palace. Below, in the courtyard, stood a massed choir, composed of 1,200 members drawn from churches and academies from across Moscow; each carried a small lantern, turning the courtyard into *"a sea of flickering lights,"* as Konstantin Konstantinovich recalled.[140] The concert concluded with the Glory Chorus from Glinka's *A Life for the Tsar* and the National Anthem, *"sung with loyal fervor"* as the Empress, dressed in white, came to the edge of the balcony and bowed to the assembled choir in appreciation.[141] As the choir slowly filed out of the courtyard, their torches created a flickering river of light. *"The night,"* recalled Grand Duke Konstantin Konstantinovich, *"was quiet and luminously soft, bathed by a new moon in the sky above."*[142]

On Thursday, 9 May, the Imperial Family made its State Entrance into Moscow.

"It was calm and warm, the sun was shining joyfully, as if wishing to join the Muscovites in greeting the Emperor," wrote Grand Duke Konstantin Konstantinovich. More than a million people turned out to witness the spectacle of the Imperial Procession. Restless, filled with anticipation, they strained their necks to gaze up and down the boulevards, watching the comings and goings of the soldiers and members of the Imperial Court. *"I did not notice a single drunk,"* noted Konstantin Konstantinovich.[143]

At two-thirty that afternoon, a twenty-one-gun salute rent the sky; the bells of the city's churches soon took up the salute, ringing from one end of Moscow to the other. The Guard of Honor snapped rigidly to attention, the gates of the Petrovsky Palace swung open and, amidst the thunderous cheers of the people lining the streets, the Imperial Procession slowly marched out, on to the broad avenue leading to the Kremlin. Konstantin and Dimitri Konstantinovich rode behind Nicholas II, in a mass of Grand Dukes, followed by the women of the Imperial Family in carriages. Dowager Empress Marie Feodorovna rode alone in the Imperial State Coach, made for Catherine the Great; Konstantin Konstantinovich noted that she cried the entire afternoon.[144]

The day of the Coronation, Tuesday, 14 May 1896, was greeted by a brilliant sunrise over Moscow, promising a golden stage upon which to enact this most spectacular of Imperial pageants. *"High up in the blue skies,"* recalled Konstantin Konstantinovich, *"the swallows darted with shrill cries. It was already hot."* By 8:45 AM, all of the Imperial Family, as well as those foreign royals attending the ceremony, had gathered in the Hall of the Order of St George, awaiting the appearance of the Dowager Empress. *"Our hearts bled when we saw her,"* Konstantin noted. *"She was wearing a crown, and a heavy purple mantle, like a victim prepared for the sacrifice. Her face expressed suffering."*[145]

The future Queen Marie of Romania left a vivid description of Grand Duchess Alexandra Iosifovna during the Coronation: *"Exceedingly tall and still astonishingly upright for her age, her hair was snow white; clothed from head to foot in silver she wore a sparkling diadem like frosted sun rays.... Having a too great wealth of pearls to wear them all round her neck, she had fixed half a dozen ropes at her waist with an enormous diamond pin; they hung down along her gown in a milky cascade. She was so pale and shining white that seen against the golden walls of the cathedral she seemed to be covered with hoar-frost."*[146] Baron Karl Buxhoeveden remembered: *"All eyes were upon her, as she stood in the front row of the Grand Duchesses in her Court dress of solid cloth of silver, with a magnificent diamond tiara and a parure of sapphires three inches in diameter."*[147] By contrast, noted one correspondent noted, Queen Olga of the Hellenes *"scowled"* throughout the service *"like Lady Macbeth."*[148]

The disaster on Khodynka Meadow, where over a thousand people were crushed to death while waiting to greet the newly crowned sovereigns, darkened the Coronation ceremonies. Grand Duke Serge Alexandrovich, who – as Governor-General of Moscow – had ultimately been responsible for security arrangements, roundly protested his innocence and refused to allow any investigation into his role. Hearing this, Grand Duchess Alexandra Iosifovna declared that similar insubordination under Nicholas I would have been met with exile to Siberia.[149]

Konstantin Konstantinovich, who had been particularly close to Serge Alexandrovich, felt the incident and its aftermath keenly. On the day following the Khodynka disaster, he wrote in his diary: *"It is sad to think that the sacred celebration of the Coronation has been blemished by yesterday's tragedy."* He noted that Serge Alexandrovich, *"who should be overcome with guilt,"* was instead trying to ignore what had taken place. *"One would have thought that Serge would cancel the ball he has scheduled for tomorrow, but he will not do so. Or, that as soon as he learned of the disaster, he would have gone to the scene. I love him, and it hurts me."*[150]

As the week progressed, Grand Duke Serge Alexandrovich's behavior increasingly alienated even those members of the Imperial Family who had been favorably inclined to him. On 26 May Konstantin Konstantinovich again wrote in his diary: *"Serge is not personally responsible, though he is to blame for the lack of planning. However, it is his fault that he finds himself showered in accusations. If he had gone to the scene of the tragedy, instead of welcoming the Emperor at the fete; if he had attended a single funeral of one of the victims; if he had told the Emperor that, because he was ultimately responsible, he no longer felt worthy of continuing as Governor-General; if he had himself requested a thorough investigation – then no one would condemn him. Instead, he would inspire sympathy. But instead of this, he does what? On the day of the tragedy, he arranged a group photograph in the courtyard of the officers of the Preobrajenzky Regiment who were staying with him; when they learned of the misfortune, the officers dispersed, believing that it was no time for commemorative photographs, but Serge summoned them back and ordered the session to proceed. The Emperor, deeply distressed and in tears, did not want to attend the French Ball; but Serge – together with his brothers – who should have been upset as was the Emperor, persuaded the Emperor to attend and remain for supper. And when the Emperor wants to establish an extraordinary committee to investigate the tragedy, Serge – through one of his officials – declares that he will resign from his post if Pahlen is appointed as chairman. This whole week, in a word, Serge has behaved quite contrary to the way he should. Throughout these days, I have suffered for him. I love him dearly, we have been friends since childhood, and now I have to listen to him being condemned on all sides, and find myself unable to say a single word in his defense. I cannot even talk to him; we would only fight, and it would serve no purpose."*[151]

In the years that followed, Konstantin Konstantinovich watched in silent horror as Nicholas II staggered from disaster to disaster, and the Empire seethed with discontent. He noted that Nicholas II's *"tendency to agree with the last opinion voiced will probably get worse over the years. How painful, how sad, and how dangerous."*[152] And again: *"If only he had more strength and self-confidence."*[153]

Nine months into the disastrous Russo-Japanese War, he wrote: *"The present mood in society is far too like that of the end of the 1870s, in 1880, or 1881. At the same time the Government has lost its way, but the presence of authority was still felt. Now, however, authority is shaky and all our misfortunes stem from the Emperor's lack of will."*[154]

The Grand Duke did not see action during the conflict. Near the end of the War, he was uncharacteristically optimistic about Russia's chances for victory, only to learn that Count Serge Witte, on Nicholas II's order, had brokered a peace treaty. To his diary, he confided his hopes: *"Our active army is increasing in size and becoming considerably more powerful than the Japanese Army and is ready for battle. Japan is short of money and now when military luck might smile upon us – sudden peace."*[155]

In 1905, when Grand Duke Serge Alexandrovich was assassinated by a terrorist's bomb in Moscow, Konstantin Konstantinovich was the only senior member of the Imperial Family to immediately rush to the side of his widow, Grand Duchess Elisabeth Feodorovna. His son Gabriel later recounted how, on the afternoon that he received the news, Elisabeth Mavrikievna found her husband in the nursery with his young son George, sobbing over the loss.[156] *"I was thunderstruck,"* he wrote in his diary. *"For the first minutes, I could not think at all. It was only as I was leaving that I realized what had been lost to me, and could not stop crying. I had to prepare my wife, who loved Serge very much. Both she and I felt that I should go to Moscow to see my poor friend's body, to see poor Ella, who has no family around her."*[157] The other Grand Dukes were forbidden to travel to Moscow, or even to attend the memorial services in St Petersburg. He assisted Ella in the funeral preparations and remained until the services had ended, at a time when other members of the

Imperial Family, including Nicholas and Alexandra, followed the advice of those who warned that the situation was too dangerous.

Konstantin Konstantinovich was strongly opposed to the concessions Nicholas II reluctantly granted in his famous October Manifesto of 1905. *"It's the end of Russian autocracy,"* he wrote sadly in his diary. *"These new freedoms are not an expression of the free will of the sovereign power, but rather concessions wrenched from this power by force."*[158] Two weeks later, he wrote: *"My comrades and I all maintain our support for an autocratic government and nurture the hope that if many peasants are elected as deputies to the State Duma, it may then be possible to return to the autocratic model, which has the undoubted support of the masses of the peasants."*[159]

Konstantin Konstantinovich joined other members of the Imperial Family at the State Opening of the Duma, on 27 April 1906, at the Winter Palace. He recorded in his diary: *"The procession moved into the Hall of St George. At its head, they bore the Imperial Regalia: the Seal, the Sword, the Standard, the Scepter, and the Orb...After Their Majesties had kissed the Cross, Metropolitan Anthony began the religious service before the icon of the Savior. To the left of the Hall stood members of the State Council, to the right members of the Duma. When everyone had taken their places, the Emperor slowly and majestically approached the Throne. On a sign from the Emperor, the Minister of the Court mounted the steps and, with a low bow, presented a paper; the Emperor took it and stood up. Loudly, distinctly, and slowly, he began to read the speech. The more he read, the more strongly I was overcome by emotion. Tears flowed from my eyes. The words of the speech were so good, so truthful, and sounded so sincere that it would have been impossible to add anything or to take anything away."*[160]

In June of 1909, Konstantin Konstantinovich joined Nicholas II as the Emperor celebrated the Bicentennial of the Battle of Poltava, commemorating Peter the Great's victory over Charles XII of Sweden. It was one of the first official appearances en masse undertaken by the Imperial Family after the disturbances of 1905, and no one was certain what the reaction would be. They arrived at the site of the battle on 25 June, Konstantin Konstantinovich joining Nicholas II in attending a dinner with officers of the Preobrajenzky Guards Regiment. The following day, there was a military review, followed by the Procession of the Cross, when Nicholas was surrounded by several thousand peasants, who cheered him and fell to their knees as he passed. It was, Grand Duke Konstantin Konstantinovich noted in his diary, *"very touching and significant."*[161] At the end of the festivities, the Grand Duke wrote, *"one could see the extraordinary spiritual power,"* adding, *"this is a feeling that none of us have experienced in a long time."*[162]

The end of this tumultuous decade brought changes to the Konstantinovichi as well. Grand Duchess Alexandra Iosifovna survived her husband by twenty years. As a widow, she continued to live in splendor at Strelna and in the Marble Palace, where she barred the introduction of electricity as a modern plague.[163] She cut a striking and impressive figure wherever she appeared, and never lost her dignified, regal bearing. Prince Christopher of Greece remembered her at the unveiling of a statue: *"I could hardly take my eyes off my grandmother, who looked as though she had stepped out of the pages of one of my fairy tales. Her dress was of cloth of gold, cut in the traditional way with a tight fitting bodice and a train that was yards long."*[164]

Baroness Buxhoeveden recalled her as *"a commanding old lady with snow white hair, beautifully coiffed. She had kept a great sense of dress and her black, tight fitting princess frocks set off her tall, erect and slim figure...the old fashioned type of princess, gracious and smiling but never forgetting her rank for a moment and was a great stickler for etiquette. She could be freezingly cold and haughty when she was displeased, peering at one through a long tortoiseshell handled lorgnette. She carefully avoided gossip."*[165] Grand Duke Kirill Vladimirovich later recalled being, *"somewhat frightened of this old lady,"* with her *"high-pitched voice"* and *"fine, white hair."* He recalled her, *"driving about in an open carriage with a kind of awning over it, which could be opened and closed like an umbrella. I have never seen anything quite the same anywhere else, and think that she was the only person in the world who had such an ingenious cover to her carriage."*[166]

On arriving at Pavlovsk, recalled Prince Christopher of Greece, *"I would be clasped in grandmother's arms and told to 'go and open the parcel you will find in your bedroom. That was a glorious moment, for although I had had the tact not to mention it I had been thinking of this particular parcel all the journey, wondering what I should find in it. Whatever it was, it was certain to be something I had wanted, for Grandmother, using that particular instinct common to all grandmothers, invariably guessed right."*[167]

Like her husband, the advance of age brought with it debilitating illness and Alexandra, as had her husband before her, suffered a severe stroke that left her confined to a wheelchair in the last years of her life. She died on Thursday, 23 June/6 July 1911 in the Marble Palace, just two days short of her eighty-first birthday. By the time of her death, a new Grand Ducal Vault had been built by Leon Benois and Anthony Tomishko, adjoining the Cathedral in the Fortress of SS Peter and Paul.[168] For her funeral, her husband was exhumed from his tomb and the pair was laid to rest, side by side, along with their son Vyacheslav, on Thursday, 30 June/13 July 1911.[169]

At her funeral, Grand Duke Dimitri Konstantinovich's poor eyesight became the source of temporary mirth in the midst of mourning. At the end of the service, Dimitri Konstantinovich followed members of his family up the steps of the dais in the Cathedral of SS Peter and Paul to pay his last respects to his mother, and to kiss the icon she held in her hands. Unable to see clearly, he misjudged the distance and, bending forward to make his farewell, missed the open coffin completely, tumbling off the steps with a loud crash as his ceremonial saber and medals struck the stone floor. Relatives rushed to his side, but the Grand Duke appeared unfazed, and went on as though nothing had happened.[170]

The death of the formidable Grand Duchess also marked great changes in the lives of her daughters. In Germany, her second daughter Vera had lived a quiet, regal life, respected and admired by those who knew her. Whatever the cause of her early childhood illness, it seems to have largely disappeared with the passing years. By the turn of the century, recalled her nephew Prince Christopher of Greece, she was *"small and dumpy, with a fat, round, spectacled face."*[171] She made herself extremely popular in Stuttgart, sponsoring and financing some thirty charitable organizations and institutions ranging from hospitals and schools to shelters for destitute women.[172]

Although her Russian relatives saw little of her, Grand Duchess Vera Konstantinovna always made an indelible impression; her great-nephew Prince Gabriel Konstantinovich later described her as a *"singularly original"* character, who believed that attendance at the theater was a sin. She was, he recalled, very religious, but had never understood the Orthodox faith, and eventually abandoned it to convert to Lutheranism in 1909, much to the consternation of her Romanov relations.[173]

In 1903, during the wedding dinner for Princess Alice of Battenberg to her nephew Prince Andrew of Greece in Darmstadt, the Grand Duchess found herself the object of much mirth. *"My brother George sat next to her,"* recalled Prince Christopher, *"and, at a pause in the proceedings, snatched off her tiara and put it on his own head. Everybody laughed, Aunt Vera included, though she vowed vengeance on the culprit. Her turn came, as she thought, a little later, when the bride and bridegroom started on the honeymoon. We were all gathered at the door throwing rice after them, when someone knocked off poor Aunt Vera's glass-*

es, which were smashed to atoms on the stone steps."[174] Mark Kerr, who happened to be standing next to the Grand Duchess, became the unfortunate subject of her wrath. "*She pulled the hat off,*" he wrote, "*and started to hit me over the head with it.*"[175] A product of this wedding would be the future Prince Philip, Duke of Edinburgh, husband of The Queen.

Grand Duchess Vera Konstantinovna suffered a stroke in October 1911, and she died in Stuttgart on 11 April 1912. Her two daughters married two brothers, Olga to Maximilian of Schaumburg-Lippe, and Elsa to his brother Albrecht. Olga had two sons, Eugen and Albrecht, while Elsa had four children, Maximilian, Franz Josef, Alexander, and Bathildis.[176]

The life of her sister Queen Olga of the Hellenes also took a dramatic turn in these decades. In October 1889, a few months after her daughter Alexandra married Grand Duke Paul Alexandrovich, her eldest son, Crown Prince Constantine, called "Tino" in the family, married Princess Sophie of Prussia, sister of Kaiser Wilhelm II. As they settled into married life in Greece, disaster struck in Russia. In April 1890, Grand Duchess Alexandra had given birth to a daughter, Marie, and in the fall of 1891, she and her husband had gone to Illinskoe, the country estate a country estate outside Moscow owned by Grand Duke Serge Alexandrovich and his wife Elisabeth Feodorovna. The Grand Duchess, who was at the time seven months pregnant, went into premature labor after suffering a fall, and gave birth to a son, Dimitri Pavlovich, before lapsing into a coma. For almost a week, doctors tried to work a miracle, but after six days Alexandra died at the age of twenty-one, leaving Paul a widower with a year-old daughter and a newborn son.[177]

The loss of her eldest daughter struck Queen Olga hard but, recalled her granddaughter Marie Pavlovna, "*she endured everything with the same patience and resignation.*" She tried to act as a surrogate mother to Marie and Dimitri on her trips to Russia, and her granddaughter, starved of affection, relished the time spent with her: "*Her caresses and her radiant, affectionate eyes made me want to go to her arms for refuge, but I was so little used to caresses that I did not know how to begin.*"[178]

Olga was an indulgent grandmother. Marie Pavlovna remembered taking tea with her, when the elderly Queen covered a drop of tea in a cup with boiling milk, "*covered with a skin-like scum. At that age, boiled milk had always been insupportable to me. Grandmother, seeing that I did not touch my 'tea,' asked why. I told her. Grandmother took the cup and tried to make me drink. I pushed the cup away so rudely as to splash milk on her dress, over mine, and all over the tablecloth. Uncle Serge was angry. Everyone else laughed, even my grandmother.*"[179]

In 1900, Olga's daughter Princess Marie wed Grand Duke George Mikhailovich, and two years later another marriage brought the Greeks and Russians even closer when Prince Nicholas of Greece married Grand Duchess Helen Vladimirovna. As the only daughter of the proud and haughty Grand Duke Vladimir Alexandrovich and his wife, the dark-haired Helen was indulged, and grew up domineering, and regal. She also caused difficulties with the young men from the Corps des Pages selected to serve as her pages. Helen picked her pages strictly according to their looks, and was known to cause more than stir with her exacting and illogical demands, which in turn led to malicious rumors started by court gossips. She once declared her priorities were, "*God first, then the Russian Grand Dukes, then the rest.*"[180]

Grand Duchess Vladimir initially arranged an engagement with Prince Max of Baden; when he abruptly changed his mind, Helen was publicly humiliated and her mother, according to Grand Duke Konstantin Konstantinovich, was "*desperate to find another husband*" for her daughter. After a proposed match with the future King Albert of

Belgium fell through, Helen met the dashing Prince Nicholas of Greece. Grand Duchess Vladimir, however, summoned the Prince and, as Grand Duke Konstantin Konstantinovich recalled, *"told him not to count on Elena, because, as the third son of a King, he was not a suitable match for her."*[181] But after two years the ambitious Marie Pavlovna was forced *"to change her mind, as her search for other suitors for her daughter has been in vain."*[182] Helen married Nicholas in the Cathedral of the Catherine Palace at Tsarskoe Selo in August 1902; one of their daughters, Marina, later married the Duke of Kent, son of King George V of Great Britain.

Greece was always something of a political hotbed, unstable and seething with conflicting aspirations. In March 1913, King George I was assassinated, a shocking blow to the now elderly Olga, who buried her mother, her sister, and her husband in the space of two years. Now, her eldest son, named for his Russian grandfather, succeeded to the throne as Constantine I, with his wife Sophie at his side. In less than a year, Sophie's brother Kaiser Wilhelm II would lead his country into war against Olga's homeland.

While his brother carried on in Tashkent in his eccentric, extravagant manner, Grand Duke Konstantin Konstantinovich had settled into a productive career that won him many admirers. In the military, he had risen to the rank of General in the Russian Infantry. In 1891, Alexander III appointed him Commander of the famed Preobrajenzky Life Guards Regiment, taking the place of the ineffectual Grand Duke Serge Alexandrovich. The latter, though he had spent decades in the Imperial Army, had left little impact; one fellow officer described him as *"indifferent to the rules,"* adding that the Grand Duke *"did not know any regulations, could not give a proper march command, and commanded on the left or right foot at random."*[183] Not surprisingly the impression he left was less than favorable. Alexis Ignatiev remembered Serge Alexandrovich at military reviews as *"awkward and, as usual, untidily clad,"* adding that he was *"a tremendous intriguer."*[184]

Konstantin Konstantinovich was determined to be a different kind of commander. He reorganized the regiment, introducing new rules and regulations designed to relieve the men of many of the odious pressures they had faced under the tenure of their former commander. *"Thoroughly understanding the soul of a peasant,"* recalled Grand Duke Alexander Mikhailovich, *"he achieved marvels in reforming the methods of teaching adopted by our Army. Nothing pleased him more than a morning spent in the military barracks where he personally conducted a class for the recruits."*[185] Konstantin, recalled his son Gabriel, *"always looked extremely elegant, sitting on his horse with his regiment."*[186]

The Grand Duke proved so adept that, in 1899, Nicholas II appointed him Chief of the Empire's Military Training Institutes. *"In three months, I shall have to give up my Regiment,"* the Grand Duke noted sadly in his diary. *"My heart aches at the thought."*[187] At the time, there were some twenty Kadetski Corps in Russia, each with roughly 600 students who now fell directly under the Grand Duke's authority. These boys, who entered the schools between the ages of nine-ten, were most often the sons of privilege: scions of the nobility, or those whose fathers had reached the eighth rank in Peter the Great's system.[188]

Konstantin did well in the position, earning the respect of both pupils and school administrators. *"He attracted the hearts not only of the students but also of their teachers,"* wrote one contemporary, *"and he influenced in a significant and positive manner the entire process of education."*[189] He had a perfect memory, and had absolute recall of the names of all the military cadets he encountered.[190] One man recorded: *"Becoming acquainted with a school gave him great satisfaction. He sincerely loves children, and they respond to his affection; their trust and openness delight him. The main identifying characteristic of the*

Grand Duke's inspections consisted in their total lack of ritual and official formalities. He did not inspect schools in a conventional and formalistic way, but he visited them for several days at a time, consorting with the students and with the entire corps of teachers."[191]

In 1910, the Emperor made Konstantin Konstantinovich Chief Inspector of the Military Training Institutes. During his tenure, said Grand Duke Alexander Mikhailovich, "he did a great deal to humanize the barbarous mentality of the tutors, who thought that a cadet should be led to his commission via fear and punishment."[192] Yet he also drew the ire of many when, in 1904, he supported a revision to the schools that would allow Jewish boys who had converted to Christianity to enter the institutions. Konstantin Konstantinovich, almost uniquely in the Romanov family, seems to have harbored few anti-Semitic prejudices, and he was genuinely shocked that the proposal should be met with such vehement opposition.[193]

Konstantin Konstantinovich held an extraordinary number of official posts in his lifetime, making him perhaps the most accomplished of all of the Grand Dukes. Nicholas II created Konstantin Konstantinovich a member of the Imperial Suite, bestowing upon him the rank of Major-General a la Suite. He also made him a member of the Imperial Senate in 1896, and the Grand Duke joined other officials in presiding over its meetings at St Petersburg's Mariinsky Palace.

On 5 December 1887, Konstantin was made an honorary member of the Russian Grand Priory Order of the Knights of St John of Jerusalem; two years later, on 3 May 1889, he became Grand Master of the Order, a post he held until his death. After Napoleon's seizure of Malta in 1798, the Order of St John of Jerusalem, or the Knights of Malta, had been dispersed; many former members fled to Russia, where Emperor Paul I was elected Grand Master of the Order. It was Paul who created a separate Russian Division to the Order, which until that time had been a strictly Roman Catholic institution; Alexander I further reinforced this, granting the Russian division financial and legal autonomy from the European institution. As Grand Master, Konstantin Konstantinovich helped organize charitable contributions and presided over its ceremonies.

The Grand Duke early on expressed a concern about the state of education in the Russian Empire. He chaired several committees that advocated the establishment of universal village schools across the country, to help educate and train the millions of peasants who ordinarily fell through the cracks in the system. In this, he made a vehement enemy of the odious Konstantin Pobedonostsev, Alexander III's closest advisor and a man who feared and mistrusted nearly all of those who sought higher education, suspecting that they would be exposed to dangerous, "liberal" tendencies. In St Petersburg, the Grand Duke put his energy to more practical use, founding the Higher Women's Course as a means for promoting the training and education of Russian women, though again not without fighting a prolonged battle with Pobedonostsev over the issue.[194]

In 1899, Grand Duke Konstantin Konstantinovich became President of the Russian Imperial Academy of Sciences, following in the footsteps of Admiral Feodor Litke, the man who had served as tutor to his father, and once installed in his post he became the chief supporter of Ivan Pavlov's revolutionary new experiments.[195] Under the Grand Duke's tenure, the Academy acquired a new and permanent home in two buildings on the spit of Vassielievsky Island, the former Customs House and the Exhibition Hall, which had lain dormant for nearly a hundred years.[196]

The Grand Duke commissioned architect Roman Marfeld to completely redesign the two buildings, linking them with a series of exhibition halls and staircase to accommodate future visitors. The work was completed in 1898, and over the course of the next three years the Grand Duke devoted himself to the organization of the

Academy's first properly researched and displayed exhibition.[197] On 6/19 February 1901, the Grand Duke welcomed Nicholas II, members of the Imperial Family, the Russian Court, the Ministers and Senators, and members of the Academy to the new re-dedication ceremony and opening of the exhibition.[198] His tenure as President of the Imperial Academy of Sciences, though, was not without its controversies. In 1902, he granted honorary membership to writer Maxim Gorky; a mere two weeks later, his membership was revoked when it was learned that he had been arrested the previous years on suspicion of printing and distributing subversive pamphlets.

In 1900, Konstantin Konstantinovich served as President of the Centennial Committee of Russian poet Alexander Pushkin's birth. To mark the occasion, the Russian Imperial Academy of Sciences sponsored a poetry contest; the Grand Duke submitted a composition entitled *The Poet's Soul Will Quiver as an Eagle Shaking Itself from Sleep*. The submission was anonymous, and won the competition. Subsequently, it formed the basis of a celebratory cantata composed especially for the event by Alexander Glazunov.[199] As a lasting legacy to commemorate Pushkin's achievements, the Grand Duke established the Pushkin Fund, a philanthropic group devoted to providing struggling young writers and poets with financial support. Among its sponsors was Leo Tolstoy, with whom the Grand Duke began a brief, but erudite, correspondence.

In 1914, the Grand Duke also founded the Polar Commission as a branch of the Imperial Academy of Sciences. This came after three Polar expeditions, organized by Russian explorers between 1912-1913, had ended in disaster. The Grand Duke recognized the need for a well-funded, coordinated effort if Russia's explorers were to reach their goal of studying conditions in the Arctic and Antarctic, and through his insistence the Government allotted funds from the State Budget to assist in their pursuit. For the inaugural meeting of the new Commission on 1/14 December 1914, the Grand Duke brought together the best and most experienced scientists and explorers in the Empire to work out a comprehensive plan of Russian expeditions. The Grand Duke also recognized the need for a comprehensive library and, with his own funds, established a special collection of books and maps, purchased from libraries all across Europe, that focused on the Polar Regions.[200]

Konstantin Konstantinovich also concerned himself with the development and promotion of the fine and applied arts. He sponsored numerous painters, providing them with studio space in St Petersburg and forming a cooperative community in which they were able to complete and exhibit their work. He was also quick to recognize and promote foreign talent. In 1891, the French jeweler Frederic Boucheron participated for the first time in an exhibition organized in Moscow. Konstantin Konstantinovich was so taken with the items shown that he personally helped organize the Franco-Russian Artistic Exhibition of the following year, asking Boucheron to return to Russia and assisting him in the opening of his first Russian branch store in Moscow.

Such extensive concerns and hard work did not go unnoticed and unappreciated. Princess Catherine Radziwill, writing under her pseudonym of Count Paul Vassili in 1913, called him *"the cleverest man in the Imperial Family."*[201] Soviet historian Peter Zaionchkovsky, who in his important work on the reign of Alexander II termed the Imperial Family as *"for the most part rather stupid individuals,"* had words of praise for only two of its members, Grand Duke Nicholas Mikhailovich, and Konstantin Konstantinovich.[202]

For all of his sensible appearance and serious approach to life, the Grand Duke loved practical jokes, and enjoyed a good laugh at the minor misfortunes of others. Once, during one of Their Majesties' Great Processions at the Winter Palace, the whole Imperial Family had gathered in all its court finery. When a young page bent over to adjust a train, his skintight breeches split; Konstantin Konstantinovich burst into loud guffaws – *"a deep-throated laugh"* – that caught everyone's attention. Fortunately, a fellow page managed to grab a cloak and wrap it round his friend's waist before he could expose more of himself.[203]

During these years, Konstantin Konstantinovich became very close to Bishop Serge of Narva, and relied on the man, born in 1853, for spiritual advice and guidance. Bishop Serge, who presided over the Trinity-Sergeievsky Monastery near Strelna, often welcomed the Grand Duke and his family for services. In 1900, at the request of Grand Duke Konstantin Konstantinovich, Bishop Serge was appointed personal confessor to his family.

The tumultuous years of War and Revolution had passed and, under the strong hand of Prime Minister Peter Stolypin, it seemed as if Russia might yet heal its wounds and move forward, albeit slowly and laboriously as it struggled against ancient traditions mingled in a world of modern expectations. Konstantin Konstantinovich allowed himself and his family the luxury of semi-private lives, lived against a backdrop of glittering palaces.

Once again, members of the Konstantin Family began to visit Oreanda, to bask in the warm Crimean sun. In September of 1894, Konstantin Konstantinovich journeyed to Livadia, where Alexander III lay dying, to discuss the purchase of Oreanda. The Grand Duke insisted that his family be allowed to retain possession of a small section of the estate that included their wooden dacha, and the Emperor agreed to this concession. The rest of the estate, including its vineyards and the ruins of Nicholas I's former Grecian Palace high above the Black Sea, was transferred to the Imperial Appanage Department. For the sale, Konstantin Konstantinovich – who had inherited the property on the death of his father in 1892 – was paid some 13 million rubles.[204]

Under Konstantin Konstantinovich, Oreanda enjoyed a new renaissance. His family lived in the wooden dacha, and entertained in the nearby Villa Tiesenhausen, which had belonged to one of the first Alexandra Feodorovna's Ladies-in-Waiting. This was a larger building than the old lodge, with a hexagonal drawing room hung with floral cretonne and a large dining room decorated with tapestries depicting scenes from the Orient. With his nine children, Konstantin Konstantinovich often used the additional bedrooms here to accommodate his eldest sons.[205]

The arrival of the Grand Duke and his family at Oreanda was always marked by a review and the ceremonial raising of Konstantin Konstantinovich's personal standard over the little summer house he had built above the Black Sea.[206] The Grand Duke and his wife frequently entertained at Oreanda, with dinners in the Villa Tiesenhausen followed by long, languid evenings spent on the terrace of the ruined Palace. Here, they and their guests would sit, the few remaining fountains playing, while a military band or symphony orchestra, hidden in the semi-circular colonnade on the hillside above, serenaded them.[207] Afterward, the Grand Duke would lead his guests round the park by torchlight, showing them the new reflecting pools he had built, laid out in the shapes of the Black Sea, the Sea of Azov, the White Sea, and the Caspian Sea.[208]

During the reign of Nicholas II, the Emperor and Empress often visited Oreanda and the family of the Grand Duke. The estate and Livadia were linked by a scenic walk laid out above the Black Sea known as the "Emperor's Path." There were frequent picnics, and carriage rides to the ruined Palace, which was a source of perpetual curiosity for the Grand Duchesses. Their nurse, Miss Eager, often took Olga and Tatiana to climb its decaying walls, and watch the large, colorful goldfish that filled the ponds. One year, they arrived to find that the fish had disappeared, much to the dismay of the young Grand Duchesses. When Miss Eager asked the gardener what had become of them, he explained, *"Alas! We wanted to clean out their little lakes, so with great care we captured the goldfish and put them into the large pond in which the swans live, but we could not find them again."*

"No," Miss Eager replied, *"of course not, the swans ate them."*

"Oh, no, Miss," the man exclaimed, horrified at the suggestion, *"those swans are particularly tame; His Majesty takes great notice of them; they would never eat anything that belonged to the Emperor."*[209]

During the Revolution of 1905, Oreanda, being a ruined estate abandoned during the unrest, and with commanding views over Yalta harbor and the Black Sea, became home to a band of Socialists. They set up their revolutionary cells in the ruins of the palace, and posted watches atop the blackened walls to observe the comings and goings in the town below. Inside the remains of the reception rooms, the stillness of the estate's former life was replaced with the rattle of their makeshift printing presses, churning out leaflets urging the Black Sea Fleet to revolt.[210]

In St Petersburg, Konstantin Konstantinovich hired architects Dimitri Zaitsev and Alexander Dzhyorguli to complete a suite of rooms in the Marble Palace in the Gothic Baronial style. They faced his Music Room in light, honey-colored oak panels, set between Gothic-style, blue and silver traceried hangings; a silver, Gothic-style chandelier hung from the center of the vaulted ceiling. The Gothic Library, hung in blue paper stenciled with gold quatrefoils and red arabesques, was lined with carved oak panels and bookcases; the vaulted ceiling, crossed by carved oak ribbing, rested on medieval-style tendrils extending down the walls like spidery fingers.[211] To soften the hushed, tomb-like Palace, Konstantin Konstantinovich filled these rooms with thick carpets, potted palms, hundreds of paintings, and comfortable, over-stuffed sofas and chairs.[212] Despite its somewhat cramped, incongruously decorated private apartments, the Marble Palace provided subtle testament to Imperial Russia's past glories.

When Konstantin Nikolaievich died in January 1892, his second son, Grand Duke Konstantin Konstantinovich, inherited Pavlovsk, and his growing family moved in to Cameron's magnificent Palace. The children occupied rooms on the Palace's Third Floor, and in the northern wing, while the Grand Duke and his wife Elisabeth redecorated rooms on the Ground Floor of the Central Block for their own use. Elisabeth Mavrikievna moved into the rooms formerly occupied by her mother-in-law, while her husband took the suite of rooms on the northern side of the Palace. Disliking the immensity of his father's Reception Room (formerly the Ballroom), Konstantin Konstantinovich had the space divided into several smaller apartments with wooden partitions. As his Study, he selected his mother's Reception Room (formerly the Green Dining Room), located directly beneath the Greek Hall.[213] The family lived in relative simplicity amidst these luxurious surroundings. They kept a staff of just eleven people, including a butler, and a former Sergeant in the Cavalry Horse Guards who taught all of the children to ride.[214]

With his appreciation of the arts, the Grand Duke adored Pavlovsk, and during his residence, he took special care to ensure its preservation. He commissioned a comprehensive inventory of its contents – the last taken before the Revolution – that was so detailed that it was later used by Soviet restorers in their work.[215] He restored several of the Halls, including the Chevalier Gallery, returning its abundance of statuary to their original locations in the Palace, and had the Rossi Pavilion constructed according to the architect's original designs. When the work was complete, he had a photographic record made, which in 1903 formed the basis of a series of illustrated articles on the Palace, and in 1913, a book.[216]

Konstantin Konstantinovich opened the majority of the State Apartments in the Palace to the public, who could enjoy its treasures before attending an evening concert at the Voksal. He built the Rossi Pavilion in the neoclassical style to shelter a bronze bust of Marie Feodorovna, and commissioned gardeners and landscape architects to restore the Park and replant its faltering trees.[217]

But, above all other residences, Konstantin Konstantinovich adored Ostashevo, a large country estate outside of Moscow that he purchased shortly after the turn of the century. Situated in the Volokolamsk District on the banks of the Ruza River, the estate had been founded at the end of the 18th Century by A. V. Urusov, who built a large, two-storeyed neoclassical mansion in the center of a forest glade. A decade later, he sold Ostashevo to N. N. Muraviev, who further developed the estate, adding several pavilions, and creating a large, serpentine lake in the surrounding gardens.[218]

In 1825, Ostashevo became infamous when the Decembrist Revolt erupted in St Petersburg. The investigation ordered by Nicholas I revealed that much of the planning for the insurrection had taken place at Ostashevo, and that Muraviev was deeply involved. Muraviev was forced into exile, and the estate was sold to N. P. Shipov, a local aristocrat. Shipov, in turn, sold Ostashevo to General A. A. Nepokoichitsky, who lived there for most of the 19th Century. In 1890, he sold it to industrial magnate A. G. Kuznetsov. It was from this industrialist – who bore the same surname as the ballerina whose affair with his father had resulted in so much shame and scandal – that Grand Duke Konstantin Konstantinovich purchased the estate in 1903.[219]

The estate lay just beyond the small village of Ostashevo, from which it took its name. At the end of the village road, a pair of tall, white stone obelisks marked the entrance to the Park. Just beyond them, at the edge of a thick forest of pine and birch trees, stood two small, brick towers, used as guard houses. Like many of the service buildings and pavilions on the estate, Muraviev had ordered them built in neo-Gothic style. He seems to have largely been influenced in this by Catherine the Great's two, similar Muscovite projects, Matvei Kazakov's Petrovsky Palace on the outskirts of the city, and Vassili Bazhenov's great, unfinished country estate, Tsaritsyno. The buildings at Ostashevo copied many elements from these two complexes, reflecting their red brick walls, pointed arches, lancet windows, and crenellated towers. Further along the main drive at Ostashevo, visitors came to the Administrator's House, a single-storeyed structure also built in the neo-Gothic style, and the expansive stable complex, erected in the 1850s.[220]

At the edge of the forest, a meadow skirted the crest of the hillside above the Ruza River. Here, ringed by a dark fringe of trees and mirrored in the placid waters of the reed-choked lake, stood the Mansion. Built at the end of the 18th Century of wood upon a Ground Floor of rusticated stone, it reflected the prevailing neoclassical taste that predominated in the last years of Catherine the Great's reign. Of two principal storeys, the center of its river and lake façades were adorned with immense, pedimented porticoes each held aloft by white Corinthian columns. Above, crowning the steeply pitched roof, a belvedere, pierced with windows, looked over the gardens and to the countryside beyond. The reception rooms and apartments for Konstantin and Elisabeth Mavrikievna were situated on the First Floor, while their children occupied a series of rooms on the floor above. Long, one storey service wings to either side of the main block contained additional rooms, as well as the kitchens.[221]

Grand Duke Konstantin Konstantinovich and his family frequently came to

Ostashevo. Here, in the depths of the country, they could relax far away from the intricacies of life in St Petersburg and, as the Grand Duke confided, it was a place to which he could remove his growing sons from the temptations of the Imperial capital.[222] Although Pavlovsk and Oreanda were suburban retreats, both were still filled with servants and etiquette. At Ostashevo, the family could temporarily abandon the intense ritual of Court life, and enjoy the peaceful, if privileged, existence of other aristocratic landowners.

On 15/28 April 1909, Grand Duke Konstantin Konstantinovich and Grand Duchess Elisabeth Mavrikievna celebrated their silver wedding anniversary at Pavlovsk, joined by her brother Ernst, who had only recently succeeded his uncle as Duke Ernst II of Saxe-Altenburg, and by most of the Imperial Family. To mark the occasion, their myriad children gave a tableaux vivant, entitled *The Union of the Sun and the Spring*, in which each was assigned a particular role. Princess Tatiana, clothed in a diaphanous white gown, played the role of "Spring," supervising her younger siblings as they scurried across the makeshift stage.[223] As the couple led their guests to dinner, Tatiana and her brother Gabriel sat together at the piano, playing them out to the sound of the Wedding March from Wagner's *Lohengrin*. Toasts were made and congratulations exchanged, and Nicholas II and Empress Alexandra presented Elisabeth with a large aquamarine brooch surrounded by diamonds.[224] Watching these happy proceedings, Konstantin Konstantinovich could temporarily believe that his world had finally settled into a comfortable existence. That, however, was not to be the case as the next few years were fraught with loss, tragedy and death.

By 1914, Grand Duke Konstantin Konstantinovich was increasingly unwell. That momentous summer, he joined his wife and family in Germany. While Elisabeth Mavrikievna and her youngest children George and Vera stayed with her mother, the widowed Duchess Auguste of Saxe-Altenburg, the Grand Duke went to Bad Nauheim to take the cure. One day, however, he received an urgent cable from his brother Dimitri Konstantinovich, announcing the Russian mobilization against Germany and Austria-Hungary. Grand Duke Konstantin Konstantinovich immediately left the spa town and reunited with his wife and two youngest children, making hasty plans to return at once to Russia. Elisabeth Mavrikievna's cousin suggested that, should hostilities erupt and the family be unable to leave, he would gladly provide them with a suitable residence where they could live quietly until the end of the war, but Konstantin was determined to return to Russia.

In the end, there was no need for such contingency plans. On the evening of 1 August 1914, they learned that Germany had declared war on Russia. When the Grand Duke expressed his wish to leave Germany, he was informed that he should consider himself and his family as prisoners-of-war. Elisabeth Mavrikievna immediately wrote out a telegraph to Kaiserin Augusta Viktoria, with whom she had been friendly before her marriage, asking that her family be allowed to depart for Russia. When she handed the cable to an official, however, he rudely informed her prisoners were not allowed to send private telegrams. It was not a "private," she replied in German, but an "Imperial message!" The official, at a loss for words, took it from her and duly dispatched it to Berlin. Within a few hours, the prisoners received word that they would be allowed to leave on the train.[225]

The following morning, the Grand Duke and his family boarded a train headed east. The journey was fraught with minor inconveniences as well as real dangers: the German military officer escorting the Russians warned them not to look out of the train windows, lest they be shot. At one halt, when the family attempted to leave the train and walk along the siding for a few minutes, soldiers armed with rifles ordered them back into their compartment. Passports were repeatedly checked and re-checked by rather surly officials, and rather too efficient Prussian officials ordered the Grand Duke and his family about according to their whims. Near the Russian border, the railway carriage in which the family had been confined was separated from the main locomotive and coupled to another engine, which would then take it back to Russia. Finally, at Eydkuhnen near the Russian border, the Grand Duke and his family were told to disembark; the rest of the journey – several miles – was to be undertaken on foot. They duly set off along a forest road, where they eventually met a motorcar bearing white flags, and were driven the rest of the distance to a contingent of Russian officers and a battalion from the Smolensk Uhlan Life Guards Regiment.[226]

At least one member of the extended Konstantinovichi family, Grand Duke Dimitri Konstantinovich, openly welcomed the outbreak of hostilities. For years, he had poured over the Bible, according to his cousin Alexander Mikhailovich, and was utterly convinced that the end of the world was near.[227] *"The war with Germany is imminent!"* he would cry, predicting disaster. When the First World War finally did erupt in 1914, Dimitri Konstantinovich was satisfied that his prophecy had been correct. Unfortunately, by this time, his intense near-sightedness kept him from participating in the conflict, and he had to content himself with a job training the Cavalry Regiments away from the field of action.[228]

His unbounded enthusiasm stood in stark contrast to the reaction from his nephews in the family, however, who found themselves called up to serve on the front lines of battle. At the beginning of the First World War, Prince Ioann Konstantinovich dutifully followed his regiment into battle, though he was reluctant to abandon his wife, Elena Petrovna. By the beginning of the War, the widowed Queen Olga of the Hellenes had taken up semi-permanent residence at Pavlovsk, where she founded a hospital for the wounded and, following her example, Elena decided to put her previous medical training to good use, funding hospital trains and field hospitals that she helped organize and run.[229]

In this work, she was joined by Grand Duchess Marie Pavlovna, who had recently divorced her husband in Sweden and returned to Russia. Together, the two women boarded one of Elena's hospital trains and set off for the Front. Aboard was a Red Cross unit, with two doctors, eight nurses, twenty orderlies, and number of officials, along with carriages filled with supplies including bandages, antiseptic, and medicines. Their journey took them to the frontier town of Eydkuhnen, where Konstantin Konstantinovich and Elisabeth Mavrikievna had only recently crossed back into Russia from Germany, and then on to an East Prussian town near the Front. *"Everywhere were soldiers in field-stained uniforms,"* recalled Marie Pavlovna; *"carts stood heaped together; smoke rose here and there from field kitchens; the air was full of mingled scents-the aromatic smell of hay and of horses, the warm smell of fresh baked bread, the smell of trampled grass, the smell of smoke. Some families had apparently decided to leave town. Their belongings were piled on wagons in front of their yards or lay scattered on the street amid hay and straw."*[230] Once they settled in and organized the field hospital, both women took up active duty as operating nurses, trained by the Red Cross, and treated young soldiers blown apart by artillery fire, helped amputate limbs, and tried their best to nurse the wounded back to health.[231]

In the midst of this work, however, Princess Elena learned that she was pregnant with her and Ioann's second child. Reluctantly, she abandoned her hospital work to return to the Russian capital, newly renamed Petrograd in a bit of misplaced patriotism by Nicholas II. Elena gave birth to a second child, Princess Catherine Ioannovna, on 30 June/13 July 1915, at Pavlovsk. The couple nicknamed her "Kissa," after the faces she made.[232] Catherine Ioannovna became the only member of the House of Romanov to bear the style of Serene Highness, in accordance with Alexander III's decree of 1886.

By the time of her birth, Prince Ioann was usually away, serving with his regiment and at Stavka, the Russian Military Field Headquarters, where he acted as Adjutant to Nicholas II. His brother Prince Konstantin Konstantinovich also followed his regiment into battle, and received several citations for bravery. *"He was an extremely modest officer of the Guard of the Izmailovsky Regiment,"* recalled one man, *"much beloved by officers and soldiers alike; along with them he was a brave soldier who distinguished himself…I personally remember seeing him in the trenches among the soldiers, risking his life."*[233] In May 1915, Prince Konstantin Konstantinovich, as his brother Gabriel recalled, left for the Front in Galicia; they would never see each other again.[234]

Prince Igor, too, served with the Izmailovsky Regiment during the conflict before his ill-health led to his unlikely appointment as an Adjutant to Nicholas II.[235] He often accompanied the Emperor to Military Headquarters at Stavka in these years, and in early 1916, Nicholas II introduced him to Countess Nina Zarnekau, encouraging the young man to pursue her. Igor, according to his brother, fell hopelessly in love, and spent most of his time at Stavka escorting her on walks, and taking tea with her. *"She was all he could talk about,"* Prince Gabriel recalled.[236]

"Igor is behaving well," Nicholas II reported to his wife, *"and seems to be on splendid terms with everybody."*[237] But eventually his poor health took its toll. In April 1916, Nicholas II wrote to his wife that, during an expedition along the Dneiper River, Igor became exhausted while trying to row. *"He says that after a few strokes, he begins to cough and spit blood,"* the Emperor noted. *"For the same reason he cannot walk quickly-poor boy! And he is only twenty-two years old."*[238] In the fall of 1916, he fell severely ill with inflammation of the lungs, which soon devolved into pleurisy, and he was forced to return to Petrograd for treatment. *"Now he is out of danger,"* Empress Alexandra Feodorovna wrote to her husband at Stavka; *"Poor boy – he lies in the Marble Palace – what bad health they all of them have. I pity poor Mavra."*[239]

Grand Duke Konstantin Konstantinovich aged prematurely in the first year of the War; it was not only the stress over the uncertainty of Russia's position within the conflict, but a series of tragic blows, one falling upon another, that together took their toll and left him morose and fatalistic. The first of these involved Prince Oleg, undoubtedly his favorite son, and the one who most resembled him in temperament and artistic abilities.

At the beginning of the First World War, Prince Oleg Konstantinovich had joined his regiment, fighting the German advance in East Prussia, and saw action on 6/19 August 1914, in the Battle of Kauschen, one of the first conflicts in the hostilities. On that day, the Guards Cavalry units attempted an advance on a German reserve brigade, but for the first time faced the superior artillery power of the Kaiser's forces. Of the twenty-four officers of the Horse Guards Regiment at the battle, sixteen were wounded or killed. Prince Oleg, who was fighting alongside his brother Prince Ioann, came under enemy fire, but both men managed to escape safely.[240]

Just six weeks later, Oleg was involved in a cavalry attack near the village of Pilviski, in present-day Poland. On Saturday afternoon, 27 September/10 October he came under enemy fire leading his Cavalry Platoon in a chase of a retreating German battalion. In the exchange that ensued, one of the German soldiers shot Oleg. *"We rode into the attack,"* the Prince later explained. *"My horse suddenly reared up. Then I was wounded, and fell.*"²⁴¹

The wound, which at first appeared minor, was bandaged, and the Prince was evacuated to the Vitebsk Red Cross Hospital in Vilna, a difficult journey of fifteen hours, during which his condition worsened. On arrival at the hospital, he was rushed straight into surgery. Physicians determined that the bullet had entered Oleg at hip-level, striking the right sciatic prominence, passing through the rectum, and lodging firmly in the left sciatic prominence. Out of fear of blood poisoning, the surgical team left his wounds open.²⁴²

Initially, it seemed that Oleg would recover. He was progressing normally until the afternoon of 29 September/12 October, when he unexpectedly lapsed into unconsciousness; thereafter, he was only periodically awake. During one moment of lucidity, he said, *"I am happy to die. It will be good for the troops to know that the Imperial House does not fear to shed its blood."*²⁴³ At seven that evening his parents arrived at the hospital. *"It was completely dark as we went in,"* Elisabeth Mavrikievna later told Grand Duke Andrei Vladimirovich. *"The driver, who had to show us the way, moved so quickly that not a moment was wasted before we were with him, yet our steps through the streets and into the hospital seemed endless. We knelt around Oleg's bed. His death was only minutes away. He was completely conscious and aware, embracing me strongly."* Konstantin Konstantinovich had brought with him the Cross of the Order of St George that Grand Duke Konstantin Nikolaievich had been awarded a half-century earlier, and presented it to his son on behalf of Nicholas II. *"Grandfather's Cross,"* the dying Prince said, *"you have brought me Grandfather's Cross."* He fell into brief unconsciousness; when he awoke, his mother recalled, he *"opened his eyes and asked, astonished, why we were all standing in a circle around him."* The doctor gently explained that his parents had not seen him for a long time, and wanted to be with him. He closed his eyes for a few minutes, and then suddenly sat up in his bed, looked toward the window, and shouted, *"See! My horse! He is jumping! See! There he is, there he is! He is jumping!"* Then, as his mother later tearfully recounted, *"he lay down again, back on his pillows, and fell asleep forever."*²⁴⁴ Prince Oleg, who finally fell victim to blood poisoning and septic shock, became the only Romanov to die in the First World War.

Konstantin Konstantinovich and Elisabeth Mavrikievna accompanied their son's body on a special train back to Russia. Their destination was Ostashevo; in life, Oleg had enjoyed reading and writing under the trees above the Ruza River, and his grieving father wished his favorite son to rest here, surrounded by tranquil solitude.²⁴⁵ Other members of the family joined the sad procession along the way: Ioann and his wife Elena; Gabriel, Konstantin, Igor, and George Konstantinovich; Princess Tatiana Bagration-Moukhransky; Dimitri Konstantinovich; Queen Olga of the Hellenes; and Grand Duchess Elisabeth Feodorovna.²⁴⁶ Only eight-year-old Princess Vera was absent. She was devastated by her favorite brother's death, and desperately wanted to attend his funeral, but her parents deemed her too young to do so. This denial stung deeply and, even as an elderly woman, it was, she said, the one decision made by her parents with which she disagreed.²⁴⁷

On the cold, windy morning of 3 October the funeral train steamed slowly into the Volokolamsk Railroad Station near Ostashevo. The siding was decorated with flowers, and draped with black bunting that flapped in the chill breeze. To one side of the platform stood members of Konstantin and Elisabeth's Grand Ducal household; across from them was a deputation from the Corps de Pages in Petrograd; representatives from the Assembly of Nobility; and delegations from the Russian Zemstvo Union, the Moscow Provincial Zemstvo, and the city of Moscow.²⁴⁸ Beyond the military guard of honor, over a thousand local peasants stood, heads bared and faces bowed in respect.²⁴⁹

The military guard of honor presented arms as the train came to a halt, and the mourners gathered on the siding as clergy from Volokolamsk, assisted by Grand Duke Konstantin Konstantinovich's Personal Confessor, sung a liturgy.[250] The Grand Duke, his brother Dimitri, and Ioann, Gabriel, Konstantin, Igor, and George Konstantinovich all carried the Prince's metal coffin from the train to a waiting gun carriage and, as a military band struck up a funeral dirge, the procession rolled off through the rain, toward Ostashevo, the Grand Duchess and the other mourners all walking behind on foot. Dimitri Konstantinovich, stooped against the wind, carried a velvet cushion on which his nephew's awards rested, including Konstantin Nikolaievich's Cross of the Order of St George that Konstantin Konstantinovich had pinned on his dying son; behind him came Oleg's favorite horse, draped in black and with the Prince's boots reversed in the stirrups.[251]

In silence, the procession passed through the gates of Ostashevo and along the avenue to a spot high on a bluff overlooking the Ruza River. When Konstantin first announced his decision to bury his son here, in unconsecrated ground, there had been an outcry from clergy of the Orthodox Church, but the Grand Duke managed to have the estate clergy bless the soil and grant his wish.[252] On reaching the site, the Prince's body was lowered into the open grave after prayers, and members of his family threw in handfuls of earth atop the metal lid.[253]

Grand Duke Konstantin Konstantinovich commissioned the Church of St Oleg and St Seraphim of Sarov as a memorial and final resting place for his son. Designed by architects M. M. Peretiatkovich and S. M. Deshevov, the structure incorporated elements of art nouveau joined with medieval Russian church architecture, with a whitewashed façade crowned by a single drum and large onion dome; in appearance, it closely resembled the Church of the Icon of the Savior, built at the Moscow country estate of Abramtsevo owned by Savva Mamontov. Work on the church continued slowly throughout the years of the First World War, but the February Revolution halted its construction, and it was never finished nor consecrated. In 1922, Prince Oleg's coffin was taken from its grave on a bluff overlooking the Ruza, and interred by the Soviets in the vault of another church on the opposite shore of the river.[254] This church was destroyed in 1935, and Oleg's body was reburied nearby, in an unmarked grave.

After Oleg's death, his parents authorized a small biographical book on their son, to *"preserve his memory,"* as his mother explained. Called simply *Knyaz Oleg*, the book included a collection of essays, as well as entries from the Prince's diaries, and a number of photographs culled from his private albums. Each copy featured two original watercolors and poems by Oleg. *"It is a wonderful history,"* Elisabeth Mavrikievna said, *"especially those parts that come from his journal. I don't want to sound like a book seller, but many people have told me that they came to know him through this book."*[255]

The loss of his favorite son fell heavily on Grand Duke Konstantin Konstantinovich, and he never recovered his former spirit. Just seven months later, disaster again struck. This time, it was his son-in-law Prince Konstantin Bagration-Moukhransky, falling victim to the horrors of war.

After his marriage to Princess Tatiana Konstantinovna, Prince Konstantin Bagration-Moukhransky had transferred to the Chevalier Life Guards Regiment, where he rose rapidly through the officer ranks, being promoted a lieutenant in 1913, and a Captain a year later. In that same year Nicholas II made him an Adjutant at the Imperial Court, which allowed him to spend a great deal of time with his wife and family at Pavlovsk. But, with the outbreak of the First World War, he was sent to the Front. He served with his regiment in Galicia and in Poland before being transferred in 1915 back to the Erivan Life Guard Grenadier Regiment. In the spring of 1915, the company was dispatched to Galicia to fight against the Austro-Hungarian forces in anticipation of a campaign in the Carpathian Mountains. On 19 May 1915, he was shot and killed during a battle at Yaroslav, near Lemberg, at the age of twenty-six. Conditions did not allow for the transportation of his body back to St Petersburg, and he was buried in the Svetitskhoveli Cathedral in Mtzkheta, the ancient capital of Georgia. In recognition of his bravery and service, Nicholas II posthumously awarded the Prince the Cross of the Order of St George. At the age of twenty-five, Princess Tatiana was a widow, left with two small children to raise.

These family tragedies struck Grand Duke Konstantin a devastating blow. His health began to break down, and more and more he could be found collapsed on a sofa in his study, suffering from chest pains. To his son Gabriel, he explained wearily, *"I feel everything in my heart, and that makes it weak."*[256] N. N. Sergeievsky, visiting the Grand Duke at Pavlovsk, noted that his face *"had visibly aged, and his features sunk."*[257]

In the spring of 1915, Prince Vladimir Paley, son of Grand Duke Paul Alexandrovich's morganatic marriage and himself a burgeoning poet, visited the ailing Konstantin Konstantinovich at Pavlovsk. The Prince had, for a year, been translating Konstantin Konstantinovich's great final work, the play *The King of Judea*, and he wanted the author's opinion of his progress. With him, he took his mother Olga, Princess Paley, Paul Alexandrovich's morganatic wife; Pavlovsk was one of the few Romanov palaces where the Grand Duke's morganatic wife was welcomed, and not subjected to petty humiliations at the hands of her husband's relatives.[258]

The pair found Konstantin Konstantinovich sitting in a chair in his study, looking tired and depressed. The Prince read his translation of the first two acts, and finished with a poem he had written and dedicated to Konstantin. When the young man finished, the Grand Duke burst into tears. *"I have had one of the greatest emotions of my life,"* he sobbed. *"I cannot say any more. I am dying. I pass on to him my lyre. I bequeath to him my talent as a poet, as thought he were my son."*[259]

The Grand Duke's fatalistic words proved only too true. A few weeks later, on Tuesday, 2/15 June 1915, he was resting on a sofa in his study at Pavlovsk, following doctors' orders that he attempt to relax; just a few months earlier, he had suffered from heart trouble, and everyone noted that with the death of his favorite son Oleg he seemed to have lost the will to live. His daughter Vera, then nine, happened to be sitting with him when, as she recalled, *"I suddenly heard Papa gasping for breath. After hearing three or four more horrible gasps, I ran to Mama's bedroom, where she was trying on a new, colorful dress, probably for our intended journey to Ostashevo as soon as Papa had recovered."* In a rush, the young girl cried, *"Papa can't breath!"* The Grand Duchess ran from her room to her husband's study, but by the time she arrived, she found him laying quietly on the sofa, his breathing silenced.[260] That afternoon, Grand Duke Konstantin Konstantinovich died. He was only fifty-six-years-old.

Because Princes Ioann, Gabriel, Konstantin, and Igor Konstantinovich were all serving with their various regiments at the Front in the War, it fell to thirteen-year-old Prince George Konstantinovich to break the news of his father's passing to the Emperor. Nicholas II was at nearby Tsarskoe Selo when, just after eight that night, the Duty Adjutant announced the young Prince's arrival. Tearfully but with composure, he broke the news of his father's death. Nicholas comforted the boy, and quickly informed his family before returning with him to Pavlovsk just after nine, where he attended the first requiem service for the Grand Duke. Aside from the Grand Duke's widow, the only members of his immediate family present were his two youngest children, George and

Vera; his brother Grand Duke Dimitri Konstantinovich; and his sister Queen Olga of the Hellenes, who had been staying at Pavlovsk at the time of her brother's death.

When the physicians autopsied the Grand Duke's body, they found that a heart attack had killed him; on examining the heart itself, the organ was found to be ulcerated and in extremely disintegrated condition. When the post-mortem had ended, the Grand Duke was embalmed; ordinarily this was not permitted in the Orthodox Church, but exceptions were made for members of the Imperial Family, who had to be on public view after their deaths for a period of time. For seven days, the body of the Grand Duke lay in state in the Palace's Italian Hall, on a bier surrounded by a guard-of-honor formed of soldiers from the Imperial Regiments in which he had served, and of the cadets from the Military Training Institutes. *"Next to the Hall where only a month before a literary morning, with lovely music and poetry, had taken place,"* recalled the Grand Duke's friend N. N. Sergeievsky, *"there was now the sound of mourning prayers over the lifeless body of our August Poet, who had left us so unnaturally early. I gazed on him, and could not take my eyes away from his kind features, which expressed, as always, so much good will. He had changed very little, and his face, in its awe-inspiring sleep, looked beautiful."*[261] Unfortunately, this appearance was not to last long. The embalmer was too rushed in his work, and the result was poorly executed. After a few days, Gabriel noticed, his father's face had already begun to show signs of decay.[262]

Every day, Nicholas II attended the requiem services at Pavlovsk; by Friday, 5/18 June, the Grand Duke's older sons had returned from the War to participate in the services, and there was a solemn family dinner that evening. On the eighth day, Sunday, 7/20 June 1915, nearly the entire Imperial Family attended a requiem for the Grand Duke, held at two o'clock in the elaborate Italian Hall, led by Nicholas II and his daughters Olga, Tatiana, and Marie. They watched as the coffin was carried down the Palace Staircase and through the Egyptian Vestibule to the courtyard, where a gun carriage waited to convey the Grand Duke's remains to the nearby Voksal Station, where a funeral train conveyed them to the Imperial capital.[263]

Grand Duke Konstantin Konstantinovich's state funeral was the last to be held in Imperial Russia. The coffin was conveyed from the Nicholas Station in St Petersburg upon a gun carriage, drawn through the streets by horses covered with white palls and led by grooms in black liveries; at its side walked a guard-of-honor of members of the Preobrajenzky Life Guards and the Izmailovsky Life Guards Regiments, as well as members of the Corps des Pages and the Cadet Corps. Nicholas II followed on foot, surrounded by the Grand Dukes; after them, in closed carriages, came Grand Duchess Elisabeth Mavrikievna and the women of the Imperial Family. Along the route, which wound from the Station along Gorokhovaya to the Fontanka Canal, through the Champs des Mars and over the Troitsky Bridge across the Neva, thousands of people waited in lines four and five people deep-there as much to see a rare appearance of the Imperial Family as to pay their respects to the retiring Grand Duke. The coffin rested on a bier in the Cathedral of the Fortress of SS Peter and Paul that night, beneath a canopy of black crepe supported by four poles covered with gold brocade and adorned with gold fringe; above, plumes of white ostrich feathers waved softly in the mild breeze.[264]

One of the few family members absent was Grand Duke Michael Alexandrovich, who remained with his regiment, much to the apparent consternation of his relatives. His morganatic wife, Countess Brassova, wrote him a stern letter in which she chided him for his decision: *"Why do you always harm yourself, and why didn't you come for Konstantin Konstantinovich's funeral? Literally all your relatives came en masse, only you didn't appear...your absence was conspicuous. Even assuming that you did not feel like showing your face at a family gathering, you could still have taken that opportunity just to come home!"*[265]

The following day, Monday, 8/21 June 1915, the Metropolitan of St Petersburg conducted the burial service, which lasted for two and a half hours. At the end of the service, Gabriel recalled, he saw his mother approach the coffin. Throughout the various ceremonies, Elisabeth Mavrikievna had kept her feelings to herself, showing no emotion, but now her actions betrayed her. As the coffin lid was slowly pulled up over the body, she bent down, attempting to see her husband's face for as long as she could before he disappeared forever.[266]

The coffin was carried from the Cathedral and out a side door, down a stone passage to the Grand Ducal Vault, built in 1908 to house the remains of lesser members of the Imperial Family. Here, a vault had been prepared, in the second row in front of the iconostasis; the Grand Duke's final resting place was directly behind those of his parents, and of his brother Vyacheslav.[267] After the coffin was lowered, Elisabeth Mavrikievna approached the open grave; in her hands she held a small wooden box that the Grand Duke had carried with him wherever he went, filled with earth taken from the garden at Strelna, the Palace where the Grand Duke had spent so much of his life. She opened the box and slowly sprinkled the contents upon the lid of the coffin as a last tribute to her husband.[268]

Grand Duke Konstantin Konstantinovich became the last member of the Romanov Dynasty to be buried in a state ceremony before the Revolution, and the last to be interred in the Grand Ducal Vault that adjoins the Cathedral in the Fortress of SS Peter and Paul. It was not until 1992 that another Romanov, Grand Duke Vladimir Kirillovich, was buried in the Grand Ducal Vault. In 1995, the bodies of his father and mother, Grand Duke Kirill Vladimirovich and Grand Duchess Victoria Feodorovna (Ducky) were brought back to Russia from Coburg and also placed in the Grand Ducal Vault. In 1998, the remains of Emperor Nicholas II, Empress Alexandra Feodorovna, three of their children, and the four members of their retinue assassinated with them by the Bolsheviks at Ekaterinburg in July, 1918, were buried in the Cathedral's St Catherine's Chapel.

There was a peculiar – and telling – footnote to the Grand Duke's death. Grand Duchess Elisabeth Mavrikievna was perplexed, on reading his will, to find that her husband had added a clause that stipulated that his diaries would remain locked away and could not be read by anyone until ninety-nine-years after his death.[269] Discussing this peculiarity with her, Grand Duke Andrei Vladimirovich wrote: *"He hadn't let anyone – even her – read them in life, and she used to tease him that he was writing all sorts of complaints and criticisms about her in there. Now she was worried that this might really have been the case, but that she was going to honor his request anyway."*[270] Grand Duke Konstantin Konstantinovich, to the last, attempted to preserve the secret of his homosexuality. Yet, preserved in the pages of his diary, is a clearer, more interesting, and profoundly more moving portrait of the man than history has yet recorded.

Back in 1886, Konstantin Konstantinovich published his first verse for the general public, under the pseudonym of "K. R." for Konstantin Romanov; the quest for anonymity was futile, however, and soon everyone knew of the Grand Duke's work. Many of his poems were widely acclaimed, and became very popular among the Russian public. More than seventy of these verses were set to music, most notably by composer Peter Tchaikovsky, who was so impressed by the Grand Duke's efforts that he spent several of his last years working on scoring accompaniment to the poems.

As a man of literary and artistic talent, the Grand Duke also wrote several plays: in contrast to his poetry, these early efforts were rather mediocre, though filled with

Konstantin Konstantinovich's soaring lyricism and studied use of language; his greatest theatrical work would only come a few years before his death. He devoted enormous energy and time to translating the works of Byron, Schiller, and Goethe into Russian – the first time that their prose and poetry could be read in complete Russian translations. His efforts were so successful that Alexander III asked him to translate the works of Shakespeare as well. This was a massive task, and it was not until 1900 that the first Russian version of Hamlet had been completed and published. To celebrate, the Grand Duke received permission from Nicholas II to stage the first Russian-language version of the play in 1900. The performance took place in the Hermitage Theater of the Winter Palace on 17 February 1900, before a specially invited audience largely composed of members of the Imperial family (including Nicholas and Alexandra), the Russian Court, and members of the aristocracy. Not content to simply provide the texts, the Grand Duke took the title role in the production, donning 16th Century costume, black tights, and a long, curly wig to perfect his appearance as the Prince of Denmark. The performance began at seven in the evening, and ended six-and-a-half hours later, interrupted by several intervals and a dinner in the halls of the Hermitage. Nicholas II termed it *"a great success,"* adding that the Grand Duke *"performed his role the best of all."*[271] But the Grand Duke, who had performed the unexpurgated version of the play, later learned that Empress Alexandra Feodorovna, with her censorious and prim morality, had been greatly displeased at some of the language and action.[272]

The performance proved a great success, and launched the prolific Grand Duke on yet another career as an amateur play write. His involvement with the theatrical world culminated in 1913 when, along with Stanislavsky and a host of other important figures in the world of Russian Theater, he helped established the Russian State Theater Museum as a center of Russian culture.

Above all else, though, it was the Grand Duke's artistic and cultural legacy that infused his existence. Baroness Buxhoeveden recalled: *"He was a perfect linguist and collector; when one crossed the threshold of his rooms one felt surrounded by an atmosphere of perfect taste."*[273] In 1914, he had his greatest triumph, when his important play, *The King of Judea*, premiered in the Imperial capital. It became Russia's first Passion Play, and mingled powerful religious imagery with a rich score by composer Alexander Glazunov.

The play had its genesis in an exchange of letters between Konstantin and composer Peter Tchaikovsky in 1889. *"I have been inspired,"* the Grand Duke wrote to his friend, *"and have written several minor poems, apparently not too unsuccessful. But it is all small change, and although I do not blame a poet for being unable to write anything more important than lyric poetry, all the same I mortally desire to write something major. But it must be that I will never find it within myself."* To this, Tchaikovsky replied with a suggestion: *"You say that you do not hope to write something major. But in view of your youth I am certain that you will write something important. As you have the happiness of possessing a live, warm, religious feeling, why not choose a theme from the New Testament for your proposed important creation?"* Konstantin Konstantinovich responded: *"I have thought about it, and some day it may please God I will undertake this work, but right now I have not yet sufficiently matured for such a great enterprise."*[274] But the seed was born, and Tchaikovsky's advice eventually found voice in the Grand Duke's *King of Judea*.

At the end of 1912, Alexander Glazunov later recalled, two men visited him at the Conservatoire in St Petersburg. One was Captain P. Daniltschenko of Grand Duke Konstantin Konstantinovich's Izmailovsky Guards Regiment; the other was Nicholas Arbatov, a distinguished producer. Both had been sent by the Grand Duke to ask if Glazunov would compose the score for *The King of Judea*. With some trepidation

Glazunov agreed. Due to the Orthodox Church's restrictions and the Grand Duke's fear of censorship, Konstantin Konstantinovich had decided that, during the staging of the play, the figure of Christ would not be seen at all. Instead, Glazunov was to convey the specter of his presence through the use of music. Throughout 1913, he labored over the orchestration and vocal score, finally settling on a leitmotif that he wove throughout the story. He traveled to Pavlovsk where he performed the score privately for the Grand Duke. Konstantin, he later wrote, *"was enthusiastic about it. As a result, I decided to arrange the orchestration in such a way that the music could be used for a concert-like performance."*[275]

The Grand Duke had hoped that the play would receive public staging and acclaim. To this end, when he had completed it, Konstantin Konstantinovich submitted a copy to the Holy Synod, whose approval was required for all religious works. They refused the Grand Duke permission to stage the play for the general public, a decision that Nicholas II himself approved, as he explained to his cousin: *"It made the deepest impression on me – more than once my eyes filled with tears and I had a lump in my throat. I am certain that to see your play on stage and to hear the beautiful paraphrasing of what each of us knows from the Gospels, all this could but produce the most profound effect on the spectator. It is for this reason that I share the opinion of the Holy Synod that it cannot be staged publicly. However the Chinese Theater of the Hermitage could be made available for it, as well as the singers who participate in the Izmailovsky celebrations. I told your wife in conversation that, as well as the lofty sentiments that it inspired in me, I was also fired by a hatred of the Jews, who crucified Christ. I think the common Russian man would feel the same thing, if he saw it on stage, and from there it would not be far to the possibility of a pogrom. These are the impressions evoked by the dramatic strength of your latest work."*[276]

The King of Judea duly premiered on January 9, 1914, in the Hermitage Theater of the Winter Palace, with nearly all of the Imperial Family present. Arbatov took charge of stage direction, Hugo Warlich conducted the orchestra, and the famed Michael Fokine choreographed the performance.[277] The Grand Duke himself played Joseph of Arimathea, and his son Prince Konstantin Konstantinovich played a Roman prefect. The pair had themselves photographed in their costumes: the Grand Duke aged, his gray beard and hair accentuated by a long wig, and dressed in a tunic, and his son slim and tall, a laurel wreath on his head and a cowl draped across his tunic. It was to be the Grand Duke's swan song.

For Grand Duchess Elisabeth Mavrikievna, life after her husband's death was fraught with sadness. She spent the war years and the revolutionary period mainly at Pavlovsk. Most material possessions were confiscated by the Bolsheviks and what Elisabeth could turn into cash, was used to feed her family.

In July 1918 three of her sons (Ioann, Igor and Konstantin) were killed by the Bolsheviks at Alapaievsk. Executed with the Konstantinovichi princes were also Grand Duchess Elisabeth Feodorovna, Grand Duke Serge Mikhailovich and Prince Vladimir Paley, Grand Duke Paul Alexandrovich's son by his second wife. It was a devastating blow for the Konstantinovichi branch of the Imperial Family, not to mention poor, heartbroken Elisabeth Mavrikievna.

One month later, however, Elisabeth Mavrikievna finally accepted an offer from the Queen of Sweden to escape. The Queen, formerly Princess Victoria of Baden, had been a childhood friend of the Grand Duchess, and had repeatedly begged her to leave Russia. For several months, Elisabeth Mavrikievna had refused, saying that without word from her sons, she did not want to leave the Marble Palace in the event that they would one day appear unannounced. Finally, after hearing rumors that Ioann,

Above left: Grand Duke Vladimir Alexandrovich of Russia (1847-1909).

Above right: Grand Duchess Marie Pavlovna (née Mecklenburg-Schwerin).

Right: The Vladimirovichi children in 1886. From top: Grand Duke Boris Vladimirovich, Grand Duke Andrei Vladimirovich, Grand Duke Kirill Vladimirovich, and Grand Duchess Helen Vladimirovna. At center is their sailor companion.

Above, from left: Grand Duke Andrei Vladimirovich, Grand Duke Vladimir Alexandrovich, Grand Duchess Helen Vladimirovna, Grand Duke Kirill Vladimirovich, Grand Duke Boris Vladimirovich and Grand Duchess Marie Pavlovna.

Left: Two cousins who at times were at loggerheads: Grand Duke Kirill Vladimirovich and Tsar Nicholas II.

Right: Grand Duke Kirill Vladimirovich, Tsar Nicholas II, and Hereditary Prince Ernst of Hohenlohe-Langenburg.

Below left: Empress Alexandra Feodorovna, Grand Duke Ernst Ludwig of Hesse and by Rhine, and Grand Duchess Elisabeth Feodorovna.

Below right: Grand Duchess Victoria Melita of Hesse and by Rhine (née Edinburgh). In her marriage with Ernst Ludwig, Empress Alexandra Feodorovna's brother, Victoria Melita soon discovered that enjoying a good laugh and the same pranks were not a solid foundation for a successful marital life. Frustrated, she sought companionship in the embrace of Grand Duke Kirill Vladimirovich, much to the ire of Tsar Nicholas II.

Above, attending the coronation of Tsar Nicholas II in 1896. From left, standing: Grand Duchess Vera Konstantinovna, Grand Duchess Anastasia Mikhailovna, Grand Duchess Marie Pavlovna Sr., Grand Duchess Helen Vladimirovna, Grand Duchess Elisabeth Mavrikievna and Princess Helene of Saxe-Altenburg (née Mecklenburg-Strelitz). Seated: Grand Duchess Alexandra Iosifovna and the Duchess of Connaught (née Princess Louise of Prussia). In the foreground is Duchess Elsa of Württemberg, daughter of Grand Duchess Vera Konstantinovna.

Right: Grand Duke Kirill Vladimirovich in Russian Naval uniform.

Attending a royal gathering in Coburg. In the carriage, from left: Grand Duchess Marie Alexandrovna of Russia (Duchess of Edinburgh and of Saxe-Coburg & Gotha) with her daughters, Crown Princess Marie of Romania, Grand Duchess Victoria Melita of Hesse and by Rhine and Fürstin Alexandra of Hohenlohe-Langenburg. Behind Marie of Romania's right shoulder is King Ferdinand I of Bulgaria in profile.

The Vladimirovichi c. 1912. Standing in back: Grand Duke Andrei Vladimirovich, Prince Nicholas of Greece, Grand Duchess Marie Pavlovna Sr., Grand Duke Kirill Vladimirovich and Grand Duke Boris Vladimirovich. Seated, middle row, same order: Princess Marina of Greece and her mother Grand Duchess Helen Vladimirovna, Princess Elisabeth of Greece, and Grand Duchess Victoria Feodorovna with her daughters Maria Kirillovna and Kira Kirilovna. In the foreground: Princess Olga of Greece.

Just before the Great War, Grand Duchess Victoria Feodorovna with her cousin Empress Alexandra.

From left to right: Princess Alexandra of Hohenlohe-Langenburg, Grand Duke Vladimir Kirillovich, Princess Irma of Hohenlohe-Langenburg, Prince Friedrich Josias of Saxe-Coburg & Gotha, Grand Duchess Kira Kirillovna, and Princess Sibylla of Saxe-Coburg & Gotha.

From left to right: Grand Duke Kirill Vladimirovich, Grand Duchess Victoria Feodorovna, Grand Duke Vladimir Kirillovich and Grand Duchess Kira Kirillovna (Ker Argonid, c. 1929)

Right: Grand Duchess Victoria Feodorovna helped with her husband's political activities. She traveled to the USA to meet with exiled Russian groups that not only supported her husband's claims in exile, but also his anti-Bolshevik political movement. A quiet personality, Victoria Feodorovna's introspective character did little to prepare her for the vicissitudes life had in store for her.

Below left: Grand Duke Vladimir Kirillovich and his cousin Prince Friedrich Josias of Saxe-Coburg & Gotha, who in 1954 succeeded his father Duke Carl Eduard as Head of House.

Below right: Grand Duchess Maria Kirillovna of Russia and her first cousin Princess Ileana of Romania. Maria's mother, Victoria Feodorovna, was a younger sister of Ileana's mother, Queen Marie of Romania.

Below right: Grand Duchess Maria Kirillovna with four of her children. From left: Princess Kira-Melita (who married Prince Andrej of Yugoslavia), Prince Karl-Wladimir (who married Princess Marie Louise of Bulgaria), Maria Kirillovna holding Margarita (who married the Fürst of Hohenzollern), and Hereditary Prince Emich (who married Duchess Eilika of Oldenburg).

Grand Duke Vladimir Kirillovich. (1917-1992)

The wedding of Grand Duchess Kira Kirillovna and Prince Louis Ferdinand of Prussia, Cecilienhof, Potsdam, 2 May 1938. Standing in back, from left: Prince Hubertus of Prussia, Hereditary Grand Duke Friedrich Franz of Mecklenburg-Schwerin, Prince Friedrich of Prussia, Prince Oskar of Prussia, Prince Burchard of Prussia, Duke Christian Ludwig of Mecklenburg-Schwerin. Front row, same order: Prince Karl Franz Josef of Prussia, Prince Louis Ferdinand of Prussia, Grand Duchess Kira Kirillovna of Russia, Grand Duke Vladimir Kirillovich, Grand Duke Dimitri Pavlovich and Prince Vsevelod Ioannovich of Russia.

While on a visit to their childhood home, Ker Argonid, Grand Duke Vladimir and his sister Grand Duchess Kira pose with their spouses for a photo. Grand Duchess Leonida stands behind Kira, while Prince Louis Ferdinand of Prussia stands next to his sister-in-law Leonida. In 1967 Kira Kirillovna suffered a massive health crisis while visiting her brother in St Briac-sur-Mer. Nothing could be done to save her.

Below left: The wedding of Grand Duchess Maria Vladimirovna and Prince Franz of Prussia.

Below right: Grand Duchess Maria Vladimirovna and her son Grand Duke George Mikhailovich.

Grand Duke Boris Vladimirovich of Russia. (1877-1943)

Grand Duke Boris Vladimirovich and his wife Zinaida Rachevsky while touring the USA.

Grand Duke Andrei Vladimirovich of Russia. (1879-1956)

Mathilde Kschessinska, Princess Romanovsky-Krassinsky, Grand Duke Andrei's wife.

Right: Grand Duke Dimitri Pavlovich in 1900. After Nicholas II banned his uncle Grand Duke Paul Alexandrovich from Russia for marrying morganatically, Dimitri and his sister Maria Pavlovna Jr. became the wards of Grand Duke Serge Alexandrovich and his wife Elisabeth Feodorovna. It was not a happy childhood for Marie and Dimitri. At least, Dimitri was the main recipient of his uncle Serge's considerable fortune after in 1905 assassins blew to pieces the hated former Governor of Moscow.

Below left: Four generations: Grand Duchess Alexandra Iosifovna, Queen Olga of Greece, Grand Duchess Alexandra Georgievna and Grand Duchess Marie Pavlovna Jr.

Below right: Grand Duchess Marie Pavlovna Jr. and her brother Grand Duke Dimitri Pavlovich, c. 1892.

Right: Grand Duke Dimitri Pavlovich spending time with his cousin Tsar Nicholas II and Grand Duchess Olga Nikolaievna, whom many expected Dimitri would eventually marry.

Below left: Grand Duke Dimitri Pavlovich on his wedding day to Audrey Emery, a wealthy American whose fortune made the groom's exile financially secure.

Below right: In due time, Grand Duke Dimitri Pavlovich became a regular visitor to the wealthy enclave of Palm Beach, Florida. His son, Paul Dimitrievich, would later become Mayor of Palm Beach.

Grand Duke Konstantin Nikolaievich of Russia. (1827-1892)

Grand Duchess Alexandra Iosifovna of Russia. (1830-1911)

Grand Duke Nicholas Konstantinovich of Russia. (1850-1918)

Grand Duke Nicholas Konstantinovich and his wife Nadezhda Dreyer.

Right: Grand Duke Konstantin Konstantinovich. Known as KR, Konstantin was among the most erudite of the Romanovs. He was a talented poet and a man of letters. His theatrical productions were legendary and well-respected, as was his translation of Shakespeare's works into Russian.

Below left: From left, Grand Duke Dimitri Konstantinovich, Grand Duke Vyacheslav Konstantinovich, Grand Duke Konstantin Konstantinovich and Grand Duchess Vera Konstantinovna.

Below right: Two inseparable friends and cousins: Grand Duke Konstantin Konstantinovich and Grand Duke Serge Alexandrovich.

Right: Grand Duchess Elisabeth Mavrikievna (née Saxe-Altenburg). Mavra, as Elisabeth was known to the Romanovs, led a happy, fulfilled and contented life in Russia. Her charmed existence was brought to a sad and tragic end by both the Great War and the Russian Revolution.

Below: The Konstantinovich were a tight-knit family group. When Grand Duchess Alexandra Iosifovna suffered a debilitating stroke, her children flocked to her side. In this image dating from 1903 she is surrounded by her descendants. From left, Grand Duke Dimitri Konstantinovich, Grand Duke Konstantin Konstantinovich, Princess Tatiana Konstantinovna, Grand Duchess Alexandra Iosifovna, Queen Olga of Greece, Grand Duchess Vera Konstantinovna, Prince Ioann Konstantinovich, Grand Duchess Elisabeth Mavrikievna, Prince Christopher of Greece, Prince Gabriel Konstantinovich. On the floor: Princes Nicholas, Igor and Oleg Konstantinovich.

Prince Ioann Konstantinovich of Russia.
(1886-1918)

Prince Konstantin Konstantinovich of Russia.
(1891-1918).

Prince Oleg Konstantinovich of Russia.
(1892-1914)

Prince Igor Konstantinovich of Russia.
(1894-1918)

Right: Prince George Konstantinovich, the youngest son of Grand Duke Konstantin Konstantinovich escaped Russia with his mother and sister. Initially, they lived in Stockholm under the protection of the Swedish Royal Family. Later Mavra took her children to Altenburg, where she lived with her brother Duke Ernst II. She died in Leipizg in 1927. George Konstantinovich settled in the USA and had a successful career as an interior decorator. It was cut short by his untimely death in 1938.

Below right: Grand Duke Dimitri Konstantinovich (1860-1919).

Below left: Grand Duke Vyacheslav Konstantinovich (1862-1879).

Grand Duke Nicholas Nikolaievich of Russia. (1856-1929)

During the Great War, Tsar Nicholas II listens to Grand Duke Nicholas Nikolaievich.

Grand Duke Peter Nikolaievich of Russia. (1864-1931)

Grand Duchess Militza Nikolaievna of Russia. (1866-1951)

Right: Grand Duke Michael Nikolaievich. A trusted advisor to his brother Tsar Alexander II, Michael served as Viceroy of the Caucasus for many years.

Bottom left: Grand Duke Nicholas Mikhailovich (1860-1919).

Bottom right: Grand Duke Michael Mikhailovich (1861-1929).

Grand Duke George Mikhailovich of Russia.
(1863-1918)

Grand Duke Alexander Mikhailovich of Russia.
(1866-1933)

Prince Serge Mikhailovich of Russia.
(1869-1918)

Grand Duke Alexis Mikhailovich of Russia.
(1875-1895)

Right: Grand Duke Michael Mikhailovich with his family. In 1891 Miche-Miche, as Michael was known within the Romanov Family circle, married in contravention of the House Laws. His wife was Countess Sophie von Merenberg, herself the morganatic daughter of a Prince of Nassau and a daughter of Alexander Pushkin. Banned from entering Russia by a furious Tsar Alexander III, Miche-Miche settled in England. In this image, originally from his private collection, Miche-Miche and Sophie are surrounded by their children: Anastasia (Zia), Nadejda (Nada) and Michael (Boy).

Below left: Grand Duke Michael Mikhailovich in full Russian uniform.

Below right: The wartime wedding of Countess Nada de Torby and Prince George of Battenberg.

Right: Grand Duke George Mikhailovich with his daughters Xenia and Nina. The girls survived the revolution, having stayed in England during the duration of the Great War. Nina married Georgian Prince Paul Chavchavadze, with whom she settled in the USA. Xenia firstly married American millionaire Willam B. Leeds Jr., whose own mother was Nancy Stewart Leeds, the first wife of Prince Christopher of Greece.

Below left: A private photo of Grand Duke George Mikhailovich.

Below right: Grand Duchesseses Marie Georgievna and Xenia Alexandrovna were not only sisters-in-law, but first cousins as well. Both were granddaughters of King Christian IX of Denmark.

Right: Grand Duke Alexander Mikhailovich. He was an early enthusiast and decided supporter of aviation.

Below: The family of Grand Duke Alexander Mikhailovich and Grand Duchess Xenia Alexandrovna c. 1909. From left: Prince Nikita Alexandrovich, Princess Irina Alexandrovna, Prince Andrei Alexandrovich, Prince Dimitri Alexandrovich, Grand Duchess Xenia Alexandrovna with Prince Vassili Alexandrovich, Prince Feodor Alexandrovich, Prince Rostislav Alexandrovich, and Grand Duke Alexander Mikhailovich.

Konstantin, and Igor Konstantinovich had been killed at Alapaievsk, she reluctantly agreed to leave Russia.[277]

Swedish diplomats managed to obtain travel passports for the Grand Duchess and her two children Vera and George, along with her grandchildren and a few members of her household. They left St Petersburg aboard the Swedish vessel *Angermanland* on what would prove a perilous voyage. A Soviet agent had managed to sneak aboard as well, and several times the Grand Duchess's luggage, as well as that of her children, was searched for valuables; suspecting that this would happen, Elisabeth Mavrikievna had given all of her jewels and other items of value to a Swedish diplomat to carry. After eight long, turbulent days spent on the stormy Gulf of Finland and in the Baltic, during which the ship was stopped and searched by both the Soviets and the Germans, the party finally reached Stockholm.[278]

The Grand Duchess lived first in Sweden, then in Belgium, accepting an offer of hospitality from King Albert and Queen Elisabeth with some reluctance, for she did not want to become a burden to her royal friends.[279] Eventually, she returned to her native Altenburg, where she spent her remaining days with her family.[280] Few members of the Romanov family had lost as much as had she: her son Oleg and her son-in-law Prince Konstantin Bagration-Moukhransky to the First World War, her husband to a heart attack, and three of her sons as well as her favorite brother-in-law to Bolshevik assassins. She died in Leipzig on Thursday, 24 March 1927, and was buried with her parents in the Agnes Memorial Chapel in Altenburg; in 1939, her remains were transferred to a new mausoleum in Trockenborn-Wolfersdorf, where she was buried near several of her siblings.

The four surviving Konstantinovichi princes escaped Russia and died in exile. Prince Gabriel Konstantinovich settled in France. His wife Antonina predeceased him, dying in 1950. One year later Gabriel remarried, his second wife being Princess Irina Kurakin. Gabriel died in Paris in 1955, his second wife survived him by nearly four decades.[281]

Once in the safety of Western Europe, Princess Tatiana Konstantinovna remarried. In 1921 Alexander Korochentzov became her second husband, however he died the following year. Years later Tatiana took Holy Orders and became a nun. As Mother Tamara she was the Abbess of the Mount of Olives Convent in Jerusalem, where she died in 1970.[282]

Prince George Konstantinovich lived with his mother until her death in 1927. Some time later he relocated to the United States, where he became a successful interior decorator. He died of complications following surgery in November of 1938.[283] George died unmarried.

After the death of her mother, Princess Vera Konstantinovna lived in Bavaria and London before returning to Germany, where she spent the difficult years of World War II. In 1951 she also settled in the United States, where she worked for the Tolstoy Foundation. *"I didn't leave Russia, Russia left me,"*[284] Vera once said. She died in Nyack, New York, in 2001. She rests next to her brother George at the cemetery of the Russian Orthodox Monastery of Novo-Diveyevo in Nanuet, New York. Vera Konstantinovna was the next to last Romanov born in Russia to die.[285]

Grand Duke Dimitri Konstantinovich
(1860-1919)

By Penny Wilson

Unlike his elder brother Nicholas, whose wayward behavior led to scandal and scorn, or even Konstantin Konstantinovich, upon whom the public smiled and offered laudatory comments, Grand Duke Dimitri Konstantinovich was the quietest of all the Konstantinovichi sons. His was a life lived on the edge of obscurity, or at least as obscure as a Romanov Grand Duke could make himself. He sought no recognition for his hard work, and disliked any public attention.

Dimitri had been born at Strelna on Wednesday, 1/13 June 1860, the third son and fifth child of Konstantin Nikolaievich and Alexandra Iosifovna. A week later, his christening was held in the Cathedral of the Winter Palace in St Petersburg. His godparents included his uncle, Emperor Alexander II, and his aunt, Grand Duchess Alexandra Petrovna, wife of Grand Duke Nicholas Nikolaievich, Sr.[1] At his christening, Dimitri Konstantinovich was named Honorary Colonel-in-Chief of the Mingrelia Grenadier Life Guards Regiment, and enrolled as an honorary member of the Izmailovsky Life Guards Regiment and of the Horse Guards Regiment.[2] A month later, he was also enrolled in the Garde Equipage, and also in the Imperial Family's 4th Rifle Battalion Life Guards Infantry Regiment.

When he reached the age of seven, Dimitri Konstantinovich's education was turned over to Alexis Zelenoy, an officer who had served under his father in the Imperial Navy. His lessons followed the usual course, with sciences, arithmetic, Russian and world history, composition, and geography, alternating with languages and the arts. As a child, the young Grand Duke learned French, German, and English, the latter widely used within the Imperial nurseries. With Konstantin Nikolaievich's love of the sea, lessons were also arranged in naval warfare and tactics, and although Dimitri Konstantinovich – like his brothers – disappointed his father's hopes and abandoned a career in the Navy in favor of the Imperial Army, he was entranced by the tales of naval battles and circumnavigation. Father Arsene Dvukarev, a monk from the Troitsky-Sergeievsky Monastery near Peterhof, taught religion, instilling in his young charge a deep reverence for the Russian Orthodox Church. There were twice-weekly lessons on the piano and on the violin, and an instructor from the Imperial Conservatoire, Professor Samus, came to Strelna and to Pavlovsk to give the Grand Duke singing lessons. Countess Nathalia Keller, a Freilina to Grand Duchess Alexandra Iosifovna, later recalled that Dimitri Konstantinovich was, *"very attentive, diligent, and curious; he studied gladly, and with a great deal of zeal. He was always polite and attentive, capable and kind. One could feel his thirst for knowledge, and he was always ready to learn. Every subject seemed to interest him, and he was always full of questions."*[3]

The young Grand Duke was also extremely modest and withdrawn; not as boisterous as his elder brother Nicholas, he – like his brother Konstantin Konstantinovich – seemed to be more of an introvert, preferring quiet time spent reading to more usual childhood pursuits. But in the company of his favorite brother, Vyacheslav, even Dimitri could become a cut-up. In the summer of 1876, the boys' oldest sister, the twenty-five year old Olga, Queen of the Hellenes, was visiting

St Petersburg, and was invited by her family to dine with them at Strelna on 20 July. Olga duly arrived at the palace at the appointed time to find her youngest two brothers engaged in a boisterous game of "Russian Tsars" that quickly became an excuse to chase their sister and tumble her to the ground. The young Grand Dukes continued their high spirits through dinner, pretending to be horses and leaping over the seated Olga and her chair as though jumping a fence in a steeplechase.[4]

At the age of fifteen, the Grand Duke was enrolled as a cadet aboard the tender Kadetski, along with his younger brother Vyacheslav. Together, the two brothers underwent the rigors of life at sea during their training cruises through the Gulf of Finland, drilling, standing watch, and taking turns leading their fellow cadets. Grand Duke Konstantin Nikolaievich selected Lieutenant Vassili Vahtin as his sons' naval governor, and it was Vahtin who trained them during their cruises.[5]

In 1877, the seventeen-year-old Grand Duke Dimitri Konstantinovich made his first official public appearance as a member of the Imperial Family. With his father, he joined Alexander II and his sons Grand Dukes Serge and Paul Alexandrovich on a journey to southern Russia, where they met and decorated troops returning from the Russo-Turkish War. After this, Dimitri Konstantinovich returned to the Imperial Naval Cadet Corps, passing his examinations as a Midshipman, but he was becoming increasingly enamored of military life, and fought against his father's plan for a naval career. Apparently, a short illness temporarily detained Dimitri Konstantinovich from active service, and he used this interval to raise his desire to leave the Imperial Navy with his father. It was a blow to Konstantin Nikolaievich to see his third consecutive son abandon his beloved Imperial Navy for the military, but in the end – allegedly after Dimitri Konstantinovich begged his father on his knees, and Grand Duchess Alexandra Iosifovna interceded on her son's behalf – he agreed to let him leave the sea and join the Horse Guards Regiment in 1879.[6]

Also in 1879, a heavy blow fell on Dimitri Konstantinovich: his younger brother Vyacheslav died suddenly in February. Dimitri was present at the deathbed, and helped his brother Konstantin in a desperate effort to administer artificial respiration to Vyacheslav. The youth had long been Dimitri's favorite brother, and of all the family, Dimitri had been the one who spent most time with him. On 1 July of that year, Dimitri wrote to his sister Olga in Greece: *"Today would have been Vyacheslav's seventeenth birthday."* He went on to tell her that he had spent the day at Tsarskoe Selo with his good friend Pereslavtsev, who reminded him of his lost brother, and who was *"as nice as Slava."*[7]

On 1 June 1880, Dimitri Konstantinovich was appointed to the Suite of Alexander II, and given the rank of Flugel-Adjutant. Six months later, having completed his initial infantry training, the Grand Duke was gazetted to the Horse Guards Regiment as a Lieutenant. He was to serve with the Horse Guards for twelve years as a junior officer; in 1892, he was promoted to senior officer, and finally, to Commander.

After completing a training course with the General Staff Academy in 1880, Dimitri Konstantinovich was promoted to Ordnance Officer, and scheduled to make his first official appearance – when he would deliver the report as an Imperial Adjutant in the Guards Sappers Cavalry Regimental – on Sunday, 1 March 1881, during a review by Alexander II.[8] These reviews, which took place on Sundays in the Mikhailovskii Manege in St Petersburg, had been customary for several years. On this particular morning, however, Alexander II was counseled – in light of heightened terrorist threats – not to attend as usual. Princess Yourievsky also advised against his attendance, worried about her husband's safety. When she learned of these discussions, Grand Duchess Alexandra Iosifovna appeared at the Winter Palace and met her brother-in-law. Apparently, she reminded Alexander II that her son Dimitri was to appear as Imperial Adjutant for the first time at the review, and urged the Emperor to keep to his regular schedule. Alexander II duly kept to his regular schedule, attending the review early that afternoon; as Dimitri Konstantinovich made his report, his parents looked on with pride. Within two hours, Alexander II would be dead, the victim of a terrorist bomb thrown at his carriage as he returned to the Winter Palace.

In November 1881, Alexander III promoted Dimitri Konstantinovich to the rank of Adjutant in the Imperial Entourage, and on 26 November of that year, the young Grand Duke had his Majority Ceremony in the Cathedral of the Winter Palace; the ceremony had been delayed owing to mourning for Alexander II, and on that day not only Dimitri Konstantinovich but also Grand Dukes Paul Alexandrovich and Michael Mikhailovich, all took their oaths of loyalty to the Emperor, followed by military oaths in the Hall of the Order of St George.[9]

Throughout the 1880s, Dimitri Konstantinovich served with his regiment with unceasing energy and an eye toward correcting grievances from his men. He built himself a two-storied dacha at Krasnoe Selo, equipping the property with stables and even a small exercise yard for his horses. Here, he spent the summers with his regiment; in spring and fall, he invariably invited his regimental officers to Strelna, which he inherited on the death of his father in 1892.[10] Here, they were lodged in comfortable flats and provided for at the Grand Duke's expense. Mornings were spent riding through the park, the Grand Duke putting his men and their horses through increasingly intricate maneuvers; after lunch, he would lead the officers on walks through the exquisite gardens.

On 6 April 1889, the Grand Duke was promoted to the rank of Captain, and given command of the 2nd Squadron of the Horse Guards. Three years later, on 10 December 1892, he was promoted to the rank of Colonel, and-owing to his distinguished service-was given command of the Horse Guards Grenadiers Regiment by Alexander III. This promotion apparently did not sit well with his cousin, Grand Duke Nicholas Mikhailovich, who complained that he had been passed over for a mere captain.[11]

Dimitri Konstantinovich was, recalled his nephew Gabriel, *"a very religious person,"* and he assumed financial responsibility for the Church of the Apparition of the Virgin near Strelna, which was the regimental church of the Horse Guards Grenadiers.[12] He commissioned both an enlargement and a renovation program, which he paid for himself, in order to better suit the regiment's needs.

Strelna, with its sumptuous rooms, provided an unlikely setting for the quiet, misanthropic Dimitri Konstantinovich, who lived there until the Revolution. He lived in a suite of rooms on the Ground Floor of the west wing that had previously been occupied by his father. The Grand Duke made a number of small but significant changes to the Palace and to the Park during his tenure: for the first time, the Palace was electrified, telephones were installed, and modern plumbing provided for the bathrooms and kitchen. He also restored the Palace Chapel, the Church of St Konstantin and St Helen, in its original location on the Ground Floor, and replaced some of the crumbling statuary in the garden with modern reproductions or with other antique pieces.[13]

Surprisingly, given Dimitri Konstantinovich's sense of morality, he allowed his cousin Grand Duke Serge Mikhailovich to purchase a villa on the grounds of

Strelna for his mistress, the ballerina Mathilde Kschessinska, in 1894. Here, Kschessinska lived quite openly with her paramour and, later, conducted simultaneous affairs with both Serge and with his cousin Grand Duke Andrei Vladimirovich. It was also here that, just after the turn of the century, Kschessinska gave birth to her bastard son Vladimir, a child of questionable paternity.

Being somewhat straight-laced, proper, dignified, and very refined in his manner, Dimitri Konstantinovich had found his father's continued affair with the former ballerina Kuznetsova an unbearable humiliation. He despised the way in which Grand Duke Konstantin Nikolaievich treated Alexandra Iosifovna, and sided completely with his mother over the liaison. The Grand Duchess, in turn, had been deeply scarred by both her husband's romantic entanglements and by the wayward, possibly deluded behavior of her eldest son, Nicholas Konstantinovich. Following Nicholas Konstantinovich's exile, Alexandra Iosifovna had gathered her remaining sons, Konstantin, Dimitri, and Vyacheslav, and – warning of the dangers of a dissolute style of life – made all three promise that they would not consume any alcohol, fearing perhaps that her eldest son's scandalous behavior had its roots in such a lack of self-control. All three gave their solemn vow to abstain from any drinking.[14] In time, however, Dimitri Konstantinovich found that his temperance pledge was adversely affecting his military career. As Commanding Officer, he was expected to join his men in regimental luncheons, dinners, and celebrations, and found it extremely uncomfortable to excuse himself from the usual rounds of ceremonial toasts and frequent evenings spent discussing regimental matters over endless rounds of drinks. It says something about the Grand Duke's honorable character that, although he was in his early thirties, he felt obliged to explain the situation to Grand Duchess Alexandra Iosifovna and ask to be formally released from his previous pledge. Recognizing that her son's military career was suffering, the Grand Duchess gave her assent and freed her son from his vow.

Dimitri Konstantinovich was a popular commander, though a demanding officer. One general later wrote that the Grand Duke "considered himself and his Horse Grenadiers Regiment as a model of everything a smart cavalry regiment must be. While on march, in order that turns could be carried out correctly, he had circles clearly whitewashed on the regimental parade ground at Peterhof, so that the flanks of the platoons as they came round had to coincide exactly. On the march, so that the squadrons opened up evenly, the trumpeter who rode behind Dimitri had to throw down a special cardboard marker at the side of the road at the command *"Gallop!"* Each of the six squadrons started in the gallop as they reached the marker.[15] He took pride in his soldiers, and was greatly concerned with their welfare. Once, spotting a rather thin new recruit, he pulled him aside and whispered, *"You're sick."* The soldier, however, denied that he was unwell. *"Ah, well, you'll soon get better once you start on the soldiers' rations,"* the Grand Duke told him. Not realizing the identity of the officer questioning him, the new recruit apparently looked at the tall, thin Grand Duke and replied, *"Looking at you, it doesn't seem that soldier's' rations will improve me that much!"*[16]

General Ignatiev later recalled encountering Dimitri Konstantinovich during the summer maneuvers at Krasnoe Selo. Early one morning, the two men distributed various divisions of the Horse Grenadiers across the plain in anticipation of a practice charge. As soon as the detachments were settled, Grand Duke Serge Mikhailovich rode up in a cloud of dust, looking distinctly disorganized, his cap askew. *"Where must I stand?"* he asked in a rather bored way. Ignatiev showed him his position, but Serge Mikhailovich protested that he wanted another position. Hearing this, Dimitri

Konstantinovich rode closer and, turning to his cousin, said gently, *"Now, now, Serge dear, the General and I have everything arranged so well, and now you come and upset it all again."*[17]

Dimitri Konstantinovich was fair, with light brown hair and blue eyes, and wore a small cavalry mustache. Baroness Sophie Buxhoeveden later wrote that the Grand Duke was, *"extraordinarily tall and thin, with legs that seemed endless in his tight cavalry breeches."*[18] The Baroness's childhood recollection of his great height seems to have been accurate: his own cousin Alexander Mikhailovich, who himself stood just over six-feet-two-inches, later called Dimitri *"a hawkish giant."*[19] General Ignatiev called him, *"the queerest of the Highnesses...tall, lean, and fair, with a very long neck."*[20] He was, said Grand Duchess Militza Nikolaievna, *"the nicest and best among the Grand Dukes."*[21] Grand Duke Alexander Mikhailovich, who counted Dimitri Konstantinovich among his friends, later referred to him as, *"a fanatically religious man."*[22]

Alexander Mosolov, head of Nicholas II's Court Chancellery, described him as, *"full of good sense,"* remarking that Dimitri Konstantinovich, *"was the one among all the Grand Dukes who was most deeply imbued with the sense of his duty as a Prince and a cousin of the Emperor."*[23] One day, the Grand Duke dispatched a hefty portion of his annual Civil List income to support a struggling church. When Mosolov learnt of this, he warned, *"If you make gifts everywhere on this scale, your revenues will not last."* But Dimitri Konstantinovich replied that the stipend was *"not intended to enable us to live as sybarites; this money is put into our hands in order that we may augment the prestige of the Imperial Family."*[24]

For all of his equanimity, the Grand Duke was a life-long bachelor and vocal misogynist. *"Beware of skirts!"* he would warn his young male relatives at every chance.[25] Alexander Mikhailovich called him, *"a confirmed and enthusiastic woman-hater,"* a characterization with which Baroness Sophie Buxhoeveden agreed completely.[26] There has been some suggestion that Dimitri may have been homosexual.[27] It is also possible that he harbored such sweeping views after having witnessed firsthand the humiliation inflicted on his mother by his father's affair with Kuznetsova.

Despite this strident position, the Grand Duke was adored by his family, and especially loved by his young nieces and nephews, with whom he would happily play and ride for hours. He was particularly close to his brother Konstantin's children; his nephew Gabriel remembered him as, *"a wonderful, kind person"* who was almost a second father, and whenever they saw him, they ran across the room, jumping up to hug him and wrap their arms around his neck.[28] Dimitri Konstantinovich also loved to tease the children and play practical jokes on them. Once, he pulled the end of the belt he was wearing out from behind his back and waved it in front of a young Ioann Konstantinovich, telling his nephew that it was his tail; Ioann erupted into screams, and it took some coaxing before the boy approached his uncle again.[29]

Under Nicholas II, the Grand Duke received further promotions. On 26 May 1896, he was raised to the rank of Major-General, and three months later, he was named a General a la Suite in the Imperial Entourage. On 19 December 1904, Dimitri Konstantinovich was promoted to Lieutenant-General, and appointed Adjutant-General to Nicholas II. The Tsar also appointed the Grand Duke General Director of the Imperial Stud in 1896, replacing Count Hilarion Vorontzov-Dashkov, then in the midst of a battle with Grand Duke Serge Alexandrovich over the Khodynka disaster at the Moscow Coronation and himself just a few weeks from resigning his post as Minister of the Imperial Court over the affair.[30] Despite his love of the military, it was this latter post that struck the deepest and most sympathetic chord in Dimitri

Konstantinovich. On learning of his appointment, the Grand Duke – whom one courtier termed *"timid beyond imagining"* – declared, *"I should eagerly have accepted the appointment if it only meant looking after horses...I am afraid I shall never get on properly with officials."*[31]

Alexander Mikhailovich declared that his cousin was, *"in love with horse flesh."*[32] According to Alexander Mikhailovich, *"no other subject touched the heart of Dimitri Konstantinovich."*[33] As a man who loved horses, the Grand Duke was entranced with this new position, one which demanded that he travel across Russia and Europe, selecting the finest horses. Acting on his advice, the Imperial Stud purchased Galtee More, who had won the Derby in Great Britain, for an astronomical 200,000 rubles; as soon as he arrived in Russia, the exquisite thoroughbred was put to stud at Tsarskoe Selo.[34] Dimitri Konstantinovich held the post until 1905, when he was replaced with Major-General Alexis Zdonovich.

He also often turned to his horses when Christmas came, giving fine pairs as presents to various relatives. His niece Princess Marie of Greece later recalled how one year she received from her uncle, *"a pair of lovely fat ponies. My joy and pride were boundless – I believe the ponies came from an island in the Baltic...The particularity of these animals was that when driven they squealed just like pigs. They were rather wild and I was not allowed to drive them that first year."*[35]

On 10 January 1904, Dimitri Konstantinovich relinquished command of the Horse Guard Grenadiers Regiment. Although he would have been happy to remain in his post, Dimitri's rapidly failing eyesight was increasingly proving a detriment to his military career; reluctantly he recognized that by remaining he was depriving another, more capable man of advancement. On leaving active service, the Grand Duke generously gave his dacha at Krasnoe Selo to the Horse Guards Regiment, to be used as an officers' mess and club.[36]

The Grand Duke's retirement allowed him to focus solely on his principal obsession: horses. Just outside the village of Mirgorod, in the Poltava Province, the Grand Duke had created a model equestrian center, the Dubrovsky Stud Farm. Comprising 11,610 acres, the Dubrovsky was divided into several sections: 2,700 acres were given over to agricultural and forestry concerns, and 5,400 acres were set aside as open meadows and pastures; the remaining 3,500 acres were rented to local farmers and peasants on extended, extremely low leases dictated by the Grand Duke, who realized that they could not afford to pay market value for the lands. The center of the operation, however, was the Stud Farm, run by Colonel Feodor Ismailov. An expansive wooden dacha, termed the Palace, provided rooms for the Grand Duke when he visited: comfortable rather than ostentatious, its rooms were furnished with chintz-covered sofas and chairs, and its walls hung with various prints and paintings of horses. At Dubrovsky, the Grand Duke established not only his own equestrian stud, but also a training facility for jockeys; a school of veterinary medicine; and workshops devoted to the creation of exquisite saddles and tack. Some four hundred horses were housed in the numerous barns, which were themselves models of modern technology and efficiency. The Grand Duke began by breeding the famous Orlov trotters, and then crossbred them with Rostopchin horses; he also kept a number of English thoroughbreds as well as a diverse mixture of American breeds, shipped to Russia from markets in the United States. *"Between breakfast and dinner,"* recalled his nephew Prince Gabriel, *"we rode horses, and talked about horses."*[37] He took the greatest care and concern over his estate, and was himself never happier than when in the saddle. *"I would like you to see my yearlings!"* he would call out to visiting relatives, leading them on a tour of the extensive stables and facilities he had built to show his *"excellent yearlings."*[38] His stud provided many of the fine thoroughbreds for his regiment and for the Imperial Cavalry.[39]

In 1911, Dimitri Konstantinovich became President of the Imperial Society of Horse Racing, and was also named Honorary President of the Russian Society of Care and Protection of Animals. In the autumn of 1913, he inaugurated the Russian Imperial Horse Exposition in Kiev, and the first All-Russian Sports Competition, a kind of Slavic Olympic Games.[40] By this time, the Grand Duke's eyesight had become so poor that he could scarcely see without the aid of glasses.

More and more often, he retreated to the Crimea, where he enjoyed the last, carefree days of the Romanov Dynasty along these rugged Black Sea shores. His was the smallest and most picturesque Romanov estates in the Crimea: Kichkine, perched at the edge of a sheer cliff high above the Black Sea. This simple yet peculiar Palace, located near Gaspara, was completely in keeping with the Grand Duke himself, an enigmatic, complex man whose inward personality remained unfathomable to even his closest relatives.

Dimitri purchased a small plot of land at Gaspara in the Crimea in 1907, some distance down the shore from Harax and Ai Todor. The property included a small mountain vineyard, and stretched to the Aurora Cliff, a dramatic wall of sheer rock rising some 500 feet above the Black Sea. The following year, he commissioned architect Nicholas Tarasov to design and build a villa in the Moorish style. The land was leveled and work began in late summer, 1908. Three years later, the little villa was completed, an exquisite structure which Dimitri called Kichkine, from the Tartar word meaning *"Tiny Jewel."* The adjacent garden was planted with roses and shaded by magnolia, palm, and cypress trees.[41]

Kichkine was loosely modeled on Moorish prototypes but Dimitri Konstantinovich was less concerned with architectural authenticity than pure style. The villa, of local whitewashed stone, contained only one main floor, with a second-storey belvedere crowned with a low dome built atop the center. The exterior was wrapped with arcades of Moorish arches supported on polylobate columns, with elaborately carved window frames that included traditional Arabic inscriptions and geometric stucco designs. Little balconies, sharply crenellated towers, and bay windows pierced the façades; rising above the building was an eight-sided, three-storey minaret, circled by a covered balcony at the top and ending in a sharply peaked roof. Although the building was, and still is, frequently derided as a theatrical pastiche, it suited the Grand Duke perfectly and Dimitri Konstantinovich was delighted with the final result.[42]

The interior of the Palace was decorated in the same mixture of eclectic Moorish, Turkish, and Gothic styles, and contained only a handful of rooms, including the Drawing Room, with large, arched French doors opening to the arcade surrounding the exterior. The largest room in the Palace, the Dining Room, was one-and-a-half stories high. Double rows of arched windows were set along one side; the upper tier windows were fitted with jalti panels over stained glass, while the lower windows opened to a terrace overlooking the garden. Along the opposite wall was an arcade of Moorish arches, decorated with mosaic tiles. Both the Drawing and Dining Rooms were lit with hanging copper and stained glass lanterns, decorated with chased designs and arabesque scrollwork. Aside from the Hall, the Library, and a small guest suite, the rest of the first floor was given over to the kitchen, pantries, and rooms for the Grand Duke's Suite and staff.[43]

Dimitri Konstantinovich's private apartments were situated in the belvedere on the second floor. He had a small bedroom, a dressing room, a bathroom, and his Study, the latter with large French doors that opened onto the terrace built along the roof. Here, wicker chairs and tables were scattered over the tile, and the Grand Duke and his guests spent many pleasant evenings watching the sunset over the Black Sea, unaware that the sun was also setting over their privileged way of life.[44]

As the Russian war effort collapsed and the Tsar's political problems increased, Dimitri Konstantinovich – alone of the various Grand Dukes – remained silent, believing that it was not his place to offer unsolicited advice to Nicholas II. He was in the Crimea, at his estate of Kichkine, when he learned that Rasputin was murdered; although he did not record his thoughts of the removal of the peasant, he did express outrage that members of the Imperial Family – among them his sister Olga – had signed and sent a plea for leniency on behalf of Grand Duke Dimitri Pavlovich to the Tsar; apparently, he did not agree with their sentiments, and is said to have declared that he himself would never have signed the letter had he been in Petrograd at the time.[44] Nicholas II returned the petition with an inscription: *"No one is permitted to engage in murder. I am surprised that you addressed yourself to me. Nicholas."*[45]

Grand Duke Dimitri Konstantinovich was also in Petrograd when the Revolution broke out. Just two months earlier, despite the uncertain times, he had purchased a large mansion on Petrogradsky Quay in Petrograd, overlooking the Malaya Nevka. Built between 1911-13 by architect L. A. Ilina as his own personal residence, it was a solid, two-storeyed neoclassical building ornamented with a portico of Corinthian columns, and comfortably elegant, though not lavish, rooms.[46] It was here, in his new house opposite Kamenostrovsky Bridge, that Dimitri Konstantinovich learned of the Emperor's abdication and the declaration of the Provisional Government. With the fall of his family's Dynasty, he lived quietly, in obscurity, depending largely on Alexander Korochentzov, his trusted Adjutant, for the necessities of daily life.

By March 1918, Dimitri received a summons from Moisei Uritsky to register at the offices of the Petrograd Cheka. Also living in the Grand Duke's palace at this time was his widowed niece, Princess Tatiana Konstantinovna, and her two children, Teymuraz and Nathalia. Tatiana had been devastated at the quick succession of deaths that had come to her family in the first years of the World War: Her brother, Oleg Konstantinovich, was killed in battle in November 1914; within the year, he was followed by his father, Grand Duke Konstantin Konstantinovich and Tatiana's husband, Prince Konstantin Bagration-Moukhransky. Dimitri Konstantinovich, always close to his niece, invited her to live with him so that he could care for her; in her turn, she helped him through his problems with is fading vision. On the morning the Grand Duke was ordered to Moisei Uritsky's office, he was accompanied by Colonel Alexander Korochentzov, his adjutant, but also was joined at the last minute by Tatiana Konstantinovna, who thought her presence would ensure that he was not subjected to any undue pressure. Heavily bundled against the chill winter, the three of them set off on foot to Cheka Headquarters on Gorokhovaya Prospekt. Here, they were taken directly to see Moisei Uritsky, the Chairman of the Petrograd Cheka, who declared that, as the Government thought it dangerous for so many Romanovs to be living in Petrograd, the male members of the former Dynasty would be sent into internal Russian exile. The Treaty of Brest-Litovsk had just been signed, and the Bolshevik

Government was in the process of preparing to move the capital to Moscow, fearing eventual German occupation of Petrograd, and the possible seizure and manipulation of members of the former Dynasty. Uritsky offered three choices for exile: Vologda, Olonets, or Vyatka, and warned that the decision would have to be made within a few weeks. Tatiana Konstantinovna asked the Chairman if she could accompany her uncle, and Uritsky agreed. After some consideration, Dimitri Konstantinovich chose Vologda. On 18 April, carrying a suitcase and accompanied by his niece, her two children, their nanny, and his Adjutant, Colonel Korochentzov, Dimitri Konstantinovich boarded a train and left Petrograd for his exile.

In Vologda, Dimitri Konstantinovich took two rooms in a house owned by a local merchant, just opposite the river: he lived in one with Colonel Korochentzov, while Tatiana and her children occupied the other. They were not restricted in their movements, and able to walk about the town at will. Shortly after their arrival in Vologda, they learned that Grand Dukes Nicholas and George Mikhailovich had also been exiled to the town. The prisoners enjoyed relative freedom; aside from having to report to Cheka Headquarters once a week, they could come and go as they wished, and took long walks around the town, visiting and dining with each other frequently. In the middle of May, Colonel Alexander von Leiming, one of Dimitri Konstantinovich's Adjutants, arrived in Vologda with news that passage had been prepared to Finland, but the Grand Duke refused to leave Russia.[48]

This quiet and somewhat uncertain situation was abruptly interrupted on 14 July, two days before the murder of Nicholas II and his family in Ekaterinburg and the subsequent murders at Alapaievsk. That morning, a cart with four heavily armed men arrived and collected the Grand Dukes from their lodgings; they were transported to a small, walled village, where he could be more easily guarded. In a letter to his wife, then living in England, Grand Duke George Mikhailovich wrote: *"We were each given a cell, and later on were joined by Dimitri. I saw him arriving through the iron bars of my window, and was struck by his sad expression. The first twenty-four hours were very hard, but after that they luckily allowed us to have our camp beds and also our clothes. There is no one in the prison but we three."* They were guarded, he explained by men he identified as Letts, soldiers from the Baltic Provinces. *"They treat us like comrades, and have not locked our cells after the second day, while they allow us to walk in the small garden in the courtyard. Our food is brought from outside."*[49]

While imprisoned, the Grand Dukes heard rumors that Nicholas II and his family had been killed; this seemed to indicate the worst, and Tatiana left with her two young children to return to Petrograd. Then, on 21 July, all of the exiled Grand Dukes in Vologda were again transferred back to Petrograd. In the former Imperial capital, the men were quickly imprisoned with six other detainees in a cell at Cheka Headquarters.[50]

Dimitri Konstantinovich – along with the other Grand Dukes – was questioned at length by Uritsky. In a letter to his wife, Grand Duke George Mikhailovich wrote: *"Dimitri asked Uritsky why we were imprisoned, and his answer was that it was to save us as the people had intended shooting us at Vologda. This, of course, is an absolute lie. He also said that when the German Government would release* [Karl] *Liebknecht and* [Victor] *Adler (two Socialist leaders), then we, too, would all be liberated."*[51] The prisoners were photographed, and then moved incarcerated in the rather pompously named House of Preliminary Arrest on Shpalernaia Street in Petrograd. Their diet, reported George Mikhailovich, consisted of *"dirty hot water with a few fish bones floating in it,"* and black bread.[52]

For a time, Gabriel Konstantinovich was in a cell adjoining those of his uncle

Grand Duke Dimitri Konstantinovich, as well as those of Grand Dukes Nicholas and George Mikhailovich and Paul Alexandrovich. In the spring of 1918, when the Bolsheviks had initially tried to arrest him, Gabriel was suffering from tuberculosis; rather than imprison him, the Bolsheviks allowed him to stay with his wife Antonina at her Petrograd flat. By the summer of 1918, however, he had recovered, and one day in July, a contingent of armed soldiers arrived at the modest apartment and took him into custody.[53]

Gabriel, younger and more resilient than his older kinsmen, found prison less of an ordeal, but he was shocked at his uncle Dimitri's appearance when they were first reunited. Until the last, Gabriel later recalled, Dimitri was the cheerful, favorite uncle of his childhood, telling him jokes, attempting to raise his spirits, and bribing prison guards to carry hopeful messages to his nephew's cell.[54] Throughout Gabriel's incarceration Antonina, as he lovingly wrote later, was tireless in her efforts to obtain her husband's release. She finally succeeded – with the intervention of Maxim Gorky, whose wife was counted among Antonina's closest friends – near the end of 1918, when Gabriel was moved to a hospital. A few weeks later – again with Gorky's assistance – the Petrograd Soviet gave the couple permission to leave Russia for Finland.[55]

The Prince's release had come just in time. During Dimitri Konstantinovich's incarceration, Colonel von Leiming regularly sent food each day for the prisoners; on 29 January 1919, it was returned to him, with a note that the Grand Duke was no longer being held prisoner. The following day, von Leiming learned that Dimitri Konstantinovich, along with Grand Dukes Paul Alexandrovich, and Nicholas and George Mikhailovich, had been executed by the Bolsheviks.

Only later did the truth of what had happened begin to filter out of Russia, and then in often – contradictory fragments. For several months before the executions, Princess Paley, wife of Grand Duke Paul Alexandrovich, had attempted to plead for his release. Eventually, Maxim Gorky took her case to Lenin in Moscow, asking that the Grand Dukes be spared. This was a dangerous and daring move on Gorky's part; in December, 1918, he had secured Prince Gabriel's release from the prison, and many Bolsheviks suspected the writer of actually being a counter-revolutionary.[56] During his interview with Lenin, Gorky is said to have pointed out that Nicholas Mikhailovich was a known liberal, and a respected historian. According to Grand Duke Alexander Mikhailovich, Lenin's response was emphatic: *"The Revolution does not need historians!"*[57]

Yet we now know that Gorky in fact succeeded in obtaining Lenin's orders for their release.[58] Grand Duchess Marie Georgievna, wife of George Mikhailovich, recalled: *"It appears that Maxim Gorky went to Lenin and told him to release the four Grand Dukes as there was no sense in keeping them in prison and to allow them to go abroad. Lenin consented, but that inhuman monster in Moscow,* [Jacob] Peters, *hearing of this decision, immediately wired to the Commissariat in Petersburg to have the Grand Dukes shot."*[59] Princess Paley, Grand Duke Paul Alexandrovich's wife, also recalled in her memoirs how Gorky's wife, Maria, had told her when she telephoned their apartment for news, that her husband had succeeded in his mission, and was returning the next day from Moscow *"with all their liberations signed."*[60] On receiving the agreement, Gorky immediately boarded a train for Petrograd, but he arrived only to find that the authorities in Petrograd had already executed the men.

What apparently took place was as follows: at 11:30PM on 28 January 1919, guards awoke Grand Dukes Dimitri Konstantinovich, and Nicholas and George Mikhailovich, in their cells at Shpalernaia Prison, telling them that they must pack their belongings to be moved. Nicholas Mikhailovich seemed optimistic, suspecting that they were about to be released, or perhaps moved to Moscow; hearing this, his brother George commented that it was more likely they were about to be shot. They had an ominous hint of this when, at the time of departure, they were told to leave their luggage. Nicholas Mikhailovich took with him only a small kitten that he had been allowed to keep in his cell. The men were herded into a truck, next to six sailors with hands tied behind their backs, and driven through the quiet city to the SS Peter and Paul Fortress. Here, they were taken to the office of the Fortress Commandant, Galkin, where they found Grand Duke Paul Alexandrovich sitting quietly. Galkin apparently read their death sentence, and the prisoners were told to remove their coats and hats, and then marched out into the courtyard, to a trench in front of the Trubetskoy Bastion. The four men embraced each other, and Nicholas Mikhailovich handed his kitten to a soldier, asking that he look after it.[61] At the last moment, one of the Grand Dukes – either Dimitri Konstantinovich or Paul Alexandrovich – said, "*God, forgive them, they know not what they do,*" before a fusillade of shots sent their bodies reeling into the trench.[62] Although the bodies of the other three Grand Dukes were thrown into a mass grave within the Fortress, that of Dimitri Konstantinovich was secretly collected the next morning by his devoted former Adjutant, von Leiming, rolled up in a rug, and taken away for a private burial in the garden of a house in Petrograd, where he remains to this day.[63]

Grand Duke Vyacheslav Konstantinovich (1862-1879)

By Penny Wilson

In the high summer of 1862, in the beautiful Polish city of Warsaw, Grand Duchess Alexandra Iosifovna, wife of Grand Duke Konstantin Nikolaievich, gave birth to her fourth son and sixth child, a little boy known in the family as "Slava." This tiny Grand Duke was christened fourteen days later at the Lazienki Palace amidst a national tempest over his chosen name: His father, Viceroy of Poland, had given him the name of Vaclav, in honor of his Polish birth, but Russian protests had driven the Imperial parents to revise their son's name to *"Vyacheslav."* The compromise name, like most compromises, pleased nobody.[1]

Within a year of Vyacheslav's birth, Konstantin Nikolaievich was back home in Russia. He had requested that his brother the Emperor remove him from the post of Viceroy; he had been unable to adequately handle the strikes and protests in the Polish capital, and this failure weighed heavily upon him. Seeing his younger brother's distress, Alexander II agreed to recall him to St Petersburg. Upon returning to the Imperial capital, Konstantin found that Alexander was ready to reverse many of the more liberal policies of his first decade of rule. Dissatisfied with this development, blaming himself for his failure in Poland, and growing away from his wife – with whom he had had little in common in the first place – his marriage to Alexandra reached its unofficial end. The Grand Duke started to stray from the marriage bed, a practice that would shortly bring him into the arms of the woman who would be his mistress for the rest of his life, the ballerina Anna Kuznetsova. Divorce was an impossible remedy for a failed Imperial marriage, so Alexandra Iosifovna – like many other royal wives before and after – sought distractions to ease her pain and humiliation. She traveled frequently to Europe, and, when at home in Russia, she became increasingly involved in religious mysticism and other spiritual activities. She largely withdrew from her children; her letters from this time show that she spent little time nurturing her last son.[2] Despite his mother's absence, Vyacheslav was not a lonely or unhappy child; he lived in the company of his two elder brothers, Konstantin and Dimitri, and he maintained a devotedly close relationship with his father, who called him *"Little Bird."*[3]

Sometime around 1870, when Vyacheslav was eight, he and his brothers were joined at home by a half-sister, Marie Condorusso, the toddler daughter of Konstantin Nikolaievich, born of a relationship with an unknown woman in the late 1860s.[4] Marie would be raised within the Grand Duke's legitimate family, a scandalous situation which was perhaps something else that served to keep Alexandra Iosifovna at a distance. In 1880, her half-sister Queen Olga invited Marie to Greece; she became a Lady-in-Waiting, a position that she held for several years until she married a wealthy Greek banker.[5]

By the time he was ten, and living in St Petersburg at the Marble Palace, the elder members of Vyacheslav's family had scattered: His mother was residing mostly at the country palace of Pavlovsk; his elder sister Olga had married and become Queen of the Hellenes; and his younger sister Vera was living with relatives in Germany, where it was hoped that she would receive better medical care than Russian experts could offer for what was then believed to be severe epilepsy. Most ominously of all, Vyacheslav's eldest brother, Nicholas, had embarked on the scandalous affair that would set Europe on its ears and result in his permanent exile to Tashkent. In the highly-charged family atmosphere following Nicholas' banishment, Vyacheslav was summoned to his mother's presence along with his two brothers, Konstantin and Dimitri, and together, Alexandra required that they take an oath of abstinence, promising that they would not drink alcohol, which substance she evidently blamed for their eldest brother's fall from grace.[6]

In 1873, Konstantin Nikolaievich and his mistress Kuznetsova celebrated the birth of their first child; eventually, they would have a family of five, three sons – all of whom died young – and two daughters. Emperor Alexander II decided that his brother's second family would bear the surname of "Kniazev," in honor of their father's title.[7] Konstantin was devoted to his second family, taking care to move them wherever he would be: They had an apartment in St Petersburg near the Marble Palace; they had a villa in the Crimea close to Oreanda; and when Konstantin was living at Pavlovsk, he moved them into a house on the estate. This additional humiliation for their mother cooled significantly the relationship between the Grand Duke and his sons Konstantin and Dimitri, but it seems that Vyacheslav remained as devoted as ever, writing frequently to his father about the events and activities of his daily life.[8] *"My dear Papa!,"* He wrote from Nice at this time, *"Thank you for the wooden spoon that you have sent me: I always eat soup for dinner, and now it seems to me that the soup tastes incomparably, because I love you very much..."*[9]

From an early age, Vyacheslav had a love for music and church choirs; one of his favorite activities was to attend choir practices at the nearby Cathedral, and once – while still very young – he wrote this considered opinion in a letter to his father: *"I was in the Cathedral today, but it was not very beautiful at all! The singing was very bad – God himself would not have known 'Izhe Kherubimi' at first."*[10] More unusually, Vyacheslav liked to imagine and lay out plans and diagrams for ceremonial occasions, most particularly for funerals. In considering the event of his own funeral, he joked to his brother Konstantin that because of his great height and the lengthy coffin he would require, his family would find it impossible to carry him around the narrow and sharp corners of the Marble Palace hallways.[11]

When Vyacheslav was thirteen, he was enrolled alongside his brother Dimitri as a naval cadet on the Imperial tender *Kadetski*. Together, the brothers faced learning a sailor's life at sea with all its attendant drills, watches and seamanship training. The city of Revel did not fare well in Vyacheslav's estimation, when compared with St Petersburg: *"The town is not very beautiful,"* he wrote to his father. *"It is dirty and neglected."*[12] The young Grand Duke went on to describe a visit to the palace in Revel, and recorded his impressions of some paintings he saw: *"…there are wonderful portraits of Aunt Maria, Aunt Adini and Aunt Olga. I like them very much, but especially the portraits of Aunt Maria and Aunt Adini. I don't like the portrait of Aunt Olga as much because her head looks very small, and her body enormous in comparison."*[13] Dimitri would soon abandon the Navy in favor of a life in the Imperial Cavalry, for which he was better suited; Vyacheslav remained a naval cadet for the rest of his short life.[14]

By the end of the 1870s, Vyacheslav had grown into a kind, caring and engaging young man. He was becoming as handsome as his eldest brother; his thick, light brown hair was cut short and carefully brushed into place, but it still sought to curl and wave over his forehead and around his ears. His oval face was straight-nosed and full-lipped, but his most arresting feature was a pair of dark and intelligent eyes. He was sixteen when his final illness struck – yet the circumstances surrounding his death are not without a touch of mystery. Vyacheslav's nephew, Prince Christopher of Greece, recorded in his memoirs a story involving Grand Duchess Alexandra Iosifovna and what happened to her one evening in February 1879 shortly before her son died, as she crossed the Gonzaga Gallery at Pavlovsk on her way to dinner: *"She was walking through it on her way to dinner one evening, followed by two Aides-de-Camp, when the three of them saw a woman coming toward them in the distance. She was dressed in white from head to foot, but there was nothing whatever out of the ordinary in her appearance and they supposed her to be one of the ladies of the household. It was only afterwards that they remembered that her footsteps had made no sound. There was still enough light from the fading day coming in through the arches for them to see her quite clearly as she approached. When she was within a few feet of them she stopped, raised her head and looked straight at my grandmother. None of them could recall her face in detail; they could only say that it was full of indescribable evil and malevolence. Meeting her eyes, Grandmother was so overcome with fear that she stood rooted to the spot, literally unable to move. Then with one swift spring the woman threw herself upon her, as if about to strike her. At that the two Aides-de-Camp, who had been petrified with surprise, were galvanized into action and immediately closed in front of grandmother, with arms outstretched. But to their amazement they found themselves clutching thin air. There was no trace of the stranger; she had vanished as mysteriously as she had come. Grandmother, who was half fainting with fright, was helped back to her apartments, where her ladies-in-waiting revived her. They shuddered when she told them of her experience. "You have seen the White Lady," one of them told her, and her heart sank. She had heard, as what princess has not, of the terrible, wandering ghost whose story is lost in antiquity and who is associated with no particular country but appears to the people of royal houses foretelling disaster. The day after the apparition of the White Lady, Grandmother's youngest son was taken ill."*[15]

This could well be an apocryphal tale – or an exaggeration of a much less dramatic premonition – but it is in accordance with what we know of Alexandra Iosifovna's interest in spiritualism and the supernatural. And undeniably, Vyacheslav did fall ill within days of his mother's experience, whatever it may have been. The first symptom discernable from the historical record of a high temperature, and at first, his illness was treated as a normal virus. Within just a few days, however, his condition had deteriorated and he had quickly become very desperately ill. Called home to the Marble Palace, an anxious Grand Duke Konstantin Nikolaievich noted ominously in his diary on 14 February: *"All night, Vyacheslav did not sleep, and moaned almost continually, sometimes falling unconscious for a few moments. Morphine did not help much. Golovin [a court doctor] came at nine, and Botkin* [Professor Serge Botkin] *at eleven. They, despite the seriousness of the illness, did not consider that all hope was yet lost."*[16]

Early the next morning, 15 February, the household was roused early from bed. Vyacheslav had taken a turn for the worse, and had sunk into an apparent coma at around five o'clock. Within two hours, his breathing had become labored, his pulse increased to 120, and he began to foam at the mouth.[17] Vyacheslav's father and brothers gathered anxiously around his bed, watching the doctors as they worked over the boy who was struggling to breathe. Vyacheslav was dying in agonizing pain; when he was able to draw enough breath, his screams and cries of pain echoed down the halls outside his bedroom. Not knowing from what he suffered, knowing only that the pain was in his head, the doctors were loathe to give him painkillers, in case they worsened the situation. At last, the attending doctor, Golovin, approached Konstantin Nikolaievich and murmured that Vyacheslav's strength was failing, and that the end was near. Konstantin Konstantinovich, in supporting his father in his grief, recorded the following impression in his diary: *"Papa could not bring himself to believe it was ending."*[18]

In a valiant attempt to fight off death, Konstantin and Dimitri Konstantinovich joined the doctors in a desperate attempt to prolong Vyacheslav's life. Together, they went through the motions of artificial respiration until it became all-too evident that life had passed from the youngest Grand Duke. Through his grief, Konstantin Nikolaievich watched his sons' actions and later that day, he wrote in his diary: *"I could see from the raising and lowering of their arms, that they were attempting artificial respiration. But there was no pulse, no breathing, and nothing was to be accomplished, and we soon recognized that it was all over, that life had gone from him, that his soul had flown from his suffering body. The Lord gives, and the Lord takes; this is His Will! There were many bitter, inconsolable tears...The day was terrible, beaten down, oppressive, and melancholy, affecting the whole family and our friends...At half-past two was the first panikhida, terrible in its tears and sobbing. I was the whole time on my knees beside the bed...Vyacheslav was entirely covered with flowers, and he wore a peaceful and quiet, almost happy, expression."*[19]

Alexandra Iosifovna did not have the chance to say good-bye to her son; she had been summoned early that morning from Pavlovsk, but despite all her efforts, she had arrived too late. Vyacheslav's parents were grief-stricken, yet they gave permission for an unusual procedure to take place: an autopsy. When Vyacheslav's skull was opened, his brain was discovered saturated with fresh blood. It would seem that he died from a cerebral hemorrhage, a diagnosis that better fit his symptoms than the malignant tumor that some have claimed for him.[20] On the morning of 16 February, Konstantin Nikolaievich visited Vyacheslav, who still lay on his deathbed, though he had been dressed for burial in his ceremonial Uhlan uniform; the heartbroken father noted in his diary that Vyacheslav's face had not been damaged by the autopsy procedure.[21] Konstantin Nikolaievich further recorded: *"All morning, I was occupied with all sorts of arrangements. At one o'clock, I – alone of my family – along with Serge and Paul and my adjutants, lifted Vyacheslav into his coffin, and bore him via the service stairs to the Hall of Columns, where the duty officers of the regiment in which he was enrolled immediately attended the coffin. At two o'clock, a panikhida service began in the presence of the Sovereign and the whole family...At five o'clock, brothers came from the Sergeievsky monastery and gave another panikhida in which we all participated..."*[22]

At the end of the day's memorials, a devastated Konstantin Nikolaievich returned to the Rotunda, where Vyacheslav's coffin awaited removal the next morning. The Grand Duke stayed with his son, so that he could, *"spend with him the last night he would pass under our roof."*[23]

On 17 February, the day appointed for Vyacheslav's remains to be taken to the Peter and Paul Fortress, the Imperial family gathered at the Marble Palace, led by Emperor Alexander II. Konstantin Nikolaievich, dressed in his General-Admiral's uniform, went alone to the Rotunda at two in the afternoon. He later wrote: *"With tears, I said goodbye to my son for the last time inside the Marble Palace, [and] closed the coffin…"*[24] Several Grand Dukes, including Serge Alexandrovich and his brother Paul, assisted by officers of Vyacheslav's honorary Uhlan regiment, carried the coffin from the Marble Palace to the hearse. Despite Vyacheslav's light-hearted predictions in years gone by, there was no trouble in maneuvering his casket through the palace halls.

Grand Duke Konstantin Nikolaievich, accompanied by his sons Konstantin and Dimitri, walked behind the hearse on foot, followed by the Emperor himself and the other Grand Dukes. They walked all the way to the Fortress, where the final funeral rites would take place the next day. The final service of the day was at nine o'clock that evening, a panikhida in the presence of the Emperor and the entire Imperial

Family. Then the Imperial Family withdrew, and Vyacheslav's immediate family were left alone with his body. *"At half-past one that night, we returned to the Fortress to say farewell in private to our own very dear Vyacheslav,"* remembered his father. *"We spent some time in prayer by the coffin and blessed him and made the cross over him on his last night above ground."*[25]

On 18 February, the funeral service took place in the Cathedral of the Fortress of SS Peter and Paul. It was, as Konstantin Nikolaievich noted in his diary, the twenty-fourth anniversary of Nicholas I's death. *"The terrible day that we bury our dear Vyacheslav, our 'Kindchen', our little bird,"* he wrote. *"My tears flowed at the final, harrowing parting. Before the lid of the coffin was closed, I kissed him for the last time on the brow."*[26]

Vyacheslav's original grave was in the Cathedral crypt. He lay there undisturbed for thirty-two years until the death of his mother, Alexandra Iosifovna, in the summer of 1911. In the years since his death, a new Grand Ducal vault had been built by Leon Benois and Anthony Tomishko, which adjoined the Cathedral of the Fortress.[27] On the occasion of Alexandra Iosifovna's funeral on 30 June 30/13 July, the authorities decided to exhume the bodies of Vyacheslav and his father, and to re-bury them in the new vault.[28]

These three Konstantinovichi were joined by Princess Nathalia Konstantinovna, who had died in 1905; she was the infant daughter of Vyacheslav's brother Konstantin, who died at the age of just two months. Konstantin Konstantinovich himself was laid to rest in the vault in 1915. They are the only members of this branch of the Imperial Family to lie inside the SS Peter and Paul Fortress.

The Konstantinovichi Grand Dukes

Sophia Dorothea of Württemberg =(2 Paul I 1)= Wilhelmina of Hesse-Darmstadt
1759–1828 / 1754–1801 / 1755–1776

- **Helen** 1784–1803 = Friedrich Ludwig of Mecklenburg-Schwerin 1778–1819
  - 3 sons, 5 daughters

- **Nicholas I** 1796–1855 = Charlotte of Prussia 1798–1860
  - **Nicholas** 1831–1891 = Alexandra of Oldenburg 1838–1900 — *Nikolaievichi Line*
  - **Michael** 1832–1909 = Cecilia of Baden 1839–1891 — *Mikhailovichi Line*
  - **Alexander II** 1818–1881 = Marie of Hesse and by Rhine 1824–1880 — *Main Line of the Russian Imperial Family*
  - **Konstantin** 1827–1892 = Alexandra of Saxe-Altenburg 1830–1911

Konstantin 1827–1892 = Alexandra of Saxe-Altenburg 1830–1911

- 3 daughters
  - George of Saxe-Altenburg = Marie 1796–1853 / 1803–1862
  - Augusta of Saxe-Meiningen = Moritz 1843–1919 / 1829–1907

- **Nicholas** 1850–1918 = Nadezhda Dreyer 1861–1929 — *Princes Iskander*

- **Olga** 1851–1926 = George I of the Hellenes 1845–1913

- **Vera** 1854–1912 = Wilhelm Eugen of Württemberg 1846–1877

- **Konstantin (KR)** 1858–1915 = Elisabeth 1865–1927

- **Dimitri** 1860–1919

- **Vyacheslav** 1862–1879

Children of Konstantin (KR) and Elisabeth

- **Ioann** 1886–1918 = Elena of Serbia 1884–1962
  - **Vsevelod** 1914–1973
    - 1)= Mary Lygon 1910–1982
    - 2)= Emilia de Gosztonyi 1914–1993
    - 3)= Valli Knust 1930–2012
  - **Catherine** 1915–2007 = Ruggiero Farace di Villaforesta 1909–1970
    - 1 son, 2 daughters

- **Gabriel** 1887–1955
  - 1)= Antonina Nesterovsky 1890–1950
  - 2)= Irina Kuryakin 1903–1993

- **Tatiana** 1890–1970
  - 1)= Konstantin Bagration-Moukhransky 1889–1915
  - 2)= Alexander Korochentzov 1877–1922

- **Konstantin** 1891–1918
- **Oleg** 1892–1914
- **Igor** 1894–1918
- **George** 1903–1938
- **Natalia** b./d. 1905
- **Vera** 1906–2001

6

The Sons of Grand Duke Nicholas Nikolaievich

Grand Duke Nicholas Nikolaievich (1856-1929)

By Greg King

In the last years of the Russian Empire, few of the Grand Dukes had any real power or exerted any real influence on political or military events. The one notable exception to this was Grand Duke Nicholas Nikolaievich, Jr., known in the Imperial Family as Nikolasha. Stubborn and far-sighted, eccentric and capable by turns, he was a prominent figure in the reign of Nicholas II, both praised for his talents and scorned for his often brutal personality. In military parades and reviews, the six-foot-six-inch Nicholas Nikolaievich literally towered over his extended family, his piercing blue eyes sweeping round for the slightest mistake. The Grand Duke was a defining figure in these years and no one, whether they admired or despised him, was ambivalent about Nicholas Nikolaievich.

Nicholas Nikolaievich Junior was born on 6/ 18 November 1856, in St Petersburg, the first son and child of Grand Duke Nicholas Nikolaievich, Senior, and his wife Grand Duchess Alexandra Petrovna. Named after his late grandfather Emperor Nicholas I, the boy was called Nikolasha to distinguish him from his father, but both father and son were destined to share more than just their names. Their military careers overlapped, both held the same positions in the Imperial Army, and both rose to prominence as commanders-in-chief when Russia when to war.

On his birth, Nicholas Nikolaievich was enrolled in His Majesty's Hussar Life Guards Regiment, setting the tone for a life that revolved around the military.[1] A series of tutors and military governors put the boy through his education paces. In addition to the usual subjects, he studied military strategy and engineering, following in his father's footsteps. When he was ten, his parents' marriage fell apart; even in the vast Nikolaievich Palace, there was no disguising the tension, and young Nicholas withdrew into himself, throwing his energies into his studies. He entered the Nikolaievskii Engineering Academy, graduating in 1873, and completed his education with a term at the General Staff Academy, from which he graduated in 1876 in the 1st Class.[2]

In 1871 he was gazetted into His Majesty's Life Guards Hussars Regiment, formally embarking on a military career that would last for the next forty-six years.[3] During the Russo-Turkish War of 1877-78, he served on the staff of his father, the Commander-in-Chief of the Russian Army in the Balkans. He came under fire when crossing the Danube in June 1877, and was awarded the Cross of the Order of St George, 4th Class, for bravery. By 1884, he had become Commander of the Life Guards Hussars Regiment, a position he held until 1890, when he became Commander of the 2nd Life Guards Cavalry Division. In 1895, he was promoted to the same post his father had held – Inspector General of the Imperial Cavalry – which he was to occupy until 1905. He was made an Adjutant-General in 1894, and rose to the rank of Cavalry General in 1901.[4]

In his private life, the Grand Duke had few passions. One was collecting old china and porcelain – a hobby starkly at odds with his pervasive military demeanor – and he was a well-known gourmand who often personally supervised his chefs during their work.[5] *"He was a real soldier and did not care about social life,"* recalled Grand Duchess Marie Georgievna. *"Sport, hunting, and shooting were his passions, and whenever he could get away from his military service he used to go to the country."*[6]

In 1887, the Grand Duke purchased a large country estate at Perchina in Tula Province, a three-hour carriage ride from the nearest railway station. Here, in a wooded valley, he extensively renovated the existing lodge, wrapping it in an Italianate façade to mirror the new formal gardens. A visitor in 1912 recalled: *"Nearly every room in the lodge is hung with hunting trophies killed by the Grand Duke and rigorously 'protected' by his clown, a dwarf about three-feet-six-inches tall, bearing on his thumb the Seigneur's signet ring, a curious relic of medieval custom."*[7] That this military giant thought it somehow amusing to have such a short counterpart as his jester, to amuse himself by mocking the (in this case literal) shortcomings of another, was indicative of a side of Nicholas Nikolaievich's character that became well known to those in the military. There was a sort of cruelty, a delight in misfortune, in humiliation, and in the torment of others. The Grand Duke once gave a horrifying example of this penchant for this cruel streak. The centerpiece of the estate were the Grand Duke's ten kennels, where he bred his prizewinning Borzois under the care of Dimitri Valtzov, his manager. Several hundred of these regal animals, along with a number of English Greyhounds, were put to regular use on Nicholas Nikolaievich's hunts for fox, wolf, and bear, and the Grand Duke won numerous awards for his magnificent animals.[8] Despite his apparent love for his kennels of animals, though, the Grand Duke was not above using them to make a point. Once, he had guests at Perchina and was pointing out his collection of antique weaponry; this talk continued during dinner, when Nicholas proudly boasted that his was the finest and sharpest sword in the empire. To prove his point, the Grand Duke called for one of his pet Borzois brought in. The animal was placed atop the dining table and, with a swift stroke, Nicholas Nikolaievich suddenly and abruptly drew his sword, brought it through the air, and cut the poor animal cleanly in half, leaving the dying, howling dog writhing in agony as his stunned, horrified, and blood-spattered guests looked on in shock.[9]

This display confirmed what many of those in the Imperial Family knew, or thought that they knew, about the Grand Duke. Dowager Empress Marie Feodorovna once declared of him: *"Il est malade d'une maladie incurable....Il est bête!"*[10] Opinions of the Grand Duke were almost universally negative. One of the few positive voices was Princess Anatole Bariatinsky, who asserted that Nicholas Nikolaievich, *"was very popular among his troops; his noble bearing had also a great effect upon the masses, as he was immensely tall and held himself very upright. He was of a very determined character and had a will of iron."*[11] Others, though, were quick to point out just how disagreeable Nicholas Nikolaievich could really be. *"One could not describe him as being particularly brilliant,"* remembered Grand Duchess Marie Georgievna, *"nor was he very popular while he* commanded the Guards before the war, because he was terribly severe and rather hard."[12] Government official Vassili Shulgin spoke of his, *"difficult character, quick temper, and rudeness,"* while Grand Duchess Marie Pavlovna recalled his *"patronizing attitude"* toward younger members of the Imperial Family.[13]

"In the Guards – the cream of the Russian regiments where only the finest traditions held sway – he was despised and detested," declared Countess Lillie Nostitz. *"He was clever enough to know it, and set himself out deliberately to appeal to the masses. He would flatter the officers of an obscure provincial regiment by appearing suddenly among them, unceremoniously joining their mess, drinking them all under the table, performing his favorite trick of crunching up the wine glass between his strong teeth. They liked his great hearty laugh, his gruff voice, his air of swashbuckling joviality. When they annoyed him, he would stand towering over them all, a gigantic figure of a man, swearing like a trooper."*[14]

Behind his back, members of the Imperial Guard regiments called him, *"the Evil One"* and *"Old Nick,"* an unsubtle reference to his Mephisthophelean reputation. He delighted, recalled one officer, in *"the dressing down of his subordinates."*[15] Prince Andrei Lobanov-Rostovsky remembered: *"He inspired us with absolute terror, for it was known that he never minced words if anything went wrong."* He recalled a review of young cadets, when the Grand Duke, *"had abused them in such language that all the ladies present blushed."*[16]

Many of the soldiers Nicholas Nikolaievich trained went off to battle in the Russo-Japanese War, but the Grand Duke was not among them; instead, he remained in St Petersburg as dissatisfaction with the conflict grew and strikes and riots became common.[17] Three weeks after the infamous Bloody Sunday massacre in the capital, one aristocrat found Nicholas Nikolaievich, along with his brother Peter and their cousins Nicholas and Serge Mikhailovich, at St Petersburg's Imperial Yacht Club, *"dreadfully frightened at the approaching revolution"* and *"throwing off all the pride and reconciling themselves to the end."*[18]

The year 1905 proved a fateful one for the Romanov Dynasty. As the months passed, and the situation all across Russia's interior deteriorated, concessions seemed inevitable. By October, Prime Minister Serge Witte was advising Nicholas II that only two options lay open to him to restore authority: a military dictatorship under marshal law, or the granting of a constitution and an elected assembly. Nicholas, ever reluctant to make any concessions, or abandon any of the privileges of the autocracy, favored the former idea and seriously considered asking Nicholas Nikolaievich – the only man he thought capable of exerting sufficient authority and cruel command – to assume dictatorial powers. In his position as Commander of St Petersburg's Military District, the Grand Duke possessed the necessary legitimacy if such a step was required, but he was also a realist: plunging Russia, at a time of such discontent and upheaval, into even greater repression and potential chaotic rebellion, seemed disastrous. In the second week of October 1905, the Grand Duke was visited by an influential labor leader in the imperial capital, who told him that although the vast majority of the factory workers remained loyal to the throne, they wanted a constitution and a say in the government that ruled them. This, Nicholas Nikolaievich replied, was easier to say than to accomplish, but the conversation weighed heavily on him and influenced his ultimate decision.[19]

A few days later, having considered the rumors floating about, the Grand Duke went to the Lower Palace at Alexandria, Peterhof, where the Tsar was in residence, and confronted Count Vladimir Fredericks, the Minister of the Imperial Court. Nicholas Nikolaievich pulled out a revolver and melodramatically shouted, *"If the*

Emperor does not accept the Witte program, if he wants to force me to become dictator, I shall kill myself in his presence with this revolver! I am going on to the Emperor! You must all support Witte at all costs! It is necessary for the good of Russia and of all of us!"[20] It was even said that the Grand Duke had actually stormed into the Emperor's study and torn the proposed manifesto from Nicholas II's hands, insisting that he sign it at once, although Nicholas II's own diary makes no mention of such a memorable occurrence.[21]

The Grand Duke's threat proved decisive: on the afternoon of 17/30 October 1905, Nicholas II finally bowed to the inevitable and signed the manifesto granting a constitution and the creation of a Duma. *"Nikolasha,"* the Emperor wrote in his diary that night, *"came to lunch. We sat and talked while we waited for Witte to arrive. Signed the manifesto at 5 o'clock. After such a day my head felt heavy and my thoughts became clouded. Lord help us, save and pacify Russia!"*[22] Most members of the Imperial Family, including Empress Alexandra, were universal in their belief that Nicholas Nikolaievich's threats had forced the Emperor's hand, and for this, he was never forgiven.

Publication of the Emperor's manifesto did nothing to quell the violence in the country and, on 27 October Nicholas II named Nicholas Nikolaievich Commander of the St Petersburg Military District in place of Grand Duke Vladimir Alexandrovich.[23] The Emperor and his family were virtual prisoners at Peterhof, unable to leave for fear of assassination or anarchist plots, and the Grand Duke's first task was to restore order to the imperial capital. Perceiving dangerous elements all around, Nicholas Nikolaievich threw in his lot with the odious Union of the Russian People, a staunchly monarchist, anti-Semitic organization that financed pogroms and rebelled at the merest hint of representative government.[24] The Grand Duke ringed St Petersburg with troops and dismissed the continuing riots in Moscow as unimportant, saying, *"Once Moscow was indeed the heart and mind of Russia, but now it is the center from which all anti-monarchist and revolutionary ideas spread. No harm would come to Russia if it were destroyed."*[25]

In the aftermath of the aborted 1905 Revolution, and the transformation of Russia from an autocracy into a kind of constitutional monarchy, Grand Duke Nicholas Nikolaievich was named chairman of the Imperial Council for State Defense, a body designed to forestall any further revolutionary outbursts and also to prepare the country for any possible future conflict.[26] The Grand Duke supervised some important army reforms but, as historian Hugh Seton-Watson noted, the committee *"proved in practice too large a body, and its members included too many irresponsible persons. It achieved little if any improvements."*[27]

The Grand Duke did himself no favors with his continuing war with military official Vladimir Sukhomlinov. Nicholas Nikolaievich hated Sukhomlinov, a career bureaucrat with little practical military experience; unfortunately, Sukhomlinov happened to be a favorite of Nicholas II, a man the Emperor considered as a possible candidate for the position of Minister of War. The first step was Sukhomlinov's promotion to Chief of the General Staff, a move vehemently opposed by Nicholas Nikolaievich. Safe in the knowledge that he had the Emperor's support, Sukhomlinov began a campaign against the Grand Duke, saying that it would be impossible for him to even consider taking the post as long as his powerful enemy held such sway. On 16/29 July 1908, therefore, Nicholas II relieved the Grand Duke of his position as Chairman of the Imperial Council for State Defense, and disbanded the committee, thus clearing the way for Sukhomlinov's promotion. In retaliation, Nicholas Nikolaievich resigned most of his military posts and offices two weeks later under the guise of retirement.[28]

Throughout these decades, Nicholas Nikolaievich had remained a bachelor, though he had carried on a number of liaisons. In his youth, he was secretly engaged to Baroness Nina Pilar, a member of Empress Marie Alexandrovna's suite, but he was refused permission to contract a morganatic marriage with her and, on their last meeting in Switzerland, the pair had romantically thrown their intended engagement rings into an Alpine lake.[29]

More enduring was his affair with Sophie Boureine, daughter of the mayor of St Petersburg.[30] The relationship, which began in the 1880s, was rumored to have produced two illegitimate children before Nicholas finally worked up the courage to seek permission to marry her.[31] Apparently in 1887, he went to his cousin Alexander III and declared that marriage was the only honorable course of action; the Emperor seems to have considered the idea, though he made clear that any union would be a morganatic one. Nicholas Nikolaievich further added that his father, Nicholas Nikolaievich Senior, had approved of the match, saying, *"I would do the same thing if your mother were not still alive."* This was no more than Alexander III, who despised his uncle Nicholas Nikolaievich Sr. for his dissolute style of life, would have expected, and was unfortunately the wrong comment for the younger Grand Duke to make. The Emperor had already tried to keep the elder Grand Duke away from the capital, away with his mistress and their illegitimate children, and he feared that Nicholas Nikolaievich Jr. was about to launch himself down the same scandalous path to ignominy. Alexander III therefore wrote to Nicholas Nikolaievich Senior explaining the situation and his son's request; he had given the matter some thought and he was inclined against such a union but he wanted to know what the father believed. Then, at least according to Alexander III, Nicholas Nikolaievich Sr. completely reversed himself and insisted that he had never told his son that he favored a morganatic union; this seems quite unlikely – or at least out of character – for the father, who had himself tried several times to annul his own marriage and contract a morganatic union, but this was what Alexander III now told Nicholas Nikolaievich Jr. Under the circumstances, the Emperor declared, he would refuse to countenance such a marriage. Although he continued to live quite openly with his mistress for several years, the ardor waned and soon enough Nicholas Nikolaievich Jr. had transferred his affections to Maria Polotsky, an actress at the Alexandrinsky Theatre in St Petersburg.[32]

In these years Nicholas Nikolaievich developed a strong bond with Anastasia, Duchess of Leuchtenberg, whose sister Militza had married his brother Peter in 1889. The Princess had several other sisters: one, Elena, later married King Victor Emanuel III of Italy; another sister, Princess Anna, wed Prince Franz Josef of Battenberg, cousin to the future Empress Alexandra Feodorovna, and set up house in Darmstadt, providing another close link with the Romanov Dynasty.[33] In their homeland of Montenegro, the sisters had been raised in the most humble of circumstances bordering on poverty. The capital of Cetinje, in the words of Hugh Montgomery-Massingberd, *"was no more than a small village,"* and the Royal Palace was a simple, two-storeyed wooden villa which lacked indoor plumbing and was furnished with threadbare carpets and moth-eaten furniture handed down by sympathetic relatives.[34]

King Nicholas of Montenegro, according to Serge Witte – who admittedly hated the sisters – was, *"notorious…widely renowned for his cupidity and lack of scruples."* Anastasia and Militza had been educated at Alexander III's expense at the Smolny Institute for Young Ladies of Noble Birth in St Petersburg. Here, Witte contended, their father, *"paid little attention to them. Because the Prince did what he could to earn Alexander III's goodwill, it was only natural that the Emperor should show some attention to these young ladies upon their graduation for the institute. And this was enough to encourage some of the young men of the Imperial Family to seek their hands in marriage."*[35]

Anastasia, born in 1868, had married George Romanovsky, 6th Duke of Leuchtenberg and a junior member of the Imperial Family in 1889 in a union arranged by Alexander III; this took place the same year that her sister Militza married Grand Duke Peter Nikolaievich. The Duke, a widower with a young son, proved to be a less than ideal husband. Anastasia gave birth to two children, Serge, born in 1890, and Helen, born in 1892, but soon the Duke had all but abandoned his wife and children and lived openly with his mistress in Biarritz, leaving Anastasia humiliatingly rejected and alone in St Petersburg.[36]

The two Montenegrin sisters earned several court monikers: the kinder appellation referred to them as *"The Black Pearls,"* drawn from their dark complexions and the name of their homeland, Montenegro, or Black Mountain.[37] Their enemies twisted this into the far more sinister *"Black Peril,"* expressing the undisguised distaste with which they were more frequently regarded.[38] In family gatherings, as Nicholas II's sister Grand Duchess Olga Alexandrovna remembered, *"The sisters were nicknamed Scylla and Charybdis, and nobody dared to make a move until the Montenegrin ladies were where they considered they should be."*[39]

After Nicholas II came to the throne, the two Montenegrin sisters embarked on a deliberate course to ingratiate themselves with the new Emperor and Empress. *"Like their father, the Montenegrins were greedy and tried to get as much money as possible out of the Emperor,"* Witte questionably asserted.[40] While there seems to be little evidence to support Witte's view, a bond did indeed form between Empress Alexandra and Anastasia of Leuchtenberg. As Elisabeth Naryshkin-Kurakin, later Alexandra's Mistress of the Robes, noted, the Empress, *"felt very sorry for her and regarded her as a neglected wife because her husband sent most of his time abroad. And as her financial condition was in a state of disorder, the Empress not only consoled her in her loneliness but also assisted her materially."*[41]

Over the next few years, only the two sisters, as Witte writes, showed Alexandra, *"the deference due an Empress. They were not only deferential but also boundlessly devoted. Thus when the Empress came down with a stomach disorder, they were right on the scene. They took over the work of the chambermaids, carrying out the unpleasant duties associated with illness. In this they gained the Empress's favor, but the Emperor paid little attention to them as long as he was under the influence of his mother, but as her influence waned, the Montenegrins' status with him grew."*[42]

In time, the bond deepened, and the two sisters began to introduce the Empress to their own particular brand of mysticism. *"From their mysterious homeland,"* writes Edvard Radzinsky, *"the Montenegrins brought an unshakable belief in the supernatural. Witches and sorcerers had always lived there, in the high mountains grown up in wild forests, and some people there could talk with the dead and predict the fates of the living."*[43] To Witte, both Anastasia and Militza were, *"infected by that disease known by such names as spiritualism and occultism."*[44] *"All kinds of spiritualistic séances went on,"* asserted one clergyman, *"and all sorts of prophets, clairvoyants, preachers, pilgrims, faith healers and miracle workers tumbled over each other."*[45] And Countess Lillie Nostitz, another harsh, often inaccurate, and somewhat hysterical critic, flatly declared that Anastasia's name, *"was a byword for intrigues. It is an open secret that she and her ambitious sister Militza played no small part in bringing Russia into the Great War, and in the subsequent downfall of the Romanovs."*[46]

There is little doubt of the influence the two sisters wielded over the easily susceptible Alexandra.[47] For the first year of their marriage, Peter and Militza lived with Nicholas Nikolaievich at Znamenka, the immense Nikolaievich palace on the Gulf of Finland adjoining the Imperial estate of Alexandria, Peterhof. The two Nikolaievich brothers and the two Montenegrin sisters all shared a great interest in the occult, mysticism, and Eastern philosophies. *"They were much interested in occultism and lived surrounded by soothsayers and questionable prophets,"* wrote Prince Felix Youssoupov, who went so far, in his typically over-wrought fashion, as to deem Znamenka *"the center of the powers of evil"* within the Russian Empire.[48]

It is certainly true that the two Montenegrins were responsible for introducing a number of prophets, pilgrims and holy fools to the Imperial couple. One of the most influential was Philippe Nazier-Vachot, the infamous French faith healer the sisters had brought to St Petersburg, who told Nicholas II that his Empire would only achieve true greatness, *"when the Double Headed Eagle spreads his wings over the Black Mountain,"* a not so subtle reference, if the story is to be believed, to the Kingdom of Montenegro, Russian involvement in the Balkans, and the role of the two Montenegrin sisters at court.[49] Nazier-Vachot, who was said to be able to control the sex of an unborn child, held sway over the Imperial couple for several years. In 1901, Nicholas II repeatedly recorded in his diary how he and Alexandra had gone to Znamenka to visit *"Our Friend."* Eventually, Nazier-Vachot's influence waned: in 1902, he falsely assured the Empress that she was with child – a debacle that ended with a hysterical pregnancy.

The efforts of the Montenegrins tragically culminated in the introduction of Grigory Rasputin to the Emperor and Empress in 1905.[50] *"He is marvelous,"* the sisters supposedly told the Imperial couple. *"He is a new saint. He cures all ills. He is a simple peasant from Siberia, but…God never entrusts His power to the spoiled children of sophistication."*[51] On 1 November 1905, Nicholas II noted in his diary, *"We went to Sergeievska* [the Leuchtenberg villa near Peterhof] *at four. Had tea with Militza and Stana* [Anastasia]. *We met a man of God, Grigory, from Tobolsk Province."*[52]

Nicholas Nikolaievich, according to the ever loquacious Count Witte, harbored an, *"abnormal interest in mysticism, from which he had long suffered and with which the Emperor had been infected by the Empress. One cannot call the Grand Duke mad. Neither can one call him normal."*[53] Nicholas Nikolaievich was a profoundly religious man, who followed the dictates of Orthodoxy but coupled them with an interest in spiritualism.[54] In keeping with Orthodox tradition, he accepted that miracles still took place, and that holy men wandered the earth-beliefs that made him susceptible to varying philosophies and even a number of charlatans.

The Grand Duke's involvement with Rasputin remains somewhat murky, though he was certainly among the peasant's early proponents in St Petersburg. Rasputin was said to have visited his drawing room one day and miraculously cured one of his ailing dogs, a move that won Nicholas Nikolaievich's favor.[55] No matter the genesis of the relationship, the peasant became a permanent fixture at Znamenka in 1905, and the Grand Duke certainly pressed Rasputin's first introduction to Nicholas and Alexandra.

The relationship between the Nikolaievichi brothers, the Montenegrin sisters, and the Siberian peasant, however, was short-lived, and by 1910 they had become Rasputin's implacable enemies, certain that he was disreputable. The turn against the peasant led to the Nikolaievich brothers' temporary fall from imperial grace, although the Montenegrin sisters would remain, at least to Empress Alexandra, untrustworthy and determined enemies.

But in the days when the Nikolaievich brothers and the Montenegrin sisters still enjoyed imperial favor, Alexandra treated them all as important confidants. According to Elisabeth Naryshkin-Kurakin, the Empress supported Anastasia's decision to leave her unfaithful husband and even urged Nicholas II to grant permission for a divorce.[56] Amidst these difficulties, Anastasia spent a great deal of time with her sister Militza and her brother-in-law Peter Nikolaievich at Znamenka, and it was here that she came to know Nicholas Nikolaievich. As her divorce was finalized in the fall of 1906, a romance blossomed, and the pair eventually sought Nicholas II's permission to marry. Again, it was Empress Alexandra who pressed her husband to bend the usual, stringent precedents and on 30 April/12 May 1907, Nicholas Nikolaievich and Anastasia were married in a quiet ceremony held at Yalta in the Crimea.[57]

Having finally settled down, Nicholas Nikolaievich commissioned a new palace, topped with a green bronze dome, at No. 2 Petrovskaya Quay on the Petersburg side of the Neva in the capital. It faced on to Troitsky Square, near the old, three-room hunt that had been Peter the Great's first house in his new capital, and was a somewhat severe, restrained, neoclassical building, in keeping with the Grand Duke's somewhat severe character.[58] There was also an estate in the Crimea, Tchair, purchased by Anastasia using the money from her divorce settlement and situated in a small valley near the Black Sea.[59]

Despite the rift over Rasputin, Nicholas Nikolaievich continued to hold a powerful influence over Nicholas II, and this proved particularly fateful when the First World War erupted in the summer of 1914. The Grand Duke had always loathed Germany, and regarded the conflict as a great opportunity for Russia to claim her rightful place on the world stage. Like many, he was overly optimistic, believing – as did his wife – that Divine Providence would lead to a quick and decisive victory. So hasty was the Grand Duke that he had urged Nicholas II to mobilize Russian troops against Germany without either man consulting – as logic dictated – the Minister of War.[60]

Nicholas II had himself wished to take Supreme Command of the Russian Army, but he let himself be talked out of such a course of action. Instead, he called upon Nicholas Nikolaievich to shoulder the responsibility. Thus, like his father before him, the Grand Duke became Commander-in-Chief of the Empire's forces in a European struggle.

Maurice Paleologue, the French Ambassador in St Petersburg, met the newly-appointed Commander-in-Chief at Znamenka a few days after the announcement. The Grand Duke, Paleologue recalled, *"received me in his enormous study, where maps were spread out on all sides. He came toward me with his quick, firm strides. 'God and Joan of Arc are with us!' he exclaimed. 'We shall win.'"*[61]

Paleologue left a vivid portrait of the Grand Duke: *"His whole being exhaled a fierce energy as he stood thus, unveiling his plans, his finger on the map. His incisive, measured speech, flashing eyes and quick, nervous movements, hard, steel-trap mouth, and gigantic stature personify the imperious and impetuous audacity which was the dominant characteristic of the great Russian strategists."* At the same time, he also noted, *"something irascible, despotic, and implacable, which places him in the true line of the Muscovite voivodes of the 15th and 16th Centuries."*[62]

Nicholas Nikolaievich was fifty-seven at the outbreak of war; he had spent forty-three years in the military, but had never commanded an army in battle. All hopes rested on the tenuous idea that his experience as a career soldier and the respect and fear he commanded from his soldiers would be enough to win the day. One British military official recalled that *"the peasant soldiers in the Russian Army"* regarded the

Grand Duke, *"as a sort of legendary champion of Holy Russia."*[63] *"Although charm and tact could win the hearts of men,"* wrote W. Bruce Lincoln, *"strategic brilliance and logistical genius were needed to win battles and these were the very elements of military command in which Nicholas Nikolaievich had the least expertise."*[64] Yet he duly took up his post, moving to the isolated forest town of Baranovichii, a Polish railway halt midway between Germany and Austria-Hungary in Western Russia, where Stavka, or General Headquarters, had been established.[65] His dedication was intense: during his tenure as Supreme Commander, Nicholas Nikolaievich saw his wife Anastasia only once, and that was only because her train happened to pass through the station.[66]

The Grand Duke had wanted to install General Feodor Palitsyn, former Chief of the General Staff from 1905-1908, as his Chief of Staff at Stavka. Nicholas Nikolaievich knew that he himself had little practical administrative experience, and he needed a strong man upon whom he could rely. But Nicholas II refused to grant his Commander-in-Chief this privilege, insisting upon the appointment of General Nicholas Yanushkevich to the post, a man who had served in the General Staff for a mere three months. Nicholas Nikolaievich agreed, despite his own desires, and thus began a slow disintegration of the Russian war effort.[67]

The millions of Russian soldiers who marched off to war were poorly trained, poorly equipped, and poorly led. He disaster of Tannenberg in the autumn of 1914 set the tone for what was to come, as the Russians found themselves hunkered down in desperate conflicts with Germany and Austria-Hungary, and as Supreme Commander Nicholas Nikolaievich shouldered most of the blame for the hasty East Prussian offensive, which cost the Empire some 100,000 men. *"We are happy to have made such sacrifices for our Allies!"* the Grand Duke told the French Ambassador.[68] The spring 1915 offensive in Galicia at first resulted in victories and the Russian capture of the important fortified town of Przemysl, but soon the Central Powers drove the Imperial Army back in retreat with enormous losses.[69] The Russians were forced to move their Stavka from Baranovichii to the town of Mogilev on the Dneiper River.

As Supreme Commander, Nicholas Nikolaievich actually had little control over the conduct of the war. Organization and questions of supply largely rested with the Grand Duke's old nemesis Vladimir Sukhomlinov, Minister of War, while commanders in the field were most often left to their own devices. There was little cooperation between Stavka, the War Ministry in the patriotically renamed Imperial capital of Petrograd, and the regimental commanders-a result of the country's faltering communication system and Byzantine layers of bureaucracy. Yet Nicholas Nikolaievich, as the figurehead, was the man who shouldered the ultimate responsibility, basking in the praise when the Russians succeeded and, more often, taking the blame when the Emperor's soldiers suffered losses.

The crisis over the state of Russia's munitions occupied much of the Grand Duke's time. One government official, visiting him at Stavka in February 1915, recalled Nicholas Nikolaievich in a confused state, pouring over various ledgers in his railway carriage. *"I am in a difficult situation,"* the Grand Duke declared. *"It says here that I'm supposed to receive so many shells this month, and so many that month. The list covers the whole year. It looks good on paper, but in reality I'm not receiving any shells at all. Quite frankly don't understand the calculations. I asked for an explanatory note and got it, but it still doesn't make any sense. I understand only one thing, either they themselves don't know what's going on or they're lying and cheating us."*[70]

There were rumors that Sukhomlinov was involved in shady armaments deals, stories that Nicholas Nikolaievich eagerly latched on to and himself helped spread in an effort to discredit his enemy. Sukhomlinov, in return, attributed the problems to the Grand Duke's ineffectual leadership. In fact, at least some of the responsibility may have rested with Grand Duke Serge Mikhailovich, Inspector General of the Imperial Artillery, who had allowed his one-time mistress (and former paramour of Nicholas II) Mathilde Kschessinska, to influence munitions deals in exchange for bribes she received.[71] Nicholas Nikolaievich certainly did nothing to stop his friends in the Imperial Duma from publicly accusing Sukhomlinov of mismanagement and incompetence, and he also promoted the idea that the Minister of War was engaged in espionage for Germany. These accusations, all later proved to be false, took hold, and in June 1915 Sukhomlinov was dismissed as Minister of War.[72] *"Informed sources state that Grand Duke Nicholas Nikolaievich played the main role in my removal from office,"* Sukhomlinov wrote. *"Russia is greatly indebted to him: for the manifesto of October 17, for the leftist movement, for removing ministers from office at the most critical moment, and for all the losses of 1914 and 1915 that he blames on others. Grand Duke Nicholas Nikolaievich had found a scapegoat in me."*[73]

The Grand Duke's position as Supreme Commander, and the loyalty he inspired, preyed upon Nicholas II and especially Empress Alexandra. When Rasputin cabled an offer to come to Stavka to bless the troops, the Grand Duke had supposedly replied, *"Yes, do come, I'll hang you."*[74] When Michael Rodzianko, President of the Duma, asked the Grand Duke directly if this was true, Nicholas Nikolaievich chuckled and said, *"Well, not exactly,"* though his reply made it clear that *"something of the sort had actually taken place."*[75]

This response – whatever it was – coupled with the Grand Duke's role in forcing the Emperor's decision to grant a constitution in 1905, earned Nicholas Nikolaievich Alexandra Feodorovna's lasting enmity, and she began a steady campaign against him, attempting to undermine his influence. In her letters to her husband, she suggested that the Grand Duke deliberately ignored the Emperor, and attempted to make him appear subordinate on his visits to Stavka. *"It seems to me you think that Nikolasha is holding me back on purpose,"* the Emperor wrote to his wife, *"with the idea of not letting me move about and see the troops. In reality that is not quite correct. About a fortnight ago, when he wrote to me advising me to come here, he said that I could easily visit three army corps, because they were grouped together in the rear."*[76]

The Emperor's faith in the Grand Duke remained intact for the time being. In June 1915, violent demonstrations broke out in Moscow, in which the crowd demanded that Rasputin be executed, Alexandra Feodorovna be sent to a convent, and that the Emperor be deposed in favor of Nicholas Nikolaievich, to be crowned as Nicholas III.[77] Such scenes, coupled with Rasputin's constant denunciations of the Grand Duke, bothered the Empress, and in her letters that summer of 1915 she made a concerted effort to shatter her husband's faith in the Supreme Commander:

"Our Friend [Rasputin] dreads your being at the Headquarters as all come round with their own explanations & involuntarily you give in to them, when your own feeling has been the right one, but did not suit theirs. Remember you have reigned long, have far more experience than they – Nikolasha has only the army to think of & success – you carry the internal responsibilities on for years – if he makes faults (after the war he is nobody), but you have to set all straight."[78]

"Please, my Angel, make Nikolasha see with your eyes – don't give in."[79]

"Would to God that Nikolasha were another man & had not turned against a Man of God [Rasputin]."[80]

"Nikolasha is far from clever, obstinate, & led by others – God grant I am mistaken &

this choice may be blest....Is he not Our Friend's enemy, as that brings bad luck?"[81]

"*I have absolutely no faith in Nikolasha – know him to be far from clever & having gone against a Man of God, his work can't be blessed, nor his advice be good....You know N's hatred for Grigory is intense.*"[82]

"*Never forget that you are & must remain autocratic Emperor-we are not ready for a constitutional monarchy, N's fault & Witte's that the Duma exists, & it has caused you more worry than joy. Oh, I do not like N having anything to do with these big sittings, which concern interior questions – he understands our country so little & imposes upon the ministers by his loud voice & gesticulations. I can go wild at times at his false position....Nobody knows who is Emperor now – you have to run to the Headquarters & assemble your ministers there, as though you could not have them alone here....It is as though N settles all, makes the choices & changes – it makes me utterly wretched.*"[83]

"*Sweetheart needs pushing always & to be reminded that he is the Emperor & can do whatsoever pleases hi – you never profit of this – you must show you have a way & will of your own, & are not led by N & his staff, who direct your movements & whose permission you have to ask before going anywhere.*"[84]

"*I loathe your being at Headquarters and many others, too, as it's not seeing soldiers but listening to N's advice, which is not good & cannot be – he has no right to act as he does, mixing in your concerns. All are shocked that the ministers go with reports to him, as though he were now the Sovereign. Ah, my Nicky, things are not as they ought to be, & therefore N keeps you near, to have a hold over you with is ideas & bad counsels...Can't you realize that a man who turned simple traitor to a Man of God cannot be blest, nor his actions be god?*"[85]

The Grand Duke never entertained any thought of disloyalty to the Emperor at this time, nor did he seek to usurp any of his authority. To Vladimir Bezobrazov, Commander of the Imperial Guard, Nicholas Nikolaievich confided, "*Should the Sovereign order me to jump out of this window, I would do so without hesitation.*"[86] He once told Serge Witte that he considered the Emperor neither human nor divine, "*but something in between.*"[87] But the accumulated effect of these missives from the Empress, coupled with Russian losses, finally convinced Nicholas II that he had been wrong to make Nicholas Nikolaievich Supreme Commander. In August 1915, he decided to relieve the Grand Duke of his post and install himself as Commander-in-Chief. In truth, Nicholas Nikolaievich had not been a success in the post: he lacked the knowledge and administrative skills necessary to the post – not that Nicholas II himself was particularly brimming with these advantages. But by making himself Supreme Commander, Nicholas II would be able to not only fulfill his personal desire to lead his troops – even if only as a figurehead – but also to consolidate the military and governmental administration in one person. He had no more practical experience than the Grand Duke upon which to draw – indeed, if anything he had less – but the move satisfied both his longings and those of his wife.

In his letter of August 23, 1915 to the Grand Duke, Nicholas II outlined his reasons for the decision:

"*At the beginning of the War, there were reasons of a political nature which prevented me from following my personal inclinations and immediately putting myself at the head of the Army. Hence the fact that I conferred upon you the Supreme Command of all the Military and Naval Forces. Before the eyes of all Russia, Your Imperial Highness has during the War displayed an invincible courage, which has given me and all Russians the greatest confidence in you, and roused the ardent hopes with which your name was everywhere associated in the inevitable vicissitudes of military fortune. Now that the enemy has penetrated far into the Empire, my duty to the country which God has committed to my keeping ordains that I shall* assume Supreme Command of the fighting forces, share the burdens and toils of War with my Army and help it to protect Russian soil against the onslaught of the foe. The ways of Providence are inscrutable; but my duty and my own desires strengthen me in a determination which has been inspired by concern for the common weal. The hostile invasion, which his making more progress every day on the Western Front, demands above all an extreme concentration of all civil and military authority, unity of command during the War, and an intensification of the activities of the whole administrative services. But all these duties distract our attention from the Southern Front, and in these circumstances I feel the necessity for your advice and help and on that front. I therefore appoint you my Lieutenant in the Caucasus and Commander-in-Chief of the brave Army operating in that region. To Your Imperial Highness I wish to express my profound gratitude, and that of the Country, for all your work in the War."[88]

Nicholas Nikolaievich was said to have received this news with relief. *"God be praised!"* he supposedly declared. *"The Emperor releases me from a task which was wearing me out."*[89]

News of the decision sent shockwaves across the country and through the Army. Grand Duke Andrei Vladimirovoch visited Dowager Empress Marie Feodorovna shortly after the decision was announced and, *"found her in a terribly worried condition. She was particularly excited over the question of Nicholas Nikolaievich. She is sure that his removal will be the ruin of N [Nicholas II] because he will never be forgiven for it. She exonerated Nicky in all of this, and laid all the blame on Alix. When Nicky came to see her before leaving, she begged and begged him to reconsider everything carefully and not lead Russia to ruin. But, to her pleas, he declared that everyone had deceived him, that he must save Russia, that it was his duty. In vain did she plead with him that he was poorly prepared for this difficult task, and that State affairs required his presence in Petrograd."*[90]

On his dismissal, Nicholas Nikolaievich immediately boarded a train and set off for Tiflis, where he was to service as Commander-in-Chief of the Southern Russian Army and as Viceroy of the Caucasus. Accompanying him was his wife Anastasia, as well as his brother Peter Nikolaievich and his family; Peter served as adjutant and Chief of Staff to his elder brother. The area was subject to incursions on the part of the Turkish Army under Enver Pasha, whose country had entered World War I on the side of the Central Powers. Most of the Ottoman efforts were directed toward the Caucasus and Georgia, with occasional threats to the Crimea and Black Sea coast. The Grand Duke successfully prosecuted the Russian war effort along these fronts, though a shortage of supplies and concentration of manpower to the European struggle meant that he often fought under less than ideal circumstances. Under his direction, Russian forces captured the fortified Turkish towns of Erzerum and Erzindzhan, the important port of Trebizond, and nearly all of Armenia and the Anatolian Peninsula.[91]

Throughout 1916, the situation in Russia rapidly deteriorated. On 7 November 1916, Nicholas Nikolaievich visited the Emperor at Stavka, warning that the country was on the verge of disaster and urging him to let the Duma select a responsible ministry. According to the Grand Duke, Nicholas II, *"sat silently and shrugged is shoulders."* Finally, in an attempt to break through this apathetic reserve, Nicholas Nikolaievich shouted, *"I would be more pleased if you swore at me, struck me, or kicked me out rather than your silence! Can't you see that you are losing your crown? Grant a responsible ministry! You just procrastinate! For the moment there is still time, but soon it will be too late."*[92] But the Emperor rejected this plea and sent the Grand Duke on his way.[93]

By the time Nicholas Nikolaievich had returned to the Caucasus, his once unflappable loyalty to the Emperor had largely faded. After the scene at Stavka, he was convinced, apparently, that Nicholas II had no interest in saving his throne, and he began, quietly, secretly, to speak with those who were already in the midst of planning a coup against the Emperor. Action was to be led by General Michael Alexeiev, the Emperor's Chief-of-Staff at Stavka, along with politician Prince George Lvov, President of the Union of Russian Zemstvos. According to this plan, the Empress was to be arrested and incarcerated in the Crimea, Rasputin killed, and Nicholas II compelled to abdicate the Throne in favor of Nicholas Nikolaievich. A. I. Khatisov, Mayor of Tiflis, was charged with informing the Grand Duke of these developments. Nicholas Nikolaievich requested a day to consider the idea before ultimately rejecting any participation. Still, it says something of the situation in Russia, and the rift between Nicholas and Alexandra and the rest of the Romanov Family, that the Grand Duke apparently gave no thought to informing the Emperor that his Chief-of-Staff was actively plotting against him.[94]

Nicholas Nikolaievich was in the Caucasus when the February revolution erupted in 1917. When General Alexeiev sought out the opinions of the various military commanders on what should be done, the Grand Duke composed a cable that helped seal the fate of the Empire. On 1/14 March 1917, he wrote to Nicholas II: *"Adjutant General Alexeiev reports to me on the unprecedented fearful situation that has developed and asks me to support his view that a victorious end to the War, so very necessary for the happiness and future of Russia and the salvation of the Dynasty, calls for the adoption of extraordinary measures. According to the duty and spirit of my oath as a loyal subject, I think it necessary to beg Your Imperial Majesty upon bended knee to save Russia and your heir, knowing your feeling of holy love for Russia and for him. Having made the Sign of the Cross over yourself, transfer your legacy to him. There is no other way out."*[95]

This, and similar cables – all unanimous in their calls for the Emperor's abdication – led Nicholas II to formally renounce the Imperial Throne the next day. Even in his semi-exile, the Grand Duke remained an enormously popular figure among the Army; he had assumed that the Emperor would abdicate only for himself, making his son Tsarevich Alexis the new sovereign. At the age of twelve, Alexis would prove a popular and sympathetic rallying point for the country; until he reached his majority, however, a regent would have to be installed, and it is probable that Nicholas Nikolaievich envisioned himself in such a role. In the end, though, Nicholas abdicated for himself and for Alexis – illegally and a violation of the Fundamental Laws of the Russian Empire; the throne passed to Grand Duke Michael Alexandrovich, who declined to accept it unless asked to do so by a future constituent assembly. With this, the 304-year-old Romanov Dynasty came to its end.

With the political and military situation in Russia still so uncertain, the Grand Duke decided to leave the Caucasus for Mogilev to offer his services. Indeed, in one of his last acts as Emperor, Nicholas II had once again installed his great uncle as Supreme Commander-in-Chief of the Russian Army. On learning of this, the Grand Duke gave an interview to the press in which he said that, *"a return to the old regime is impossible, and I would never consent to such a retrograde step."*[96] On arriving at Stavka, the Grand Duke immediately pledged his loyalty to the Provisional Government and prepared to assume his duties as Commander-in-Chief, but the next day a letter arrived from Prince George Lvov, the country's new Premier, declaring that *"the National feeling is decidedly and insistently against the employment of any members of the House of Romanov in any official position,"* and relieving Nicholas Nikolaievich of his position.[97]

With no expectation of any future role, Nicholas Nikolaievich and his wife

Anastasia retreated to their Crimean estate, Tchair, a move that undoubtedly saved their lives. With them came Anastasia's children from her first marriage to the Duke of Leuchtenberg, and the Grand Duke's adjutants Prince Vladimir Golitsyn and Prince Nicholas Orlov, Dr. Malama, the Grand Duke's personal physician, and Boldarev, the Grand Duchess's secretary. While Nicholas and Anastasia lived in the main house, Serge and Helen Leuchtenberg, Prince Golitsyn, Dr. Malama, and Boldarev all lived in the adjoining children's wing. Prince Nicholas Orlov, the Grand Duke's other adjutant, moved into a small guesthouse at Harax, the neighboring estate of Grand Duke George Mikhailovich and his wife Grand Duchess Marie Georgievna.[98]

"Uncle Nikolasha lived a cloistered life in his Tchair estate," his nephew Prince Roman Petrovich recalled, "and refused to receive any visitors from the North, no matter who they were. I visited my Aunt Stana [Anastasia] and Uncle fairly frequently. He often went down to the seashore with his hunting rifle to shoot."[99] It became the once mighty Grand Duke's sole diversion. Very quickly, other members of the former Dynasty sought refuge in the Crimea, including the Dowager Empress, her two daughters Xenia and Olga Alexandrovna, and their families, who lived at both Grand Duke Alexander Mikhailovich's estate of Ai-Todor and later at Harax; and Nicholas Nikolaievich's brother Peter and his family at their estate, Dulber.

The quiet interlude at Tchair was temporarily broken when Anastasia's daughter Duchess Helen of Leuchtenberg married Count Stepan Tyshkevich, an officer in the Imperial Horse Guards. As the bride was Orthodox and the groom Catholic, two services took place: the first, Catholic rite was performed in a Church at Mishkor, while the Orthodox service took place at St Nina's Chapel at Harax. The wedding was deliberately kept a secret to avoid attracting the attention of the public and of any revolutionary officials, an ominous sign of the increasingly uncertain atmosphere surrounding members of the former Dynasty.[100]

In the early morning hours of 26 April/8 May 1917, a contingent of a hundred soldiers from the Sevastopol Soviet sailed to Yalta, and drove in a convoy of motorcars through the gates of Ai-Todor, Dulber, and Tchair, to search the Romanovs and assert their authority. At Tchair, Senior Lieutenant Verkhovsky, Commissar of the Provisional Government, arrived with an armed convoy of sailors and demanded entrance to the house. When Nicholas Nikolaievich appeared in his dressing gown, Verkhovsky presented him with a search warrant, signed by Rear Admiral Lukin, Commander of the Black Sea Fleet.[101] Diaries, letters, and papers were seized, and the Grand Duke's collection of English shotguns was confiscated. There was also a telegram, signed by Prime Minister Prince Lvov of the Provisional Government and Alexander Kerensky, the Minister of Justice, which announced that the Romanovs in the Crimea were henceforth to consider themselves prisoners.[102]

Eventually, all of the Romanovs in the Crimea were moved to Grand Duke Peter Nikolaievich's estate at Dulber, including his brother Nicholas Nikolaievich and his family at Tchair.[103] Here, they lived under increasingly strained conditions, guarded by members of the local Yalta Soviet. This situation changed the next year, when the Germans took control of the Crimea after the signing of the Treaty of Brest-Litovsk in the spring of 1918. On the Kaiser's orders, the Romanovs in the Crimea were all released from their confinement, and Nicholas Nikolaievich and Anastasia returned to Tchair. But now the former Supreme Commander-in-Chief of the Russian Army became the focus of intense German interest. At first, the Germans suggested that a guard composed of their own troops should surround his estate to protect him, but the Grand Duke refused, saying he would only allow Russians to act as his guards on his own estate. The Germans bowed to this request, but installed their own set of guards as well, to patrol the exterior of the park at regular intervals.[104]

Within a few days, a German general in full dress uniform covered with medals arrived at Tchair and formally requested an audience with the Grand Duke. Nicholas, suspecting that the Kaiser wished to coerce him into some sort of collaboration agreement, refused to meet his caller. Instead, he sent Anastasia down to the front gate, where, armed with a broom, she literally swatted away at the poor man, driving him hastily back to his waiting motorcar.[105] Later, the Grand Duke sent a letter to the general, informing him that if he wished to take him captive as a formal prisoner-of-war, he was prepared to surrender; if not, the Grand Duke said, he had no wish to meet with a representative of the Empire which he still regarded as being at war with Russia.[106]

The Germans were not the only ones who regarded the Grand Duke as a possible savior in an increasingly chaotic Russia. Donald Thompson, a news photographer who had spent time in Russia during World War I and had met the Grand Duke, declared in 1918: *"The one man who, in my judgment, could bring order out of chaos and stand the nation on its feet, is the Grand Duke Nicholas, the biggest man in all of Russia, the man that German intrigue could never buy, the man who was deposed as Commander-in-Chief of the Russian Armies and sent to the Caucasus because the German armies could not whip him. Every true friend of Russia should pray for the day when he shall start his march…toward the capital, for millions of loyal Russians will flock to his standard and the Bolshevikii, the Socialists, and the anarchists will be crushed under the Russian steamroller with Grand Duke Nicholas at the throttle."*[107]

Nicholas Nikolaievich only remained at Tchair for a few weeks. With no income from his former estates, nor his regular annual stipend as a Grand Duke, Tchair was simply too expensive to maintain. In May, Anastasia sold the estate to a wealthy industrialist from the Urals, and the pair returned to his brother's estate at Dulber to live.[108]

By the fall of 1918, the Romanovs in the Crimea once again faced imminent danger. Nicholas II and his family had been killed in Ekaterinburg that summer; Grand Duke Michael Alexandrovich had been assassinated in Perm; and a group of other Romanovs, including the Empress's sister Grand Duchess Elisabeth Feodorovna, had been cast down a mineshaft in Siberia and left to die there. The mood in the country was ugly, the Red Terror was in force, and Imperial Germany – the only force that had guaranteed the continued safety of the Romanovs in the Crimea – was crumbling. The Kaiser made one last attempt to negotiate an offer of asylum for the motley collection of displaced and dispossessed Romanovs, but before it could be delivered to them he was forced to abdicate and driven into exile in Holland.[109] The signing of the Armistice on 11 November 1918, meant the immediate evacuation from the Crimea of thousands of German soldiers who, unwelcome though they may have been, had ultimately helped spare the lives of the Romanovs and keep them safely out of the hands of the Bolsheviks.

Through these long months, Nicholas Nikolaievich remained a spectral figurehead for monarchists and members of the White Army fighting the Civil War against the Bolsheviks. Once they took the Crimea, the Volunteer Army made straight for Grand Duke Nicholas Nikolaievich. The monarchist elements hoped to entice the Grand Duke to assume his position as Supreme Commander in the Civil War, while others were more direct, insisting that he assume the position of Military Dictator of the Volunteer Army. Yet others offered the enticement of re-established monarchy, with the Grand Duke as Emperor Nicholas III. Much of the literature concerning these overtures is contradictory, and in exile, monarchists went to great lengths to protect the Grand Duke's reputation, reporting that he had always refused such offers.[110]

Yet evidence remains that suggests the Grand Duke gave the idea of crowning himself Nicholas III a great deal of thought. George Shavelsky, the last Chaplain of the Imperial Army, arrived at Dulber on Grand Duke Nicholas Nikolaievich's birthday, to find a party in progress. In addition to Anastasia, Peter, Militza, and their families, there was a group of White Russian officers present. As the evening wore on, Shavelsky learned that the group was awaiting word from Rumania. At that time, a conference of monarchist officers was taking place at Jassy; among the items on the agenda was the potential offer of a restored Imperial Russian Throne to the Grand Duke. Shavelsky himself certain got the impression that Nicholas Nikolaievich was anxious, and prepared to accept if the offer arrived.[111]

The question, though, brought with it certain difficulties. The Grand Duke had not endeared himself to many when he had openly pleaded for the Emperor to abdicate, and the reputations of his wife Anastasia and her sister Militza who had been responsible for introducing Rasputin to Nicholas and Alexandra, further tinged his record. Nor was the Grand Duke himself averse to these mystical leanings. Nicholas Nikolaievich introduced Shavelsky to a certain Captain A. A. Svechin, describing him as a mystic and interpreter of prophecy. The Grand Duke had met Svechin through Duke Serge of Leuchtenberg, his stepson, who was apparently quite convinced of his abilities. Shavelsky further learned that Svechin had taken the Grand Duke to Yalta to meet with a second mystic, an elderly woman known as Mother Eugenia, who told Nicholas Nikolaievich that she had seen a vision of him as Russia's savior. Shavelsky was startled by these revelations: he was horrified when the Grand Duke himself told the chaplain that he, too, should visit Mother Eugenia and submit himself to her powers. It all stank too much of the Rasputin scandal again, and when Shavelsky reported that the Grand Duke should not look for miracles where none were to be found, Nicholas stormed out of the room. Shavelsky later recalled that his teeth were clenched and that he had seemed almost delirious with rage. The following morning, Svechin told Shavelsky that he was no longer welcome at Dulber, and the chaplain abruptly left, convinced that handing the Grand Duke any power would prove disastrous. In the end, the talk and the scenes came to nothing: at Jassy, the delegates overwhelmingly selected General Denikin as their preferred leader.[112]

In April 1919, a convoy of British warships, led by the battleship *HMS Marlborough*, finally arrived at Yalta on the orders of King George V to rescue the remaining Romanovs. On the evening of 11 April, the members of the Imperial Family stood on deck as the ship slowly eased out of the harbor. Nicholas Nikolaievich was at the railing as former officers in the Imperial Army sang *God Save the Tsar*.[113] Watching on deck, Prince Roman saw the Grand Duke raise his hand in salute, while the Dowager Empress crossed herself.[114] None of those aboard knew that this would be their last glimpse of Russia.

At Constantinople the two Nikolaievich brothers and their families transferred to another British ship, *HMS Nelson*, which took them on to Genoa, where they were welcomed by Anastasia and Militza's sister Queen Elena, consort of Victor Emmanuel III of Italy. Eventually Nicholas Nikolaievich and his wife took up residence in France, living in an isolated villa at Choigny some twenty miles outside Paris. Here, recalled Grand Duchess Marie Pavlovna, *"they led an extremely modest and retired existence, so retired that they would hardly see anybody. The French police and a bodyguard of Russian officers carefully watched over their safety. Their seclusion was so complete that under ordinary circumstances it was impossible to penetrate farther than the entrance to the park; only upon special orders from the house would the sentinels open the gate to visitors."*[115]

In exile, the Grand Duke became one of the principal figureheads of the monarchist movement. He lived in constant fear of Soviet plots and kidnapping attempts, aware that his prominent role in the last years of the Dynasty made him a person of interest. Nicholas Nikolaievich made a great show of disinterest in the question, but secretly he often received delegations imploring him to step into the void created by the Revolution and exile of the Romanovs. The Russian émigré Supreme Monarchist Council, formed in Berlin in 1921, began to make overtures to the Grand Duke, although he remained a deeply divisive figure to many.[116]

Soviet agents, fearful that the Grand Duke would prove too irresistible a banner for the monarchist exiles to rally round, actively began to plot his kidnapping and death. In the process, they managed to infiltrate the Grand Duke's inner circle, and thus learned his plans, which included authorizing the political assassinations of Bolshevik officials and financing agents who would betray the Soviet regime.[117]

In 1924, Grand Duke Kirill Vladimirovich, as the next legitimate male heir to the Imperial Throne, issued a manifesto in which, according to Article 29 of the Fundamental Laws of the Empire, he declared himself Emperor in exile. Although most surviving members of the Imperial Family recognized Kirill as the rightful claimant, Nicholas Nikolaievich protested. *"I am no pretender,"* Nicholas declared, *"nor am I an émigré in the old French interpretation of the term. I am merely a citizen and a soldier, anxious to return home in order to aid his fellow citizens and his country."*[118] Yet he did everything he could to make himself the center of monarchist attention, publicly denouncing Grand Duke Kirill as an alcoholic and Grand Duke Dimitri Pavlovich as *"a womanizer."*[119] Perhaps these remarks were meant to undermine their own claims upon the throne, for each ranked, by law, much higher than did Nicholas Nikolaievich. According to the Fundamental Laws of the Empire, there were nearly a dozen legitimate male claimants who stood ahead of the Grand Duke. His few supporters took his side, however, and the issue fractured not only the monarchist cause in exile and the émigré community but also the Romanov Family.

Nicholas Nikolaievich spent his last years alternating between Choigny and the Villa Thénard at Cap d'Antibes in the South of France, where he went each fall to escape the chill Parisian winter. In December 1928, he came down with pneumonia, and for several weeks was plied with oxygen in the hope that he would recover.[120] On 5 January 1929, Nicholas Nikolaievich died at the age of seventy-two. After a ceremonial funeral, he was interred in the crypt of the Russian Orthodox Cathedral of St Michael the Archangel in Cannes.

Grand Duchess Anastasia lived on in France. She would visit her sister Queen Elena of Italy in Rome when possible, but her universe was now much reduced from the glories and luxuries of the past. Anastasia died at Cap d'Antibes on 15 November 1935. She rests by her husband.

Grand Duke Peter Nikolaievich
(1864-1931)

By Greg King

The life of a Russian Grand Duke, particularly in the last decades of the Romanov Dynasty, was scarcely one of anonymity. Their positions, power, and prestige set them apart from their European counterparts. Many of these men relished – and openly relished – these privileges, and the publicity that stemmed from their fortunate births. But in these years, a few Grand Dukes stood apart, lingering in the shadows; one was a quiet, gentle, thoughtful man, hampered by ill health and seemingly untouched by scandal, content to live on the periphery of power and in the almost overwhelming shadow of his legendary brother.

Grand Duke Peter Nikolaievich was born in St Petersburg on 10/22 January 1864, the second son of Grand Duke Nicholas Nikolaievich Sr. and his wife Alexandra Petrovna. He was the first Romanov in a century to be named after his illustrious ancestor Peter the Great; at birth he received the Order of St Andrei, an honor accompanied by the bestowal of knighthoods in the Orders of St Alexander Nevsky, of the White Eagle, of St Anna, and of St Stanislav.[1] He may have carried this illustrious string of awards and the name of Russia's greatest Emperor but, from the first, Peter Nikolaievich shared little of his namesake's rugged vigor: young Peter was a delicate child, plagued by weak lungs recurrent bouts of pneumonia – a situation undoubtedly exacerbated in the long, cold northern winters of St Petersburg. He grew up in his father's immense Nikolaievich Palace in the imperial capital; in summer, the family retreated to Znamenka, their country estate on the Gulf of Finland, and in both houses Peter lived a kind of isolated existence. His only brother Nicholas was eight years older, and the two siblings were separated by taste and attitude as well as age: where Nicholas was confident and boisterous, Peter seemed uncertain and quiet; one brother seemed bold, rash, the other quiet and contemplative. Nicholas was already in the schoolroom when Peter was born, and age and the passage of time only emphasized the temperamental gulf that existed between the brothers. This is not to say that any real dissention existed, for Peter always treated his brother with great respect and a kind of worshipful deference; but Nicholas Nikolaievich's almost overpowering personality had the unintentional effect of reducing his younger sibling to a kind of shadow figure, a sort of unofficial auxiliary, a mere aide apparently content to bask in whatever reflected glory came his way.

There was more at work in Peter Nikolaievich's early years, more turmoil picking apart at the fragile fabric of his life, than mere differences of personality with his brother. Peter was just a year old when his parents' marriage irrevocably crumbled. Nicholas Nikolaievich Senior, gruff, energetic, ambitious, and vivacious, shared absolutely nothing in common with his wife, the rather plain, serious, and mystically minded Alexandra Petrovna and, like Romanovs before and after him, he had taken a mistress, ballerina Catherine Chislova, with whom he lived off and on quite openly in St Petersburg. It was humiliating, and the wounded wife struck back, taking her own lover and bearing him a son just a year after Peter's birth.[2] The strain within the Nikolaievich Palace must have been overwhelming, particularly for a child as sensitive as young Peter: there was no real parental affection or even interest, just suspicions and betrayals, accusations and arguments that consumed the selfish Nicholas Nikolaievich Sr. and his equally unpleasant wife whenever circumstance forced them together. Too distant and angry to offer their youngest son comfort or concern, the parents left Peter to the care of nurses and nannies, tutors and military minders.[3]

Peter Nikolaievich's comfort, when it came, was found alone, in books, in a passion for the arts, and in a growing fascination for architecture. He had no better tutor than his father's own palace, a silent testament to the power of beauty in a world of ugliness. He was fascinated by the suites of gilded rooms, with their rows of columns and stuccoed ceilings, but it was in an exotic hall that he first discovered the enchanting Middle East. At the southwest corner of the palace's ground floor stood the Moorish Study, a perfect little jewel of Eastern splendors. Rich blue walls ringed with polylobate columns were set with mosaic tile inlays, traditional Islamic geometric designs of gold and crimson, arches with multi-colored carved wooden muqarnas, and panels with stylized gilded Arabic inscriptions from the Koran.[4] The Moorish Study became for Peter a favorite place, an exotic escape, a refuge from the turmoil around him. It also became something more, a vivid and visible introduction to the evocative, enchanting world of the Ottoman Empire, a lasting and powerful influence when Peter Nikolaievich built his own house thirty years later.

Escape was certainly welcome. With the passing years Nicholas Nikolaievich Sr. was increasingly gone, living with his mistress and with their growing brood of illegitimate children in St Petersburg and in the Crimea, while Alexandra Petrovna had settled into a more or less permanent, self-imposed exile in Kiev with her own favorite, a dubious priest named Lebedev.[5] Relatives tried to step into this void, particularly Peter's uncle Grand Duke Konstantin Nikolaievich, whose invitations to join his own family at St Petersburg's Marble Palace were so frequent that, for a time, it became a second home for the young Grand Duke. Peter befriended his cousin Grand Duke Dimitri Konstantinovich, but was probably closest in both these and later years to Grand Duke George Mikhailovich.[6]

Peter was left to his education, to course after course, year after year, an education frequently interrupted – despite his sharp mind and wide interests – by exhaustion, pneumonia, and most seriously, tuberculosis, a disease whose symptoms became impossible to ignore as the young Grand Duke matured.[7] At sixteen he reached his majority, and on completing his studies the young Grand Duke did as all Grand Dukes did, and were expected to do, entering the military and serving in Her Majesty's Lancer Life Guards Regiment with his cousin and friend Grand Duke George Mikhailovich. Although Peter rose to the rank of Lieutenant-General, recurring bouts of pneumonia and the battle with tuberculosis meant that – even had he been militarily inclined – he found it difficult to serve as he would have wished, and as tradition demanded.[8]

Peter grew up a tall, thin young man with a high forehead and a dashing little cavalry mustache. He was, by all accounts, genial and shy, a talented painter and a great reader, liked and respected but believed by some to suffer from feelings of inadequacy when compared with his imposing and accomplished older brother.[9] Serge Witte called him *"a very nice young man,"* but decreed him to be – on precisely what basis is not known – someone of *"limited ability,"* incapable *"of performing any useful functions."*[10] This judgment was not fair: owing to his recurring illnesses, Peter was never able to deploy his talents and abilities to their best, and his weak lungs forced an early resignation from the Lancer Life Guards Regiment. Constantly seeking relief from the cold, he roamed through the South of France, Egypt, and Palestine, hoping to stave off another illness.

Then, in 1888, Peter Nikolaievich met the twenty-two-year-old, beautiful and brilliant Princess Militza of Montenegro. One of several daughters of King Nicholas I, Militza and her sisters had been sent to Russia, to be educated in St Petersburg at the Smolny Institute for Young Ladies of Noble Birth at Alexander III's expense and under his care. Tall and refined, with dark features and a quick mind, Militza was a force to be reckoned with, and Peter was drawn to her beauty, to her strength of character, to her passion for knowledge, and to her intellect. Militza was certainly unique in the ranks of the last Romanovs: she was an Orthodox princess, with the advantage of not having to convert to marry into the Imperial Family, and possessed a deep knowledge of and passion for the faith. She loved history, especially that of the East, and spoke Russian, Serbian, German, and French well; could converse well in English; and was fluent enough in Persian, Arabic, and Sanskrit that she was able to translate a number of ancient texts into Russian.[11] Encouraged by Alexander III and Empress Marie Feodorovna, Peter proposed to Militza, and she accepted.[12] Alexander III, recorded State Senator Alexander Polovtsov in his diary, was *"extremely happy that a German princess will not enter his family, but an Orthodox one, not unattractive, albeit a Montenegrin."*[13] Peter and Militza were duly married in the cathedral of the Great Palace at Peterhof on 26 July/7 August 1889.

Marriage came just as a new family drama unfolded. In her isolation at Kiev, Peter Nikolaievich's mother established the Kievo-Pechersky Convent of Nursing Sisters in Kiev and, in a move that surprised few but was nonetheless unusual within the modern Romanov Family, took holy orders, becoming Mother Superior. Alexandra Petrovna had for many years been gone from the vast Nikolaievich Palace in St Petersburg, at first to avoid her husband, but by this time he, too, no longer lived in the capital: Alexander III, disgusted by the flaunted affair with Chislova and the string of illegitimate children, had advised the Grand Duke that it might be better if he remained out of the public eye, in the Crimea. And so it was there, just five weeks after his hated wife voluntarily abandoned the world and retreated into religious seclusion, that things took an unexpected turn and Chislova died unexpectedly, a tragedy that completely unhinged Nicholas Nikolaievich Sr. With their mother abandoning any vestige of earthly responsibility, it fell to Peter and his older brother to order their increasingly demented father locked away at Alupka, the former palace of Prince Michael Vorontzov, in the Crimea.[14]

Grand Duke Nicholas Nikolaievich Sr. died in 1891 at the age of sixty, and his two sons were left to sort out his extremely complicated and indebted estate. The Grand Duke had, for many years, been borrowing heavily from both banks and from private individuals, obtaining loans based on property and assets he no longer owned. Most of this money had gone to the avaricious Chislova and her children, leaving his sons to face a mountain of unsettled debts.[15] The remaining contents of the Nikolaievich Palace were sold, and the building purchased by the Ministry of the Imperial Court in an effort to pay off the long list of creditors: once these outstanding sums were settled, very little – at least according to Romanov standards – remained to be shared between the Grand Duke's two legitimate sons.[16]

Peter and Militza were often away in these years, driven into a kind of extended tour owing to concerns over the Grand Duke's tuberculosis and the need to avoid the cold of St Petersburg.[17] They traveled through Italy, the Mediterranean, Egypt, North Africa, and Palestine, touring churches and mosques, museums and ruins, with a growing shared appreciation for the art and architecture of the ancient Middle East. In Europe, they gravitated to the Riviera, to Nice. Both Peter and Militza adored France and, contrary to the vogue for all things English among many Russian aristocrats, loathed England. Peter, unlike most Russian Grand Dukes, had no interest in Monte Carlo's casino, but he often joined in pigeon shoots organized by the principality's Société des Bains de Mer, having become enamored of the sport during his Caucasian holidays with George Mikhailovich. His main interest, though, was sailing, and he kept a small yacht, *Mechta*, in Villefranche. This offered not only diversion but also the occasional opportunity to annoy visiting English naval squadrons, for he took his yacht to sea proudly sporting his Grand Ducal pennant; according to the gentlemanly rules of naval command, this display demanded that the visiting British ships recognize the Russian Grand Duke's presence and honor him with a salute, a cumbersome bit of petty business that delighted the Anglophobic Peter.[18] It was during one of their frequent stays in the South of France that, in March 1892, Militza gave birth to the couple's first child, a daughter, Princess Marina; four years later came a son, Prince Roman Petrovich.

But the Grand Duke could not – nor did he wish to – remain in a state of endless medical exile, roaming Europe and the ruins of the classical world. His desire for a permanent house eventually took form in the tropical warmth of the Crimea, where this propitious union of two educated and artistic people resulted in the largest of all the Romanov palaces on the peninsula. Dulber, the villa Peter and Militza built, was an appealing, emotional house perched on a high slope above the Black Sea, an enchanted palace that owed its charmed existence to the personal vision of its gifted owners and served as a visible expression of their passions shared.

In 1893 Peter purchased a plot of land from the neighboring Youssoupov estate of Koreiz, some fifteen miles west of Yalta, and set about planning a house.[19] As the new house was to become their main residence for the greater part of each year, the couple needed something more substantial than a mere holiday villa: Dulber was, from the first, intended as a true palace, designed to accommodate not only Peter and Militza and their family, but also their own suites and household. It was no surprise, in this warm southern climate and with their love of all things Eastern, that they quickly decided to build their new house in the Moorish style. During their travels the couple had toured architectural marvels and ruins, taking careful note of ornament and antiquities; now, this accumulated wealth of was to be given concrete form in the most substantial Romanov residence ever built on the peninsula. Though other holiday villas had copied elements of Persian and Moorish architecture, Dulber was to become the first of the Crimean palaces to faithfully incorporate and utilize these elements, not as mere decorations but as integral aspects of form and form.

For all of their talents, though, Peter and Militza needed an architect, someone with the training to transfer their vision from sketches to final form, and they soon gravitated to Nicholas Krasnov, awarding him the commission in 1895. At the time Krasnov worked as City Architect for the Yalta Municipal Authority, and had previously designed a number of small villas for members of the aristocracy along the Black Sea Coast; he had also taken commissions from the Imperial Family for their estates of Livadia and Massandra. But it was his restoration of the Khan's Bakhchisarai Palace that won him the Dulber project. At Bakhchisarai, Krasnov had shown both insight and care in working with Moorish and Islamic architecture, and moved sympathetically among this alien world of design with a convincing ability that convinced Peter and Militza that he could bring their dreams to fruition.

"*Dulber,*" wrote Prince Roman Petrovich, Peter and Militza's only son, "*was quite a complicated project.*" The scheme, as worked out by the Grand Duke and his wife, called for more than a hundred rooms spread over two principal floors and around three-storeyed wings following the slope of the hillside site to embrace a main entrance court. Initially Krasnov was intimidated at the sheer size of the plan. "*He looked at my father's sketches and notes,*" Roman recalled, "*and said that he was not familiar with the Arabic style. He asked for some time to think about the project, and consider how he could realistically make the plans work. My father liked the conscientious way in which Krasnov worked. He found him to be a very pleasant man and over the years they became firm friends.*"[20] Eventually Krasnov overcame his hesitations. His exterior design, following Peter Nikolaievich's sketches, drew inspiration from a number of existing structures, including the loggias and entrance portal of the mausoleum of Kait-Bey in Cairo. Other details were copied from Bakhchisarai itself, where Peter spent a number of days photographing and sketching, and Militza herself added ideas drawn from her knowledge of Persian architecture and culture.[21]

Construction took three years. When the new palace was completed Peter and Militza christened it Dulber, a Tartar word meaning beautiful; rarely was a house so aptly named. Standing tall atop the cliffs above the Black Sea, shimmering white against the tree-clad mountain slopes, Dulber seemed to have emerged from some Arabian fantasy, a building ringed with expansive terraces and cool, shadowed loggias, proud blue domes and fierce-looking crenellations. Stained glass windows, surrounded by blue and white mosaic decorations, opened to little balconies shaded by tall palm trees, and towers reached from the flat roofs toward the deep blue sky. "In the rays of the setting sun," Prince Roman recalled, "*the white palace assumed a rosy glow, whilst in the moonlight it appeared to be silver.*"[22]

Entrance to this enchanted vision was equally dramatic: a two-storey Moorish arch opened to an apse adorned with blue, white, and gold mosaic tiles. Above the portal rose a large blue dome; below, crowning the door, a carved panel greeted visitors with its gilded, stylized Arabic script: *Allah! Bless All Who Enter This House!* Within, most of the rooms were decorated in the Moorish style, with colorful mosaic tiles, arches, carved jalti screens over windows, and rainbow-hued stained glass, although there were a handful of rather heavy, Jacobean-inspired halls. Everywhere the eye looked was some extraordinary detail: an elaborately carved wooden cornice; heavy, deeply paneled doors beneath pierced brass grills that allowed air to circulate; lintels adorned with arabesques; and marble floors inlaid with intricate geometric designs.[23]

Life at Dulber was leisurely. The family always celebrated their safe arrival with a service in the drawing room, an interminable ordeal for the children were quick to rush outside as soon as the prayers had ended, chasing each other over the exquisitely manicured gardens and swinging wildly in hammocks slung between the trunks of lofty palms. There were visits from other Romanovs, young cousins from the neighboring estates of Livadia, Harax, and Ai-Todor who happily played as their parents sat on the terrace, writing, reading, and visiting as the sun sank against the horizon. Bengal lights and a shimmering moon offered illumination for informal dinners served on the terrace; only if important guests were present did the family take their meals in the formal dining room.[24]

In its first years of life, Dulber witnessed an event of both profound happiness and great despair. In the spring of 1898, Militza was again pregnant, and Grand Duchess Alexandra Petrovna, Peter's mother, left her convent in Kiev to come and stay at Dulber to help look after her daughter-in-law. On 2/15 March, Militza went into premature labor; much to her surprise, and that of her doctor, she gave birth to twin daughters. From the first moments after birth it was obvious that while one was strong, the other girl was desperately clinging to life. Peter sent for a local priest and had the girl baptized, giving her the name of Sophia; a few hours later, she died, leaving her stronger sister Nadezhda perfectly healthy and her parents desolate with grief. With Nicholas II's permission, Alexandra Petrovna took the small oak coffin back to Kiev and buried her granddaughter in the Kievo-Pechersky Convent cemetery.[25]

In these years Peter Nikolaievich was something of a phantom presence at the Russian Court. He and Militza occasionally journeyed north to St Petersburg to make appearances but the majority of their time, in the first years of their marriage, was spent in the Crimea and abroad. Then, in 1904, Nicholas II appointed Peter Nikolaievich Inspector General of the Military Engineering Department. In this post, the Grand Duke followed in his father's footsteps, but frequent ill health meant that his tenure was often interrupted with personal concerns; he did his best, but was unable to fully utilize his talents and effect lasting practical change. As the post required his presence in St Petersburg, Peter began to plan for a new palace; in the interim, the family first rented the Von Dervitz mansion on the English Embankment, and later leased an apartment in the Wonlar-Larsky mansion at No. 22 Fontanka Canal. They continued to spend summers at Znamenka and their winters in the Crimea. But the planned new St Petersburg palace was never built: the Grand Duke had inherited little, and had been plagued with financial troubles, a situation exacerbated by the cost of building Dulber. Things became so serious that, according to his grandson Prince Nicholas Romanov, Peter Nikolaievich even seriously considered selling his Crimean palace.[26] Peter was forced to appeal to Nicholas II for additional funds from the Imperial Appanage Department to cover both the losses and his ordinary expenses.[27]

But the time in St Petersburg was marked by something of greater importance than any building. Empress Alexandra Feodorovna, disliked and herself so disapproving of others, found in Militza and her sister Anastasia two dedicated friends, at a time when she was most in need of confidants. Four times Alexandra had been pregnant, and four times she had delivered girls, to the growing disappointment and disbelief of the Romanov Family and of the Empire. The Emperor and Empress needed a son, an heir, and desperation drove them into a netherworld of mystical intrigue peopled by wandering pilgrims, reputed holy men, and saintly fools of dubious character. And this overwhelming desire, coupled with an almost pathetic credulity, drove the Imperial couple straight into the influential orbit of Grand Duchess Militza.

At first, the relationship was innocent enough: Militza and her sister treated the Empress with the deference Alexandra liked and expected, and a friendship formed between the trio. Militza and Alexandra spent hours together, playing duets on the piano and talking.[28] Somewhere along the way, though, these talks began to transcend the mundane matters of family and court life and entered the realm of religion and philosophy. Alexandra Feodorovna, as a convert, appreciated Militza's knowledge of Orthodoxy, and her ability to explain seemingly arcane doctrines, a spiritual bond that helped draw the two women together.[29] Militza had always had a passionate interest in Eastern mysticism, thought, and medicine, and she shared these ideas with the Empress who, despite her narrow mind, seems to have been quite open to divergent theologies. The difference-and it was an important one – was that Militza approached such topics from an intellectual level, driven by her deep respect for esoteric subjects, while

Alexandra flung herself into this world with unrestrained emotion.

There was nothing particularly odd about this dabbling in Eastern thought and in mysticism, especially in turn of the century, aristocratic St Petersburg. It was all the rage to hold séances, host traveling philosophers at soirees, and meet would-be pilgrims. And so it was with Militza and her sister Anastasia, particularly when it came to a dubious little Frenchman named Philippe Nazier-Vachot, a former butcher from Lyon who claimed a number of extraordinary powers for himself, including the ability to calm the seas and – most importantly for the Empress – to predict the gender of an unborn child. Perhaps the two sisters were impetuous in welcoming Monsieur Philippe, as he came to be called, into their drawing room, and in apparently thinking him genuine in his declarations. That both believed in him for a time is without doubt, though to what extent is not known. Later, Prince Felix Youssoupov, in his rather typically overwrought and melodramatic style, related an alleged incident that seems to always be quoted whenever Militza's name is mentioned. One day, Youssoupov insisted, he met the Grand Duchess and her French protégé out driving in a carriage; he bowed to her, but she evinced no recognition. When he later asked why she had ignored him, Militza supposedly declared that, as she was with Monsieur Philippe and he was wearing a hat that gave him – and those with him – powers of invisibility, Felix could not possibly have seen her.[30]

The rather large issue of Felix Youssoupov's reliability aside, the story simply sounds too absurd to be believed: Militza may have been many things, but stupidity was not an attribute anyone attributed to her. What is certain, though, is that when Monsieur Philippe left Russia in disgrace, the two sisters soon discovered a replacement, a new, altogether more dangerous holy man, the infamous Rasputin, a man they eventually brought to the attention of Nicholas and Alexandra. For this, the two Montenegrin sisters, and particularly Militza, were to be forever condemned by the Romanov Family and by history, but it is a verdict not entirely fair. The Rasputin of 1905 was different than to the Rasputin of 1914, the Rasputin of legendary excesses and disrepute; of the pair, it was Anastasia – the usual portrait to the contrary – who was far more fanatical about the Siberian peasant and who eagerly promoted him: indeed, Militza tried unsuccessfully to limit Rasputin's growing contact with the Imperial couple. In the end, it took her only a few years to see through the Siberian peasant, and soon enough she was complaining to Empress Alexandra about his behavior, about his sordid personal life, and about his dubious character – opinions that were met with silence in the Alexander Palace.[31] Eventually, when Militza and Anastasia tried to push the issue, Alexandra Feodorovna responded by dismissing them from her presence; thereafter, she deemed them *"the black family,"* Rasputin's – and those her own – enemies.[32]

It was just as well, with this turn of events, that in 1909 Peter Nikolaievich's poor health finally forced him to relinquish his post as Inspector General of the Military Engineering Department and settle into a quiet existence with his family at Dulber, away from the capital and from the angry and powerful partnership formed by the Empress and Rasputin. This allowed him to follow his greatest passion aside from architecture: horses. The Grand Duke owned an extensive stud farm near Voronezh, where he bred trotters that won numerous awards and races in Russia. When the First World War erupted, the Grand Duke's family left the Crimea, devoting themselves to Russia's victory: Peter Nikolaievich joined his brother Nicholas at Stavka, acting as the Supreme Commander's aide, and frequently attempting to calm his ever-excitable brother following military setbacks or victories; increasingly, he could act only as a voice of reason against a growing sea of nervous uncertainty. Surrounded on a daily basis by struggling commanders and desperate soldiers, he again sought escape in his love of architecture, sketching religious symbols and even designing a commemorative chapel to mark the sacrifice of the troops that was erected at the great Valaam Monastery on an island in Lake Ladoga.[33] Prince Roman, having graduated from the Nikolskii Engineering Academy in Kiev, served in the Imperial Army along the Turkish front; and Militza funded and supervised hospitals and ambulance trains for the wounded. In 1915, when Nicholas II relieved Nicholas Nikolaievich Jr. of his command and made him Viceroy of the Caucasus and Commander-in-Chief of the Southern Armies, Peter and Militza accompanied him to Tiflis.

They were there when the February Revolution erupted, following sketchy reports from distant Petrograd as the chaos spread and Nicholas II abdicated. They might have remained in Tiflis, but the new Provisional Government asked most of the Romanovs to travel south, to the Crimea: in addition to Peter and his family, this included his brother and his family; Dowager Empress Marie Feodorovna, who had been living in Kiev; and her two daughters Grand Duchesses Xenia and Olga Alexandrovna and their families.[34] Dulber was the destination for Peter and Militza; when they arrived, as Prince Roman recalled, they were surprised to find that Demidov, the Estate Manager, as well as their old servants, were all still in place. "*At first sight,*" Roman said, "*nothing had changed at Dulber.*" The Palace was in perfect condition, the lawns manicured, the gardens planted and watered, the avenues of linden trees and tall yew hedges perfectly clipped. This Moorish paradise was completely peaceful, a tranquil bastion against the onslaught of the Revolution.[35]

In these early months following the Revolution, life was not unpleasant and the Romanovs enjoyed considerable freedom. Roman took regular carriage rides along the coast, visiting friends and neighbors, while his mother sat for hours with the estate gardener, discussing plantings for the coming season. The few soldiers charged with guarding the family were friendly, and Roman sat with them in the park, discussing politics, philosophy, and his family, sharing cigarettes from his golden engraved Fabergé case. In April Princess Nadezhda quietly married Prince Nicholas Orlov in St Nina's Chapel at Harax and the newlyweds took an apartment in Yalta. Grand Duke Peter painted scenes of the Crimea, assisting his daughter Marina with her technique as they worked together in his studio. The Grand Duke, always a thwarted architect, even sketched proposed churches and villas for future construction.[36]

This domestic tranquility was not to last very long. Early on the morning of 26 April/8 May, an armed contingent of hundreds of soldiers from the Sevastopol Soviet sailed to Yalta and drove in a convoy of motorcars to the various Romanov estates to search the prisoners and assert their authority. "*I was woken by the door into my bedroom being opened,*" Roman later wrote. "*I turned the light on and saw a sailor with a gun. Behind him, I noticed someone who was strangely dressed, lighting up the walls of the room with a hand-held torch. This person, who had a red band on his sleeve, ordered me to remain in bed while he searched my two rooms. The sailor with the gun stood guard next to my bed.*"[37]

Soon, the entire household was roused, told to get dressed and stand silently by as soldiers ransacked the house. They searched through cabinets and wardrobes, desk drawers and bookshelves, leaving a trail of debris in their wake. They confiscated Peter Nikolaievich's hunting rifles and even Militza's gardening books, where she had listed the names and addresses of the Russian, French, and German firms from which she regularly ordered plants and seedlings. "*No doubt,*" Roman commented dryly, *"these were of immense importance to those seeking the plans of counter-revolutionaries."* Letters, papers, and diaries disappeared into boxes, to be carted out to waiting trucks that stood in the courtyard. As dawn came, Prince Roman happened to look out a window to watch them being loaded; the family's maids, he now saw, were standing around the grounds, smoking and happily chatting with the armed mob.[38]

The days of indulgent captivity were over. Food grew short and was rationed, electricity became erratic, and the soldiers guarding the prisoners seemed increasingly nervous. In the fall of 1917, the smell of blood was in the air: in the wake of the Black Sea mutiny, the Yalta Soviet issued an order calling for the immediate execution of every Romanov and aristocrat on the Crimean coast.[39] The lives of everyone at Dulber hung in the balance. It was now that the sympathetic Commander Zadorojny from the Sevastopol Soviet intervened, ordering all of the Romanov prisoners in the Crimea to Dulber, whose *"high walls,"* as he explained, made it the easiest of the peninsula's houses to defend against any attack or rescue attempt.[40] A car was sent to Ai-Todor for the Dowager Empress, Grand Duchess Xenia, and her youngest sons, who were then driven to Dulber; the rest of the Crimean prisoners – Grand Duke Alexander Mikhailovich and his elder sons, and Grand Duke Nicholas Nikolaievich and his wife, Militza's sister Anastasia – walked to the estate between rows of Zadorojny's armed sailors. Because Grand Duchess Olga Alexandrovna and Grand Duke Peter's daughter Nadezhda had both married morganatically, they were not included among the prisoners and allowed to remain free.[41]

Peter and Militza awaited their new guests in the main hall; Prince Roman later recalled that his mother was extremely anxious, having never been on friendly terms with the Dowager Empress, and worried how Marie Feodorovna might behave toward her as she nervously paced back and forth.[42] When the Dowager Empress finally arrived, Peter swept her a bow while his wife dropped a deep curtsy, both kissing her hand as Militza promised that she would do all in her power to make Marie Feodorovna welcome and comfortable. True to her word, she and Peter gave up their own rooms, so that the Dowager Empress could have a bedroom, a boudoir, a dressing room and a bathroom, in addition to adjoining rooms for her accompanying ladies-in-waiting.[43] The rest of the prisoners slept where they could: Xenia Alexandrovna and Alexander Mikhailovich were given a second floor study, into which camp beds had been moved; Prince Roman converted the Arabian Room into a dormitory for himself and his three eldest Mikhailovichi cousins, Andrei, Feodor, and Nikita, while the three youngest sons, Dimitri, Rostislav, and Vassili, took Roman's old bedroom; Militza and Peter moved into his study on the ground floor; and Nicholas Nikolaievich and his wife Anastasia were given a large, adjoining sitting room with a balcony that looked out over the Black Sea. Only Princess Marina Petrovna kept her old room.[44]

"We had often chaffed Peter about his unscalable walls," Grand Duke Alexander Mikhailovich recalled. *"Now we knew that he had unwittingly built a prison for himself and for us. This gave rise to innumerable jokes at Peter's expense. Our sense of humor enabled us to endure the terrific tension under which we were living."*[45] Security at Dulber was stringent. Members of the family were only allowed to exercise in the open courtyard of the Palace, where they could easily be watched.[46] Zadorojny constantly worried about the safety of his prisoners. One day, he took Grand Duke Alexander Mikhailovich aside and, with a map of Dulber, together the two men plotted the best defensive positions for machine guns.[47] Along with Zadorojny and his assistants Batuk and Zabolotny, Grand Duke Alexander, his sons, and Prince Roman helped affix seven machine guns

to the balconies, roof, and gates of Dulber.[48]

The Treaty of Brest-Litovsk in the spring of 1918 brought German occupation, and it was only a matter of time before the Kaiser's soldiers reached the Crimea. News of this impending invasion sent the Yalta Soviet into a panic. Fearing that the Germans would somehow reach the Romanovs before they could seize them, they passed a resolution to attack Dulber and execute all the prisoners.[49] The next day Zadorojny, called the prisoners at Dulber together and explained the tenuous situation. He declared that if the Yalta Soviet made an attempt on the Palace, he was uncertain that his men would be able to hold out. According to Grand Duke Alexander Mikhailovich, Zadorojny, *"exerted himself in every possible way to delay the bloody sentence of the Red Court."*[50] The prisoners were unanimous in saying that they would remain at Dulber and take their chances against the Yalta Soviet.[51]

Hearing this, Zadorojny returned to the family all of their confiscated pistols and rifles. *"We equipped ourselves with an extraordinary variety of weapons,"* Alexander Mikhailovich recalled. *"We were resolved not to permit our wives, our children, or ourselves to fall alive into the fiendish hands of the Bolshevik mob."*[52] Zadorojny helped the prisoners set up a twenty-four-hour watch.[53] A rocket fired in the garden would be the sign for everyone to move to an assigned place if an attack began. The young princes, as well as servants and suite, were all assigned to the roof of the palace, where they worked in watch shifts. Later, Prince Roman would remember those long, dark nights spent on the roof at Dulber, a cigarette in one hand and a rifle in another, nervously peering into the distance for any sign of headlights on the road winding up from Yalta.[54]

When Peter and Militza learned that their daughter, then living in an apartment in Yalta with her husband Nicholas Orlov, was in labor, Zadorojny allowed the Grand Duke and Duchess, accompanied by Prince Roman, to leave Dulber under minimal guard so that they could attend the birth.[55] Almost immediately after, fearing for their safety, Zadorojny asked Nadezhda, her husband and their new baby as well as Grand Duchess Anastasia's daughter Duchess Helen of Leuchtenberg and her husband, to leave their apartments in Yalta and quietly move to Nicholas Nikolaievich's former estate, Tchair, where he could install a small guard of his own, reliable men to protect them from the Yalta Soviet.[56] Over the next several evenings, convoys of sailors from the Yalta Soviet arrived at the heavily armed gates of Dulber. As it happened, Zadorojny was always waiting for them, shouting at them to turn back and waving his gun in the air. Then, early one morning, a telephone call from a German officer informed them that the Kaiser's Army had taken the Crimea in the night and were on their way to Dulber.[57] Kaiser Wilhelm II's first order to his troops on landing in Yalta was to head straight for Dulber and ensure the protection of the Romanovs, but the Yalta Soviet was still intent on reaching the prisoners first and executing them all. On several nights the prisoners were kept awake by the sounds of gunfire and angry shouts: a group of loyal Tartars had joined with Zadorojny's men to keep both the Yalta Soviet and the Germans at bay. Then, just as a gun battle erupted at the palace gates, the Germans arrived, pulled out their heavy artillery, and sent the sailors from Yalta scurrying for cover in the night.[58]

The arrival of the Germans probably saved the prisoners. Technically, the Romanovs were now free. They interceded with the Kaiser's soldiers not to execute their Soviet captors, and soon the Bolsheviks were welcomed back to Dulber, installed as trusted family guards. These Soviets were allowed to patrol the park and guard the palace, while the Germans were still forbidden entrance. Grand Duke Peter even allowed Zadorojny to move into a little villa on the hillside above the palace, but the mixture of Bolsheviks and imperial German soldiers soon proved contentious, and the Kaiser's men demanded that the sailors from Sevastopol be dismissed. On the day they left, the entire Imperial Family lined up in the Reception Hall to bid them farewell. Zadorojny and his men bowed to their former prisoners, addressing them by their former titles and kissing the hands of the Dowager Empress and the Grand Duchesses. Many in the group, both former prisoners and guards, were in tears.[59] Each man was presented with some small souvenir by a member of the family – a cigarette case, a lighter, a gold coin, a hand-painted watercolor, or a signed photograph.

In late May, the Dowager Empress finally took leave of Peter and Militza, thanking them for their hospitality and drove to Harax, where she was to live for the next eleven months. Throughout the long ordeal of Bolshevik imprisonment at Peter's palace, the Dowager Empress's antipathy toward the two Montenegrin sisters had visibly lessened. She later told Prince Roman how much she admired his parents and the sacrifices they had made on her behalf.[60]

The collapse of Imperial Germany in the autumn of 1918 and further chaos in Russia led to renewed worries. Peter and Militza learned that Nicholas II had been executed an ominous development that threatened the worst. The Kaiser had made on last attempt to negotiate an offer of asylum, but before it could be delivered he himself was forced to abdicate and flee to Holland.[61] The signing of the Armistice on November 11, 1918, meant the immediate evacuation from the Crimea of thousands of German troops who, unwelcome though they may have been, had ultimately spared the lives of the Romanovs and kept them alive and out of reach of the Yalta Soviet.

The next five months were the most uncertain, an escalation of threats and conflicting reports that came to an end only when King George V dispatched *HMS Marlborough*, a British Iron-Class Dreadnought that had been involved in the Battle of Jutland, to the Crimea in April 1919 on a mission to rescue the Romanovs. Although the Dowager Empress spent several days dithering between remaining and leaving, most of the Imperial Family recognized the danger and on 8 April, they began their reluctant evacuation. A small flotilla of boats conveyed them from a makeshift pier out to *HMS Marlborough*, which lay anchored several hundred feet of the coast. First came Peter and Militza and their children, followed by Nicholas Nikolaievich and his wife Anastasia. The elder Youssoupovs along with Prince Felix, Princess Irina and their daughter, arrived with the Mikhailovichi Princes Feodor, Nikita, Dimitri, Rostislav, and Vassili. Last to appear was the Dowager Empress, accompanied by Grand Duchess Xenia and members of her suite.[62]

Throughout the night, the embarkation continued, until *HMS Marlborough* had taken on some fifty passengers, including a number of servants. One officer attached to *HMS Marlborough* recalled Peter Nikolaievich as *"tall, thin, and quite unlike his brother," "not in good health,"* and a man who, *"was rarely seen on deck."*[63] On the evening of 11 April 1919, *HMS Marlborough* weighed anchor and steamed out of the harbor at Yalta away into the night, carrying the Romanovs into an exile from which they would not return.

Peter and Militza transferred in Constantinople to another British vessel, which took them to Genoa, where they stayed for a time as guests of her sister Queen Elena and her husband King Victor Emmanuel III of Italy. Eventually they settled – as did Nicholas Nikolaievich – in France. But how to live? It was a problem faced by all émigrés, and while most of the Romanovs in exile were never quite reduced to impoverishment, most of their assets had been lost to the Revolution. In 1919, shortly after arriving in France, Peter and his brother attempted to sell one of their estates, a wooded tract called Borissovo that, luckily, happened to be in White Russia and still out of Soviet hands. An eager buyer made an offer, and paid the pair a sizable advance, but difficulties with the new Polish Government meant that the sale ultimately fell through; the would-be buyer, though, allowed the two Grand Dukes to keep the first installment of funds, a bonus that helped them survive in some comfort these first uncertain years of exile.[64]

But the money did not last forever, and like so many other Grand Duchesses, Militza was reduced to selling off her personal jewelry to provide for her family. Her most valuable pieces, stored in a St Petersburg bank vault, were seized by the Soviets, and she had no opportunity to retrieve them, but she had taken many pieces with her to Kiev and Tiflis that she managed to claim, and there were also some jewels at Dulber: a collection of rings and brooches and, most importantly, six strings of perfectly matched, fresh-water pearls that reached to her knees. And in exile, Militza again proved her intelligence, for she sold off these pieces before many other exiled relatives and émigré aristocrats flooded the market with their own collections, and was thus able to raise a sizable sum of money.[65]

Half of the proceeds from these sales, recalls Prince Nicholas Romanov, Peter and Militza's grandson, went toward the purchase of a residence, the Villa Donatello, set in a five-acre park at Cap d'Antibes on the Riviera, whose warm climate was so beneficial to the Grand Duke's health. Militza's sister Queen Elena of Italy also provided financial assistance, though certainly they lived in reduced circumstances, at least for a Russian Grand Ducal couple. *"How they managed to survive, I do not really know,"* says Prince Nicholas. But life was not unpleasant: Peter still enjoyed attending the races when his health permitted, and most Sundays the Grand Duke presided over luncheon, sitting at the head of the table. It was *"a very Russian atmosphere,"* according to Prince Nicholas, replete with an Orthodox priest attached to the villa's small private chapel, General Baron Alexis de Stahl und Holstein, who served as the Grand Duke's equerry, and a contingent of visiting aristocrats.[66]

In his last years, Peter Nikolaievich battled not only tuberculosis but nephritis, a disease whose symptoms ultimately claimed his life. He died at Cap d'Antibes on 17 June 1931, at the age of sixty-six. Like his more famous brother before him, Peter Nikolaievich was interred in the crypt of the Russian Orthodox Cathedral of St Michael the Archangel in Cannes.

Grand Duchess Militza eventually settled in Tuscany, where she was in closer contact with her sister Queen Elena. During the German invasion of Italy, Militza received asylum from the Vatican, but not her children, who had to move, *"from house to house in an attempt to stay beyond the reach of the Germans."*[67] The American liberation of Rome brought an end to the family's ordeal. However, Italian politics were to be the cause of yet another exile. In 1946 King Vittorio Emanuele III abdicated the throne and was succeeded by his only son Umberto II. A plebiscite was held to decide the future form of government, but the Italian monarchists lost. Thirty days after becoming king, Umberto II led his family into exile. Militza joined her Savoy relations and settled in Alexandria, Egypt, where King Farouk welcomed them. She died there on 5 September 1951. Her earthly remains were taken to France and buried next to her husband's in the same crypt where her sister and brother-in-law lay.

The Nikolaievichi Grand Dukes

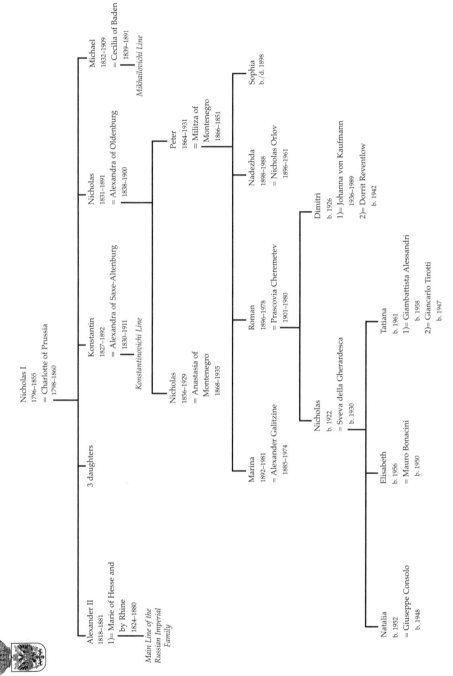

7

The Sons of Grand Duke Michael Nikolaievich

Grand Duke Nicholas Mikhailovich (1859-1919)

By Janet Ashton

The prime purpose of a ruling dynasty is to rule. If its members stand out, they tend to do so for feats that are military or administrative. This was particularly true in earlier centuries, when infant mortality and dynastic laws took their toll on numbers, making Grand Dukes and Princes to be in short supply. As in most ruling families, male Romanovs born before around 1850 knew very well that their role in life would be to work in support of the Emperor, as a soldier or occasionally as a sailor. For surviving daughters, the function was to marry well. This they all did punctiliously, whatever their own talents or inclinations, and some excelled at it. Peter the Great, the young Catherine the Great and Alexander I; Nicholas I; Alexander II and Grand Duke Konstantin Nikolaievich: for all their differences in policy and despite instances of openly tyrannical behaviour in some cases all these people were noted for their ability as rulers. They made Russia a power to be reckoned with.

Few earlier Romanovs had the opportunity to make their mark in an artistic or intellectual sphere, except insofar as they wrote theoretically on government or corresponded with notable intellectuals of the day, as Catherine II did. In the generations after Catherine, however, as the dynasty grew larger and larger and Grand Dukes proliferated to the point that Alexander III eventually felt the need to place a limit on the title, a small number of individuals emerged who were able to find the time and the persistence to make a name for themselves beyond the traditional imperial sphere.

In small German states such as those from which the Grand Duke's ancestors came, and into which their sisters married, there was by the middle of the nineteenth century a long tradition of patronizing the arts and providing direct help to struggling writers or musicians. These tiny states, often shorn of their political importance, developed into cultural centres of international significance. Maria Pavlovna, daughter of Tsar Paul and sister of the first Alexander and the first Nicholas, shares her tomb in Weimar with Goethe and Schiller, whom her family protected across several generations. Her son, Carl Alexander of Saxe-Weimar-Eisenach, corresponded with Hans Christian Andersen and other writers. But few of these princes, intellectual and intelligent as they were, became artists or original thinkers in their own right.

The first Romanov to make it the main business of her life to encourage artistic development was Helen Pavlovna, born Charlotte of Württemberg, the neglected wife of the single-mindedly military Michael Pavlovich. In the next generation, her beloved nephew Konstantin Nikolaievich, the gifted administrator and Naval reformer, was a patron of musicians and artists and also a notable musician himself, a Renaissance man who used his naval journal, *Morskoi sbornik*, as a vehicle for the dissemination of new ideas and writing. But it was not until the generation after his that the Romanov dynasty was to produce two men who could hold their own not just intellectually but also in terms of reputation with other noted names of their era. The first of these was Konstantin's own son, Konstantin Konstantinovich, who under the pen-name "KR" wrote poetry and plays which won him the respect of noted writers of the age, and the second was Konstantin's cousin, Nicholas Mikhailovich, whose reputation as historian arguably eclipses that of KR's as a poet, and earned him more lasting respect.

Nicholas Mikhailovich was born on the 14 April 1859 (O.S.), twenty months after the marriage of his parents, whose first child he was. Like all of his first-born male cousins he received their late grandfather's name in preference to his father's. The shade of Nicholas I and his conception of the Grand Ducal role and obligations hung very heavily over that Tsar's descendants, but "Nikolai" was also the name of the new baby's youngest uncle – his father's closest brother – so the name could be seen as a double tribute to both grandfather and uncle.

Unlike his cousin Konstantin Konstantinovich, Nicholas had little in his background to suggest that he would grow into an obstreperous intellectual, and little active encouragement to do so. Nicholas' father, Michael Nikolaievich, Nicholas I's youngest son, was noted for his calm, loyal, dutiful nature but certainly not for his intelligence. The most notorious appraisal of him came from the lips of the French Empress, Eugenie, who said of him that he was *"not a man but a horse."*[1] Michael's wife Olga, the former Princess Cecilie of Baden, was the source of their son's intelligence. She liked to read widely, but was also a sharp-tongued, harsh woman who enjoyed complaining endlessly about other people and offered most of her children little maternal warmth. She criticized Michael freely too, but he and his career were the centre of her life and gave it meaning, and his educational plans for the children went unquestioned. Like it or not, the new-born "Niki" was going to be in the Army, as a true Romanov.

Military education apart, Nicholas had a childhood that was quite radically different from that of any of his other cousins or forebears. He spent his infancy conventionally enough in the St Petersburg/Tsarskoe/Peterhof area, where his parents were having several houses built for them, and where his only sister Anastasia and his brother Michael – the first of five more boys born to their parents – soon joined him in the nursery. Then, when he was three years old, his father was appointed viceroy of the Caucasus, and from that point Niki would be a colonial child.

Michael Nikolaievich's task in the Caucasus was to subdue the volatile native Islamic tribes, driving them off to Turkey where necessary, and to imbed Russia's rule in these areas which had only recently been conquered and were still apt to rebel against her. He was selected specifically for his status as a Grand Duke. A member of the dynasty, with authority over civil government and military administration, potentially carried far more weight in the eyes of a native population still immersed in places in a patriarchal warrior culture. By extension, young Niki would grow up with a status rather different from that enjoyed by other young Grand Dukes. He was no mere nephew of the Tsar: here, in the Caucasus, he would play the role of the Heir, accompanying his parents on trips around the country and celebrating his birthdays with big, public church services.

In April 1863 the family took up residence in Tiflis (Tbilisi), capital of Georgia, the ancient Christian kingdom which had voluntarily acceded to Russian rule in 1801 and was considered an invaluable ally against the Islamic rebels. Russia recognized Georgian titles, and treated the nobility and military with respect; Georgians were, furthermore, socially acceptable as companions, being white. But the Caucasus still had no railway, so travel involved lengthy and often uncomfortable journeys over narrow mountain roads, and Tiflis was undeniably exotic in appearance. *"Tiflis contains 30,000 inhabitants,"* wrote a contemporary Russian visitor. *"It may be compared to Prague for its aspect and to Cairo for its concourse and daily life, of which it is the theatre. The streets are not so fine as the places or squares. There are forty-three churches, but Georgian and Armenian cupolas are conic and not round like those of Russian churches. The palace of the Governor-General, in the new town, is a fine edifice; it was built with the arches of the ancient palace of the kings of Georgia...There is a botanic garden, but it requires great improvement to deserve that name. The bazaar, which is rendezvous of a numerous population, composed of many races, is very attractive and excites curiosity of the highest degree; there you meet the Georgian and the Armenian, the Imeretian and the Circassian; the Russian warrior and the Tartar, all distinguished from one another by their various costumes. There Europe and Asia intermix through commerce...The Turk, the Jew who speaks Spanish...carry on there also their commercial transactions...The Georgian woman, with black eyes, a curved nose and painted cheeks, with or without a veil, looks, when seen from a distance, more beautiful than when surveyed closely...Russian morals have invaded Tiflis, and the virtue of Georgian women is not the better for it."*[2] On the south side of the dramatic, rushing river Kur stood the old town, with its fortifications, towers and walls. North of the river was the new town, predominantly western in style, featuring a museum and theatre, hotels, and eventually a Russian cathedral. *"As far as the eye can wander in every direction the horizon is bounded by ridges of mountains,"* observed another, more romantic traveler. *"Here the steep hills of rock that rise in the immediate neighbourhood; there the snow peaks of the great range of the Caucasus, faint against the blue sky."*[3] The palace in which the family would take up residence was a, *"handsome building of great size...amply suited to its purpose, and cannot fail to impress the native of the country, but also the civilized traveler, with the magnificence of the Russian court. Within it is gorgeously decorated: great clusters of palms, innumerable glass chandeliers and a quantity of gold paint give it the most brilliant appearance, a fitting setting for the semi-European, semi-oriental crowds that flock it salons on reception nights."*[4] The contrast between this ancient city on the mountainous fault line between Europe and Asia, and neoclassical St Petersburg, built amid the flat marshes and huge Scandinavian sky barely a hundred and fifty years before, cannot be over-emphasized. Michael Nikolaievich's children would grow up with a self-consciously different outlook to their "northern" cousins, and felt that they in turn were looked upon as different. To the Petersburg Romanovs, the Mikhailovichi, or Michels, as they called Grand Duke Michael's offspring, were "liberals" – though some of their attitudes barely suit that description in the modern sense. They were, however, rather radical in some ways, and Nicholas was particularly so.

Michael's mantra was obedience without question; but Nicholas and several of his brothers felt themselves duty-bound to criticize when they perceived a problem, and they expected to be treated as equals by the Tsar. This was their way of showing their loyalty, and they attributed it to their Caucasian background without overtly analyzing what it was about that background which made them this way. In Nicholas' case, above all, the reasons seem fairly clear: it was his upbringing almost as an heir which gave him the confidence to speak his mind. Then, too, he felt he had seen more of the world than those raised in Europe; he had lived at the edge of conflict and met people whose clothes and language and lifestyle were quite alien to his sheltered, northern relatives. For ten years after their arrival, his family remained in the Caucasus, and his parents built another, private country home there. Borjomi, constructed of red-brown wood and stone and adorned with balconies and cupolas, stood amid heavily wooded mountains cleaved by fast-flowing muddy rivers, stunningly beautiful and ideal for hunting and for all manner of scientific expedition. Like many young boys of the nineteenth century, Nicholas developed a keen interest in collecting butterflies and insects. *"I walk about all day making my search for butterflies,"* he once happily recorded in a letter to his mother[5] Later, as an adult, he would go on long expeditions, climbing the Caucasus's highest peaks, where snow lay even in mid-summer, to find the rarest of species, and traveling abroad to the Canary Islands and other exotic places in pursuit of others.

Here at home, out of the public eye, however, his daily schedule as a boy was little different to the one he would have enjoyed had he stayed in the north. From the time they left the nursery, he and his brothers slept together in a room like a dormitory on iron beds and rose at 6 a.m. for a rigorous program of academic studies and exercise that included much practice with firearms. Whereas their father had been raised with other young cadets as companions in addition to his brother, they were isolated from cadet contemporaries and had only each other for company. Perhaps, despite his apparent mildness and tolerance, Michael feared contamination by non-Russian elements. From time to time, the Grand Duke himself came to the schoolroom or parade area and watched their exercises, recalled his fourth son Sandro, *"with a critical eye."*[6] The consequence of this sequestered upbringing with no other friends was that all the younger brothers looked up to and hero-worshipped Nicholas as a leader, and possibly as a buffer against their sharp-tongued mother, whose acknowledged favourite he was to the absolute exclusion of all the rest of them. *"If it will be of any consolation to you, my dear son, I have loved you more than my other children,"* she wrote to him shortly before her death.[7] Anastasia, the second child and only daughter, was Michael's obvious favourite in turn, and all her brothers adored her too and looked forward eagerly to Sundays, when there were no lessons and they could all be together.

Nicholas Mikhailovich's education differed from his father's in another respect besides his isolation: he was taught classical languages. Perhaps this was the influence of his German mother, for it certainly broke the rule established by his grandfather, Nicholas I's, nationalistic prejudice against a classical education. The late Tsar deemed Latin and Greek unsuitable topics for Russian youths, whose culture, he felt, owed nothing to the classical world and western Europe.[8] For Nicholas Mikhailovich, though he may have complained about them as a boy, these languages would furnish the important background to his interest in science and classification. They would also act as his introduction to the world of west European ideas – the politics, the art, the whole theoretical framework of its civilization. For this, he would have cause to be grateful later.

Young Niki also learned modern languages, becoming extremely proficient in French and German, though he had less interest in English. His religious education again bore his grandfather's imprint: it would be comprehensive, comparative, designed to make him think what he was learning rather than repeat without question. Then there was music, mathematics, history and literature: the full education required by Russia's grammar schools to equip a young man for university entry, and he excelled at everything he learned, earning the highest grade of 5 or 5 plus in most subjects, and proudly reporting these to his mother.[9]

In Nicholas' case, however, university was out of the question, even though he wanted to go. Instead, he would return to St Petersburg at last, to enter the military academy. But even before this could happen, the eighteen-year-old Grand Duke saw military service. In 1877, Russia went to war with the Ottoman Empire over the complicated situation in the Balkan territories, where recent Bulgarian uprisings against the Empire had been ruthlessly suppressed. Some of the soldiers the Sultan's government used for this were Muslims expelled by Russia from the Crimea or Caucasus not long before, and Russia again stepped up to the plate as the defender of Orthodox Christians in the region. Despite negotiations, and despite strong warnings from Russia's liberals that the war would be as much of a disaster as the Crimea had been nearly a generation before, neither side was willing to compromise. As a Grand Duke now eighteen years old, and in particular as the eldest son of the Viceroy of the Caucasus where much fighting took place, Nicholas was unequivocally expected to take part in the fighting.

The young Grand Duke served under his father, of whom he wrote with the same dutiful, admiring distance that had characterized his childhood relationship with this parent. *"Papa continues to be content with me, I have spoken with him often,"* he assured his mother.[10] While Michael was in supreme command of the Caucasian troops, his first-born was allocated a role with the wounded. Whether the intention was that he should be kept in relative safety, or whether the idea was to show him that war was not all about winning battles and getting medals is not clear, but if it was the latter it succeeded only too well. He found the experience deeply disturbing, and wrote long graphic descriptions home. When his mother complained that she was upset by these, he countered ambiguously with, *"You have been unhappy with my description of my day; I am destroyed by it."*[11]

The war was over in a year, and great economic depression came from it. If Nicholas was starting to doubt the wisdom of a military career, this fact can only have underscored his instincts that war was a bad idea. Nevertheless, he had no choice but to go to Petersburg and enter the Nicholas General Staff Academy – named, of course, in honour of his grandfather, and thus coincidentally emphasizing the reason for his own lack of choice about his fate. Nevertheless, he enjoyed the academic rigour of the education he was to receive at the Academy, and graduated with top honours. During these years in Petersburg, he also enjoyed the social life of a wealthy young aristocrat, and became very friendly with Marie Feodorovna, wife of his cousin Alexander and from 1881 Empress of Russia. She was far from being his intellectual equal – and as matter of fact his mother resented giving precedence to her for exactly this reason – so it was probably a shared love for dancing and court gossip that drew them together. Her husband, his cousin Alexander III, was far less entranced: Nicholas Mikhailovich soon had an unenviable reputation for an acid tongue. One of the most famous and damning descriptions of him is provided by A.A. Mosolov, who served at Nicholas II's court and was admittedly a man given to hyper-critical judgments himself. Nicholas was, Mosolov wrote: *"Fairly good-looking and very intelligent,* [but] *he spun intrigues wherever he went. He was always criticizing, but never did anything himself. He wrote numberless letters to the Tsar; they show that he knew how to please and to make himself amusing. But one would search in vain through the letters for a single practical idea."*[12] Another society acquaintance accused him of, *"employing his leisure time by engineering quarrels between his friends,"* and alleged that he *"never felt so happy"* as when he learned that he had managed to make two old friends fall out or had caused an estrangement between a husband and wife.¹³

Nicholas undoubtedly had some very unpleasant characteristics. For all his exotic, Georgian upbringing may have left him with a curiosity about the world and a great confidence in his own wisdom as a man of broader experience than some of his relatives, it did nothing to inspire a love of the local culture. Nicholas Mikhailovich liked colorful stories of brigands and tribesmen at large in the Georgian mountains, and Borjomi was his favourite home all his life, but he had the typical prejudices of a European abroad, who is forever complaining about the 'natives'. He apparently despised the Georgians and certainly the Jews, despite rumours that his true, biological grandfather on his mother's side had actually been one of the latter. With his dark eyes and hair, inherited from his mother, Nicholas could have passed for a Georgian – and his appearance was certainly cited by his own enemies as evidence of Jewish forebears – but this did nothing to alleviate his prejudice against *"mongrels"* and *"International Jewry,"* who he blamed for all of Russia's problems.¹⁴ He enjoyed the privileges of his rank without qualm or guilt, winning and losing vast sums of money at gambling in various casinos around Europe, and he had numerous love affairs. Nicholas' relationship with Maria Feodorovna was not a romance: the young Empress was far too strait-laced for such a thing; but his family believed that he sired several illegitimate children by other society women.¹⁵ As a young man, he fell in love first with his cousin "Vicky" of Baden (later Queen of Sweden), and then with a French Princess named Amelie (future Queen of Portugal), but neither was deemed suitable as a bride. Vicky was forbidden him by the Church due to their degree of consanguinity; Amelie by parental disapproval of her ancestors and by Alexander III's marriage laws, which demanded that she convert to Orthodoxy – something the Catholic Princess's family refused to allow her to do. Thenceforth, Nicholas seems to have resigned himself to remaining single while availing himself of the extensive extra-marital romantic opportunities available to a rich, tall, entertaining and reasonably good-looking man.

Despite his acid tongue and the harm it did them, Nicholas Mikhailovich did not actively dislike many people. His criticisms of his relatives and of their role in government had a serious point, but they were often the product of momentary jealousy or of frustration, and many of his comments about his own associates were probably non-serious and came from the desire to entertain an audience. He was, remembered his sister-in-law later, *"a strange mixture. He was a highly cultured man and a mischievous child at once."*¹⁶ Nicholas was as generous with his money when it came to others as he was to himself, spending most of his casino winnings on presents for his sister, his sister-in-law and his young nieces.¹⁷ He had a genuine instinct to treat the people around him as equals, regardless of age or status. In the Army, he was called "Nicolas Egalite" for his attitude to the troops, and later, as a single man otherwise alone in his apartments, he invited his valet for breakfast every day. When his family objected to his carrying on the same arrangement on visits to their own houses, he chose to eat breakfast separately, still accompanied by his friend.¹⁸ His niece, the future Crown Princess of Prussia, recalled that he, *"took me seriously and never teased me, and to a sensitive child or schoolgirl that means a great deal!...He could talk entrancingly of his studies, and made me keenly interested in history and family history in particular."*¹⁹ These were the pleasant aspects of his personality.

One relative for whom Nicholas did, however, harbour an intense, life-long animosity was his cousin Nicholas Nikolaievich, the elder son of his father's favourite brother. Mystic, excitable, and single-mindedly devoted to his military career, "Nikolasha" was in many ways the antithesis of his cynical namesake and cousin. When both were in the Army, disagreements over military policy added to their catalogue of issues with one another, and some of these were most likely due to jealousy. Despite his brains and success in exams, Nicholas Mikhailovich was not popular with the other officers. This was partly due to his outspoken manner and reputation as a gossip, as well as his egalitarian style with the men and his cerebral pursuits in themselves. *"His intellectual superiority,"* recalled his brother Sandro, *"took all enjoyment out of his regimental contacts."*[20] Nicholas Nikolaievich Jr., on the other hand, was adored by all his colleagues, notwithstanding his reputation for extreme harshness with the troops and his difficulties passing the necessary exams. He was an advocate of an aggressive foreign policy, and as a commander he never seemed to know when to draw the line and simply retreat. His tendency to get huge numbers of men killed can not have endeared him to the other Nicholas, with his burgeoning conscience.

In 1903, Nicholas Mikhailovich finally resigned his Army commission and left to pursue interests to which he was more suited. He continued, however, to observe the actions of his cousin Nikolasha, and to voice his views on these without restraint. Even during his years in the Army, the Grand Duke had begun to publish scholarly works. His first was scientific, the product of his boyhood days in the hills around Borjomi: *'Memoires sur les Lepidopteres'*, a nine-volume work on butterflies, was published in 1884 under the name "N.M. Romanoff." Nicholas was general editor, and not all contributions were authored by him, but it was a work which earned him the respect of scientific contemporaries. He was also fascinated by fruit-growing, and became president in time of the Russian Society of Pomology. Even his hunting had a scholarly aspect: Nicholas wrote a book on it that displayed a broad knowledge of the species of birds.[21]

His most productive interest, however, was in history, and it was here that he was to make his enduring reputation. He had, of course, no formal historical training, but he had a deep interest in people – as evidenced by his fondness for gossip – combined with the desire to make sense of his family's place in the world, and with a passion for France, and all of this gave him his first impetus. The majority of his original works were to be on the Napoleonic era, and he admired that monarch greatly, much as his relations Alexander and Konstantin Pavlovich had done, at least until he invaded Russia. Nicholas did not even allow the invasion to change his opinion of his historical hero: in 1912, at a military review for the centenary commemoration of Alexander's driving Napoleon from Russian soil, he dismounted and strolled around smoking insolently behind his patriotically saluting relatives.[22] The Grand Duke was well aware that the current Tsar, Nicholas II, rarely did anything about such displays of recalcitrance on the part of relatives. Alexander III, however – a much tougher customer who did not at all like his cousin Nicholas II – once had him arrested for appearing in public with a cigar clenched between his teeth and with his coat unbuttoned.

Nicholas' most renowned display of all – one which reflects well on him in addition to perhaps convincing him that he might do anything he felt inspired to do without fear of repercussion – took place very early in Nicholas II's reign. At the coronation in May 1896 an infamous tragedy occurred, when up to four thousand people were crushed to death at a popular celebration organized for peasants and workers in Khodynka meadow, near Moscow. The field had been used in the past for military maneuvers, and as the crowd grew larger and larger and rumours circulated that the supply of beer, food and coronation mugs was running low the wooden boards placed across the trenches and holes used by the army gave way in the crush, causing many people to fall under the feet of the other revelers, where they were killed or seriously wounded. The Tsar was due to attend a ball that evening at the French Embassy, and Nicholas was adamant that he should not go, and that the Governor of Moscow – Grand Duke Serge Alexandrovich – be dismissed as recognition of his ultimate responsibility for arrangements. *"The blood of those five thousand men, women and children will remain forever a blot on your reign,"* he told the Tsar, evoking France as usual as he reminded Nicholas that the French sovereigns Louis XVI and Maire Antoinette had danced while the storm broke about them.[23] Serge Alexandrovich and his brothers – the young Emperor's uncles – were naturally of a different view, arguing that Russia could not afford to offend their French ally by canceling anything, and their view prevailed. The Romanov family duly presented themselves at the ball, but Nicholas Mikhailovich, with his loyal brothers in train, left as soon as the dancing began. According to Sandro's albeit always melodramatic memoir, their cousin Alexis Alexandrovich exclaimed audibly as he watched them: *"There go the four imperial followers of Robespierre!"*[24]

Every year, starting in 1885, Nicholas went to France twice, staying in at the Hotel Vendôme in Paris or on the Riviera, where both his father and his sister Anastasia had villas. He visited archives, read documents or books and made contacts, the most notable of whom was the French historian Frederic Masson, with whom he kept up a constant correspondence. Masson was rather of the French right, a monarchist who shared Nicholas' anti-Semitism and had sympathy for the revengeful, anti-German spirit at large in the Third Republic. Although generally more liberal in his political leanings – his brother Sandro remembered that he was, *"an enthusiastic admirer of the parliamentary regime"*[25] – Nicholas was happy to adopt a similar stance toward Germany, from which so many of his ancestors hailed. On one occasion, he gave an interview to a newspaper which came close in spirit and effect to the infamous *Daily Telegraph* incident of his personal bugbear, Kaiser Wilhelm II. In the interview, a champagne-fuelled Nicholas told the world that he hoped for war between France and Germany, and that the Tsar, Alexander III, was anti-German too. On that occasion, the furious Alexander sent him to lie low at Borjomi for several months.[26]

The most significant product of Nicholas' work in France was the vast *Relations diplomatiques de la Russie et de la France d'apres les rapports des ambassadeurs d'Alexandre et de Napoleon*. This ran to seven large volumes and was finally published in 1915. In the meantime, the Grand Duke had also written biographical studies of several eminent figures from the era, starting with Alexander's friend, Paul Stroganov, which he completed even before he left the Army. He then moved on to the Empress Elisabeth Alexeievna, and to Alexander himself. These biographies were no dry, academic works, inaccessible to the general reader. Nicholas was fascinated by that ever-enticing theme of popular history, the claimant, and his interest in Alexander originally stemmed in large part from a desire to discover whether the Tsar had really died in 1824, or whether he had actually gone underground and continued life as the hermit Feodor Kuzmich, as the legend suggested. Nicholas set to work on a book about this legend, making full use of his status to gain access to every possible primary source, and even taking papers away from the imperial library or from archives to study them in the comfort and privacy of his own home. Ultimately, he decided that the legend was nonsense, and published his conclusions in a book with the untranslatable title: *"Legend o konchine Imperatora Aleksandra I v Siberi v obraz staritsa Feodora Kos'micha"* [Literally, The legend of Alexander I's end in Siberia into the Holy Man Feodor Kuzmich]. In the face of the published conclusions, however, members of his own family continued to question him about the story, and to believe that he secretly gave credence to it and knew more than he was letting on.[27]

Nicholas was apparently also the author of another book on a claimant, this one concerning his maternal ancestors, the House of Baden. Nicholas' grandfather, Leopold I of Baden, scion of a morganatic line, succeeded to the Grand Duchy when the older line failed to leave a legitimate heir. This caused something of a scandal in the royal houses of Europe, and the story gained ground that Leopold's mother had actually kidnapped the legitimate heir at birth in order that her own son might succeed. That true heir was alleged to have resurfaced eighteen years later as the mysterious foundling Kaspar Hauser. According to Nicholas' niece, Cecilie, he himself *"firmly believed"* this tale and wrote a book on it with the aid of family archives.[28] The book, however, was never published. Nicholas undoubtedly knew of tales which questioned whether his mother was the biological daughter of Leopold or of an American Jew, and this might have lent credence to further scandalous gossip concerning this side of the family; but whether as a rigorous historian he actually found evidence which backed up the identification of Kaspar Hauser as royal heir is another matter.[29] Much as he enjoyed gossip, Nicholas was committed to publishing the whole truth, whatever it might be, and once complained in print about Nicholas I having "systematically destroyed" or otherwise hidden papers relating to Alexander I.[30] He once announced that he meant to publish warts and all biographies that took account of their subjects' *"vices, weaknesses and consequences"* while constructing a convincing *"psychology of the individual."*[31] More to the point, it was also his aim to make public as many documents as he could, so as to "provide material for the historian of the future" in forming their own assessment.[32] *"It is not our role to ask here whether the Emperor comes out of this as a bigger or smaller man,"* he claimed in the foreword to his biography of Alexander.

Unsurprisingly, given his reputation for gossiping, Nicholas' no-holds-barred approach to the primary evidence earned him some scathing assessments from those who likely did not even read what he wrote. One society lady called him *"a scandalmonger, who ransacked history for the sake of gossip. The eighteenth century was his happy hunting ground, but he did not neglect either the nineteenth or the twentieth centuries. He felt very happy, for instance, when he discovered that his great-aunt Elisabeth Alexeievna, the wife of Alexander I, whom Russia revered as a saint, had had a lover, and he published with loving care every item of information he could find concerning the young officer."*[33] Others, however, saw the value in his approach, and he received honorary doctorates from the Universities of Moscow and Berlin, as well as the thoroughly prestigious gift of membership of the French Academy.

To back up his primary research, Nicholas kept two enormous libraries full of books. The first was at his Petersburg home, the New Mikhailovsky Palace, and the latter at Borjomi. His beloved mother, Olga Feodorovna, died of heart disease in 1891, but Michael Nikolaievich remained alive until 1909, the straight-backed but benevolent paterfamilias of the Romanov family, whom everyone admired and usually obeyed. Nicholas and several of his brothers shared their father's homes, there being plenty of room for them all. Only Alexander – *Sandro* – who married Alexander III's daughter and alone amongst his brothers produced multiple Romanov dynasts moved out into his own Petersburg palace. Unmarried Nicholas and Serge continued to live under their father's roof, as did George, even after his own marriage to Princess Marie of Greece, which produced two daughters. The remaining brothers were Alexis, who died at twenty, and *"Misha the Fool,"* as the last two Tsars contemptuously dubbed Michael Mikhailovich, a man compelled to live in England after making a morganatic marriage. Alexander III's restrictive marriage laws had worked only too well: unable to find suitable, Orthodox brides, two-thirds of Michael Nikolaievich's six sons left no descendants eligible for the Romanov name or funds.

In adulthood, his younger brothers continued to look up to Nicholas, whom they now called usually "Bimbo" rather than his childhood name of "Niki", for advice or sometimes for mediation with their father. It is a mark of his role in the family that he was asked to be godfather to Prince Andrei Alexandrovich, the eldest son of his brother Sandro, and the first male child born in the next generation of the Mikhailovichi with the name Romanov.[34] He also felt himself compelled to counsel and guide other young members of the family, from Nicholas II to the latter's youngest brother, another runaway, morganatically-married Grand Duke named Michael. These were the sons of his great friend Marie Feodorovna, so he may have felt an almost uncle-ish protectiveness toward them, though he was not really a full generation older. *"You should try and settle everything before the end of your holidays, namely, permission for Natalia Sergeevna to come to Russia,"* he once wrote, referring to the young Grand Duke Michael's new wife. *"I showed your letter to Xenia* [Michael's sister] *and Sandro* [Xenia's husband who was also Nicholas' own brother]. *You should first talk to them because they are going to England and they could together influence* [your] *Mama* [the Dowager Empress Marie Feodorovna] *to persuade His Majesty to allow Natalia Sergeevna to visit Russia…..I send my regards to Natalia Sergeevna and embrace you three times from the bottom of my heart. Next year about 19th June I am going to move to Marienbad, then I will have the greatest pleasure to go to the ever-beautiful Paris….From your ever-loving old Bimbo"*[35] Inevitably, Michael had no success in persuading either his mother or his brother to receive his unacceptable wife, and Nicholas' well-meant advice simply added to his own reputation as the family trouble-maker.

As a historian and a liberal, Nicholas observed the political changes of Nicholas II's reign with great interest. In the turbulent revolutionary year of 1905, he believed that the initiative for reform should come from the government, and was disgusted by the Tsar's vacillations and constant changes of plan, leading to reforms that were effectively forced from him and left him looking weak and reactionary. Neither did Nicholas much like the look of the Duma that emerged from these events, but he attended sessions frequently, and was an ardent supporter of the strong conservative Prime Minister Peter Stolypin, who knew how to control it, to the extent of interceding with the Tsar to keep Stolypin in office when he planned to resign. A few weeks later Stolypin was assassinated, and Nicholas' many detractors were thus able to name him as the murderer!

When war with Germany broke out in 1914, the Grand Duke was working hard on setting up Russia's Archival Commission, whose function was to provide central assistance to struggling local archives. He was also President of the Imperial Historical Society and was in charge of planning the celebrations for the centenary of his uncle, Alexander II, the Tsar-Liberator, which were due to take place in 1918. All of this work he continued to do, adding in a series of visits to hospitals and tours of the front to observe the conditions of the wounded. Since he had resigned from the Army, Nicholas could be given no active command, but he acted as an effective ambassador of the Imperial Family, doing his best to raise morale among those he spoke to by putting on a cheerful face. Even his family won his praise at this stage. *"Our Emperor is indefatigable,"* he told his friend Frederic Masson, reporting on Nicholas II's own visits to the troops. *"He went all the way to ...the Turkish frontier, where he personally distributed the St George Cross to soldiers, almost under the nose of the enemy. These voyages, like those to Russia's interior, make the best impression, as do those that Their Majesties make to the many wounded in the hospitals...Even the Grand Duchess Vladimir* [Maria Pavlovna, the infamous "Miechen", who Nicholas did not much like] *is admirable. Empress Alexandra bandages the wounded herself, having taken along with her two eldest daughters the exams of a nurse."*[36]

In reality, behind his cheerful and patriotic front, Nicholas found the war as searing as he had found the Russo-Turkish War all those years ago. *"I understand so well what you mean about a soul worn out with human suffering,"* he admitted to Masson when the war had been going on for a year. *"One tries to help the wounded and their unfortunate families, one comforts them in their suffering, but one shares it too, and sometimes a deep sadness takes over the whole of one's soul. I have to echo your cry of sorrow: 'Everything is lost, everyone is dead, everything is broken!' It's so true..."* [37] In his usual style, he looked around for someone to blame, and his first target was the Commander-in-Chief, his hated cousin Nicholas Nikolaievich Jr., "Nikolasha," of whom he had nothing good to say even in the most optimistic early days of the war. The historian felt – with some justification – that the military man was too triumphal over his early victories and territorial gains, and would rue it when Russia was forced to give the land back. This duly came to pass, and Nicholas' letters to friends and family switched into still angrier mode, heaping criticisms both personal and professional on the military staff around his cousin and warning the Tsar that the Commander-in-Chief's popularity *"alarms me in a dynastic sense."* Nikolasha's wife, Nicholas declared, had *"carefully manufactured"* her husband's popularity by, *"spreading among the people brochures, popular prints, brochures, calendars, etc."*[38] He was actively implying that the Emperor should doubt their cousin's loyalty and should fear that he had designs on the throne.

In due course, as set-back followed set-back, Nikolasha was relieved of his post, and Nicholas – who correctly perceived that the chaotic state of Russia's supply system would create terrible hardship among the civilian and military populations before long, with the associated likelihood of a *"gigantic uprising"* – turned his attention to the government itself. He lambasted Russia's diplomats as *"German, Jewish, senile or colourless;"* he described various ministers as *"snobbish,"* *"a canary"* and men given to *"venomous analyses"* [which was rather ironic on the whole] and he laid into members of the imperial family as well, with particular attention for the Grand Duchess Marie Pavlovna and the *"international band of pederasts and parvenus"* who surrounded her, and who were also fond of criticizing the government. Ultimately, he decided *to blame the Empress Alexandra ("the Hessian tigress"; "the patron of the occult"* as he snidely called her) for the whole mess, despite the fact that she and he agreed on more things than either of them fully realized, from the imperative necessity of sorting out the supply problem to the need for Russia to have a strong presence at post-war peace conferences.

Nicholas did not confine his comments to letters. *"In his club, where he was always the centre of a group,"* wrote a member of the Tsar's household, *"his mordant criticisms, essentially destructive, did much damage to the regime; sarcasms coming from so high a quarter affected society with a morbid tendency that helped to deprive the Sovereign of all moral authority."*[39]

When Grigory Rasputin – whom Nicholas sarcastically dubbed *"the great* apostle" – was assassinated in December 1916, the Grand Duke rushed at once to the side of the suspected murderers. One, the ringleader Felix Youssoupov, was married to his niece; furthermore, given his reputation for broadcasting everything he heard, it is possible that the killers sought him out knowing that he would protest their innocence to all who listened once they had assured him of it. Later, when it became all too clear that they had done it after all, he was one of the ringleaders in the Romanov family letter which begged the Tsar not to punish them. Nevertheless, he and his brothers felt that both the killing and the letter were futile gestures; they even felt a certain pity for the *"miserable Grigory"* who had been made a scapegoat for the Tsarist regime's desperate condition. There is some evidence that meetings about the pointless letter masked a more desperate purpose: the Romanov family was planning to unseat the Tsar in some way, and Nicholas was a ring-leader, acting with the eager cooperation of one of his least favourite relations, Grand Duchess Marie Pavlovna.[40] The plot, even if it even got that far, came to nothing, but the atmosphere of suspicion and treachery played its part, as Mosolov noted, in undermining the Emperor.

Then Nicholas II finally acted. Well aware of the things his cousin was saying, he ordered Nicholas to, *"leave the capital and to stay for two months at your property at Grushevka."*[41] Grushevka, in the Ukraine, was the vast tract of land whose farms had supported the Mikhailovichi when their father was alive, though he himself had never set foot in it. Nicholas by contrast, often went there, but its small estate house was not a particularly convenient place to be in winter.

By March, Nicholas was back in Petrograd, just in time to witness the riots and disorder which led to Nicholas II's abdication. He was with Nicholas's brother, Michael Alexandrovich, when the Grand Duke heard that the throne was to pass to him rather than the Tsar's son, and deliberated what to do. In the past, Nicholas had counseled Michael on his morganatic marriage, offering advice on how to return to the Emperor's and the Dowager Empress's favour. His experience during these revolutionary days, however, soured him on the young Grand Duke and his wife forever. Michael's dithering renunciation of the throne seemed to convert Nicholas to an ardent republican. Gloomily, he explained this in a letter to Masson, laying out the defects of all possible Emperors, according to the order of succession. *"First, Grand Duke Mikhail. He's a carbon copy of his brother, but without Nicholas's learning, without the least suspicion of personality, and he's married to a Moscow whore who's been married twice before, let alone how many lovers she's had. This Natalie Sheremetevskaia is intelligent, but she's evil and she's surrounded by a bunch of social climbers. Next is Kirill, a pompous imbecile.....then the music-hall man, Boris, so well known in Paris; and then finally the gigolo Andrei, lover of my brother's mistress. Then the Konstantin branch, nice guys, but stupid and sickly, and then Nicholas and Peter* [his hated cousin Nikolasha and brother], *with their disgusting Montenegrins* [their wives, whom Nicholas believed to have encouraged Nikolasha in designs on the throne]. *Dreadful! I would have liked Nicholas II better, but since he completely refused to get rid of the Hessian, then no."*[42]

The Grand Duke now described himself as *"an authoritarian liberal"* in his beliefs – perhaps thinking that a benevolent dictatorship in the French Bonapartist mold was the best form of government for Russia. He loathed what he saw of the Bolsheviks whose power was growing in the soviets in Russia's main cities: to him, they were all, predictably, *"Jews and Germans"* who had *"infected"* the army with their *"pacifist"* ideas and *"served the enemy."*[43] Lenin, their leader, commandeered the house of the ballerina Kschessinska, who was his brother Serge's mistress (also, as Nicholas contemptuously pointed out, that of their cousin Andrei), and was now effectively living on Serge and Kschessinska's bounty. Ever-cynical, Nicholas advised Serge to abandon the dancer to her fate, since in his view she had been using him for years anyway. This led to something of a rift between the brothers, though Serge moved into the New Mikhailovsky Palace alongside Nicholas, and continued to look out for Kschessinska and for her son, whom he regarded as his own.[44] Sandro went to the Crimea with his family and the Dowager Empress, but their brother George, whose daughters and semi-estranged wife had been in England since the war began and who wanted to join them there, was also obliged to remain in the capital. It was clear that England, their ally, didn't want to take him.

Nicholas carried on working for the Historical Society – now shorn of its adjective "Imperial" – living in his palace on the Neva and forging links with the new Provisional Government, notably Alexander Kerensky, the de facto head. To his chagrin and bitterness, the French Ambassador and staff, representatives of the Republic he had so loved and admired, distanced themselves from him now that he seemed just a remnant of a fallen regime, just as Britain cold-shouldered his brother George.

During the summer of 1917, Nicholas became the only member of the Imperial Family to consider standing for the Constituent Assembly on a semi-conservative ticket called "The Union of peasants and Landlords" based near his estate at Grushevka. Late in the day, however, he was warned by Alexander Kerensky that as a former Grand Duke he would not be allowed to do so.

For several months after the fall of the Provisional Government to the Bolsheviks, members of the Imperial Family remained in Petrograd, subject to ever more harassment and restriction. Their post was opened, their belongings pillaged; Nicholas was evicted from the New Mikhailovsky Palace and took an apartment on the river Moika.

In March of 1918 the Grand Dukes and imperial princes were all arrested and ordered to leave the capital. With his cook and his valet, Nicholas went to the ancient town of Vologda, carrying as one final remnant of his old life his prize bottles of Chablis from his cellar.[45] George went first to Finland, but after a few months of difficulties with local Bolsheviks joined him at Vologda. Their cousin Dimitri Konstantinovich, a tall, silent, shy man, arrived at around the same time. And Serge, who had a presentiment that they would never meet again, went to Viatka, from where he was taken to Alapaievsk and murdered not long afterwards along with the Konstantinovich princes (Dimitri's nephews), a son of Grand Duke Paul, Grand Duchess Elisabeth Feodorovna and a nun who had accompanied her there.

That same month of July, Nicholas, George and Dimitri were taken from their simple lodgings with local families to the prison at Vologda, where they were admittedly treated quite well. Belatedly, the French government attempted to intercede on behalf of this member of the French Academy, but the Bolsheviks turned them down on the grounds that to release a member of the Imperial Family would be impossible due to *"public opinion."* At the same time, a newspaper story alerted Nicholas to the fact that his cousin the Tsar had been shot in Ekaterinburg. *"My God, my God – is it possible that they really have committed this crime!?"* he cried in horror, unaware that his brother Serge was also dead.[46]

Then came the order that the Grand Dukes were to return to Petrograd, where they were incarcerated, an ironic reversal of the fate that had befallen so many others in that city at their ancestors' hands – particularly those of Nicholas' grandfather and namesake. Yet he himself had also been several times under arrest for his opinions in Romanov days, albeit in the comfortable surroundings of his own estates, and it was in deference to his reputation as a scholar that Maxim Gorky now intervened on his behalf. Nicholas was aware of this; pathetically, he began to plan a visit to his sister Anastasia's daughter, Queen Alexandrine of Denmark, as a stopover on his way to his intended new home in his beloved France.

Before Gorky could speak to Lenin, the Petrograd Cheka intervened. On 28 January 1919, the Grand Dukes were taken from their cells and driven to the Fortress of SS Peter and Paul, where some of them crossed themselves in passing the cathedral where their ancestors were interred. Another of their cousins, Paul Alexandrovich, the last surviving son of Alexander II, was carried out to join them, on a stretcher as he had been ill for a long time. There was no time for reunions; the soldiers lined the Grand Dukes up before a ditch in which thirteen bodies already lay. Nicholas, who was carrying a cat he had been caring for in prison, famously passed it to one of the guards and asked him to care for it. Then the four Grand Dukes were shot and interred in the ditch, whose exact location on that site of so much death over the course of three centuries has never been pinpointed.

Nicholas Mikhailovich was an outsider all his life, a man who by accident of birth did not really fit in anywhere. Had he been born in an earlier age, when the Tsarist government showed commitment to reform, he might have contributed in the mode of his equally outspoken uncle Konstantin Nikolaievich, but there is some justice in the criticisms of those who felt that in his own era he was simply a destructive force who attacked without offering solutions. His personality would have harmed him, whatever era he lived in: he was indiscreet and sarcastic, and his opinions were inconsistent and changed with great regularity. Professedly a "liberal", he was violently intolerant of certain nationalities or races, and his personal vendettas against some of his relatives often deprived him of objectivity in assessing situations. Hated by Alexander III and mistrusted by Nicholas II and Alexandra, he was nevertheless shot by the government that came after them simply because of what he represented as a member of the Imperial Family. But when the murdered Romanovs were canonized as "martyrs" by the Orthodox Church Abroad in 1981, it forgave all earthly sins except those of Nicholas Mikhailovich, who was excluded for his purported opinions.

It is as a historian that Nicholas made his most lasting and honourable mark. His books are masterfully researched and eminently readable; even the Soviet historian Peter Zaionchovsky, a fair and respected source, thought well of his work, and it gained him an entry in the Great Soviet Encyclopedia, an honour accorded few Romanovs who had not played a role in government. Whatever his motives, Nicholas' determination to expose his ancestors *"warts and all"* made a wealth of restricted material available to future historians, and his activities through the Archival Commission were carried on by later generations of historians eager to assist local archives in caring for their irreplaceable material. Whatever his faults, it was in his commitment to scholarly openness and unadulterated honesty that Grand Duke Nicholas Mikhailovich stood out.

Grand Duke Michael Mikhailovich
(1861-1929)

By Marlene Eilers-Koenig

Grand Duke Michael Mikhailovich of Russia broke with Imperial tradition and the Family Law when he married Countess Sophie von Merenberg. As Sophie was not a member of a reigning or ruling house, the marriage was considered morganatic. Although Grand Duke Michael would retain his title – and his right to succeed to the throne – his wife and their children were not considered members of the Russian Imperial Family, and thus were not entitled imperial titles or the right of succession to the Russian throne.

The Fundamental Laws required that members of the Imperial Family were to marry equally and with permission of the Emperor. Those who chose to violate this caveat faced serious consequences.

Michael's marriage caused great concern and strain for the Grand Duke's immediate family, and for Emperor Alexander III, whose permission had not been sought. The consequences of Michael's marital choice were immediate, and included exile from Russia. In hindsight, this marriage was the catalyst that saved Michael's life. If Grand Duke Michael had married a German princess, he would have remained in Russia, where he might have suffered the same fate as other Romanovs. Three of his brothers, Nicholas, George and Serge, were imprisoned during the revolution. All would be executed by the Bolsheviks. But Michael, exiled in England, was safe from the Russian revolution and its blood-thirst.

Grand Duke Michael's marriage may not have been a grand alliance, but it was a marriage that survived the initial scandal, exile, and, eventually, financial insecurity. Today, Michael and Sophie's descendants live in the United Kingdom, and include two future dukes (Abercorn and Westminster), a future Earl (Dalhousie), and a current Marquess (Milford Haven). One great-granddaughter has married into a historic Scottish family, and another is the wife of a Hungarian count.

The second son of Grand Duke Michael Nikolaievich of Russia and his wife, Princess Cecile of Baden, Grand Duke Michael Mikhailovich was born at Peterhof on 16 October 1861. Most of his childhood was spent in Tiflis[1], Georgia, where his father was the Viceroy of the Caucasus. It was common for a Romanov to be known by a nickname. Young Michael was known by the family nickname, "Miche-Miche." His mother, Princess Cecile Auguste, was a pious Lutheran, who took the name Olga Feodorovna when she converted to the Orthodox faith. She was the youngest of eight children of Grand Duke Leopold of Baden, who, in 1819, had married his great-niece, Princess Sophie of Sweden. Although her paternal grandmother was born a von Geyersberg, Cecile's ancestral lines were largely impressive. Her mother was a member of the Holstein-Gottorp dynasty that had ruled Sweden from 1751-1818.[2] Most important, for the Russians, she was a descendant of Rurik, the founder of Russia's first dynasty.

In his book, *The Grand Dukes*, Prince David Chavchavadze describes Grand Duchess Olga as *"intelligent, sharp-tongued, and very critical of others, and she dominated her family."* The marriage, according to Prince David, *"was very close and very fruitful."*

Between 1859 and 1875, Grand Duchess Olga gave birth to six sons and one daughter. But the Grand Duchess' motherly instincts were virtually non-existent.[3] Although she was *"something of a bluestocking,"* Olga could be rather *"critical of others"* and a *"neurotic hypochondriac who complained endlessly about her health."*[4]

It was a strict, military-regime upbringing: cold baths and sleeping on army cots. The young grand dukes were taught Greek and Latin, and avoiding a military career was not an option. The young Grand Dukes saw their sister, Anastasia, once a week on Sunday. The couple's fourth son, Grand Duke Alexander Mikhailovich, wrote that his mother, *"came of age in the days when Bismarck kept all Germany spellbound by his sermon of iron and blood."*[5]

This branch of the Romanov family, known as the Mikhailovichi, was close-knit. Although the Grand Ducal family maintained a residence in St Petersburg and a palace on the Black Sea, the family considered the Caucasus their home. The family estate, Borjomi, near Tiflis, was larger than the Netherlands. The young grand dukes were *"rebellious, preferring the relative independence of life so far away from St Petersburg."* Grand Duke Michael's father, Grand Duke Michael Nikolaievich, served as Viceroy of the Caucasus for nineteen years. He was described as able and intelligent, a keen solider and a strict disciplinarian. Thus, Miche-Miche lived for most of his childhood away from the Imperial Court, which may have contributed to a streak of independence that led to his morganatic marriage.

Unlike his elder brother, Nicholas, a historian who was described by many as an intellectual, Grand Duke Michael was a more carefree chap and not very bright. Grand Duchess Olga once described him as *"stupid,"*[6] and Emperor Alexander III, at least twice, referred to his cousin as a *"fool."*[7] According to Grand Duke Nicholas biographer, Jamie H. Cockfield, Michael would repay in spades his mother for her emotional abuse toward him.

Michael and his five brothers were among the tallest members of the family, all more than six feet tall. A handsome man, he was also rather *"solemn-faced, charming, a good dancer, but lacked some of the intelligence of his brothers."*[8] Military service was expected of all Grand Dukes, and Grand Duke Michael was no exception. He served for a time in the Chausseur Regiment of the Guards. It was said that he "adored the military, but not the responsibilities of a Russian Grand Duke.[9] Grand Duke Michael said his brother, Grand Duke Alexander, *"had none of Nicholas Michailovich's talents... His good looks, generous heart and dancing ability endeared him to St Petersburg society, and very soon "Miche-Miche" became a recognized favorite in the capital."*[10]

He sowed his wild oats, but unlike other cousins who preferred their mistresses to weddings. Michael's desire to find a wife was *"an extraordinary, indeed frenetic obsession,"* according to Raleigh Trevelyan, the author of *Grand Dukes and Diamonds*. When he turned 20-years-old, he came into his munificent inheritance, and, he used his wealth to build a magnificent palace. *"We must have a decent place to live."* Not the royal we. Michael was referring to himself and his future wife. He didn't know who the lady would be, but *"he wanted to marry someone as soon as possible."*

One of the Grand Duke's first marital prospects was Princess May of Teck, whose mother, Mary Adelaide, was a British princess and a first cousin to Queen Victoria. In the spring of 1886, the young Grand Duke was in London. Perhaps excited by the prospect of a grand marriage, May's grandmother, the Duchess of Cambridge eagerly hoped that her granddaughter would marry Michael.[11] The Duke of Cambridge was against it, and May's father, the Duke of Teck, would not hear of it. His daughter was not going to marry a Russian grand duke, as he considered the

Romanovs to be *"notoriously bad husbands."*¹² He was not *"sacrificing his child"* for a Russian marriage. It is also doubtful if Alexander III had approved Michael's marriage to Princess May, whose father was the son of a morganatic marriage between Duke Alexander of Württemberg and a Hungarian countess.

That same year, Princess Irene of Hesse and by Rhine, the third daughter of Grand Duke Ludwig IV and his British-born wife, Alice, was also mooted as a possible bride. Two years earlier, her older sister, Ella, had married Grand Duke Serge Alexandrovich, a younger brother of Alexander III.¹³ But Irene was in love with her first cousin, Prince Heinrich of Prussia, and their engagement was announced at the end of the year.

Undaunted by Irene's rejection, Michael turned his attention elsewhere. In 1887 he proposed to Princess Louise, the eldest daughter of the Prince and Princess of Wales. She turned him down, as she was already aware that Michael had been rejected by her first cousin, Irene. Michael admitted to Louise that he could never love her. He only wanted to marry her.

He then embarked on a brief affair with Princess Walewski before falling *"frantically in love,"* with Countess Catherine Ignatiev, the daughter of a Russian minister. Neither Grand Duchess Olga nor the Empress Marie Feodorovna¹⁴ thought much of the *"little commoner,"* and it was made clear to Michael that he would not be permitted to marry Katya. Thus, he was sent abroad to *"cool off."* Michael's relationships with such unsuitable women led to *"painful scenes"* between him and his parents.

It is not known where Grand Duke Michael was first introduced to Countess Sophie von Merenberg, although the meeting probably took place in Biarritz, France. For Michael, however, it was love at first sight, although most of the stories about their romance appear not to be true, such as *"snatching the bride off her horse as it bolted through the flower market at Nice."* The exact date and place of their marriage are also shrouded in mystery. Most likely, the couple were married on 26 February 1891, in a Russian Orthodox ceremony in San Remo, Italy.¹⁵ This is the date that is accepted by Grand Duke Michael's descendants, and which appears in the *Almanach de Gotha*. The date cannot be verified because the marriage was not registered with civil authorities in Italy or in France, and there are no vital records to corroborate any of the possible wedding dates.

The decision to marry in San Remo would not have been a difficult one because the Riviera community was a popular resort for members of the Russian aristocracy and Imperial Family. Grand Duke Michael's youngest brother, Grand Duke Alexis, suffered from tuberculosis and had died there in 1895. Another brother, Grand Duke Serge, often spent winters in San Remo, staying at the Villa Flora. At the time of Michael's marriage, San Remo did not have a Russian Orthodox Church, although several families had private chapels in their villas. It is entirely possible that the marriage took place at one of these villas, such as the Strelakovas Villa Gloria. Russian Orthodox services were also celebrated in a building at 22 Via Roma, in San Remo.

On 7 April 1891, a Cannes newspaper, *Courrier*, reported that the marriage had taken place in Genoa. The next day, the same newspaper reported that the couple had left Cannes on 3 April and were married in San Remo. A German newspaper, the *Kölnische Zeitung* concluded on 14 April that Michael and Sophie had married in Venice on 26 February. On 9 April 1891, *The Times* included a report about Michael's marriage. *"Today's official military gazette [8 April], the Invalide, contained three important Imperial decrees, addressed to the Minister of War, peremptorily excluding the Imperial Grand Duke Michael Mikhailovich, the Emperor's cousin, from the Russian military service, and* ordering that the infantry regiment of Brest and the 4th Battery of the Mounted Artillery of the Guard, which have hitherto been under the honorary command of the Grand Duke, shall no longer bear his Imperial Highness's name. The news account also reported that this severe punishment was due to the Grand Duke, who had been abroad for the last two or three years, having secretly married, five weeks ago, without the permission of the Tsar and the Imperial Family. This incident has caused much grief in the highest circles," according to *The Times* correspondent.

The date of Alexander III's decree was 7 April the same day as his response to a letter from the bride's father, Prince Nicholas of Nassau. He informed Nicholas that the marriage was without authorization and family approval, and was, thus, not legal. On the same day, the Russian emperor also wrote to the Grand Duke of Luxembourg to inform him that he had written to Prince Nicholas to express his disapproval with Grand Duke Michael's marriage. One day earlier, Grand Duke Konstantin Konstantinovich noted in his diary, *"I have known that Misha married...in unknown place ... and wrote about His marriage to Lord* [Emperor] *and parents."*

The couple were certainly married before 12 April, when Grand Duchess Olga succumbed to a heart attack en route to Ai-Todor, the family residence in the Crimea. It was at Ai-Todor where Olga could always find peace. The Grand Duchess died in the waiting room at the Kharkov train station. A few days earlier, the Grand Duchess and her husband were in tears as they had received a letter from Michael, informing them of his marriage to Countess Sophie von Merenberg. Grand Duke Alexander described his brother's wife as a *"lovely girl,"* but the marriage brought the *"wrath of the Emperor and of our parents on his head."*[16] Michael's father blamed the marriage for hastening Olga's death. This is a view shared by others, including Queen Victoria. Marie Mallet, one of Queen Victoria's Maids of Honour, was in Cannes with Queen Victoria in April 1891. In an entry in her journal dated 15 April 1891, Marie wrote: *"The secret marriage of the Grand Duke Michael* [to Countess Torby] *has created great excitement in Cannes. The shock killed his poor mother who had heart disease and all are agreed that the Tzar is a terrible tyrant."*[17] It is possible that the telegram that Grand Duchess Olga received shortly before her death provided the details of her son's marriage. But the telegram was probably crumbled up and thrown into a fire, and not saved for the family archives. Neither Michael nor Sophie confided the details of their marriage to their three children, or to anyone else. Sophie's father, Prince Nicholas of Nassau, who attended the wedding, never confirmed the exact date.

Countess Sophie von Merenberg was not a commoner. Neither was she a royal, which was a prerequisite for a Grand Ducal marriage. Her father was His Highness Prince Nicholas of Nassau, the eldest son of Duke Wilhelm of Nassau and his second wife, Princess Pauline of Württemberg. Sophie was closely related to many of Europe's royal families. Her uncle, Adolphe, was the Grand Duke of Luxembourg. Shortly after Sophie's marriage Grand Duke Adolphe created his niece as the Countess Torby. One of Sophie's aunts, Princess Therese, was married to Prince Peter of Oldenburg, and their grandson, Peter, was to be the first husband of Grand Duchess Olga Alexandrovna of Russia, youngest child of Alexander III and future sister-in-law of Michael Mikhailovich's brother Alexander. Sophie's first cousins included Queen Emma of the Netherlands, widow of Willem III, and mother of the young Queen Wilhelmina; Princess Helen, Duchess of Albany, Queen Elisabeth of Romania, the consort of King Carol I; King Gustaf V of Sweden, who was married to Michael's first cousin, Victoria of Baden; Friedrich, Fürst of Waldeck-Pyrmont; and Marie of Württemberg, who, in 1882,[18] had died following the birth of a stillborn daughter.

Despite their father's princely status, Sophie and her siblings were not recognized as members of the Nassau ducal family. To add to the controversy, Sophie was born before her parent's marriage. Duke Nicholas and Natalia Alexandrovna Pushkin[19] were married in London on 1 July 1868 before Natalia received a divorce from her first husband, Michael von Dubelt. In 1864, Natalia had been granted the right to separate from her husband, by whom she had two daughters and one son. Natalia committed bigamy when she married Nicholas. Thus, the marriage was not valid and their three children were illegitimate. Not long after the wedding, Natalia was given the title Countess von Merenberg, in the principality of Waldeck. This lesser title would also be borne by the couple's three children: Sophie, who was born in 1868, Alexandrine in 1869,[20] and a son, George,[21] who was born in 1871.

Michael's morganatic marriage meant that he would not be able to move into the fabulous palace that he had built for his family. Alexander III stripped him of his military rank, and he was banned from returning to Russia. He was also unable to attend his mother's funeral. Sophie begged him not to leave France because she feared that the marriage would be annulled. Her fears were largely unfounded. The marriage would not be annulled, although Michael and Sophie were not welcome in Russia. The first years of their marriage were spent in Wiesbaden, where Sophie gave birth to their first child, Anastasia was born in 1892. Throughout her life, Anastasia de Torby was known as Zia. She was named for Michael's only sister, Grand Duchess Anastasia, the wife of Grand Duke Friedrich Franz III of Mecklenburg-Schwerin. Baroness Agnes de Stoeckl described Zia's christening in her memoirs, *Not All Vanity*. *"The christening was a grand function, little Zia being carried on a white satin cushion. The Grand Duchess Anastasie was Godmother. The Russian Church with all the glittering lights was new and strange to me; the singing was pathetic and at the same time filled the church with melodies of joy."*[22] Four years later, Sophie gave birth while in Cannes to a second daughter, Nada. A son, Michael, known as Boy, was born in Wiesbaden in 1898.

In 1899, the family moved into a new home in Cannes, the Villa Kazbeck, a *"great white terraced structure full of jardinières with ferns hanging from the walls."*[23] Grand Duke Michael, whose personal wealth derived largely from the income from estates in the Caucasus and from a factory that bottled mineral water, continued to live in Imperial style. The staff at the villa, which was named for the highest mountain in the Caucasus, consisted of *"five footmen, a butler, a valet, a lady's maid, a governess, a nursery maid and six chefs."*[24] In Cannes, the Grand Duke and his wife were at the apex of the social strata. It was at their home in Cannes in 1898 where the Prince of Wales (the future Edward VII) was introduced to Alice Keppel.[25] Other members of the Imperial Family also maintained residences at Cannes. Michael's sister, Grand Duchess Anastasia, whose husband had died at Cannes in 1897, lived at the Villa Wenden. The Grand Duchess, known to her Torby nieces and nephew as Aunt Stassie, was the mother of three children: Grand Duke Friedrich Franz; IV, Alexandrine, whose marriage to the future Christian X of Denmark took place at Cannes, and Cecilie.[26] During the social season, which took place during the winter, the Riviera was awash with Grand Dukes and Grand Duchesses, Princes and Princesses, and, the Prince of Wales, who became a firm friend to Michael and his wife. The season included dinner parties; visits to the Golf Club, where one had to wear a red and white blazer; the Battle of Flowers; and the Casino at Monte Carlo. The Grand Duke was also active in the local Russian Orthodox Church, where he *"passed the plate on Sundays."*[27] Each summer, Michael and his family traveled to England where he rented Keele Hall, near Newcastle in Staffordshire with occasional trips to London. Autumn was spent in

Paris, and when winter returned, it was time, once again, to return to the South of France.

From 1897 through 1908, Baron Alexander (Sasha) de Stoeckl served as Michael's equerry. Baron de Stoeckl came from an important Russian noble family. His father had negotiated the sale of Alaska to the United States in 1867. He was married to Agnes Barron, whose Irish parents had settled in Paris shortly after their marriage. Baroness de Stoeckl wrote several books, including her memoirs, *Not All Vanity*, in which she described in detail the lives of Grand Duke Michael and his family. She described her years with the family as *"gay,"* but the friendship ended following a disagreement with Sophie.

Mrs. Keppel was a guest at Villa Kazbeck when Agnes de Stoeckl first met her. Alice was, according to the Baroness, *"entertaining, handsome, and very refreshing."*[28] Agnes believed that Mrs. Keppel *"might amuse the Prince,"* so a luncheon was arranged in the Prince's honor. The guest list was limited to Michael, Sophie, the Baron and Baroness, Alice Keppel, and the Prince of Wales. Edward VII was fond of Sophie Torby, but he was a stickler for protocol. He was disturbed unreasonably when Countess Torby, whom he liked, and who was the morganatic wife of the Grand Duke Michael of Russia, seated herself on the Duchesses bench at a Court Ball.[29]

Sophie Torby has been described as gracious, refined, and *"unfailingly kind-hearted."*

The Lady's Realm, a popular woman's magazine, described Sophie as having a delicately molded face and penciled eyebrows. She was also always laughing. Although she moved in the highest of social circles, Sophie remained an outsider at the Imperial Court. It was not until 1903, when she was finally introduced to her father-in-law. Grand Duke Michael Nikolaievich had suffered a stroke, and was transported by train to Cannes to recuperate. The Grand Duke was charmed by Sophie and her children. Zia was Grandpapa's favorite, described by the elder Michael as *"délicieuse."* Baroness de Stoeckl did not include the incident or incidents in her memoir that led to a rupture in her relationship with the Countess de Torby. She wrote: *"after many happy years, our relations with Countess Torby became difficult, for reasons of no interest except to ourselves. The Grand Duke Michel, always so kind and pacific, thought that perhaps if we did not come to Keele Hall for a time things might calm down....But matters did not improve, and finally it was decided that we had better part....At once people took our part and it created a big stir amongst many friends. Even King Edward sent word he was absolutely on our side."*[30] Grand Duchess Marie,[31] the wife of Michael's brother, George, offered Sasha de Stoeckl the position as her Chamberlain. Sophie de Torby was *"very upset and refused to speak"* to the de Stoeckls for some time.

In 1902, the decree of exile was lifted, and Michael returned to Russia for the first time in many years. He returned to take part in the commemorations celebrating the 100th anniversary of the Battle of Borodino. Nicholas II also restored his cousin to the honorary colonelcy of the 49th Brest Regiment. But Michael had no plans to reestablish a presence at the Imperial court because, according to *The Lady's Realm*, "the position of the charming lady whom he had made his wife would be less pleasant in Russia than it is over here or on the Riviera, where he and Countess Torby are the uncrowned king and queen of Cannes society."[32] This was echoed by H.C. Bainbridge's comment that the Michaels had *"forged for themselves a unique place in Edwardian Society."*[33] Their social circle included members of the Greek Royal Family and the British-born Princess Daisy of Pless. The Princess, the former Mary-Theresa Cornwallis-West, described the Countess de Torby as *"dear Sophy,"* visited Michael and Sophie at their homes in England and Cannes.

Grand Duke Michael's father died at Cannes on 18 December 1909. Following the funeral, the late Grand Duke's coffin was taken by a Russian cruiser to Sebastopol, and then to the SS Peter and Paul Fortress, where the Grand Duke would lie in state. Michael attended the second funeral in Russia, although he was not accompanied by his wife, as she had refused to ever visit Russia due to the controversy over her marriage.

There is no doubt his wife's inferior status rankled Michael. During a visit to Moscow in 1912, Michael sought out his cousin, Nicholas II, in an attempt to curry favor. He wanted the Emperor to ask George V if he could create a title for Sophie. Nicholas, who was not happy with Michael's demands, did broach the subject with his British cousin. George V responded in a letter dated 23 September 1912: *"As to our friend, that good fool of Michael, who I am sure bores you with his many grievances as he does me. He has lived here in England for many years and dear Papa was always most kind to him....I do not know what he may have said to you at Moscow with regard to his wife being given a title by me, to the acceptance of which you gave your consent. Unfortunately however I have not the power to grant a title for a foreign subject and still more impossible in the case of the wife of a Russian Grand Duke."*[34] George V went on to say that he did not look forward to meeting with Michael because he would have to refuse Michael's demand that Sophie be given another title.

After he had signed a 21-year lease, Grand Duke Michael and his family moved into Kenwood House, an 18th-century mansion largely designed by Robert Adam on 1 March 1910. The house, on Hampstead Lane, was originally owned by the Earls of Mansfield, whose primary residence, Scone Palace, is in Scotland. The Earls of Mansfield and their families continued to use Kenwood as their London home until the early part of the 20th century. The sixth Earl of Mansfield preferred to reside at Scone, thus, renting the house to tenants. The rent was £2,200 per year. Kenwood, with its Imperial tenants, moved once again to the forefront of high society. *"The Grand Duke has been a stranger in his own country, but here he is a personal favorite with the Royal Family, and his elder daughter Countess Anastasia (Zia), born in 1892, is to be one of the debutantes of the present season."*[35] At Kenwood, the Grand Duke and Countess Torby entertained on a grand scale with dinner guests ranging from King George V and Queen Mary to other members of the Imperial Family. But Michael and Sophie did not consider themselves aloof from the Hampstead neighborhood. Michael became the President of the Hampstead General Hospital in 1912; a year later, he gave the hospital an ambulance. When war broke out, the family started a campaign to collect a half million pairs of socks and mittens for soldiers heading to the front. Kenwood, with the support of the Grand Duke and Lord Mansfield, served as a division of the Royal Naval Anti-Aircraft Mobile Brigade, which was established in the stables.

Michael and Sophie's children, despite their lack of imperial titles and status, were largely expected to marry among the higher echelons of British or European society. In 1916, Nada, the younger daughter, announced her engagement to Prince George of Battenberg, the elder son of Prince and Princess Louis of Battenberg. The Battenbergs, too, were of a morganatic streak. George's mother, the former Princess Victoria of Hesse and by Rhine, was a granddaughter of Queen Victoria. News of the engagement was made known to relatives in Russia as the Battenberg had their own ties to the Russian court. George's maternal aunt was the Empress Alexandra. On April 7, 1916, Nicholas II sent his wife a telegram, where he mentioned Misha's letter. *"Misha the ass wired to announce engagement of his second daughter with George Bat. Shall answer from us both."* Alexandra's response came the next day *"Is it possible that Georgi [son of] Victoria, is getting engaged? Seems quite improbable. He is all of 23 and has been at sea all the time."*[36]

Prince George's parents were also worried about money, as most of Prince Louis' property was in Germany. Due to these straitened circumstances, he could give George only £350 per year as a wedding gift. Michael was able to purchase a small home for the newlyweds at Rosyth, as George was attached to Admiral Beatty, Commander-in-Chief of the Grand Fleet. Countess Nada and Prince George were married in two ceremonies on 15 November1916. The first wedding was a Russian Orthodox ceremony at the Russian Embassy. The only guests at this wedding were immediate family, *"most of them being Russian,"* according to *The Times*. After the ceremony, Prince George and his best man, Lord Burghersh,[37] were the first to leave the embassy, and were *"heartily cheered."* The bridesmaids followed with Countess Zia, and her cousins, Princesses Nina and Xenia of Russia, in one car, and Princess Louise of Battenberg and her parents, in another car, all heading toward the Chapel Royal at St James's Palace.

The crowds gathered on Welbeck Street *"loudly cheered"* the bride and her father as they emerged last from the Embassy. *"A charming simplicity,"* is how *The Times* correspondent described the Anglican service that followed at noon. The second ceremony took place in the presence of King George V and Queen Mary, Queen Alexandra and other members of the Royal Family. The bride was escorted toward the altar on the arm of her father. Her gown was, *"a cloth of silver, worn with a Russian headdress,"* and, the four bridesmaids' dresses were deep blue velvet and tulle. The newlyweds, Prince and Princess George of Battenberg, emerged from the chapel to the strains of Mendelsohn's Wedding March. More than 2000 thousands guests, including King George V and Queen Mary, attended the reception at Kenwood House.[38]

No doubt that conversation at the reception centered on Russia as Michael had met earlier with King George V, at Buckingham Palace, where the king informed him about the deteriorating situation in Russia. Michael was told that British intelligence believed that Russia was hurling toward revolution. Alarmed by this news, Michael immediately wrote to the Tsar, telling him that "Georgie" was upset by the news; he warned the Emperor to take appropriate action to save Russia – and the monarchy – before it was too late. Grand Duke Michael's letter to his cousin, Nicholas II, on 31 October 1916 was one of his last letters to the Tsar. Michael was concerned about the news in Russia, and he hoped his cousin, *"will find it possible to satisfy the just demands of our people before it is too late."* This letter also included news of Nada's marriage to Prince George of Battenberg, and a request for money as his financial situation was difficult due to the war, and now he had to pay for his daughter's wedding. He asked "Nicky" to send him money from his Russian account.

The revolution and the fall of the Romanov dynasty also meant the end of a rich and glorious lifestyle for the surviving members of the family. Michael's estates were lost, and he no longer had the means to maintain an imperial lifestyle. In April 1917, he wrote to A.J. Balfour at the Foreign Office, stating (in the third person) that he was, *"entirely without means for his living requirements and has no capital or money here."*[39] Michael also hoped that the British ambassador to Russia, Sir George Buchanan, would arrange for his securities to be placed at Drummonds Bank in order to affect a temporary loan. When this request was refused, Michael had to move out of Kenwood House.

Sir Frederick Ponsonby, one of the Grand Duke's close friends, wrote to King George V and Queen Mary about Michael's financial predicament. In a letter to Michael, Fritz Ponsonby wrote: *"Their Majesties, who appeared to feel very deeply for you in this cruel situation in which you have been placed, expressed their willingness to help you in every possible way."*[40] The King had agreed to advance Michael £10,000. *"The King has* put every penny he has in the War Loan and has left me little margin,"⁴¹ Sir Frederick wrote. Sophie's jewels, which were kept in a London bank, were worth approximately £40,000, and were considered as nominal security.⁴² No legal documents were drawn up for this transaction. *"May and I are only too happy to help you and your wife at such a moment as this and thus to prove our friendship to you,"* King George V wrote to Grand Duke Michael. But this friendship did not extend to Michael's relatives. He would not permit Michael's brother, Grand Duke George, to come to England, even though George's wife, Marie, and their two daughters, Nina and Xenia, were already in the country. Michael's son, Boy, was denied a commission in the British Army. His Romanov blood was only one reason for the denial. Boy suffered from headaches and fits of depression, which grew more intense as the years went on.

According to the Princess of Pless, Michael and Sophie, who *"had never known what it was to be poor, found the greater part of their income gone."*⁴³ With few resources beyond the gracious loan from the king, Grand Duke Michael was forced to leave Kenwood. They moved into 3 Cambridge Gate, Regent Park, described as, *"part of a brown limestone block put up in Edwardian times."*⁴⁴ A year later, Kenwood was rented by Nancy Leeds, the American millionaire, who in 1920 married Prince Christopher of Greece. Mrs. Leeds' rent provided the Michaels with an income. The house was purchased by the 1st Earl of Iveagh, who bequeathed the house and his magnificent art collection to the nation. In 1925, the house was opened to the public by George V. The loss of the family's fortune meant that Zia, who was her father's favorite child, would have to marry well. In 1917, she became engaged to Harold Wernher, the younger son of the late Sir Julius Wernher, Bt. Sir Julius, who had died in 1912, had left the bulk of his fortune £11,500,000 to his younger son. The baronetcy was inherited by Harold's older brother, Derrick. (In 1948, Harold succeeded to the baronetcy, when his older brother died without male issue.)

To the Princess of Pless, Zia was *"a charming girl."* There was no doubt in anyone's mind that she would marry well. In 1913, she was involved in a "flirtation" with her cousin, Prince George of Greece, who had visited Kenwood several times. He seemed taken with Zia. He wrote to her: *"....I have been thinking of you since a whole year without knowing you well and now that we have become good friends (at least I think so!) I even dream about you. With best love and kisses from your devoted Georgie."*⁴⁵

Queen Sophie of the Hellenes was aware of the correspondence between her eldest son and Zia, and she wrote to Countess Sophie: *"I hear some rumours are going about concerning our son and your daughter Zia, and as this alarms and distresses me I should like to say the following. It seems so hard and cruel if your daughter as any false hopes on this question."*⁴⁶ The Queen continued to say, *"that there can be no possibility of marriage between them....I am awfully sorry if our son has given false hopes to your daughter or shown her too many attentions."*⁴⁷ Despite Zia's Romanov and Nassau blood, Queen Sophie did not consider her to have the right stuff – genealogically speaking – to be the future Queen of the Hellenes. Countess Sophie's response was *"tactful"* and *"ironic."* *"To my knowledge there is no serious feeling underlying the friendship with my daughter, with whom I always speak openly on many subjects, and she with me wishes me particularly to mention that your son has never in any way led her to believe that he wishes to marry her."* The Countess also informed the queen that *"the only wish Micha and I have, and which is shared by my daughters, is that they may yet get married in England."* Crown Prince George and Zia continued their correspondence, remaining close friends. In the spring of 1914, Zia, planning a ball at Kenwood, read in the *Tatler* magazine that George was engaged to marry his cousin, Princess Elisabeth of Romania. She wrote immediately to George, asking for confirmation of the story. He responded that, *"there is not a word of truth in it."* He described Elisabeth as *"awfully nice,"* but *"we got on quite well together, but only as a guest would with his host."*[48/49]

Zia had known Harold Wernher for nearly her entire life. Harold would later tell friends that he had fallen in love with Zia when he was only fifteen. *"It's funny our being engaged. Although I have known you for so long I never thought of you in that way,"* Zia wrote to Harold after their engagement had been announced by their families. The wedding took place quietly, owing to the war, on 20 July 1917 at the Chapel Royal, St James's Palace. Earlier in the day, the couple were married in a Russian Orthodox service at the Russian Embassy's chapel, *"which was decorated with masses of white flowers and an arch of white rambler roses over the doorway."*[50] After the marriage, it was decided that she could not be called Mrs. Wernher. She would be styled as The Lady Zia Wernher, the title and precedence of an earl's daughter, following the example set by the former Countess Valda Gleichen who had been styled as The Lady Valda Machell following her marriage. Valda was a granddaughter of Queen Victoria's half-sister, Princess Feodora, the wife of the Fürst of Hohenlohe-Langenburg.

Lady Zia and Sir Harold were the parents of three children: George Michael Alexander, "Alex," born in 1918; Georgina "Gina," a year later, and Myra born in 1925. Alex was killed in the Second World War. The late Alex Wernher was a close friend of Prince Philip, Duke of Edinburgh, who got to know the Wernhers through George and Nada Mountbatten. Gina and Myra, who married Harold Phillips and David Butter, respectively, were childhood friends of Queen Elizabeth II. The Queen and Prince Philip spent a part of their honeymoon at home of Lady Zia and Sir Harold, and remained lifelong friends, sharing a common interest in horseracing.

Grand Duke Michael's son, Count *Boy* Torby's life was largely devoid of promise, although he was much loved by his family. Young Michael was a cause of *"a great deal of anxiety"*[51] to his family. Health problems, which plagued *Boy* for most of his life, began following an attack of measles when he was still at Eton. He spent some time in Switzerland, recuperating, but he developed into a manic depressive. He was a talented artist, especially interested in women's fashion. Although he was close to Zia, *Boy's* relationship with his parents was fraught with difficulties. As a young adult, he was described as *"constantly rude"* to his parents, and appeared not to understand their anxieties concerning the fate of Michael's brothers and other family members trapped in Russia after the Revolution.

For a time, *Boy* worked for Vickers, but the job didn't last long. A heavy drinker, he downed a bottle of port each day. His mother complained that *Boy* cared only for himself, not for others. He would paint, but was out of the house for most of the time, spending evenings at the clubs, coming home at four in the morning, only to be up again at eight. Grand Duke Michael was in despair, believing that his son would soon suffer a complete breakdown. In the early 1920s, living in Paris, *Boy* was becoming *"more gaga than ever."* He was eventually placed in a mental home near Uxbridge, which was paid for by his brother-in-law, Harold Wernher. Harold visited *Boy* several times, and thought him normal, except when *Boy's* parents were mentioned. *"He has all the peculiarities of his parents only a thousand times accentuated....he has the G.D.'s* [Grand Duke] *nervousness and his mother's mania for thinking they are being persecuted by the Government."*[52] *Boy* was released after a few months, and rooms were found for him in London. A job, drawing fashion illustrations for the newspapers, was secured, and an allowance was provided by Harold's family. Sadly, it was soon learned that *Boy* was spending the money in Soho nightclubs. He lived for a time with Zia and her family at Thorpe Lubenham, and later at Luton Hoo. He was described at that time as, *"decidedly odd, mooching about,"* but was always *"courtly,"* and polite. He continued to paint, mostly on rice paper or silk. In 1938, he became a naturalized British subject.

Count Michael Torby also suffered from depression. He would write to Zia from his hospital – he spent time at Roehampton – telling her about *"all these terrible pills fighting inside me."* He would stay at Luton Hoo for a few days at a time, only to say that he felt his depression returning, and would then be rushed back to Roehampton, where he died on 25 April 1959. He was 60-years-old at the time of his death. *The Times* noted that Michael was a gifted artist with a pleasant sense of colour and a free style: in particular he liked to paint on rice paper in the delicate Chinese manner.[53] The writer also noted that the Count had retained the manner and appearance of his ancestors: his white, pointed face, high forehead and large eyes, with his elegant taste in dress, recalled the tradition of the Grand Dukes.[54] He was buried with his parents in Hampstead.

Grand Duke Michael kept in touch with his relatives who had survived the Russian Revolution, and were now in exile. He was invited to visit with the Dowager Empress Marie, when she arrived in London. He also maintained a close relationship with his British cousins. At Buckingham Palace, he saw his sister-in-law, Grand Duchess Xenia, and kept in touch with Grand Duchess Marie and her two daughters, Princesses Nina and Xenia. But he, *"was becoming edgy and cantankerous, and he took to railing against other surviving members of the Imperial Family."*[55] Sophie had become so fat that she *"could not see her feet over her bosom."*

Countess Sophie Torby died at her home in Regent's Park on 14 September 1927. The impressive funeral took place three days later at the Russian Church on Buckingham Palace Road. The Prince of Wales represented King George V at the funeral. She was, according to her obituary, a lady of much charm and many social gifts, and she occupied a position of her own among the most notable hostesses.[56]

Sophie's will was largely concerned with the disposition of her jewels. Queen Mary received a ruby brooch and ruby pendant, which had been given to Sophie by her brothers-in-law, a gift originally chosen for Empress Alexandra. The pearl necklace, which Sophie wore every day, was sold to pay death duties. Other pieces of jewelry were inherited by her daughters and other relatives. Her Fabergé collection was to be divided by Zia, Nada and *Boy*. Villa Kazbeck was sold to pay death taxes, and the Grand Duke moved to a house on York Terrace where he died, intestate on 26 April 1929. His estate was limited to property valued at $371,515.

Michael's death, according to *The Times*, was *"deeply regretted by numerous attached friends."*[57] The obituary also noted that, *"like so many other Russians of rank, he and his wife suffered severely from the Revolution but they remained unshaken by* adversity." His son-in-law, Harold Wernher, upon learning of Michael's final illness, did not appear saddened by the news. He said of Michael: *"He has never showed any gratitude or one single endearing quality since I have known him."* The *New York Times* reported that with the death of Grand Duke Michael, *"an unusual cosmopolitan figure passed. He was one of Russia's royalty who made history in Occidental capitals and on the Riviera a generation ago."*[58] May Birkhead, a Paris-based correspondent for the paper, wrote that the Grand Duke, *"was notable for his huge bulk and physical strength, his hands being so large and his body so tall that he had to have special golf clubs with long shafts and thick grips."*[59] He was also known for his irritable outspokenness.[60] Sophie, Birkhead noted, *"was much loved for her radiant kindness and multiple charms*[61] *and her extraordinary popularity combined with Michael's imperial rank made this couple the social arbiters*[62] *in Cannes."*

Sophie and Michael are interred in an *"appropriately Imperial tomb"* at the West Hampstead cemetery, largely concealed by rambler roses. Grand Duke Michael was the author of one book, *Never Say Die*, which was about a morganatic marriage. He dedicated the book to *"his beloved wife."* *"What is the greatest happiness in the world? Surely love for a woman – the choice of our future wife and family life. And even in this we have not the facilities of providing individuals. We have less choice, and there is often the question of religion. So it will be easily understood what a terrible lottery marriage in our position is, and why, consequently, there are so few happy unions."*[63]

Grand Duke George Mikhailovich (1863-1919)

By Coryne Hall

Grand Duke George Mikhailovich, the third of Grand Duke Michael Nikolaievich's six sons, was born at Bielyi Kliuchi, near Tiflis, on 11 August 1863. In the family he was known as 'Gogi'.

Like his brothers he endured a regime of hard beds and cold baths, coupled with a rigorous training for the army under an exceptionally severe group of tutors. His mother, Grand Duchess Olga Feodorovna, considered him intelligent but preferred his older brother Nicholas and younger brother Alexander.

Holidays formed a welcome relief and were usually spent at their summer palace at Borjomi, about three hours from Tiflis. The huge estate, roughly the size of Holland, was set in the mountains with spectacular scenery all around. Here the boys went riding, enjoyed climbing the mountains, *"and generally were left to their own devices."*[1]

George became a talented painter. Confessing his liking for this profession one day at dinner, his reward was to be deprived of a delicious-looking ice-cream dessert. His younger brother Sandro later described him as, *"a modest boy of not too many words, who wanted to be left alone with his paintings."*[2]

George grew up to be over six feet tall and sported an imposing moustache, although he became prematurely bald. Very early on he developed a passion for the Caucasus, that lasted all his life. He also developed a youthful passion for a young Georgian girl, Princess Nina Chavchavadze, a descendant of the Kings of Georgia. Unfortunately, she was not considered to be of equal birth to the Grand Duke. Any idea of marriage was vetoed by Nina's mother, who would not allow her daughter to enter into what would have to be a morganatic marriage. Both Nina and George were heartbroken.

When he was eighteen the family returned to St Petersburg to support Tsar Alexander II, who had recently been the victim of several attempts on his life. They moved to the enormous New Mikhailovsky Palace in St Petersburg, whose halls were so vast that in later years the brothers used bicycles to visit each other. In 1881 George was present at the death-bed of Alexander II when the final attempt on his life succeeded.

Grand Duke George served in the Horse Artillery of the Guards in St Petersburg, where he became friendly with Grand Duke Peter Nikolaievich, to the detriment of his own personality according to his brother Sandro. Unfortunately, his military career was somewhat blighted when he sustained an injury to his knee. He probably did not regard this as much of a loss, as he was more of a scholar than a military man.

George had the normal interests of a Russian Grand Duke – drinking, gambling and, of course, women. During the reign of Alexander III, he became friendly with the Tsarevich, later Nicholas II. Together with his brothers Serge and Sandro, he accompanied Nicholas to the house of his mistress, the ballerina Mathilde Kschessinska, where they sang Georgian songs and drank champagne.

In 1892 he wanted to marry Princess Marie of Edinburgh. 'Missy' was the eldest daughter of Grand Duchess Marie Alexandrovna, Alexander III's sister, who in 1874 had married Queen Victoria's son Alfred, Duke of Edinburgh. When informed about the plan the Tsar said that Missy must be prepared to convert to Orthodoxy. Finally, George went to see the Duchess, bringing a letter from the Tsar asking her to persuade Missy to convert. George was not permitted to see Missy, although the Duchess promised to reply to the letter. The marriage did not take place and Missy later became the flamboyant Queen Marie of Romania.[3]

His military career curtailed by the knee injury, in 1897 George was appointed Director of the Alexander III Museum in St Petersburg. The organisation of this new institution gave the Grand Duke a great deal to do but it was work he enjoyed. He was passionately interested in numismatics and assembled an impressive collection of Russian coins stretching back to ancient times. He also wrote ten monographs on the subject. When his own collection became too large to keep at home it was transported to the museum, where he constantly worked to catalogue and organise it.

In April 1896 he travelled to Athens and proposed to Princess Marie, only surviving daughter of King George I. Marie accepted the Grand Duke reluctantly, as she was already in love with a member of her father's court. The engagement was of long duration. Marie dreaded the thought of being away from Greece and when the Greco-Turkish war broke out in 1898 she broke off the engagement, using the excuse that Russia was not doing enough to support Greece in the struggle.

George was devastated but continued to press Marie. He suffered two unhappy years before she changed her mind. *"We made it up,"* Marie telegraphed to her aunt the Dowager Empress Marie Feodorovna, as if they had merely made up after a short quarrel. *"Far too ridiculous, really,"* the Dowager Empress wrote to her sister Queen Alexandra, *"and then nevertheless to take him finally after saying that she couldn't stand him etc – I hope he will forget all that now and not bore her with his endless stories about it, because then it could end in fun and games again."*[4]

Marie insisted that the marriage ceremony be in Greece and not Russia. The wedding on 30 April, in a small church in the old Venetian fortress on Corfu, was followed by a honeymoon in Italy. As neither spoke the other's language they communicated in French.

They lived initially at Mikhailovskoe, Grand Duke Michael Nikolaievich's Italianate-style villa at Strelna on the Baltic, and in an apartment in the New Mikhailovsky Palace in St Petersburg. Two daughters were born. Nina, on 7 June 1901 (named after the love of George's youth), and Xenia on 9 August 1903 (named after Marie's sister-in-law and best friend, Grand Duchess Xenia Alexandrovna), called 'Tommy' by the family.

George was a quiet, withdrawn man but liked to joke and tease his friends. His main interests were art, coins and his daughters, to whom he remained devoted. Although Marie described him as kind-hearted, she remained thoroughly Greek and their marriage was never really happy.

In 1901 they went to Tiflis for the centenary celebrations of the union of the Caucasus with Russia. The festivities began with a Te Deum in the cathedral, attended by all the Caucasian clans wearing their colourful national costumes. Later there was a huge outdoor feast in a field outside the town. Hundreds of people sat at enormous long tables to participate in the meal. Kahetinsky, a Caucasian wine, was distributed to all the guests with a long silver ladle from an ox's skin and a toast was proposed to the health of everyone present. The round of celebrations ended with a gala performance at the opera and a state ball in Tiflis palace.

At the end of all these festivities George and his wife returned to Borjomi, where they stayed in a small wooden house on a hill above the River Kura. The estate provided plenty of opportunity for shooting stags, bucks and ibex and every morning George left at 4 o'clock in the morning with the guns, returning to their house during the afternoon.

During a visit to Egypt, Greece and Odessa in the spring of 1902 the Tsar asked them to pay a courtesy visit to Sultan Abdul Hamid II of Turkey. When their boat docked at Constantinople, George had to don full-dress uniform to receive one of the Sultan's officials, sent on board to welcome them. They were then taken by carriage to the Yildiz Kiosk where the Sultan and his officials, all in full-dress with a Turkish fez, were waiting. While drinking Turkish coffee, they conversed through an interpreter as the Sultan could not, or would not, speak a foreign language. Later they were taken to another palace, to await the Sultan's return call and an invitation to dinner.

During the three-day visit the Grand Duke and Duchess were shown many of the wonderful sights of Constantinople and taken to see the Arab horses in the Sultan's stables. They were each asked to choose a horse for themselves, but when the horses eventually arrived in Russia they bore no resemblance to the magnificent animals George and Marie had picked.

After George's father suffered a stroke in 1903 they paid many visits to Cannes, where he was recuperating. Here they were reunited with other members of the family, all keen gamblers. There were many trips to the Casino at nearby Monte Carlo, where George liked to play roulette.

During the Russo-Japanese war George rented a house on the outskirts of St Petersburg and turned it into a small hospital for soldiers who had lost limbs in the conflict. The Grand Duke ensured that they were well supplied with musical instruments of every kind so that there would be plenty of entertainment.

A great worry for George during these years was his wife's health. During the winter of 1904/5 Marie suffered a heart attack and the doctors advised her to take a cure in Homburg. This was not the only worry. Discontent over the handling of the war had led to revolution. All over the country strikes and riots erupted. In August George took his family to the Crimea. In 1900 he had purchased a small plot of land at Alupka, three miles west of his brother Sandro's estate of Ai-Todor. This land had once been the site of a Roman fortress and, in honour of this Marie called the estate Harax, the Greek word for fortress. They planned to build an English cottage on the site and had asked the architect Nicholas Krasnov to draw up plans. So that they could see how work was progressing, they went to stay with Sandro and Xenia at Ai-Todor.

As there was no room in the main building, George and his family lived in a flat over Sandro's wine cellar in the park. Later in the year Xenia's brother Michael and sister Olga arrived and they all met for meals. It was a depressing time. Postal and telegraph services were cut, they were guarded by soldiers because of riots on the ships at nearby Sevastopol and they were more or less cut off from the rest of the world. One day George and Marie were sitting in their flat when they heard people singing the Marseilles outside. George immediately opened the window and, in some very colourful language, gave them a piece of his mind. Not until January was it considered safe to leave Ai-Todor.

In the autumn of 1907 they were finally able to move into their own home. Harax was built from the blue-grey granite stones literally lying about on the site and the roof was of red tiles. The first-floor rooms led directly onto terraces overhung with roses and honeysuckle, cascading down to the Black Sea. The house was small by Imperial standards but the interior was very English. Nearby was a playhouse for George's daughters. The small houses which surrounded the main building all had red roofs like an English country village and the Grand Duke also built the small Church of St Nina.

George had a passion for trees and planted them all over the estate. Marble benches and statues were brought back from Italy, roses and other flowers thrived. Water was at first a problem, until he discovered a spring in the hills about eight miles away and arranged to buy it. Pipes were laid to Harax and neighbouring estates and in this way they were kept well supplied with water. Fruit from the orchard, as well as milk and butter from the farm he built nearby, were sold. Soon it was regarded as a model estate.

The family were never happier than when they were at Harax and they had many visitors. Every autumn George organised a shoot, to which the Tsar was invited, with an entire regiment of soldiers acting as beaters. Other Romanovs also arrived from their neighbouring estates and as they assembled in front of the house servants handed round silver mugs filled with port.

Sometime George loaded his family into his closed Renault car and they set off into the mountains for a picnic. The Grand Duke liked to drive recklessly, at great speed. Luckily his daughters' nanny always came provided with a small porcelain bowl in case either of her charges was overcome by car sickness.

In the years before the First World War the Tsar and his elder daughters Olga and Tatiana were regular visitors to Harax. They usually arrived for tea, often stayed to dinner and afterwards played whist or charades. George and Marie also gave a series of tea-dances, dinner and balls which necessitated much re-arranging of the furniture to accommodate everyone. After dinner, dances were held in the drawing-room or on the loggias. In 1914 electricity was introduced onto the estate and for the party that May the balconies and loggias were hung with tiny electric lights. At the request of the Grand Duke, the Choir of the Cossack Convoy entertained the guests after dinner.

In June 1914 Marie took her daughters to England, ostensibly for health reasons. However, her grandson Prince David Chavchavadze wrote that it was probably a trial separation. A few weeks later war broke out. Marie then said that she could not return to Russia and poor George never saw his wife and daughters again.

On the outbreak of war George became a lieutenant-general in the army. He was sent by the Tsar to report on morale and conditions in the army, and he inspected Red Cross units and hospitals. He also organised a private hospital in St Petersburg.

In 1915 he was sent on a mission to Japan, travelling back via the Far East. At Vladivostok he received an order from the Tsar to visit German and Austrian prisoners of war, to ensure they were being well-treated. *"I wire every day to Nicky as I know how interested he is,"* George told his wife. *"I only tell him the truth and my good impressions of this far-away land, where everything is in good order. Our peasants are prosperous and rich and one sees no beggars or people in need."*[5] In his reports he refused to overlook the dishonesty of various military commanders, insisting they be punished or even removed from command. This earned him many enemies.

In between his work George was still trying to persuade Marie to return to Russia. In May 1916 he sent his private secretary, Mr Maichrowsky, to London to convince the Grand Duchess to return with him. Marie continued to make excuses and the plan did not materialize.

Early in 1917, living in daily expectation of revolution, George went to see the Dowager Empress Marie Feodorovna who had taken refuge in Kiev, in order to discuss the worrying situation. From there he travelled to Romania to visit the Russian army corps, and he also saw Missy (now Queen of Romania), to whom he had wanted to propose all those years before. He arrived back in Petrograd one night toward the end of February and went immediately to bed. The next morning he was told that there were barricades in the streets, firing had been going on for days and cars were being attacked by the mob. He decided to go to Gatchina, thirty miles away, to see the Tsar's brother Grand Duke Michael Alexandrovich, but he was still in the capital. George remained at Gatchina with Michael's morganatic wife Natalia.

A few days later came news of the Tsar's abdication and the refusal of the throne by Grand Duke Michael. A Provisional Government was formed and George joined a group of Romanovs who submitted a formal statement waiving their appanage income.[6]

"...Our fate, that is, the fate of the Grand Dukes, has not yet been decided," George told his wife at the end of March. *"...There are only three things to be done, ie, first to try and escape, which none of us tried to do, secondly, to commit suicide, thirdly to recognize this provisional government, which we have done, instinctively, without even consulting each other, because there is no doubt that the old regime could not work any more."*[7] In the meantime he stayed at Gatchina with Michael. All letters addressed to the Grand Dukes were confiscated and communications with England were becoming more difficult as the British Ambassador refused to forward letters in the diplomatic bag. George and Michael were given a guard of revolutionary troops, which at least protected them from the excesses of the mob. George was now anxious to leave Gatchina, as he could not stand many more of Natasha's outbursts against the Romanovs.

In the summer of 1917, having been refused a visa to join his family in England, the Grand Duke travelled to Finland, still part of the Russian empire. From there it would be easy to reach Scandinavia as soon as he was given permission to go abroad. He rented a villa near the lake at Retiervi, where he remained until the winter, continuing to write daily letters to his wife. When the villa became too cold George moved to a small hotel in Helsingfors, where he befriended some British officers including General Poole. The General tried to take George with him as part of the departing British mission but the plan was frustrated.

In Helsingfors there was fighting in the streets. Early one morning George was woken by loud knocking on his bedroom door. He was confronted by three sailors. A revolver was put to his head, a bayonet to his chest and they demanded he surrender his weapons.

One day the hotel was raided by a band of sailors who asked for identity cards. One of the band, a student, became interested when he discovered that George was a Grand Duke and George asked his help to obtain a document to leave the country. Friends implored him to keep quiet, saying that soon Finland would gain independence from Russia and he would automatically be abroad but he refused to listen. George would pay dearly for this mistake.

Shortly afterwards he was thrown into prison in Helsingfors and, on 3 April, taken to Petrograd under escort. The following day Commissar Uritsky gave him a choice of three towns in which he could spend his exile – Vologda, Viatka and Perm. George chose Vologda, where his brother Nicholas and cousin Grand Duke Dimitri Konstantinovich were already living. Before leaving, he went to see his mother-in-law Queen Olga to persuade her to leave the country as soon as possible. *"Thank God you are not in this country which was once called Russia and now does not exist any more,"* he wrote to Marie.[8]

Arriving in Vologda George was billeted with a family in a tiny house with little room. Luckily he was able to obtain a permit to change quarters so moved into the house of a rich merchant. Letters to England were now forwarded by the Japanese mission, who seemed eager to help, although he rarely received news from his family.

He often visited Nicholas and Dimitri, the only two people he knew in the town. Nicholas later described his brother as being *"in a pitiful state of nerves."* They had little food and their clothes were in tatters. Most of George's luggage had remained in Finland as he was given no time to pack. He now wore, *"a civilian overcoat and a chauffeur's cap"* and looked, as one writer expressed it, *"like a member of a yacht club."*[9] It was impossible to buy more clothes as prices had shot up. Even the mattress from his army camp bed had been stolen.

On 1 July Grand Dukes George and Nicholas were having lunch together when two cars stopped in front of the house. Informed they were under arrest, George sensibly asked permission to stop at his own house so that he could get his coat. The cars then went to pick up Grand Duke Dimitri.

At Vologda prison Grand Duke George was thrown into cell no. 14. After the first 24 hours he was allowed his camp bed and clothes. He reported that their Lettish guards were decent men who, after the second day, did not lock the cell doors and permitted them to walk together in the small garden. Food was brought in from outside and George's devoted valet smuggled letters out. After a fortnight George had still been given no reason for his arrest. The guards were becoming friendlier, sensing that the Grand Dukes were imprisoned without any real reason. Then, just as George was becoming hopeful that they might be released, the three men were suddenly informed that they would be taken to Petrograd the next day.

On 20 July they received news that the Tsar had been murdered. Now none of them could be sure that they would not suffer the same fate. Only uncertainty about the fate of the rest of the Tsar's family, and rumours that some had survived, kept them going. George probably never knew that his brother Serge had been murdered with other Romanovs at Alapaievsk soon afterwards.

They arrived in Petrograd under guard on 21 July and were immediately taken to the Kresty prison, where inmates were confined six to a cell. Two days later the three Grand Dukes were moved to the notorious Shpalernaia prison, where they were later joined by Grand Duke Paul Alexandrovich. Prince Gabriel Konstantinovich was another inmate.

George's cell was on the 5th floor, roughly 7 feet by just over 3 feet, with one window high up in the wall. It had a fixed iron bed, a small table, a bench, a washstand and a tube where heating came through. They were allowed little exercise and the food was poor.

At the urgent request of the Allied Ambassadors in Petrograd (and without waiting for instructions from his government in Copenhagen), the Danish Minister Harald Scavenius visited the Bolsheviks to demand the safety and decent treatment of the Grand Dukes, two of whom were the uncles of Queen Alexandrine of Denmark. He then visited the Grand Dukes in prison to see for himself that they were all physically well and afterwards sent them food bought with money deposited at the Danish Legation by their friends. The Grand Dukes asked Scavenius to try and secure their release.

After a while the Grand Dukes were allowed to meet and walk in the courtyard twice a day and to use the prison library. George wrote to his wife that he had never read so much in his life. He read many historical books and also the novels of Dostoyevsky.

"Yesterday it was my 55th birthday and, strangely enough, my 55th day in prison,"

he wrote on 25 August. *"Imagine my joy when the dear kind nurse of this prison brought me a whole packet of letters from you and the children. It has warmed my heart and given me new courage in my miserable plight and loneliness."*[10] Every evening he had to sweep out his own cell and keep it clean, and everything he collected was taken away the next morning. The lights were turned on at 7 o'clock in the evening but, by September, it was dark so early that in the afternoons he lay on his bed in the dark unable to see, read and write. One of the most terrible occurrences was the nightly disappearance of prisoners, whose fate he never knew. Usually they were shot.

Harald Scavenius and his wife Anne Sofie visited regularly during the autumn of 1918 and remained in constant contact. They continued to bring provisions to supplement the prison rations, which usually consisted of *"dirty hot water with a few fish bones floating in it"* and black bread.[11] George's stomach constantly suffered from eating cold food. Eventually the kindly prison nurse brought him a small spirit lamp to enable him to warm his food.

On 12 September Uritsky was murdered and the Red Terror began. Scavenius reported that innocent hostages were shot daily and Bolshevik newspapers were crying out that the four Grand Dukes should be executed. In London, George's wife again became alarmed, fearing that her husband and his relatives were being held as hostages in case of attempts against the lives of other Bolshevik leaders. Henrik Castenskiold, the Danish Minister in London, asked his government on her behalf if anything could be done for Grand Duke George. Once again the request was passed to Scavenius in Petrograd. The Norwegian and Swedish governments were also approached, with no result.

By the autumn Scavenius felt that George's only real hope of freedom was an approach to the German Kaiser. When the Grand Duke was advised to seek assistance from the German Consul he refused, saying that he would not ask a favour from a Hun. By this time Germany's allies were collapsing, defeat was imminent and there was little the Kaiser could do but he instructed his Consul in Petrograd, Hans Karl Breiter, to take the Grand Dukes under his protection.

At the beginning of October the Bolsheviks began to make things even more unpleasant. They tried to remove the kindly nurse, although the director of the prison managed to keep her a little longer. Soon afterwards, the Danish King and Queen received another appeal for help from the Grand Dukes. King Christian X informed his foreign minister that the Danish royal family would take care of them if their release and journey to Denmark could be negotiated. This offer reached the Grand Dukes in prison and Scavenius also arranged to have their few valuables sent to Denmark.

George's health was now really suffering from the lack of warm food, despite the help of the spirit lamp. His valet brought food in three times a week but George shared even these meagre rations with other prisoners who were not so fortunate. He was now so thin that he had tied his rings together with a piece of string so that they would not get lost.

Rumours now circulated that the Grand Dukes would be set free on the first anniversary of the Bolshevik take-over, or as Grand Duke George called it, *"Lenin's accession to the throne."*[12] Then the men were informed that they could purchase their freedom – but they had no money. Soon afterwards the prison director and the nurse were removed for being too kind.

It was becoming more and more difficult to smuggle letters out. George's last letter to his wife was dated 27 November but he continued to write because pouring his feelings out on paper provided some consolation. He even asked Marie to keep his letters, as he hoped to be able to write his memoirs at some time in the future.

By early December there were no more matches to light the spirit lamp and George was complaining about his stomach. A desperate appeal reached Harald Scavenius, who telegraphed the foreign ministry asking them to tell the Queen so that she would know her uncles were still alive. Shortly afterwards a parcel of warm clothes arrived for the Grand Dukes, sent from Grand Duchess George via the Legation.

At this point, just as it seemed that the Grand Dukes' release might be obtained by payment of a ransom, Harald Scavenius was recalled. He protested against leaving the people who needed his help, especially as their lives could depend on him remaining in Russia. His pleas fell on deaf ears. He would leave Petrograd on 15 December.[13]

Before Scavenius left Petrograd he deposited extra provisions at the prison for the Grand Dukes *"until further notice."*[14] Toward the end of January, Queen Alexandrine sent a letter to her uncles with a Danish businessman who was travelling to Petrograd. Whether the Queen's letter reached them is unclear.

In January 1919, the writer Maxim Gorky apparently succeeded in securing Lenin's signature on a document ordering the Grand Dukes' release. He hurried to the station to catch the night train from Moscow to Petrograd. On the station platform he caught sight of a newspaper headline. He was too late.

On the night of 27/28 January the Grand Dukes were woken in their cells and told to bring their baggage, as they were leaving. George seems to have had a premonition that they were to be shot, allegedly asking a prison guard to tell the Grand Duke's family, if he ever met any of them, that he kissed them. Then, without their baggage, they were put into a lorry with some other prisoners, driven to the Fortress of SS Peter & Paul and pushed into the notorious Troubetzkoy Bastion.

Although the temperature was 20 degrees below freezing, the Grand Dukes were ordered to strip to the waist. By now they had no illusions about what would happen next and, after Nicholas had made what one informant called an affecting speech, the men embraced one another. Then, with a soldier holding each arm, they were led out into the courtyard. As they passed the SS Peter & Paul Cathedral, the Grand Dukes removed their hats and made the Sign of the Cross.

They stopped in front of a trench which already contained thirteen bodies. George began to pray quietly as the executioners made their preparations. *"I have already decided that if I am to be shot, I will refuse to have my eyes bandaged as I wish to look at the rifles which will shoot me,"* George had written to Marie some months earlier.[15] He, Nicholas and Dimitri died in the same hail of bullets. Paul, apparently too weak to stand, was shot on a stretcher. In payment, the executioners received half a loaf of bread and a book. The following day one of the men boasted in the street that he had taken George's boots.[16]

The reason for their deaths remains a mystery. George, certainly, had never played any part in politics. One theory is that it was in retaliation for the killing of Karl Liebknecht and Rosa Luxemburg, prominent Communists, in Berlin earlier in January.[17] The bodies of George and the other Grand Dukes were thrown into a common grave only yards from the Cathedral where they should by rights have been buried. Their remains have never been found.

Grand Duchess Marie Georgievna eventually returned to Greece, where she spent her last years. Both her daughters married and gave her grandchildren. Nina and Xenia eventually settled in the USA and died here in 1974 and 1965 respectively. In 1922, Marie married Greek Admiral Pericles Ioannides, 'Perks', who was very popular with his Greek in-laws. She died in Athens in 1940. Perks survived her until 1965.

Grand Duke Alexander Mikhailovich
(1866-1933)

By Coryne Hall

A salute of 101-guns greeted the birth of a fifth child to the Viceroy of the Caucasus, Grand Duke Michael Nikolaievich and his wife Olga, in Tiflis, Georgia, on 1 April 1866. The baby Grand Duke was christened Alexander, in honour of his uncle Tsar Alexander II, and within 24 hours of his birth was honorary colonel of several regiments. In the family, and to history, he was known simply as Sandro.

On his seventh birthday Sandro left the nursery for the harsh world of his brothers' tutors. From that moment, until he was fifteen, he lived with his brothers in surroundings more like a barracks, sleeping on hard iron beds with only a thin mattress. Their education resembled the training of a regiment, with particular attention being paid to firearms, riding, fencing and bayonet fighting. Every day the boys visited their father's study, *"an enormous room laid with Persian rugs and decorated with Caucasian swords, rifles and pistols."*[1] From here they could watch the colourful costumes of the natives in the main thoroughfare and look up to the snow-covered peak of the Kasbek mountain beyond. This was their one treat in the daily grind of lessons with tutors who were unnecessarily severe, where even a small mistake in the spelling of a German word would deprive the offender of dessert. Starved of parental love, the boys lavished all their affection on their only sister Anastasia ('Stassie') whom they were only allowed to see on Sundays.

Every year there was a six-week summer holiday, spent either at Borjomi, Grand Duke Michael's enormous country estate about 90 miles from Tiflis or in the Crimea where, in 1869, Grand Duchess Olga purchased Ai-Todor ('St Theodore'). This was to become Sandro's most beloved home.

The outbreak of the Russo-Turkish war in 1877 gave the boys a break in the dull routine. Their father was appointed Commander-in-Chief of the Russian army and every day Sandro and his brothers accompanied him as he inspected the troops. Then came the day when the 73rd Krimsky Infantry passed through Tiflis on their way to the battlefield and their eleven-year-old colonel, Grand Duke Alexander, proudly reviewed his regiment. Their father's enforced absences also enabled them to venture beyond the palace walls and learn that life outside was not all luxury and privilege.

In 1878 Sandro made his first trip to European Russia, to attend the marriage of Stassie and Prince Friedrich Franz of Mecklenburg-Schwerin. Sandro and his brothers were devastated by this first breaking-up of the family circle, and he cursed the heartless rules that forced Grand Duchesses of that period to marry abroad.

Then in 1880 Sandro's life changed forever. After an attempt on the life of Alexander II, Grand Duke Michael decided to take his family back to St Petersburg. Sandro had no liking for the grey fogs of the north, much preferring the wide open plains of the Caucasus to the vast, rambling New Mikhailovich Palace in St Petersburg or the Italianate Mikhailovskoe at Strelna.

When terrorists finally succeeded in killing Alexander II the following year, Sandro was present at his deathbed. With the accession of Alexander III the *"Wild*

Caucasians", as Grand Duke Michael's sons were called, became playmates of his elder children Tsarevich Nicholas, Grand Duke George and Grand Duchess Xenia.

It was made clear that Sandro's career choices lay between the cavalry, the artillery and the fleet. Yet with a father who was a devoted artilleryman, it came as somewhat of a shock to the family when Sandro announced he wanted to enter the navy. It was Alexander III who interceded with his father. Prevented by his position from attending the Naval College, Sandro studied for four years with tutors at home and spent three summers on training ships before passing his exams as a midshipman in 1885. No favouritism was shown to him on these training voyages and he was never allowed ashore unless accompanied by his tutor – Grand Duchess Olga had given strict instructions that he was to return with his 'morals' intact.

In April 1886 Sandro came of age and gained financial independence. Shortly afterwards he left on the *Rynda* for his first long voyage as a sub-lieutenant with the Pacific Fleet. By Christmas they had reached Rio de Janeiro, where Sandro had his first taste of romance. The ship sailed on to South Africa, Singapore and Hong Kong where, inevitably, he lost his virginity in a brothel. In Japan the Grand Duke acquired an official 'wife' in Nagasaki. Later he was obliged to call on the Mikado and reduced the Empress to almost hysterical laughter by trying out his only words of Japanese – some wholly inappropriate phrases learnt from his geisha.

It was the summer of 1889 before Sandro returned to St Petersburg. Six-foot two inches tall, dark-haired and handsome, Sandro was restless, bored and ambitious. He resumed his old friendship with Tsarevich Nicholas and quickly noticed that his sister Xenia, now fourteen, was growing up fast. That summer Sandro visited the Exposition Universelle in Paris and he sent her a postcard: *"My lovely Xenia, I am writing to you from the top of the Eiffel Tower... Goodbye, I am kissing your dear little hand."*[2]

The following season at the small private balls he danced only with her. In May 1890 he asked his brother George whether he thought Xenia preferred him or their brother Serge and, more importantly, whether he considered the Tsar would allow either of them to marry his daughter. Despite the fact that neither Alexander III nor Empress Marie Feodorovna were particularly impressed with Sandro at this time, both feeling that he was too restless to settle down, he was invited to join the imperial family on their annual Finnish cruise. He took advantage of the invitation to spend as much time as possible with Xenia.

In September Sandro left on his new yacht *Tamara* for a voyage round the world, scheduled to last for two years. In Egypt he met up with Tsarevich Nicholas and Grand Duke George Alexandrovich. Reaching Bombay, Sandro learnt of his mother's death brought on, it was said, by news of his brother Michael's unsuitable marriage and subsequent banishment by the Tsar. After only nine months away, Sandro returned to St Petersburg.

By now Sandro and Xenia were in love. Sandro confided his feelings to Xenia's brother George, now living in the Caucasus for health reasons. The Tsar, however, disapproved. Xenia sulked and Sandro left to serve with the Baltic Fleet.

After Xenia's eighteenth birthday in the spring of 1893 Sandro saw no need to wait any longer. He approached the Tsar with two requests – a transfer to the *Dimitri Donskoi*, soon to leave for America, which was granted, and a request for Xenia's hand in marriage, which was refused. The Tsar advised him to wait. The Empress did not want Xenia to marry so young.

In 1893 Sandro arrived for the first time in America. The *Dimitri Donskoi* was part of a great international fleet taking part in a Naval Review in New York Harbour in May, as part of the celebrations for the 400th anniversary of America's discovery by Columbus. Sandro was also to convey Alexander III's thanks to President Cleveland for aid given during the recent famine in Russia. The Grand Duke was impressed with America, despite the financial crisis and industrial depression, and he began to work out a plan for the 'Americanization' of Russia.

On his return home, and after some persuasion from Grand Duke Michael Nikolaievich, the Empress finally agreed to Xenia and Sandro's betrothal, which was announced in January 1894. Then, with the betrothal of Nicholas to Princess Alix of Hesse and by Rhine in April, Sandro and Xenia found their wedding pushed into the background. No decision was even made about the date and Sandro's protests brought the reply that the dressmakers would need six months to make Xenia's trousseau.

Preparations were overshadowed by worry over the Emperor's failing health. Sandro's behaviour, criticised by Grand Duke Konstantin Konstantinovich as *"demanding and tactless,"* also upset the Imperial couple. According to Konstantin, Sandro complained about the accommodation allotted at Ropsha for their honeymoon and demanded the apartments of the Emperor and Empress. Then he found fault with the decoration of their rooms in the Winter Palace, *"although he will only have to live there one winter, as the Emperor has bought them Princess Vorontsov's house on the Moika [canal], which will have been completely redecorated in a year's time. All this is upsetting and does nothing to bring parents and son-in-law closer."*[3] By the time the Imperial family viewed the lavish trousseau a few days before the wedding, the tensions were beginning to show.

At 3 p.m. on 25 July Sandro and Xenia followed the Tsar and Tsarina in a long procession to the Cathedral of SS Peter & Paul in the Grand Palace at Peterhof. Despite the Tsar's obvious ill-health the wedding was followed by a lavish banquet and it was after eleven o'clock before Sandro and his bride were able to leave for Ropsha.

The Palace of Ropsha and the adjoining village had been brilliantly illuminated. Unfortunately, the nervous coachman, blinded by the lights, overlooked a small bridge and deposited the carriage, horses and bridal couple in a brook. No-one was hurt, but Xenia's ostrich-feathered hat and ermine-trimmed coat were covered in mud, while Sandro's face and hands were black. On reaching the palace, General Wiazemsky diplomatically said nothing as he received them at the entrance.

They spent the main part of their honeymoon at Ai-Todor, which Sandro had inherited on his mother's death. The young couple settled into the Old House, its outside walls covered with climbers and grapes. Everything remained as it was in Sandro's childhood, he permitted no alterations. When ivy began to poke through the bathroom floorboards, he simply let it flourish until it covered the walls. Sandro and Ai-Todor had grown up together. *"With the passing of years it became a flourishing country estate covered by gardens, vineyards, lawns and coves,"* he recalled. The estate stretched right down to the sea. *"A lighthouse was built on its grounds to enable us to find our way on a foggy night."*[4]

Their idyll was disturbed by worrying news of the Tsar's health as the doctors diagnosed nephritis. In September, Sandro and Xenia were on the quayside at Yalta to meet the rest of her family as they disembarked for a stay at Livadia. At first the Crimean air seemed to do the Tsar good. Then, as he weakened, Xenia and Sandro joined the family's vigil and were present when Alexander III died. According to Sandro, Nicholas II turned to him in despair in his first moments as Tsar.

With the death of Alexander III, Sandro was now brother-in-law to the new

Tsar. He and Xenia moved into apartments at the Winter Palace and were soon expecting their first child. Irina was born at The Farm Palace at Peterhof on 3 July 1895. As the great-granddaughter of a Tsar through the male line she held the rank of Princess. Xenia and Sandro often spent evenings with the newly-married Tsar Nicholas and Tsarina Alexandra. Sandro even helped the Tsar to christen his new billiard room.

After the birth of their son Andrei on 12 January 1897 they moved into their new St Petersburg home, 106 Quai de la Moika. At first they remained close to the Tsar and Tsarina, but the birth of one son after another (Feodor in 1898, Nikita in 1900, Dimitri in 1901 and Rostislav in 1902), while the Empress produced only daughters, put a strain on this relationship. In 1896, after disagreements with Grand Duke Alexis Alexandrovich, Grand Admiral of the Russian Navy, who he regarded as old-fashioned in his views, Sandro resigned. He undoubtedly coveted Alexis's position as Grand Admiral but between 1896 and 1900 he was given no significant naval duties and spent most of his time at Ai-Todor.

Sandro was a passionate collector of naval books and amassed a large library on the subject. Under the name of VKAM [Grand Duke Alexander Mikhailovich] he also wrote some himself, including *The Navies of Foreign Countries* and *The Naval Reference Book*, "*the first reference books on foreign fleets in the Russian language.*"[5]

In 1900 Sandro was promoted to captain of the *Rostislav* stationed in the Black Sea (his son, born two years later, was named after the ship) describing this as "*the dream of my life.*"[6] In 1902, now promoted to Rear Admiral, he became Minister of Merchant Marine and the youngest member of the Cabinet. His interest and aptitude for technical innovations, usual for a Grand Duke, had also become apparent, as had his interest in the growth of commercial shipping. He was strongly in favour of Russian expansion in the Far East and (buoyed up by his own ambitions, both political and monetary) encouraged the Tsar to buy forestry concessions near the Yalu River in Korea. This was the first step toward Russia's disastrous war with Japan.[7]

In 1904 the Japanese attacked Port Arthur, without a declaration of war. The Dowager Empress ensured that Sandro remained firmly in St Petersburg as the Russians marched from debacle to debacle. The surrender of Port Arthur early in 1905, with a loss of 28,000 men, started a howl of criticism at the government's management of the war. Unrest spread, as the people began to agitate for a say in the running of the country. Sandro was strongly opposed to sending the Russian Baltic fleet to Japan and the annihilation of this fleet at Tsushima in May 1905 with the loss of many lives left the Imperial family stunned.

As the country erupted in a riot of revolutionary activity Sandro found peace at Ai-Todor, where two of the villas in the park had been converted into hospitals. The estate was enlarged as his family grew. New buildings were added including the New House (where the younger boys had their bedrooms) and a house for the Suite. Sandro planted trees and supervised the production and marketing of his wine, fruit and flowers. The area around Ai-Todor had once been the site of a Roman fortress and Sandro began a series of archaeological digs. The property remained completely unspoilt. When it was proposed to extend the railway line, Sandro and Xenia were determined to ensure it would not go through their estate.

Finally news came that the Tsar had signed a Manifesto giving the country a parliament (Duma). The Tsar no longer reigned as an Autocrat but as a Constitutional Monarch. To Sandro this was the end of everything. When telegraphic communication was finally restored he resigned his ministerial post in protest. They remained at

Ai-Todor protected by a company of soldiers. Even though they were 1,500 miles away from the capital it was not safe to leave until after Christmas. Both were present at the opening of the Duma in April 1906. Although all the ladies wore Court dress and the men were resplendent in uniforms, most of them agreed with Sandro that *"deep mourning would have been more appropriate."*[8]

After the war Sandro was appointed to the command of the new torpedo boat *HIMS Almaz* but returned to Gatchina on hearing that Feodor was dangerously ill with scarlet fever. While he was away his crew mutinied, planning to seize the Grand Duke as hostage on his return. The Tsar immediately told Sandro he would have to resign his command.

Now all Sandro wanted to do was to leave hated Russia. As soon as Feodor was well enough they all went to Biarritz, a fashionable resort on the border between France and Spain. Sandro enjoyed mixing with the 'smart set' and threw himself with zest onto the golf course opposite their temporary home, the Villa Espoir. They had originally planned to stay for three months but when Christmas came Sandro had no desire to return to Russia. They spent a carefree Christmas holiday, their happiest for twelve years. Then the hunting season arrived, with its luncheons in the country and dinners in Biarritz. Still they remained.

As the Tsar's brother-in-law Sandro was naturally the centre of attention and although he had never looked at another woman up to now, suddenly forbidden fruits began to appeal. Gradually he became infatuated with Maria Ivanova, a woman of Spanish-Italian ancestry who often visited their villa. Xenia's diary refers to her only as "M.I." The affair lasted several years and at the same time Xenia was having her own affair, with an Englishman named Fane. Xenia and Sandro conducted their liaisons discreetly, in the meantime maintaining their marriage and family life. There is no truth in the often-quoted statement that Xenia's lover was the husband of Sandro's mistress.[9] Only in the spring of 1907 did Sandro and Xenia reluctantly return home, in time for the birth of her seventh and last child, Vassili, in June.

During his stay in Biarritz Sandro became interested in flying. In 1909 he founded Russia's first Military Aviation School just outside Sevastopol in the Crimea. He and Xenia continued to spend long periods away from Russia, disillusioned at the way things were going in the country, the influence of Rasputin, and their increasingly cool relations with Empress Alexandra. By this time Xenia and Sandro were leading separate lives. There were serious disagreements and Sandro moved out of the marital bedroom. In 1910 he tried to persuade Maria Ivanova to go with him to live in Australia. She refused.

In the summer of 1914, as Europe tottered on the brink of war, Sandro and Xenia were in London. At the end of July, having failed to impress upon Xenia and the Dowager Empress the seriousness of the situation, Sandro left for Constanza. It was an eventful journey. Travelling through Austria, the Orient Express was stopped at Vienna where the passengers were forced to wait for several hours while negotiations proceeded. Finally, permission was given for the train to proceed to the Romanian border. Sandro then had to walk for several miles to meet the special train provided for him by the Romanian government. Finally he reached Constanza, from where his old ship the *Almaz* took him to the Crimea.

Sandro was assigned first to headquarters. He was then created Head of Military Aviation and left for Kiev, where he was later joined by the Dowager Empress Marie Feodorovna, eager to get away from the oppressive atmosphere in the capital, and her daughter Olga who was working as a nurse in a nearby hospital. In November

1916 he was one of the handful of witnesses when Olga, whose first marriage had been annulled, married Nikolai Kulikovsky, a Colonel in the Life Guards Cuirassiers.

In December 1916 news arrived that Rasputin had been murdered by a group of right-wing conspirators, who included Prince Felix Youssoupov (husband of Sandro's daughter Irina) and Grand Duke Dimitri Pavlovich. Sandro left hurriedly for the capital, where he asked the Tsar not to treat Felix and Dimitri like common murderers but as misguided patriots with a desire to help Russia. The family then presented a joint letter to Nicholas asking for clemency, which Sandro thought was about the stupidest thing ever written. The plea was refused. Felix was exiled to one of his remote estates; Dimitri was sent to the Persian front.

Sandro made one final effort to make the Tsar and Tsarina see sense. He visited Tsarskoe Selo, where for nearly two hours he spoke heatedly with Alexandra while Nicholas stood nearby, smoking but saying nothing. The Grand Duke tried to persuade them to appoint a government which would have the confidence of the people – to no avail. He then wrote to Nicholas giving his own advice about political reform, saying that the Tsar himself was actually promoting the cause of revolution. *"We witness the unprecedented sight of a revolution carried out not from below, but above,"* his letter concluded.[10]

Frustrated in his endeavours, Sandro returned to Kiev where he remained throughout the revolution. After Nicholas' abdication on 2 March, Sandro accompanied the Dowager Empress to Moghilev where the former Tsar had gone to say goodbye to his army. Nicholas and his mother had a long conversation alone. When Sandro was finally summoned he found the Dowager Empress *"sobbing aloud,"* while Nicholas *"stood motionless, looking at his feet and, of course, smoking."*[11]

After Nicholas left under escort for Tsarskoe Selo, Sandro and the Dowager Empress returned to Kiev. They were greeted by civilians wearing red armbands and forced to drive to the palace in hired cabs. Sandro had already seen the way things were going, writing to his brother Grand Duke Nicholas Mikhailovich, *"I personally see that the Provisional Government has lost its balance, being completely in the power of the Soviet of workers' deputies. And if the Provisional Government does not prevail, total anarchy and the collapse of Russia will follow."*[12]

At first Sandro, the Dowager Empress and Olga remained in Kiev but then the situation turned ugly. Sandro was forced to resign his commission, Kiev became dangerous and at the end of March the Romanovs secured permission to leave for the Crimea.

They left Kiev secretly at night on 23 March. During the four-day journey refugees tried to board the train at every stop, but were repelled by a group of loyal sappers. Finally, at Sevastopol, the Imperial party transferred to cars provided by still loyal officers of the Military Aviation School. They drove straight to Ai-Todor, where Sandro was reunited with his younger sons. Xenia and the older boys joined them a few days later, while Irina and Felix went to one of the Youssoupov estates nearby. With the younger boys' rooms in the New House occupied by Xenia's mother and sister, Sandro and his wife now shared his bedroom. This enforced cohabitation put a further strain on the already fragile state of their marriage and long uncomfortable periods of silence were now interspersed with prolonged scenes in front of their startled sons.

For the first few weeks they had comparative freedom, although Sandro was asked to stop his archaeological digs. Soon he became taciturn, deprived of his work and with nothing important to do. He tried to occupy himself with his coin collection, the study of astronomy and wine growing. Money was also a problem. The Imperial estates were nationalised and all the family ceased to receive their incomes from the Imperial appanages. Xenia and Sandro were forced to send many of their servants away as they could not afford to keep them.

Then in April the revolution reached the Crimea. Early on the morning of 26 April, Sandro and Xenia were woken by a party of sailors, who said they had come to arrest them in the name of the Provisional Government and the Soviet of Workers and Soldiers' Deputies. Sandro was ordered to show them around the house. After ransacking the building and taking away personal correspondence and diaries the sailors left. Sandro lodged a complaint with the Provisional Government and a commission was sent to Ai-Todor to investigate. The Dowager Empress' old Danish bible, seized as a 'revolutionary book' was returned a few weeks later.

Soon afterwards the Provisional Government's Special Commissar moved into Ai-Todor with twenty heavily armed Soviet sailors. The Romanovs were placed under house arrest and subjected to various petty humiliations. Between late August and mid-October they were all confined to the limits of Ai-Todor. News that the former Tsar and his family had been moved to Siberia did nothing to help the family's peace of mind.

Then on 25 October the Bolsheviks seized power in Petrograd. At Ai-Todor the family were again arrested and Zadorojny, a representative of the Sevastopol Soviet, moved into the house. They were now under threat from the Sevastopol and Yalta Soviets who were arguing over whose right it was to execute them.

After Russia and Germany signed the separate peace of Brest-Litovsk on 3 March 1918 the occupants of Ai-Todor were moved to nearby Djulber, the Arabian-style villa of Sandro's cousin Grand Duke Peter Nikolaievich and his wife Militza. They were joined by Peter's brother Nicholas and his wife. Grand Duchess Olga and Irina Youssoupov, married to 'commoners' were allowed to go free. There were forty-five people in all, including servants, and conditions inside Djulber were cramped.

As the Germans marched toward the Crimea, Commissar Zadorojny was warned that the Yalta men planned to execute the Romanovs before they could be liberated. Bands of Yalta men now descended on Djulber but Zadorojny refused to let them inside. Every gate and exit was locked and machine-guns were positioned as they prepared for a major attack. Zadorojny returned their weapons and Sandro helped him position the searchlights. It could only be a matter of time before the Yalta men returned and Zadorojny decided to go to Sevastopol to summon help. That evening Sandro and the other men took turns on the night watch.

They were saved by an advance party of German soldiers sent personally by the Kaiser. The Dowager Empress, considering Russia still at war with the Germans, declined an invitation to go to Germany. Sandro was angry, fearing they would all be killed when the Germans left. He wanted to know if he and his family could travel to Switzerland and he spoke to one of the Germans at Ai-Todor, a move that caused a rift with the Dowager Empress. He also pleaded for the release of Zadorojny, who had tried to help them during their captivity.

In June Sandro and his family returned to Ai-Todor, where they settled down to a more peaceful existence. Soon alarming rumours about the murder of the Tsar, and of Sandro's brother Serge at Alapaievsk, reached the Crimea. Nobody knew what to believe.

With the collapse of Germany and the signing of the armistice on 11 November the Germans had to evacuate the Crimea. As the allied fleets arrived there was great debate over what the family should do. The Dowager Empress and Xenia thought it was unnecessary to leave. Sandro disagreed and was angry with Xenia.

By now he was anxious to go to Paris to see the heads of the Allied governments and impress upon them the seriousness of the situation. On 26 December he left on *HMS Forsythe*. With him went his eldest son Andrei and his bride Elisabetha (née Ruffo), who had been married barely a month before at Ai-Todor. Elisabetha was expecting Andrei's child.[13]

Sandro arrived in Paris at the end of January 1919 and moved into the Ritz Hotel, where he learnt from a newspaper that his brothers Nicholas and George had been shot by the Bolsheviks. Money was a problem and Sandro bitterly regretted not taking earlier advice to invest some of his fortune abroad. He was forced to sell his coin collection to make ends meet.

His efforts to gain a voice for Russia at the Versailles Peace Conference were unsuccessful. None of the allied statesmen would see him. The British Foreign Secretary was so anxious to avoid the Grand Duke that he fled down the hotel fire escape. To add insult to injury, when Sandro applied for a British visa his request was refused.

Having failed to persuade his family to start a new life with him in Fiji, Sandro was reunited with Xenia in Biarritz in the summer of 1919, where they celebrated their silver wedding anniversary. Nevertheless, their marriage was over. Xenia made her home in England, Sandro settled in France. It seems that he still hoped that things could be mended, pouring out his feelings in an emotional letter from Paris in 1922. *"Sweet Xenia, I write again with hope to touch your soul and your heart! Tomorrow you will celebrate New Year and maybe will think about me and that with your refusal you pushed me away for ever."*[14] It seems that Xenia had finally reached the limits of her tolerance.

Sandro's life in exile was a nomadic existence. He settled for a while in Princess Paley's house in Biarritz, helped with her charity work, attended Boy Scout reviews, became interested in Freemasonry and in 1928 was appointed Grand Prior of the Order of Malta. He began to frequent the golf course hoping to find Maria Ivanova. Instead he met a young English girl whom he pursued for three years. She refused to run off with him to Australia. There were other women, including Helene Yourievich, wife of a sculptor.

While staying in Monte-Carlo Sandro met an Ethiopian diplomat, who asked him to act as emissary in an effort to recover the property of a monastery in Jerusalem. During a six months' stay in Ethiopia Sandro succeeded in organising the country's aviation.

He remained one of the most outspoken opponents of Anna Anderson's claim to be Grand Duchess Anastasia. In America, where he undertook several lecture tours speaking about spiritualism, he found that the reporters were only interested in 'Anastasia'. *"…I told everyone the same, that I know she is not Anastasia and do not wish to go into details,"* he told Xenia.[15]

Sandro remained devoted to his family and was particularly fond of his grandson Prince Michael Feodorovich. He took the little boy for walks along the beach at Biarritz, he spoke of the waves and of the stars – but he never ever said a word about Russia.

Sandro's first volume of memoirs, *Once a Grand Duke*, was published in 1931. That autumn he returned to Europe after a lecture tour of New York. Shortly afterwards he fell seriously ill with a lung malady. Tuberculosis of the spine was also suspected, although it may have been cancer. During his illness he wrote *Twilight of*

Royalty and *Always a Grand Duke*, the last published posthumously. In the autumn of 1932 he moved to the Villa St Therese at Carnolés in the South of France, the home of Captain Nicholas and Mme Tchirikoff, formerly Olga Vassilievna. She had been with the family in the Crimea and left Russia with Xenia's party. Now she nursed Sandro. In November 1932, as his condition worsened, Xenia arrived. By the New Year he was clearly dying.

On the evening of 25 February Xenia was to be guest of honour at a ball. She left Sandro's bedside at 11 p.m. and Irina kept him company. At 3 a.m. on 26 February he suddenly complained of terrible pains. Irina immediately sent for her mother and the doctor but Xenia arrived too late. He died peacefully at 3.45 a.m.

Despite his wishes, he was given a religious funeral at the small Orthodox Church of Vierge, Joie des Tous les Affligés et St Nicolas le Thaumaturge nearby. He was buried with military honours on 1 March in the cemetery at Roquebrune-Cap-Martin.

Sandro's grandson Michael later described him as one of the most lucid members of the Imperial family – *"but alas, in advance of his time."*[16]

The Other Grand Dukes

THE MIKHAILOVICHI GRAND DUKES

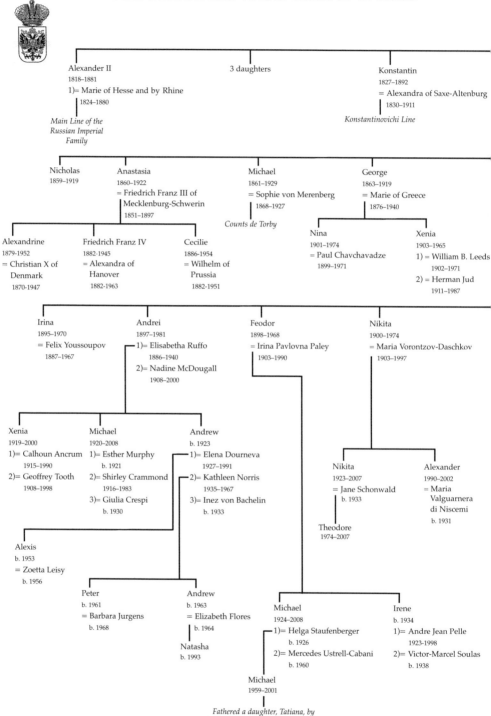

Chapter 7 – Grand Duke Alexander Mikhailovich

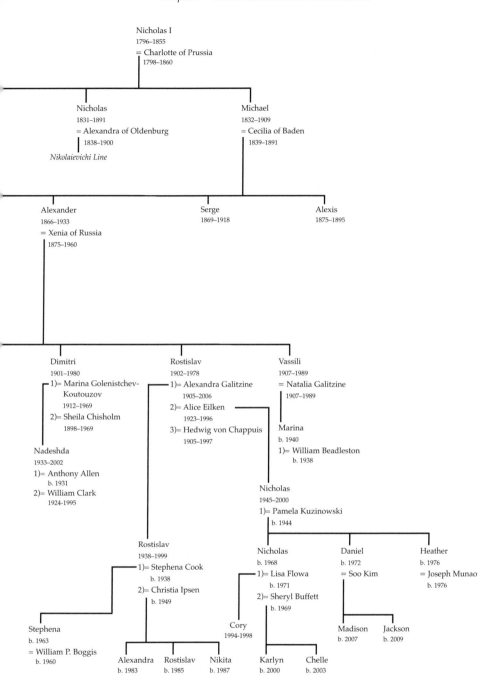

Grand Duke Serge Mikhailovich
(1869-1918)

By Coryne Hall

Serge Mikhailovich is one of the most impenetrable of the Russian Grand Dukes. He never married and his private life remains an enigma. Even his burial place is a mystery.

The fifth son of Grand Duke Michael Nikolaievich was born at Borjomi, his father's estate in the Caucasus, on 25 September/7 October 1869. He shared the same harsh upbringing as his brothers, a barrack regime of hard beds and cold baths coupled with a rigorous training for the army. Under his tutor Colonel Helmerson, Serge developed a *"defeatist, pessimistic, nature."* His favourite saying was *"tant pis!"* (So much the worse!)[1]

In 1880 the family returned to St Petersburg and moved to the enormous New Mikhailovsky Palace, whose halls were so vast that in later years the brothers used bicycles to visit each other. Serge grew up to be tall with blue eyes and blond hair but unfortunately became prematurely bald. Described as *"the least handsome"* of a very good-looking family, he liked mathematics, physics and, much to his father's delight, the artillery. Although he was clever, with a keen sense of the ridiculous, he had a tendency to be moody.[2] A graduate of the Mikhailovsky Artillery School, he joined the Life Guards of the Cavalry Artillery Brigade, becoming an ADC to the Emperor in 1891. He remained close to his brother Alexander (Sandro), sailing with him on a voyage round the world scheduled to last for two years. In Bombay they learnt of their mother's death and, after only nine months away, returned home.

Relations between the brothers cooled in 1894, when Sandro won the hand of their cousin Grand Duchess Xenia Alexandrovna, with whom Serge was in love. Serge was also a close friend of Xenia's brother Tsarevich Nicholas and attended the lively gatherings at the house of Nicholas' mistress, the ballerina Mathilde Kschessinska.

Serge was immensely wealthy. Besides his Grand Ducal allowance of 200,000 rubles a year he received the income from vast personal estates which included a hunting lodge 60 miles from St Petersburg. When Nicholas broke with Mathilde on his betrothal to Princess Alix of Hesse it was the Mikhailovichi Grand Dukes who lent him money to buy the house on the English Prospekt for Mathilde.[3]

Twenty-five-year-old Serge then became Mathilde's protector. Although Serge was devoted to Mathilde, she was not in love with him and *"used him as a tool to get what she wanted."*[4] Serge showered her with jewels and bought her a dacha at Strelna which, thanks to his lavish spending, was soon considered one of the best seaside villas in Europe. He also acted as Mathilde's go-between when she needed something from the Tsar.

As President of the Imperial Theatrical Society, Serge's main aim was to benefit Kschessinska. In 1899 Mathilde was furious when the Director of the Imperial Theatres gave one of her ballets to a guest ballerina. When he refused to reconsider, Serge summoned him, saying that the matter must be considered, *"not with official dryness, but with humanity and heart."*[5] The Director put the reasons for his refusal in writing. In reply he received an incoherent letter from Serge, which ended: *"You write that you answer me after mature deliberation. I, too, did not address myself to you without it. By wronging Matilda Felixovna [sic] you insult me."*[6] A cipher telegram was then sent to the Tsar in Darmstadt. A few days later the Director was ordered to leave the ballet with Kschessinska. This is but one instance of Serge's interference. There were many others.

In 1900 Mathilde fell in love with Grand Duke Andrei Vladimirovich, yet 'all' St Petersburg knew that Serge was sharing Kschessinska's bed. So, by now, was Andrei, and the two men frequently shared her dacha.[7] The ménage à trois became the talk of St Petersburg.

According to Mathilde, during the winter of 1901-02 Serge began *"courting a young and pretty Grand Duchess"* and rumours spread of their eventual marriage. Mathilde selfishly asked him to put an end to this romance, claiming she found the gossip unpleasant.[8] This is a mystery. After Serge's unrequited love for Xenia, his name was only linked with Kschessinska. A more likely explanation is that Mathilde invented the story to show that Andrei was definitely the father of the child she was expecting and that Serge's affections were engaged elsewhere.

In June 1902 a son, Vladimir ('Vova') was born to Mathilde. But who was the father? Prince David Chavchavadze, Serge's great-nephew, said that *"Vladimir claimed in later life that he did not know who was his father, Grand Duke Sergei or Andrew [sic]."*[9] In her memoirs, Mathilde maintained that the child was Andrei's, despite the fact that Serge had been her official 'protector' for the past eight years. Lydia Kyasht stated that the father was Serge. *"That picture of father and son will long linger in my memory',* she wrote after watching them together."*[10] Although both Grand Dukes were at first 'convinced' they were Vova's father, it was Serge who looked after Mathilde and her son. Andrei *"kept a much lower profile."*[11]

The baby received the name and patronymic of Vladimir Sergeievich. Vova's original birth certificate gave Serge as the father and he certainly treated him like his own son. All his life Vova had a sincere attachment to Serge and some sources say that the Grand Duke offered to adopt him.[12]

Although Mathilde kept Serge dangling on a string, it was *"Andrei the Gigolo, the lover of my brother's mistress,"*[13] as Grand Duke Nicholas Mikhailovich called him, who accompanied her when she travelled abroad. Yet the faithful Serge regularly transferred money to pay her expenses. When Mathilde and Andrei were in Cannes in 1905 poor Serge was desolate when she did not return home for Christmas. *"The holidays are getting closer. It is so difficult to spend them without you and Vova,"* he lamented. *"There is not going to be a Christmas tree… This is my favourite holiday and I am crying like a baby."* He instructed his sister Anastasia, who was staying on the Riviera, to send presents from him to Mathilde and Vova.[14]

It has generally been assumed that Serge accepted this ménage à trois, happily vacating the bedroom for Andrei and paying Mathilde's bills when called upon. This may not always have been the case.

In 1908 Countess Barbara Vorontzov-Dashkov gave birth to a son, Alexander, in Switzerland. However, the baby's father was not her husband Count Ivan Vorontzov-Dashkov, who had died in 1898. Alexander's father seems to have been Grand Duke Serge Mikhailovich. Little Alexander was adopted by Sophia von Dehn and brought up in Italy, where her husband Dimitri was naval attaché.[15]

In January 1907 Mathilde moved into a magnificent newly-built mansion on Kronversky Prospekt. Estimates of the cost range from half a million to a million rubles, at a time when one rouble would purchase a gross of eggs. Lydia Kyasht said it was paid for by Grand Duke Serge; while Prince David Chavchavadze said the money came from Andrei.[16]

Rumours of shady financial dealings involving Serge and Mathilde had circulated since the early 1900s. One night in December 1910 the police searched her mansion. According to the wealthy socialite Count Alexis Bobrinsky they found 'secret artillery documents and underground revolutionary literature' in the cellar. She claimed that Serge had placed the artillery contracts in her custody and offered to wake him so that he could confirm her story. The angry Grand Duke corroborated Mathilde's statement but gave no explanation for the presence of the revolutionary literature. *"One version was that Kschessinska had wheedled the documents out of her patron for purposes of selling them to foreign intelligence agents."*[17]

In the years before the First World War, Serge did everything in his power to persuade the Tsar and the government that war with Germany was inevitable. When war was declared in 1914 Serge was confined to bed at his family's Mikhailovskoe dacha near Strelna, with either rheumatic fever or arthritis. In early autumn he returned to the capital where his illness, now complicated by pleurisy, took a very severe form. He spent five months in bed in constant pain before resuming his duties as Inspector General of Artillery.

In the spring of 1915 all Russia's western fortresses, all of Poland and part of Lithuania were lost, together with three million men. The War Minister, General Vladimir Sukhomlinov and the Artillery Department were blamed for the shortage of ammunition. Serge and his brother Sandro *"have not hesitated to say in public that Sukhomlinov is a criminal,"* Grand Duke Andrei recorded in his diary. *"…Maybe it is due to the fact that the war has shown how poorly we are provided with artillery, and Grand Duke Serge is trying to draw attention away from himself and therefore accuses Sukhomlinov? This is quite unjust."*[18]

It was now said that Serge was so far under Kschessinska's influence that he allowed her to meddle in his affairs. The dishonesty and cupidity of the Artillery Department was a common topic of conversation, *"but as a Grand Duke was at its head, no-one dared say a word,"* commented Princess Radziwill.[19] Mathilde was rumoured to be accepting huge bribes from arms contractors and was said to have persuaded Serge to purchase materiél from various friends.

In June 1915 Grand Duke Paul asked, *"whether Serge would be relieved of his post as all are so much against him, right or wrong – and Kschessinska is mixed up again – she behaved like Mme Sukhomlinov it seems with bribes and the Artillery orders…"*[20] Michael Rodzianko, the President of the Duma, considered Serge's appointment a disaster and insisted that his resignation be insisted on. *"…the thieving gang operating under cover of the Grand Duke's name must be got rid of,"* he added.[21]

Serge was away, receiving painful treatment for his illness. A special commission investigated the Artillery Department and in January 1916 Serge 'resigned' on the grounds of ill health. He was ordered to Stavka as Field Inspector-General of Artillery where, although he had daily contact with the Tsar, he seems to have done little more than grow a vegetable garden. The scandal over the bribes had not died down and in private letters Serge became more cautious in an attempt to distance himself from Kschessinska, who, his brother Nicholas Mikhailovich warned him, had used him *"in her quest for financial profit."*[22]

Soon it was rumoured that a scheme was being drafted at Stavka *"for the establishment of a dictatorship in the rear to deal with all matters concerning internal government and war supplies"* and that Serge would be dictator. Rodzianko was appalled, seeing the appointment of the Grand Duke as *"tantamount to the ruin of the whole war supply organisation."* Rodzianko added that if the Grand Duke did not cease his intrigues in the sphere of munitions supplies, his activities would be exposed in the Duma. *"I have more than sufficient evidence concerning them in my possession."*²³

By September 1916 Sukhomlinov was under arrest, facing charges of peculation and treason against the State. *"Why should he* [Sukhomlinov] *suffer and not... Serge who on account of her* [Kschessinska] *has just as much fault,"* the Empress complained in December.²⁴

Under the Empress' government the situation was going from bad to worse and by the end of 1916 Serge could see that revolution was coming. His *"meticulous mathematical mind was never engaged in guesswork,"* recalled Sandro.²⁵

Revolution came in February 1917. After the Tsar's abdication Serge remained at Stavka in 'voluntary exile' on the advice of his brother Nicholas, because of the *"cloud of corruption that hung over him as a result of the Kschessinska scandals."*²⁶

Early in March Serge received a letter from Nicholas Mikhailovich demanding he break off all relations with Mathilde and make no attempt to see her or Vova again. Serge refused, unable to contemplate life without Malechka, who had *"provided him with a substitute of family life."* Serge was distressed that his brother had not helped Mathilde when she had to flee from the mob. *"I thought I could count on your friendship, and... your support....,"* he wrote. *"What a terrible disappointment for my brotherly feelings... I really do not know what to think."*²⁷

Nicholas had spared nothing when telling Serge what he thought of Mathilde. Serge came to her defence. He would not abandon his civil wife, yet his main concern was for Vova, who he still called his son. He had always been upright and honest and insisted he would remain that way.²⁸

On 20 March all court property was transferred to the State. The Romanovs now ceased to receive their incomes from the Imperial Appanages. A civil list was to be drawn up – one report estimated 30,000 rubles a year for Grand Dukes.²⁹ Serge's income in 1917 was 280,000 rubles a year, plus revenue from his estates. He complained that he would *"now have only 41,000* [rubles]*."*³⁰

Serge returned to Petrograd at the beginning of June, wearing unaccustomed civilian clothes. Soon afterwards he proposed to Mathilde. She refused. He moved into the New Mikhailovsky Palace with his brother Nicholas but spent a lot of time with Kschessinska. They urgently needed to calculate their budget and make plans for the future. Serge estimated their loss as at least half a million rubles, *"maybe even more."*³¹ The most urgent matter was Mathilde's mansion, still in the possession of the Bolsheviks. On 5 June Serge, Mathilde's lawyer and a squadron of loyal cavalry went to evict them by force. The matter went to armed conflict but after negotiations the mansion was left to the Bolsheviks.³²

Early in July the Bolsheviks very nearly pulled off a successful coup and Mathilde decided to take Vova to join Andrei in the Caucasus. Serge refused to go, believing that a sudden exodus of Grand Dukes would endanger the lives of the Tsar and his family. On 13 July Serge went to the Nicholas Station to say goodbye. The parting was meant to be temporary.

Serge remained at the New Mikhailovsky Palace, concentrating his efforts on regaining Mathilde's property. Her letters begged him to leave but, despite an offer from Count Cheremetev to let him stay in his Kislovodsk house, Serge refused. In October Mathilde's stage partner Pierre Vladimirov obtained a permit for Serge to leave for Finland, but there was no mention of his manservant and secretary Feodor

Remez, who had joined his service in 1905.[33] The Grand Duke was ill and unable to travel alone. He remained in Petrograd and by the time he had dealt with all Mathilde's affairs it was too late. The Bolshevik take-over in October removed any hope Serge may have had of leaving.

In March 1918 all the Romanov males were ordered to register with the Cheka. On 4 April Serge and Remez were sent into exile. A train journey of two days and two nights took them east to Viatka, a small town barely touched by the revolution. With them went Princes Ioann, Konstantin and Igor Konstantinovich, Ioann's wife Princess Elena (going of her own free will) and Prince Vladimir Paley, 21-year-old son of Grand Duke Paul's morganatic marriage. They were allowed to find their own lodgings and the townspeople gave them gifts and prepared meals.

Eleven days later they were moved to Ekaterinburg, where they arrived on 3 May and were lodged in an hotel. As it was Holy Week they were allowed to attend religious services. Soon they were joined by the Empress' sister Grand Duchess Elisabeth Feodorovna, sent from her Moscow convent with two of her nuns.

The Bolsheviks soon decided that it was inadvisable to have so many Romanovs living near the Tsar, who was imprisoned in the Ipatiev House. Serge and his relatives were moved 120 miles north-east to Alapaievsk.

After a twelve hour train journey, they were taken to the Napolnaya School, a red brick building on the outskirts of town. The place was dirty and they spent the first night on benches, until beds arrived. Serge shared a room with Vladimir Paley. It became the communal dining room, where their cook Alexandra Krivovna served meals. At first they were allowed to walk into town, plant vegetables and talk to the children who came to play football with the younger princes. On Sundays they attended church. The evenings were passed reading Russian novels delivered from the local library. Serge was in severe pain from rheumatism and a doctor came to look after him.

Serge became close to Vladimir Paley, a talented poet and playwright. *"What a beautiful soul, what intelligence, what a memory, what culture!"* Vladimir wrote to his family. *"…He talks quite openly with me and I know now that this man, who outwardly is so cold and haughty, is a man of tender heart and that all his life has been profoundly unhappy."*[34]

Serge also chatted to the guards, giving his views on equality and the impossibility of equal land distribution. Some were friendly and sympathetic, others were coarse and enjoyed bursting into the rooms in the middle of the night to conduct 'searches'. Although Serge protested, no notice was taken.

Princess Elena, worried about her children, returned to Petrograd. Soon afterwards, on the night of 12 June, Grand Duke Michael Alexandrovich disappeared from Perm. Rumours of his "escape" (he had been murdered) were now used as an excuse to impose a more severe regime at Alapaievsk. A barbed wire fence was erected, they were put on soldier's rations, and the excursions and games of football were stopped. Their belongings were confiscated and they were forbidden to write letters.

On 21 June Serge sent a telegram to the head of the Ekaterinburg Soviet asking for the lifting of the prison regime, as they had done nothing wrong. It had no effect but their servants were permitted to leave. Remez chose to share Serge's fate and Sister Barbara remained with Grand Duchess Elisabeth.

As the White army closed in the Bolsheviks decided to act. During the afternoon of 17 July the guards were replaced by Bolshevik workers from Ekaterinburg, who took the prisoners' remaining money and told them they would be transferred that night to the Verkhne-Sinyachikhensky works about 10 miles away. After a hurried supper the prisoners were blindfolded and put into carts outside with their hands tied behind their backs. When Serge barricaded himself behind a cupboard one of the guards shot him in the arm. He offered no further resistance. As the carts rumbled out of town, Serge repeated that he knew they were going to die. *"Tell me why?"* he asked. *"I have never been involved in politics. I loved sport, played billiards…. was interested in numismatics…"*[35]

At about one o'clock in the morning of 18 July, Serge's name day, the carts approached Sinyachikha, where the prisoners were made to walk several hundred yards to the disused Nizhny Seliminsky mineshaft. There they were hit on the head with blunt instruments before being thrown down the mineshaft. Serge resisted and was shot in the head. It was officially announced that the prisoners had been *"abducted."*[36]

When the White Army entered Alapaievsk on 25 September excavations began at Sinyachikha and the bodies were brought up. All were washed, placed in coffins and taken to St Sergius Cathedral where funeral services were held before they were placed in the crypt.

The saga did not end there. As the Bolsheviks advanced in July 1919, Father Seraphim moved the eight coffins by train to Chita in the Far East. They remained in the Holy Protection Convent until February 1920, when for safety they were moved by rail via Harbin. In April they reached Peking but it was forbidden to bring dead bodies into the city. The coffins were taken to the Russian Spiritual Mission and placed in the crypt of the St Seraphim of Sarov chapel in the Russian cemetery outside the city's north gate. The bodies of Grand Duchess Elisabeth and Sister Barbara were later taken to Jerusalem. During the Japanese invasion of 1938, the coffins were transferred to the All Saints' Martyrs Chapel in the Mission's cemetery, then moved back to St Seraphim's in 1947. After the Chinese Communists seized power in 1949 this territory was handed over to the Soviet Union. In 1954 the churches were destroyed to make way for a new Russian Embassy and the coffins were transferred to the Russian cemetery. This was destroyed in 1988 to make way for a park.[37]

During recent excavations a bronze tablet bearing Serge's name was apparently found. Latest research indicates that the Grand Duke's final resting place is probably underneath the golf course.[38]

Grand Duke Alexis Mikhailovich
(1875-1895)

By Arturo E. Beéche

Loss of life always brings much sadness, particularly when it is one still in the flower of youth. And yet, at times, even young life brought to an end is more deliverance than tragedy. Such is the case of Grand Duke Alexis Mikhailovich, youngest of the Mikhailovichi sons. He was born in Tiflis on 28 December 1875, last of the "Caucasian" grand dukes. The child, described by one author as an *"after thought,"* arrived *"when his mother was nearly forty."*[1] By the time of Alexis' arrival, Olga Feodorovna was thirty-six, while her husband had already celebrated his forty-third birthday. The boy was sixteen years junior to his eldest brother, Nicholas Mikhailovich. As the baby of the family, Alexis is said to have received much attention from doting parents and solicitous siblings.

In his memoirs, *Once a Grand Duke*, Alexander Mikhailovich remembered his brother's birth as one of the events in a year that marked, *"a significant date in my childhood: my brother Alexis was born shortly after Christmas, and I met two persons who were destined to become my lifelong friends."*[2] Perhaps keeping with the Victorian approach to the facts of life, Alexander also recalled that his parents, *"took all possible precautions to conceal from us the real circumstances accompanying the birth of a child. We were expected to combine a thorough knowledge of modern artillery with a sincere belief in the stork."*[3] Given the sexual shenanigans and exploits that Sandro and some of his close male relations were involved in later in life, one can see, perhaps, why the circumspection coming from his parents concerning certain, private matters.

Raised away from the oppressive court atmosphere of St Petersburg, with its adulation and sycophancy, the Mikhailovichi were raised alongside barrack-like and very strict guidelines. Someone who had contact with Michael Nikolaievich's children remembered them as *"exceedingly friendly toward nonaristocratic"* people.[4] Francis Vogel, the director of the coach line that transported the Mikhailovichi during their many years in the Caucasus, also said that Michael Nikolaievich and his sons, he *"learned to have an altogether different view"* of the Romanovs. *"Friendliness and affability itself,"* were terms Vogel thought of when reminiscing about these grand dukes. Furthermore, Vogel concluded, *"if everyone of them* [the Romanov's] *subjects felt toward them as he, a foreigner, did, there would not* (be) *a disloyal subject in all of Russia."*[5]

Perhaps this affability, a natural and unaffected approach to others, is what made Alexis become such a popular cousin within the Imperial Family. Because of his age, the young Mikhailovichi naturally fit in with the second group of Alexander III's children, Grand Duchess Xenia and Grand Duke Michael Alexandrovich, being tied to both by strong bonds of friendship. Tsar Alexander III is said to have been very fond of Alexis. The Tsar, *"took an interest in him and suggested that he come to him with any marital questions."*[6] Offering this fatherly advice, Alexander III, must have thought, could prevent the boy from making the mistakes that his "cretin" older brother Michael Mikhailovich had made.[7]

Alexis' siblings were permitted to see their newborn brother two days after *"the Almighty deemed it necessary to send another son to Their Imperial Highnesses."*[8] Alexis was destined to enter a realm in which, at least by the accounting of one of his brothers, the child must be the object of *"sympathy…I hoped for his sake that by the time he grew up, all our teachers would have passed out of existence."* Furthermore, Alexander Mikhailovich said *"looking at the wrinkled reddish face of the baby, I felt distinct pity."*[9]

In spite of the unaffected environment in which Alexis was raised, the birth of a grand duke demanded a degree of pomp and ceremony. In Alexis' case, his first contact with the power within the hands of his family was provided by his baptism, which took place three weeks after his birth. *"The ceremony of baptism took place three weeks later and was preceded by a mammoth parade of the garrison,"* recalled Alexander Mikhailovich. In the background imperial music played and the crowds cheered, while a lady-in-waiting carried the baby to a ceremony that, according to Orthodox tradition, his parents could not attend. *"Poor Alexis rested quietly on a silk cushion, kin his long white-lace robe, with a blue ribbon of St Andrew – the highest decoration in Russia – attached to his tiny breast. The touch of cold water made him shriek at the top of his voice."*[10]

Not many images of Alexis have survived through the turbulent times since his birth. One in particular, shows a strapping, tallish young man with well-proportioned ears, a high forehead, sensitive blue eyes and an exquisitely shaped nose and mouth. He was tall, thin and cut a striking figure in uniform. Yet, within the beauty of his outside body was concealed an illness that would bring his life to an early life.

Alexander Mikhailovich described his brother as *"a brilliant boy of liberal heart and absolute sincerity,"* who also happened to *"suffer acutely in the atmosphere of the palace."*[11] another contemporary with uncanny insight into the Romanov dynasty, recalled Alexis as *"an intelligent especially dear child,"* who unfortunately was influenced negatively by contact with some family members, *"especially the elder Nicholas,"* who somehow *"was ruining his character."*[12]

Grand Duke Kirill Vladimirovich, a contemporary of Alexis Mikhailovich, also had many reminiscences of his cousin. They were born months apart; both boys were destined to serve in the Imperial Navy. During a holiday with Tsar Alexander III and his family, who were vacationing in the Gulf of Finland, Kirill and Alexis engaged in a friendly sailing race. *"I spent two delightful days with them, and had, to use the schoolboy expression, a real treat. Uncle Sasha* (Alexander III) *arranged a boat race for cousins Misha* (Michael Alexandrovich), *Alexey Mikhailovich, and myself,"* Kirill remembered. Furthermore, *"The race was to be rowed in dinghies, one dinghy to each of us with naval officers at the tillers. I won easily by several lengths, and on our return to the yacht received a handsome prize from Uncle Sasha."*[13]

It was to be the last time that Kirill saw his Mikhailovichi cousin, for soon after that Alexis' illness forced the boy to be taken from Russia. Kirill remembered that the circumstances leading to the boy's death were *"interesting,"* and had much to do with parental stubbornness. Alexis was finishing his naval training when his health gave way. *"he was of delicate health, and when he caught a chill it was suggested to his father…that he should interrupt his course of training to get over his illness,"* Kirill said.[14] Unfortunately, Grand Duke Michael Nikolaievich seems to have ignored better advise and would not consider an interruption of Alexis' training. Consequently, Alexis' chill took a turn for the worst and by then little could be done to save the boy's life.

Symptoms of the illness responsible for bringing an early end to Alexis' promising life first became apparent as the family mourned the loss of Grand Duchess Olga Feodorovna. Alexis, as was mentioned in a separate chapter, lost his mother in 1891. By then the early signs of tuberculosis must have been present inside the young man's body. What was believed to be a chill, turned out far worse. When the illness turned virulent, Alexis Mikhailovich was sent to warmer climates, as it was believed that a change in temperature would accelerate his recovery, or perhaps cure him of such a dreaded disease. San Remo, on Italy's Mediterranean coast, and just some thirty-five miles up the road from Nice, where so many Romanovs had residences, was thought to enjoy a climate propitious for combating tuberculosis. Desolately, it was not to have a curing effect on Alexis' illness. He died in San Remo on 2 March 1895.[15]

Alexis' body was taken to Russia by sea. From Kronstadt the coffin reached St Petersburg by train. His brother Serge Mikhailovich, apparently, was in charge of organizing the funeral, *"which featured military units everywhere, especially those featuring the artillery."*[16] Kirill recalled, somewhat forlornly that *"the first time he wore his midshipman's uniform was in his coffin."*[17] Grand Duke Alexander Mikhailovich's parting words concerning the death of his brother were most telling, *"Although attached to him stronger than to any other member of my family, I never regretted his passing away ... he suffered acutely in the atmosphere of the palace."*[18]

In a letter she wrote to her daughter Crown Princess Marie of Romania, Grand Duchess Marie Alexandrovna remembered her first cousin Alexis' brief passing through life, *"My poor cousin Alexis is who is dead. So young and I am afraid not much regretted."*[19]

Sad as Alexis Mikhailovich's early death was, perhaps it also provided a silver lining. At least it spared this young boy of a far more harrowing end, like the one suffered by three of his brothers.

End Notes

Chapter 1

Grand Duke Kirill Vladimirovich

1. *Almanach de Gotha 1878* (Justus Perthes, Gotha), p. 68.
2. Kirill, Grand Duke of Russia. *My Life in Russia's Service Then and Now.*(Selwyn & Blount, 1939), p. 38.
3. Ibid., p. 31.
4. Ibid., p. 53.
5. Ibid., p. 54.
6. Ibid.
7. Ibid., p. 56-57.
8. Ibid., p. 63.
9. Ibid., p. 62.
10. Ibid., p. 69.
11. *Almanach de Gotha 1880* (Justus Perthes, Gotha), p. 30.
12. *The New York Times*, March 31, 1899.
13. Kirill, p. 112.
14. Bülow, Prince Bernhard von, *Memoirs 1897-1903* (Putnam, 1931), p. 483.
15. Kiste, John van der & Coryne Hall. *Once a Grand Duchess – Xenia Sister of Nicholas II.* (Sutton Publishing, 2002), pp. 52-53.
16. Kirill, p. 123.
17. Ibid., p. 80.
18. Ibid., p. 152.
19. Sagrera, Ana de. *Ena y Bee – En defensa de una amistad.* (Velecío Editores, 2006), p. 110.
20. Ibid.
21. Ibid.
22. Ibid., pp. 110-110.
23. Bing, Edward J. (ed.), *The letters of Tsar Nicholas and Empress Marie* (Ivor Nicholson & Watson, 1937), 157-8.
24. Sagrera., p. 118.
25. *The New York Times*, 28 February 1904.
26. *The New York Times*, 21 April 1904.
27. *The New York Times*, 14 May 1904.
28. Kirill, p. 174.
29. Ibid., p. 169.
30. Ibid., p. 174.
31. Bing, pp. 187-188.
32. Kirill, p. 175.
33. Ibid., p. 181.
34. *The New York Times*, 30 July 1905.
35. Kirill, p. 183.
36. . Bülow, *Memoirs 1903-9* (Putnam, 1931), pp. 168-170.
37. Kleinpenning, Petra H. (ed.) *The Correspondence of the Empress Alexandra of Russia with Ernst Ludwig and Eleonore Grand Duke and Duchess of Hersse* (Books on demand, 2010), pp. 284-285.
38. Kiril, p. 184.
39. Previously unknown letter written by Grand Duchess Maria Pavlovna to her daughter Grand Duchess Helen Vladimirovna (Tsarskoe Selo, 16 January 1907) – Imperial Russia File, Eurohistory Archive.
40. Kirill., p. 185.
41. Ibid.
42. Ibid., p. 189.
43. Previously unknown letter written by Grand Duchess Maria Alexandrovna to her daughter Fürstin Alexandra of Hohenlohe-Langenburg (St Petersburg, 27 May 1913) – Imperial Russia File, Eurohistory Archive.
44. Kirill, p. 193.
45. *The New York Times*, 18 December 1910.
46. *The New York Times*, 23 July 1913.
47. Kirill, pp. 194-195.
48. Previously unknown letter written by Grand Duchess Victoria Feodorovna to her sister-in-law Grand Duchess Helen Vladimirovna (Tsarskoe Selo, 21 December 1914) – Imperial Russia File, Eurohistory Archive.
49. Ibid.
50. Ibid.
51. Previously unknown letter written by Grand Duchess Victoria Feodorovna to her sister-in-law Grand Duchess Helen Vladimirovna (Tsarskoe Selo, 31 July 1915) – Imperial Russia File, Eurohistory Archive.
52. Previously unknown letter written by Grand Duchess Victoria Feodorovna to her sister-in-law Grand Duchess Helen Vladimirovna (Tsarskoe Selo, 30 April 1916) – Imperial Russia File, Eurohistory Archive.
53. Ibid.
54. Paléologue, Maurice. *An Ambassador's memoirs* (Hutchinson, 1923-5), III, 232.
55. Vorres, Ian. *The Last Grand Duchess – Her Imperial Higness Grand Duchess Olga Alexandrovna* (Charles Scribner's Sons, 1964). p. 185.
56. Van der Kiste. *Princess Victoria Melita* (Sutton, 1991), p. 137.
57. Hall, Coryne. *Little Mother of Russia* (Shepheard-Walwyn, 1999), p. 339.
58. http://www.angelfire.com/realm/gotha/gotha/leiningen.html
59. Beéche, Arturo E. & David McIntosh. *In Memoriam.... Prince Louis Ferdinand of Prussia & Grand Duchess Kira of Russia* (Eurohistory, 2005), p. 15.
60. *The New York Times*, 9 April 1931.
61. *The New York Times*, 30 December 1937.
62. *The New York Times*, 4 May 1938.
63. Vorres, p. 182.
64. Pakula, Hannah. *The last Romantic* (Weidenfeld & Nicolson, 1985), p. 392.
65. *The New York Times*, 3 March 1936.
66. Van der Kiste, p. 177.
67. *The New York Times*, 13 October 1938.

Grand Duke Boris Vladimirovich

1. Elsberry, Terence. *Marie of Romania..* (Cassell, 1973), p. 59.
2. Pakula, pp. 107-108.
3. Gelardi, Julia. *Born to Rule.* (St Martin's Press. 2004), p. 92.
4. Elsberry, p. 59; Pakula, p. 411.
5. Perry, John Curtis & Pleshakov, Constantine. *Flight of the Romanovs.* (Basic Books, 1999), pp. 126 & 265.
6. Ibid., p. 70.

7. Kirill, pp. 124-127; Perry & Pleshakov, p. 71.
8. Kirill, p. 170.
9. Noel, Gerard. *Ena. Spain's English Queen.* (Constable, 1984), pp. 22-23.
10. Ferrand, Jacques. *Descendances Naturelles des Souverains et Grands-Ducs de Russie de 1762 à 1910.* (Paris, 1995), p. 408.
11. Chavchavadze, Prince David. *The Grand Dukes.* (Atlantic International Publications, 1990), pp. 235-236.
12. Perry & Pleshakov, p 126.
13. Fuhrmann, Joseph T (ed). *The Complete Wartime Correspondence of Tsar Nicholas II and the Empress Alexandra.* (Greenwood Press, 1999), p. 388.
14. Paleologue, Maurice. *An Ambassador's Memoirs.* Vol 2. (Hutchinson, 1924), p. 78; Dobson, Christopher. *Prince Felix Yusupov. The Man Who Murdered Rasputin.* (Harrap, 1989), p. 119.
15. Anonymous. *The Russian Diary of an Englishman.* (Robert M. McBride, New York, 1919), p. 90.
16. Ibid., p. 139.
17. Beal, Erica. *Royal Cavalcade.* (Stanley Paul. 1939), p. 347.
18. Dobson, pp. 118-119.
19. Perry & Pleshakov, pp. 265 & 341.
20. Ibid., pp. 265-256.
21. Hall, Coryne. *Imperial Dancer: Mathilde Kschessinska and the Romanovs.* (Sutton Publishing, Stroud. 2005), p 217.
22. Crawford, Rosemary & Donald. *Michael & Natasha.* (Weidenfeld & Nicolson, 1997) [hereafter M&N],p. 30; Hall, p. 248.

Grand Duke Andrei Vladimirovich

1. Kurth, Peter. *Anastasia: The Life of Anna Anderson.* (Johnathan Cape, 1983), p. 164; Chavchavadze, p. 241.
2. Chavchavadze, p. 241
3. Ibid., p. 242.
4. Fuhrmann, p. 424.
5. Andrei's diary, 21 Dec 1916. In Atlantis, vol 5 no. 1.
6. Diary, 4 March 1917. Ibid.
7. Kurth, p. 114.
8. Kurth, p. 146
9. Kurth, pp. 369-370 & 205-206.
10. Kurth, pp. 277, 231 & 337.
11. Summers, Anthony & Tom Mangold. *The File on the Tsar.* (Gollancz, 1977), paperback edition., p. 355.

Chapter 2

Grand Duke Vladimir Kirillovich

1. Kirill, p. 204.
2. Ibid., p. 212.
3. Ibid., p. 213.
4. *Almanach de Gotha 1926* (Justus Perthes, Gotha), p. 102.
5. Ibid.
6. Ibid., p. 112.
7. Fenyvesi, Charles. *Splendor in Exile - The Ex-Majesties of Europe.* (New Republic Books, 1979). p. 253.
8. Kirill, p. 240.
9. Sagrera, p. 389.
10. Kirill, pp. 243-244.
11. Perrys & Pleshakov, p. 318.

12. Ibid., p. 319.
13. Leonida, Grand Duchess of Russia. *Chaque matin est une grâce.* (JC Lattès, 2000), p. 190.
14. Fenyvesi, p. 257.
15. Enache, Nicolas. *La Descendance de Pierre le Grand, Tsar de Russie* (Sedopolis, 1983), p. 162.
16. Leonida, p. 175.
17. Ibid., p. 176.
18. Ibid.
19. Sagrera, p. 484.
20. Ibid.
21. Beéche & McIntosh, *Louis Ferdinand...*, pp. 34-35.
22. Leonida, p. 215.
23. Ibid.
24. Sagrera, p. 483.
25. Fenyvesi, p. 261.
26. Curley, Walter J.P. Jr. *Monarchs-in-Waiting* (Dodd, Mead and Company, 1973), pp. 81-82.
27. Ibid.
28. http://www.angelfire.com/realm/gotha/gotha/prussia.html
29. Ibid.
30. Leonida, p. 247.
31. Ibid., p. 248.
32. Ibid., p. 249.
33. Mateos Sainz de Medrano, Ricardo. *La familia de la reina Sofía* (Esfera de los Libros, 2004), p. 462.
34. *Royalty Digest*, Volume 1, p. 360.
35. Leonida, pp. 269-270.
36. Ibid., p. 270.
37. *The New York Times*, 30 April 1992.
38. Ibid.
39. http://www.imperialhouse.ru
40. Fenyvesi, p. 259.
41. Arturo E. Beéche, *Obituary: Grand Duchess Leonida of Russia (1914-2010),* The European Royal History Journal, Issue LXXV (June 2010), p.15.

Chapter 3

Grand Duke George Mikhailovich

1. http://www.imperialhouse.ru/eng/imperialhouse/chipdom/georgiy.html
2. http://en.wikipedia.org/wiki/Grand_Duke_George_Mikhailovich_of_Russia
3. Massie, Robert K. *The Romanovs – The Final Chapter.* (Random House, New York, 1995), p. 270.
4. Leonida, p. 248.
5. Ibid., p. 249.
6. Massie, p. 270.
7. Tash, Edwina, *A Royal Wedding in Potsdam,* The European Royal History Journal, Issue LXXXII (August 2011), pp. 19-22.
8. Leonida, p. 277.
9. Ibid., pp. 278-279.
10. Ibid.
11. Ibid., p. 278.
12. Ibid.
13. http://www.imperialhouse.ru/eng/imperialhouse/chipdom/georgiy.html
14. Beéche, Arturo E. T*he Passing of An Era – The Death of Madame, the Countess of Paris,* The European Royal History Journal, Issue XXXIV (August 2003), pp. 3-8.

Chapter 4

Grand Duke Dimitri Pavlovich

1. Russia, Grand Duchess Marie of. *Education of a Princess* (Viking Press, New York, 1931), pp. 9–10, 11, 32.
2. The Glitter and the Gold [hereafter Glitter], pp. 163–164.
3. Once a Grand Duke [hereafter OGD], p. 139.
4. Before the Storm, p. 189.
5. M&N, p. 175.
6. A Lifelong Passion, p. 471.
7. M&N, p. 248.
8. Diary of a Diplomat in Russia, p. 29.
9. EoP, p. 263.
10. Ibid., p. 266.
11. OGD, p. 277.
12. EoP, p. 277.
13. Glitter, pp. 201–01
14. Always a Grand Duke, p. 124.
15. This King Business, pp. 5–7.
16. Ibid., pp. 12–23.
17. In Search of Complications, pp. 303–305.

Chapter 5

Grand Duke Nicholas Konstantinovich

1. Konstantin Nikolaievich and Alexander II, p. 17.
2. Kleinmichel, pp. 63-64.
3. Kleinmichel, p. 64.
4. Kleinmichel, p. 65.
5. Konstantin Nikolaievich and Alexander II, p. 19.
6. Konstantin Nikolaievich and Alexander II, p. 17.
7. Kleinmichel, p. 65.
8. See numerous letters from Grand Duke Nicholas Konstantinovich to Henrietta Blackford, 1873-74, in RGIA, F. 435, Op. 1.
9. See numerous letters from Grand Duke Nicholas Konstantinovich to Henrietta Blackford, 1873-74, in RGIA, F. 435, Op. 1.
10. Brayley-Hodgetts, 2:143.
11. Naryshkin-Kurakin, p. 98.
12. Private information.
13. Blackford, pp. 51-54.
14. Chavchavadze, p. 138.
15. *Philadelphia Public Ledger* and *Daily Transcript*, March 31, 1847.
16. Smylie, p. 2
17. PHS, Record Group 317, Box 1, Folder 3, Legal Papers, the Carswell Estate and Property in Missouri, 1836.
18. Virtual American Biographies, at www.famousamericans.net; "Blackford Research Report," compiled for the authors by Stephanie Hoover, 2005.
19. Beach, p. 300; 1880 US Census Records, in NA.
20. Blackford, p. 17.
21. Ibid., p. 12.
22. Philadelphia Public Ledger and Daily Transcript, April 22, 1864.
23. Beach, 421; 1870 US Census Records, in National Archives.
24. Syracuse Herald, August 3, 1937.
25. The Constitution, Atlanta, Georgia, March 22, 1876.
26. "Fanny Lear," Notes by Alexandre Tarsaidze, 8, in Hoover Institution of War, Revolution and Peace, Papers of Alexandre Tarsaidze, Box 7, Folder 24.
27. The Constitution, Atlanta, Georgia, March 22, 1876.
28. "Fanny Lear," Notes by Alexandre Tarsaidze, 5, in HI, Papers of Alexandre Tarsaidze, Box 7, Folder 24.
29. Blackford, p. 21.
30. "Fanny Lear," Notes by Alexandre Tarsaidze, 2, 8-9, in HI, Papers of Alexandre Tarsaidze, Box 7, Folder 24.
31. Blackford, 47.
32. Ibid., p. 48.
33. Ibid.
34. Ibid.
35. Ibid., p. 49.
36. Ibid., p. 50.
37. Ibid.
38. Ibid.
39. Ibid., p. 55.
40. Ibid.
41. Ibid.
42. Ibid., pp. 79-92.
43. Ibid., pp. 63-67.
44. Tarsaidze, Czars and Presidents, 316-17.
45. Blackford, pp. 104-105.
46. Grand Duke Nicholas Konstantinovich to Henrietta Blackford, undated letter, in RGIA, F. 435, Op. 1, D. 2.
47. Blackford, p. 118.
48. Ibid., pp. 125-131.
49. Ibid., pp. 149.
50. Ibid., p. 164.
51. Grand Duke Nicholas Konstantinovich to Henrietta Blackford, undated letter, 1873, in RGIA, F. 435, Op. 1, D. 2.
52. Blackford, p. 190.
53. Ibid., p. 186.
54. Ibid., p. 206.
55. Ibid., p. 207.
56. Grand Duke Nicholas Konstantinovich to Henrietta Blackford, undated letter of summer 1873, in RGIA, F. 435, Op. 1, D. 2.
57. Blackford, pp. 270-271.
58. Blackford, pp. 275-277.
59. Kleinmichel, pp. 65-66; Private Information to Penny Wilson and Greg King.
60. Tarsaidze, Czars and Presidents, pp. 316-17.
61. Grand Duke Konstantin Nikolaievich, Diary, April 12/24, 1874, in Radzinsky, p. 245.
62. Blackford, pp. 283-84.
63. Ibid., p. 284.
64. See Eugene Schuyler, Dispatch No. 61 from the Legation of the United States in St Petersburg, December 29, 1874, to the United States Department of State, Washington, D. C., File Microcopies of Records in the National Archives, Washington DC; #77, Roll 137, Diplomatic Instructions of the Department of State, 1801-1906, RUSSIA Volume 15, January 1, 1865-March 9, 1877.
65. Kleinmichel, p. 67.
66. Grand Duke Konstantin Nikolaievich, Diary, April 15/27, 1874, in Radzinsky, p. 245.
67. Blackford, p. 287.
68. Ibid., p. 291.
69. Ibid., pp. 293-294.
70. Ibid., p. 297.
71. Ibid., p. 299.
72. National Archives, Washington DC; Microcopy 35,

Dispatches from United States Ministers to Russia, 1808-1906, Roll 26, Volume 26. April 3-September 24, 1874. Dispatch #69 dated 4 May 1874 from Marshall Jewell, the American Ambassador to Hamilton Fish, Secretary of State.
73. National Archives, Washington DC; Microcopy 35, Dispatches from United States Ministers to Russia, 1808-1906, Roll 26, Volume 26. April 3-September 24, 1874. Enclosure "A" to Dispatch #69 dated 4 May 1874 from Marshall Jewell, the American Ambassador to Hamilton Fish, Secretary of State.
74. National Archives, Washington DC; Microcopy 35, Dispatches from United States Ministers to Russia, 1808-1906, Roll 26, Volume 26. April 3-September 24, 1874. Enclosure "B" to Dispatch #69 dated 4 May 1874 from Marshall Jewell, the American Ambassador to Hamilton Fish, Secretary of State.
75. National Archives, Washington DC; Microcopy 35, Dispatches from United States Ministers to Russia, 1808-1906, Roll 26, Volume 26. April 3-September 24, 1874. Dispatch #69 dated 4 May 1874 from Marshall Jewell, the American Ambassador to Hamilton Fish, Secretary of State..
76. National Archives, Washington DC; Microcopy 35, Dispatches from United States Ministers to Russia, 1808-1906, Roll 26, Volume 26. April 3-September 24, 1874. Dispatch #69 dated 4 May 1874 from Marshall Jewell, the American Ambassador to Hamilton Fish, Secretary of State.
77. National Archives, Washington DC; Microcopy 35, Dispatches from United States Ministers to Russia, 1808-1906, Roll 26, Volume 26. April 3-September 24, 1874. Dispatch #69 dated 4 May 1874 from Marshall Jewell, the American Ambassador to Hamilton Fish, Secretary of State.
78. National Archives, Washington DC; Microcopy 35, Dispatches from United States Ministers to Russia, 1808-1906, Roll 26, Volume 26. April 3-September 24, 1874. Dispatch #69 dated 4 May 1874 from Marshall Jewell, the American Ambassador to Hamilton Fish, Secretary of State.
79. Blackford, pp. 309-12.
80. Ibid., p. 327.
81. Ibid., p. 328.
82. Kane and Leclerc, V.
83. Tarsaidze, Katia, p. 165.
84. Eugene Schuyler, Dispatch No. 61 from the Legation of the United States in St Petersburg, December 29, 1874, to the United States Department of State, Washington, D. C. File Microcopies of Records in the National Archives, Washington DC; #77, Roll 137, Diplomatic Instructions of the Department of State, 1801-1906, RUSSIA Volume 15, January 1, 1865-March 9, 1877.
85. Tarsaidze, Katia, p. 165.
86. Grand Duke Konstantin Nikolaievich, Diary, April 18/30, 1874, in Radzinsky, p. 246.
87. RGIA, F. 435, Op. 1, D. 5, report dated May 30, 1874.
88. RGIA, F. 435, Op. 1, D. 141, report of August 12, 1874; RGIA, F. 475, Op. 66, D. 675.
89. Witte pp. 224-25; Poliakoff, p. 87.
90. RGIA, F. 1405, Op. 539, D. 89, Memorandum from Minister of the Imperial Court Count V. A. Adlerberg to the Minister of Justice, September 12, 1874.
91. RGIA, F. 472, Op. 23, D. 68, report dated December 11, 1874; RGIA, F. 472, Op. 23, D. 6, Memorandum from Minister of the Imperial Court Count V. A. Adlerberg, December 9, 1874.

92. Kleinmichel, pp. 66.
93. Eugene Schuyler, Dispatch No. 61 from the Legation of the United States in St Petersburg, December 29, 1874, to the United States Department of State, Washington, D. C., File Microcopies of Records in the National Archives, Washington DC; #77, Roll 137, Diplomatic Instructions of the Department of State, 1801-1906, RUSSIA Volume 15, January 1, 1865-March 9, 1877.
94. Various medical reports in RGIA, F. 472, Op. 41, D. 223/2846, D. 140-145, D. 153-156, and D. 158.
95. RGIA, F. 472, Op. 23, D. 68, report dated December 11, 1874; RGIA, F. 472, Op. 23, D. 6, Memorandum from Minister of the Imperial Court Count V. A. Adlerberg, December 9, 1874.
96. RGIA, F. 1282, Op. 3, D. 1019, order dated July 6, 1875.
97. RGIA, F. 435, Op. 1, D. 6, various reports December 9, 1875-December 30, 1876.
98. Ferrand, Descendances Naturelles, p. 359.
99. RGIA, F. 1614, Op. 1, D. 63.
100. Ferrand, Descendances Naturelles, p. 359.
101. Order from Alexander II, 1879, in RGIA, F. 1282, Op. 3, D. 1020.
102. Kleinmichel, p. 68.
103. Ferrand, Descendances Naturelles, 358; RGIA, F. 796, Op. 205, D. 238, document from Alexander II to the Minister of Justice, dated March 3, 1878, declaring the union to be illegal; RGIA, F. 974, Op. 1, D. 11, Correspondence of N. A. Krzyzanowski with the Minister of Imperial Court on the morganatic status of the marriage, June 21, 1878.
104. RGIA, F. 776, Op. 5, D. 130; RGIA, F. 614, Op. 1, D. 526, Letter from A. P. Davidov, Councilor of the Russian Embassy in London to Minister of Foreign Affairs Nicholas de Giers, May 12, 1880.
105. RGIA, F. 851, Op. 1, D. 52, Letters of Grand Duke Nicholas Konstantinovich to A. V. Golovnin, 1882; Perry and Pleshakov, 348; Naryshkin-Kurakin, p. 98.
106. Letter of Grand Duke Nicholas Konstantinovich to A. V. Golovnin, April 8, 1880, in RGIA, F. 851, Op. 1, D. 52.
107. Perry and Pleshakov, p. 103.
108. Perry/Pleshakov, 103; www.washington.edu/ark2/archtm/dw1186; tashkent.freenet.uz; www.uzbek-travel.com/cities_guide/tashkent_history_3
109. Perry and Pleshakov, p. 347.
110.. Ferrand, Descendances Naturelles, p. 358.
111. Ferrand, Descendances Naturelles, p. 361.
112. Ulstrup, p. 146.
113. Chavchavadze, p. 140.
114. Bariatinsky, p. 168.
115. Ibid., pp. 168-69.
116. Ibid., pp. 169.
117. Perry and Pleshakov, p. 347.
118. Tarsaidze, Katia, p. 259.
119. see Perry and Pleshakov, p. 194.
120. Ferrand, Descendances Naturelles, p. 359.
121. Ferrand, Toujours, p. 253.
122. Ferrand, Descendances Naturelles, pp. 358-59.
123. Ibid. p. 359.
124. Ibid., pp. 358-359. Ferrand gives these two varying dates without comment.
125. Ibid., p. 359.
126. Ibid., p. 361.
127. Perry and Pleshakov, p. 348.
128. Ferrand, Toujours, p. 253; Ferrand, Descendances Naturelles, p. 361.

129. Perry and Pleshakov, p. 349.
130. Ibid.
131. ibid.

Grand Duke Konstantin Konstantinovich

1. Konstantin Nikolaievich, Pisma, Dnevnik, p. 65.
2. Court Calendar, issued by the Ministry of the Imperial Court, September 27/October 9, 1858; cited, Nunes, Volume Two, No. 3, p. 96.
3. Romanov, Dimitri Konstantinovich.
4. Zeepvat, Camera, p. 77.
5. Cited in Nunes, Atlantis Volume Two, No. 3, 97.
6. Korshunov, p. 229.
7. Ibid., p. 233.
8. Chavchavadze, p. 145.
9. Windsor and Bolitho, p. 217.
10. Korshunov, p. 242.
11. Cited in Nunes, Atlantis Volume Two, No. 3, p. 97.
12. Court Calendar, issued by the Ministry of the Imperial Court, St Petersburg, November 27/December 9, 1878.
13. Russian Court Memoirs, p. 166.
14. Ibid.
15. Ibid.
16. Brayley-Hodgetts, 1:143.
17. Buxhoeveden, Before, p. 218.
18. Russian Court Memoirs, p. 167.
19. Gabriel Konstantinovich, p. 9.
20. Ibid., p. 11.
21. Grand Duke Konstantin Konstantinovich, Diary, April 9, 1884, cited in Barkovets, Federov, and Krylov, 120.
22. Gabriel Konstantinovich, p. 101, p. 289.
23. Grand Duke Konstantin Konstantinovich, Diary, April 10, 1884, cited in Barkovets, Federov, and Krylov, p. 120.
24. Ibid.
25. Ibid.
26. Ibid.
27. Ibid., p. 122.
28. Barkovets, Federov, and Krylov, pp. 122-23.
29. Grand Duke Konstantin Konstantinovich, Diary, April 15, 1884, cited in Barkovets, Federov, and Krylov, pp. 124-25.
30. Barkovets, Federov, and Krylov, p. 127.
31. Benckendorff, 138; Chavchavadze, p. 146.
32. Buxhoeveden, Before, p. 146.
33. Marie Pavlovna, p. 85.
34. Gabriel Konstantinovich, pp. 8-9.
35. The Tatler, January 24, 1906.
36. Gabriel Konstantinovich, p. 60.
37. Grand Duke Konstantin Konstantinovich, Diary, November 26, 1908, in GARF, F. 660, Op. 1, D. 67.
38. Grand Duke Konstantin Konstantinovich, Diary, March 30, 1912, in GARF, F. 660, Op. 2, D. 74.
39. Smirnoff, p. 25.
40. Gabriel Konstantinovich, p. 18.
41. Ibid., p. 11.
42. Ibid., p. 9.
43. Ibid., p. 22.
44. Grand Duke Konstantin Konstantinovich, Diary, June 23/July 5, 1886, in Barkovets, Federov and Krylov, p. 136.
45. Gabriel Konstantinovich, p. 27.
46. Brayley-Hodgetts, 2:139.
47. Grand Duchess Elisabeth Mavrikievna, Letter of March 6, 1885, in Barkovets, Federov, and Krylov, pp. 132-33.
48. Court Calendar, issued by the Ministry of the Imperial Court, St Petersburg, July 4/16, 1885.
49. Court Calendar, issued by the Ministry of the Imperial Court, St Petersburg, July 12/24, 1885.
50. Gabriel Konstantinovich, p. 22.
51. Ibid., p. 43.
52. Court Calendar, issued by the Ministry of the Imperial Court, St Petersburg, January 7/20, 1908.
53. Gabriel Konstantinovich, p. 421.
54. Princess Elena of Serbia and Russia, Memoirs, in BA, MS Collection, Box 42, 39-40.
55. Gabriel Konstantinovich, p. 211.
56. Bing, p. 263.
57. Ibid.
58. Gabriel Konstantinovich, p. 139.
59. Zeepvat, Camera, 56; Information from Konstantinovichi family descendants to Penny Wilson.
60. Ukase of Nicholas II, January 8/21, 1914, published in the Court Calendar, issued by the Ministry of the Imperial Court, St Petersburg.
61. Court Calendar, issued by the Ministry of the Imperial Court, St Petersburg, January 13/26, 1914.
62. Court Calendar, issued by the Ministry of the Imperial Court, St Petersburg, July 6/19, 1887.
63. Court Calendar, issued by the Ministry of the Imperial Court, St Petersburg, July 30/August 9, 1887.
64. Gabriel Konstantinovich, p. 51.
65. Ibid., p. 43.
66. Court Calendar, issued by the Ministry of the Imperial Court, St Petersburg, January 7/20, 1908.
67. Kyasht, p. 239.
68. Bobrov and Kirikov, pp. 34-37.
69. Nijinska, pp. 46-47.
70. Chavchavadze, p. 216.
71. Teliakovsky, p. 242.
72. Gabriel Konstantinovich, p. 152; Vassiliev, p. 285.
73. Kyasht, p. 128.
74. Cited, Hall, Imperial Dancer, p. 106.
75. Cited in Vassiliev, p. 287.
76. Kyasht, pp. 131-32.
77. Gabriel Konstantinovich, pp. 152-55.
78. Kyasht, pp. 129-30.
79. Gabriel Konstantinovich, p. 167.
80. Ibid., p. 299.
81. Ibid., p. 157.
82. Brayley-Hodgetts, 2:139.
83. Gabriel Konstantinovich, p. 101.
84. Ibid., p. 95.
85 Marie Pavlovna, p. 86.
86. Grand Duke Konstantin Konstantinovich, Diary, May 28, 1907, in GARF, F. 660, Op. 1, D. 64.
87. Gabriel Konstantinovich, p. 115.
88. Russian Court Memoirs, p. 165.
89. Information and documents provided to Greg King by Brien Horan; See also Horan, the Russian Imperial Succession, at http://www.chivalricorders.org/royalty/gotha/russu-clw.htm
90. Chavchavadze, p. 150.
91. Gabriel Konstantinovich, pp. 113-15.
92. Information and documents provided to Greg King by Brien Horan; See also Horan, the Russian Imperial Succession, at http://www.chivalricorders.org/royalty/gotha/russu-clw.htm
93. Ibid.
94. de Diesbach, p. 331.

95. Information and documents provided to Greg King by Brien Horan; See also Horan, the Russian Imperial Succession, at http://www.chivalricorders.org/royalty/gotha/russu-clw.htm
96. Marie Alexandrovna, Duchess of Edinburgh, to Crown Princess Marie of Romania, letter of May 24, 1911, in Zeepvat, Camera, p. 102.
97. Grand Duke Konstantin Konstantinovich, Diary, November 30, 1910, in GARF, F. 660, Op. 1, D. 70.
98. Gabriel Konstantinovich, p. 115.
99. Letter of Baron Vladimir de Freedericksz on behalf of Nicholas II, June 14, 1911, in GARF, F, 601, Op. 1, D. 2143.
100. Decree of Nicholas II, August 11, 1911, in GARF, F. 601, Op. 1, D. 2187.
101. Gabriel Konstantinovich, p. 141.
102. Decree of Nicholas II, published by the Ministry of the Imperial Court and the Imperial Senate, in GARF, F. 610, Op. 1, D. 2218; Court Calendar, issued by the Minister of the Imperial Court, St Petersburg, August 25, 1911.
103. Information and documents provided to Greg King by Brien Horan; See also Horan, the Russian Imperial Succession, at http://www.chivalricorders.org/royalty/gotha/russu-clw.htm
104. Ibid.
105. Court Calendar, issued by the Ministry of the Imperial Court, St Petersburg, January 14/26, 1891.
106. Gabriel Konstantinovich, p. 302.
107. Nostitz, p. 136.
108. Gabriel Konstantinovich, p. 43.
109. Letter from Marie Alexandrovna, Duchess of Edinburgh, October 17, 1911, in Zeepvat, Camera, p. 103.
110. Gabriel Konstantinovich, p. 26.
111. Court Calendar, issued by the Ministry of the Imperial Court, St Petersburg, January 4/16, 1893.
112. Gabriel Konstantinovich, p. 92, p. 118.
113. Gabriel Konstantinovich, p. 118, pp. 121-23, p. 183.
114. Court Calendar, issued by the Ministry of the Imperial Court, St Petersburg, June 22/July 4, 1894.
115. Gabriel Konstantinovich, p. 302.
116. Kyasht, p. 127.
117. Gabriel Konstantinovich, p. 297.
118. Kyasht, p. 127.
119. Petrochenkov, p. 225.
120. Gabriel Konstantinovich, p. 295.
121. Court Calendar, issued by the Ministry of the Imperial Court, St Petersburg, May 30/June 12, 1903.
122. Gabriel Konstantinovich, p. 43.
123. Grand Duke Konstantin Konstantinovich, Diary, November 26, 1908, in GARF, F. 660, Op. 1, D. 67.
124. Kniaz Oleg, p. 43.
125. Grand Duke Konstantin Konstantinovich, Diary, November 26, 1908, in GARF, F. 660, Op. 1, D. 67.
126. Felix Medvedev, "Daughter of a National Poet," in Argumenty v fakty, No.898-99, 1998.
127. Information from Konstantinovichi Family descendants to Penny Wilson.
128. Ibid.
129. Hall, Little Mother, 160.
130. Grand Duke Konstantin Konstantinovich, Diary, November 15, 1894, in GARF, F. 660, Op. 1, D. 41.
131. Buxhoeveden, Life, p. 60.
132. Mosolov, p. 75.
133. Cited, Hall, Imperial Dancer, p. 19.
134. Hall, Imperial Dancer, p. 32.
135. Alexander Mikhailovich, Once, p. 142.
136. Vassili, p. 247.
137. Grand Duke Konstantin Konstantinovich Diary, March 18, 1899, in GARF, F. 660, Op. 1, D. 42.
138. Grand Duke Konstantin Konstantinovich, Diary, October 29, 1894, in GARF, F. 660, Op. 1, D. 41.
139. Grand Duke Konstantin Konstantinovich, Diary, November 14, 1894, in GARF, F. 660, Op. 1, D. 41.
140. Grand Duke Konstantin Konstantinovich, Diary, May 8, 1896, in GARF, F. 660, Op. 1, D. 43.
141. Hickley, p. 10; Maude, p. 34.
142. Grand Duke Konstantin Konstantinovich, Diary, May 8, 1896, in GARF, F. 660, Op. 1, D. 43.
143. Grand Duke Konstantin Konstantinovich, Diary, May 9, 1896, in GARF, F. 660, Op. 1, D. 43.
144. Grand Duke Konstantin Konstantinovich, Diary, 9 May, 1896, in GARF, F. 660, Op. 1, D. 43.
145. Grand Duke Konstantin Konstantinovich, Diary, May 14, 1896, in GARF, F. 660, Op. 1, D. 43.
146. Queen Marie of Romania, 2:79.
147. Buxhoeveden, Before, p. 153.
148. Davis, p. 61.
149. Naryshkin-Kuryakin, p. 151.
150. Grand Duke Konstantin Konstantinovich, Diary, May 19, 1896, in GARF, F. 660, Op. 1, D. 43.
151. Grand Duke Konstantin Konstantinovich, Diary, May 26, 1896, in GARF, F. 660, Op. 1, D. 43.
152. Grand Duke Konstantin Konstantinovich, Diary, July 12, 1896, in GARF, F. 660, Op. 1, D. 43.
153. Grand Duke Konstantin Konstantinovich, Diary, April 21, 1899, in GARF, F. 660, Op. 1, D. 45.
154. Grand Duke Konstantin Konstantinovich, Diary, November 18, 1904, inGARF, F. 660. Op. 1, D. 53.
155. Westwood, p. 145.
156. Gabriel Konstantinovich, p. 112.
157. Grand Duke Konstantin Konstantinovich, Diary, February 4, 1905, in GARF,F. 660, Op. 1, D. 54.
158. Grand Duke Konstantin Konstantinovich, Diary, October 8, 1905, in GARF, F. 660, Op. 1, D. 55.
159. Grand Duke Konstantin Konstantinovich, Diary, October 26, 1905, in GARF, F. 660, Op. 1, D. 55.
160. Grand Duke Konstantin Konstantinovich, Diary, April 27, 1906, in GARF, F. 660, Op. 1, D. 56.
161. Grand Duke Konstantin Konstantinovich, Diary, June 26, 1909, in GARF, F. 660, Op. 1, D. 68.
162. Grand Duke Konstantin Konstantinovich, Diary, June 27, 1909, in GARF, F. 660, Op. 1, D. 68.
163. Bergamini, p. 421.
164. Prince Christopher of Greece, p. 22.
165. Buxhoeveden, Before,pp. 219-20.
166. Kirill Vladimirovich, pp. 17-18.
167. Prince Christopher of Greece, p. 21.
168. Gendrikov and Senko, p. 27.
169. Ibid., pp. 70-71.
170. Prince Christopher of Greece, p. 32.
171. Ibid., p. 61.
172. McIntosh, in Beéche. p. 70.
173. Gabriel Konstantinovich, p. 122; McIntosh, in Beéche, p. 70.
174. Prince Christopher of Greece, p.61.
175. Kerr, p. 131.
176. Zeepvat, Camera, p. 117; McIntosh, in Beéche, p. 71.
177. Marie Pavlovna, p. 9.
178. Ibid., p. 79.
179. Ibid., p. 15.
180. Vickers, p. 69.
181. Grand Duke Konstantin Konstantinovich, Diary,

May 24, 1900, in GARF, F. 660, Op. 1, D. 47.
182. Grand Duke Konstantin Konstantinovich, Diary, June 19, 1902, in GARF, F. 660, Op. 1, D. 49.
183. Cited, Belyakova, Way it Was, p. 91.
184. Ignatiev, pp. 132-33.
185. Alexander Mikhailovich, Once a Grand Duke, p. 142.
186. Gabriel Konstantinovich, p. 13.
187. Grand Duke Konstantin Konstantinovich, Diary, August 12, 1899, in GARF, F. 660, Op. 1, D. 46.
188. Ignatiev, pp. 38-39.
189. Quoted in Sergeievsky.
190. Gabriel Konstantinovich, p. 15.
191. Quoted in Sergeievsky.
192. Alexander Mikhailovich, Once a Grand Duke, p. 142.
193. Gruzenberg, p. 185.
194. Chavchavadze, p. 147; Vassiliev, p. 285.
195. Kolchinskii, pp. 189-96.
196. Bunin, p. 36.
197. Sobolev, pp. 18-21; p. 63.
198. Novoe Vremia, February 7/20, 1901, No. 8962: 12.
199. Sergeievsky.
200. Sobolev, p. 107; pp. 168-72.
201. Vassili, p. 33.
202. Zaionchovsky, p. 117.
203. Kyasht, pp. 60-61.
204. Zemlyanichenko and Kalinin, pp. 20-21.
205. Botkine, p. 86.
206. Fromenko, p. 28.
207. Zeepvat, Romanov Memories, p. 134.
208. Fromenko, p. 28; Zeepvat, Romanov Memories, p. 135; and information provided by Marion Wynn.
209. Eager, p. 126.
210. Dehn, pp. 34-35.
211. Belkovskaia, pp. 20-21; Uspensky, p. 288.
212. Kennett and Kennett, pp. 4-75; Brumfield, pp. 274-75.
213. Information from Konstantinovichi family descendants to Penny Wilson.
214. Massie, p. 128.
215. Ibid., p. 140.
216. Ibid., p. 315.
217. Flit, Guzanov, Koval, and Mudrov, p. 181.
218. Chizhkov, p. 14.
219. Ibid.
220. Ibid., pp. 15-16.
221. Ibid., pp. 15-17.
222. Information from Konstantinovichi family descendants to Penny Wilson.
223. Information from Konstantinovichi family descendants to Penny Wilson.
224. Gabriel Konstantinovich, p. 101.
225. Russian Court Memoirs, p. 164.
226. Chavchavadze, p. 149; Russian Court Memoirs, p. 164.
227. Alexander Mikhailovich, Always a Grand Duke, p. 88.
228. Alexander Mikhailovich, Once a Grand Duke, 143.
229. Marie Pavlovna, pp. 165-66.
230. Ibid., pp. 168-69.
231. Ibid., p. 177.
232. Smirnoff, p. 87.
233. Serfes, p. 41.
234. Gabriel Konstantinovich, p. 287.
235. Ibid., p. 295.
236. Ibid., p. 298.
237. Nicholas II to Empress Alexandra Feodorovna, April 25/May 8, 1916, in GARF, F. 640, Op. 1, D. 110.
238. Nicholas II to Empress Alexandra Feodorovna, April 26/May 9, 1916, in GARF, F. 640, Op. 1, D. 110.
239. Empress Alexandra Feodorovna to Nicholas II, October 9/24, 1915, in GARF, F. 601, Op. 1, D. 1149.
240. "They Were the First to Die in World War I," by Andrei Rimsky-Korsakov, in Moscow Times, March 10, 2004.
241. Grand Duke Andrei Vladimirovich, Diary, October 10, 1915, in GARF, F. 650, Op. 1, D. 2.
242. "The Death of Prince Oleg Konstantinovich," in Novoe Vremia, No. 13849, October 1, 1914.
243. Gabriel Konstantinovich, p. 267.
244. Grand Duke Andrei Vladimirovich, Diary, October 10, 1915, in GARF, F. 650, Op. 1, D. 2.
245. Gabriel Konstantinovich, p. 276; Svet, No. 259, October 1, 1914, Page 1.
246. Novoe Vremia, No. 13851, October 3, Page 4.
247. Information from Konstantinovichi family descendants to Penny Wilson.
248. Novoe Vremia, No. 13851, October 3, Page 4.
249. Gabriel Konstantinovich, p. 275.
250. Novoe Vremia, No. 13851, October 3, Page 4.
251. Ibid.
252. Gabriel Konstantinovich, p. 276; Information from Konstantinovichi descendants to Penny Wilson; Novoe Vremia, No. 13852, October 4, Page 4; "Funeral of Prince Oleg Konstantinovich," in Moscow Chronicle, October 3, 1914; "The Death of Prince Oleg Konstantinovich," in Svet, No. 264, October 7, 1914, Pages 2-3.
253. Novoe Vremia, No. 13852, October 4, Page 4; "Funeral of Prince Oleg Konstantinovich," in Moscow Chronicle, October 3, 1914.
254. Chizkov, pp. 17-18.
255. Grand Duke Andrei Vladimirovich, Diary, October 10, 1915, in GARF, F. 650, Op. 1, D. 2.
256. Gabriel Konstantinovich, pp. 286-92.
257. Sergeievsky.
258. Paley, p. 173.
259. Ibid., p. 175.
260. Gabriel Konstantinovich, pp. 288-89.
261. Sergeievsky.
262. Gabriel Konstantinovich, pp. 286-92.
263. Court Calendar, issued by the Ministry of the Imperial Court, Petrograd, June 8/21, 1915.
264. Court Calendar, issued by the Ministry of the Imperial Court, Petrograd, June 9/22, 1915; Gendrikov and Senko, 127.
265. Crawford and Crawford, pp. 188-89.
266. Gabriel Konstantinovich, p. 291.
267. Gendrikov and Senko, p. 73.
268. Gabriel Konstantinovich, p. 271.
269. Ibid., p. 11.
270. Grand Duke Andrei Vladimirovich, Diary, October 10, 1915, in GARF, F. 650, Op. 1, D. 2.
271. King, Greg and Prenny Wilson, Gilded Prism – The Konstantinovich Grand Dukes (Eurohistory, 2006), p. 185.
272. Ibid., p. 186.
273. Ibid.
274. Ibid.
275. Ibid., p. 190.
276. Ibid., p. 187.
277. Ibid., p. 190.
278. Ibid.
279. Ibid., p. 191.

Grand Duke Dimitri Konstantinovich

1. Court Calendar, issued by the Ministry of the Imperial

Court, St Petersburg, June 9/21, 1860.
2. Romanov, Dimitri Konstantinovich, citing "Russkij Invalid No. 8, Veliki Kniaz Dimitri Konstantinovich."
3. Ibid.
4. Obaturova and Pompeiev, p. 17.
5. Gabriel Konstantinovich, p. 88.
6. Mosolov, p. 87.
7. Obaturova and Pompeiev, p. 21.
8. Tarsaidze, Katia, p. 243.
9. Court Calendar, issued by the Minister of the Imperial Court, St Petersburg, November 26, 1881.
10. Spiridovich, 1:68.
11. Polotsvov, 2:459.
12. Gabriel Konstantinovich, p. 368.
13. Gerasimov, pp. 126-27.
14. Mosolov, p. 84.
15. Ignatiev, p. 131.
16. Romanov, Dimitri Konstantinovich.
17. Ignatiev, p. 132-33.
18. Buxhoeveden, Before, p. 218.
19. Alexander Mikhailovich, Always, p. 88.
20. Ignatiev, p. 131.
21. Romanov, Dimitri Konstantinovich.
22. Alexander Mikhailovich, Once a Grand Duke, p. 334.
23. Mosolov, pp. 83-85.
24. Ibid., p. 85.
25. Alexander Mikhailovich, *Once a Grand Duke*, p. 143.
26. Alexander Mikhailovich, *Always a Grand Duke*, p. 88; Buxhoeveden, Before, p. 218.
27. See Perry and Pleshakov, p. 41.
28. Gabriel Konstantinovich, p. 368.
29. Ibid., 22.
30. Romanov, Dimitri Konstantinovich.
31. Mosolov, pp. 84-85.
32. Alexander Mikhailovich, *Always a Grand Duke*, p. 88.
33. Alexander Mikhailovich, *Once a Grand Duke*, p. 143.
34. Romanov, Dimitri Konstantinovich.
35. Grand Duchess George, p. 39.
36. Romanov, Dimitri Konstantinovich.
37. Gabriel Konstantinovich, pp. 95-96.
38. Alexander Mikhailovich, *Once a Grand Duke*, p. 143.
39. Alexander Mikhailovich, *Always a Grand Duke*, p. 88.
40. Chavchavadze, p. 153.
41. Zemlyanichenko and Kalinin, p. 142.
42. Bikov, pp. 47-48.
43. Ibid.
44. Ibid.
45. Cockfield, pp. 236-39.
46. Grand Duchess George, p. 227.
47. Cockfield, p. 239.
48. Grand Duchess George, p. 230.
49. Ibid., p. 237.
50. Gabriel Konstantinovich, pp. 325-40.
51. Ibid., p. 368.
52. Ibid., pp. 362-70.
53. Grand Duchess George, p. 237.
54. Alexander Mikhailovich, *Once a Grand Duke*, p. 334.
55. See Cockfield, p. 242.
56. Grand Duchess George, p. 239.
57. Paley, p. 295.
58. Perry and Pleshakov, p. 209.
59. Alexander Mikhailovich, *Once a Grand Duke*, p. 334; Gabriel Konstantinovich, p. 368.
60. Private family information to Penny Wilson.

Grand Duke Vyacheslav Konstantinovich

1. Van Der Kiste, 35
2. see Motsardo, 227 et seq.
3. Motsardo, 227
4. see Ferrand, 361
5. ibid.
6. Mosolov, 84
7. see Ferrand, various; Chavchavadze, 60-61
8. Motsardo, 227
9. ibid.
10. Motsardo, 228
11. Vostruishev, 177; Chavchavadze, 257
12. Motsardo, 227
13. Motsardo, 227-228
14. Gabriel Konstantinovich, 88; Motsardo
15. Prince Christopher of Greece, 24-25
16. Konstantin Nicholaievich, Diary, 14 February 1879; see also Motsardo 228
17. Konstantin Nicholaievich, Diary, 15 February 1879; see also Motsardo 228
18. ibid.
19. ibid.
20. Motsardo, 230; Chavchavadze, 158
21. Konstantin Nicholaievich, Diary, 16 February, 1879; see also Motsardo
22. ibid.
23. Konstantin Nicholaievich, Diary, 17 February 1879; see also Motsardo
24. ibid.
25. Konstantin Nicholaievich, Diary, 18 February, 1879; see also Motsardo
26. ibid.
27. Gendrikov and Sentro, 27
28. Gendrikov and Sentro, 70-71

Chapter 6

Grand Duke Nicholas Nikolaievich

1. Marvin Lyons, Editor. *Diary of Vladimir Mikhailovich Bezobrazov, Commander of the Russian Imperial Guard, 1914-1917*, Boynton Beach, Florida: Dramco Publishers, 1994, Notes, p. 3.
2. Lyons, Notes, p. 3; Valerii Sokolovoi and I. V. Kondratiev, Dom Romanovykh. St Petersburg: Lio Redaktor, 1992, p. 142.
3. Sokolovoi and Kondratiev, p. 142.
4. Robert Timms, Editor. *Nicholas and Alexandra: The Last Imperial Family of Russia*, New York: Harry N. Abrams, Inc., 1998, p. 339; Lyons, Notes, p. 3; Sokolovoi and Kondratiev, p. 142.
5. Russia, Grand Duchess Marie Georgievna of. *A Romanov Diary*, New York: Atlantic International Publications, 1988, p. 84; Prince David Chavchavadze, *The Grand Dukes*, New York: Atlantic International Publications, 1990, p. 161.
6. Marie Georgievna, p. 84.
7. Joseph B. Thomas Jr., Observations on Borzois, Boston: Houghton Mifflin, 1912, p. 46.
8. Joseph B. Thomas Jr., A Trip of 15,000Miles for a Brace of Russian Wolfhounds, in The Rider and Driver, February 9, 1907, p. 21.
9. John W. Davis, The Ambassadorial Diary of John W.

End Notes

Davis, Edited by Julia Davis and Dolores Fleming, Morgantown, West Virginia: West Virginia University Press, 1993, p. 184; A. A. Ignatiev, A Subaltern in Old Russia, Translated by Ivor Mantagu, London: Hutchinson, 1944, p. 97.
10. A. V. Bogdanovich, Tri oslednikh Samoderzhsta: Dnevnik A. V. Bogdanovich, Moscow/Leningrad: Frenkel, 1924, p. 454; Count Serge Witte, The Memoirs of Count Witte, Edited by Sidney Harcave, Armonk, New York: ME Sharpe, 1990, p. 752.
11. Princess Anatle Bariatinsky, My Russian Life, London: Hutchinson, 1923, p. 268.
12. Marie Georgievna, p. 84.
13. Vassili Shulgin, The Years, New York: Hippocrene Books, 1984, p. 224; Marie Pavlovna, Grand Duchess of Russia, A Princess in Exile, New York: Viking, 1932, p. 240.
14. Countess Nostitz (Lillie Bouton de Fernandez-Azabal), Romance and Revolution, London: Heinemann, 1937, p. 157-58.
15. Ignatiev, p. 81.
16. Prince Andrei Lobanov-Rostovsky, The Grinding Mill: Reminiscences of War and Revolution in Russia, 1913-1920, New York: Macmillan, 1935, p. 14.
17. Timms, p. 339; Sokolovoi and Kondratiev, p. 142; Lyons, Notes, p. 3.
18. Count Alexis Bobrinsky, Diary entry of January 31, 1905, in Krasnii Arkhiv, 1928, Volume XXVI, p. 132.
19. Howard D. Mehlinger and John M. Thompson, Count Witte and the Tsarist Government in the 1905 Revolution, Bloomington, Indiana: Indiana University Press, 1972, p. 44; Witte, p. 486.
20. Alexander Mosolov, At the Court of the Last Tsar, London: Metheun, 1935, p. 88; Witte, 186.
21. Witte, p. 486.
22. Nicholas II, Diary entry of October 17/30, 1905, in Gosudarstvennyi Arkhiv Rossiiskoi Federatsii (State Archives of the Russian Federation, hereafter GARF), F. 601, Op. 1, D. 249.
23. Ibid.
24. Witte, p. 520.
25. Ibid, p. 536.
26. Sokolovoi and Kondratiev, p. 142.
27. Hugh Seton-Watson, The Decline of Imperial Russia, 1855-1914, New York: Praeger, 1964, p. 266.
28. Shulgin, p. 224.
29. Lili Dehn, The Real Tsarista, London: Thornton Butterworth, 1922, p. 22.
30. Witte, p. 780.
31. Count Paul Vassili (pseudonym of Princess Catherine Radziwill), Behind the Veil at the Russian Court, London: Cassell and Company, 1913, p. 248.
32. See Jacques Ferrand, Descendances Natureles des Souverains et Grands-Ducs de Russie de 1762 a 1910, Paris, Repertoire Genealogique, 1995, pp. 159-62.
33. Baroness Sophie Buxhoeveden, The Life and Tragedy of Alexandra Feodorovna, London: Longmans, Green, 1928, p. 91.
34. Hugh Montgomery-Massingberd, Royal Palaces of Europe, New York: Chartwell Books, 1983, p. 134.
35. Witte, p. 356.
36. Alexander Leuchtenberg, born in 1881, died in exile in France in 1942; Serge died in Rome in 1974; and Elena died in Rome in 1971.
37. Nostitz, p. 144.
38. Prince Felix Yusupov, Lost Splendor, New York: Putnam's, 1954, p. 52.
39. Ian Vorres, The Last Grand Duchess, London: Hutchinson, 1964, p. 100.
40. Witte, p. 357.
41. Princess Elizabeth Naryshkin-Kurakin, Under Three Tsars, New York: Dutton, 1931, p. 163.
42. Witte, p. 356-57.
43. Edvard Radzinsky, The Life and Death of Nicholas II, New York: Doubleday, 1992, p. 63.
44. Witte, p. 301.
45. Iliodor (Serge Trufanov), The Holy Devil, Garden City, New York: Garden City Publishing Club, 1928, p. 115.
46. Nostitz, p. 144.
47. See Robert Warth, Nicholas II, Westport, CT: Praeger, 1997, Chapter Nine, for further discussion of the Imperial Couple's mysticism.
48. Yusupov, p. 52.
49. Nostitz, p. 145.
50. See Edvard Radzinsky, The Rasputin File, New York: Doubleday, 2000, pp. 51-55.
51. Alexander Mikhailovich, Grand Duke of Russia, Once a Grand Duke, New York: Farrar, 1932, pp. 183-84.
52. Nicholas II, Diary entry of November 1/14, 1905, in GARF, F. 601, Op.1, D. 249.
53. Witte, p. 518.
54. Anonymous, Russian Court Memoirs, 1914-1916, New York: Dutton, 1916, p. 135; Vassili, p. 249.
55. R. J. Minney, Rasputin, London: Cassell, 1972, pp. 32, 42-43.
56. Alexandre Tarsaidze, Katia, Wife Before God, New York: Macmillan, 1970, p. 52; Empress Alexandra Feodorovna to Nicholas II, November 4/17, 1916, in GARF, F. 601, Op. 1, D. 1157.
57. Naryshkin-Kurakin, p. 163; Witte, p. 404; Tarsaidze, p. 52; Empress Alexandra Feodorovna to Nicholas II, November 4/17, 1916, in GARF, F. 601, Op. 1, D. 1157.
58. Princess Katya Galitzine, St Petersburg: The Hidden Interiors, New York: The Vendome Press, 1999, pp. 202-04.
59. Zoia Belyakova, The Romanovs: The Way It Was, St Petersburg: Ego, 2000, p. 109; Prince Roman Petrovich Romanov, Am Hof des Letzen Zaren, 1896-1919, Munich: Piper, 1994, p. 405.
60. Richard Pipes, The Russian Revolution, New York: Knopf, 1991, p. 200.
61. Maurice Paleologue, An Ambassador's Memoirs, New York: Doran, 1925, pp. 1:60-61.
62. Ibid., p. 1:62.
63. Alfred Knox, With the Russian Army, New York: Dutton, 1921, p. 43.
64. W. Bruce Lincoln, Passage Through Armageddon, New York: Simon and Schuster, 1986, p. 51.
65. Knox, p. 46; Paleologue, p. 1:56.
66. John Curtis Perry and Constantine Pleshakov, The Flight of the Romanovs, New York: Basic Books, 1999, p. 120.
67. Lincoln, p. 52.
68. Knox, p. 90.
69. Sir Bernard Pares, The Fall of the Russian Monarchy, New York: Vintage, 1961, pp. 228-29.
70. Shulgin, pp. 227-28.
71. See Coryne Hall, Imperial Dancer, Stroud: Sutton, 2005, pp. 160-61.
72. On the falsity of the Sukhomlinov charges, see Pipes, p. 220.
73. Shulgin, p. 230.
74. Knox, p. 334.

75. Michael Rodzianko, The Reign of Rasputin, Gulf Breeze, FL: Academic Press International, 1973, p. 118.
76. Nicholas II to Empress Alexandra Feodorovna, Letter of March 7/20, 1915, in GARF, F.640, Op. 1, D. 105.
77. Paleologue, p. 2:13.
78. Empress Alexandra Feodorovna to Nicholas II, Letter of June 10/23, 1915, in GARF, F. 601, Op. 1, D. 1149.
79. Ibid, letter of June 11/24, 1915, in GARF, F. 601, Op. 1, D. 1149.
80. Ibid, letter of June 12/25, 1915, in GARF, F. 601, Op. 1, D. 1149.
81. Ibid., letter of June 12/25, 1915, in GARF, F. 601, Op. 1, D. 1149.
82. Ibid., letter of June 16/29, 1915, in GARF, F. 601, Op. 1, D. 1149.
83. Ibid., letter of June 17/30, 1915, in GARF, F. 601, Op. 1, D. 1149.
84. Ibid., letter of June 24/July 7, 1915, in GARF, F. 601, Op. 1, D. 1149.
85. Ibid., letter of June 25/July 8, 1915, in GARF, F. 601, Op. 1, D. 1149.
86. Lyons, p. 117.
87. Witte, p. 519.
88. Paleologue, pp. 2:70-71.
89. Ibid., p. 2:63.
90. Grand Duke Andrei Vladimirovich, Diary entry of August 24/September 6, 1915, in GARF, F. 650, Op. 1, D. 2.
91. Lincoln, p.168.
92. Cited in Warth, p. 230.
93. Pipes, p. 256.
94. See Pipes, p. 269; Serge Melgunov, Na Putyak k Dvortsovomu Perevorotu, Paris: Conrad, 1931, pp. 98-101.
95. Cable from General Michael Alexeiev to Nicholas II, March 2/14, 1917, in GARF, F. 601, Op. 1, D. 2102.
96. The New York Times, March 23, 1917.
97. Sir John Hanbury-Williams, The Emperor Nicholas As I Knew Him, New York: Dutton, 1923, p. 179.
98. Romanov, pp. 405-409.
99. Ibid., p. 410.
100. Belyakova, p. 124; Charlotte Zeepvat, Patriots and Just Men, Part 2, in Royalty Digest, October 2000, No. 112, Volume X, No. 4, pp. 121-22.
101. Belyakova, p. 137.
102. Romanov, pp. 412-14.
103. Belyakova, p. 148.
104. Perry and Pleshakov, p. 199.
105. Vladimir Poliakoff, Mother Dear: The Empress Marie of Russia, New York: Appleton, 1926, p. 322.
106. General Alexis Wrangel, General Wrangel, Russia's White Crusader, New York: Hippocrene Books, 1987, pp. 95-97.
107. D. C. Thompson, Donald C. Thompson in Russia, New York: The Century Company, 1918, p. xviii.
108. Belyakova, p. 161.
109. Perry and Pleshakov, p. 201.
110. Ibid., p. 211.
111. Ibid., p. 213.
112. Ibid., pp. 212-13.
113. Sir Francis Prideham, Close of a Dynasty, London: Wingate, 1959, p. 73.
114. Romanov, p. 456.
115. Marie Pavlovna, p. 239.
116. Perry and Pleshakov, p. 270.
117. Ibid., pp. 279-82.
118. The New York Times, October 11, 1925.
119. Perry and Pleshakov, p. 283.
120. Time Magazine, December 31, 1928.

Grand Duke Peter Nikolaievich

1. Information from Prince Nicholas Romanov to the author
2. See Jacques Ferrand, Descendances Natureles des Souverains et Grands-Ducs de Russie de 1762 a 1910, Paris, Repertoire Genealogique, 1995)
3. Information from Prince Nicholas Romanov to the author
4. Zoia Belyakova, The Romanov Legacy: The Palaces of St Petersburg, London: Hazar, 1994, p. 150; Princess Katya Galitzine, St Petersburg: The Hidden Interiors, New York: Vendome, 1999, p. 100
5. Count Serge Witte, The Memoirs of Count Witte, Edited by Sidney Harcave, Armonk, New York: ME Sharpe, 1990, pp. 77-78
6. Information from Prince Nicholas Romanov to the author
7. Ibid.
8. Aleksandr Bikov, Pyuti Na Golgofii: Mronika Gibeli Velikii Knizei Romanovik, Vologda, Russia: Izdatelbstvo, Musei Diplomatischeskogo Korpiusa, 2000, p. 99; Valerii Sokolovoi and I. V. Kondratiev, Dom Romanovykh. St Petersburg: Lio Redaktor, 1992, pp. 142-43; Alexander Mikhailovich, Grand Duke of Russia, Once a Grand Duke, New York: Farrar,1932, p. 145
9. Bikov, 99; Prince David Chavchavadze, The Grand Dukes, New York: Atlantic International Publications, 1990, p. 167; Sokolovoi and Kondratiev, p. 142
10. Witte, p. 78
11. Bikov, p. 99; Information from Prince Nicholas Romanov to the author
12. Coryne Hall, Little Mother of Russia, London: Shepheard-Walwyn, 1999, p. 119
13. Alexander Polovtsov, Diary entry July 1, 1889, from the archive of Prince Nicholas Romanov
14. Count Paul Vassili (pseudonym of Princess Catherine Radziwill), Behind the Veil at the Russian Court, London: Cassell and Company, 1913, p. 33
15. Ibid., p. 33
16. Belyakova, Romanov Legacy, pp. 153-54
17. Alexander Mikhailovich, p. 143; Sokolovoi and Kondratiev, p. 142
18. Information from Prince Nicholas Romanov to the author
19. Marina Zemlyanichenko, The Romanovs and the Crimea, Moscow: Rurik, 1993, pp. 138-39
20. Prince Roman Petrovich Romanov, Am Hof des Letzen Zaren, 1896-1919, Munich: Piper, 1994, pp. 136-38
21. Zemlyanichenko, pp. 138-39; Bikov, p. 100
22. Romanov, pp. 139-40
23. Romanov, pp. 142-44; Bikov, pp. 100-01; Zemlyanichenko, pp. 138-39
24. Romanov, p. 145
25. Romanov, pp. 144-45; Charlotte Zeepvat, Djulber, in Royalty Digest, September 1999, No. 99, Volume IX, No. 3, p. 68
26. Information from Prince Nicholas Romanov to the author
27. Witte, p. 357
28. Bikov, p. 99; Baroness Sophie Buxhoeveden, The Life and Tragedy of Alexandra Feodorovna, London: Longmans, Green, 1928, p. 91

29. Information from Prince Nicholas Romanov to the author
30. Prince Felix Yusupov, Lost Splendor, New York: Putnam's, 1954, p. 62
31. Iliodor (Serge Trufanov), The Holy Devil, Garden City, New York: Garden City Publishing Club, 1928, p. 216-20
32. See Joseph Fuhrmann, Rasputin: A Life, New York: Praeger, 1990, p. 62
33. Information from Prince Nicholas Romanov to the author
34. George S. Viereck, Glimpses of the Great, London: Duckworth, 1930, p. 124; Iulia Kudrina, Imperatritsa Maryia Fedorovna, Moscow: Mokba Olma Press, 2001, pp. 169-70
35. Romanov, pp. 405-07
36. Ibid., pp. 402-10
37. Ibid., 410-11
38. Ibid.
39. Alex Shoumatoff, Russian Blood, New York: Vintage Books, 1990, p. 227
40. Alexander Mikhailovich, p. 305
41. Zoia Belyakova, The Romanovs: The Way It Was, St Petersburg: Ego, 2000, p. 148
42. Romanov, p. 414
43. Belyakova, The Romanovs: The Way It Was, p. 148; Zeepvat, p. 70; Romanov, pp. 414-15
44. Romanov, p. 415
45. Viereck, pp. 126-27
46. Countess Ekaterina Petrovna Kleinmichel, The Departure of an Empress, in Michael Glenny and Norman Stone, The Other Russia: The Experience of Exile, New York: Viking, 1990, p. 161
47. Alexander Mikhailovich, p. 305
48. Harrison Salisbury, Black Night, White Snow: Russia's Revolutions, 1905-1917, New York: Doubleday, 1977, p. 582
49. General Alexis Wrangel, General Wrangel, Russia's White Crusader, New York: Hippocrene Books, 1987, pp. 95-97
50. Viereck, p. 128
51. Belyakova, The Romanovs: The Way It Was, p. 160
52. Viereck, p. 128
53. Belyakova, The Romanovs: The Way It Was, p. 160
54. Romanov, p. 418
55. Ibid., p. 418
56. Belyakova, The Romanovs: The Way It Was, p. 160
57. Viereck, p. 129
58. Wrangel, p. 95
59. Yusupov, p. 187
60. Romanov, p. 423
61. John Curtis Perry and Constantine Pleshakov, The Flight of the Romanovs, New York: Basic Books, 1999, p. 201
62. Sir Francis Pridham, Close of a Dynasty, London: Wingate, 1959, pp. 67-68
63. Ibid., p. 67
64. Information from Prince Nicholas Romanov to the author
65. Ibid.
66. Ibid.

Chapter 7

Grand Duke Nicholas Mikhailovich

1. Quoted by Piotr Zaionchovsky, and cited in Cockfield, p. 7.
2. Golovin, p. 112.
3. Harris, p. 38.
4. Ibid., p. 42.
5. Cockfield, p. 76.
6. Alexander Mikhailovich, p. 23.
7. Cockfield, p. 63.
8. Grimm, pp. 103-4.
9. Cockfield, p. 23.
10. Cockfield, p. 54.
11. Ibid.
12. Mosolov, p. 93.
13. Kleinmichel, p. 161.
14. Cockfield, p. 50.
15. Ibid., p. 63.
16. Maria, Grand Duchess George, p. 83.
17. Ibid., p. 113.
18. Cockfield, p. 47.
19. Cecilie, pp. 88-89.
20. Alexander Mikhailovich, p. 167.
21. Cockfield, p. 77; the book is Nabludeniia po okhote na dukikh gusei, 1917.
22. Gabriel Konstantinovich, pp. 150-155. (With thanks to Katrina Warne for hunting this anecdote down as I awaited my own copy!)
23. Alexander Mikhailovich, p. 172.
24. Ibid.
25. Ibid., p. 168.
26. Cockfield, pp. 59-60.
27. Cockfield, p. 81.
28. Cecilie, p. 89.
29. Recent tests on the mitochondrial DNA found in strands of Hauser's hair failed to find a match with that of known matrilineal descendants of the real heir's mother's family, as would be expected if he were the heir. A relationship could not be 100% excluded, due to the possibility of a mutation in either Hauser or the later descendants, but seems unlikely.
30. Nikolai Mikhailovich, Alexandre I, v.
31. Cockfield, p. 81.
32. Nikolai, Alexandre I, vi.
33. Kleinmichel, p. 161.
34. It is remarkable that although Sandro was the fourth son of the prolific Michael Nikolaievich, he became the first to have a son of his own named Romanov. Any son of Nicholas would have been illegitimate (as was also the case with the fifth brother Serge, who acknowledged one illegitimate child, Vladimir Romanovsky-Krassinsky, and fathered at least one other, Alexander Den); their second brother Michael's son bore the morganatic title Torby; and George (no.3) was the father of daughters who were born after Sandro's eldest children. The first known male grandchild of Michael Nikolaievich was actually Anastasia's son, who carried the name Friedrich Franz of Mecklenburg Schwerin.
35. Nicholas Mikhailovich to Michael Alexandrovich, 13/26 June 1913, at www.iconastas.co.uk, accessed July 18 2009.
36. Nikolai to Frederic Masson,, 9/22 December 1914, in Fin du tsarisme [author's translation].

37. Ibid., 1/14 October 1915.
38. cited in Lieven, 212.
39. Mosolov, 93.
40. The existence of this "plot", or at least of wild talk about the need to get rid of Nicholas II and Alexandra, is mentioned in the memoirs of the French diplomats Paleologue and Chambrum, and discussed at length in Cockfield.
41. Cockfield, p. 87.
42. Nikolai to Masson, 29 June/12 July, 1917, in Fin du tsarisme [author's translation].
43. Cockfield, p. 210.
44. Hall, pp. 177-8.
45. Cockfield, p. 229.
46. Ibid., p. 238.

Grand Duke Michael Mikhailovih

1. Now Tblisi.
2. The Holstein-Gottorp dynasty came to power in 1751 following the death of King Fredrik I of Sweden, a member of the Hesse-Cassel family. (Fredrik was the husband of the Swedish princess Ulrika Eleonora, who had abdicated her rights in favor of her husband, the Landgrave Friedrich I of Hesse-Cassel. This marriage was childless. When Friedrich/Fredrik died in 1751, he was succeeded by Adolf Fredrik of Holstein-Gottorp, who had been elected as heir to the throne in 1743. He was a Vasa descendant in the female line. The present Swedish royal family, the Bernadottes, also have a Vasa line of descendant. Duke Leopold and Duchess Sophie's eldest son, Friedrich I and his wife, Luise of Prussia, had only one child, a daughter, Victoria, who, in 1881, married King Gustaf V of Sweden.
3. White Crow by Jamie Cockfield. Praeger (Wesport, CT: 2002) p. 10.
4. Ibid.
5. Once a Grand Duke by Grand Duke Alexander of Russia (Farrar & Rhinehart (New York: 1932).
6. Ibid.
7. Ibid.
8. Grand Dukes and Diamonds. The Wernhers of Luton Hoo by Raleigh Trevelyan (Secker & Warburg: 1991).p. 205.
9. Ibid.
10. Once a Grand Duke. P. 149.
11. Princess Augusta of Hesse-Cassel who in 1818 married Prince Adolphus, Duke of Cambridge.
12. Trevalyan. P. 205. Also Pope-Hennessey, James. Queen Mary. (Knopf: 1960). p. 153.
13. In 1894, the new Tsar Nicholas II married Irene and Ella's younger sister, Alix.
14. Née Princess Dagmar of Denmark. Younger sister of Alexandra, the Princess of Wales, whose daughter Louise had said no to Michael's marriage proposal.
15. Baroness de Stoeckl, in her autobiography, Not all Vanity, refers to the marriage having taken place at the Russian Church in San Remo. However, a Russian Orthodox church was not built until 1908. The Baroness may have been referring to a ceremony in a chapel at one of the villas owned by Russian aristocrats.
16. Once a Grand Duke. p. 119.
17. Life With Queen Victoria. Marie Mallet's letters from Court 1887-1901 edited by Victor Mallet (John Murray; 1969). P. 52.
18. Michael's eldest brother, Nicholas, who in his youth, fell in love with Princess Victoria of Baden. Alexander II would not give his permission for a marriage between first cousins, as such marriages were not permitted by the Russian Orthodox Church. Nicholas never married. According to his brother, Grand Duke Alexander, "he stayed alone in his very large palace, surrounded by books, manuscripts and botanical collections."
19. Daughter of the Russian poet Alexander Pushkin, and his wife Natalia Nikolaievna Goncharoff.
20. Alexandrine was married in 1914 to an Argentine Don Massimo de Elia. The marriage was childless, and she died in Buenos Aires in 1950.
21. George's first wife was HSH Princess Olga Yourievsky, the daughter of Alexander II of Russia and his morganatic second wife, Princess Catherine Yourievsky.
22. de Stoeckl, Baroness Agnes. Not All Vanity. (Scribner's: 1952).
23. Trevelyan. P. 207.
24. Ibid.
25. Michael and Sophie were godparents to Alice's daughter, Sonia.
26. In 1905, Cecilie married Crown Prince Wilhelm of Prussia.
27.. The Grand Dukes. p. 178.
28. Not All Vanity, p. 67.
29. King Edward the Seventh by Philip Magnus (John Murray: 1964). P. 405.
30. Not All Vanity. P. 74.
31. Princess Marie of Greece and Denmark.
32. Bryant, Julius. The Iveagh Bequest Kenwood. (English Heritage: 1990).
33. Bainbridge was Carl Fabergé's London Partner.
34. Maylunas, Andrei & Mironenko, Sergei. A Lifelong Passion. (Weidenfeld & Nicolson: 1996). P. 354.
35. The Graphic. March 11, 1911.
36. The Complete Wartime Correspondence of Tsar Nicholas II and Empress Alexandra April 1914-March 1917. Edited by Joseph T. Fuhrmann. P. 445.
37. Vere Anthony Francis St Clair Fane (1893-1948), who in 1922, succeeded his father as the 14th Earl of Westmoreland. Married in 1923 to the Hon. Diana Lister.
38. In July 1917, Prince Louis of Battenberg renounced his German titles, and was created the Marquess of Milford Haven. His only son was styled as the Earl of Medina, and succeeded as the 2nd Marquess of Milford Haven. The present 4th Marquess was born in 1961, and is George and Nada's grandson.
39. Grand Dukes and Diamonds. P. 276.
40. Ibid.
41. Ibid.
42. Queen Mary bought Sophie's sapphire and diamond necklace, which she then gave to her daughter, Mary, when she married Lord Lascelles in 1922.
43. Daisy, Princess of Pless by Herself. E.P. Dutton: 1929.
44. Ibid. p. 278.
45. Grand Dukes and Diamonds. P. 261.
46. Ibid
47. Ibid
48. Ibid
49. Prince George married Princess Elisabeth in 1921. The marriage ended in divorce in 1935.
50. The Times, July 21, 1917.
51. Grand Dukes and Diamonds. p. 274.
52. Grand Dukes and Diamonds. P. 297.
53. The Times. April 27, 1959.
54. Ibid.

55. Grand Dukes and Diamonds. P. 287.
56. The Times. April 27, 1929.
57. Ibid
58. Russian Grand Duke was Exile for Love. The New York Times. May 5, 1929.
59. Ibid.
60. Ibid.
61. Ibid.
62. Ibid.
63. Never Say Die (Collier and Co: 1908)..

Grand Duke George Mikhailovich

1. Hall & King, in Atlantis, p 67
2. Alexander, *Always*, p 88
3. Chavchavadze, p 184
4. Marie Feodorovna to Queen Alexandra, 4 May 1900. Ulstrup, p 164
5. George, p 176
6. Perry & Pleshakov, p 166
7. George, p 182
8. Ditto, p 219
9. All quotes, Cockfield, p 233
10. George, p 230
11. Ditto, p 237
12. Ditto, p 236
13. Jensen, p 118
14. Jensen, p 120
15. George, p 232
16. This account of the execution is taken from Cockfield, p 244/5.
17. Cockfield, p 243

Grand Duke Alexander Mikhailovich

1. Alexander, Once a Grand Duke, p 18.
2. Van der Kiste & Hall, p 27.
3. Constantine's diary, 25 July 1894, in Maylunas & Mironenko, p 87.
4. Alexander, Once, p 133.
5. Nunes, in Atlantis Magazine, vol 2, no. 4. p 78.
6. ditto, p 80.
7. Perry & Pleshakov, p 80.
8. Alexander, Once, p 252.
9. Van der Kiste & Hall (paperback edition), p 69
10. Perry & Pleshakov, p 140
11. Alexander, Once, p 320/1
12. Perry & Pleshakov, p 161
13. Van der Kiste & Hall, p 140
14. ditto, p 162
15. ditto, p 188
16. Domin, p 13

Grand Duke Serge Mikhailovich

1. Chavchavadze, Prince David. The Grand Dukes. (Atlantic International Publications, New York. 1990), p 203; Hall, Coryne. Imperial Dancer: Mathilde Kschessinska & the Romanovs. (Sutton Publishing, Stroud, 2005, and paperback 2006), p 45.
2. Chavchavadze, p 203; Cockfield, Jamie. White Crow. (Praeger, Connecticut, 2002), pp 20/21; George, HIH Grand Duchess, A Romanov Diary. (Atlantic International Publications, New York.1988), p 83.
3. Cockfield, pp 212 & 53; Hall, Imperial Dancer, p 46 .
4. Hall, Imperial Dancer, p 47.
5. Volkonsky, Prince Serge. My Reminiscences. (Hutchinson, 1925.) Volume 2, p 95.
6. Volkonsky, volume 2, p 97.
7. King, Greg. Glory & Adornment. Kschessinska, The Romanov Men and a Mansion. In Atlantis Magazine, USA. Volume 4, no. 3.
8. Kschessinska, Mathilde (Princess Romanovsky-Krasinsky). Dancing in Petersburg. (Gollancz, 1960. Reprinted by Royalty Digest 1999), p 89.
9. Chavchavadze, p 216.
10. Kyasht, Lydia. Romantic Recollections. (Brentano, New York, 1929) p. 242.
11. Information from Prince Nicholas Romanov.
12. Hall, Imperial Dancer, p. 86.
13. Gray, Pauline. 3 The Grand Duke's Woman. (Macdonald & Janes, 1976), p.83.
14. GARF, Fond 684. Op 1, D 25. L5-6. Quoted in Hall, Imperial Dancer, p 100.
15. Ferrand, Jaques, Noblesse Russe: Portraits d'Exil. (Paris 2001), p 67.
16. Kyasht, p 204; Chavchavadze, p 242
17. Bobrinsky diary, 19 December 1910, in Krasni Arkhiv (1928), p 142; Salisbury, Harrison E. Black Night, White Snow. (Da Capo, 1977), p 200.
18. Grand Duke Andrei's diary, 12 May 1915, on The Alexander Palace Time Machine website.
19. Radziwill, Princess Catherine. Nicholas II, Last of the Tsars. (Cassell, 1931), p 230.
20. Fuhrmann, Joseph (ed), The Wartime Correspondence of Nicholas & Alexandra. (Westport, Connecticut, 1999), p 169. 25 June 1915.
21. Rodzianko, M.V. The Reign of Rasputin. (Philpot, 1927), p 130.
22. Cockfield, p 139; King, Glory & Adornment.
23. Rodzianko, pp 194/5
24. Fuhrmann, p 677. 10 December 1916.
25. Alexander, Grand Duke. Once a Grand Duke. (Cassell, 1932), p 276.
26. Cockfield, 204.
27. Alexander, p 150; Krasni Arkhiv. Iz Perepiski S M & N M Romanovov za 1916-17gg. (Russia, 1932), p 141. 9 March 1917
28. Krasni Arkhiv, Iz Perepiski…., p 143
29. Stopford, Hon. Albert. The Russian Diary of an Englishman. (Robert M McBride, New York. 1919), p 151.
30. Krasni Arkhiv, Iz Perepiski…, p 144. 19 March 1917.
31. Ditto, p 146, 149.
32. Bobrov, V D & Kirikov, B M. Osobnyak Kschesinskoi. (Beloe i Chernoe, St Petersburg, 2000), p 102.
33. Hall, Imperial Dancer, p 190; Sáenz, Jorge F. A Poet Among the Romanovs. (Eurohistory.com. California 2004), p 65.
34. Paley, Princess Olga. Memories of Russia 1916-1919. (Herbert Jenkins 1924), p 206.
35. Sáenz, pp 83/84; Maylunas, Andrei & Mironenko, Serge. A Lifelong Passion. (Weidenfeld & Nicolson, 1996), p 676.
36. Sáenz, p 85/88; Warwick, Christopher. Ella: Princess, Saint & Martyr. (John Wiley, 2006), p 307/8.
37. Sáenz, pp 91/94.
38. www.orthodox.cn/news/050304romanov-en.htm "Burial site of members of the Imperial Romanov Family Found in Beijing."

Grand Duke Alexis Mikhailovich

1. Cockfield, James. White Crow. (Praeger, 2002), p. 21.
2. Alexander, *Once*, 23.
3. Ibid.
4. Cockfield, p. 15.
5. Ibid.
6. Ibid., p. 21.
7. Chavchavadze, Prince David. The Grand Dukes. (Atlantic International Publications, New York. 1990), p. 207.
8. Alexander, *Once*, p. 23.
9. Ibid., pp. 23-24.
10. Ibid., p. 24.
11. Ibid.
12. Cockfield, p. 21.
13. Kirill, p. 54.
14. Ibid.
15. *Almanach de Gotha 1896*. (Justus Perthes, Gotha), p. 1307.
16. Cockfield, p. 22.
17. Kirill, p. 54.
18. Alexander, *Once*, p. 24.
19. Mandache, Diana. *Dearest Missy – The letters of Marie Alexandrovna, Grand Duchess of Russia, Duchess of Edinburgh and Saxe-Coburg and Gotha, and her daughter, Marie, Crown Princess of Romania 1879-1900*. (Rosvall Royal Books, 2011), p. 217.

Bibliography

Books and Exhibition Catalogues

Alekseev, A. I. *Fedor Petrovich Litke*. Fairbanks: University of Alaska Press, 1996.
Alexander (Mikhailovich), Grand Duke. *Once a Grand Duke*. Farrar & Rinehart, 1932.
Alice, Princess, Countess of Athlone. *For My Grandchildren: Some Reminiscences of Her Royal Highness Princess Alice, Countess of Athlone*. London: Evan Brothers Limited, 1966.
Almanach de Gotha 1858, Justus Perthes, Gotha.
Almedingen, E.M. *Emperor Alexander II*. Bodley Head, 1962.
Almedingen, E.M. *The Romanovs. Three Centuries of an Ill-Fated Dynasty*. Bodley, Head, 1966.
Almedingen, E.M. *The Empress Alexandra 1872-1918: A Study*. London: Hutchinson of London, 1961.
Almedingen, E.M. *An Unbroken Unity*. London: The Bodley Head, Ltd, 1964.
Alville [pseud.] *La vie en Suisse de S.A.I. Anna Feodorovna, née Princesse de Saxe-Cobourg-Saalfield*. Lausanne: Librairie Rouge, 1942.
Alville [pseud.] *Des cours princières aux demeures helvétiques*. Lausanne [s.n.], 1962.
Anolic, Tamar. *The Russian Riddle – Grand Duke Serge Alexandrovich of Russia (1857-1905)*. Eurohistory, East Richmond Heights, CA 2009.
Barkovets, Olga. *Peterhof ist ein Traum: deutsche Prinzessinen in Russland*. Berlin: Edition Q, 2001.
Barkovets, Olga. *Nixa, Minny & Sacha*, in *Marie Feodorovna, Empress of Russia*. Exhibition catalogue, Copenhagen, 1997.
Barkovets, Olga. 'Proshaite Dushenka!' in *Sred shunova bala*. Exhibition catalogue, GARF, Moscow. 2001.
Bassin, Mark. *Imperial visions: nationalist imagination and geographical expansion in the Russian far east, 1840-1865*. Cambridge: Cambridge University Press, 1999.
Beéche, Arturo E. *DEAR ELLEN – Royal Europe Through the Photo Albums of H.I.H. Grand Duchess Helen Vladimirovna of Russsia*. East Richmond Heights, CA: Eurohistory, 2012.
Beeche, Arturo E. (Editor) *The Grand Duchesses – Daughters and Granddaughters of Russia's Tsars*. Eurohistory, Oakland, CA, 2004.
Belyakova, Zoia. *Grand Duchess Maria Nikolaevna and her palace in St Petersburg*. St Petersburg: EGO, 1994.
Belyakova, Zoia. *Honour and Fidelity. The Russian Dukes of Leuchtenberg*. Logos Publishers, St Petersburg 2010.
Belyakova, Zoia. *The Romanov legacy: the palaces of St Petersburg*. London: Hazar, 1994.
Belyakova, Zoia. *Velikii Kniaz Alexei. Za I Protiv*. St Petersburg. Logos 2004.
Bloomfield, Georgiana. *Reminiscences of court and diplomatic life*. London: Kegan Paul, 1883.
Bogdanovich, A.V. *Tri poslednikh samiderzhtsa*. 1924.
Bohanov, A. N. *Nicholas II*. ACT Press, Moscow. 2000.
Bokhanov, Alexander, et al., *The Romanovs Love Power & Tragedy*. London: Leppi Publications. 1993.
Bott, I. and V. Faybisovich. *The Alexander Palace*. Tsarskoe Selo: State Museum Preserve Tsarskoe Selo, 1997.
Bourke, Richard Southwell. *St Petersburg and Moscow: a visit to the court of the Czar*. London: Henry Colburn, 1846.
Breyfogle, Nicholas B. *Heretics and colonizers: forging Russia's empire in the south Caucasus*. Ithaca, Cornell University Press, 2005.
Buchanan, Meriel. *Queen Victoria's Relations*. London: Cassell & Co Ltd, 1954.
Buxhoeveden, Baroness Sophie. *Before the Storm*. London: Macmillan and Co., 1938.
Buxhoeveden, Baroness Sophie. *The Life and Tragedy of Alexandra Feodorovna Empress of Russia*. Ticehurst: Royalty Digest, 1996.
Byrnes, Robert. *Pobedonostsev, His Life and Thought*. Indiana University Press, Bloomington, 1968.
Crawford, Rosemary & Donald. *Michael and Natasha*. London: George Weidenfeld and Nicholson, 1997.
Cecilie, Crown Princess of Germany. *The memoirs of the Crown Princess Cecilie*. London: Gollancz, 1931.
Cherniavsky, Michael. *Tsar and people: studies in Russian myths*. Yale: Yale University Press, 1961.
Choiseul-Gouffier, Sophie de. *Historical memoirs of the Emperor Alexander I and the court of Russia*. London: Kegan Paul, 1904.
Cockfield, Jamie H. *White crow: the life and times of the Grand Duke Nicholas Mikhailovich Romanov*. London: Praeger, 2002.
Correspondance Grand-duc Nicolas Mikhaïlovitch et Frédéric Masson 1897-1914. Bernard Giovanangeli: Paris, 2005.
Corti, Count Egon. *The Downfall of Three Dynasties*. Freeport, New York: Books for Libraries Press, 1970.
Cronin, Vincent. *Napoleon*. Harmondsworth: Penguin, 1973.
Custine, Astolphe de. *Journey for our time*. New York: Pellegrini and Cudahy, 1951.
Czartoryski, Adam Jerzy. *Mémoires du prince Adam Czartoryski*. Paris: [s.n.], 1887.
De Robien, Louis. *Diary of a Diplomat*. Michael Joseph, London, 1969.
Dimitri Pavlovich, Grand Duke of Russia. *Diaries*. 1920.
Dimsdale, Elizabeth. *An English lady at the court of Catherine the Great*. Cambridge: Quest, 1989.
Eagar, Margaretta. *Six years at the Russian court*.

London: Hurst and Blackett, 1906.

Edling, Roxandra. *Mémoires de la comtesse Edling, née Stourza, demoiselle d'honneur de l'impératrice Elisabeth Alexeevna*. Moscow: [s.n.], 1888.

Elchaninov, Andrei Grigorievich. *The Tsar and his people*. London: Hodder and Stoughton, 1914.

Enache, Nicolas. *La Descendance de Pierre le Grand Tsar de Russie*. Sedopols, Paris, 1983

Epton, Nina. *Victoria and her Daughters*. New York: W.W. Norton & Company, Inc., 1971.

Ernst Ludwig, Grand Duke of Hesse and by Rhine. *Erinnertes. Aufzeichnungen des letzten Grossherzogs Ernst Ludwig von Hessen und bei Rhein*. Darmstdt: Roether, 1983.

Eugénie, Princess of Greece. *Le Tsarevich, enfant martyr*. Paris: Perrin, 1990.

Ferrand, Jacques. *Aperçus genealogique sur quelque descendances naturelles des grands ducs de Russie au XIX siecle*. Paris: Jacques Ferrand, 1982.

Ferrand, Jacques. *Descendances Natureles des Souverains et Grands-Ducs de Russie de 1762 a 1910*. Paris, Repertoire Genealogique, 1995.

Ferrand, Jacques. *Le Grand-Duc Paul Alexandrovitch de Russie, sa famille, sa descendance*. Paris, 1993.

Ferro. Mark. *Nicholas II: The Last of the Tsars*. Oxford University Press. 1993.

Figes, Orlando. *A People's Tragedy*. Johnathan Cape, London. 1996.

Florinsky, Miachel T. *The end of the Russian Empire*. New York: Collier Books, 1961.

Fricero, E. *The Grand Duke Nicholas Alexandrovich, Crown prince of Russia*, (English Edition). Nice, France.

Fulford, Roger. *Your Dear Letter - Private Correspondence of Queen Victoria and the Crown Princess of Prussia 1865-1871*. Charles Scribner's Sons, New York, 1971.

Gelardi, Julia. *From Splendor to Revolution – The Romanov Women 1847-1928*. St. Martin's Press: New York, 2011.

George, Grand Duchess (Maria Georgievna). *A Romanov diary: the autobiography of H.I. and R. H. Grand Duchess George*. New York: Atlantic International, 1988.

Gerasimov, V. V. *Bolshoi dvorets v Strelne*. St Petersburg: Almaz, 1997

Grand Duke Konstantin Nikolaevich [book produced to accompany an exhibition]. St Petersburg: Abris, 2002.

Grebelsky, Petr, and Aleksandr Mirvis, *Dom Romanovykh: Biograficheskie svedeniia o chlenakh tsarstvovavshego doma, ikh predkakh i rodstvennikakh*. St. Petersburg, 1992.

Grey, Pauline. *The Grand Duke's Woman*. London: Mac Donald and Jane's, 1976.

Grimm, August Theodor von. *Alexandra Feodorowna, Empress of Russia*. Edinburgh: [s.n.], 1870.

Grunwald, Constantin de. *Tsar Nicholas I*. London: Douglas Saunders, 1954.

Hall, Coryne. *Little Mother of Russia*. Shepheard Walwyn. London, 1999.

Hall Coryne. *Imperial Dancer – Mathilde Kschessinska and the Romanovs*. Sutton Publishing, Stroud, 2005.

Harcave, Sidney. *Years of the Golden Cockerel*. Robert Hale, 1970.

Hartley, Janet M. *Alexander I*. London: Longman, 1974

Hennessy, Una Pope [ed.]. *A czarina's story: being an account of the early married life of Nicholas 1 of Russia*.

London: Nicholson & Watson, 1948

Hertsen, Alexander. *Biloye i dumi*. Leningrad, 1978

Hibbert, Christopher, ed. *Queen Victoria in Her Letters and Journals*. New York: Viking, 1985.

Hodgetts, Edward Brayley. *The court of Russia in the nineteenth century*. [s.l.]: Methuen, 1908.

Hough, Richard, ed. *Advice to My Grand-daughter Letters from Queen Victoria to Princess Victoria of Hesse*. New York: Simon and Schuster, 1975.

Ignatiev, Aleksei A. *Pyatdesyat let v stroyu*, Gosudarstvennoe izdatel'stvo khudozhestvennoi literatury, Moscow, 1950, vol. 1.

Jackman, Sydney Wayne [ed.] *Romanov Relations*. London: Macmillan, 1969

Jerrmann, Eduard. *Pictures from St Petersburg*. [s.l.]: Longman, Brown, Green and Longmans, 1852.

Jersild, Austin. *Orientalism and empire: north Caucasus mountain peoples and the Georgian frontier, 1845-1917*. Montreal: McGill-Queen's University Press, 2002.

Karnovich, Evgenii Petrovich. *Tsesarevich Konstantin Pavlovich*. St Petersburg: [s.n.], 1899

King, Greg. *The Last Empress: The Life & Times of Alexandra Feodorovna, Tsarina of Russia*. New York: A Birch Lane Book: Published by Carol Publishing Group, 1994.

King, Greg, and Penny Wilson. *Gilded Prism – The Konstantinovich Grand Dukes & the Last years of the Romamov Dynasty*. Eurohistory, East Richmond Heights, CA, 2006.

King, Greg, and Penny Wilson. *The Fate of The Romanovs*. Hoboken: John Wiley and Sons, 2003.

Klausen, Inger-Lise. *Dagmar, Zarina fra Danmark*. Lindhardt & Ringhof, Copenhagen, 1997.

Kleinmichel, Countess Marie. *Memories of a Shipwrecked World*. Roryalty Digest Reprint, Ticehurst, from 1923.

Kleinpenning, Petra H. (Ed.) *The Correspondence of the Empress Alexandra of Russia with Ernst Ludwig and Eleonore Grand Duke and Duchess of Hesse 1878-1916*. Herstellung und Verlag: Norderstedt, 2010.

Komarovsky, Nikolai Egorovich. *Zapiski*. Moscow: Obschestvo revnitelei russkago istoricheskago provsyschenya, 1912

Kozlianinoff, W. *Manuel Commemoratif de la Garde a Cheval, Edition de Son Altesse Imperiale Mgr. le Grand Duc Dmitri de Russie*. Paris, 1931.

Kurth, Peter. *Tsar: The Lost World of Nicholas and Alexandra*. Boston: A Madison Press Book produced for Little Brown and Company, 1995.

Kwiatowski, Marek. *Lazienki and Belweder*. Warsaw: Arkady, 1986.

Kyrill, Grand Duke of Russia. *My Life in Russia's Service: Then and Now*. Ticehurst: Royalty Digest, 1995.

Letters of Feodora Princess of Hohenlohe-Langenburg from 1828-1872. Spottiswoode & Co., London, 1874.

Letters of Tsar Nicholas and Empress Marie. Edited by Edward J. Bing. London: Ivor Nicholson and Watson Ltd, 1937.

Lincoln, W. Bruce. *Nicholas I: Emperor and autocrat of all the Russias*. London: Allen Lane, 1978.

Londonderry, Frances Anne Vane, Marchioness of. *Extracts from the Russian journal of Lady Londonderry, 1835-1837*. London: Royal College of Art, 1980.

Mandache, Diana. *Dearest Missy: The Letters of Marie Alexandrovna Grand Duchess of Russia and of Saxe-Coburg and Gotha, and her daughter Marie, Crown Princess of Romania 1879-1900*. Enasen: Rosvall Royal Books, 2011.
Maples, William. *Dead Men Do Tell Tales*. New York: Doubleday. 1994.
Maria Feodorovna, Empress of Russia, Exhibition catalogue, 1997.
Marie, Grand Duchess of Russia. *Education of a Princess*. New York: Viking Press, 1931.
Marie, Princess of Erbach- Schönberg (Princess of Battenberg). *Reminiscences*. Ticehurst: Royalty Digest Reprint, 1996.
Marie, Queen of Romania. *The Story of My Life* (vol.1). London: Cassell & Co Ltd, 1934.
Markham, Felix. *Napoleon*. London: Weidenfeld and Nicolson, 1963.
Martin, Marie. *Maria Féodorovna en son temps, 1759-1828*. Paris: Harmattan, 2003.
Massie, Robert K. *Nicholas and Alexandra*. New York: Atheneum, 1967.
Massie, Robert K. and Suzanne Massie. *Journey*. London: Gollancz, 1975.
Masson, C.F.P. *Memoirs of Catherine II and the Court of St. Petersburg : During Her Reign and that of Paul I, By One of Her Courtiers*. London: The Grolier Society, 1904.
McLean, Roderick R. *Royalty and diplomacy in Europe, 1890-1914*. Cambridge: Cambridge University Press, 2000.
Michael, Prince of Greece. *Imperial palaces of Russia*. London: Tauris, 1992.
Milford Haven, Victoria. *Recollections 1863-1914*. ms. not published Eingang 4. XII 1969. Hess. Staatsarchiv Darmstadt D 24 64/1.
Millar, Lubov. *Grand Duchess Elizabeth of Russia: New Martyr of the Communist Yoke*. Richfield Springs, New York: Nikodemos Orthodox Publication Society: 1991.
Miller, Ilana D. *The Four Graces – Queen Victoria's Hessian Granddaughters*. East Richmond Heights, CA: Eurohistory, 2011.
Miliutin, D A. *Dnevnik DA Miliutina*, Moscow: Gosudarstvenaya Ordena Lenina Biblioteka, 1947.
Miller, Forrestt A. *Dmitrii Miliutin and the reform era in Russia*. Nashville: Vanderbilt University Press, 1968.
Moriolles, Alexandre. *Mémoires du comte de Moriolles sur l'émigration, la Pologne, et le cour du grand duc Constantin*. Paris: [s.l.], 1902.
Mosolov, Alexander. *At The Court of the Last Tsar*. London: Methuen, 1935.
Narishkin-Kurakin, Elizabeth. *Under Three Tsars*. E.P. Dutton & Co., Inc., 1931
Nichols, Robert L. "The Friends of God: Nicholas and Alexandra at the canonisation of Serafim of Sarov", in *Religious and secular forces in late Tsarist Russia: essays in honour of Donald W. Treadgold*, edited by Charles E. Timberlake, 206-223.
Nicholas and Alexandra: the last imperial family of Tsarist Russia [exhibition catalogue], edited by Robert Timms. London: Booth-Clibborn, 1998.
Nicholas, Prince of Greece. *My Fifty Years*. East Richmond Heights: CA, Eurohistory, 2006.
Nikolai Mikhailovich, Grand Duke. *L'impératrice Elisabeth, épouse d'Alexandre I*. St Petersburg: [s.n.], 1908-9.
Olga Nikolayevna. *Son Junosti. Zapiski docheri imperatora Nikolaya I*. Paris, 1964.
Olga, Queen of Wurttemberg (Grand Duchess Olga Nikolaevna). *Traum der Jugend goldner Stern*. Pfullingen: [s.n.], 1955.
Paléologue, Maurice. *An Ambassador's Memoirs: Last French Ambassador to the Russian Court*. Translated by F.A. Holt, 1923. (AlexanderPalace.org).
Paleologue, Maurice. *La Russie des Tsars*. Librairie Plon, Paris, 1922.
Palmer, Alan. *Alexander I, Tsar of war and peace*. London: Weidenfeld and Nicolson, 1974.
Pienkos, Angela T. *The imperfect autocrat: Grand Duke Constantine Pavlovich and the Polish Congress Kingdom*. New York: Colombia University Press, 1987.
Ponsonby, Sir Frederick. *Letters of the Empress Frederick*. Macmillan, 1928.
Radzinsky, Edvard. *Alexander II: The Last Great Tsar*. New York: Simon and Schuster, 2005.
Raeff, Marc. *Understanding imperial Russia*. New York: Columbia University Press, 1984.
Ragsdale, Hugh. *Tsar Paul and the question of madness*. New York: Greenwood Press, 1988.
Rasputin, Valentin. *Siberia, Siberia*. Evanston, Ill.: Northwestern University Press, 1996.
Trewin, JC. *Tutor to the Tsarevich: an intimate portrait of the last days of the Russian imperial family*. London: Macmillan, 1975
Roberts, Ian W. *Nicholas I and the Russian intervention in Hungary*. London: Macmillan, 1990.
Seaman, W. A. L. and J. R. Sewell, Editors. *The Russian Journal of Lady Londonderry, 1836-37*. London: John Murray, 1973.
Schnitzler, Johann Heinrich. *Secret history of the government and court of Russia under the Emperor Alexander and Nicholas*. London: [s.n.], 1847.
Sáenz, Jorge F. *A Poet Among the Romanovs – Prince Vladimir Paley 1897-1918*. Eurohistory, Oakland, CA, 2004.
Semennikov, V.P. ed. *Nikolai II I velikie kniaz'ia: rodstvenn'ie pis'ma k poslednemu tsariu, Gosudarstvennoe Izdatel'stvo*. Leningrad, 1925.
Sheremetev, S.D. *Memuari grafa S.D.Sheremeteva*. Moscow, Indrik, 2001.
Sokolovoi, Valerii and I. V. Kondratiev. *Dom Romanovykh*. St. Petersburg: Lio Redaktor, 1992.
Soloveva, T.A. *Paradnye rezidentsii Dvortsovoi naberezhnoi*. St Petersburg: Evropeiskii Dom, 1995.
Steinberg, Mark D. and Vladimir Khrustalev, Editors. *Flight of the Romanovs*. New Haven: Yale University Press. 1995.
Strukov, Dmitri Petrovich. *Avgustischii General-Feldtseikhmeister Velikii Kniaz Mikhail Nikolaevich*. St Petersburg: P.P. Soikina, 1906.
Teliakovsky,V.A. *Dnevniki Directora Imperatorskih Teatrov*. Moscow, 2002.
The complete wartime correspondence of Tsar Nicholas II and the Empress Alexandra, edited by Joseph T. Fuhrmann. Westport, CT.: Greenwood Press, 1999.
Tiutcheva, Anna. *Pri dvore dvuh imperatorov*. Moscow, 1990.

Trotsky, Leon. *A History of the Russian Revolution*. New York: Simon and Shuster. 1932.
Tsesarevich: dokumenty, vospimananiia, fotografii, edited by A. Iu. Maliutin. Moscow: Vagrius, 1998.
Tuomi-Nikula, Jorma & Päivi. *Kejsaren i Skärgården*. Schildts Förlags Ab, Esbo. 2002.
Ukhtomskii, Esper Esperovich. *Puteshestvie na Vostok' Ego Imperatorskago Vysochestva Gosudaria Nasliednika Tsesarevicha, 1890-1* [Puteshestvie Gosudaria Imperatora Nikolaia II na Vostok']. S-Peterburg: Brokgauz [i.e. Brockhaus of Leipzig], 1893-7.
Ular, Alexander. *Russia From Within*. New York: Henry Holt and Company, 1905.
Van der Kiste, John & Hall, Coryne. *Once a Grand Duchess: Xenia, Sister of Nicholas II*. Sutton Publishing, Stroud. 2002.
Van der Kiste, John. *The Romanovs:1818-1959*. Stroud: Sutton, 1998.
Vassili, Count Paul (pseudonym of Princess Catherine Radziwill). *Behind the Veil at the Russian Court*. London: Cassell and Company, 1913.
Verner, Andrew M. *The Crisis of Russian Autocracy: Nicholas II and the 1905 Revolution*. Princeton New Jersey: Princeton University Press, 1990.
Vostryshev, Mikhail. *Avgusteishee semeystvo*. Moscow, 2001.
Waliszewski, K. *Paul The First of Russia, The Son of Catherina The Great*. William Heinemann, London 1913.
Welch, Frances. *The Romanovs and Mr Gibbes: the story of the Englishman who taught the children of the last Tsar*. London: Short Books, 2002.
William II, Emperor. *My Early Life*. Methuen, 1926.
Wood, Ruth Kedzie. *Honeymooning in Russia*. Fisher Unwin, London, 1911.
Wortman, Richard. *Scenarios of power: myth and ceremony in Russian monarchy*. Princeton: Princeton University Press, 1995.
Wassenaer, Cornelie de. *A visit to St Petersburg, 1824-1825*. Norwich: Michael Russell, 1994
Whelan, Heide W. *Alexander III and the State Council*. New Brunswick: Rutgers University Press, 1982.
Witte, Count Serge. *The Memoirs of Count Serge Witte*, edited by Sidney Harcave, Armonk, New York: M. E. Sharpe, 1990.
Witte, Sergei Iulevich. *Vospominaniia*. Moscow: Izdvo sotsnalnoekon. litry, 1960.
Youssoupoff, Prince Felix. *Lost Splendor*. Translated from the French by Ann Green and Nicholas Katkoff. New York: G.P. Putnam's Sons, 1953.
Zaionchkovsky, P A. *Krizis samoderzhavia na ribezhe 1870-1880 godov, Moscow*. Moscow University Press, 1964.
Zamoyski, Adam. *The last king of Poland*. London: Cape, 1992.
Zeepvat, Charlotte. *Romanov Autumn – Stories from the Last Century of Imperial Russia*. Sutton, Publishing, Stroud 2000.
Zeepvat, Charlotte. *From cradle to crown*. Stroud: Sutton, 2007.
Zeepvart, Charlotte. *The Camera and the Tsars*. Sutton Publishing, Stroud, 2004.
Zherve, V. V. *General-Feldmarshal Velikii Kniaz Nikolai Nikolaevich Starshii*. St Petersburg: [s.n.], 1911.

Articles, Periodicals, Grey literature and other media

Ashton, Janet. "The coronation of Tsar Alexander II: a translation from a book by Joachim Murat." In the European Royal History Journal, issues 9:4 and 9:5, 2006.
Ashton, Janet and Greg King. "*Political dramas and private traumas*": the Romanovs in the palaces of the Warsaw region. Royalty Digest Quarterly, 4: 2006.
Hall, Coryne. *The Madness of Youth*. In The European Royal History Journal. Nov/Dec 2002.
King, Greg. "*A tyrant's menacing memorial*": the Mikhailovskii Castle. Atlantis Magazine, volume 5 issue 2, 72-79.
Kipp, Jacob W. and Maia Kipp. *Grand Duke Konstantin Nikolaevic [sic]: the making of a Tsarist reformer*. In Jahrbucher fur Geschichte Osteuropas, Band 34, Heft 1, 1986, p. 4- 18.
Konstantin Pavlovich to Alexander I, 14th January 1822. [Copy of the letter held in the British Library: Misc. Official Publications of the Russian Empire.]
Kucherskaya, Maya. "*Grand Duke Constantine Pavlovich in Russian cultural mythology.*" Unpublished PhD thesis, University of California, Los Angeles, 1999.
Lee, William. "*Grand Ducal Role and Identity as a Reflection on the Interaction of State and Dynasty in Imperial Russia.*" Unpublished PhD thesis, University College, London, 2000
Sbornik Imperatorskago Russkago Istoricheskago Obshchestva [S.I.R.I.O.]. Moscow: Russkaia Panorama, 1999-
Charlotte Zeepvat, *Djulber*. I*n* Royalty Digest, September 19999, No. 99, Volume IX, No. 3, page 66

Websites

www.iconastas.co.uk
www.hermitagemuseum.org
http://www.angelfire.com/realm/gotha/gotha/wied.html
http://andrejkoymasky.com/liv/fab/fab21.html
http://macedonsky.narod.ru/agnates/a10.html
http://www.orthodox.net/russiannm/nicholas-ii-tsar-martyr-and-his-family.html
http://www.alexanderplace.com
http://www.angelfire.com/realm/gotha/gotha/gotha.htm
http://erhj.blogspot.com/

Name Index

A

Adler, Viktor 130
Aleksy, Patriarch of Russia 43
Alexeiev, General Michael 151
Anderson, Anna (aka Franziska Schankowska, "Faux"
Anastasia, Frau Tchaikovsky) 30, 31, 210
Andersen, Hans Christian 169
ANHALT
Catherine, Princess of (See Russia, Catherine II, Empress of)
Edward, Prince of 97
Marie, Princess of (See PRUSSIA, Marie, Princess of)
Arbatov, Nicholas 120
Arseni, Father 95
Asquith, Herbert 55
AUSTRIA
Franz Ferdinand, Archduke of 36
Maria Theresa, Empress vii
Marie Antoinette, Archduchess of (See FRANCE, Marie Antoinette, Queen of)
Rudolf II, Holy Roman Emperor vii

B

BADEN
Cecilie (Cecile), Princess of (See RUSSIA, Olga Feodorovna, Grand Duchess of)
Leopold I, Grand Duke of 177, 183
Louise, Princess of (See, RUSSIA, Elisabeth Alexeievna, Empress of)
Max, Prince of 104
Sophie, Grand Duchess of (née Sweden) 183
Victoria, Princess of (See SWEDEN, Victoria, Queen of)
Bainbridge, H. C. 188
Bakst, Leon 25
Balinsky, Doctor Ivan 73
Balsan, Jacques 55
Baratoff, General 53
Barbara, Sister 218, 219
Bariatinsky, Princess Anatole 76, 140
BATTENBERG
Alice, Princess of (See GREECE, Alice, Princess of)
Anna, Princess of (née Montenegro) 143
Franz Josef, Prince of 143
George, Prince of (2nd Marquess of Milford Haven) 189, 190
Louis, Prince of (1st Marquess of Milford Haven) 189, 190
Louise, Princess of 190
Victoria, Princess of (Marchioness of Milford Haven, née Hesse and by Rhine) 189, 190
Batuk, Mr. 164
BAVARIA
Elisabeth, Duchess in (See BELGIUM, Elisabeth, Queen of)
Ludwig II, King of 86
Bazhenov, Vassili 110
Beatty, Admiral 190
BELGIUM
Albert, King of the Belgians 105, 121
Elisabeth, Queen of (née Bavaria) 121

Benois, Albert 75
Benois, Leon 103, 137
Bernadotte, Count Lennart (former Prince Lennart of Sweden) 58
Bezobrasov, Vladimir 149
Birkhead, May 193
Blackford, Harriet (aka Fanny Lear, née Henrietta Ely) 61, 62, 63, 64, 65, 66, 67, 68, 69, 70, 71, 72, 76
Bobrinsky, Count Alexis 216
Boldarev, Mr. 152
BONAPARTE
Eugenie, Empress (née de Montijo) 170
Napoleon I, French Emperor ix, 106
Bothmer, Countess von 48
Botkin, Dr. Serge 135
Boucheron, Frederic 107
Boureine, Sophie 143
Brassov(a), Countess Natalia Sergeievna (née Cheremetvsky) [Natasha] 10, 47, 51, 52, 54, 57, 92, 117, 178, 180, 199
Buchanan, Sir George 190
BULGARIA
Ferdinand I, King of 27
Margarita, Queen of 44
Simeon, King of 44
Burghersh, Lord 190
BURGUNDY
Charles, the Bold, Duke of vii
Philip, the Good, Duke of vii
Butakov, Rea Admiral Grigory 81
Butter, David 192
Buxhoeveden, Baron Karl 100
Buxhoeveden, Baroness Sophie 82, 98, 102, 119, 126
Byron, Lord 119

C

Castenkiold, Henrik 201
Chanel, Gabrielle "Coco" 47, 56, 57
Chasovitinov, Nicholas 76
Chasovitinov, Sviatoslav 76, 78
Chasovitinova, Darya 75, 76, 77, 78
Chasovitinova, Darya (Jr.) 76, 77, 78
Chavchavadze, Prince David 183, 198, 215, 216
Chavchavadze, Princess Nina 195
Cheremetev, Count 217
Chernavin, Vsevelod 20
Chernavin, Vyacheslav 20
Chislova, Catherine 156, 158
Churchill, Lord Randolph 55
Cockfield, Hamie H. 184
Collins, Frederick L. 55, 56
Comte, Professor Baily 85
Condorusso, Marie 133
Crofts, Millicent 20, 25
Cunard, Emerald, Lady 55

Index

D

Daller, General Alexander 20
Daniltschenko, Captain P. 119
Davelli, Marthe 56
Davydova, Lydia 28
Delevskaya, Mademoiselle 20
Demidov, Alexander 74
Demidov, Mademoiselle 21
Demidov, Mr. 163
Demidov, Nicholas (aka Nicholas Volinsky) 74, 78
Demidova, Alexandra Abaza 74, 77, 78
Demidova, Olga (aka Olga Volinsky) 74, 78
Dehn, Sop
DENMARK
Alexandra, Princess of (See GREAT BRITAIN, Alexandra, Queen of)
Alexandrine, Queen of (née Mecklenburg-Schwerin) 19, 182, 187, 200, 202
Christian X, King of 19, 187, 201
Henrik, Prince of (né de Monpezat) 46
Dernoff, Protopresbyter Alexander 34
Deshevov, S. M. 115
Diaghilev, Serge 22, 90
Diernoff, Father Alexander 20
Djunkovskaya, Yelena 48
Dolgoroukaya, Princess 72
Dostal, Nicholas 79
Dostoyevsky, Feodor 200
Dreyer, Nadezhda 74, 75, 76, 77, 78
Dubelt, Michael von 187
Dvukarev, Father Arsene 122
Dzhyorguli, Alexander 109

E

Eager, Miss 109
Egypt, Farouk, King of 167
Egypt, Khedive of 21
Elissiev, Nicholas 23
Emery, Audrey [Princess Romanovsky-Ilynsky] 56, 57
Ermolinsky, Major-General N.N. 96
Eugenia, Mother 154

F

Ferrand, Jacques 58
Figanniere, Viscount de 71
Findeisen, Father 84
Fokine, Michael 120
FRANCE
Amelie, Princess d'Orléans (See PORTUGAL, Amelie, Queen of)
Chantal, Princess of (Baroness François-Xavier de Sambucy de Sorgue) 46
Isabelle, Countess of Paris 45
Louis XVI 55, 176
Marie Antoinette, Queen of (née Austria) 176
Franco, General Francisco 39
Fredericks, Count Vladimir 9, 94, 141
Fry, Nannie 48, 49

G

Galkin, Fortress Commander 132

GEORGIA
Bagration-Moukhransky, Prince George 38
Bagration-Moukhransky, Prince Irakly 40
Bagration-Moukhransky, Prince Konstantin Alexandrovich 92, 93, 94, 115, 116, 121, 129
Bagration-Moukhransky, Prince Teymuraz Konstantinnovich 94, 95, 129
Bagration-Moukhransky, Princess Nathalia Konstantinovna 95, 129
George XII, King of 92
Irakly II, King of 92
Gibson, Charles Dana 55
Gilliard, Pierre 58
Glazunov, Alexander 107, 119, 120
Gleichen, Countess Valda (Lady Valda Machell) 192
Goethe, Johann Wolfgang von 119, 169
Goldschmidt, Commander 29
Golitsyn, Prince Vladimir 152
Golovin, Doctor 135
Golovina, Lubov 54
Gorky, Maxim 107, 131, 182, 202
GREAT BRITAIN
Adolphus, Prince of (Duke of Cambridge) 184
Alexandra, Princess of (and Saxe-Coburg & Gotha, Fürstin of Hohenlohe-Langenburg) 9, 12, 35, 37
Alexandra, Queen of (née Denmark) 190, 196
Alice, Princess of (See HESSE AND BY RHINE, Alice, Grand Duchess of)
Alfred, Duke of Edinburgh and Saxe-Coburg & Gotha, Prince of 3, 20, 37, 68, 196
Beatrice, Princess of (and Saxe-Coburg & Gotha, Infanat of Spain) [Baby Bee] 5, 6, 37, 38, 39
Edward VII, King of 21, 187, 188
Edward VIII, King of 193
Elizabeth II, Queen of 104, 192
George V, King of 24, 32, 105, 154, 166, 189, 190, 191, 193
George, Duke of Kent, Prince of 32, 37, 105
Louise, Princess of (Duchess of Fife) 185
Marie, Princess of (Edinburgh and Saxe-Coburg & Gotha) (See Romania, Marie, Queen of)
Marina, Princess of (Duchess of Kent) 32, 37, 105
Mary, Queen of (née Teck) [May] 184, 189, 190, 191
Mary Adelaide, Princess of Cambridge (See Teck, Mary Adelaide, Duchess of)
Philip, Prince of (Duke of Edinburgh) 104, 192
Victoria, Queen of 3, 4, 9, 41, 189, 192, 196
GREECE
Alice, Princess of (née Battenberg) 103
Anastasia, Princess of (née Leeds, aka Princess Christopher of Greece) 191
Christopher, Prince of 102, 103, 135, 191
Constantine I, King of the Hellenes 44, 104, 105
Elisabeth, Queen of (née Romania) 95, 192
George I, King of the Hellenes 89, 105, 196
George II, King of the Hellenes 191, 192
George, Prince of 99
Maria, Princess of (See Russia, Maria Georgievna, Grand Duchess of)
Marina, Princess of (See GREAT BRITAIN, Marina, Princess of (Duchess of Kent)
Nicholas, Prince of 99, 104, 105
Olga, Queen of the Hellenes (née Russia) 48, 66, 75, 76, 84, 87, 91, 98, 99, 104, 105, 112, 122, 123, 129, 133, 199
Philip, Prince (See GREAT BRITAIN, Philip, Prince of (Duke of Edinburgh))
Sophie, Queen of the Hellenes (née Prussia) 104, 105, 191
Grove, Lizzie 48, 49

Index

H

HANNOVER
Marie, Queen of (née Saxe-Altenburg) 95
Hauser, Kaspar 177
Helmerson, Colonel 214
HESSE AND BY RHINE
Alice, Grand Duchess of (née Great Britain) 185
Elisabeth, Princess of (See RUSSIA, Elisabeth Feodorovna, Grand Duchess of)
Ernst Ludwig, Grand Duke of 3, 4, 10
Irene, Princess of (Princess Heinrich of Prussia) 185
Ludwig IV, Grand Duke of 185
Victoria, Princess of (See BATTENBERG, Victoria, Princess of)
Hitler, Adolf 37, 58
Hmelnitskuju, Valerie 76
Hohenberg, Sophie, Duchess of 36
HOHENOHE-LANGENBURG
Ernst, Fürst of 9, 36
Feodora, Fürstin of (née Leiningen) 193
HOLSTEIN-GOTTORP
Karl Peter, Duke of (Tsar Peter III) xi
Hungary, St Stephen of viii

I

Ignatiev, General 125, 126
Ignatiev, Catherine [Katya] 185
Ilina, L. A. 129
Ioann, Archimandrite 84
Ioannides, Pericles 202
Iskander, Prince Alexander 75, 77, 78
Iskander, Prince Artemi 75, 78
Ismailov, Colonel Feodor 127
ITALY
Elena, Queen of (née Montenegro) 143, 154, 155, 166, 167
Umberto II, King of 167
Victor Emanuel III, King of 143, 154, 166, 167
Ivanova, Maria 207
Iveagh, 1st Earl of 191

J

Jewell, Marshall 69, 70, 71

K

Kazakov, Matvei 110
Kedrinsky, Father 88
Keller, Countess Nathalia 122
Keppel, Alice 187, 188
Kerensky, Alexander 28, 77, 152, 181
Kerr, Mark 104
Khanykova, Nathalia Konstantinovna 78
Khatisov, A. I. 151
Khiva, Khan of 66, 67
Kirby, Helen 39, 41
Kirby, Sumner Moore 39
Klein, Angelika 86
Knox, General Sir Alfred 22
Konstadt, Father Ioann of 98
Korochentzov, Alexander 121, 129, 130
Kossikovskaya, Alexandra 10
Krasnov, Nicholas 159, 160
Krivovna, Alexandra 218
Krymov, Vladimir 90
Kschessinska, Mathilde Felixovna (Princess Romanovsky-Krasinsky) 22, 23, 24, 25, 26, 28, 29, 30, 31, 32, 33, 89, 90, 98, 125, 180, 181, 195, 214, 215, 216, 217, 218
Kube, F.F. von 29
Kulikovsky, Nikolai 11, 49, 208
Kurakin, Princess Irina 121
Kuznetsov, A.G. 110
Kuznetsova, Anna Vassilievna 60, 81, 98, 126, 133, 134
Kuzmich, Feodor 176, 177
Kyasht, Lydia 89, 90, 96, 215

L

Lacroix, Jean Boris 21
Lacroix, Jeanne 21
Laiming, General Paul Alexandrovich 50
Leeds, Nancy (See GREECE, Anastasia, Princess of)
Leiming, Colonel Alexander von 130, 131, 132
LEININGEN
Emich, Fürst of 17
Feodora, Princess of (See HOHENLOHE-LANGENBURG, Feodora, Fürstin of)
Karl, Fürst of 17, 36
Lenin, Vladimir Ilych Ulianov, known as 47, 55, 131, 180, 182, 201, 202
Leonid, Abbot 80, 81
Lestchinsky, Commissar 28, 29
LEUCHTENBERG
Eugenia Maximilianovna, Princess of (See OLDENBURG, Eugenia Maximilianovna, Duchess of)
George Romanovsky, Duke of 31, 144, 152
Helen Georgievna Romanovsky, Princess of 144, 152, 165
Serge Georgievich Romanovskt, Duke of 144, 152
Zinaida, Duchess of 26
Liebknecht, Karl 130, 202
Lincoln, W. Bruce 147
LITHUANIA
Gediminas, Grand Duke of viii
Mindaugas, Grand Duke of viii
Litke, Admiral Fedor 106
Lloyd George, David 16
Lobanov-Rostovsky, Prince Andrei 141
Loftus, Lord Augustus 71
Lukin, Rear Admiral 152
Luxemburg, Rosa 202
Lvov, Prince George 151, 152

M

Madsen, Axel 56
Maichrowsky, Mr. 198
Maintenon, Madame de 64
Malama, Dr. 152
Mamontov, Savva 115
Mannerheim, General Baron Carl Gustaf 35
Mansfield, Sixth Earl of 189
Marfeld, Roman 106
Marling, Sir Charles 54, 55
Masson, Frederic 176, 179, 180
Mateos-Saínz de Medrano, Ricardo 42
MECKLENBURG-SCHWERIN
Alexandrine, Grand Duchess of (née Prussia) 25
Friedrich Franz III, Grand Duke of 187, 203

243

Mendes, Gonçalo vii
Merenberg, Count George of 187
Merenberg, Countess Sophie of (See Torby, Countess Sophie of)
Mikhailov, Varvara 80
MONACO
Grace, Princess of (née Kelly) 57
Pierre, Prince of (né de Polignac) 57
MONTENEGRO
Anastasia, Princess of (See RUSSIA, Anastasia Nikolaievna, Grand Duchess of)
Anna, Princess of (See BATTENBERG, Anna, Princess of)
Elena, Princess of (See ITALY, Elena, Queen of)
Militsa, Princess of (See RUSSIA, Militsa Nikolaievna, Grand Duchess of)
Nicholas I, King of 88, 143
Zorka Lyubika, Princess of 88 (Princess Peter of Serbia)
Montgomery-Massingberd, Hugh 143
Mossolov, Alexander 98, 126, 173
Murat, Joachim, King of Naples ix
Muraviev, N.N. 110
MUSCOVY
Ivan I, Kalita, Prince of Moscow x
Ivan III, Tsar of x
Ivan IV, the Terrible, Tsar of x, xi
Theodor I, Tsar of x

N

Narva, Serge, Bishop of 108
Naryshkin-Kurakin, Elisabeth 60, 144, 146
NASSAU
Adolf, Duke of (later Grand Duke Adolphe of Luxembourg) 186
Nicholas, Prince of 186, 187
Pauline, Duchess of (né Württemberg) 186
Therese, Princess of (See OLDENBURG, Therese, Duchess of)
Wilhelm, Duke of 186
Nazier-Vachot, Philippe 145, 162
Nepokoichitsky, General A.A. 110
Nesterovskaya, Antonina Rafailovna [Nina] 90, 91, 121, 131
NETHERLANDS
Emma, Queen Mother of the (née Waldeck-Pyrmont) 186
Juliana, Queen of the 57
Wilhelmina, Queen of the 46
Willem III. King of the 186
Nevsky, Alexander, Prince of Novgorod, Grand Duke of Vladimir-Suzdal x
Nostitz, Countess Lillie 141, 144

O

Obolensky, Prince Serge 22
OLDENBURG
Alexander Petrovich, Duke of 95
Elisabeth, Grand Duchess of (née Saxe-Altenburg) 95
Eugenia Maximilianovna, Duchess of (née Leuchtenberg) 96
Peter, Duke of 186
Peter Alexandrovich, Duke of 10-11, 49, 96
Therese, Duchess of (née Nassau) 186
Orlov, Prince Nicholas 152, 163, 165

P

Paléologue, Maurice 15, 54, 146, 147
Paley, Princess Olga Valerianovna (née Karnovitch)10, 49, 54, 116, 131
Paley, Prince Vladimir Pavlovich 49, 55, 116, 120, 218
Palitsyn, General Fedor 147
PAPACY
Pius V vii
Pasha, Enver 150
Pavlov, Ivan 106
Pavlova, Anna 22
Peretiatkovich, M. M. 115
Perovskaya, Sophie 60
Peters, Jacob 131
Phillips, Harold 192
Pilar, Baroness Nina 143
Pistolkhors, Eric von 10, 54
Pless, Daisy, Princess of (née Cornwallis-West) 188, 191
Pobedonostsev, Konstantin 106
Polotsky, Maria 143
Pompadour, Madame de 64
Poonsonby, Sir Frederick [Fritz Ponsonby] 190, 191
Poole, General 29, 199
PORTUGAL
Amelie, Queen of (né Orléans) 174
Prokopovich, Feofan 96
PRUSSIA
Augusta Viktoria, German Kaiserin (née Schleswig-Holstein-Sonderburg-Augustenburg) 111
Cecilie, Crown Princess of (née Mecklenburg-Schwerin) 57, 174, 177
Franz Josef, Prince of 41
Franz Friedrich, Prince of 41
Franz Wilhelm, Prince of (aka Grand Duke Michael Pavlovich of Russia) 41, 42, 44-45
Friedrich III, German Kaiser 25
Georg Friedrich, Prince of 45
Heinrich, Prince of 185
Hermine, German Kaiserin (née Reuß, also Princess of Schönaich-Carolath) 41
Joachim, Prince of 41
Karl Franz Josef, Prince of 41
Louis Ferdinand, Prince of 19, 42, 44, 57
Marie, Princess of (née Hesse-Kassel) 95
Sophie, Princess of (See GREECE, Sophie, Queen of the Hellenes)
Wilhelm I, German Kaiser 20
Wilhelm II, German Kaiser 19, 35, 41, 57, 104, 105, 153, 165, 166, 176, 201, 209
Pushkin, Alexander 91, 107, 187
Pushkin, Natalia Alexandrovna 187
Putiatin, Prince Serge 54, 55, 56

R

Rachevsky, General Serge 23
Rachevsky, Zinaide Sergeievna [Zina] 23, 24, 28
Radzinsky, Edvard 144
Radziwill, Princess Catherine 99, 107, 216
Radziwill, Prince Konstantin 89
Rasputin, Grigory 22, 26, 27, 47, 52, 53, 54, 55, 57, 145, 148, 149, 154, 162, 179, 180, 207, 208
Rasputin, Maria 57
Remez, Feodor 217, 218

Index

REUß
Caroline, Princess 20
Heinrich VII, Prince 9
Ricard, Monsieur 59, 60
Robien, Count Louis de 52
Rodzianko, Michael 148, 216
Rogovskaya, Olga Iosifovna 77, 78
ROMANIA
Carol I, King of 21, 186
Elisabeth, Princess of (See GREECE, Elisabeth, Queen of)
Elisabeth, Queen of (née Wied) 186
Ferdinand I, King of 20, 21
Marie, Queen of (née Great Britain) [Missy] 10, 19, 20, 21, 24, 37, 93, 100, 196, 199, 222
Michael I, King of 46
Nicholas, Prince of 17
Romanov, Prince Michael Feodorovich 210, 211
Romanov, Prince Nicholas Romanovich xv, 161, 167
Romanovsky-Ilynsky, Paul, Prince 57
Romanovsky-Iskander, Prince Kirill 77, 78, 79
Romanovsky-Iskander, Princess Nathalia 77, 78, 79
Romanovsky-Krasinsky, Prince Vladimir Andreievich 25, 28, 29, 30, 32, 33, 89, 125, 215
Ruffo Donna Elisabetha 210
Rurik, Prince of Novgorod ix-x
RUSSIA
Alexander I, Tsar of xiii, 45, 106, 169, 175, 176, 177
Alexander II, Tsar of 3, 20, 25, 44, 56, 59, 60, 66, 71, 72, 73, 74, 80, 82, 123, 124, 133, 134, 136, 167, 178, 182, 195, 203
Alexander III, Tsar of xii, xiv, 2, 10, 20, 74, 75, 77, 78, 80, 83, 84, 87, 88-89, 95, 96, 98, 105, 106, 108, 113, 119, 122, 124, 143, 144, 158, 173, 174, 175, 176, 177, 178, 182, 183, 184, 185, 186, 187, 195, 196, 203, 204, 205, 220, 221
Alexander Mikhailovich, Grand Duke of [Sandro] xv, 50, 53, 55, 80, 98, 105, 106, 112, 126, 127, 152, 164, 165, 175, 177, 178, 181, 184, 186, 195, 197, 203, 204, 205, 206, 207, 208, 209, 210, 211, 214, 216, 220, 221, 222
Alexander Vladimirovich, Grand Duke of 1
Alexandra Feodorovna, Empress of (née Hesse and by Rhine) 2, 4, 5, 6, 9, 10, 14, 15, 22, 26, 53, 54, 86, 88, 92, 94, 97, 102, 108, 111, 113, 118, 119, 142, 143, 144, 145, 146, 148, 149, 150, 151, 153, 154, 161, 162, 179, 182, 189, 193, 205, 206, 207, 208, 214
Alexandra Georgievna, Grand Duchess of (née Greece) 10, 48, 95, 104
Alexandra Iosifovna, Grand Duchess of (née Saxe-Altenburg) 20, 59, 60, 68, 80, 83, 89, 95, 96, 97, 98, 99, 100, 102, 103, 122, 123, 124, 125, 133, 135, 136, 137
Alexandra Petrovna, Grand Duchess of (née Oldenburg) 25, 95, 139, 156, 157, 158, 160
Alexis Alexandrovich, Grand Duke of 9, 11, 59, 60, 81, 95, 206
Alexis Mikhailovich, Grand Duke of 2, 185, 220, 221, 222
Alexis Nikolaievich, Tsarevich of 6, 17, 27, 30, 86, 91, 97, 151
Anastasia Mikhailovna, Grand Duchess of (Grand Duchess of Mecklenburg-Schwerin) [Stassie] 170, 182, 184, 187, 203, 215
Anastasia Nikolaievna, Grand Duchess of (née Montenegro) [Stana] 88, 143, 144, 145, 146, 152, 153, 154, 155, 161, 162, 164, 165, 166, 179
Anastasia Nikolaievna, Grand Duchess of (daughter of Nicholas II) 210
Anastasia Romanova xi
Andrei Alexandrovich, Prince of 164, 178, 210
Andrei Vladimirovich, Grand Duke of 1, 2, 7, 14, 20, 22, 23, 24, 25, 26, 27, 28, 29, 30, 31, 32, 89, 90, 114, 118, 125, 150, 180, 215, 216
Anna I, Empress of 66

Boris Vladimirovich, Grand Duke of 1, 2, 4, 6, 7, 11, 20, 21, 22, 23, 24, 26, 28, 29, 32, 34, 180
Catherine II, the Great xi, xii, xiii, xiv, 46, 66, 93, 100, 110, 169
Catherine Ioannovna, Princess of xii, 113
Dimitri Alexandrovich, Prince of xv, 166, 206
Dimitri Konstantinovich, Grand Duke of 80, 81, 84, 88, 89, 96, 100, 103, 111, 112, 114, 115, 117, 122, 123, 124, 125, 126, 127, 128, 129, 130, 131, 132, 133, 134, 136, 157, 181, 199, 200, 202
Dimitri Pavlovich, Grand Duke of 13, 14, 17, 22, 26, 27, 47, 48, 49, 50, 51, 52, 53, 54, 55, 56, 57, 58, 85, 104, 129, 155, 208
Dimitri Romanovich, Prince Romanov xv
Elena Petrovna, Princess of (née Serbia) 88, 112, 113, 114, 218
Elisabeth I xi, 46, 66
Elisabeth Alexeievna, Empress of (née Baden) 176
Elisabeth Feodorovna, Grand Duchess of (née Hesse and by Rhine) 49, 50, 51, 55, 92, 97, 101, 104, 114, 120, 153, 181, 185, 218, 219
Elisabeth Mavrikievna, Grand Duchess of (née Saxe-Altenburg) [Mavra or Lilinka] 83, 84, 85, 86, 87, 88, 91, 92, 95, 101, 109, 110, 111, 112, 114, 115, 116, 117, 118, 120, 121
Feodor Alexandrovich, Prince of 164, 166, 206, 207
Gabriel Konstantinovich, Prince of 83, 85, 86, 87, 89, 90, 91, 92, 93, 95, 96, 103, 105, 111, 113, 114, 115, 116, 117, 118, 121, 126, 127, 130, 131, 200
George Alexandrovich, Grand Duke of 4, 204
George Konstantinovich, Prince of xv, 97, 101, 111, 114, 115, 116, 117, 121
George Mikhailovich, Grand Duke of xiv, 42, 43, 44, 45, 46, 80, 97, 104, 130, 131, 132, 152, 157, 159, 178, 181, 183, 188, 191, 195, 196, 197, 198, 199, 200, 201, 202, 204, 210
Helen Pavlovna, Grand Duchess of (née Württemberg) 170
Helen Vladimirovna, Grand Duchess of (Princess Nicholas of Greece) 1, 11, 13, 14, 20, 25, 37, 39, 104, 105
Igor Konstantinovich, Prince of 96, 113, 114, 115, 116, 120, 121, 218
Ioann Konstantinovich, Prince of [Ioannchik] 85, 86, 87, 88, 97, 112, 113, 114, 115, 116, 120, 121, 218
Irina Alexandrovna, Princess of [Princess Youssoupov] xii, 33, 166, 209
Kira Kirillovna, Grand Duchess of (Princess Louis Ferdinand of Prussia) 11, 17-18, 34, 36, 37, 39, 40, 57
Kirill Vlarimirovich, Grand Duke of xiv, xv, 1, 2, 3, 4, 5, 6, 7, 8, 9, 10, 11, 12, 13, 14, 15, 16, 17, 19, 20, 21, 22, 24, 25, 27, 30, 32, 34, 35, 36, 37, 38, 40, 57, 103, 118, 155, 180, 221, 222
Konstantin Konstantinovich, Grand Duke of [Kostia/Kostya] 17, 43, 50, 76, 80, 81, 82, 83, 84, 85, 86, 87, 88, 89, 91, 92, 93, 94, 95, 97, 98, 99, 100, 101, 102, 105, 106, 107, 108, 109, 110, 111, 112, 113, 114, 115, 116, 117, 118, 119, 120, 122, 125, 126, 129, 133, 134, 135, 136, 137, 170, 186, 205
Konstantin Konstantinovich, Prince of [Kostia] 95, 96, 114, 115, 116, 120, 121, 218
Konstantin Nikolaievich, Grand Duke of 59, 60, 66, 68, 69, 72, 73, 74, 80, 81, 84, 87, 91, 95, 98, 103, 109, 114, 122, 123, 125, 133, 134, 135, 136, 137, 157, 169, 170, 182
Konstantin Pavlovich, Grand Duke of 175
Leonida Georgievna, Grand Duchess of (née Bagration-Moukhransky) 38, 39, 40, 41, 42, 43, 44, 45, 46
Maria (Marie) Alexandrovna, Empress of (née Hesse and by Rhine) 80, 143
Maria (Marie) Alexandrovna, Grand Duchess of (Duchess of Edinburgh and Saxe-Coburg & Gotha) 3, 5, 7, 9, 11, 12, 16, 35, 36, 37, 68, 93, 95, 196, 222
Maria (Marie) Feodorovna, Empress of (née Württemberg) 88, 110
Maria (Marie) Feodorovna, Empress of (née Denmark) 5, 8, 14, 17, 19, 30, 40, 84, 88, 95, 99, 100, 140, 150, 152, 158, 163, 164, 166, 173, 178, 181, 185, 193, 196, 198, 204, 206, 207, 208, 209, 210

245

Index

Maria (Marie) Georgievna, Grand Duchess of (née Greece) 95, 104, 127, 131, 133, 140, 152, 178, 188, 193, 196, 197, 198, 199, 202

Maria Kirillovna, Grand Duchess of (Fürstin of Leiningen) 11, 17, 34, 36, 37, 39

Maria (Marie) Nikolaievna, Grand Duchess of (daughter of Nicholas II) 117

Maria (Marie) Pavlovna (Jr.), Grand Duchess of (Princess Wilhelm of Sweden, Princess Putiatin) xiii, 12, 14, 47, 48, 49, 50, 51, 53, 54, 55, 56, 57, 58, 85, 92, 104, 112, 141, 154

Maria (Marie) Pavlovna (Sr.), Grand Duchess of (née Mecklenburg-Schwerin) [Grand Duchess Vladimir] 1, 2, 7, 9, 11, 13, 14, 16, 20, 22, 23, 24, 25, 26, 27, 28, 29, 30, 33, 34, 35, 84, 104, 105, 179, 180

Maria Pavlovna, Grand Duchess of (Grand Duchess of Saxe-Weimer-Eisenach) 169

Maria Vladimirovna, Grand Duchess of xiv 40, 41, 42, 43, 44, 45, 46

Marina Petrovna, Princess of 159, 164

Michael I, Tsar of xi, xv

Michael Alexandrovich, Grand Duke of xii, 2, 4, 5, 6, 7, 10, 16, 17, 20, 27, 30, 37, 49, 51, 52, 54, 92, 94, 117, 151, 153, 178, 180, 197, 199, 218, 221

Michael Mikhailovich, Grand Duke of 80, 124, 177, 178, 183, 184, 185, 186, 187, 188, 189, 190, 191, 192, 193, 194, 220

Michael Nikolaievich, Grand Duke of 32, 87, 95, 170, 171, 172, 173, 178, 183, 188, 189, 195, 203, 204, 205, 214, 220, 221

Michael Pavlovich, Grand Duke of 170

Militza Nikolaievna, Grand Duchess of (née Montenegro) 88, 96, 126, 143, 144, 145, 146, 154, 158, 159, 160, 161, 162, 163, 164, 165, 166, 167, 209

Nadezhda Petrovna, Princess of 96, 163, 164, 165

Nathalia Konstantinovna, Princess of 97, 137

Nicholas I, Tsar of 31, 66, 68, 100, 110, 137, 139, 169, 170, 172, 177

Nicholas II, Tsar of xii, xv, 2, 3, 4, 5, 6, 7, 8, 9, 10, 11, 12, 14, 15, 16, 17, 22, 23, 25, 27, 28, 30, 34, 49, 50, 53, 54, 78, 79, 87, 88, 89, 91, 92, 93, 94, 95, 96, 97, 98, 99, 100, 101, 102, 105, 106, 107, 108, 111, 113, 114, 115, 116, 117, 118, 119, 120, 126, 129, 130, 139, 141, 142, 144, 145, 146, 147, 148, 149, 150, 151, 153, 154, 161, 162, 163, 166, 175, 178, 179, 180, 182, 188, 189, 195, 204, 205, 206, 208, 214, 215, 217

Nicholas Konstantinovich, Grand Duke of 59, 60, 61, 64, 65, 66, 67, 68, 69, 70, 71, 72, 73, 74, 75, 76, 77, 78, 81, 83, 122, 125, 134

Nicholas Mikhailovich, Grand Duke of [Niki] 27, 80, 99, 107, 124, 130, 131, 132, 141, 170, 171, 172, 173, 174, 175, 176, 177, 178, 179, 180, 181, 182, 183, 184, 195, 200, 202, 208, 210, 215, 216, 217

Nicholas Nikolaievich (Jr.), Grand Duke of [Nikolasha] 17, 19, 26, 28, 139, 140, 141, 142, 143, 145, 146, 147, 148, 148, 150, 151, 152, 153, 154, 155, 156, 163, 164, 166, 175, 179, 180, 209

Nicholas Nikolaievich (Sr.), Grand Duke of 80, 122, 139, 143, 156, 157, 158

Nikita Alexandrovich, Prince of 164, 166, 206

Nina Georgievna, Princess of (Princess Paul Chavchavadze) 190, 192, 196

Oleg Konstantinovich, Prince of 95, 96, 97, 113, 114, 115, 121, 129

Olga Alexandrovna, Grand Duchess of xii-xiii, 10-11, 14, 16, 19, 30, 49, 51, 144, 152, 163, 164, 186, 197, 207, 208, 209

Olga Feodorovna, Grand Duchess of (née Baden) 170, 177, 183, 184, 185, 186, 195, 203, 204, 220, 221

Olga Nikolaievna, Grand Duchess of (Queen of Württemberg) 87, 134

Olga Nikolaievna, Grand Duchess (daughter of Nicholas II) 109, 117

Olga Konstantinovna, Grand Duchess of (See GREECE, Olga, Queen of the Hellenes)

Paul I, Tsar of xii, xiii, 38, 40, 46, 66, 87, 91, 93, 106, 169

Paul Alexandrovich, Grand Duke of 10, 48, 49, 54, 80, 104, 116, 120, 123, 124, 131, 132, 136, 181, 182, 200, 202, 216

Peter I, the Great, Tsar of x, xi, xv, 66, 146, 156, 169

Peter III, Tsar of xi, xii, xiii, 46

Peter Nikolaievich, Grand Duke of 17, 40, 80, 95, 96, 143, 144, 146, 150, 152, 154, 156, 157, 158, 159, 160, 161, 162, 163, 164, 165, 166, 167, 180, 195, 209

Roman Petrovich, Prince of xv, 17, 152, 154, 159, 160, 163, 164, 165, 166

Rostislav Alexandrovich, Prince of 164, 166, 206

Serge Alexandrovich, Grand Duke of 3, 8, 48, 49, 50, 80, 99, 100, 101, 104, 105, 123, 126, 136, 176, 185

Serge Mikhailovich, Grand Duke of 23, 25, 30, 89, 120, 124, 125, 130, 141, 177, 180, 181, 183, 204, 209, 214, 215, 216, 217, 218, 219, 222

Tatiana Konstantinovna, Princess of xii, 91, 92, 93, 94, 97, 111, 114, 115, 116, 121, 129, 130

Tatiana Nikolaievna, Grand Duchess of 109, 117

Vassili Alexandrovich, Prince of xv, 164, 166

Vera Konstantinovna, Grand Duchess of (Duchess Eugen of Württemberg) 84, 89, 99, 103, 104

Vera Konstantinovna, Princess of xv, 97, 98, 111, 114, 116, 117, 121, 133

Victoria Feodorovna, Grand Duchess of (née Edinburgh) [Ducky] 1, 3, 4, 5, 6, 7, 8, 9, 10, 11, 12, 13, 14, 15, 16, 17, 19, 20, 22, 32, 34, 35, 36, 37, 38, 118

Vladimir Alexandrovich, Grand Duke of 1, 2, 4, 5, 7, 9, 11, 20, 22, 25, 95, 99, 104, 142

Vladimir Kirillovich, Grand Duke of xiv, xv, 16, 19, 34, 35, 36, 37, 38, 39, 40, 41, 42, 43, 44, 45, 57, 118

Vsevelod Ioannovich, Prince of 88

Vyacheslav Konstantinovich, Grand Duke of 118, 122, 123, 125, 133, 134, 135, 136, 137

Xenia [Ksenia] Alexandrovna, Grand Duchess of 4, 14, 152, 163, 164, 166, 178, 192, 196, 197, 204, 205, 206, 207, 208, 209, 210, 211, 214, 215, 220

Xenia Georgievna, Princess of [Mrs William B. Leeds] 31, 190, 192, 196

Ruzsky, General 26

S

Sagrera, Ana de 6
Sainty, Guy Stair 40
Sambucy de Sorgue, Baron Axel de 46
Samus, Professor 122
Sartak Khan x
Sarov, St Seraphim of 219
Savitsch, Dr. Eugene de 58

SAXE-ALTENBURG
Agnes, Duchess of (née Anhalt-Dessau) 89
Auguste, Princess of (née Saxe-Meiningen) 83, 89, 95, 96, 111
Elisabeth, Princess of (See OLDENBURG, Elisabeth, Grand Duchess of)
Elisabeth, Princess of (See RUSSIA, Elisabeth Mavrikievna, Grand Duchess of)
Ernst I, Duke of 87
Ernst II, Duke of 111
Louise, Princess of 95
Marie, Princess of (See HANNOVER, Marie, Queen of)
Moritz, Prince of 83, 87
Marie Anne, Princess of (See SCHAUMBURG-LIPPE, Marie Anne, Princess of)

Index

SAXE-COBURG & GOTHA
Carl Eduard, Duke of [Charlie] 36
Friedrich Josias, Prince of 36
Hubertus, Prince of 36
Johann Leopold, Hereditary Prince of 36
Sibylla, Princess of 36
SAXE-MEININGEN
Anna, Dowager Duchess of (née Saxe-Meiningen) 87
Ernst, Prince of 95
Friedrich, Prince of 95
Georg II, Duke of 89, 97
Marie, Duchess of (née Hesse-Kassel) 89
SAXE-WEIMAR-EISENACH
Carl Alexander, Grand Duke of 95, 169
Scavenius, Anne Sofie 201
Scavenius, Harald 200, 201, 202
SCHAUMBURG-LIPPE
Alexander, Prince of 104
Albrecht, Prince 104
Albrecht (Jr.), Prince of 104
Bathildis, Princess of 104
Eugen, Prince of 104
Franz Josef, Prince of 104
Marie Anne, Princess of (née Saxe-Altenburg) 87, 95
Maurice, Prince of 97
Maximilian, Prince of 104
Maximilian (Jr.), Prince of 104
Schiller, Friedrich , 119, 169
SCHLESWIG-HOLSTEIN-SONDERBURG-AUGUSTEN-BURG
Augusta Viktoria, Princess of (See PRUSSIA, Augusta Viktoria, German Kaiserin)
Schönaich-Carolath, Henriette, Princess of 41
Schuyler, Eugene 70, 71, 72, 73
Sergeivsky, N.N. 116, 117
SERBIA
Elena Petrovna, Princess of (See RUSSIA, Elena Petrovna, Princess of)
Peter I, King of 88
Seton-Watson, Hugh 142
Shakespeare, William 119
Shipov, N.P. 110
Shuvalov, Count Peter 68, 69, 70, 71, 72, 73
Simpson, Wallis Warfield 51
Smirnov, Serge 86
Sobchak, Anatoly 42, 43
Sokolov, Nicolai 30
SPAIN
Alfonso XIII, King of 21, 40
Alfonso, Infante of (né Bourbon-Orléans) 37
Antonio, Infante of (né Bourbon-Orléans) 37
Eulalia, Infanta of 37
Juan Carlos I, King of 44
María de las Mercedes, Infanta of (also Princess of Bavaria) 40
Sofía, Queen of (née Greece) 42, 44
Victoria Eugenia, Queen of (née Battenberg) 6, 21
Stahl und Holstein, General Baron Alexis de 167
Stalin, Joseph 58, 79
Stoeckel, Baron Alexander de [Sasha] 188
Stoeckel, Baroness Agnes de (née Barron) 187, 188
Stolypin, Peter 26, 108, 178
Stopford, Albert [Bertie] 23
Stroganov, Count Paul 176
Sukhomlinov, Vladimir 142, 147, 148, 217
Sumarokov-Elston, Count Felix (Prince Yussoupov) 78
Sumarokov-Elston, Count Paul 78
Svechin, Captain A. A. 154

SWEDEN
Charles XII, King of 102
Gustaf V, King of 12, 30, 35, 51, 186
Lennart, Prince of (See Bernadotte, Count Lennart) 58
Sophie, Princess of (See BADEN, Sophie, Grand Duchess of)
Victoria, Queen of (née Baden) 97, 120, 174, 186
William, Prince of 12, 50

T

Tarasov, Nicholas 128
Tarsaidze, Alexandre 65
Tchaikovsky, Peter Ilych 50, 118, 119
Tchirikoff, Captain Nicholas 211
Tchirikoff, Olga Vassilievna 211
Teck, Franz, Duke of 184
Teck, Mary, Princess of (See GREAT BRITAIN, Mary, Queen of)
Teck, Mary Adelaide, Duchess of (née Cambridge) [May] 184, 185
Teliakovsky, Vladimir 89
Thailand, King Vajiravudh of 22
Thompson, Donald 153
Thornhill, Major 22
Tolstoy, Count Leo 107
Tomishko, Anthony 103, 137
Torby, Countess Anastasia de (Lady Zia Wernher)[Zia] 187, 188, 189, 190, 191, 192, 193
Torby, Count Michael de [Boy] 187, 191, 192, 193
Torby, Countess Nada de (Marchioness of Milford Haven) 187, 190, 192
Torby, Countess Sophie of (née von Merenberg) 183, 185, 186, 187, 188, 189, 190, 193, 194
Trepov, General Fedor 68, 70, 71, 72
Trevelyan, Raleigh 184
Turkey, Abdul Hamid II, Sultan of 197
Tyshkevich, Count Stepan 152

U

Uritsky, Moisei 129, 130, 199, 201
Urusov, A.V. 110

V

Valentino, Rudolph 55
Valtzov, Dimitri 140
Vanderbilt, Consuelo (Duchess of Marlborough, Mrs Jacques Balsan) 49, 55, 56
Velde, François 40
Verkhovsky, Senior Lieutenant 152
Vladimir, Metropolitan 32
Vladimirov, Pierre 217
Vogel, Francis 220
Vorontzov, Prince Michael 158
Vorontzov, Princess 205
Vorontzov-Dashkov, Count Alexander (aka Alexander von Dehn) 215
Vorontzov-Dashkov, Count Hilarion 126
Vorontzov-Dashkov, Count Ivan 215
Vorontzov-Dashkov, Countess Barbara 215
Vorpovsky, Captain Victor 61, 68, 69
Vyroubova, Anna 54

W

WALDECK-PYRMONT
Emma, Princess of (See NETHERLANDS, Emma, Queen Mother of)
Friedrich, Fürst of 186
Helen, Princess of (See GREAT BRITAIN, Helen, Duchess of Albany)
Marie, Princess of (See WURTTEMBERG, Marie, Princess of)
Waleski, Princess 185
Warlich, Hugo 120
Wernher, Alexander [Alex] 192
Wernher, Sir Derrick 191
Wernher, Georgina [Gina] 192
Wernher, Sir Harold 191, 192, 193
Wernher, Sir Julius 191
Wernher, Myra 192
Westmann, M. de 71
Westminster, Duke of 57
Wiazemsky, General 205
WIED
Elisabeth, Princess of (See ROMANIA, Elisabeth, Queen of)
Witte, Count Serge 101, 141, 142, 143, 144
Wrangel-Rokassowsky, Baron Carl von 52
WURTTEMBERG
Alexander, Duke of 185
Elsa, Duchess of 96, 99, 104
Marie, Princess of (née Waldeck-Pyrmont) 186
Olga, Duchess of 96, 99, 104
Pauline, Princess of (See NASSAU, Pauline, Duchess of)

Y

Yanishev, Father Ioann 85, 87, 89, 95
Yanushkevich, General Nicholas 147
Yeltsin, Boris 42, 43
Yourievsky, Princess Catherine (née Dolgoruki) 123
Youssoupov, Prince Felix 47, 51, 52, 53, 54, 55, 57, 162, 166, 180, 208
Youssoupov, Princess Irina Felixovna 166
Youssoupov, Princess Zenaide 78

Z

Zabolotny, Mr. 164
Zadorojny, Commander 164, 165, 166, 209
Zaionchkovsky, Peter 107, 182
Zaitsev, Dimitri 109
Zarnekau, Countess Marianne 54
Zarnekau, Countess Nina 113
Zdekauera, Doctor Nicholas 73
Zdonovich, Major-General Alexis
Zelenoy, Alexis 122
Zelenoy, Lieutenant N. A. 81
Zlotnicka, Elena 38